Baedeker

Canada

Contents

Baedeker Specials

Principal Sights of Tourist Interest

4

(Continued on page 631)

Preface

This guide to Canada is one of the new generation of Baedeker guides.

These guides, illustrated throughout in colour, are designed to meet the needs of the modern traveller. They are quick and easy to consult, with the principal places of interest described in alphabetical order, and the information is presented in a format that is both attractive and easy to follow.

This guide covers the whole of Canada and also includes the Waterton Glacier International Peace Park, the major part of which is in the north-west of the United States of America.

The guide is in three parts. The first part gives a general account of the country, its political and geographical divisions, its landscape, climate, flora and fauna, population, educational systems, government and administration, economy, history, famous people, art and culture. A number of suggested itineraries provide a transition to the second part, in which the country's places and features of tourist interest – towns, provinces, regions, rivers – are described. The third part contains a variety of practical information. Both the sights and the practical information are listed in alphabetical order.

The new Baedeker guides are noted for their concentration on essentials and their convenience of use. They contain numerous specially drawn plans and colour illustrations; and at the end of the book is a large map making it easy to locate the various places described in the "A to Z" section of the guide with the help of the co-ordinates given at the head of each entry.

How to use this book

Following the tradition established by Karl Baedeker in 1844, sights of particular interest and hotels and restaurants of particular quality are distinguished by either one ★or two ★★stars.

To make it easier to locate the various sights listed in the "A to Z" section of the Guide, their co-ordinates on the large country map are shown in red at the head of each entry, e.g. ★Montréal P 8.

Only a selection of hotels and restaurants can be given; no reflection is implied, therefore, on establishments not included.

The symbol ⓘ on a town plan indicates the local tourist office from which further information can be obtained. The post-horn symbol indicates a post office.

In a time of rapid change it is difficult to ensure that all the information given is entirely accurate and up to date, and the possibility of error can never be completely eliminated. Although the publishers can accept no responsibility for inaccuracies and omissions, they are always grateful for corrections and suggestions for improvement.

Facts and Figures

Foreword

Canada has long enjoyed great popularity as a holiday destination. World famous natural beauty (the Niagara Falls and the impressive mountain scenery in the Banff and Jasper National Parks are just examples), immense areas of vast countryside, but also the cities rich in tradition such as Québec and Montréal and the vibrant developing cities including Toronto, Calgary, Edmonton and Vancouver with outstanding examples of modern architecture are all worth the journey. Canada has something for everyone – for those who enjoy strolling around town centres, lovers of nature and wildlife or those seeking adventure.

In the limited space of this volume only a selection of the countless sights of interest to the visitor in this vast North American country can be included.

General

Location and area

Canada, the largest country in the world, with an area of 9,997,000sq.km/3,859,845sq.miles occupies the northern half of the North American sub-continent. The most southerly point of Canada is latitude 41°41'N, the most northerly point 83°7'N, the most easterly longitude 52°37'W and the most westerly 141°W. This vast country stretches over approximately 5500km/3417 miles from the Atlantic to the Pacific Ocean (six time zones). From Ellesmere Island in the north to the Niagara Falls in the south is a distance of 4600km/1840 miles. Its area is comparable to that of Europe as far as the Urals. Canada's highest point is Mount Logan (6050m/19,849ft) in the north-west.

Leading economic power

Canada belongs to the world's leading economic nations. An enormous wealth of mineral and vegetable resources, fertile land for agriculture and forestry along with an immense potential for hydro-electric power have contributed to Canada becoming one of the world's leading economic powers. Practically all minerals essential to modern industry can be extracted in Canada. This North American country ranges among the world's leading producers of potash, nickel, zinc, copper, gold and iron.

◀ The St Lawrence River near Québec (city)

Geography

This gigantic country possesses considerable quantities of coal, oil and gas (especially in the province of Alberta). Water power, available in excess, is harnessed by the huge hydro-electric stations. Providing enormous amounts of energy (particularly electricity) to the neighbouring USA contributes to the Canadian export surplus.

Hydro-electricity constitutes about 70% of electricity produced in Canada. Almost 50% of the country is covered in forests. The boreal pine forests, which stretch from the Atlantic far into the northwest (Yukon), are an almost inexhaustible source of wood pulp and cellulose for the paper industry. Two-fifths of the world's newspaper comes from Canada! The forests in the west, where there is more rainfall, provide the best quality wood for felling and building in large quantities.

Not much more than 7% of the country is suitable for agriculture. Yet the Canadian Prairies, where four fifths of Canada's arable land is found, are one of the most important granaries in the world. In the west of Canada cattle rearing and fattening take place on a vast scale. Milk production is concentrated in the St Lawrence Lowlands where vegetable growing is also important.

Canadian industry is highly developed. Technology and research in the areas of energy production, mining, forestry and food production as well as telecommunications and transport have earned international prestige.

Population density

More than four fifths of the total area is uninhabited. In sharp contrast the population is concentrated in an almost 500km/310 miles wide strip in the south of the country, parallel to the US border. Almost 80% of Canada's population live here. Two thirds of all Canadians are concentrated in the south-east of the country (southern areas of Ontario and Québec provinces), especially in the highly industrialised areas – Toronto–Hamilton–London–Windsor and in the conurbation of Montréal. Other densely populated areas are the Edmonton–Calgary axis in the plains of the eastern slope of the Rocky Mountains, around the Pacific harbour of Vancouver, the region around the capital Ottawa and the St Lawrence Lowlands with the historical city of Québec.

Geography

Geographical framework

The geographical framework of Canada encompasses the geology, the topography, the soil, the rivers and lakes, the climate, and forms the basis for human settlement. The extreme conditions in Canada are apparent from only 11% of the total area being populated and cultivated. Minerals, soils, rivers, lakes and woods have potential economic value. These natural resources influence both human settlement and the economy but the size of the country also determines their development and economic value.

Six time zones with between 3½ and 8 hours difference from Greenwich Mean Time, a distance of 5500km/3417 miles from east to west coast and 4600km/1840 miles from north to south provide striking evidence of the size of the country. Five different zones of "northerness" are identified according to the degree of development: the Central Zone or Okumene which is divided into four by mountain ranges and in which 90% of all Canadians live, the Near North which directly adjoins it and is characterised by the boreal wood with little settlement apart from mining towns, the Mid-North, which is almost completely uninhabited and essentially comprises the Yukon Territory, the Northwest Territories and Labrador (mostly tundra and forests), and finally the Far North, which is generally inaccessible, heavily glaciated with only very few isolated settlements.

Some Canadian geographers include the Extreme North, the Arctic, in this category.

Geological formation, Ice Age morphology

The oldest core of Canada and the whole North American continent is the Canadian Shield, comparable with the Baltic Shield in Europe. It stretches out in a circle from Hudson Bay. This "Ukraton" consists of several layers of ancient folded rocks dating back to the Archean period, with the newest fold being Pre-Cambrian 800 to 1100 million years ago. Over long geological periods of time rock from the Canadian Shield formed part of the neighbouring areas.

The "Border Lands" surround the lowlands and plateaux of the Canadian Shield. They are made up of the Arctic Lowland in the north, the Interior Plains in the west and St Lawrence Lowlands in the south. These tablelands consist of horizontal layers of sedimentary rock, deposited over long periods from the Cambrian to the Tertiary. The Pre-Cambrian stratum below is called the "Buried Platform".

This ring of lowlands and plateaux is encircled by an outer ring of mountains interspersed with high plateaux.

This upland ring begins in the south-east with the Appalachians which were formed during the Caledonian (about 450 to 390 million years ago) and Varistian (c. 300 million years ago) periods and, like the Varistian mountains of Central Europe, were later folded.
These older mountains, which only reach heights of around 2000m/6562ft, face the Rocky Mountains (Cordilleras) in the west, which are Alpidian i.e. 190 to 2 million years ago, are similar to the Alps and were formed from the Mesozoic to the Tertiary periods. The Laramic and Nevadian mountain formation was most significant here with mountain chains and enclosed plateaux.

The third outer ring of mountains are the Innuitians in the north, the so-called Franklin Orogen, folded in the Palaeozoic period and heavily glaciated owing to their northerly position with high Alpine features.

Apart from the geological structure, i.e. the rock formation, another important element in the shaping of the landscape was glaciation. As in Europe North America was subject to four phases of glaciation. They are the Nebraska Ice Age (beginning 600,000 years ago), the Canada Ice Age (beginning 480,000 years ago), the Illinois Ice Age (beginning 230,000 years ago) and the Wisconsin Ice Age (beginning 72,000 years ago). During the Pleistocene era 97% of Canada's present-day landmass was covered in ice. The only exceptions were the southernmost parts of Alberta and Saskatchewan and small areas of the Yukon. Almost all evidence of the first three ice ages was erased by the most recent ice age, the Wisconsin Ice Age, which corresponds to our Quaternary Ice Age.
The term "glacial series" refers to the land formations left behind after the ice has melted following a fairly long static period. There is a regular sequence of glacial accumulation (deposition):
1. the icing over inland from north to south left undulating, rounded ground moraines, belts of hilly terminal moraines, sand plains and glacial valleys,
2. the local Alpine-type glaciation left corries, terminal moraines and glacial drift.
With inland glaciation reaching as far as the present-day USA the prevalent form of landscape in Canada is that of ground moraines.

In Canada there were several isolated centres of glaciation. The Laurentide Ice Sheet had such a centre to the east and one to the west of Hudson Bay in Keewatin. The eastern centre divided into various bodies of ice during the Wisconsin Ice Age, which were active independently at times. Among these were the Arctic Islands in the

Margin notes

Canadian Shield

Border Lands

Buried Platform

Mountains

Appalachians

Rocky Mountains

Innuitians

Glacial evidence

Centres of glaciation

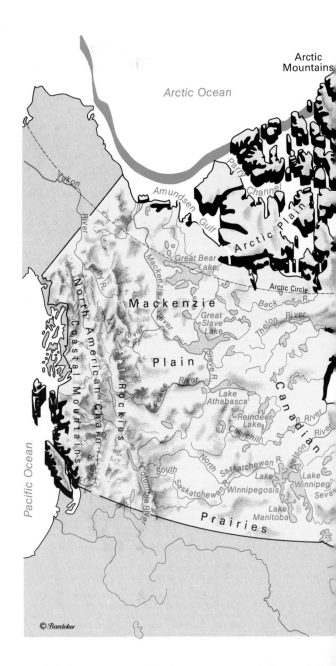

Mountains
Rivers and Lakes

Baffin
Bay

Davis Strait

Baffin
Island

Foxe
Basin

Atlantic

Labrador

Sea

Ocean

Hudson Strait

Ungava
Bay

son
ay

Rivière Caniapiscau

Labrador

Churchill R.

James
Bay

La Grande Rivière

Appalachians

Cabot Strait

ny River

Shield

Lake
Nipigon

Lake
Superior

Ottawa River

St. Lawrence River

Lake
Huron

Lake
Ontario

Plain of
St Lawrence

Lake
Erie

On the edge of the Arctic

north. The Appalachians were also independently glaciated, and a further large centre of glacial activity was situated in the mountainous zone of the Cordilleras. South of the 48th line of latitude, which roughly corresponds to Canada's southern border, the glacial complexes of the Cordilleras breaks down into smaller complexes.

This perspective shows already that the centres of glacial activity are located in the upland areas because of the wet winters with abundant snow. This applies to the Cordilleras, the Appalachians and also to Labrador, whereas various theories have been discussed regarding Keewatin, which is not of a high altitude.

The terminal moraines are situated just beyond the Canadian Border where older ice ages are identifiable. The Illinois Ice Age near St Louis, on the same latitude as Sicily, pushed south. The main thrust of the Wisconsin Ice Age reached the New York area about 20,000 years ago. Since then the ice has oscillatingly withdrawn and left behind numerous glacial features, as well as a whole drainage network for the meltwater.

Apart from the upper areas of the Cordilleras parts of Baffin, Devon, Axel Heiberg and Ellesmere Islands are permanently covered in snow and ice.

Glacial lakes

The huge glacial lakes are an outstanding feature, among these Lake Agassiz was by far the largest with an area of 500,000sq.km/ 193,050sq.miles. This lake, twice the size of Germany, had a maximum depth of 200m/656ft. As the ice withdrew it created Lake Ojibway-Barlow with an area of 175,000sq.km/67,567sq miles, i.e. 350 times the size of Lake Constance. Finally, the whole series of Great Lakes belongs to the group of lakes beyond the boundary of the mighty sheets of ice, which were already tectonically formed. Lake Athabaska, the Great Slave Lake and the Great Bear Lake also mark the boundary of former ice sheets.

Hudson Bay underwent great changes and after the post-glacial rise of the land in the south was encircled with a layer of marine clay (Clay Belt). Similarly to the Baltic Shield in Europe the disappearance of the massive ice cover caused an isostatic rise to the Canadian Shield in North America, while the melting of the glaciers led to an eustatic rise in sea level. This interplay of isostasis and eustasis has affected the morphology of vast areas of Canada.

All in all it must be said that the Ice Age has transformed this region. An extensive network of rivers, uneven gradients with fast-flowing rivers and waterfalls are widespread. Drumlins and osers (see below) are to be found in many places, particularly west of Hudson Bay and North Québec. In regions of raised marine clay the soil is fertile as in the Clay Belt.

Drumlins are elongated ground moraines – between 100m and 2km long – with a steeply sloping rear side and dropping away gently on the other in the direction of the flow of ice; they have an elliptical outline. They were formed in places where the glacier met an obstacle.

The so-called "oser" (eskers) are very long embankments, vertical to the edge of the ice, formed by the debris deposited by glacial melt-water before it flows from the glacier, when the glacier is stationary.

Oser

The Canadian Shield – the dominant geological feature of Canada – encompasses an area of over 5 million sq.km/1,930,501 sq.miles and covers about 43% of the total land surface. It stretches as far as the great glacial lakes in the west; its highest points in the east are on Baffin Island and in Labrador. Some of its geological formations date back to the earliest geological periods of time. The characteristic rocks are granite and gneiss, in which grey boulder clay or metamorphised sandstones are present. Conglomerates, sandstones and limestones are not so common.

Canadian Shield
Ukraton

As granite and gneiss are the most resistant to erosion, numerous flat crests with rocks scraped smooth by the ice and hollows can be recognised. The sea level is relatively low, between 200–600m/656–1968ft. The Shield adjoins Hudson Bay, which is surrounded by a clay belt.

Hudson Bay itself has only an average depth of 100m/328ft and a maximum depth of 230m/745ft and was therefore subject to severe changes caused by the isostatic and eustatic fluctuations. Former beaches can be easily identified indicating a phased withdrawal of the sea. The debris from weathering which had accumulated in hollows was cleared out by the ice and the rock crests worn down.

Hudson Bay

Although the Canadian Shield is of little agricultural value its mineral wealth, its giant forests and water power are of great importance to the economy. The minerals comprise chiefly metal ores, but asbestos, spar, mica and graphite are found. The most important reserves, according to output, are iron, nickel, copper, zinc, gold, uranium, plati-nium and silver. The mines are situated on the southern edge of the Shield and were discovered from the 1890s onwards with the de-velopment of the railways. Other sites are in the north-west of the Canadian Shield and in the Labrador-Trog with its iron reserves. The many deep rivers with their numerous falls were ideal rafting routes, today they are used as sites for hydro-electric power stations.

Mineral wealth

The "interior plains" are bordered by the Canadian Shield in the east, the Cordilleras in the west and in contrast to the Canadian Shield are the ideal wheat-growing region of Canada. They stretch from the Arctic Ocean over 2600km/1615 miles to the border with the USA and in the south are turned over to fertile land for cultivation. They occupy about 15% of Canadian territory. The underlying rock consists of massive

Interior Plains
General

sediments, deposited on the base rock of the Shield which slopes gently to the east. Devonian and chalk series are most common, where the abundant reserves of oil and gas are to be found. Strata of chalk and Tertiary material form the final layer of sediment, prevalent in the south and west. The present-day surface was mainly a consequence of the Pleistocene Ice Age when material was deposited in changing forms.

Steppes

As in the USA the southern area of the Canadian Plains consists of stepped countryside, which has three areas (steppes) clearly separated fom each other by two prominent tiers. In the east – bordering on the Canadian Shield – the first area is lowland which is referred to, from south to north, as the Manitoba, Saskatchewan and Slave Lowland with an average height of 300m/984ft. Large areas of this fertile lowland were once part of Lake Agassiz and are still subject to flooding today. It is an extremely flat, monotonous landscape with massive delta-like deposits.

Manitoba Escarpment

The lowland is bordered in the west by a prominent tier, the Manitoba Escarpment, formed from harder deposits of chalk. The tier faces east and rises 200–500m/656–1640ft above the lowland, with a height of 800m/2624ft in places. This steppe is broken up by rivers into individual ranges of hills (National Park "Riding Mountains" with a variety of fauna).

Manitoba Escarpment, Saskatchewan Plain

In the west the Manitoba Escarpment adjoins the Saskatchewan Plain, which rises to a height of 300–600m/984–1968ft and displays a variety of relief. Here are higher areas with undulating ground moraines and extremely flat areas of former glacial lakes (in the surroundings of Regina, for example). The surface is modified by glacial activity with sandy crests, kettle holes, fields of dunes, drainage channels among others.

Alberta Plain

A third tier is formed by the Alberta Plain, which lies at a height of 600–900m/1968–2952ft. Its relief is prominent with hilly ground moraines and plateaux, formed partly form Tertiary material.

Cypress Hills

The Cypress Hills in the south are an unusual feature rising to 1470m/5708ft and regarded as nunataks, which were not covered in ice. The Mackenzie Lowland takes over from the Alberta Plain in the north-west, a huge alluvial plain which is drained by Canada's longest river, 4240km/2634 miles long, with a drainage area of 1.8 million sq.km/694,980sq.miles.

Economic potential

The Interior Plains are of great economic potential. In the south the soils favourable to agriculture are of particular importance. In the north there are giant forests. There are also abundant reserves of tar sands in North Alberta and of oil and gas in the south. Brown coal and potash are also present.

St Lawrence Lowland General, Morphology

The St Lawrence Lowland only covers 3% of the Canadian landmass but it is one of the most important areas of the country for the economy. Its geological construction consists primarily of Palaezoic sediments which overlay the Canadian Shield. A special feature are the volcanic intrusions, which occurred during the Mezoic period and now remain as projections in the region. Among these projections is Mont Royal, in the centre of Montreal, at a height of 234m/767ft the most well known. In Southern Ontario there are many examples of resistant Silurian limestone deposits carved into steps.

Niagara Escarpment

The Niagara Escarpment is responsible for the formation of the Niagara Falls and the Niagara Gorge. At Niagara Falls Goat Island separates the Canadian Horseshoe Falls (49m/160ft high, 790m/2591ft wide) from the USA Falls (51m/167ft high, 350m/1148ft wide). Niagara Gorge is 11km/7 miles in length and was caused by retrograde erosion of about 1.4m/4½ft per annum (over the last 200 years).

The variety of minerals ranges from smaller reserves of oil and gas to salt, gypsum, limestone, gravel, sand and asbestos. Ancient lake beds provide ideal soils for agriculture. Below the Great Lakes the St Lawrence River crosses the Canadian Shield by a series of waterfalls necessitating the technical extension to the St Lawrence Seaway.

Minerals

The fertile clays of the Champlain Sea are also of importance. It extends from the St Lawrence River through the Champlain Valley to the Hudson and is all that remains today of the Champlain Lake.

Champlain Valley

Only the most northerly slopes of the Appalachians are inside Canadian territory. They cover an area of 500,000sq.km/193,050sq.miles, yet only cover 4% of Canada. During the Caledonian and Varistian periods of mountain building chiefly old Palaeozoic sedimentary rock was folded and metamorphised. Granite intrusions can also be found. Later this region was folded and in the Tertiary broken up into a mosaic of fragments.

The Appalachians
General

As a result of this development there are numerous morphological units with complicated rock formations consisting primarily of limestones, sandstones, quarzite, conglomerates and granite. There are three distinct areas – the upper mountain ranges, the Highlands – the undulating plateaux, the Uplands – the lower-lying areas, the Lowlands. The highest points are 1268m/4160ft in the Gaspé peninsula, 814m/2670ft in Newfoundland and 532m/1745ft on Cape Breton Island of Nova Scotia. They are continued in the New England states where the highest point in the Green Mountains of Vermont is 1339m/4393ft and the White Mountains in New Hampshire reach 1917m/6289ft. The plateaux are on an altitude of between 150 to 300m/492 to 984ft.
    Below 150m/492ft lie the Lowlands, which include regions of Newfoundland situated on the Gulf, areas of New Brunswick and Nova Scotia including Prince Edward Island. The rounded shapes of the Highlands were formed during the Pleistocene period when the Appalachians were covered in ice. Another result of the Ice Age were the thin coverings of loam debris in the valleys and coastal plains, the fluvioglacial deposits, which gave rise to settlement strips in New Brunswick and New Scotland. The Annapolis and St John's Valleys are examples.

Highlands,
Uplands,
Lowlands

The economic importance of the Appalachian region lies in its extensive mixed woodlands which cover 70% of the surface area. The Lowlands and the regions around Fundy Bay and Prince Edward Island offer the right conditions for arable land. The specialist crops in the Annapolis Valley are famous. The coastline with its many bays has numerous fishing ports and some important ports such as St John's, Halifax and Sydney.

Economy

There is a wide variety of minerals but they are not particularly important to the economy. Asbestos is to be found in the Eastern Townships and coal found near Sydney, was extracted back in 1825. Zinc, lead and copper ores occur in the strata of the older Palaeozoic era. Less important are deposits of iron, gypsum, salt, barite and oil.

Minerals

The considerable difference between tides is of economic potential. Those in Fundy Bay reach 16m/52ft and at spring tide 21m/68ft making them the highest in the world.

Tides

The Cordilleras encompass an area of 1.6 million sq.km/ 617,760sq.miles, that is 13% of Canada's landmass. They form part of the gigantic 14,000km/8699 mile long chain which stretches from

Cordilleras
General

Central Purcell: Mountain range in British Columbia

Tierra del Fuego to Alaska. In Canada they extend for 2200km/ 1367 miles varying in width from 400 to 800km/248 to 497 miles. Since Pre-Cambrian times a geosyncline developed here which was folded during the Alpidian mountain formation from the Mezoic period to the Tertiary. The Cordilleras have a very complicated geological formation with folds, faults, tectonic rising and sinking accompanied by volcanic activity and plutonic intrusions. The Ice Age provided the final layer with glaciation during the Pleistocene period.

Geographical construction

As in the neighbouring USA three zones can be distinguished: the eastern Rocky Mountains, the intermontane high basins and the Pacific coastal mountains. North of the 60th latitude the high mountain chain of the Rocky Mountains becomes a series of high plateaux.

The Rocky Mountains are bordered in the east by the foothills and in the west by the Rocky Mountains Trench. To the north they become the Mackenzie and Porcupine Mountains. The mountainous zones are formed from folded sediment of the Cambrian and Palaeozoic, with widespread limestones and quarzite. In the foothills Mezoic sandstones predominate. The Rocky Mountains are especially impressive in southern Alberta, where they soar up to 3000m/9842ft above the foothills. The highest mountain of the entire chain is here, Mount Robson 3954m/12,972ft. The Mackenzie Mountains almost reach 3000m/9842ft, the Porcupine Mountains about 1500m/4921ft. The often horizontal strata and glacial evidence can be made out on the massive mountain blocks which differ from the Alps in having less sharp ridges and peaks.

Columbia Icefield

The biggest icefield of the Rocky Mountains is the 337sq.km/ 130sq.miles and about 1000m/3280ft deep Columbia Icefield. It feeds three great rivers: the North Saskatchewan River which flows into Hudson Bay, the Athabasca River which joins the Mackenzie River and then the North Polar Sea, and the Columbia River, which ends up in the Pacific. It is apparent that the Rocky Mountains are the main watershed of the continent.

The Rocky Mountain Trench is a pronounced depression which continues into the region of the Yukon Plateau where there are several faults in the trench in the north-west. It consists of long depressions up to 20km/12 miles wide with steep slopes that are often terrassed. This tectonic feature was deepened by river and glacial erosion and deposited elsewhere by meltwater. Many rivers such as the Cootenay, the Columbia River, the Fraser River among others follow this trench for a while, before escaping laterally through neighbouring mountain chains.

Rocky Mountain
Trench

Two plateaux make up the intermontane zone: the Nechako-Fraser Plateau in the south and the Yukon Plateau in the north.
   The Nechako-Fraser Plateau lies at a height of about 1200m/3937ft and is filled with glacial deposits, which are dissected by the dammed rivers (Fraser, Thompson, Okanagan) that resemble lakes in places.
   The Yukon Plateau, which continues into Alaska, is 1000m/3280ft high and surrounded by mountains more than 2000m/6560ft high. The western part of the Yukon Plateau is unusual in that it was not glaciated.
   The Yukon Plateau is drained by the Yukon River and its tributaries which in parts cut in up to 600m/1968ft deep. The breaking away of the ice often leads to massive flooding.

Intermontane
Zone

The Pacific chains of the Cordilleras border the interior basin zone in the west. Three longitudinal zones can be distinguished: the coastal mountains on the mainland, the outer mountain ranges on the offshore islands, which run into the St Elias Mountains on the mainland and the trench lying between both chains including the narrow strip of coastal lowland.

Coastal mountains

The interior zone is divided by the extreme northern part of the Cascades, the Pacific and Kitimat chains and the Boundary Mountains on the border with the Alaskan Panhandle. It continues into the Alaska Range, where Mount McKinley is the highest mountain in North America at 6193m/20,318ft. In contrast to the Rocky Mountains the Pacific Mountains are predominantly made up of granite and gneiss. There are many volcanic deposits and intrusions. Sharp ridges, jagged peaks and heavy glaciation are common characteristics of these coastal ranges.

Interior ranges

The outer range of mountains begins on Vancouver Island, stretching north to the Queen Charlotte Islands and the Alexander archipelago, including the St Elias Mountains on the mainland. This range, reaching heights of 2200m/7217ft on Vancouver Island, 1000m/3280ft on Queen Charlotte Islands, culminates in the St Elias Mountains with the highest point in the whole of Canada (Mount Logan 5951m/19,524ft). The Elias Mountains are surrounded by massive ice-fields from which surge huge glacial rivers.

Outer ranges

Individual glaciers have joined together to cause glaciation in the foothills. The 42km/26 mile long Malespina glacier which stretches as far as Alaska is one of the largest and most famous in the world.

The parallel ranges of the coastal mountains surround a depression known as the coastal trough. It runs from the Puget Sound between the mainland and the islands and includes the coastal lowland. This depression is also one of the most important areas of settlement in the far west of Canada, because it is at its widest on the north and south

Coastal Trough

Geography

side of Vancouver Island and is enlarged in the south by the Fraser River and its delta.

Volcanic activity, earthquakes

The geological make-up of the Cordilleras would be incomplete without the inclusion of the frequent earthquakes and the volcanic activity. Large areas of the intermontane basins are covered in lava, which rose from separate chimneys during the Miocene and Pliocene periods. There are 150 active volcanoes in British Columbia and the Yukon region for the Quaternary. They are mostly shield volcanoes but with some smaller volcanic peaks running along the lines of weakness. The last lava eruption is said to have taken place around 200 years ago in northern British Columbia. At present there are no active volcanoes in the Canadian Cordilleras. However, Mount St Helens, which erupted in 1980, is situated not far south of the US border in the state of Washington.

Economy

As in the Appalachians the forests are an important economic resource in the Cordilleras, covering 70% of the area with valuable species such as fir, spruce and cedar. Another important resource is the wealth of fish in the coastal waters and the waterfalls on the rivers favour salmon fishing. There are only relatively narrow strips of land along the coastal depression suitable for agriculture on the lower reaches of the Fraser River and in the Okanagan Valley with its well known special crops.

Minerals are also a source of significant economic potential. Even before the turn of the century the gold reserves attracted numerous settlers to isolated parts of the Rocky Mountains. Nowadays copper, lead and zinc ores play an important role. Iron ore, coal and molybdenum are other important minerals. The hydro-electricity reserves are of great economic value. As the rivers contain a great deal of water because of the high precipitation levels and have high waterfalls the water power can be directly harnessed. A world-famous example of this economic exploitation are the aluminium works at Kitimat.

Tourism

Finally tourism is of great economic importance, inspired on the one hand by the dramatic scenery with huge mountains, glaciers, lakes and wonderful coastlines and cultural highlights on the other. The towns of Vancouver and Victoria captivate the visitor with their attractive locations. The impressive craftwork of the coastal Indians is recognised throughout the world.

Arctic Lowland and the Innuitians
Arctic Lowland

The Arctic region of Canada includes the archipelago of islands north of the mainland, which is separated from the rest of Canada by several waterways including the Amundsen Strait and the Hudson Strait. It falls into the Arctic Lowland which, with an area of 1 million sq.km/386,100sq.miles, covers 8% of Canada's landmass. Both regions are divided from another by the Parry Channel.

In the Arctic Lowland there are horizontal sediments of the older Palaeozoic period. Limestones and dolomite overlay the deeper subsoil of the adjoining Canadian Shield. A narrow coastal strip also makes up the Arctic Lowland stretching as far as the Mackenzie delta. It is formed mainly from Tertiary and Pleistocene sands and is characterised by numerous river courses and lakes.

Innuitians

Bordering the Arctic Lowland, which from north to south rises from 100m/328ft to 700m/2296ft, are the Innuitians. The range was folded during the Palaeozoic period and consists of two chains, which encircle deeper semi-circular areas. The Innuitians soar over 1000m/3280ft reaching their highest peaks on Baffin Island with a height of 2591m/8500ft and Ellesmere Island with 2926m/9599ft. The Innuitians are covered in extensive ice-fields from which single mountains protrude as steep-sloped nunataks.

Glacial morphology

The geomorphology of the Arctic regions is particularly interesting. Pleistocene glaciation and the present-day glaciers created high-

Alpine chains of mountains with deeply incised fiords and far-reaching valley systems. The micro relief displays a multitude of small features. There are frost-patterns on the earth with stripes, circles and polygons, each pattern depending on the inclination of the slope.

These ice formations created by the high pressure of groundwater producing earth hills are widespread and rely on an ice lens in the centre for their dome shape. These thufure can be 1m high and 2m radius and are mostly extensively distributed.

Palsas are larger and can be between 2–30m radius and over 8m high. They have an ice centre which is protected by an insulating peat cover. If the cover is destroyed the ice centre melts and the hill collapses in on itself. Only hollows remain which fill up with water in summer. The existence of these so-called thermokarst has only recently been the subject of research.

The most interesting feature are pingos which occur in large numbers in the Mackenzie delta. They are cone-shaped hills with a radius of over 400m and a maximum height of over 50m. They were formed by groundwater coming under hydrostatic pressure caused by the advancing permafrost breaking onto the surface. Small craters may form in the pingos as the ice thaws.

The Arctic region of Canada is not of prime economic importance as the minerals present – coal, gas and oil – can only be exploited at tremendous cost. However, the discovery of oil at Prudhoe Bay in North Alaska (1968) was significant and was continued on Canadian soil to the east. In 1970 larger oil and gas fields were discovered on the Mackenzie delta.

In conclusion the geological and geomorphological construction is relatively distinct. Of a total area of 12.2 million sq.km/4,710,424 sq.miles including 2.2 million sq.km/849,420sq.miles of water (Hudson Bay, Gulf of St Lawrence, Arctic Seas) the Canadian Shield comprises 5.3 million sq.km/2,046,332sq.miles (43%), the Lowlands 4.1 million sq.km/1,583,011 sq.miles (34%), the Mountains 2.7 million sq.km/1,042,471sq.miles (22%) and the coastal plains 0.1 million sq.km/38,610sq.miles.

Thufure

Palsas

Pingos

Economy

Climate

Overall Canada has a cold winter climate with long winters and short, temperate summers. 60% of the land area, 75% according to some figures, has average annual temperatures below 0°C/32°F. 70% of the country has mid-January temperatures of below −10°C/14°F and 30% does not exceed an average temperature of 10°C/50°F even in July. Only in the populated south of the country is the climate more varied and changes over a small area.
    The following factors determine the climate:
1. The northern location – only a small tip of Canada on Lake Eerie reaches 42° north (latitude of Rome). The largest part of the country lies between 48° north (western border with US): and 70° north (mainland coast on the Mackenzie estuary, still south of North Cape in Europe!). The northern location increases the differences in sunlight, daylight and temperature between summer and winter considerably. For over 90% of the country the seasonal temperature range is over 30°C/86°F.
2. The size of the continent: the vast interior of the country is only marginally affected by maritime influences, which is reflected in the continental climate with low rainfall and high ranges of temperature.
3. The surface features: the Rocky Mountains, lying across the direction of the prevailing west winds, act as a barrier to the influence of the

General

Pacific Ocean on the interior, contributing to the formation of the Prairies. On the other hand they favour the north–south exchange of air masses and extreme changes in the weather (e.g. blizzards).

4. The temperature and currents in the adjoining seas: the fringes of the Curo-Shio current, comparable with the Gulf Stream in Europe, bring relatively warm water along the Pacific coast to the north creating even temperatures along the coast and high rainfall in the coastal ranges. On the east coast of Canada the Labrador current, in contrast, brings cold water south; in the whole of eastern Canada and around Hudson Bay, the "ice-box" of North America, the temperatures are significantly lower than those of a similar latitude in the west or in Europe – with far-reaching consequences for vegetation, population and land use.

On the basis of these factors the following climatic divisions can be made:

in the south following each other from west to east:

1. the mild winter-warm summer climate of the Pacific coast
2. the cold winter-dry summer climate of the Prairies
3. the cold winter-warm summer climate between the Great Lakes and St Lawrence River

In the north, which covers the greatest area:

4. the boreal snow-forest climate
5. the polar-arctic climate

Distribution of land and water

The distribution of land and water has an important influence on the temperature. Owing to the vast landmass Canada has a predominantly continental climate. The annual range of mean daytime temperatures extends from 38°C/100°F in Winnipeg, 44.6°C/111°F at Yellowknife, sinking to 15/50°C°F in Vancouver on the Pacific coast. Whereas the January temperatures in Vancouver are on average 2.4°C/36°F, in the Arctic north they sink to −28.6°C/−19°F (Yellowknife) and −32.6°C/−26°F (Resolute). Even close to the coast in Labrador temperatures fall to −22.7°C/−9°F in Schefferville and in the relatively favourable climate of the St Lawrence Lowlands the January temperatures are −8.9°C/16°F in Montréal and −11.6°C/12°F in Québec.

Along the Pacific coast a relatively narrow zone enjoys a milder climate caused by the warm Curo Current (Pacific North Equatorial Current). Hudson Bay has the opposite effect acting as an "ice box". On the Atlantic coast the maritime climate of the Gulf Stream is countered by the cold Labrador current, which carries the icebergs as far south as Newfoundland. Whereas the July temperatures, for example, Winnipeg 19.7°C/67°F and even Yellowknife at 16°C/60°F, are comparable with central European temperatures, the winter temperatures are much lower. This is apparent at Winnipeg in the Prairies, which lies on the same latitude as the German towns Mainz and Frankfurt am Main, but the average January temperature is −18.3°C/−1°F, compared with +1°C/34°F of the above two towns.

Mountain ranges

The lack of east to west mountain ranges has a significant influence on the climate of Canada. In Europe the Pyrenées, Alps and Dinaric Alps act as the "fur caps" of Spain, Italy and Dalmatia but the wide open spaces of Canada lack such protection. It allows uninterrupted exchange of air masses between north and south to take place, which can transport cold masses south in winter and hot air northwards in summer. The dominant north–south direction of the mountain zones is conducive to this exchange of air causing windward and lee effects in a west to east cross-section of Canada, especially in the Cordilleras. These windward and lee effects are characterised by the precipitation, with heavy rainfall on the western slopes and relative dryness on the eastern side. An example is Vancouver Island, where a 14 year average of 6633mm/261in. was recorded on Henderson Island with a record

8222mm/324in. in 1931. On the other hand Penticton in the rain shadow of the mountain chains in the intramontane zone receives only
296mm/12in. of rainfall and Regina in the Prairies 398mm/16in.

Canada lies in the area of westerlies which are governed by air pressure formations. Such areas of low pressure are found in the Aleutians
and near Iceland whereas conversely a flat high is formed in the Arctic.
Areas of high pressure are also found near the Azores or Bermuda; in
summer they can move north and influence the Pacific coast or eastern
Canada.

West wind zone

There are five major cyclonic paths which cross Canada. In the west
there are ridges on the Pacific coast, in Alberta the leeward location
causes a pronounced "cyclone genesis", brought about by the air
masses from the north and south. A further cyclonic path follows the
Great Lakes and the St Lawrence Lowlands, another the Atlantic coast
in a north-easterly direction. In addition there are Arctic cyclones which
rarely reach the lower latitudes.

Cyclonic paths

High air pressure and extremes of temperature often cause dangerous
storms which develop in the country itself or come up from the south.
Blizzards are the most common, i.e. sudden blasts of cold Arctic air
accompanied by snowstorms and wind speeds of more than
40kph/25mph. Such a blizzard can last several hours with limited visibility. The Prairies are most affected by them. An example of a devastating blizzard was December 15th, 1965 when there was a snowstorm
with speeds of 88kph/55mph and temperatures of −35°C/−31°F. In
1966 in Winnipeg a blizzard reached 118kph/73mph bringing a snow
cover of 35cm/14in. in a very short time. When air masses from the
south are present sleet and long periods of snowfall can occur.

Cold air advances,
blizzards

Hurricanes which originate in tropical latitudes and, somewhat
weaker, cause incessant rainfall on reaching eastern Canada, are particularly dreaded. Examples include Hurricane Beth that brought
300mm/12in. of rain within two days in August 1971, or Hurricane
Hazel which caused floods and destruction and even claimed lives in
October 1954.

Hurricanes

Unlike hurricanes tornados occur only relatively infrequently. There
are about five per year. But there have been horrific examples: in
Regina 41 people were killed and enormous damage was caused in
1912. A tornado in Windsor in 1974 left eight dead.

Tornados

The Chinook is a well known local wind, a foehn wind in Alberta.
Adiabatically warmed air results in melting snow and a sudden rise in
temperature. In Pincher Creek in southern Alberta a temperature increase from −18°C/0°F to +3°C/37°F within an hour was recorded.

Chinook

The northern light or polar light appears in the form of ribbons, arches,
bundles of rays and crowns and may be red, greenish or bluish-white.
It is between 100 to 1100km/62 to 683 miles high at the most, increasing
towards the equator. It is created by "corpuscles" (electrically charged
particles given off by the sun at high speeds) in the earth's magnetic
field being attracted to the poles. On meeting the atmosphere they are
ionised by its gases; causing the air molecules to glow. The spectrum
mainly consists of atoms of oxygen and bands of nitrogen.
    The zone of northern light encircles the magnetic North Pole at some
distance and is very narrow. Over a cycle of 27 days and in a time span
of 11 years a certain periodicity in strength and frequency of appearance can be observed.

Northern light,
polar light

Meteorologists assume a worldwide warming of 3°C/5°F on average
over the next 50 to 100 years, which will result in serious changes in the
Arctic regions more than anywhere. Whereas a rise of 1°C/2°F is pre-

Greenhouse
effect

The "Northern Lights" – an impressive natural phenomenon

dicted for the tropics the temperature in the Polar regions is set to rise by 12°C/21°F. The acknowledged reasons for the general warming of the earth's atmosphere are, among others, the increased amounts of carbon dioxide.

Such a development would completely unbalance the sensitive tundra landscape. If the permafrost floor melts rivers of mud will carve out so-called "thermo-limestone scenery". In the short Arctic summers the tundra vegetation still insulates the underlying ground. The dramatic final stage of the process would be the melting of the ice cap.

Destruction of the ozone layer

As the ozone layer is at its thinnest at the poles, it is here where it can first be destroyed. The influence of sunlight on the increased concentration of fluorochlorocarbons in the upper layer of the mantle of air around the earth results in the release of chlorine atoms which attack the vital ozone layer.

Permafrost
General

The reasons for the permafrost floor are the limited amount of sunlight, low winter temperatures and a thin covering of snow. The underlying ground is cooled down greatly and the earth only thaws superficially in summer. There is a distinction between continuous and discontinuous permafrost. The continuous covers an area of 3 million sq.km/1,158,301sq.miles, which is twelve times the size of Great Britain, the discontinuous an area of 1.3 million sq.km/501,930sq.miles. The limits of the permafrost concur with −1°C/30°F and −7°C/19°F annual isotherms. The lack of vegetation in the tundra is conducive to cooling. The depth of the permafrost therefore increases northwards reaching 366mm/15in. in the Mackenzie delta, 548mm/21in. in Melville Island, with the depth to which thawing occurs seldom being more than a metre.

The discontinuous permafrost is mostly formed in the forest belt where it is not so cold, the vegetation cover resulting in thawing.

Owing to the greater degree of thawing the permafrost is restricted to northern slopes or bogs.

The permafrost has far-reaching consequences for people. Mining is not possible because of flooding. When laying surface pipelines cold aggregate has to be added to prevent the supports from sinking when the upper layer thaws. Roads are damaged as the frost causes the subsoil to break up and parts of the road sink and airfields become uneven. Houses sink down so that recently a method of building on pillars is being tried to provide circulation of air below the house. Insulation and cooling systems are often effective but electricity and water supplies are continually threatened. Waste and sewage disposal is problematic as biological and chemical breakdown is not possible. Even though many problems can be solved by technology it is at great expense and is a clear disadvantage of the north compared with the southern regions. This becomes extreme during the cold season.

Effects

Winter influences human life in many ways. The fight against the cold and storms, against darkness and snow demands a lot of energy. Coupled with this the size of the country brings additional problems. In the towns the houses and shopping malls need to be protected against the frost and weather. Transport is hampered by permafrost in summer and by snow in winter, with snowfalls obstructing traffic in the towns as well. On the other hand winter is the chief travel period in the north as the rivers and bogs are frozen and do not present an obstacle.

General effects in winter

The following paragraphs examine more closely the climatic details of these climatic zones with reference to graphs taken at typical climatic stations. In the graphs on pages 24/25 the annual range of temperature and precipitation is shown. The months are represented by letters. Temperatures are shown by a red band: the upper limit corresponds to the highest average daily temperature, the lower the lowest night. The mean daily temperature for each month can thus be read from top to bottom with a fair degree of accuracy.
    The height of the blue columns indicates how many millimetres of rainfall were recorded on average in each month.
    These graphs provide the answers to many of the particular questions of the individual traveller. Some examples: the visitor to Ottawa in the middle of July can ascertain from the upper and lower graph limits of the temperature curve that the night temperatures are as low as in Germany, but the daytime temperatures are 6°C/11°F higher. However, the visitor to Ottawa in February must be prepared for day time temperatures between −16 and −9°C/3 and 16°F, much lower than in Great Britain. The precipitation curve is equally informative: the rainfall levels from November to March in Vancouver are twice as high as in central Europe, whereas the temperatures are about the same.
    For places between the stations the climatic conditions can be estimated by applying simple rules, which follow.

Climatic graphs

Six climatic zones can be distinguished on the basis of temperature, precipitation, wind conditions. They are the Pacific coastal region, the Cordilleras, the Prairies, the St Lawrence Lowlands, the Atlantic region and the Arctic region.

Climatic regions

Canada's west coast has a maritime climate with high levels of precipitation and low daily and annual temperature variations. It is comparable with the climate of western Europe and very different from the climate of Canada's east coast (see below). The prevailing west winds carry the warmth from the ocean onto the land. At the same time the air humidity turns to precipitation in the form of rain in the mountain slopes. The amount of rainfall decreases from south to north. It depends heavily on the location on the coast with its fiords, bays, inlets and peninsulas and height. In the lee of the mountains and islands and

West coast (Vancouver climatic station)

Climate

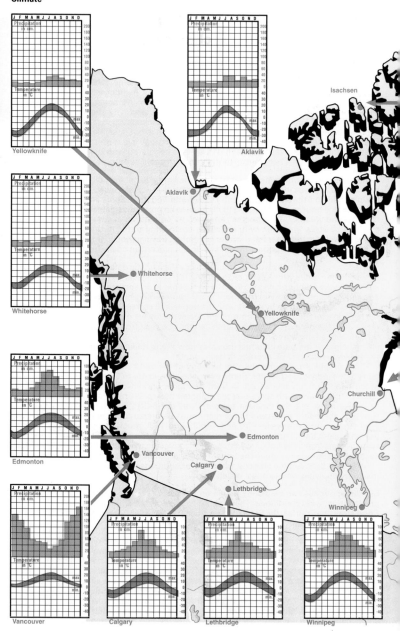

Yellowknife

Aklavik

Whitehorse

Edmonton

Vancouver

Calgary

Lethbridge

Winnipeg

Isachsen

Churchill

24

Thirteen typical regional climatic stations in Canada

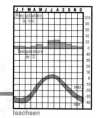

Isachsen

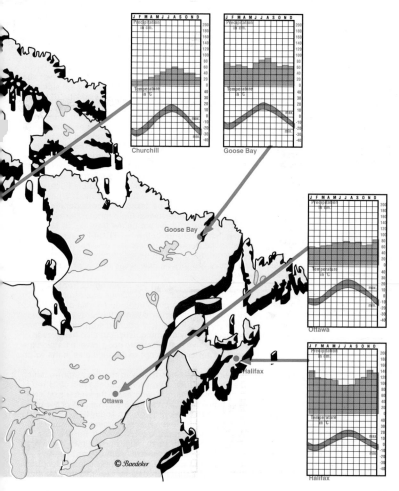

Churchill

Goose Bay

Goose Bay

Ottawa

Halifax

Halifax

© Baedeker

25

inside the bays the rainfall is considerably higher than on the outer edges of the coast or high altitudes in the mountains.

No other region of Canada has such mild weather. The temperature band for Vancouver is correspondingly narrow and only curves gently.

There is a distinct range of precipitation with maximum rainfall in winter and minimum in summer. The influence of the Mediterranean climate further south on the Pacific coast is felt here. Heading north the temperatures drop (annual mean temperature in Vancouver 10.2°C/50°F, in Prince Rupert on the north end of the Canadian coast 7.6°C/46°F). Further north, as far as US territory (Panhandle), temperatures fall and precipitation increases until widespread glaciation is found with glacier tongues forming down to sea level.

There is a more pronounced difference in climate inland than northwards. A narrow strip in the eastern hinterland of Vancouver has a cool temperate climate, comparable with that of the southerly St Lawrence region. Towards the east a cold temperate and increasingly dry climate follows. The climatic station Whitehorse at 65° north and about 300km/186 miles from the coast only experiences 257mm/10in. annual rainfall. In comparison the Rocky Mountains are only partially glaciated.

The cold winter and dry summer climate of the Prairies (Lethbridge climatic station)

The damp Pacific air masses are dried out after passing over the coastal mountains and Rocky Mountains, so that on the lee side only scarce amounts of rainfall occur, with the foehn-like sinking of the air masses in the eastern-sloping plains being an additional factor. So Lethbridge only has 439mm/17in. of annual precipitation with maximum amount falling in June. Compared with the west coast the annual and daily fluctuations in temperature are much greater. It can be seen on the climatic graph that the mean daily difference in temperature is about twice as great as in Germany. The actual temperatures can be even more extreme than those given. The absolute minimum for February in Calgary is −45°C/−49°F, the absolute summer maximum +35°C/+95°F. Nobody should underestimate the possible fluctuations in daily temperatures or those from one day to the next. When planning outdoor activities this must be taken into consideration with regard to equipment. The absolute lowest night temperatures in Lethbridge, even in summer, up to July, are below freezing. In May and again in September temperatures below −10°C/14°F have been recorded, a factor being the tremendous heat loss on clear nights. However, the weather is the dominant influence on temperature fluctuations: east of the Rocky Mountains new areas of low pressure form which move west.

Each low sucks up air masses from the south on its front, cold air masses from the north on its back. The exchange of air from north to south can, unlike in Europe, take place unhindered east of the Rocky Mountains. At the extreme it gives rise to winter blizzards with drops in temperature of over 20°C/68°F in a few hours disrupting traffic and economic activity, occasionally claiming lives, but also heatwaves of tropical air. As crops sensitive to the frost are not grown in Canada the effect of the blizzard on agriculture is not so damaging as in the south of the United States.

In this climate prairie grass turns to hay in the dry autumn, which with quickly falling temperatures is preserved under a thin covering of snow (minimum winter precipitation), whereas in the wetter east it rots or freezes. In earlier times this hay was the preferred diet of the great herds of buffalo which migrated here from afar. Today this region is the granary of Canada. Summer wheat requires a growing season of 100 days over 10°C/50°F, which cannot be achieved if harvested after August 20th and is not at all possible in the north (limit of cereals). Barley needs 90 days and so can be grown further north.

The decreasing temperatures and increasing precipitation recorded by the climatic stations in Edmonton and Winnipeg mark the boundary with the boreal snow forest climate. In this region there are projecting tongues and islands of arable land where the cultivation of cereals has advanced.

In the corner between the Great Lakes and St Lawrence River lies Canada's most southerly region. The Great Lakes have a mitigating influence on temperature. The winter temperatures are higher than in the Prairies, the daily fluctuations somewhat less, the growing period reaches 160 days. Precipitation is evenly spread throughout the year; the weather is changeable owing to the areas of low pressure converging in the Great Lakes region and being "revitalised".

The following statistics illustrate the temperature increase from Ottawa in the direction of Detroit: annual mean temperature of Ottawa 5.7°C/42°F (Detroit 9.9°C/50°F), average July temperature in Ottawa 20.7°C/69°F (Detroit 23.3°C/74°F), average temperature fluctuation in January in Ottawa from −16 to +16°C/3 to 61°F (Detroit −7°C to −0.6°C/19 to 30°F). In the opposite direction towards the north—east of Ottawa the temperatures fall: annual mean temperature in Québec 4.4°C/40°F, average July temperature 19.3°C/67°F, mean temperature fluctuations in January from −16.7 to −7.7°C/2 to 18°F. The annual precipitation levels rise from Detroit (787mm/31in.) to Ottawa (850mm/33in.) and 1058mm/47in. in Québec.

The estuarine region of the St Lawrence River along with Novia Scotia and Newfoundland have a wet, temperate but cool climate. Northwards along the coast the temperatures fall, particularly in winter: annual mean temperature of Halifax 7.4°C/45°F, of St John's, Newfoundland 5.4°C/42°F; January average in Halifax −3.3°C/26°F, in St John's −6.9°C/20°F. The cause of this is the northern cold Labrador current which brings icebergs far south (up to 40°N; Titanic disaster). Fog is common in the sea area off Newfoundland as the mixing of the cold waters with the warm water of the Gulf Stream current results in the cooling of the air and condensation. Temperatures continue to fall northwards along the coast (compare Goose Bay climatic station).

North of the climatic zones already described the growth period is too short for deciduous trees. This is the beginning of the boreal coniferous tree belt which extends monotonously and endlessly beyond Canada, around the northern hemisphere into Eurasia. Adequate warmth in summer (mean July temperatures over 12°C/54°F) and low winter temperatures provide the ideal conditions for this type of forest in a broad belt right across the continent. There is a continental high centred between Hudson Bay and the Alaskan border with annual fluctuations in the monthly mean temperatures of over 40°C/104°F. In the interior the precipitation is low (Whitehorse 257mm/10in. per annum), but owing to low evaporation and being in the form of snow, adequate for tree growth, unlike the southern Prairie regions.

In the regions where the temperature is not above 10°C/50°F for more than 30 days (which corresponds to a July mean temperature of 12°C/54°F) the forest cannot survive and it gradually becomes tundra (barren grounds). This applies in eastern Labrador, near Goose Bay, in a narrow coastal strip quite far south, as the temperatures are suppressed by the Labrador current. Around Hudson Bay, the "icebox" of America, the tundra climate penetrates further south than anywhere else in the world on the same latitude (50°). Further inland north of the Great Slave Lake (Yellowknife climate station) the limit is much further north. The Great Slave Lake is frozen up to a depth of 2m/7ft, the Great Bear Lake 2.7m/9ft. Below the Great Slave Lake the River Mackenzie freezes over between November 17th and 30th until between May 1st and 14th when it thaws. Only heaths, mosses and possibly shrubs can thrive in the tundra climate. The limiting factor is the summer warmth and not the cold winters or low precipitation.

The cold winter warm summer climate between the Great Lakes and St Lawrence River (Ottawa climate station)

The Canadian Atlantic provinces (Halifax climatic station)

Boreal snow forest climate (Goose Bay, Whitehorse climatic stations)

Polar Arctic climate (Yellowknife, Innuvik climate station)

27

Formation of Icebergs

As it drops towards the sea large blocks of ice break off from the 'tongue' of the glacier; the glacier 'calves'; icebergs are formed and drift out into the open sea.

© Baedeker

Permafrost is present where the annual mean temperatures are below −7°C/19°F. This can reach depths of several hundred metres, limited only by the heat from the earth's core. On the surface it thaws in summer to a depth of 1.5m/5ft. As the meltwaters cannot seep away or evaporate at such low temperatures the ground is covered in bogs and waterlogged, despite the low level of precipitation (below 250mm/10in. per annum).

With annual mean temperatures down to −3°C/27°F the permafrost only has vegetation in places. Coniferous trees can grow in the areas of summer thaw, the permafrost also occurs in the boreal snow forest. It can be recognised from the varied ground patterns; circles (on flat land) and stripes (on slopes).

Ice climate (Isachsen climatic station)

In the region of the numerous islands of the Canadian archipelago, the area around the magnetic North Pole, where average temperatures in July are below 6°C/42°F, there is no vegetation (average July temperature in Isachsen 3.7°C/37°F) with the ground cover consisting of bare rock and scree. Although this Polar region is so easily flown over en route to Japan it remains inaccessible to the land traveller. It is a climate of extremes with either summer Polar days or winter Polar nights and only a short transition phase in between the two. As the climatic graph of Isachsen station shows the daily fluctuations in temperature are slight compared with the more southerly located stations, yet the annual temperature differences are great.

Pack ice, icebergs

The limit of the pack ice reaches the northern islands. The largest part of the Arctic Ocean is always frozen. The icebergs have jagged, irregular shapes. Mostly they have broken away from the Greenland glaciers. The surface of the sea also freezes causing floating ice.

Flora and fauna

Flora and fauna

The flora and fauna are closely related to the geology, relief, soil conditions and climate. Roughly described Canada consists of 40% treeless tundra and 40% forest belt. Between the two is the zone of shrubs and small trees, known as forest-tundra. The grasslands with their fertile brown and black soils together with the mountain vegetation in the west and east make up a further 12%.

General

The boreal coniferous forest comprises about 82% of Canada's forests, with the forests of the Cordilleras making up 9% and the forest in the south-east a further 9%. This dense zone extends 5000km/3107 miles from east to west and is over 1000km/621 miles wide. It is a region where summer temperatures (July) reach 10°C/50°F to 17°C/63°F and the mean January temperature does not drop below −30°C/−22°F. Precipitation only amounts to 350mm/14in., but which is sufficient as there is little evaporation. Unlike northern Europe there are few pine trees but predominantly white and black spruce (*picea glauca, picea mariana*). In places tamarack (*larix laricina*) and in the east balsam fir (*abies balsamea*) occur. There is the occasional jack pine (*pinus banksiana*) in the south-east. The most common species of deciduous trees are birch (*betula*) and poplar (*populus*).

Forest
Boreal coniferous forest

The spruce are of considerable dimensions. White spruce reach heights of 25m/82ft with a diameter of 60cm/24in., black spruce grow to 10–15m/33–50ft and have a diameter of 15–25cm/6–10in.

In the north forest and tundra merge with the boundary following the 10°C/50°F July isotherm. This transitional zone is the habitat of the caribou. The herds graze on the open tundra in the summer, migrating

Forest-tundra

Columbian pines

29

over 1000km/620 miles south in the autumn and returning north in the spring. They are continually pursued by packs of wolves which ensure natural selection takes place.

Park belt

In the south the boreal forest belt becomes the park belt where only smaller wooded areas are found, mostly along the rivers. The park belt is the transition zone to the open grasslands. The most common tree is the trembling aspen (*populus tremuloides*) reaching a height of 10m/33ft and a diameter of up to 40cm/16in. Manitoba's lake region provides favourable habitat for bur oak (*querus macrocarpa*). Depending to their habitat they grow between 4–10m/13–33ft high and 2–40cm/1–16in. diameter.

Soils in the boreal coniferous forest

The soils of the boreal coniferous forests are generally heavily leached, consisting mainly of acidic podsoils which are unsuitable for agricultural cultivation. The grey-wooded soils are more fertile with some cultivation possible. More favourable soils may form on former glacial deposits.

Fauna of the boreal coniferous forest

Many different species of animals are to be found in the boreal coniferous forest. As well as the caribou and wolves already mentioned there are black and brown bears and deer, the most well known being the wapiti. This is also home to the bison. Smaller mammals include beaver, marten, foxes, muskrat and skunk. It is not surprising that trapping has been an important source of revenue for centuries and is still practised today.

Beaver

The close relationship between the animal and plant kingdom is demonstrated by the beaver and beaver meadows which should therefore be examined in more detail.

Canadian beaver

Also much sought after for its fur the beaver (*castor canadiensis*) lives mainly in the water. When the water level is not high enough it builds dams from tree trunks, branches, stones and earth. Sometimes these dams can be up to 100m/330ft long blocking the streams and forming 1–2km/¾–1¼ mile long lakes which gradually fill up with sediment.

The build-up of water causes the forest to flood and die. This loss is much greater than that caused by the beaver to poplar, birch, alder and willow in its search for food. Having exhausted its food supply the beaver is forced to move on. The result is the destruction of the dam at the next high water. The reservoir overflows and "beaver meadows" form with luxuriant grass providing ideal pasture for elk, deer and buffalo which therefore remain for a long time.

Beaver meadows are widely dispersed. Before the arrival of the Europeans the number of beaver was estimated at more than 10 million. Around 1800 hundreds of thousands of furs were exported from Québec alone. Over 200 dams were counted along a six mile long river and elsewhere about 70 beaver ponds in a 2 square mile area. The beaver meadows were also important for the first settlers. Land could be ploughed and hay produced and the woodcutters could find food for their animals. This short description illustrates the long-term effect that the beaver has had on Canada's original countryside.

The upland forests of the Cordilleras, which comprise 9% of the total forest area, are more varied and sturdier, because of the terrain, than the monotonous forests of the boreal coniferous zone. The Cordillera can be subdivided into four regions: the sub-Alpine region, the montane region, the Columbia forest and the coastal region.

Upland forests in the west

The sub-Alpine forest covers the largest area. It extends along the eastern slopes of the Rocky Mountains, the slopes of the coastal ranges and along the edges of the interior plateaux. Spruce, fir and pine grow here, among them the engelmann spruce (*pica engelmanni*) which can reach heights of 60m/196ft and a trunk diameter of 1.8m/6ft. Other important species of the sub-Alpine region include alpine fir (*abies lasiocarpa*) and lodgepole pine (*pinus contorta*). The firs and pines grow up to 30m/98ft with a trunk diameter of 80cm/31in.

Sub-Alpine forest

The montane forest region includes primarily the interior high plains and is made up of pine, poplar and douglas fir. Dense pine woods (*pinus ponderosa*) are especially widespread, often the result of large forest fires whereby the seeds fall from the opened cones. In the more southerly river valleys of the montane region steppe grass and plants are an indication of the aridity.

Montane forest

In contrast the Columbia forest region around the Kootenay, Fraser and Thompson Rivers receives considerably higher levels of precipitation and has different species of trees. Western hemlock (*tsuga heterophylla*) and western red cedar (*thuja plicata*) are widespread.

In British Columbia 60% of the land is wooded and only 1% cultivated. Only the alluvial soils found in the river valleys are suitable for cultivation.

Columbia forest

The coastal region is characterised by particularly high precipitation and luxuriant plant growth. There is also a wide variety of species with a predominance of hemlock fir, cedar and douglas fir and especially sitka spruce (*picea sitchensis*). Spruce, fir, poplar, oak, maple and alder are also in evidence. The four most important types, hemlock and douglas fir, sitka spruce and cedar, are the major timber producers reaching heights of 50m/164ft along the coast, with douglas fir even 100m/330ft, and trunk diameter of 4–5m/13–16ft.

Coastal region

The upland forests are the habitat of many animals. Hunting is, however, strictly controlled by the Wildlife Act. Big game include wapiti

Fauna of the coastal range

Flora and fauna

deer, elk, wild sheep and mountain goats as well as numerous mammals prized for their fur and predators such as black and grizzly bears.

There are many different species of birds and fishes, of which salmon and trout are the most common.

Salmon

Salmon up to 1.5m/5ft long and weighing 35kg/77lbs climb up to the upper reaches of many rivers on their journey from the sea to their spawning grounds, where they each lay up to 30,000 eggs in the gravelly river bed. Many of them then die of exhaustion. The young salmon stay in the freshwater for up to five years before returning to the sea.

Mixed and deciduous woodland in south-east Canada

The diverse species of mixed woodland make up the remaining 9% of forest and can be divided into three regions owing to the mild, wet climate: the belt around the Great Lakes and St Lawrence River, the extreme south of Ontario between Lake Erie and Lake Ontario, the Acadian woodlands that surround the southern Atlantic provinces.

In this region the conifers are mainly red spruce (*picea rubens*), eastern hemlock (*tsuga canadensis*) and pines. The deciduous trees comprise birch, oak, beech, elm, aspen and maple. The red maple (*acer rubrum*) and sugar maple (*acer saccharum*) enjoy particular importance. The maple trees grow over 30m/98ft tall and have a diameter of 60 to 90cm/24 to 35in. Their hard wood is prized for the manufacture of furniture and the sap produces maple sugar and syrup.

Sugar maple, maple syrup

For several species of tree the summer-green deciduous forests of southern Ontario are their northernmost limit. These include lime, walnut, hickory, oak, chestnut, tulip, magnolia, jasmine and sassafra, the softwood of which contains a heavily scented oil. The variety of species in this region is most apparent in September and October, when the "Indian Summer" reveals the colourful make up of the forest. This area attracts many tourists in autumn who come to see the rich colours of the foliage.

Indian Summer

Salmon going upstream to the breeding grounds

The varying proportion of woodland is interesting; in southern Ontario and on Prince Edward Island it is about 15%, in northern Ontario about 90%, in Nova Scotia 75% and in New Brunswick 85%.

The soil formation is patchy and varies between sands and loams. It consists mostly of podsols, which near the Atlantic are often rich in debris and difficult to cultivate. Narrow enclosed areas of arable land with favourable soil conditions are found in the St John River Valley and Annapolis Valley.

Soils

The grass steppes and the park belt which surrounds them are only one third of the area of the neighbouring forest but are of great economic importance. Unlike the forest belt the natural vegetation has been completely displaced by cultivation. Old descriptions of the countryside make it possible to imagine how it was prior to 1870. Vast grasslands, which were easy to clear and fertile soils, created favourable conditions for farming from the start.

Grass steppes,
Prairies
General

The tall grass, true grass prairie covers a relatively small area around the former Lake Agassiz, a former glacial lake. Grasses (*stipa spartea*) grow in dense formation up to 2m/6ft high. Copses of elm trees (*ulmus americana*) are only found along the rivers.

Tall grass,
true grass prairie

The flora of the mixed grass prairie is varied, with stipa and festuga being the prevalent grass species. The grass is less than 1m/3ft and there is the occasional copse of trees which continue into the park belt or north into the forest belt.

Mixed grass
prairie

Many xerophilous plants are found in the short grass prairie, among them opuntia polycantha. As much of the land is used for grazing, owing to the low precipitation (6–7 arid months), many species of grass have been preserved. Woodlands are scattered in the Cypress Hills, which reach 1470m/4822ft and tower 675m/2214ft above the surrounding area.

Short grass prairie

The fertility of the prairies lies in the soils. They were heavily glaciated and are made up of up to 70% medium grain, of which 15% is sand or clay. Finer sands are located near former glacial lakes. They range from brown, through dark brown to black soils (*chernozems*). The proportion of cultivated land falls between 40 and 80%, depending on the type of soil.

Soils of the
grass steppes

The animal world has undergone great changes in the Prairies. This used to be the home of the buffalo or bison, that migrated in great herds north in spring and south with the snowfall in the autumn. In the forest belt these migrations extend as far as the Great Slave Lake. Prior to European settlement the buffalo numbers were estimated at 60 million, with about 40 million left by 1830. By 1900 this magnificent beast had almost been wiped out with only 1000 left at the turn of the century. The virtual extermination of the buffalo had disastrous consequences for the Prairie Indians whose way of life was dependent on buffalo hunting. Efforts have been made to reintroduce and distribute these animals, requiring much patience and hard work. The numbers of antelope (*antilocapra americana*) were also much higher. Prairie dogs and numerous rodents are also found in the steppes.

Fauna of the
grass steppes

The third type of vegetation in Canada, after the forest belt and the grasslands, is the tundra zone, which the visitor coming to Canada flies over for hours. Even from the air it presents a chilly and monotonous picture, justifying its name, the "barren grounds". This description, however, is not competely true as it is carpeted with colourful flowers for a few short weeks in summer before they die off.

Tundra
General

Flora and fauna

Climatic conditions

The vegetation of the tundra zone is exposed to extreme climatic conditions. Summer only lasts three months and biting and sharp winds prevail in winter as well as being extremely dry. The above climatic factors and the permafrost hamper soil formation with bare rock being common. Regosols are widespread with underlying tundra soils.

Flora

The range of vegetation is narrow and limited to lichens and reindeer moss, with occasional dwarf heathers and ericacae. Larger areas of vegetation are situated on the warmer southern slopes. In general the vegetation thins out from north to south.

Fauna in the tundra

The extreme Arctic conditions also affect the habitat of the animal kingdom. Large herds of caribou move twice a year between the tundra and the forest belt usually covering 1300km/over 800 miles. The caribou is essential to the Indian way of life, providing both food and clothing. It also provides some variety in the diet of the Innuit who live mainly on fish.

Unfortunately the caribou herds have been decimated in the last decades, from 2.5 million in 1938 their numbers had declined to 800,000 in 1970. This drop is due to hunting with modern rifles. Packs of wolves are also responsible for killing herds of caribou; a wolf kills an average of 16 caribou during its lifetime. Road construction and forest fires have also affected the caribou population.

The largest animals of the north are the musk-ox, found on the Arctic islands where they feed on the sparse vegetation. Their numbers also decreased dramatically until a hunting ban in 1917 stabilised the population so that there are about 15,000 today. Unlike the caribou the musk-ox only wanders over a limited area.

Wolves, Arctic foxes, Arctic hares, lemmings and squirrels (which hibernate for eight months) are common. Their white colouring

A seal, ideally suited to the Arctic

camouflages them with their surroundings. There are 80 species of bird which prefer to nest around the Mackenzie delta. Around Baffin Island and Southampton Island the indigenous Innuit hunt seals and polar bears.

Conservation

Canada is not a "land of unlimited opportunies", therefore it is essential to conserve resources and protect the environment. The destruction of the balance of nature began with the displacement of the long-established lifestyles of the natives and continued with the slaughter of the buffalo herds – whose numbers fell between 1831 and 1900 from 60,000,000 to 1000 – and the decimation of the caribou and increase in forest fires.

Destruction of the balance of nature

In the farming areas soil erosion and dust storms reduce crop yields so attempts are made to increase yields by "dry farming" (the ground is regularly worked but not tilled every year) and "strip farming" (100–200m/110–220yd wide strips of land are interspersed with cereals or left fallow). In eastern Canada overworked soils resulted in widespread desert-like conditions, whereas excessive modernisation and rationalisation has led to a reduction in the number of farms in the Prairies.

Erosion in the farming areas

Canada's unilateral decision to extend its fishing limits to 200 miles (from 1977) attracted international criticism. The violence often associated with seal-hunting also provoked worldwide outrage.

Over-fishing, seal-hunting

The timber industry, which used to provide timber for the construction industry and fuel, today specialises in paper and cellulose production, with the result that because of the low growth intensity of the trees the new growth is not always ensured. Thus in many places further exploitation is only possible after 100 years.

Excessive tree-felling

Another disadvantage is that in Canada wholesale felling is the norm, unlike the selective felling in Europe. This causes severe soil erosion particularly in upland areas with high precipitation. Granting consent to set up logging camps with high levels of production therefore has environmental implications.

Other problems are water pollution by the cellulose industry and damage to the forests by acid rain. To put a stop to this danger the harmful emissions must be stopped at source. In Sudbury, a prime example of environmental destruction because of its iron and nickel mining, a 360m/1182ft high giant chimney stack, the highest in the world, has been built. Pollution in the immediate vicinity of the town has certainly been reduced but in north Québec and Labrador, 1000–1500km/620–930 miles away, acid rain has been detected which has adverse effects on the vegetation, soil systems, water quality, etc. Acid snow is also harmful with Shefferville having 48% of its annual precipitation in the form of snow. Toxins collect in the snow cover during the winter causing high levels of acidity after the snowmelt.

River pollution acid rain

The degree of the air pollution can be measured from the emissions, which were originally 3600t per day, later reduced to 2200t and now down to 700t. Sudbury is only one of many places producing emissions, others are in northern Québec and southern Ontario (Hamilton).

However, the Canadian polluters are overshadowed by the giant industrial concerns in the United States (Chicago-Gary, Indianapolis, Pittsburg, etc.).

The detrimental effects of acid rain on the fishing and forestry industries and the recreational value of the Great Lakes have been the subject of negotiations which have been taking place for years with the USA and are keenly followed by the population living around the Great Lakes. Reduction of coal-burning to lower air pollution is the main issue.

The dramatic effects of acid rain

Other agreements between the neighbouring countries concern the Great Lakes, near which no less than 40 million people live, which together with the concentration of industry creates great problems. Canada's ability to influence the agenda is, however, weakened by the fact that a large proportion of its industry is dependent on US capital. Further subjects of conflict are the transcontinental and sub-Arctic pipelines and roads. The Mackenzie Pipeline and Dempster Highway have altered the paths of the caribou and weakened the native economy to the extent that the very existence of the inhabitants is threatened.

Environmental problems caused by mining

Extensive open-cast mining, slag heaps and difficult access routes are the conflict areas created by the mining industry. The huge mining areas of the oil sands in north Alberta present problems of world importance. At St James Bay and at other gigantic hydro-electric power stations the land treaties with the Indians were infringed resulting in delays lasting years and even decades.

A particular problem is presented by the off-shore oil-fields off the coast of Newfoundland. These oil rigs lie in the path of the cold Labrador current, which causes hundreds of icebergs to drift annually south from Greenland. A collision would have disastrous environmental consequences as some of the world's most important fishing grounds are located here. A surveillance and warning system operates with tugboats guiding the icebergs away from a collision course.

National parks

In order to minimise the above problems the Department of the Environment was established in 1971 in Canada, earlier than in other countries, and was given responsibility for national parks in 1979. The first signs of a change of direction were at the end of the 19th c. when the national parks in Canada were founded in conjunction with the development of the transcontinental railways and following the national park idea in the USA (Yellowstone Park was founded in 1872).

In contrast to the popularly held opinion that in Canada conservation would be more strictly implemented than in the neighbouring USA, as far as the national parks are concerned, the opposite is true: legislation is less forceful. The impression is given that tourism is valued more highly than actual conservation. In the well known parks of the Canadian Rocky Mountains whole towns have grown up, and on the Athabasca glacier it is considered advisable to use powerful snowmobiles.

In 1885 an area of 25sq.km/10sq.miles was placed under protection on the east slope of the Rocky Mountains. The idea behind the national parks was to provide recreation and pleasure for people at the same time educating them to respect nature. Development is restricted to visitors' centres, pathways, camping and picnic sites with restrictions on exhibitions, hotels, petrol stations and shops.

The first seven parks were established between 1885 and 1914 in the Cordilleras. They are Banff (opened 1885; 6641sq.km/2563sq.miles at present), Yoho (opened 1886; 1313sq.km/507sq.miles) and Jasper (opened 1907; 10,878sq.km/4199sq.miles) on the vertex of the Canadian Pacific Railway and Canadian National Railway (formerly "Canadian Northern") in the Rocky Mountains, as well as Waterton Lakes National Park (opened 1895; 526sq.km/203sq.miles) which is connected with the US Glacier National Park, Mount Revelstoke Park (opened 1914; 263sq.km/ 102sq.miles) in the Selkirk Mountains. Away from the Cordilleras are Elk Island Park, founded before 1920, (194sq.km/75sq.miles) east of Edmonton and the smaller national parks St Lawrence Islands (4sq.km/1½sq.miles) and Pointe Pelée (16sq.km/6sq.miles) in Ontario.

Since 1920 national parks have been opened in nearly all regions of Canada. In the Cordilleras these were Kootenay Park (1378sq.km/532sq.miles) and the Pacific Rim Park (389sq.km/150sq.miles), along with the huge Kluane National Park (22,015sq.km/8498sq.miles) with Canada's highest mountains (Mount Logan, 5951m/19,531ft; Mount St Elias, 5489m/18,015ft; Mount Lucrania 5226m/17,152ft) and the Northern Yukon National Park (6050sq.km/2335sq.miles).

In the sub-Arctic and Polar north there are no fewer than five national parks of enormous areas such as Wood Buffalo Park (44,807sq.km/17,296sq.miles), Ellesmere Island Park (39,500sq.km/15,247sq.miles) and Baffin Island Park (21,471sq.km/8288sq.miles). Today there are 32 national parks distributed over all provinces and territories. The majority are situated in the Cordilleras (6), the Northwest Territories (5) and on the Atlantic coast (9).

In addition to the national parks there are another 63 national historic parks, of which 42 alone are to be found in the Atlantic provinces and in the St Lawrence Lowland. For example, they include Louisburg and Annapolis Royal in Nova Scotia or Upper Canada Village in Ontario. For the planning of future national parks Canada has been divided into 39 natural regions each with different geological and morphological structures and ecosystems.

Monuments, historic parks

Apart from the 32 national parks at present there are about 1200 provincial parks totalling 300,000sq.km/115,800sq.miles. Whereas the national parks come under central government jurisdiction the provincial parks come under control of the provinces. These are more equipped for larger crowds of visitors and often have sport and recreational facilities. Popular provincial parks include the Laurentides in Québec, the Cypress Hills and the Dinosaur Park in Alberta. All nature parks referred to have an increasing importance for tourism.

Provincial parks

Population

Population density

In area Canada is the largest country in the world, but in terms of its population it is in 31st place. According to the 1994 census there were approximately 27.6 million people living in Canada. The population density of about 3 inhabitants per sq.km compares with 227 per sq.km in Great Britain.

Population distribution
Regions

In Canada the vast expanses of the north are almost uninhabited compared with the relatively uninterrupted densely populated narrow strip along the border with the USA. The "empty spaces" in the north – Yukon and Northwest Territories – with their severe weather conditions and poor soils are only inhabited by 0.3% of the population.

Province or territory	1961		1986	
	population		population	
	absolute	in %	absolute	in %
Newfoundland	457,853	2.5	563,349	2.2
Prince Edward Island	104,629	0.6	126,646	0.5
Nova Scotia	737,007	4.0	873,199	3.4
New Brunswick	597,936	3.3	710,422	2.8
Québec	5,259,211	28.8	6,540,276	25.8
Ontario	6,236,092	34.2	9,113,515	36.0
Manitoba	921,686	5.1	1,071,232	4.2
Saskatchewan	925,181	5.1	1,010,198	4.0
Alberta	1,331,944	7.3	2,375,278	9.4
British Columbia	1,629,082	8.9	2,889,207	11.4
Yukon	14,628	0.1	23,504	0.1
Northwest Territories	22,998	0.1	52,238	0.2
Canada total	18,238,247	100.0	25,354,064	100.0

About 62% of the population live in Québec and Ontario, where the population density in the south of the provinces along the St Lawrence River and north of Lake Erie and Lake Ontario is 60 per sq.km. This is the highest concentration of population in the country. A mild climate, good soils and favourable communications have contributed to the economic development of this region. The land to the west is relatively thiny populated owing to the unfavourable physical conditions – the rocky substratum of the Canadian Shield produces poor agricultural soils. The fertile wheat-growing area of the prairie is heavily populated to the west of Winnipeg.

There a few clusters of population in the upland areas of the Cordilleras with higher concentrations around Vancouver and along the Edmonton-Calgary axis. The increasing popularity of this region can be attributed to its cosmopolitan attitudes and beautiful countryside. Unlike the east it does not have the burden of historical tradition and is more cosmopolitan. Instead of fighting against each other, ethnic groups have worked together here to create a new society inspired by the pioneering spirit.

City-country

Since the end of the Twenties, relatively late in comparison with Europe, the population has been chiefly urban. Reasons for this were the later onset of industrialisation and the importance of agriculture especially in the Prairies. In recent years there has been an increase in the rural population. This has not taken place among the farm workers, on the contrary, their numbers have declined. It is caused by the increase in areas in relative proximity to the cities. Ecological reasons and lower prices along with well developed communications are responsible for people leaving the cities. Urban lifestyles and working patterns are thus transferred to the outskirts of conurbations.

The demographic changes are dependent on two factors: the natural increase in population (births less number of deaths) and the net immigration (immigration less emigration).

Population development

In the period 1986–94 the population increased by 8% – still a particularly high rate of increase for an industrialised country. Well over half this increase was accounted for by natural growth.

Natural population development

The baby boom of the Fifties was followed by a drastic fall in the birth rate in the Sixties, generally attributed to the contraceptive pill but also because of people marrying at a later age, economic prosperity, social security and other factors. Even in Catholic Québec, where the birth rate was always higher than in other provinces, population growth has been low in recent years.

The mortality rate is 7/1000. Increasing life expectancy – 80 for women and 73 for men – has resulted in an increase in the number of old people in the population. The proportion of those under 15 fell to 21% in 1986, in 1961 it was 34%. Those over 65 increased from 8% to 11% in 1986.

Canada is still a country where immigration takes place. In 1994 immigrants made up one sixth of the population. From the historical point of view immigration is a key factor in the population development of this country. It went in cycles and was dependent on economic processes. At the beginning of the century and after the Second World War immigration was particularly high running parallel with economic upturn. Having over a long period stabilised at 120,000 per annum, recent years have seen a dramatic increase in the level of immigration, with an estimated inflow in 1994 of 250,000. Previously immigration policy was subject to frequent revision. At times restrictions were placed on the numbers of Chinese and Japanese, preference being given to applicants from Britain, Ireland, America and France. Nowadays these distinctions have been lifted in favour of a greater ethnic mix. During the Sixties and Seventies there was a shift in the proportion of Europeans and Asians: in 1975 40% of immigrants still came from Europe and 25% from Asia, in 1980 the proportion of Asians was up to 50%. With the obligation to take refugees and keep families together the preference was for well educated workers. The immigrants settled mainly in the conurbations around Toronto, Montréal and Vancouver; in 1994 over half of all immigrants were living here.

Immigration

In recent years there has been an increase in migration to British Columbia. There is a more even balance of population in the west although the main areas of population are still in the central provinces.

Migration within Canada

According to the 1986 census 711,720 people belong to the original population: 3% of the total population. Among this group are 27,000 Inuit and 300,000 Indians. The remainder are mixed race, such as the Métis – descendants of Indians and French. In addition there are large numbers of Canadians who have given up their status as Indians. Most of the original inhabitants live in the north and west. In the Northwest Territories they comprise 59% of the total population, in the Yukon Territory 21%, in Manitoba and Saskatchewan 8%, with only 1% on Prince Edward Island. Both groups display mongoloid features. They came to Canada from northern Asia over the Bering land bridge or via Greenland on the edge of the Polar ice cap during the Ice Ages 15,000 to 10,000 B.C.

Ethnic mosaic
Original population

This group of the population is the only one not to have prospered through the economic development of the country. Following the arrival of the white man the number of Indians was heavily decimated by wars, expulsion and the introduction of diseases. For two hundred years contact between them consisted chiefly of fur trading. Skins and furs were exchanged for weapons, etc. The Indians became socially and economically dependent.

In adapting to the modern world they gave up a way of life that was perfectly in harmony with the land to copy the white man's way of life. Unemployment is twice as high as it is among the immigrants; the average income is only ⅔ that of the rest of the population. Moving to the cities frequently brings the well known problems of alcoholism and crime; crime rates are between three and five times higher than the national average.

Various measures have been introduced to combat the social disadvantage faced by the original inhabitants: special education programmes with teacher training for their own schools, air-lifted medical aid in remote areas, financial support and greater participation in decision-making through local government and involvement on political committees.

Ethnic groups (a selection)	Total number	Percentage
Single race	18,035,665	72.1
French	6,087,310	24.3
English	4,742,040	18.9
Scottish	865,450	3.5
Irish	699,685	2.8
German	896,715	3.6
Italian	709,585	2.8
Ukrainian	420,210	1.7
North American Indian	286,230	1.1
Dutch	351,765	1.4
Chinese	360,320	1.4
Scandinavian	159,335	0.6
Jewish	245,860	1.0
Polish	222,260	0.9
Mixed race	6,986,345	27.9
Total	25,022,005	100.0

Indians

There are over 50 different Indian languages and dialects which belong to ten linguistic groups: in order of importance they are Algonquin (60%), Athabasca, Iroki, Salish, Wakasha, Tsimischian, Sioux, Kutenai, Haida and Tlingit. 70% of registered Indians live in reservations on their own land. Nearly every Indian belongs to one of the 576 so-called bands, administrative and political units with their own property and historic associations.

The reservations which were allotted to the Indians by the Europeans are only of limited economic potential. They are usually handicapped by a peripheral location, poor communications and infrastructure. Most of them have developed a basic subsistence economy. Those with minerals or forestry reserves or else are in locations with tourist appeal are the exceptions. Although the Indians were not dealt with as ruthlessly in Canada as in the USA there are still countless incidences of unfair treaties. A recent conflict occurred in Montréal in 1991 with plans to turn land which was regarded as sacred by the resident Indians into a golf course.

Inuit

The word "Inuit" means "person", whereas "eskimo" means "eater of raw meat" in the language of the Algonquin Indians. The latter term is not used by the Inuit themselves but rather regarded as discriminatory. Altogether there are about 100,000 Inuit in the Arctic regions of the

Original distribution of population

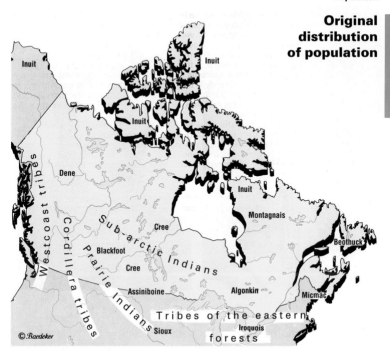

world, i.e. Greenland, Alaska, Russia and Canada. Their language is called Inuktitut. Seven different groups can be distinguished on the basis of economic and cultural practices: the Mackenzie, the Copper, the Netselik, the Caribou, the Iglulik, the Baffinland and Labrador Inuit. These are not tribes; the Inuit did not have tribes as such. Historically three cultures have been identified: the Pre-Dorset culture (2500–800 B.C.), the Dorset culture (up to 1300 A.D.) and the Thule culture (up to 1750). The Inuit live in small communities on the Mackenzie delta, on the Arctic islands and on the mainland coasts of the Northwest Territories, in Labrador, on Hudson Bay and the Ungava Bay. Their location on river estuaries, fiords and in other coastal areas reflects their original economic activity – fishing.

The classical picture of their life – canoe trips, living in an igloo, fishing at a hole in the ice, walking on snowshoes and hunting caribou with sledges pulled by dogs – belongs to the past. The modern world has arrived even here with all its comforts and complications: aeroplanes (not many settlements are without a runway), snowmobiles, motor boats, permanent houses with every possible kind of technology from video to refrigerator (strangely necessary as the milk flown in from the south has a limited shelf life and the hole in the ice is no longer fashionable as a means of storage). The houses are prefabricated in the south and simply assembled here. Apart from fishing, employment is found in the extraction of oil, gas and minerals. The interests of the Inuit are represented by various organisations – the Inuit Tapirisat of Canada or the Inuit Development Corporations; two Inuit have seats in the Senate.

An Indian of the forests   *An Inuit girl*

Mother tongue (a selection)	Total number	Percentage
Mono-lingual	24,345,390	96.2
English	15,334,085	60.6
French	6,159,740	24.3
No offical language	2,860,565	11.3
Italian	455,820	1.8
German	438,675	1.7
Ukrainian	208,410	0.8
Chinese	266,560	1.1
Aboriginal languages	138,060	0.5
Other languages	1,353,040	5.3
More than one answer	954,940	3.8
English and French	332,610	1.3
Other bilingualism	622,330	2.5
Total	25,309,330	100.0

Immigrants and language areas

In Canada there are 82 ethnic groups with 72 different languages, of which the founder nations Great Britain (40%) and France (27%) plus inhabitants of English or French descent make up over 80%. A long way behind are the Germans (5%), followed by the Italians (3%), who came after the Second World War, then the Ukrainians with 2.6%. The number of Russian and East Europeans is expected to rise in the future following the opening up of the borders.

Smaller ethnic groups – as already mentioned especially the Asians – have grown in size at the expense of the British influx. However, the remaining nations speak English rather than French. 61% of the population have English as their mother tongue, 24% French, the remaining 5% other languages. The ethnic composition is rather more heterogenous than the linguistic structure.

Those of French descent are concentrated around Québec, where 81% of the population have French as their mother tongue. The rest of the Francophone population live in the neighbouring regions of New Brunswick and Ontario. In the upper classes of some cities an affected form of old-fashioned English is deliberately cultivated. More than 80% of the economic elite belong to families which came from Great Britain. However, 15 years under the French Canadian prime minister Pierre Trudeau contributed to breaking down the traditional hierarchy of nationalities.

In 1977 French became the only official language in Québec – for which the Separatists had fought hard and has caused much resentment. Not only in schools and government but also in business French has become important. Québec has formed a linguistic enclave, as it were.

16% of the population speak English and French. This bilingual group lives primarily in south Ontario and south Québec and at the so-called Soo-Moncton-Line separates both the main language areas. According to the Constitution Act 1982 both languages have the same status, rights and privileges in all parliamentary and government institutions. Both language areas have been reinforced; instead of the sought-after bilingualism there is separation. Cultural dualism brings problems as well as enrichment.

This is the in-word of the last two decades, although the idea has been around for much longer. Canada is not so much of a melting-pot, as, for example, the ideology of the United States was represented until recently. It is more a kaleidoscope of nations who preserved many of their characteristic ethnic features. There is even a ministry for multicultural affairs. It is a question of maintaining people's links with their homelands through preserving manners and customs in clubs and through the media as well as promoting cultural pluralism and intercultural communication.

Multi-culturalism

Religion

The dominant religion in Québec was Roman Catholicism, influencing politics and society, whereas Anglican Protestantism was prevalent in the other provinces. Traditional religious and ethical values were promoted and the rural conservative society was protected from change.

It was not until after the Second World War that religious pluralism developed with the new wave of immigrants. Mennonites and Hutterer settled mainly in the Prairie states, Jews were more at home in the big cities, Japanese Buddhists in the west and Buddhists from south-east Asia in Toronto, Hindus and Sikhs in the conurbations. Para-religious groups are growing in influence.

Today the three most important religious groups are the Roman Catholic church, the United Church of Canada and the Anglicans. Next in importance are the Presbyterians, Lutherans and Baptists.

The religious communities create a very vivid picture because of their history of colonisation. They are influential in many spheres on account of their socio-economic structures, their different lifestyles, their mentality and marriage lines, and also their international associations.

In addition to the numerous communities there are numerous sects with between 5000 and 30,000 members, of which the most important

Religious communities

Menonnites in Ontario

are the Nazarenes, Dukoborzen, Hutterer, Moravian Brothers and Unitarians. In 1981 245,000 people were members of the numerous other Protestant splinter groups. A total of 1,788,995 people did not belong to any religious group, though only 4455 described themselves as atheists.

Several churches and sects are even further fragmented making the overall picture even more colourful. This is the case among the Anglicans, Presbyterians, Baptists as well as the Reformed and Orthodox churches which have different relationships with their mother church and even celebrate their festivals according to different calendars.

According to the 1981 census Christian denominations are in the majority in keeping with the European background of the Canadian population.

Among the Christian population there are three main groups, the Catholics with just 50%, the Protestants with over 40% and the Orthodox with 2% of the faithful.

The largest Protestant religious communities in Canada are the United Church (almost 4 million members), the Anglicans (2.5 million members), the Presbyterians (about 800,000), the Lutherans (about 700,000), the Baptists (around 70,000) and the Pentecostalists (about 350,000).

There are interesting regional differences between the denominations reflecting the ethnic backgrounds. The French dominated provinces of Québec and New Brunswick have with 90% and 50% respectively the highest percentage of Catholics, all other provinces have a Protestant majority, but throughout all provinces and territories (with the exception of British Columbia) the Catholic church is the strongest religious community. It is less dominant in the Prairie provinces.

In Newfoundland, Québec and both territories the Anglicans are the dominant branch of the Protestant church, in the other provinces it is the United Church. The Catholic church has more members in the provinces of Québec (5.6 million) and Ontario (3 million), the United Church of Canada in Ontario (1.7 million), British Columbia (600,000) and Alberta (550,000), the Anglican church in Ontario (1.2 million), British Columbia (400,000) and Alberta (200,000), the Presbyterians in Ontario (500,000 followers) and British Columbia (100,000 followers) and the Lutherans in Ontario (260,000 followers), Alberta (150,000 followers) and British Columbia (130,000 followers).

Even on a communal basis there are regional differences. All communes of the province of Québec have a Catholic population of more than 50%, often more than 90%. The same applies to communes in New Brunswick, on Prince Edward Island, in Nova Scotia and in south-west Newfoundland, as well as towns in northern Ontario (provincial average 30%) and north Saskatchewan. In various parts of Newfoundland, northern Ontario, Manitoba and northern Alberta Catholicism is still in first place but only includes 25 to 50% of the population.

In almost all other areas the United Church of Canada is in top position. It reaches over 50% in some parts of southern and western Ontario and Manitoba, in almost all the remaining towns in southern Ontario, the south of the Prairie provinces and in British Columbia it lies between 25 and 50%.

The Anglican church of Canada represents between 25 and 50% of Vancouver Island and the sparsely inhabited regions of Yukon Territory, Labrador and Newfoundland (up to 50% here in places!). Baptists are found in the south of Nova Scotia and New Brunswick. Apart from the main denominations mentioned above the Mennonites in south Manitoba surpass 50%.

In second place are the United Church of Canada in Manitoba and Saskatchewan (each with between 25 and 40%) and the Ukrainian Catholics and Greek Orthodox in Manitoba (10 to 40%), together with the Mormons in southern Alberta. The situation is most simple in Québec province, most complicated in the Prairie provinces where as many as six different religious communities are significantly represented.

Many Protestant communities feel more closely involved with each other than with their mother churches in Europe. This explains how the Methodists, Congregationalists and Presbyterians came together to form the United Church of Canada in 1925.

Non-Christian communities also are found in certain regions. Half of the Jewish population live in Ontario, with a further third in Québec, where they make up 2% of the population.

The distribution of those not belonging to any religious group forms an interesting pattern. It is at its lowest in Newfoundland comprising 1% and in Nova Scotia 4%, average in Ontario and Manitoba with 7% and numbering 12% in Alberta, 20% in the Yukon Territory and 21% in British Columbia. Their numbers more or less doubled between 1971 and 1990.

The individual groups are all showing different patterns of development. Within the last ten years the Unitarians fell by 30%, the Presbyterians by 6% and the Anglicans by 3%. On the other hand the United Church grew 1%, the Jews almost 10% and the Catholics by 13%. Largest increases were among the Mormons with 36% and the Pentecostalists with 54%. The most significant increase of all, however, was among the Buddhists whose numbers rose by 223% to 52,000.

Education and Science

The Canadian educational system is equally as diverse as its multicultural society. Education is highly regarded at national and provincial level.

Education and Science

Finance

Education is in second place after social security on the scale of government responsibilities. Funding of education is derived from 7% of Canada's gross national product and 8% from private income. The major proportion of the education budget comes from county and municipal government.

Development

Up until the end of the 1960s the Canadian education system experienced tremendous expansion through a constantly growing population and increasing economic capacity. Huge universities were built and new courses introduced to meet the demands created by the rise in student numbers. By the beginning of the Seventies this period seemed to be at an end with the falling birth rate. This wave spilt over into the entire education system but underwent further growth in the middle of the Seventies. The Eighties are characterised more by stagnation in the educational sphere as demographic trends and a reduction in economic capacity indicate.

Federal presence

Following the amalgamation of the four former provinces in 1867 education became the responsibility of the provinces. The Canadian constitution does not recognise (since 1981/82) federal control over the education system. The state is only responsible for marginal groups which do not come under the jurisdiction of the provinces: original settlers, personnel and relatives of the Canadian armed forces and offenders in penal institutions are subject to federal authority. The state, however, has indirect influence over financial transactions concerning provincial educational policy, especially where further education, direct funding for employees or support for bilingual education is involved.

While the provincial education departments are legally associated with the state, the day-to-day activities of public (i.e. state) schools are the responsibility of the regional administrative bodies, which are composed of elected and/or appointed representatives. The commune is responsible for school buildings, transport, employment of teachers and for setting the local taxes to maintain the schools.

Basic schools and high schools

All pupils have to attend basic school; different schools have the same curriculum. Pupils of the Junior High schools can choose some of their subjects. The colleges are not only institutions which prepare pupils for university, they also offer vocational courses. The Canadian school system incorporates various types of schools: private schools, denominational schools and further education colleges.

Private schools

The private schools are an alternative to the state schools. They normally have a religious, linguistic, social or academic bias. The extent to which a provincial government supports such schools depends upon the individual province.

Denominational schools

There are denominational schools in five of Canada's provinces. Traditionally Newfoundland's state schools are controlled by ecclesiastical Roman Catholic religious groups which are subdivided into school areas. The main Protestant groups (Anglicans, United Church, Salvation Army) founded their schools and administration in the mid-Sixties. Even the Pentecostalists and the Adventists maintain schools. Québec has a dual school system: one for Roman Catholics and one for non-Catholics.

Ontario, Saskatchewan and Alberta have a majority of Catholic schools, with fewer Protestant schools.

Further education

For many years the only form of further education was at university. Now there are further education and technical colleges in all provinces.

University-type institutions

Canada has several institutions which award university degrees:
There are colleges where study in various disciplines can lead to a

doctorate, or institutes of art, religion and theology as well as engineering and education colleges. Military academies also feature among the tertiary institutions.

Admission to university is conditional on having completed prescribed courses and having studied at an appropriate high school.

The "Community Colleges" are an alternative to university which are distributed throughout all the Canadian provinces; there are specialist schools for art, science, technology, agriculture and fishing, marine and paramedical technology, even nurses are trained here. Applicants must have successfully completed a course of study at a secondary school.

Community colleges

Business and technology are essentially covered by public and private schools of business and commerce, courses in specialist schools and related institutions.

Business and technology schools

Adult education in Canada enjoys particular regard. These courses are financially supported by trade unions, communal organisations, churches, public libraries, government departments, trade and industry. The courses can lead to recognised qualifications or they can just be taken for personal interest.

Adult education

About ½ million students are matriculated at Canada's 70-odd scientific universities with an equally sizable teaching body. The leading universities are in Montréal (Université de Montréal, McGill University), in Toronto (University of Toronto), in Edmonton (University of Alberta) and Québec (Université de Québec).

Science and research
Universities

Canada's rich supply of minerals, the absolutely immense, sustainable resources (forest, cereals) and the enormous potential of hydro-electric power have greatly inspired science and research. Thousands of scientists are employed in mining, energy, electronics, forestry, transport and communications.

Research

During the last two decades great achievements were made in the area of news transmission (e.g. construction of news satellites), data transmission and communication, long-range reconnaissance and geo-physical exploration).

Advances have also been made in medical research, especially in the field of laser surgery, radiology and remote-control dentistry. Pioneers in medical research are the university clinics in Montréal and Toronto.

Canadian research in the areas of plant and animal breeding, pest control and soil science has achieved international recognition. It is not without reason that Canada exports wheat and other vegetable and animal products to the value of 6 billion dollars per annum.

More recent subjects of Canadian technological research are nuclear energy and transport systems. Canada is in the forefront of the aeroplane construction and space industries. Considerable success has also been achieved in researching new forms of energy and energy conservation.

Canadian researchers are at the forefront of environmental research. Since 1986 they have been using fluorescence line imagers (FLIs) which measure chlorophyll fluorescence. Using this equipment the growth of algae in seas and lakes or even damage to forests caused by acid rain or other environmentally harmful factors can be measured. This equipment has already been used successfully in the Black Forest in Germany. Other projects are being planned or else about to be put into operation, partly in connection with the European Space Agency (ESA).

Environmental research

The Canadian "Natural Science & Engineering Council" is responsible for, promotes and supervises research projects. This involves exchanges between scientists of similar associated institutions abroad and the organisation of scientific congresses and meetings.

NSERC

47

Canada
State divisions

Government

Canada is a federation of states with a parliamentary monarchy consisting of ten provinces and two territories.

The national flag is the "Maple Leaf". Since 1980 it has had its own national anthem and in 1982 the first Canadian constitution, the Canadian Act, replaced the British North America Act of 1867. The British parliament is no longer responsible for Canadian parliamentary affairs.

Head of state

The head of state is the British Queen Elizabeth II. She is represented by a governor general, recommended by the Canadian cabinet and appointed by her. Apart from representative duties and signing laws he officiates at the appointment or dismissal of ministers or at the dissolution of parliament.

Executive

The executive power is shared between the prime minister and the cabinet, which is accountable to the lower chamber and whose members are also usually members of parliament. Should the lower chamber withdraw its confidence in the prime minister then he must resign from office and elections take place. The prime minister also can call a general election during his five year period of office.

Legislature

The legislative power is shared between the governor general, the senate (upper chamber) and the "House of Commons" (lower chamber).

The upper chamber consists of 104 senators from the provinces and territories, who are appointed by the governor general on the recommendation of the prime minister. It is the lower chamber of 282 delegates elected by a first-past-the-post system which is decisive in the legislative process: it is responsible to the prime minister and only here can financial laws be introduced. In general both chambers have an equal say in legislative matters. For its part the senate can simply delay the final passing of laws.

The Canadian constitution does not recognise the existence of parties. An exception is the "Election Expenses Act". Yet parties do exist within the framework of the parliamentary monarchy. The "National Liberal Federation of Canada" emphasises social security and foreign and economic independence, while the "New Democratic Party", a member of the Socialist Internationale, represents moderate socialism. The "Parti Québecois" exists only in Canada and represents the movement for autonomy in this province. Also there is the "Social Credit Party", found mainly in Alberta and British Columbia, the "Progressive Conservative Party of Canada", which supports membership of NATO and the Commonwealth and the preservation of the present economic system, and the Creditists (protagonists of social credit) representing the underprivileged classes.

Parties

Canada is made up of ten provinces and two territorial regions. The provinces have their own constitution and their governmental procedures are more or less identical to that of central government. Central government is represented by a provincial governor who is appointed for five years by the governor general on the recommendation of the prime minister. The provinces have their own legislative bodies with the exception of the Supreme Federal Courts. Legislative authority is not categorically defined; state and province compete with each other in this area. It is the responsibility of the province to raise its own taxes, to pass laws relating to civil rights or communal administration and to organise social welfare. The provinces also have control over the health service, education and use of natural resources. The administration of the Yukon Territory and the Northwest Territories is directly accountable to the federal government but is becoming increasingly independent.

Provinces

Administration of the courts lies with the provinces, apart from matters which concern the Supreme Federal Court. The Canadian laws are laid down in the "Common Law". Québec has its own civil laws based on the French "Code Civil". The highest courts in Canada are the Supreme Court and the Federal Court in Ottawa.

Courts

The judges of the federal and provincial courts are appointed by the relevant federal or provincial parliament. Canadian justice is thereby independent of the legislature and executive.

Conscription does not exist in Canada. Volunteers must serve at least five years. The total size of the army is about 90,000 men. Basic and specialised training courses are run by signals command and the Canadian Forces Training System. In 1968 formal divisions between the army, air force and navy ceased to exist.

Armed forces

The British North American Act of 1867 gave the provinces the right to form their own police authorities.

Police

In 1873 the Royal Canadian Mounted Police (RCMP) came into existence. The function of these "redshirts" was not only to keep law and order but also to see that federal laws were observed. Nowadays about a 20,000-strong force operates in the sparsely populated regions of the country. They are found in eight provinces and the two territories which come under the jurisdiction of the federal government.

RCMP

Royal Canadian Mounted Police on Parade

Financially better off provinces such as Québec and Ontario as well as individual regions and towns maintain their own police forces ("Sûrté", "Security").

Security Service

The Security Service, which controls the secret service, complements the activities of the RCMP in protecting public property and important personalities.

The Québec Problem (see Baedeker Special p. 393)

The national unity of Canada is most threatened by the situation in Québec, the francophone region of the country.

Origin

The cause is rooted in the historical tug-of-war between the British and French Canadians which began when the British took over New France in 1763.

On the one hand the influence of the French Canadians in social and economic areas was severely restricted. The consequences were that, forced by the process of economic development, these areas became dominated by the British Canadians: they occupied the key positions, whereas the French Canadians had no part in decision-making and their average income was far below that of the British Canadians. This disparity existed until quite recently.

On the other hand, however, the French-speaking inhabitants of Canada set about gradually populating the areas which were exclusively settled by the British Canadians. An easy undertaking, for these regions were insecure land for the anglophone population on account of the USA bordering in the east and the French Canadian region situated in the west.

"Silent revolution"

In 1960 the Liberal party got into provincial parliament with the French Canadian candidate Jean Lesage. This signalled a turning-point in history known as the "silent revolution". It was Lesage who forcefully demanded independence for the francophones and succeeded in not only getting the federal government to tolerate the struggle for cultural independence but also to set up a commission to solve the problem of bilingualism and twin culturalism. The result was the recognition throughout the country of French as the second official and equal language alongside English.

The independence movement did not always run so smoothly. Not long after the election of Lesage the FLQ (Front de Libération de Québec), a freedom front, was formed which sought attention through terrorist attacks, demonstrations, revolts, acts of spying and bomb attacks.
   The political tension came to a head in 1964 with the visit of the British queen. The consequence of these disturbances was the start of the migration of English-speaking population from this province; this caused the loss of the business directors with their entire management staff and left Québec in an ecomonic impasse.

"Saturday of the rubber truncheons"

When General de Gaulle publicly proclaimed his demand for a free Québec in 1967 the vehement defenders of separatism and the with-drawal of Québec from the Canadian federation regarded themselves as completely justified: the nationalist wing of the Liberals split from the party and founded the "Parti Québecois". They made a break-through in 1976 when René Levesques became the new president of Québec. However, they lost in a referendum in 1980 which was to have been the basis for negotiations on sovereignity within the confeder-ation; 60% of the population of the province of Québec voted against it. Since then serious efforts have been made to make Québec more French. Another referendum was defeated in 1995.

New wave of nationalism

In 1977 the famous Law 101 was passed which made Québec a mono-lingual francophone province with considerable restrictions on the use of other languages. The "Office de la Langue francaise" (Office of the French language) has since set about systematically changing every-thing to French.
   English expressions which are used and recognised worldwide, ad-vertising, names of companies and street names have all been trans-lated into French. A "hot-dog" is referred to as a "chien-chaud".

Law 101

Not only has there been a reduction in the British Canadian population in this province through migration as a consequence of Law 101. The traditional order, centred on the church, collapsed. Indicative of this is the abrupt decline in the birth rate since 1960; it is the lowest in Canada, whereas the traditional francophone family structure reflects a particu-larly high birth rate. 1960 is also the year when migration of French Canadians from the country to the towns began. In the province of Québec four out of five inhabitants live in urban conurbations.

Collapse of traditional order

The cultural identity also altered. Today they are proud of their heavily accented language, "québecois"; there is a French Canadian literary movement independent from France and its literary classics, which also influences music and art.
   Nowadays French Canadian politicians hold office in nearly all government departments.
   The separatist movement of Québec is not just an isolated problem within the Canadian confederation. Other provinces such as Alberta, British Columbia and Newfoundland are seeking to break away from the federation.
   Québec is merely the most visible example of one of Canada's basic problems.

Formation of its own national identity

Economy

Land of
superlatives

There are only a few countries in the world where a summary of the economy contains such a high number of superlatives as for Canada. One of the richest countries in the world, in 1994 it ranked 31st among the world's economies, with a population of 27.3 million and gross national product per head of 20,500 $. Its economic structure has been shaped for years by productive agriculture and the extraction and processing of its own raw materials. Canada is one of the largest producers of wheat and barley and possesses enormous forests (4.4 million sq.km/1.7 million sq.miles) which supply the giant cellulose and paper industries. It is a leading producer of uranium and zinc ores. Not least Canada has massive supplies of energy, especially gas and oil, as well as ideal conditions for producing hydro-electric power. Together with other factors this contributed to Canada having the highest rate of energy consumption in the world (about 9700kg/21388lb oil units per head in 1992) and the lowest energy prices of all industrial nations.

Geographical
conditions

The advantages and disadvantages of the geographical conditions in this northern country are reflected both in its geomorphological features and surface features (natural vegetation and soils) and in the climatic difficulties of distinct regions. Exploitation of the diverse range of natural resources is often problematic and can only be overcome by employing the most modern technology and involving considerable investment. The climate, in particular, exerts a lasting influence on the agriculture, mining and transport. Climate and permafrost do not only hinder tree-felling and mining in the north, but also – through snow-falls and blizzards – the centres of population in the south of Canada. Examples of the natural favourable and unfavourable conditions and their effects on the economic suitablility or exploitation are: mineral wealth of the Canadian Shield and the Cordilleras, abundant oil reserves in the Interior Plains stretching north, the giant forests of the boreal coniferous zone in the north and the mountains in the west (Cordillera) and east (Appalachians), the former grass steppes of the Prairies or the St Lawrence Valley as the fertile site of one of the most important granaries in the world, finally, the Atlantic and Pacific coastal regions and the inland lakes as fishing grounds and the water-falls in the mountains and of the Canadian Shield, which provide hydro-electric power at an increasing ecological cost.

Historical
development of
the economy

Following the discovery of Canada by the Europeans, in the first instance Jacques Cartier, who sailed up the St Lawrence River in 1534, colonisation began which continued into the 20th c. Canada's original population of about 200,000 Indians and Inuits in the 16th c. were equally as unable to defend themselves as those of the USA, but the massacres and wars did not take place to the same extent. Influential in the early economic development were four staple goods: fish, animal skins, wood and cereals. From the beginning of the 17th to the middle of the 19th c. fur-trading was organised by the powerful Hudson's Bay Company with economic proceeds being less relevant than exploration of the country by hunters, traders and surveyors. The widespread takeover of the fur trade by the increasingly prosperous wood trade was caused by the value of wood as building material for the British fleet and also more and more for settlements and companies at home. Settlement was quickly followed by cultivation and at the beginning of this century 60–70% of the Prairies were turned over to wheat, with Canada being the prime exporter of wheat. The discovery of mineral wealth in the middle of last century combined with the parallel opening

"Cathedrals of the Prairie" and a silo train ▶

up of the country by the railways gave the economy further support which brought industrialisation to the doorsteps of the exploding American markets and determined typical attitudes and outlook for a long time.

Political
influence,
Mulroney era

The period of development that follows is very similar to that of many European countries and if this is omitted and the present day political economy examined then it can be seen that on the one hand Canada has thrown off its old image and has remarkable high technology capable of competing on international markets, on the other hand, in accord with the US economy, it has been in recession since 1990 and is confronted by debt mountains, empty cash desks and unemployment, as never known before in the country.

The development of the Canadian economy has always been closely linked with political challenges. From the founding of the dominion in 1867 with the British North America Act the situation was characterised by the breaking away from England. When despite granting extensive cultural sovereignity the new constitution in 1982 failed to integrate the francophone province of Québec, a growing uncertainty arose from the complex situation. Although Brian Mulroney, leader of the government, still had a clear majority in parliament with 159 seats out of 295, surveys showed increasing support among voters for the Liberals and Social Democrats. Out of the close economic relationship with the USA, accompanied by heated discussions in Canada, the free trade agreement came into operation on January 1st, 1989, which foresees the dismantling of all reciprocal trade restrictions. Mulroney's election promises of 1988, such as, for example, the creation of new jobs through access to the USA, were not exactly fulfilled and even led to jobs being exported, to a certain extent, to the low wage regions of the American southern states. The national debt exceeded the 400 billion Can.$ mark in mid-1991, with annual interest of 43 billion Can.$ or 6.2% of the gross national product in the current financial year. High mortgage rates and overpriced consumer credit caused bankruptcies from 1989 to 1990 to rise by 44% and disturbed the high living standards of the Canadians, which were financed by budget deficits. Not until 1993 did economic growth rise above 2%; even then, while inflation fell below the 3% mark, the unemployment rate that same year reached a historic high of 11.3%.

NAFTA,
Chrétien era

The North American Free Trade Agreement (NAFTA), signed by the governments of Canada, the USA and Mexico which came into force on January 1st 1994, created the largest internal market in the world, with a total population of 365 million and an annual economic output of some 6 billion US dollars. The Chrétien government has promised a much needed boost for Canadian industry, particularly in the fields of telecommunications, computer software, space and aeronautics, agriculture and forestry, environmental conservation technology and mining (see Outlook).

Agriculture

On account of geographical conditions the most productive agricultural area is concentrated in a 300km-/186 mile-wide strip along the border with the USA. Employing almost 560,000, in 1988 this corresponded to 4.5% of the working population in almost 300,000 farms (average farm size more than 200ha), agriculture and forestry produced 2.9% of the gross national product in 1990. In the same year agricultural exports amounted to 8.8%, forestry products 14.3%. In total about 70 million ha/173 million acres (7% of the land) is used for agriculture. Different type of farms are found in different regions.

The large cereal farms dominate the three Prairie provinces (Manitoba, Saskatchewan and Alberta), where about 50% of the agricultural income is generated on about 80% of the land thereby forming the backbone of agriculture.

Dairy farms are found mostly in Québec, Ontario and Nova Scotia, cattle rearing farms in Alberta and Ontario and specialised crop farms (vegetables, fruit, tobacco and potatoes) in Ontario, Québec and British Columbia.

The main crops include (1990) wheat 56.8 mill. tonnes, barley 13.2 mill. tonnes, maize 6.8 mill. tonnes, oats 3.5 mill. tonnes, rape seed (1989) 3.1 mill. tonnes, beef (1989) 980,000 tonnes, pork 1,184,000 tonnes, poultry 693,000 tonnes and milk 8.3 mill tonnes.

The high productivity results from intense mechanisation and the degree of specialisation on the farms. A predominance of almost exclusively family concerns is a further guarantee of responsible accounting and profitability. High productivity has, however, also necessitated a corresponding level of capital investment and an increase in debt. Therefore it is not surprising that even in Canada the number of farms is decreasing and farming is increasingly concentrated in the hands of the top giant concerns. In 1988 low precipitation resulted in a low wheat yield of 33.7 mill. tonnes.

Canada is one of the leading fish exporters in the world. From catches of 1.5 mill. tonnes in 1987 about 600,000 tonnes was exported, 62% to the USA. Lucrative fishing grounds are situated off the Atlantic coast, especially for cod, plaice, mussels and lobster. Herring and salmon are caught off the Pacific coast. On account of the drop in the fishing quotas in the Seventies Canada decided to expand its fishing zone to 200 miles and to restrict the quotas for the north-west Atlantic in its negotiations with the EU. The crisis of the Atlantic fishing industry with factory closures and further reductions in quotas is exacerbated by the overfishing of the North Atlantic by the large Spanish and Portuguese fishing fleets. By 1993 the situation had deteriorated to such an extent that a total ban had to be imposed on fishing in the waters around Newfoundland. Several thousand Canadian fishermen and workers in ancillary industries lost their jobs as a result. — *Fishing*

In the early phase of economic development the trade in furs was of great importance and a trade mark of the Canadian economy. Worldwide protests against the fur hunters (especially against the cruel seal hunting), the introduction of fur farming and the general fall in demand have led to the downturn of this branch of the economy and at best it is a specialised market. — *Fur trade*

For many years Canadian forestry has been in the centre of critical economic discussions. On the one hand in 1989 890,000 jobs were directly or indirectly dependent upon it and with around 23 billion Can.$ it represented 14.3% of all Canadian exports, on the other "clear cutting" and simple reafforestation make for a permanent bad press. — *Forestry*

Canada has been over-felling its forests for years, resulting in deforestation. A "Green Plan" was initiated to carry out reafforestion, but the secondary forest, predominantly high-yielding spruce monoculture, is susceptible to insect attack and winter storms. It does not replace the sensitive ecosystem of the previous forest.

In view of this situation and the struggling wood and paper industry Canada is a long way from efficient forest management or replacing environmentally harmful chlorine bleach as in Europe. Mexico's free environment laws in view of the free trade agreement for the reprocessing of cellulose do not suggest any future change in clearing techniques, unless there is a new decline in the newsprint industry. In addition four-fifths of all forests are owned by the provinces which does not make for meaningful national control which is necessary to co-ordinate the various environmental laws.

Canada has the most productive and richest deposits of minerals and fuels in the world. Canada is at the top of the league in the production of uranium and zinc (Noranda and Canadian Pacific are the two leading companies). In 1989 11,000 tonnes and 1.2 mill. tonnes respectively were produced, which represents 30% and 17% of world production. — *Mining*

Economy

The fall in uranium production by 1400 tonnes, compared with the previous year, (Uranium City in the north of Saskatchewan province) was caused by a decrease in uranium's importance for energy and military requirements. As a result of overproduction and the fall in price the existence and profitability of some mines is in doubt.

In 1989 Canada fell into second place behind the Soviet Union in nickel production, but still produced 25% of the world's supply. Canada's position as one of the world's leading producers of minerals is illustrated by the following figures which relate to 1989 for production and position: lead 275,000 tonnes (5th), gold 4.1 mill. ounces (5th), copper 732,000 tonnes (4th), silver 1306 tonnes (5th) and a major producer of iron ore.

Canada is also an important producer of fossil fuels such as gas 107 billion cu.m (3rd), oil and coal. Mining accounts for 3.9% of the gross national product in 1990. A fall in prices on the commodities market, expanding recycling initiatives and substitute materials, falling demand in key industries such as construction and automobile industries, specialised developments (uranium) or unprofitable conditions for exploitation have caused output to fall in many areas of the industry.

Energy

Canada produced 490 billion kWh in 1989 and occupied 5th place, 70% of which was hydro-electric power, a remarkable percentage by world standards. In recent years there has been a restructuring in fossil fuel production from oil in favour of gas. A large part of the increased energy exports goes to the USA.

The Gulf crisis in 1990 brought the Canadian energy companies high export returns. The largest hydro-electric power stations in the world are in the provinces of Québec and Newfoundland. Both Churchill Falls (5320 MW) and St James Bay Project (I), which has been under consstruction since 1973 with a planned capacity of 10,000 MW, produce cheap electricity. Nevertheless, Hydro Québec, Québec's own company, the second largest energy concern in Canada after Ontario Hydro, on account of its debts is rapidly coming into conflict with its customers, state environmental authorities and conservationists through its price policy, its projected requirements and its plans to build new water power stations in the north.

Industry, trade and services

The dependence of industry on its own agricultural and mineral resources is reflected in the sectoral structure of the processing industries. This sector of the economy accounts for 25% of the gross national product in 1990 and occupied about the same percentage of the total workforce. Of the 1.8 million employed in the industry the majority are occupied in automobile construction (214,000; both General Motors of Canada and Ford Motors of Canada alone, the largest companies in the country in terms of turnover, employed over 70,000 in 1988 with a turnover of 19.3% or 15.9 billion Can.$; both companies have their headquarters in Oshawa and Oakville, Ontario). In terms of numbers of employees the food industry is in second place (195,000). The growth of industries producing items of capital expenditure was stimulated by the tax allowances enjoyed by the American automobile industry in return for greater investment since the mid-Sixties.

In addition the liberal economic policy of the Mulroney government "promoted" direct foreign investment (although not always uninterrupted), which was channelled into the service sector and increased the dependence on the US economy. Between 1970 and 1989 alone the number of employees in the private service sector rose by 7% to 33% and in 1990 the service sector made up 51% of the gross national product and 18% for commerce and transport together, a quantative indication of the change in economic structure.

The processing industries are concentrated in the provinces of Québec and Ontario in the commercial centres of Montréal, Toronto and

Ottawa. 15 of Canada's 20 largest companies had their head office in Montréal or Toronto in 1988, as well as banks, insurance companies and other service industries.

Only during the last decade have other regional centres such as Edmonton, Calgary or Vancouver become important regional centres. In the provinces of Alberta and British Columbia the growth rates of the oil and construction industry and the varied raw material industry provided for an upturn in and in part beyond their respective centres.

For 1991 a fall in the gross national product of 0.1% is expected in the two main industrial centres of Canada (around 80% of industrial net product), for the Prairie provinces of Saskatchewan and Manitoba as much as 0.7 and 0.8% respectively (Alberta +0.1%, British Columbia −0.5%). Only for the Atlantic provinces is growth of 0.5% to 2.8% predicted and oil exploitation seen as a further positive signal. Perhaps the economic community of the three (or four) Atlantic provinces will be realised in the medium term.

Future economic development could include the continuation of the St James Bay project II in Québec with massive investment, the expansion of mining of the tar sands in Alberta and the bilateral free trade treaty with the USA could finally bring clear signs of economic growth in Ontario.

The figures for 1990 demonstrate the close economic involvement with and dependence on the USA, amounting to 76% of exports (tax value 146.1 billion Can.$) and 69% of imports (tax value 135.3 billion Can.$). Japan, Great Britain and Germany (6–2%) lag far behind as exporters and importers to and from Canada. The main goods for export are cars (23%), manufactured goods (21%), machinery and equipment (20%). Imported goods include machinery and equipment (31%), cars (23%) and manufactured goods (19%). On balance Canada had an export surplus of 10.8 mill. Can.$, but with a balance of payments deficit rising to 22 billion Can.$.

Foreign trade

Tourism has been a successful part of the economy. In 1993 some 40 million visitors came to Canada spending about 5 billion Can.$. 90% were from the USA. The number of visitors who stayed longer than 24 hours totalled 16 million (including 1.7 million from Europe) spending approximately 5 billion Can.$. These statistics underline the importance of excursions, shopping and business trips between Canada and the USA especially for the main destinations in Québec, Ontario and British Columbia.

Tourism

Even greater numbers travelled in the opposite direction. Figures for 1993 show close on 50 million visits by Canadians to the USA, with total spending of 8 billion Can.$. The high expectations formed by the Canadian tourist industry in the 1980s, especially the rapidly expanding hotel and catering sectors, remain largely unfulfilled except here and there on a local scale following intensive promotion.

In the last few decades Canada's economy has been trapped in a seemingly interminable "vale of darkness", the outward manifestations of which have been and remain a massive burden of national debt and a huge budget deficit. Since 1993 however there have been tentative signs of recovery. In the third quarter of 1993 the rate of economic growth reached 3.8% for the first time in many years, reflecting on the one hand increased consumer spending and on the other hand a particularly buoyant export performance. Within a year exports rose 15.6% to 181 billion Can.$, as a result of which the balance of trade surplus in 1993 reached almost 12 billion Can.$. Expectations are for a further expansion in exports contributing to a lasting reduction in the budget deficit (which dropped from 27.7 billion Can.$ to 25.2 billion Can.$ in a single year). Giving less cause for optimism however are the exorbitantly high level of national debt (which in the 1994/95 financial year reached a record high of 661 billion Can.$), the continuing up-

Outlook

heavals in currency markets, the failure to dismantle internal economic barriers between the provinces, and the costs associated with relatively high wage levels and the expensive network of social provision.

In view of these negative factors it is difficult to predict whether, in the face of stiff international competition, the ambitious targets set by Canada's government leader – the creation of around 2.5 million new jobs and an improvement of 25% in real incomes by the year 2000 – can be met.

Nor can the economic uncertainties and possible threat to employment associated with participation in NAFTA (the recently established free trade zone, the largest in the world, involving Canada, the USA and Mexico) be ignored. The extent to which Canadian economic policy continues to be helpful towards Mexico with its pool of surplus labour but shortage of capital remains to be seen.

In conclusion the following problem areas exist from an economic point of view:

reduction in the disparity between east and west and the difference between central and peripheral development (for example Alberta with the establishment of growth industries on the outskirts);

solving the conflict between development and conservation (further opening up of the north);

defusing idea of cultural dualism as a threat but as a source of enrichment instead (Québec problem);

format of relations with the USA, Mexico and the EU;

conservation of the unique natural environment (co-ordination and consolidation of the environmental laws, reinforcement of conservation measures, national parks).

Transport and telecomunications

General

In the huge country of Canada which embraces the entire north of the American continent and whose population is traditionally very mobile a well organised transport and communication network must be guaranteed. This is particularly the case in view of the fact that Canada belongs to the leading industrial nations of the world. Owing to its sheer size it is imperative for the development of the Canadian economy and to maintain a high standard of living that well developed transport facilities and routes and the most up-to-date communication systems are available.

The technical problems presented in building an effective transport and communications infrastructure have motivated numerous Canadian entrepreneurs, scientists and engineers to great achievements. The innovative skills of Canadian technicians are in demand wherever there are problems with telecommunications, pipeline and road construction over rough terrain and civil aviation.

Shipping
Sea ports
St Lawrence
Seaway

Shipping is of paramount importance to this huge North American country. A large percentage of export goods (especially ores, building material, wood and cereals) are transported by ship. The St Lawrence Seaway was widened to allow regular maritime harbours to be built on the Great Lakes in the middle of the country and along the St Lawrence River. Thunder Bay on Lake Superior is one of the main ports for the export of cereals. Huge quantities of minerals are exported from Sept Îles/Pointe Noire and Port Cartier (all in Québec province). On the other hand the ports of Québec (town), Montréal, Toronto and Hamilton are important for the import of oil products, coal, vehicles, etc. Situated out on the Atlantic coast are other major ports (Halifax in Nova Scotia, St John in New Brunswick, and St John's in Newfoundland) and on the Pacific coast (Vancouver in British Columbia). In the Pacific port of Vancouver alone more than 64 million tonnes of goods are handled annually.

Alongside the continually expanding volume of freight traffic passenger services also operate, but on a smaller scale. The ferry services around Inside Passage (from Vancouver to Alaska) and among the Atlantic Islands in the east (especially Prince Edward Island, Newfoundland, New Brunswick, Nova Scotia) are of regional importance.

The main destinations of cruise ships are Vancouver and the Inside Passage, the Atlantic port of Halifax and the ports of Québec (town) and Montréal on the St Lawrence River.

Passenger services

The major Canadian railway companies, "Canadian National" (CN) and "Canadian Pacific" (CP), maintain a network of almost 100,000km/ 62,139 miles of track. The railway lines of the east–west routes (on some routes north–south) are primarily used to transport freight. Extra long goods trains with 100 and more wagons, often pulled by up to six locomotives, move the freight between the cereal producing areas or ore deposits and the nearest sea ports and in return distribute the goods imported through these ports. There is considerable rail freight crossing over into the USA and vice versa.

Railways
CN, CP

Passenger rail services are provided by the company "VIA" Rail, founded in 1978. It rents the infrastructure from the major railway companies and is concentrated on profitable lines with large numbers of passengers (e.g. the "racetrack" Toronto–Montréal) and tourist routes. In areas where passenger numbers are low provincial authorities or large companies fund passenger services (e.g. Ontario Northern or the Algoma Railway) for politically environmental reasons.

Passenger trains
VIA Rail

As in the neighbouring USA the motor car controls everyday life in Canada. The road and motorway network is particularly well developed in the heavily populated south and in tourist areas. At the end of the Eighties there were almost 450 cars to every 1000 people. There are 1 million kilometres (about 600,000 miles) of long distance roads which are used not only by tourists, but predominantly by whole caravans of gigantic trucks. At 7871km/4890 miles long the TransCanada Highway is the longest road in the world connecting St John's on the Atlantic with Vancouver on the Pacific.

Roads
Road networks and volume of traffic

In the long, harsh Canadian winters the importance of the caterpillar snowmobile cannot be underestimated. In the far north whole snow trains (trucks on caterpillars) are formed to make a path through the snow. In winter some of the frozen rivers function as roads. On the Mackenzie in particular and northern rivers this transport is common.

Snowmobile

Passenger air traffic is important because of the distances and morphology of the country. The main airports are at Toronto (17 million passengers per annum), Montréal, Edmonton, Vancouver, Calgary, Winnipeg and Halifax.

Air transport
International airports

Numerous larger and smaller airline companies operate from the above Canadian airports (almost 600 altogether). They serve the less populated regions and the far north, which is being opened up. These airlines use mostly smaller planes which can operate from the difficult runways on the 200 or more airfields.

Regional transport

Canada, the home of Alexander Bell, possesses the most intensive telephone network in the world. For every 100 inhabitants there are nearly 53 connections. The Canadian telephone companies maintain the largest microwave transmission system in the world, which is capable of not only transmitting telephone conversations but also radio and television programmes and electronic data.

Recent applications include surgical operations in hospitals in other cities being monitored and assisted by remote transmission. Similar monitoring can take place in prospecting for raw materials and for land and sea travel guided by satellite.

Telecommunications
Telephone, radio, television, data transmission, remote monitoring

History

c. 15,000 to 12,000 B.C.	Archaeological discoveries indicate that the predecessors of the present day Indians and Inuits were hunter-gatherers who filtered in over the Beringia land bridge in three waves from the north-east Asia to North America: first the predecessors of the northwest coast Indians, then the Inuit and finally the Paleo Indians.
c. 10,000 B.C.	Beginning of settlement in south Ontario.
c. 4000 B.C.	The west coast Indians' culture flourishes.
c. 3000 B.C.	The Inuit populate the northern regions of Canada.
c. 875 A.D.	Irish monks are said to have landed in the Gulf of St Lawrence.
c. 1000 A.D.	Vikings stop temporarily in Newfoundland and Labrador. They build a short-lived township, evidence of which exists at L'Anse-aux-Meadows.
14th c.	Portuguese, English, Normans and Bretons come to the rich fishing grounds of Newfoundland.
1497	John Cabot – probably born Giovanni Caboto in 1449 in Genoa and later entered the service of the English crown – reaches the eastern tip of Canada. He claims the country for England (Henry VII). Cabot contributes to the opening up the northwest Atlantic fishing grounds.
Early 16th c.	Spanish, Portuguese and French fish off Newfoundland.
1523	Verrazano reconnoitres present day Nova Scotia for the king of France.
1534	The Breton Jacques Cartier lands in Newfoundland after a long sea journey. He sails up the St Lawrence River to the Indian settlement Hochelaga (Montréal today). He opens the way into the interior for French colonists and fur hunters.
1576	Frobisher looks for the Northwest Passage and claims his discoveries in the Canadian north for the English crown.
1604	The first Hugenots settle here.
from 1608	Samuel de Champlain founds the settlement of Québec. It becomes the first successful white settlement and main town of New France. Champlain builds up an extensive trading network (fur trade) and becomes the first governor of French Canada.
1609/1610	Henry Hudson, on behalf of the Dutch East India Company, also searches for the Northwest Passage. He names the great inland lake in north-east Canada.
1625	Jesuits arrive in Québec and begin missionary work among the Indians.
1642	French pioneers found Montréal. The Iroquis attack the settlement for 20 years.
1663	Louis XIV of France declares New France to be a royal province. Troops are dispatched to defend the colony and further colonisation by France is encouraged.

The Hudson's Bay Company is founded by royal charter in London in 1670. The English king Charles II awards the company the fur trading monopoly for 8 million sq.km/3 million sq.miles of land.
    The English controlled company competes with French traders for favour with the Indians. The French extend their sphere of influence west along the St Lawrence River to the Great Lakes and from there to the Prairies and to the Mississippi. The English move southwards down the North American east coast.

from 1670

Louis Jollet and Father Marquette reach Lake Michigan and probably the Mississipi.

1672

The French found numerous settlements along the St Lawrence River and in Acadia (area south-east of the mouth of the St Lawrence, nowadays Nova Scotia, New Brunswick, southern part of Québec). Acadia is ruled by the French and English at different times.

17th c.

The French explorer Pierre de Vérendrye extends the French fur trading posts to Saskatchewan and Missouri.

1690–1713

As a counterpart to the inheritance wars in Europe war breaks out again between the French and English in North America.

1745–48

Shortly before the outbreak of the Seven Years' War several thousand French settlers are expelled from Acadia by the English governor for not being prepared to swear an oath of allegiance to England.

1755

The period of power struggles between France and England in North America ends with the defeat of Montréal and Québec by British troops.

1759/1760

Following the Paris peace agreement all colonies become British. France only retains the islands of St Pierre and Miquelon off Newfoundland.

1763

Samuel Hearne, commissioned by the Hudson's Bay Company, undertakes expeditions into the interior in order to increase the opportunities for trade. He is the first white man to reach the Arctic Ocean.

1770–72

In the Québec Act England guarantees the Québecois, who far outnumber the British settlers, the right to the French language, French civil law and to practise Catholicism.

1774

In the American War of Independence, in which 13 British colonies break away from the motherland and form the United States of America, Canada retains its neutral loyalty to Great Britain. Many loyal to the Empire (about 40,000 to 60,000) move north at the end of the war and settle in Nova Scotia, New Brunswick and in southern Ontario. This immigration changes Canada from a French colony of England to a predominantly English-speaking country.

1775–83

The first Europeans, led by James Cook and George Vancouver, land on the coast of present day British Columbia.

1778

In the Paris peace treaty the USA–Canadian border is established.

1783

The British government passes the Canada Act (the name Canada appears officially for the first time), which divides the old province of Québec into Upper Canada (nowadays Québec province) and Lower Canada (nowadays Ontario province), mainly English-speaking.

1791

George Vancouver, who took part in the expedition along the Pacific coast with James Cook in 1778, sails round the island which today bears his name.

1792

An overland expedition led by Alexander Mackenzie reaches the Pacific Ocean.

1793

History

1808	On one of the biggest expeditions of all time Simon Fraser travels 1368km along the river named after him, from its source in the Rocky Mountains to its estuary in the Pacific. He names the region west of the Rockies New Caledonia, after his homeland, Scotland.
1812–14	The United States of America attempts to assert its influence over Canada by force. It results in war with Great Britain which ends in defeat for America.
1823	Great Britain initiates a campaign among its poor population, particularly in Ireland and Scotland, to encourage them to emigrate to the North American colonies.
1830–50	After 1830 chiefly Irish, Scottish and Germans emigrate to Canada. Numbers are estimated at 800,000 for this period.
1837	Uprisings take place in Upper and Lower Canada in protest against the authoritarian government, but are quickly put down.
1841	Upper and Lower Canada are united in the British colony of Canada. They receive a governor, an executive council, and an elected lower chamber, in which both the former provinces are strongly represented.
1846	The 49th parallel becomes the border between the USA and the British colonies from Ontario to the Pacific coast.
1858	The British create the colony British Columbia, which is united with the separate colony of Vancouver Island in 1866.
1867	The present day provinces of Ontario, Québec, New Brunswick and Nova Scotia form the autonomous dominion of Canada.
1869	The huge northern and western territories, which until now have been administered by the Hudson's Bay Company, join the new state.
	The Métis (French Indians), under the leadership of Louis Riel, rebel against the Canadian government.
1870	The province of Manitoba is established.
1871	British Columbia joins the Canadian federation.
1873	Prince Edward Island also becomes part of Canada.
1875	Russian Mennonites settle in Manitoba.
1885	The Métis, led by Loius Riel, rebel again. Riel is hung. The transcontinental stretch of the Canadian Pacific Railway is completed.
1896	The Gold Rush erupts on the Klondike/Yukon. On account of the increased population the Yukon is made a separate province from the Northwest Territories.
1899–1902	Canadian troops fight for the British in the Boer War.
1905	Alberta, Saskatchewan and the Northwest Territories are recognised as Canadian territories.
1914–18	Canada joins the First World War on the side of England. It results in further industrialisation and in Canada earning new international status through being an independent signatory of the treaty of Versailles and as a member of the League of Nations.

Search for gold in the Klondike

The most serious disturbances in Canadian industrial history: workers strike to support their demands for social justice. Even the farmers are dissatisfied with their financial situation.	1919–25
William Lyon Mackenzie King becomes prime minister. He determines Canadian politics for 27 years.	1921
Millions of immigrants from the USA, the British Isles and many regions of continental Europe populate Canada. The two main waves of immigrants are during and after both world wars.	1st half of the 20th c.
The world economic crisis reaches Canada. In 1933 unemployment peaks at about 20%.	1929–33
The statute of Westminster grants Canada full autonomy.	1931
Canada fights against Germany in the Second World War.	1939–45
The Alaska Highway to Alaska is completed.	1942
Canada becomes a member of the United Nations.	1945
Canada becomes a member of the North Atlantic Treaty Organisation (NATO). Newfoundland becomes the tenth province of the Canadian Federation.	1949
The St Lawrence Seaway, an American-Canadian project, is opened.	1959
Parliament passes the first Bill of Rights. It gives the Indians and Inuit the right to vote in federal elections.	1960
The red maple leaf becomes the national flag.	1965

1967	Canada celebrates its centenary. Expo '67 takes place in Montréal. On July 24th Charles de Gaulle calls out from the balcony of Montréal Town Hall "Vive le Québec libre!" (= Long live free Québec).
1968	Pierre Trudeau becomes prime minister. The Québecois party is founded. Its aim is a separate, francophone state of Québec.
1969	Parliament passes the Official Languages Act, in which both English and French are recognised as official languages.
1970	Revolutionaries from the Front de Libération de Québec (FLQ) kidnap a British diplomat and a Canadian minister. Pierre Trudeau declares martial law.
1976	The Olympic Games take place in Montréal.
1980	In a referendum about 60% of the population of Québec reject separatism. The Province remains in the Canadian Federation.
1982	Canada receives a new constitution and a "Charter of Rights and Freedoms", in which human rights are guaranteed.
1983	Demonstrations take place throughout the country against the government's decision to allow American cruise missiles in Canada. They are unsuccessful.
1985/1986	Bilateral meetings between prime minister Brian Mulroney and Ronald Reagan. Main topics are acid rain and the expansion of trade between the two countries. In Vancouver Expo '86 is opened.
1988	Canada is the first country in the world to establish in law multiculturalism. In the elections of November 21st the Progressive Conservative party achieves an overall victory, but loses its two-thirds majority. Brian Mulroney is re-elected prime minister. Canada and its biggest trading partner, the USA, ratify a free trade agreement. The Winter Olympics are held in and around Calgary.
1990	At a conference of foreign ministers of NATO and the Warsaw Pact in Ottowa the four super powers together with both German states declare their support for German unity. The Meech Lake Agreement, which grants Québec province special status, collapses partly owing to the Cree chiefs in the Manitoba parliament, who vote against granting the descendants of French immigrants special status. As a result the activities of the separatist movement in Québec increase. In Oka and in Montréal militant Iroquois resist the extension of a golf course which would violate the cemetery of their ancestors. A policeman is killed in the disturbances. Canadian police are sent in against the Indians. In the Indian reservation of St Regis (north-east of Lake Ontario) members of an Iroquois tribe fight each other. Supporters and opponents of an organised gambling game fight bitterly with weapons causing deaths.
1991	In the summer a strike by postal workers disrupts public life. In the autumn discussions on the reform of Canada's constitution come to a head. Once again the main issue is the granting of special status to the francophone province of Québec.

In the spring the native inhabitants of the Canadian north opt for the creation of a new province, to be carved out of the existing Northwest Territories. 1992

A referendum organised by the federal government decides against a new Canadian constitution.

The majority of Canadian troops stationed in Germany are withdrawn, returning to their North American homeland. 1992/1993

In May Prime Minister Brian Mulroney signs the Nunavut agreement in Iqaluit granting self-government to the native inhabitants of Canada in the approximately 2 million sq.km/772,000 sq.mile eastern section of the Northwest Territories, stretching from the North Pole to the southern Hudson Bay. In June Mulroney resigns after nine years in office; he is succeeded by Canada's first woman prime minister, Kim Campbell. In subsequent parliamentary elections in October the Liberal Party emerges the clear victor; the Québec separatists, the Bloc Québécois, also make gains, becoming the second most powerful opposition group. The Liberal leader Jean Chrétien takes over as prime minister. 1993

Responding to the crisis in fish stocks resulting from over-fishing, the federal government bans fishing in the waters around Newfoundland. Several thousand fishermen and employees in the fish industry lose their jobs.

On the Pacific coast of Canada strong resistance develops to further destruction of the remaining, still largely virgin, temperate rain forest eco-systems, threatened by continuing expansion of the paper and cellulose industries.

On January 1st the North American Free Trade Agreement (NAFTA), signed by Canada, the USA and Mexico, comes into force. With some 365 million inhabitants and annual economic output of approximately 6 billion US dollars, the NAFTA countries constitute the most viable internal market in the world. The Chrétien government launches a billion dollar programme aimed at reducing unemployment which has now reached double figures. 1994

In September the provincial election in Québec is won by the separatist Parti Québécois.

Summit meeting of the G 7 group of seven major industrial nations in Halifax. 1995

Famous People

Note

The following alphabetical list of names includes personalities who are associated with Canada through birth, visit, influence or death and have achieved international importance.

Sir Frederick Grant Banting
Medical researcher
(14.11.1891 to 21.2.1941)

Born in Alliston/Ontario Frederick Grant Banting began to practise in 1920 after studying medicine and specialising in orthopaedics. A year later he carried out research at the University of Toronto with J. J. R. Macleod and with C. H. Best into the secretions of the pancreas. Although his thesis could not be substantiated, his research stimulated more extensive studies which finally led to the discovery of insulin in 1921/22 by a team made up of Macleod, Banting, J. B. Collip and Best.

Insulin immediately became effective as a life-saving treatment for diabetes. Banting was acknowledged as its main discoverer, because his idea had given rise to the research, because he was well known for having made early use of insulin, and because he and his friends led a smear campaign against their former colleagues, Macleod and Collip. When he was awarded the Nobel Prize for physiology or medicine he gave half of the prize money to Best. Banting received a life pension from the federal government and was appointed the first Canadian professor of medical research at Toronto university. In 1934 he was knighted. He was killed in an air crash in 1941.

Alexander Graham Bell
Inventor
(3.3.1847 to 2.8.1922)

Alexander Graham Bell was born in Edinburgh and arrived in Brantford/Ontario, where he and his father worked as speech therapists for the deaf-mute. Between 1874 and 1876 Bell developed equipment which constituted the first usable telephone. Bell patented his discovery and promoted the commercial use of the telephone in the USA, through which he grew rich. He finally settled in Baddeck/Nova Scotia.

Bell spent the remainder of his life on scientific research and financed other research. He worked on the photo cell, the iron lung, the desalification of seawater and tried to breed a "super race" of sheep. His wife Mabel Gardiner Hubbar (1857–1923) shared his scientific interests. She was a member of the Aerial Experiment Assn., carried out gardening experiments and supported women's right to vote.

The Aerial Experiment Assn. was founded by Bell together with J. A. D. Mccurdy, F. W. Baldwin and others. They built some successful, petrol-driven double deckers. The flight of the Silver Dart on February 23rd, 1909 was regarded as the first manned flight in Canada. The company also worked on hydrofoils. The HD-4 set a world record in 1919 with a speed of 114kmh/71mph.

J. Armand Bombardier
Inventor
(1908 to 18.2.1964)

Right from being a teenager J. Armand Bombardier attempted to realise his idea of making an all-terrain vehicle, for bog or snow. In 1937 he was successful with his machine which was chain-driven and steered by skis. In 1959 Bombardier's firm brought a Ski-Doo onto the market, a vehicle which created a new type of sport. The size, which was about the same as that of a motorcycle, was new and it was driven by a single large track. Within a short time the vehicle changed the lives of the Inuit and Arctic communities.

Paul-Émile Borduas
Painter
(1.11.1905 to 22.2.1960)

Ozias Leduc encouraged the young Paul-Émile Borduas to study at the École des Beaux-Arts in Montréal (1923–27) and helped him with his first visit to Paris (1928–30) in the studio of the Art Sacré, which was led by Maurice Denis.

On returning to Canada he had to give up his dream of becoming a church artist like Leduc, as he had to earn his living as an art teacher. In

Alexander Graham Bell

Jacques Cartier

Glenn Herbert Gould

1937 he became professor at the École du Meuble. During this time he painted very little and destroyed much of his work. His painting was figurative and gradually became more influenced by Renoir, Pascin, James Wilson Morrice and later Cézanne. In 1942 influenced by the Surrealism of André Breton he completed several abstract guaches.

Borduas was increasingly influential with younger painters, especially his students, and he became leader of the Automatist movement. In 1948 he published the manifesto "Refus Global" in which he denounced the oppressive power of established thought in Québec and proclaimed total freedom in art. As a result he had to give up teaching.

From 1953 to 1955 Borduas lived in New York where he was influenced by Action painting. Next he went to Paris. In his painting he concentrated on the contrast between black and white ("L'Étoile noire" of 1957 is considered his masterpiece). Although he was successful in Canada he had difficulty in getting into the art scene in Paris. He dreamed of returning to Canada, but died in 1960.

Examples of his work hang in the National Gallery of Canada, the Musée d'Art Contemporaine and in the Musée des Beaux Arts in Montréal.

Born Giovanni Caboto (John Cabot) in Genoa, he was the first to prove that his expedition reached North America. Independent of Columbus he seemed to have the idea of reaching Asia by travelling west over the Atlantic.

John Cabot
Discoverer
(1449/50 to 1489/99)

In 1484 Giovanni Caboto moved to London with his family. In 1496 Henry VII granted him and his sons permission to undertake expeditions of discovery. With a small ship and a crew of 18 men he set sail on May 2nd. In June he landed on the coast of North America, probably either in Newfoundland, South Labrador or Cape Breton Island. He claimed the land in the name of Henry VII and returned home convinced that he had discovered the north-east coast of Asia. The following year he sailed along the east coast of Greenland, which he named Labrador. Later the name was given to a part of the Canadian coast, because it was believed that it belonged to Greenland.

Cabot's journeys formed the basis for England's claim to North America and led to the opening-up of the fishing grounds in the Northwest Atlantic.

Emily Carr, born in the small island town of Victoria to English parents, studied art at the California School of Design in San Francisco after she was orphaned. When she returned home after 2½ years she set up a studio and gave children art lessons. Study leave in England did little for her creativity. A visit to France in 1910/1911 had a stronger impact

Emily Carr
Painter, author
(13.12.1871 to
2.3.1945)

which was expressed in a post Impressionist style, marking the end of the early English water colour fashion.

In 1908 she began to look for Indian towns to paint the diminishing number of settlements, houses and totem poles.

At 57 she took part in a national exhibition in eastern Canada and met members of the Group of Seven. This was the period of maturity and individual work on which her reputation was later to be founded. From 1932 onwards she gradually received critical acclaim, had national exhibitions and occasionally sold a painting. After 1932 the Indian theme was replaced by subjects from nature and forests, beaches and the sky were freely represented in her paintings. Following a heart attack in 1937 her health began to deteriorate and she devoted more time to writing. In 1941 "Klee Wyck" was published and received the Governor General's Award. She died four years later in her hometown, Victoria.

Jacques Cartier
Discoverer
(1491 to
1.9.1557)

Jacques Cartier can only be credited with discovering the small area of Québec, which was then called Canada by the Indians. In 1534 he was commissioned by François I to search for the passage to Asia and find gold. He reached Newfoundland and attempting to find a way through the continent discovered the Gulf of St Lawrence. He undertook further expeditions in search of gold and diamonds and came across the St Lawrence River. He was held in high regard when he died in 1557 and was buried in the cathedral of his home town, St Malo.

Samuel de Champlain
Discoverer
(c. 1570 to
25.12.1635)

The central role played by Samuel de Champlain in discovering the St Lawrence region brought him the nickname "Father of New France".

Little is known of his childhood and youth. He was born c. 1570 in Brouage, Normandy, the son of a fisherman. In 1603 he sailed up the St Lawrence River with François Gravé Du Pont. He made the first detailed description of the river since Jacques Cartier's discoveries. A year later Champlain sailed with De Monts to Acadia, where they founded Port-Royal (Annapolis Royal) and Ste-Croix. As a cartographer he was commissioned to find the ideal site for a settlement on the coast. He explored the coast of New England and finally, on De Monts' instruction, founded Québec.

Champlain built up an extensive trade network, forming links with the Montagnais on the St Lawrence, the population around Ottawa and the Huron of the Great Lakes.

Despite the resistance of several trading companies only concerned with the profitable fur trade, Champlain planned to make Québec the centre of a powerful colony. His dream seemed to come true with the founding of the "Compagnie de Cent-Associés" in 1627. But then Québec was occupied by the English from 1629 to 1632. Appointed lieutenant by Cardinal Richelieu, Champlain returned to Québec in 1633, where his plans gradually took shape. He died, however, on December 25th, 1635.

Champlain left various writings about his travels. His works contain the only account of colonisation of the St Lawrence River in the first quarter of the 17th c. He illustrated his descriptions with many maps which record all contemporary knowledge of North America.

Leif Erikson
Discoverer
(10/11th c.)

The Viking Leif Erikson, son of Erich the Red, was probably the first European to set foot, around the year 1000, on North American soil. His father came to Greenland in 982, where he founded two settlements, which disappeared without explanation in the 14th c.

He probably landed in the north of Newfoundland "Vinland", where the Norwegian archaeologist Helge Ingstad discovered eight houses with workshops and forges in L'Anse-aux-Meadows between 1960 and 1969.

Two further discoveries, Helluland (land with flat stones) is Baffin Island and Markland (land of forest) is present day Labrador.

Sandford Fleming was Canada's leading railway inspector in the 19th c. and an outstanding inventor and scientist.

When he arrived in Canada from Scotland in 1845 he continued studying engineering. After gaining professional expertise in railway construction he finally became involved as an engineer in the planning of the line from Québec City to Halifax and Saint John and in 1871 in the planning of the new Canadian railway from Montréal to the Pacific coast. Although his suggested routes for the last project were not adopted, his extensive reports on the various stretches, e.g. Kicking Horse Pass, through which the main route of the Canadian Pacific was built, greatly assisted the construction of the Canadian railways. He resigned from the CPR when the government awarded the project to a private syndicate in 1880.

Fleming turned his interest to other areas. He was an ardent defender of the long distance cable from Canada to Australia, laid in 1902. He was a participant in the International Prime Meridian Conference in Washington in 1884, when standard time was introduced, which still operates today. Fleming also designed the first Canadian stamp, the "3-penny beaver", which came out in 1851.

Sir Sandford Fleming
Engineer
(1.1.1827 to 22.7.1915)

Simon Fraser was born in Mapletown near Bennington in 1776. He was the youngest son of an officer in the government troops, who was taken prisoner by rebels and died in captivity. His mother brought him to Montréal where he was brought up by his uncle.

In 1801 Fraser became a partner in the Athabaska Dept. He was responsible for business beyond the Rockies and founded the earliest settlement in that region, which he named New Caledonia. He established Fort McLeod in 1805, Fort St James and Fraser in 1806 and Fort George (today Prince George) the following year. In 1808 he set off to discover the river which he assumed to be the Columbia. He crossed unknown land fighting his way through dangerous country, today called Fraser River Canyon. On realising that it was not the Columbia he returned deeply disappointed. He wrote a report on his expedition entitled, "The Letters and Journals of Simon Fraser, 1806–08", which are still published today.

Fraser then turned his attention to the fur trade. He was one of the NWC officers, taken prisoner by Lord Selkirk in 1816 and charged with complicity in the Seven Oaks Incident; Fraser was finally acquitted. He died in 1862 in St Andrews.

Simon Fraser
Discoverer,
Fur trader
(1776 to 18.8.1862)

The works of Glenn Herbert Gould, born on 25.9.1932 in Toronto, are of unique importance in the history of music.

He received his musical education at the Royal Conservatorium of Music in Toronto. At the age of 14 he was already a concert soloist with the symphony orchestra there. Solo concerts, performances with many Canadian orchestras and broadcasts on CBC along with his predilection for unusual piano pieces (Bach, 16th c. English piano pieces, modern composers such as Hindesmith and Schönberg) soon made him into one of Canada's leading musicians. His first appearances in Washington and New York in January 1955 and his first recording in the USA that year (Bach's Goldberg variations) brought him international acclaim. Concerts in England, Australia, Germany, Israel and the USSR (where he was one of the first Canadians to go on tour) followed. In 1964 Gould withdrew from the concert stage: he wanted to devote himself to producing records and television programmes.

Gould's talent on the piano was characterised by exceptional linear details and strong movements. His classical interpretations were often provocative and sometimes eccentric in tempo and expression. His repertoire of records contained practically all piano works by Bach and Beethoven, many from the first half of the 20th c. but few from the 19th century.

Glenn Herbert Gould
Pianist, composer
(25.9.1932 to 4.10.1982)

Gould wrote articles about all aspects of concert life including such admired pop stars as Barbara Streisand and Petula Clark. He also composed scores for US and Canadian films.

Through his unusual views, his unconventional style and his philosophical observations on music Gould became an institution in the world of pianists.

Anne Hébert
Author
(born 1.8.1916)

Anne Hébert's father Maurice, a provincial state official and author, accompanied her in the initial stages of her literary career. Through her mother she was related to the historian François-Xavier Garneau (19th c.). She continued the literary tradition of her family in a spectacular manner.

Hébert grew up in Québec and studied there. From 1950 to 1954 she worked on Radio Canada and wrote plays for NFB. Then she received a scholarship to work in Paris where she lived for a few decades.

In 1942 she published her first collection under the title "Les Songes en équilibre". Her first volume of prose "Le Torrent", which appeared in 1950, shocked the public but became a classic. In 1970 she demonstrated her impressive virtuosity in her major novel "Kamouraska" in which she skilfully combined two plots, set in 19th c. Québec. The novel received the French Prix des Libraires and was filmed by Claude Jutra. She has written many plays, published under the title "Le Temps Sauvage". Hébert's literary career, distinguished by several awards, e.g. the Molson prize, was founded on a life completely devoted to writing. Her literature was a model for other writers.

Henry Hudson
Discoverer
(c. 1550
to 1611)

Little is known about Henry Hudson from the time before his journeys of 1607 to 1611. During the years 1607 and 1608 he twice searched for a route across Norway and Russia to Asia. Commissioned by the Dutch East India Co. he travelled up the Hudson River in 1609. He sailed to Iceland and then into the Hudson Strait. He travelled along the east coast to James Bay which he criss-crossed in a vain attempt to find a passage to the Spice Islands. When he wanted to continue the search in the spring of 1611 his crew mutinied. The leaders of the uprising put Hudson, his son and seven others in a boat on the open sea. Nothing is known about his fate. Hudson did not discover the Hudson Strait – it was Frobisher and Davis – but by taking the dangerous option he left his predecessors far behind and discovered a route into the interior which was of incalcuable importance to England.

René Robert
Cavelier Sieur
de LaSalle
Discoverer
(22.11.1643 to
19.3.1687)

Born in Rouen, France René Robert Cavalier de LaSalle was brought up by Jesuits and practised the priesthood for several years until giving it up in 1667. Then he came to Canada and settled in Montréal. He acquired a piece of land, which he later called Lachine, because of his ambition to reach China by crossing the western oceans.

Fur trading and exploration lead LaSalle to Lake Erie and the Ohio River in 1669 and in 1771 to the region south of the Great Lakes. In 1673 he led the construction of Fort Frontenac and eventually became its commander. The following year he was enobled. In 1678 he began the search for the mouth of the Mississippi; in 1682 he travelled down the river from Illinois to the Gulf of Mexico and called the land Louisiana. Two years later he led an expedition by boat to found a colony in Louisiana. As the mouth of the Mississippi was not discovered the colonists went ashore on the coast of present day Texas. After vain attempts to find the delta from the sea, led his group overland to the river. However, some settlers mutinied and murdered him.

Wilfrid Laurier
Politician
(20.11.1841 to
17.2.1919)

Sir Wilfrid Laurier was born in Laurentides north of Montréal. After studying he became a lawyer. His political career began in 1874: Laurier became a Member of the Canadian parliament; in 1887 he took over the leadership of the Liberal Party. From 1896 to 1911 he was prime minister, the first French-Canadian to hold this office.

Laurier devoted his entire life to the service of Canadian unity. Under his leadership Canada prospered. It was he, above all, who oversaw mass immigration and the settlement of the Canadian west.

John Alexander Macdonald was brought by his parents to Kingston/ Upper Canada when he was five. At 15 he was articled to a prominent lawyer and opened his own legal practice at 19. He was a practising lawyer all his life, specialising in economic law. From the 1840s he was engaged in various business activities. He dealt in real estate, bought land in many parts of the province and was director of some companies.

Sir John Alexander Macdonald Lawyer, politician, businessman (10/11.1.1815 to 6.6.1891)

He played an increasingly active role in conservative politics and in 1844 was elected to the legislative body of the province of Canada. Together with Étienne-Paschal Taché he became prime minister of the province in 1856. He was involved in the plan for a federal system, in which the central government had clear control over the provincial governments. Through his constitutional expertise, his abilities and his knowledge he won the recognition of the British colonial government. He was knighted and elected the first Canadian prime minister in 1867.

During his first period in office from 1867 to 1873 Manitoba, the Northwest Territories (now Saskatchewan and Alberta), British Columbia and Prince Edward Island joined the first four provinces. His government had to resign under suspicion of corruption in connection with planning the Canadian Pacific Railway and suffered defeat in the 1874 election.

Four years later he became prime minister again and remained in office until the end of his life. In 1879 he introduced his National policy, whereby high import taxes were applied to foreign goods to protect the domestic economy. The major national project of his second period of office was the completion of the transcontinental Canadian Pacific Railway, an extremely difficult and expensive undertaking, which required enormous public subsidies. The first steps towards greater autonomy in international affairs were taken. Against his intentions the central government lost power in the federal system.

The second longest river in North America and an enormous area of northern Canada (District of Mackenzie) are named after the explorer Alexander Mackenzie.

Alexander Mackenzie Discoverer (1755? to 11.5.1820)

Mackenzie is thought to have been born in Inverness/Scotland; at the age of 10 he came with his father to New York. He quickly took over control of the Montréal Company – later North West Company – which he joined in 1779. The company's aim was to explore the north-west of Canada, and Mackenzie was obsessed with the idea of finding a way from eastern Canada to the Pacific. Under his command an expedition set out on June 30th 1798, which after 100 days and 3000 kilometres terminated not at the Pacific but at the Arctic Ocean. Mackenzie did not give up and set off again in July 1792 with a team to find the Northwest Passage. This time he was successful: on July 22nd 1793 Mackenzie and his team reached the coast of the Pacific Ocean north of Vancouver Island. In so doing Mackenzie succeeeded in making the first known crossing of the North American continent; he made a huge contribution to the geographical and cartographical opening up of the country. His diaries (Voyages from Montréal, on the River St Lawrence, through the continent of North America), first published in London in 1802, are filled with impressions and extraordinarily detailed observations.

William Lyon Mackenzie, journalist, first mayor of Toronto and leader of the 1837 rebellion, was a central figure in political life before the confederation.

William Lyon Mackenzie Journalist, politician (12.3.1795 to 28.8.1861)

He was born in Dundee, Scotland on March 12th 1795. He came to Upper Canada in 1820 and after a few years in Dundas moved to Queenston. In May 1820 he published the first edition of "Colonial

Advocate", which became a leading voice in the new reform movement. In 1824 Mackenzie went to York (Toronto). In 1828 he was elected to the assembly of York district.

Mackenzie's severe attacks on the local oligarchy resulted in libel cases against him, threats and physical injury and led to his repeated expulsion from the assembly; yet his rural voters remained loyal to him. In 1834, when the Reform party won the majority in the newly constituted town council of Toronto, Mackenzie was elected the first mayor. However, he lost the 1836 election. In 1837 he led an armed revolt. After its defeat he fled to the USA, where he continued to campaign to "Free Upper Canada" until he was imprisoned for violating the neutrality laws. Mackenzie spent the next ten years in exile in the USA. Finally he found a position as correspondent for the "New York Daily Tribune".

Marquis Louis
Joseph de
Montcalm
Officer
(28.2.1712 to
14.9.1759)

Louis-Joseph de Montcalm, born in Candiac, France, who joined the army at the age of nine, was appointed commander of the French troops in North America. He conquered Fort William Henry in 1757 and resisted a British attack on Fort Carillon in 1758.

In 1759, owing to a miscalculation by the French, Wolfe landed with 4500 soldiers on the Plains of Abraham, less than 2km/1½ miles from Québec. Montcalm quickly stationed his troops for the defensive battle. The French were beaten and Montcalm fatally wounded.

Historians are of the opinion that Montcalm achieved some worthy victories but also suffered the worst defeat in Canadian military history.

Louis Riel
Leader of the
Métis,
founder of
Manitoba
(22.10.1844 to
16.11.1885)

Louis Riel, born in the Red River Settlement, first studied for the priesthood then law.

He played a crucial role in the North West rebellion of 1869/1870. He supported the cause of the Métis even when it came to armed struggles. At the finish he fled to the USA but soon returned. He was successful in the 1874 election but was sentenced to two years imprisonment and the loss of his political rights for his part in the rebellion. In 1875 he was granted an amnesty on condition that he stayed in exile for five years.

Shortly afterwards he suffered a nervous breakdown and was taken to a psychiatric clinic. By nature introspective and strictly religious he was obsessed by the thought of introducing a new Catholicism to Canada. On his release from the clinic he went to the Upper Missouri region of Montana where he traded. He joined the Republican party, became an American citizen and married a Métis. In 1883 he became a teacher in the St Peter mission on the Sun river. As he was asked by a group of Canadian Métis to support their struggle for rights in Saskatchewan he moved to Batoche, the centre of the Métis. This conflict also ended in armed resistance in 1885 and ended with defeat for the Métis. A formal charge of treason was then made against him and he was sentenced to death.

Politically and philosophically the execution of Riel had a long-lasting effect on Canadian history. In the west many Métis were disillusioned, whereas in Central Canada French Canadian nationalism was strengthened. Even after a century Riel is still the topic of heated debate, especially in Québec and Manitoba. His execution is a controversial subject and there are still those who demand retrospective compensation.

Gabrielle Roy
Author
(22.3.1909 to
13.7.1963)

Gabrielle Roy, winner of the Governor General's Award (1947, 1957, 1978) and many other literary commendations in Canada and abroad (Lorne Pierce Medal 1947; Prix Duvernay 1956; Prix David 1971), is one of Canada's most important post-war female writers.

She was the youngest of eight children in a francophone family in St Boniface and lived until 1937 in Manitoba. She was strongly influenced by the Prairie landscape and the cosmopolitan thinking of the immigrants who had settled in western Canada in the early 20th c.

When Roy had finished her studies she taught in school for twelve years. In 1937 she went to Europe. During the two years she was in France and England she began to write. The imminent war forced her to return to Canada. She became a freelance journalist in Montréal.

Her novel "Bonheur d'occasion" (The Tin Flute), published in 1945, in which the lives of the working class in the early period of the war are described, won the Prix Fémina in Paris and the Literary Guild of America Award in New York. It was translated into more than 15 languages and established her literary fame. Following another visit to France she settled in Québec. She wrote about the loneliness of modern life ("Alexandre Chenevert", 1954), the obsessive creativity of the artist ("La Montagne Secrète", 1961), the conflict between traditional and modern values ("La rivière sans repos", 1970), the poetry of nature ("Cet été qui chantait", 1972), immigration ("Un Jardin au bout du monde", 1975) and specially about her own youth ("Rue Deschambault", 1955; "La Route d'Altamont", 1966; "Ces enfants de ma vie", 1977). Roy's works, written in a plain and simple style, have a varied public, both in Canada, where her books are translated into English, and abroad. Her central theme concerns people in pain and loneliness which are eased by the love implicit in creation, and the hope for a world in which all people live together in harmony.

George Simpson from Lochbroom, Scotland was sent by the Hudson's Bay Company of London in 1820 to take over the post of the managing director, who had been captured by the North West Company. On the amalgamation of the two companies in 1821 he first was in control of the large Northern Department and five years later took over the whole trading territory in British North America. He retained this position until his death. Simpson wrote extensive reports, e.g. "Narrative of a Journey Round the World, During the Years 1841 and 1842". He was knighted at this time for his contribution to Arctic exploration.

Sir George Simpson
Managing director or the Hudson's Bay Company
(c. 1787 to 7.9.1860)

Simpson knew the fur trade like nobody else. He was a capable administrator and indefatigable traveller who, at the same time, did not lose sight of his own interests.

Born in King's Lynn, England on June 22nd 1757, George Vancouver accompanied James Cook to the South Seas (1772–75) and to the Northwest coast (1776–80).

George Vancouver
Discoverer
(22.6.1757 to 12.5.1798)

He had two missions: he was to win back the British possession Nootka Sound, conquered by the Spanish, and explore the Californian coast as far as Cook Inlet. His negotiations with the Spanish were unsuccessful. He spent three summers exploring the coast.

In 1795 he returned to England and three years later published "A Voyage of Discovery to the North Pacific Ocean and Round the World". He claimed to have removed all doubt about the existence of a northwest passage from the Atlantic to the Pacific.

James Wolfe rose to fame through his victory over Montcalm in 1759, which marked the start of British rule over Canada.

James Wolfe
Officer
(2.1.1727/1728 to 13.9.1759)

He came to North America in 1758 and took part as leading officer in the campaign by Jeffery Amherst against Louisbourg, in which he played a major role. He was therefore named commander of the campaign against Québec, which was planned for the following year. Here he had little success. His stormed attack on Montmorency was a big mistake, and neither the bombardment of Québec nor the destruction of neighbouring settlements had any effect. On the suggestion of his officers he planned to land above the town to cut off supply lines and to bring about a battle. So after a nocturnal trip on the St Lawrence, he led his army on to the Plains of Abraham, where Montcalm's troops were attacked and beaten by the British. Wolfe was fatally wounded.

Art and culture

Art history

Note

There are three main multicultural influences on Canadian art history. Firstly, the Inuit, the original inhabitants of the north, who still today play a major part in artistic creativity (especially sculpture and painting). In second place are the Indians, but whose influence is constantly diminishing. Thirdly are the immigrants (Europeans in particular, but also Asians of different backgrounds) who have been streaming into the country since the 17th c.

Inuit

Although it is not possible to define the various Inuit cultures exactly, five periods can be determined:

Pre-Dorset

The pre-Dorset culture began with the arrival of people who had crossed the Bering Strait from Siberia 4000 years ago. Only a few works of art have been found from this period, but they are outstanding. They mostly consist of harpoon tips and spears from carefully selected stones, which were not only functional but were also of considerable aesthetic value and were also attributed magical properties. The pre-Dorset culture lasted over 1000 years.

Dorset

Dorset culture began to develop between 600 and 500 B.C. and can be described as the first indigenous, Canadian-Arctic culture. It spread from Coronation Gulf to the southern tip of Newfoundland and to the west coast of Greenland. The highly developed Dorset culture seems to have had extensive magical and religious aims. For example, there were harpoon tips in the shape of impaled bears and falcons. The pattern on the carved animals must have had some special significance.

Other types of art objects were discovered: faces carved from antlers or wood, wooden masks, human figures, animal paintings and objects of various birds and mammals. While their purpose is for the main part unknown they share certain features: most are carved in ivory; they are very small (about 1 to 10 centimetres/½ to 4in.), and all are very expressively worked.

Thule culture

The Thule culture from north Alaska began to penetrate the Canadian Arctic after 1000 A.D. and reached east Greenland about 1200.

It is the most united Inuit culture and was spread across the Arctic to the eastern tip of Siberia.

The most common evidence of Thule culture in Canada are combs, needle cases, "swimming figurines" (birds, spirits and people) which were probably intended as amulets or had similar magical and religious properties, together with assorted female statues and utensils. Unlike the Dorset culture, the objects of art of the Thule culture are female in nearly every detail. The female figurines and statuettes are small, finely worked and often beautifully decorated, yet interestingly have no carved face.

Historic period

The Historic period began in the 16th c. as more Europeans advanced into the Arctic. At the beginning of the 19th c. quality dolls, toys and carved animals were produced for barter. Around 1920 the works of art made primarily from ivory or bone had lost all their magical and religious significance. Although the Inuit maintained a traditional lifestyle before the Second World War, their artistic forms – but not their technique – adapted to suit the taste of the potential buyers.

This phase coincided with the gradual opening up of the north after the Second World War and especially with the interest of Europe and North America in the art of prehistoric and early societies. Contemporary Inuit art can be traced back to the initiatives of the painter and writer James Houston, who was supported by the Canadian government. It was not least because of his decisive involvement that Inuit craftwork became remarkably successful within a short space of time.

In the north of Québec province, later also on Baffin Island, the Inuit have become familiar with different printing techniques (lithography, copper engraving, etching) and have continued carving in soapstone, ivory and antler bone and prepared decorative pelts (wall hangings, coats made of different furs and with borders), appliqué and embroidery in silk and cotton.

Inuit art is mainly of a narrative or illustrative nature. Traditional lifestyles, survival techniques, animals of the north (and their souls) and myths are reflected in their art. Exceptional artists are: Aqguhadluq, Aqjangajuk Shaa (b. 1937), Qaqaq Ashoona (b. 1933), Pauta Saila and Parr (1893–1969).

Today the works of the Inuit are regarded as an important contribution by Canada to the development of modern art, although the motifs are, for the main part, taken from traditional Arctic life.

The contemporary phase developed and changed very quickly. Collectors and museums pay exceptionally high prices for older objects and prints, and the production of new art is increasing to a great extent but leading to a fall in quality.

The most significant collection of contemporary Inuit art is housed in the Winnipeg Art Gallery.

The history of Indian art began about 25,000 years ago with the immigration of the original North American population across the Bering Strait into modern day Canada. Whereas the Indians' first contact with the French occurred in the early 16th c. in the Lake provinces and in the St Lawrence Valley, the Indians of the west coast did not see any Europeans until the late 18th c. The earliest evidence are rock drawings, which are still visible on some lakesides (especially in southern Ontario).

Prehistoric art varies in genre, style, function, imagery and meaning, not only from region to region, but has changed from period to period. These changes were apparent throughout Canada from *c.* 1000 B.C. onwards as a consequence of different factors: the introduction of pottery, the beginning of land cutivation and settling down.

There were some outstanding periods of prehistoric art in Canada. The Marpole culture (*c.* 500 B.C. to 500 A.D.), which was concentrated around the Fraser delta and the nearby islands in southern British Columbia, produced a wide variety of stone and bone carving (ceremonial containers, portraits and utensils).

The early Iroquois culture (*c.* 900–1600 A.D.) in southern Ontario is characterised by pottery of technical quality and with symbolic geometric patterns. The Iroquois art of the upper St Lawrence Valley is known for its decorated clay and stone pipes which display a fascinating wealth of form and iconographic variety. These miniature masterpieces had a sacred function: the ritual smoking of tobacco as part of the Indian system of cultural beliefs.

The art of the eastern sub-Arctic is the most archaic in Canada; a large part of prehistoric and early rock painting was found in this region. Most of the Algonquin-speaking tribes – the Ojibwa, Cree, Algonquin, Ottawa, Montagnais, the Naskapi of Ontario and Québec together with the Mic-Mac and Maliset of the southern lake provinces – continued to lead a nomadic life, based on hunting and gathering food.

The Mic-Mac were famous for their embroidery with elk hair and for engraving with porcupine quills on birch bark as well as basket-making

Totem poles of the Indians of the north-west coast in Vancouver and Kisplox, B.C.

and leather and textile clothing. Glass pearls, brought by the European traders, replaced the elk hair and feathers, which were difficult to work, but changed the patterns.

The Naskapi made exquisite coats from caribou leather (carved or painted linear and geometric patterns).

The works of art of the Ojibwa women were similar to those in the sub-Arctic region: decorations of feathers and beads on clothes and basket-weaving with geometric and floral patterns. The men were responsible for ceremonial objects.

The work of the Cree was noted for its exquisite feather and elk hair embroidery, regarded for its technical perfection and colour harmony. As these nomadic hunters carried their possessions with them, articles of clothing, especially their decorated and embroidered coats, mocassins and hunting gloves, were an expression of their own aesthetic taste.

Among some tribes of the western sub-Arctic decoration of personal possessions was the most important art form. These tribes decorated caribou and elk leather using porcupine quills, elk hair embroidery, beads and stitching (also geometric and floral patterns).

As the Iroquois speaking people of the south Great Lakes and the upper St Lawrence Valley (Hurons, Neutals, Petuns and Iroquois among others) were practically settled farmers, living in villages, this was reflected in their artistic forms of expression. Whereas there was considerable homogenity on the whole with the bead and feather work in the sub-Arctic and at the Great Lakes, Huron art became distinctive in the later historic periods. Their "personal art" displayed a preference for elk hair embroidery with flower motifs on black coloured leather of exceptional beauty. The most remarkable art form of the Iroquois consisted of "false masks" , wooden masks with metal eyes used for healing ceremonies. Other objects with "political" function were the wampum cords and belts made of purple and white shells. These wampums with their symbolic motifs denoted treaties and important events.

The culture of the Prairie Indians was a synthesis of native and white culture. Their most important art form was painted leather and the most important architectural form the "tepee" tent. Buckskin shoes (moccasins), jackets, clothes, leggings and shirts were decorated with feathers and beads. Painted cooking pots, containers from uncured leather were produced throughout his region.

The plateau region in central British Columbia is often overlooked in descriptions of Indian art, but in many ways it is unique. The Salish left behind a mass of prehistoric pictographs. The Lillooet, Thompson, Okanagan, and Shuswap of the historical period were renowned for their finely worked waterproof baskets (weaving technique, geometric patterns).

The Indian art of the prehistoric period and the colonial period was to a certain extent "traditional". Although it was widely influenced by European materials, techniques and patterns in the historic periods, it was still much characterised by Indian cultures.

As with the Inuit after the Second World War contemporary Indian art developed which employed modern techniques, but also fell back on traditional subjects from mythology, tribal history and hunting and everyday customs. *Contemporary art*

Contemporary Indian art has two main centres, the west coast and the forest lands of eastern Canada. The latter became famous through the success of Ojibwa Norval Morisseau (b. 1932). Most forestland artists are influenced by Morisseau. They are known as the "legend painters" as they represent stories and mythology in their works (Carl Ray, Daphne Odjig, Blake Debassige).

The international artists regard themselves as being independent of every "school". However, their pictures clearly illustrate in their form and content the connection with their Indian origins. Outstanding artists from this group are: Alex Janvier, Arthur Schilling (famous Ojibwa portraits) and Sarain Stump (symbolic Surrealist works). The images of life in the reservations by Allen Sapp are reminiscent of 19th c. realism and are typical of the conservative trend among Indian artists.

Paintings, prints and sculptures by Canadian Indians have meanwhile become expensive collectors' items.

Many historical artefacts of the Cree, Ojibwa, Shoshone, Blackfoot, Chipewyan, Kwakiuti, etc. are exhibited in Ottawa, Toronto and Calgary. Contemporary works are on display in the National Gallery in Ottawa and Calgary.

Early Canadian art followed European traditions. The first representations of natives on maps were shaped more by imported prejudice than knowledge of the discoverers. Illustrations in the first books about Canada were more accurate. Some sketches in the works of Samuel Champlain convey meaningful insights into the life of the Hurons. **Immigrant art**

Exploration period

French mercantile activity impeded the development of painting in Canada. With the exception of votive pictures and some portraits of nuns and officers, paintings were imported during French rule. *17/18th century*

The arrival of the British in North America had a direct effect on the development of painting. English officers demonstrated their enthusiasm for Canada in their topographical drawings and ornamental landscapes. Thomas Davies was one of the earliest and most important of these English water-colour painters.

The influence of new waves of immigrants was felt on Canadian art. The English preferred Georgian style for a long time, which even later still symbolised the association with the English crown. The Loyalists brought works of art and ideas from the USA, e.g. silver, engravings and paintings.

Around 1900 increasing prosperity promoted education of the middle classes and the development of some garrison communities. Portraits of businessmen and their families, of soldiers, government officials and clerics were in demand. Robert Field was a brilliant artist, who was familiar with contemporary styles and techniques.

The turn of the century marked the beginning of the so-called Golden Age of Québec painting. The artists there went to Europe to study, and European artists came to Canada. Antoine Plamondon and Théophile Hamel (1817–70) belonged to the first group, William Berczy (1744–1813) and Cornelius Krieghoff (1815–72) to the second. Educated in Düsseldorf Krieghoff painted romantic scenes from everyday life and landscapes. Joseph Légaré also created landscapes and portrayed dramatic events from the history of Québec.

Stylistically the European influence in Canada continued to be dominant, but the spectrum of subjects in painting widened. Peter Rindisbacher (1806–34) depicted his experiences as an immigrant in small pictures. Paul Kane (1810–71) can be described as an artist/adventurer: on a journey through Canada in 1846 he recorded the Indians and countryside in 240 sketches and 100 pictures.

Among the portrait painters was G. T. Berthon (1806–92), landscape artists included Robert R. Whale and discoverer/painter William Hind (1833–89). They were all predecessors to the more notable Lucius O'Brien (1832–99), John A. Fraser (1838–98) and Allan Edson (1846–88), who favoured romantic landscapes.

With the confederation in 1867 art was to express the new feeling of unity. Robert Harris (1849–1919) was commissioned to paint his famous group portrait "The Fathers of Confederation" (1882). In 1880 the National Gallery of Canada was founded by the Marquis de Lorne.

Around the turn of the century painting was represented by such important artists as James Wilson Morrice (1865–1924), the father of Canadian modernism; Ozias Leduc (1864–1955), who created ambitious church decorations and exquisite still lifes and landscapes around St Hilaire; Homer Watson (1855–1936), who conveyed an intimate observation of landscape; as well as George Reid (1860–1947) and Paul Peel (1860–92), who were closer to academic tradition. The early Twenties were a great time for Canadian painting. The "Group of Seven", who saw it as their task to give Canada a real national style of painting, regarded the Canadian countryside as source of their inspiration. They used strong colours to represent this decoratively. Tom Thomson (1877–1917), despite his short career, left behind a surprising number of pictures and sketches in oil.

Emily Carr (1871–1945), influenced by the Fauvists, was the first female artist to receive high acclaim in Canadian art.

John Lyman (1866–1967) tried to set up an artistic movement from the École de Paris in the early Thirties. In 1939 he founded the Contemporary Arts Society and organised a modern offensive in Canadian painting.

During the Second World War painting in Canada advanced in an exemplary way. Shortly after his return from Paris Alfred Pellan (b. 1906) made the effects of Cubism (especially of Pablo Picasso) felt. Paul-Émile Borduas (1905–60) collected a group of young painters around him, among them, Jean-Paul Riopelle (b. 1923) and Fernand Leduc (b. 1916), and formed the so-called Automatists. The manifesto "Refus Global", which appeared in 1948 and had considerable ideological influence on Québec, marked moderate thinking, free from religious and other conformism. As a reaction to the Automatists the sculptors Guido Molinari (b. 1933) and Claude Tousignant (b. 1932) freed painting from its surrealist constraints and focused on formal styles.

The painters in Toronto followed similar aims. The Painters Eleven, of whom the most famous were Harold Town (b. 1924) and Jack Bush (1909–77) changed from abstract Expressionism, as practised in New York, to Formalism.

The general problem of Canadian painting was to maintain its originality faced with the strong American influences. Michael Snow (b. 1929) with his outstanding film contributions and the "London, Ont. Group" with Greg Curnoe and Jack Chambers (1931–78) partly succeeded in standing apart from American art.

Contemporary art in Canada was and is, as is elsewhere, characterised by the question of what constitutes art. This questioning was accompanied by experimentation and innovation. The resulting works varied from the entirely personal to public disagreement with social and political problems. Contemporary art analyses the relationship between means and ends, distinguishes art from reality and defines art in its aesthetic, social and economic contexts. In Canada the multitude of contemporary trends was a consequence of the separation of art centres from each other and their different developments.

Fusion des Arts in Montréal (founded. 1964) and Intermedia in Vancouver (founded 1967) originated in this period. They were loose associations of artists who worked in a variety of media (film, music, dance, poetry) as well as in the traditional areas of painting and sculpture. The resulting happenings and performances, which combined touch and sound, watching and movement, were performed in art galleries and elsewhere. They were carried by the optimism surrounding the social gain brought about by art, as they now spoke a common language. Iain (b. 1936) and Ingrid Baxter demonstrated their own multi-media and interdisciplinary principles.

Concept-art represented the view that if traditional forms of painting and sculpture had become meaningless, then the aim was to bring out the essential "art content", which exists independent of all form. More important than the works were the ideas of concept-art. Michael Snow was representative of this direction in art. He experimented with the possibilities of the camera. His work, which won international recognition, inspired many other artists.

Whereas concept-art was concentrated in eastern Canada, body art was the applied form which had the farthest-reaching effects. According to this genre the artist as a person was regarded simultaneously as the source of all ideas and interpreted as the final means of their realisation. In environmental art the perception of the person is expanded to the perception of the environment. The reality "outside" is awarded more weight than its reproduction in painting or other traditional medium. Since the late 1960s this long-lasting artistic direction has been practised (Irene Whittome, Bill Vazan, Rita McKeough).

Collage is celebrating its rediscovery. There should be no more discrimination between objects of art. Everything should play a part in the way we view the world. This idea is also part of structuralism and represented in the works of Michael Morris, Vincent Trasov, Glenn Lewis.

In the late 1970s metaphor re-appeared in art. An intellectual analysis of how modern art can develop and what meaning it can have is featured in the work of Jeff Wall and Ian Wallace.

Performance art was one of the most significant combined art forms. Bruce Barber critically examined the socio-political content of the mass media. The performances were a good medium for conveying feminist ideas (Elizabeth Chitty, Marcella Bienvenue).

Many native artists from all parts of the country were searching for forms, which combined the elements of traditional art and mythology with their own responses to the present. A large number of artists wanted to use all means of finding an uncompromising answer to the "disastrous" world, including traditional painting. Two of these artists are Jamelie Hassam and Ron Benner.

Carol Condé and Karl Beveridge tried, through their photography, to answer the question how, in his compromised position restricted by his privilege, the artist can work. Brian Dyson and Paul Woodrow believed that direct social activities were the only effective way for artists to realise their ideas.

Sculpture

The earliest Canadian sculpture was sacral art found in the churches and chapels of New France. In the late 17th c. sculptors were commissioned to decorate the churches with carved and gilded altars in wood. As the sculptures, unlike the church paintings, could not be transported by ship very easily, they were produced where they were wanted. The most important artists were the Baillaigrés in Québec and Louis Quévillon (1749–1823) in Montréal. These sculptors followed, with a time delay, the predominant styles of Europe: Louis XV, Rococo, Neo-Classicism.

Following the Naploeonic Wars England expanded its fleet in Canada. Wood carving (figureheads, ship decorations) flourished in Québec and in the Atlantic provinces.

Around the turn of the century sculpture, which until then had followed traditional styles, began to change. New materials were discovered, wood was replaced by bronze and plaster. There was a demand for historic monuments in city centres. After the First World War many towns erected war monuments. The façades of new buildings were decorated. The prime example of this is the façade of the parliamentary building in Québec by Louis-Phillipe Hébert (1850 to 1917). New subjects were absorbed such as Indian and characters from folklore and Canadian history. As in the past styles emerged which copied European trends: Academism, Art Nouveau, Symbolism (Alfred Laliberté; 1878 to 1953) and later Art Deco.

In the 1960s sculptors, like painters, attempted to emphasise their own originality as a reaction to the strong American influences. Examples include: Armand Vaillancourt (b. 1932), Robert Roussil (b. 1925) and Robert Murray (b. 1936).

Michael Snow and numerous other experimented with modern materials. Companies, banks and government departments promoted sculpture in their new buildings.

Evening on the coast of Newfoundland ▶

Suggested routes

TransCanada Highway

Note

It is possible to drive from east to west (or vice versa) on the 7500km/4660 miles-long TransCanada Highway which runs from St John's, the capital of Newfoundland, on the Atlantic coast in the extreme east through the Atlantic provinces of Newfoundland, Nova Scotia and New Brunswick, past Québec city to Montréal. It continues via Ottawa, North Bay, Thunder Bay (all three in Ontario province), Winnipeg (Manitoba), Regina (Saskatchewan), Calgary (Alberta) and finally through the Rocky Mountains to Vancouver in the far west on the Pacific coast.

Between five and six weeks should be allowed for the trip from coast to coast. This leaves time to take in the wonderful scenery with all its natural beauty as well as the interesting towns and places of historical significance.

Along the TransCanada Highway from the Atlantic to the Pacific

St John's
(Newfoundland)–
Clarenville
(160km/99 miles)

The TransCanada Highway begins in the far west of Newfoundland on the Avalon peninsula at the provincial capital St John's. It then follows a westerly, then northern direction to Clarenville where a detour can be made along the south-west pointing peninsula to Burin or Bonavista on the north-eastern cape.

Clarenville–
Grand Falls
(270km/168 miles)

From Clarenville it heads northwards through the 400 sq.km/ 154 sq.miles Terra Nova National Park to Gander, famous in the past for its international airport where north Atlantic air traffic refuelled. The route turns off to the west to Grand Falls.

Grand Falls–Deer
Lake (225km/140
miles)

After Grand Falls it continues north again past Notre Dame Bay. Near Springdale turn off in a south-west direction towards Deer Lake. A detour north-west to Gros Morne National Park in the Long Range Mountains is recommended.

Deer Lake–
Port-aux-Basques
(272km/169 miles)

From Deer Lake proceed south-west to St George's and further along St George's Bay, which is part of the Gulf of St Lawrence. The southern slopes of the Long Range Mountains sink down at the channel port of Port-aux-Basques into the Cabot Strait.

Port-aux-Basques
–North Sydney
(ferry journey)

The 170km/105 mile-long ferry journey (5 to 6 hours duration) from the Newfoundland channel port of Port-aux-Basques across the Cabot Strait to North Sydney in Nova Scotia is best undertaken overnight.

North Sydney–
Truro (323km/
201 miles)

The initial stage on the Canadian mainland leads first from the ferry port of North Sydney on the north-east tip of Nova Scotia to Sydney. A short detour south-east to the fortifications at Louisbourg is suggested.

From Sydney the TransCanada Highway continues south-west past Antigonish to New Glasgow. From here it is possible to take a boat excursion to the northern off-shore Prince Edward Island. It is not far from New Glasgow to Truro.

A branch road leads from Truro to Halifax, the capital of Nova Scotia, situated in the south.

From Truro head north-west to Amherst on the border of Nova Scotia and New Brunswick. It is only ¾ hour to Moncton in the historic region of Acadia.

Truro–Moncton
(177km/110 miles)

From Moncton continue south-west to Sussex (possible detour to New Brunswick port of St John) and then north-west past Grand Lake to Fredericton, the capital of New Brunswick.

An alternative to this direct route is a scenic drive along the Bay of Fundy with the Fundy National Park to Sussex. From Sussex drive via St John and then on road 7 north to Fredericton.

Moncton–
Fredericton
(200km/124 miles)

From Fredericton the route proceeds along the valley of the St John river, past several major hydro energy complexes and along the border with the US state of Maine. Charming places en route are Woodstock and Hartland (with the longest wooden bridge in the world). The road to Grand Falls crosses "Potato country" (immense potato-growing region). The gorge carved out by the St John river and the reservoir at Grand Falls should not be missed.

Fredericton
Grand Falls
(210km/130 miles)

From Grand Falls head north to Edmundston, where many French-speaking Acadians live today. Just before reaching Edmundston it is worth a visit to Restigouche in a north-east direction, and the Baie des Chaleurs with the port of Campbellton.

Not far north of Edmundston the road crosses the border between the provinces of New Brunswick and Québec.

A few kilometres further lies Cabano with Fort Ingall. Continue through the foothills of the American Appalachians, countryside similar to the Black Forest, and down to the St Lawrence river (Bas-St-Laurent) to Rivière-du-Loup.

Grand Falls–
Rivière-du-Loup
(122km/76 miles)

From Rivière-du-Loup drive along the south bank of the St Lawrence upstream through fertile farmland and past friendly fishing villages to Lévis, the heavily industrialised suburb of the provincial capital Québec, on the other bank of the St Lawrence river. A visit to Québec and the region demands at least one or more days.

Rivière-du-Loup–
Lévis/Québec
(195km/121 miles)

From Lévis/Québec continue in a south-westerly direction to Drummondville, the centre of Estrie (=long-established settlement east of Montréal). From here past St Hyacinthe to Montréal, the second largest French-speaking city in the world. A visit to this east Canadian metropolis also requires one or more days.

Lévis/Québec–
Montréal
(265km/165 miles)

From Montréal follow the Ottawa river upstream to the Canadian capital city, Ottawa, situated on the border between the provinces of Québec and Ontario. There is a lot to see here so sufficient time should be allowed.

A visit to Ottawa's neighbouring town, Hull, and to Gatineau, the countryside extending northwards is to be recommended.

Montréal–Ottawa
(200km/124 miles)

The TransCanada Highway follows the Ottawa river from Ottawa and borders on the north side of the Algonquin National Park, finally reaching the prettily situated settlement of North Bay (Ontario) on Lake Nipsissing.

Ottawa–
North Bay
(368km/229 miles)

From North Bay the route leads into the north of Ontario province, past the mining town of Cobalt and the romantic Esker Lakes to Iroquois Falls and beyond to Cochrane, Ontario. Here the road turns in a north-west direction passing Greenwater Park to Smoky Falls. Destination of this stage is Kapuskasing, Ontario.

North Bay–
Kapuskasing
(490km/305 miles)

Leaving Kapuskasing the road continues through seemingly endless forests west to Lake Nipigon, where there is a beautiful provincial park. It now runs south-west to Nipigon, to the bank of the Upper Lake. This stage ends in Thunder Bay.

Kapuskasing–
North Bay
(620km/385 miles)

TransCanada Highway

Thunder Bay–Kenora
(510km/317 miles)

National road 17 leads from Thunder Bay through a thinly populated area and through massive forests past Ignace and Dryden to Kenora.

A 570km/354 mile-long but attractive alternative route runs west past Kabakeka Falls to Atikokan on the northern edge of Quetico Park protected area. It continues west along the small river Seine to the Canadian–US border at Fort Frances. Beyond Fort Frances the national road 17 turns north to Lake of the Woods with the settlement Sioux Narrows. Kenora is a little way ahead.

Kenora–Winnipeg
(210km/130 miles)

To the west of Kenora it crosses the border between Ontario and Manitoba, continuing along the southern edge of the Whiteshell Nature Park towards Winnipeg, where a longer stay is suggested. South of Winnipeg, in an area populated by Mennonites, are several German place names (e.g. Steinbach, Winkler, Altona).

Winnipeg–Virden
(286km/177 miles)

The TransCanada Highway continues west from Winnipeg. Near Brandon it is possible to make an excursion to the extremely interesting Riding Mountain National Park, 80km/50 miles north. This stage, however, finishes at Virden.

Virden–Regina
(300km/186 miles)

From Virden the route proceeds north-west reaching the border between Manitoba and Saskatchewan after about an hour. It then passes Moosomin, Whitewood, Grenfell and Indian Head before coming to Regina, the capital of Manitoba province, which is worth visiting.

Regina–Swift Current
(246km/152 miles)

The well constructed TransCanada Highway continues west, first to Moose Jaw. At last it becomes obvious that this is the Canadian Prairies. There is a possible detour from Swift Current to the snaking South Saskatchewan river further north and Lake Diefenbaker. Recreational and sports facilities are available here.

The skyline of Calgary

From Swift Current the Highway heads west-south-west for the border between the provinces of Saskatchewan and Alberta. The Cypress Hills National Park, which is well worth a visit, extends south over the border. Medicine Hat is the destination for this stretch.

Swift Current–
Medicine Hat
(223km/138 miles)

Travelling north-west from Medicine Hat the landscape becomes rather uninviting. North-east of Brooks a detour leads to the Dinosaur Provincial Park.

North-west of Brooks is Bow river and finally Calgary, the world-famous city of southern Alberta.

Medicine Hat–
Calgary
(295km/183 miles)

West of Calgary begins the splendid upland section of the TransCanada Highway. An hour's drive from Calgary is Canmore, famous for the Olympics and winter sports. Beyond Canmore the route enters the Banff National Park. Banff is a sport and outdoor recreation centre.

Calgary–Banff
(130km/81 miles)

The highway winds on from Banff, past the romantic Lake Louise and over Kicking Horse Pass to Yoho National Park and beyond into the wild Kootenay Valley, where the world-famous winter sports resort Golden is situated.

From Golden it climbs steeply uphill and over the chain of the Purcell Mountains, crosses the Glacier National Park and borders on Mount Revelstoke National Park at Revelstoke.

Past Revelstoke the Monashee Mountains have to be traversed. The road finally descends south past Shuswap Lake to Kamloops, in the wild valley of the Thompson River.

Banff–
Kamloops
(500km/310 miles)

From Kamloops the road descends along the valley of the Thompson River to Cache Creek, where the river turns south before the Cascade Range. At Lytton about 1½ hours by car downstream the Thompson River joins the Fraser River, flowing fast from the north. A breathtaking road leads down to the Fraser Valley to Vancouver on the Pacific coast.

Plenty of time should be allowed to visit the city of Vancouver. There are numerous memorable excursions to be made from here: Victoria on Vancouver Island, the Inside Passage, a steam train journey to Squamish and a car journey to Whistler, and not least a visit into the neighbouring United States where Seattle and the Olympic National Park are within easy reach.

Kamloops–
Vancouver
(433km/269 miles)

Alternative route Montréal–Thunder Bay

From Montréal take the Macdonald Parkway (motorway; Highway Nr. 401) in a south-westerly direction along the Saint Lawrence Seaway to Kingston allowing time to visit this town. It is also possible to visit the area around the St Lawrence Islands (Thousand Island) National Park (Kingston).

From here continue along the northern bank of Lake Ontario, past the pretty, little towns of Cobourg and Oshawa, to Toronto. It is worth spending a few days in the provincial capital and also making a detour to Kitchener-Waterloo and the region where the Mennonites live. More spectacular is the trip from Toronto to the Niagara Falls, situated between Lake Ontario and Lake Erie. It passes the industrial town of Hamilton and crosses the Welland Channel.

Montréal–Toronto
(about 500km/
310 miles)

Leave Toronto on Highway 400 heading north. After just 100km it comes to Lake Simcoe and the town of Barrie, followed by the charming little town Orilla. It proceeds north-west to the south-east tip of Georgian Bay, part of Lake Huron. The small town of Midland and St Mary-among-the-Hurons National Site (rebuilt mission station and large pilgrimage church) can be seen here.

Toronto–Sudbury
(375km/233 miles)

From St Mary-among-the-Hurons proceed north through the popular recreation area "Muskoka", a "land of thousand lakes and islands". National road Nr. 69 runs parallel to the eastern bank of Georgian Bay north to the mining town of Sudbury, where the largest nickel mine in the world is situated.

From Sudbury a 130km/81 mile stretch crosses east to North Bay (see above).

Sudbury–Sault Ste Mary (552km/343 miles)

From Sudbury national road Nr. 17 leads west to the North Channel of Lake Huron and passes areas of natural beauty before coming to the port and lock town Sault Ste Marie, Ontario. A visit to the locks leading to the Upper Lake is essential. Time permitting an excursion on the Algoma Railway into the imposing mountain countryside north of Sault Ste Marie is recommended.

Sault Ste Marie–Thunder Bay (595km/370 miles)

From Sault Ste Marie follow the east bank of the Upper Lake, through Lake Superior Park to Wawa. Further north is the town of White River from where the Pukaskwa National Park can be visited to the west.

The main route (route Nr.17) continues past Marathon and Terrace Bay on the north coast of the Upper Lake to Nipigon where it rejoins the TransCanada Highway and comes to Thunder Bay.

Alternative route Calgary–Kamloops

Calgary–Edmonton (300km/186 miles)

From Calgary express road Nr. 2 leads north to Edmonton. There is much to see in the provincial capital of Alberta. Time permitting an excursion from Edmonton north to the Lesser Slave Lake and the Pelican Mountains is recommended, as is a visit to the Northern Woods and Water Route in the north of Alberta.

Edmonton–Jasper (360km/223 miles)

From Edmonton the Yellowhead Highway (national road Nr. 16) heads west to the Rocky Mountains. Passing the towns of Edson and Hinton it reaches the valley of the Athabasca River. Proceed upstream to the Jasper National Park with the recreation area of the same name.

From Jasper the 287km/178 mile-long panoramic Icefields Parkway leads south along a long valley, crossed by steps and barriers, to Banff, to rejoin the above mentioned route.

Jasper–Kamloops (430km/272 miles)

From Jasper the route crosses Yellowhead Pass into the upper Fraser Valley near Valemont. From here Highway Nr. 5 leads over another pass southwards into the valley of the North Thompson River finally reaching Clearwater and Kamloops, the destination of this stage.

Alternative route Medicine Hat–Vancouver

note

A southern variation on the route, the "Crowsnest Highway", runs from Medicine Hat, Alberta, more or less parallel to the Canadian/US border westwards to the Pacific coast

Medicine Hat–Cranbrooke (480km/298 miles)

The Crowsnest Highway (national road Nr. 3) runs from Medicine Hat westwards through the southern Canadian prairie. Via Lethbridge and Fort MacLeod it leads to the Rocky Mountains, where the first major incline is negotiated by Crowsnest Pass.

To the south of the pass the Waterton-Glacier International Peace Park extends over the border. It is well worth a visit and comprises the Waterton Lakes National Park and the US Glacier National Park.

Cranbrooke–Trail (236km/147 miles)

From Cranbrook follow the Crowsnest Highway (national road Nr, 95) south-west as far as Erickson and Creston. North of Creston the winding Kootenay Lake is worth a detour.

From Creston the routes closely follows the Canadian–US border and continues to Trail.

Not far north from Trail, near Castlegar, the Crowsnest Highway (now national road Nr. 3) turns south-west and comes to the border town Grand Fork (from here a road leads to Spokane in Washington, USA). The Crowsnest Highway heads west along the border Osoyoos in the Okanagan Valley.

Trail–Osoyoos
(227km/141 miles)

West of Osoyoos, still on road Nr. 3, it crosses the high upland mountains of the Cascade Range and descends into the Fraser Valley near Hope. It continues descending down the Fraser Valley to Vancouver on the Pacific coast.

Osyoos–
Vancouver
(403km/250 miles)

Suggested round trips by car

Distances given are approximate

Atlantic provinces

Round trip (2–3 weeks; 2000km/1243 miles):
Halifax–Lunenburg–Yarmouth–Annapolis Valley–Amherst–Cape Tormentine/New Brunswick–by ferry to Borden, Prince Edward Island (¾ hour)–Charlottetown (possible day tours of Canada's smallest province)–Wood Islands–return by ferry to Caribou, Nova Scotia (1½ hours)–Cape Breton Island–Cabot Trail–Sydney–Louisburg–Port Hastings–Halifax.

Nova Scotia, Prince Edward Island

Round trip (4 weeks; 3100km/1926 miles without the ferry crossings):
Halifax–Lunenburg–Liverpool–Digby–by ferry to Saint John, (New Brunswick; 2–3 hours)–St Andrews–Fredericton–Moncton–Cape Tourmentine–by ferry to Borden, Prince Edward Island (¾ hour)–Summerside–Cavendish–Charlottetown–Wood Islands–by ferry to Caribou, Nova Scotia (1½ hours)–Baddeck–Cabot Trail–Sydney–Louisburg–North Sydney–by ferry to Port-aux-Basques (Newfoundland; 6 hours)–Cornerbrook–Gander–St John's (through Terra Nova National Park)–Argentia by ferry to North Sydney, Nova Scotia (18 hours)–Port Hastings–Sherbrooke–Halifax.

Nova Scotia, New Brunswick, Prince Edward Island, Newfoundland

Québec

Round trip (1 week; 1100km/683 miles):
Montréal–Trois Rivières–Québec (city)–visit to Île d'Orleans–return via Québec along the south side of the St Lawrence River to Montréal.

Montréal-Québec

Round trip (2 weeks; 2000km/1243 miles without the ferry):
Québec (city)–St Foy–Charry–Montmagny–Ste-Jean-Port-Joli–Rivière-du-Loup–Trois-Pistoles–Rimouski–Grand-Métis–Matane–Cap-Chat–Forillon National Park–Gaspé–Percé–Port-Daniel–Bonaventure–Carleton–Oak-Bay–Mann Settlement–Causapscal–Sayabec–Ste Angèle-de-Merci–Ste Flavie–Rimouski–Trois-Pistoles–Rivière-du-Loup–by ferry to Saint-Siméon (1¼ hours)–La Malbaie–Clermont–St-Tite-des-Caps–St-Anne-de-Beaupré–Québec.

Québec–
St Laurent–
Gaspésie

Ontario

Round trip (1 week; 1000km/621 miles):
Toronto–Midland–St Mary-among-the-Hurons–Muskoka region–Huntsville–Algonquin National Park–Ottawa–Kingston–Upper Canada Village–Toronto.

Ontario I

Suggested round trips by car

Ontario II	Round trip (1 week; 1000km/621 miles): Toronto–Midland–Muskoka Region–Huntsville–North Bay–on the TransCanada Highway to Ottawa–Kingston–Upper Canada Village–Toronto.
Ontario III	Round trip (1–2 weeks; 2200km/1367 miles): Toronto–Hamilton–St Catherines–Niagara on the Lake–Niagara Falls–Brandford–Guelph–Kitchener-Waterloo–Stratford–London–Point Pelee–Windsor–Chatham–Sarnia–Ipperwash–Pinery–Southampton–Owen Sound–Tobermorey–Manitoulin–Sudbury–Parry Sound–Wasaga Beach–Toronto.
Ontario IV	Round trip (5–6 weeks; 6300km/3937 miles): Toronto–Hamilton–St Catherines–Niagara on the Lake–Niagara Falls–Brantford–Kitchener-Waterloo–Stratford–London–Point Pelee–Leamington–Amhersburg, Windsor–Chatham–Sarnia–Ipperwash–Pinery–Southampton–Owen Sound–Tovermorey–Manitoulin–Sault St Marie–Wawa–Thunderbay–Fort Francis–Lake of the Woods–Kenora–Dryden–Thunderbay–Hearst–Cochrane–Iroquois Falls–North Bay–Huntsville–Barry's Bay–Pembroke–Ottawa–Morrisburg–Brockville–Kingston–Belleville–Toronto.

Manitoba, Saskatchewan

Manitoba, Saskatchewan I	Round trip (2 weeks; 2000km/1243 miles): Winnipeg–Brandon–Regina–Saskatoon–Prince Albert National Park–Yorkton–Dauphin–Portage la Prairie–Winnipeg.
Manitoba, Saskatchewan II	Round trip (2–3 weeks; 2500km/1553 miles): Winnipeg–Flin Flon–The Pas (through Grass River and Clearwater Parks)–Prince Albert, Saskatchewan–Regina–Yorkton–Dauphin–Winnipeg.
Manitoba, Saskatchewan III	Round trip (2–3 weeks; 2500km/1553 miles): Winnipeg–Portage la Prairie–Dauphin–Clear Lake (through Riding Mountain National Park)–Brandon–Regina–Moose Law–Prince Albert Waskesiu Lake in Prince Albert National Park–Saskatoon–Yorkton–Winnipeg.

West Canada

Rocky Mountains	Round trip (1 week; 1100km/683 miles): Calgary–Banff–Jasper–Edmonton–Calgary.
Yukon–Alaska–Highway	Round trip (3–5 weeks; 2500km/1553 miles without ferry crossings) From Edmonton to Dawson Creek, the start of the Yukon-Alaska Highway, Whitehorse–Fairbanks–Haines Junction–Haines, Alaska, by the Alaska State Ferry to Prince Rupert–from there by ferry to Port Hardy, Vancouver Island (30½ hours)–Vancouver. Alternative (2100km/1304 miles): Prince Rupert–land route to Prince George–Williams Lake–Cache Creek–Jasper–Edmonton (2100km).
British Columbia, Alberta I	Round trip (3–4 weeks; 3000km/1864 miles): Vancouver–Okanagan Valley–Rogers Pass–Glacier National Park–Emerald Lake–Lake Louise–Banff–Columbia Icefield–Jasper–Prince George–Clinton–Vancouver.
British Columbia, Alberta II	Round trip (3–4 weeks; 3000km/1864 miles without ferry crossings): Calgary–Banff–Lake Louise–Yoho National Park–Golden/Glacier

National Park–Revelstoke National Park–Shuswap Lake–Okanagan Valley (Vernon–Kelowna–Penticton) Princeton–Manning Provincial Park–Hope–Vancouver–car ferry to Victoria (1 hour 40 mins.)–Duncan–Nanaimo–Courtnay Cumberland–Strathcona Provincial Park–Campbell River–Port McNeill–Port Hardy–car ferry to Prince Rupert (18 hours, must be booked in advance!); from Prince Rupert on the Yellowhead Highway to Terrace–Smithers–Houston–Burns Lake–Fraser Lake (Fort Fraser)–Vanderhoof–Prince of George–Mount Robson Provincial Park–Jasper–Columbia Glacier–Banff–Calgary.

Round trip (3–4 weeks; 3000km/1864 miles):
From Vancouver on the TransCanada Highway along the Fraser River to Lillooet. Proceed along the trail of the gold diggers and trappers to the 100 Mile House, in the direction of Quesnel. Here there is an interesting detour to the ghost town of Barkerville and to the Bowron Lake Park. Continue to Prince George–Jasper National Park–Banff National Park–Lake Louise–Banff–Kootenay National Park–return along the TransCanada Highway through the Yoho National Park–Glacier National Park–Rogers Pass–Okanagan Valley–Vancouver.

Cariboo-Rocky Mountains

Round trip (3–4 weeks; 2800km/1738 miles):
Vancouver–Penticton–Banff–Jasper–Prince George–Prince Rupert–by ferry back to Port Hardy Vancouver Island (18 hours)–Vancouver.

Totem-Circular tour

Canada by rail

Owing to the sparsely distributed population the rail network is also widespread and only comparable with European services in the corridor Windsor–Toronto–Ottawa–Montréal–Québec. Here there are several pairs of trains operating daily on parallel routes which link up in Montréal and Toronto. Express trains (LRC trains = Light-Rapid-Comfortable Trains) with first class service (hot meals, wine) operate between Québec and Windsor.

General

Outside of this corridor the only other integrated network is in southern Ontario. Apart from the railway lines in Ontario and Québec, the only other stretches with more than one train service a day are in New Brunswick (Moncton–Campbellton/Moncton–St John), Nova Scotia (Halifax–Moncton) and in British Columbia (Kamloops–Vancouver). Similarly the number of connections between the individual towns varies. Whereas in Montréal and Toronto 20 to 30 long distance trains arrive and depart daily (even to and from New York), in Calgary or Edmonton – both cities the size of Manchester – there is only one train a day.

At the termini of transcontinental rail connections – Halifax or Vancouver – three to four train services start or terminate. In any case nearly all big cities have the advantage of being on one of the major long distance lines. That does not apply to international connections: there is only one service between Toronto–Chicago, Toronto–New York and Montréal–New York. Other international connections have completely disappeared, such as the service Montréal–Montpellier–New York (USA), only brought into use a few years ago, or have been replaced by buses as in the case of trains between Windsor and Detroit (USA) and Vancouver and Seattle (USA).

The difference between the "Main Street" (Québec-Windsor-corridor) and the periphery is apparent not only from the number of trains and comfort but also from the speed. The Montréal–Toronto route is served by LRC trains at over 100kph/62mph so that the 539km/334 miles-long stretch takes 4½ hours. The construction of a high speed route Montréal–Toronto, modelled on the French or German system, is planned. On the otherhand the average speed on connecting lines to Québec and London in the north-east and south-west is below 100kph/62mph.

Bottom of the league is the recently opened Edmonton–Fort McMurray line, which is served weekly by two "Mixed Trains" (i.e. half freight train, half passenger train). The 473km/293 miles-long route takes twelve hours from north to south and no less than 23 hours from south to north (on account of a stopover at Lac La Biche).

There are many interesting and long routes where there is only one train on certain days. These routes include Jasper–Vancouver (855km/531 miles) and Jasper–Prince Rupert (1160km/720 miles), Prince George–Lillooet (305km/189 miles), Winnipeg–Churchill (1697km/1054 miles) or Sudbury–Capreol–Winnipeg (1498km/930 miles), each with three trains a week, and the Edmonton–Fort McMurray line with one train a week. Despite these differing services it must be stressed that all Canadian towns with a population over 50,000 are connected to the rail network. The only exceptions being Kelowna and, since the closure of the Newfoundland narrow-gauge railway some years ago, St John's.

The backbone of the Canadian railway network are the transcontinental lines of the privately owned CP (Canadian Pacific) and the state owned CN (Canadian National), upon which the operating company VIA-Rail run their transcontinental express trains.

Outstanding experience

The journey across the continent from the tidal Atlantic coast, past the huge cities in the St Lawrence Lowland and the natural landscape of the Canadian Shield to the vast expanses of the Prairies and the mountain chain of the Cordilleras is one of the most fantastic in the world. The experience is increased by the high degree of comfort on the "coach" carriages and especially on the "Dayniter" and sleeping cars, "lounge" and "dome" cars.

Careful planning essential

However, crossing Canada by train needs to be carefully prepared. As there is only a limited service reservations need to be made. There is not the same flexibility as with the bus companies which operate a parallel service and so the value of a rail pass is questionable. A further disadvantage is that the exceptionally beautiful countryside is crossed during the night, which with the Cordilleras, more than anywhere, is regrettable.

Even the timetable is problematic. For example, if it states that the train departs from Montréal at 9.55am, arriving in Calgary at 12.45pm and shortly afterwards in Banff at 3.45pm, it must be remembered that two days and two nights are in between and that it extends over three different time zones (Eastern Time, Central Time, Mountain Time).

Itinerary

From Halifax (Nova Scotia) or St John's (Newfoundland) to Moncton and Québec

The east–west journey by Canadian railways begins in Halifax, the scenically located largest town of the Atlantic provinces. Starting from Newfoundland is also advantageous. Buses depart from St John's for the ferry port Port-aux-Basques, from where it is seven hour boat trip to North Sydney. A train leaves from here for Truro connecting with Moncton, the largest rail junction in eastern Canada. The express train "Océan" follows the coastline of New Brunswick and the St Lawrence valley to Québec (1350km/838 miles). At best the scenery is varied. Adjacent areas of touristic interest such as Gaspé peninsula, Prince Edward Island or even Newfoundland can be reached by connecting trains, ferries and buses.

Québec–Montréal

From the picturesque old town of Québec the route crosses over to the right side of the St Lawrence river. The stretch through the St Lawrence

Lowland to Montréal, the city rich in tradition and the second largest French-speaking town in the world, is relatively monotonous.

The flagship of Canada's railways is the trans-continental express train "Canadian" which covers the 4645km/2886 miles between Montréal and Vancouver in almost exactly four days and nights. Comfortably equipped for long journeys this train connects with a sprinter train from Toronto, 426km/264 miles distant, after 711km/441 miles at Sudbury and after 2274km/1413 miles in Winnipeg connects with the second flagship, the "Super Continental", which operates on a 140km/86 miles longer CN route via Edmonton to Vancouver.

Montréal–
Sudbury–
Winnipeg–
Regina–Calgary–
Banff–Fraser–
Vancouver

The journey across Canada on the "Canadian", on the Canadian-Pacific railway with its notable history and spectacular countryside, or on the "Super Continental", which runs on the equally interesting Canadian-National routes, still remains an overwhelming experience. On such a journey the contrast between Franco-Canadian and Anglo-Canadian cultural landscapes makes a marked impression as well as that between the densely populated regions in the St Lawrence Lowland and the wild isolation of the Canadian Shield, where the mining country around Sudbury is typical of many mining towns in north Ontario.

The magnificent stretch along Lake Superior, in places dynamited out of the cliffs, leads to Thunder Bay, the largest port for exporting cereals in the world. Beyond Kenora there is a sudden change in scenery from the wild rocky hills of the Canadian Shield to the flat agricultural plain near the former Lake Agassiz before reaching Winnipeg.

A stopover in this fascinating town should include a visit to the Museum of Man and Nature, the old cultural centre of St Boniface and the neighbouring Mennonite settlements.

The next section is through the vast and monotonous countryside of the Prairies past Swift Current to Regina, the provincial capital of Saskatchewan. This stretch provides a bold contrast between the vast fertile Prairies with their colourful grain elevators, the charming foothills and the wild mountain chains of the Rocky Mountains. From here on superlative follows superlative. After Calgary, the rich metropolis with its modern skyline, the eastern range of the Cordilleras appear and Banff. Other highlights of this high mountain world of 3600m/11,811ft are: Lake Louise, the two spiral tunnels of the CP line, Kicking Horse Pass in the Rocky Mountains, Rogers Pass in the Selkirk Mountains with its two long tunnels – the 9km/5½ mile-long Connaught Tunnel completed in 1916 and the almost 15km/9½ mile-long Mount McDonald Tunnel completed in 1988 – and the 94m/308ft high Stoney Creek Bridge.

The next section is through the dry, warm basin of Kamloops, which recalls the Mediterranean, and the wild gorges of the Thompson River and Fraser River to Yale. The last 100km/62 miles follow the highly cultivated Fraser Valley to Vancouver, after a total of 4645km/2886 miles.

The "Super Continental", which connects with the "Canadian" in Winnipeg, offers a very interesting alternative. After travelling through flat, monotonous land it reaches the almost European-looking town of Saskatoon with its many bridges.

Variations:
Winnipeg–
Saskatoon–
Edmonton–
Jasper–Vancouver

The rest of the journey is through the Park Belt adjoining the Prairies. Here, too, as on the southern route, the massive grain elevators – the "cathedrals of the Prairies" – stand out near the huge farms. Edmonton is worth a day's visit or more. Sights of the capital of Alberta, high above the Saskatchewan River, include the Parliament and newly-built government quarter, the modern high-rise architecture of the inner city, the old Fort Edmonton and, in contrast, the "Edmonton West Mall", the largest and most modern shopping centre in the world.

Continuing the journey the train comes to the Rocky Mountains chain in the spectacular Jasper National Park by evening.

Situated on the CN line, Jasper, together with Banff on the more southerly CP line, is the most popular tourist destination in the Rocky Mountains. Continuing on the "Super Continental" (beyond Jasper it only operates two to three times weekly) there is a panoramic view of Mount Robson, at 3954m/12,972ft the highest mountain on this stretch through the Rocky Mountains. The next stage of the journey through the gorges of the Thompson River and the Fraser River leave a powerful impression. Finally it reaches Vancouver, the western metropolis on the Pacific.

Further tourist rail routes

Skeena

Apart from the above routes which make up the backbone of the Canadian railway network, there is a whole range of other connections of interest to the traveller in Canada. Among these is the "Skeena" (sleeping and dining cars) which operates on the magnificent mountain route between Jasper and Prince Rupert and takes 22 hours to cover 1160km/720 miles. Equally varied, but much shorter, is the 225km/139 mile-long trip from Victoria to Nanaimo and Courtenay on Vancouver Island.

Hudson Bay Line

A completely different experience is to be had on the 1697km/1054 mile-long Hudson Bay Line which runs from Winnipeg to Churchill through forests, bogs, and tundra and over permafrost and normally takes about 35 hours. Climatic delays are made bearable by comfortable provision (sleeping and dining cars).

B.C. Railway
Cariboo Dayliner

In addition to the long-distance trains already mentioned – without exception operated by VIA-Rail on the Canadian Pacific (CP) and Canadian National (CN) rail networks – there are several private lines of interest to the tourist. The first is the scenic and technically remarkable 742km/461 mile-long line of the British Columbia Railway from Prince George to North Vancouver. A historic steam train drawn by the legendary "Royal Hudson 2860" engine plies the 61km/37 mile southern section along the Howe Sound (Vancouver–Squamish) daily in summer, a journey which takes about two hours.

Algoma Railway

The Algoma Railway offers an extremely popular 183km/114 mile-long train excursion, especially in autumn when the leaves are changing colour, on the "White Bear Express" through the Algoma Wilderness to the Agawa Canyon north of Sault Ste Marie.

Ontario Northland
Railway, Polar
Bear Express

An unusual railway experience is provided by the 300km/186 mile-long journey on the Ontario Northland Railway from Cochrane to Moosonee, a historic fur-trading centre on James Bay (Hudson Bay). Apart from the rocky and boggy landscape the travelling public is in itself remarkable: the "Polar Bear Express" carries Indians, trappers and adventurers.

Museum trains

For railway enthusiasts there is a whole range of steam train journeys. In addition to the above-mentioned "Royal Hudson" (North Vancouver–Squamish) steam trains operate in Calgary (Heritage Park), in Edmonton (Fort Edmonton), in Winnipeg (Prairie Dog) and Ottawa (Gatineau Park). There is also a notable railway museum in Delson near Montréal.

Rocky Mountaineer

Special train
throuth the
Rocky Mountains

A new offer from the Canadian railway and airline companies is the journey by the special train "Rocky Mountaineer", which can be booked in Europe as an air and rail package tour. It comprises trans-

Atlantic flight to Calgary (Alberta) or Vancouver (British Columbia) with overnight stay at destination. The following day the luxuriously equipped express "Rocky Mountaineer" departs from Calgary (or Vancouver) across the Canadian part of the North American Rocky Mountains, through Banff and Jasper National Parks to Vancouver (or Calgary). Overnight stays in first class accommodation en route are possible in scenically situated hotels near Banff and Lake Louise.

The return flight to Europe can be from either Calgary or Vancouver.

Silver & Blue Class

Thrice weekly, "Silver & Blue Class" trains make the long journey from Toronto via Winnipeg, Edmonton and Jasper to Vancouver. Recently overhauled and refurbished, the silvery aluminium carriages, manufactured originally in the 1950s, offer the ultimate in luxury rail travel for passengers who can afford the fare. The trains are equipped with a Dome Car and a Park Car from which the grandeur of the Canadian scenery can be viewed. Catering and service likewise leave nothing to be desired.

Luxury service on the Toronto–Vancouver line

VIA Rail Canada (see Practical Information, Rail Travel).

Information

Canada from A to Z

Note

The following selected places to visit are arranged in alphabetical order. English and French are the official languages used in Canada. Each place is shown in the form normally used locally; in other words, the English name is used in those regions where English is the main language, and French spellings in the French-speaking areas.

Abbotsford · Clearbrook   E 8

Province: British Columbia. Population: 75,000

See British Columbia   Information

Abbotsford and Clearbrook, two parishes which have grown together and now number 75,000 inhabitants, lie in the shadow of the 3285m/10780ft high Mount Baker which forms part of the Cascade Range of mountains south of the state border. These two towns form the centre of the Fraser Valley, where the exceptionally mild climate has led to its development as an agricultural region which, for example, produces more than 90 per cent of Canada's total raspberry crop. The high point of the year is the Abbotsford Berry Festival held every June. As well as fields of fruit bushes and narcissi – the latter being a magnificent sight in spring – large chicken farms also dominate the landscape; some 80 per cent of British Columbia's eggs are produced in this region.

Every August the Abbotsford International Air Show, one of the largest of its kind in North America, is held here.

The Matsqui-Sumas-Abbotsford Museum, housed in Tretheway House, 2313 Ware St., which was built in 1919 and has recently been lovingly restored, is rather out of the ordinary. It is open Mon.–Sat. 10am–noon and 1pm–4pm, and offers the opportunity to study exhibits of items used by the Red Indians who originally inhabited the country as well as memorabilia from the pioneering period. Particularly interesting are the documents about Sumas Lake, which was drained in 1924, thus producing 12,140ha/30,000 acres of fertile grazing and farmland which lie almost one metre below sea-level and are protected by means of a dyke from the risk of being flooded by the Fraser River.

Abbotsford
Matsqui-Sumas-
Museum

The Museum of the Mennonite Historical Society of British Columbia will be found in the Clearbrook Community Centre at 2825 Clearbrook Road. It is open Mon.–Fri. 9am–4.30pm, Sat. 9am–noon, and provides information about the history and life-style of the Mennonites in British Columbia.

Clearbrook
Mennonite
Historical
Society Museum

Acadia National Park   Q/R 8/9

Provinces: New Brunswick, Nova Scotia, Prince Edward Island, Québec

Tourist information offices in the above provinces.   Information

The areas south-east of the Lower St Lawrence River and on the Bay of Fundy, once called New France, are now known as "Acadia". Many sections of this land which has been developed by man over the centuries

Location

◀ *Rideau flight of locks and Château Laurier*

now belong to the Canadian Atlantic Provinces of New Brunswick, Nova Scotia and Prince Edward Island – in some parts of which old French is still spoken – and to the French-speaking province of Québec and the US state of Maine.

History

In 1604 Samuel de Champlain (see Famous People) and his companions landed on Docher's Island, now Maine in the United States. They founded a colony here, which was moved the following year to a sheltered bay on the eastern side of the Bay of Fundy (now Annapolis in Nova Scotia). The new colony was named Port Royal.

This new, rapidly developing French colony was attacked as early as 1613 by British troops, and subsequently ownership alternated between France and England. In 1632 it was returned to France and remained so for some time. Civil war-like conditions provided the opportunity for the British to take it over again between 1654 and 1667. Under the Treaty of Breda Acadia was returned to France. In 1710 British and Scottish troops seized Port Royal and renamed it Annapolis, after the Scottish Queen Anne Stuart.

Under the Treaty of Utrecht in 1713 the larger part of Nova Scotia was ceded to England, while Cape Breton Island, New Brunswick and Prince Edward Island remained French. Shortly before the outbreak of the Seven Years' War the 10,000 or so French settlers were deported from Acadia by the English governor and scattered in small groups in other British possessions. Some made a new home for themselves in Louisiana or in the West Indies. Finally, under the terms of the Treaty of Paris in 1763, the whole of Canada came under the rule of the British monarchy.

Acadia today

The French-speaking descendants of the Acadian settlers are now scattered in pockets in Canada. Some still live in the Edmundston area and along the middle course of the St John River, as well as along the boundary with the USA, with many others scattered along the Atlantic coast between Moncton (see entry) and the Baie des Chaleurs and the Gaspésie (see entry). Small settlements are also to be found on the south-west coast of Cape Breton (see entry), on the Île Madame, near Chéticamp on the northwest coast of Nova Scotia, in the west of Prince Edward Island and on the Îles de la Madeleine.

Cajun music

Cajun music combines elements of American "hillbilly" and square dance tempos with music introduced by settlers from Normandy and Brittany. This music has become very popular in Canada and is now spreading to Europe as well. The main instruments used are the accordion and violin with suitable song accompaniment.

Cajun music is basically French-American folk-music which originated in Louisiana in the early 19th c. "Cajuns" is the name given to those French-Canadians who, after 1775, left their homeland of Acadia (the present Canadian provinces of Nova Scotia and New Brunswick) and moved to Louisiana.

Originally cajun music was purely French folk-music, but it has absorbed an increasing number of English and West African elements and is now strongly influenced by "blues" music from the southern states of the USA. For a long time the fiddle was the dominant instrument, but the accordion and triangle now play an increasingly important role. Modern cajun bands, influenced by commercial country and western trends, often add electric guitars and percussion instruments.

The first records were made in 1928, when the accordionist Joe Falcon played "Allons à Lafayette". With that title he paid tribute to one of the most important centres of cajun music in Louisiana, the town of Lafayette. Cajun music spread further afield mainly through the influence of Clifton Chenier (1925–87) who, in the opinion of the musical magazine "Rolling Stone", was the best Acadian accordionist in the world. At the end of the 1970s Chenier and his "Red Hot Louisiana Band" went to Europe and played at the Montreux Festival.

Elements of cajun music can be found today mainly in the mainstream country and western style.

Alaska Highway

The Alaska Highway (Alaska–Canada Military Highway; Alcan), 2430km/1500 miles long, is the main route from Dawson Creek in British Columbia through the Yukon Territory to Fairbanks in Alaska. The following distances are measured from the starting point at Dawson Creek.

Location and distances

Fort Nelson: 480km/298 miles
Watson Lake: 1015km/630 miles
Whitehorse: 1473km/915 miles
Fairbanks: 2444km/1515 miles

Distances

Although the highway is open to traffic all the year round, there is always the possibility, especially in the Canadian section, that weather conditions such as melting snow in spring and heavy rainfall in summer can lead to some stretches being blocked.

The speed limit is 80kph/50mph, and higher speeds are definitely not recommended. Filling stations will be found at regular intervals along the road, and they can also carry out running repairs. Also along the whole length, but particularly on the section between Watson Lake and White-horse, motels, service areas and camp-sites can be found close to the highway.

The main reason for building the Alaska Highway was the Japanese occu-pation of the Aleutian Islands off the coast of Alaska during the Second World War in 1941. In a record time of eight months between March and October 1942, equivalent to 10km/6 miles a day, Canadian and American soldiers constructed a marked-out route in the extreme north of the states which provided safe transport for troops and provisions to Alaska, which until then had been almost unprotected in a military sense. Originally built solely to meet military needs, after the end of the war the Alaska Highway was opened to civilian traffic and since then has become the major access road and tourist route into the Yukon Territory and southern Alaska.

Importance

★★Route followed by the Alaska Highway

The Alaska Highway begins in the town of Dawson Creek, in the fertile corn-growing plain of Peace River (see entry), on the border with Alberta. Beyond Fort Nelson some 500km/310 miles to the north the road approaches the Rocky Mountains. There are two notable nature parks along this stretch, Stone Mountain and Muncho Lake Provincial Park.

Dawson Creek

The first community of any size in the Yukon Territory is Watson Lake, also known as the "Gateway to the Yukon", with some 1200 inhabitants. Founded in the 1890s, it developed into an economic and cultural centre during the building of the Alaska Highway, when up to 25,000 troops were stationed here. The newly-established information centre will provide the visitor with background information on the construction of this giant high-way. The most famous landmarks in Watson Lake, the Watson Lake Sign-posts, are also linked to the building of the road; following the example set by a homesick building worker, thousands of tourists have erected signs at the junction of the highway and Campbell Highway (see entry) showing the name of and distance to their own home town, producing a veritable "forest of signs" over the years.

Watson Lake

For some miles between Watson Lake and Whitehorse the Alaska Highway hugs Teslin Lake which, although 125km/78 miles long, is only some 3km/2 miles wide on average. From the road there are magnificient views to be had of this uniquely-shaped lake and also of the heights of the Yukon Plateau (see Yukon Territory). In the George Johnston Museum in Teslin can be seen exhibits illustrating the period of the gold-diggers and the way of life and culture of the native Indians.

Teslin Lake

From Jakes Corner it is worthwhile branching off southward for some 100km/60 miles to Atlin. This little township, a settlement dating from the time of the gold-rush, is charmingly situated on the shore of Lake Atlin. Between Jakes Corner and Whitehorse (see entry), the capital of the Yukon Territory, the highway stays parallel for some 15km/9½ miles to Marsh Lake, with its shimmering turquoise waters framed by mountains beyond. Because of its proximity to Whitehorse larger crowds must be expected here than at other lakeside areas.

Beyond Whitehorse the Alaska Highway turns westward towards the coastal range of the St Elias Mountains. Passing the little township of Haines Junction the road leads to Kluane National Park (see entry) in the western corner of the Yukon – a unique nature conservation area with Canada's highest peak, Mount Logan (5951m/20,130ft), which should definitely be on the itinerary.

Haines Junction
Kluane National
Park

In Haines Junction will be found the National Park Visitors Center, which provides an informative multi-media show about the park. There is excellent fishing to be had at Kluane Lake, some 60km/37 miles north of Haines Junction.

This little place, with about 100 inhabitants, was founded as a supply station when the highway was being built, and can claim to be the most westerly settlement in Canada; it has a few motels with bars and cafés.

Beaver Creek

A few miles beyond Beaver Creek, and about 1950km/1210 miles after starting out from Dawson Creek, we leave Canadian territory. It is a further 500km/300 miles or so to Fairbanks in Alaska.

Alberta (Province)   F/G 6–8

Geographical location: latitude 49°–60° north/longitude 110°–120° west
Area: 661,200sq.km/255,290sq.miles
Population: 2,469,000. Capital: Edmonton

Alberta Tourism, Main Level, City Center, 10155–102 St., Edmonton, T5J 4L6; tel. (403) 427–4321.

Information

Alberta covers 6.6 per cent of Canada's total area, and is its fourth largest province. The longest distance north–south is an impressive 1206km/750 miles at longitude 114° west, while the maximun east–west is 660km/410 miles at latitude 55° north. The longitudinal and latitudinal borders are parallel, except in the Rocky Mountains where it follows the line of the watershed. Manitoba, Saskatchewan and Alberta together form what are known as the Prairie States of Canada, over 70 per cent of the total area being taken up by the Alberta Plain, a high-lying prairie mainly between 900 and 1000m/2950 and 3300ft above sea-level. 570 million years ago this entire region formed part of a giant inland lake. 70 million years ago the folding of the Rockies began to take place in the west (see British Columbia) and on the main ridge, Mount Columbia at 3747m/12,300ft being the highest mountain in Alberta. The prairies now consist largely of material released and deposited during the period of the structural deformation of the Rockies, with rich black and brown soil predominating, ideal for agriculture. Alberta can be divided into three sections: South Alberta, covering the southern third of the province and with a slightly hilly prairie landscape, the "rolling prairies"; the "parklands" of Central Alberta, with their wide valleys and mountain-chains, numerous rivers and lakes, and criss-crossed with forests; and Northern Alberta, covering almost a half of the whole, characterised by large areas of coniferous forest divided up by the Peace and Athabasca Rivers. Less than three percent of the total area is taken up by lakes and waterways, a relatively small amount compared to nearly nineteen per cent in Manitoba. The largest areas of water are Little Slave Lake (1150sq.km/444sq.miles) and Peace River (1916km/1190 miles).

◀ *Alaska Highway: milepost "0"*

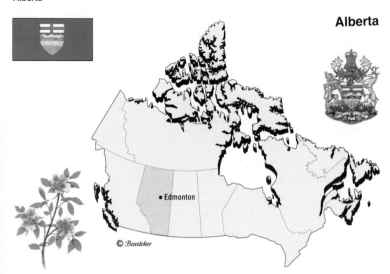

Alberta

© Baedeker

• Edmonton

Climate

As the Rocky Mountains follow the meridian and consequently the western edge of the mountain ridge is protected from rain, Alberta by and large enjoys a continental climate. Where the mountains afford protection from wind and rain the average annual precipitation is only 400–500mm/16–20in. The lack of an east–west mountain barrier results in an interchange of Arctic and tropical air masses. This means that in winter dry polar air pushes far into southern Alberta, while in summer tropical air masses can result in heavy falls of rain. On the prairies this results in hot summers with frequent thunder storms and winters with little snow but low temperatures. Even as late as April the average minimum in Alberta is below freezing point, and there are signs of impending winter in October. As an example, Lethbridge in the south of the province enjoys an average maximum temperature in July of 26°C/79°F and over ten hours sunshine each day. A unique feature of Alberta is the "chinook", a warm dry wind coming from the Rocky Mountains, which frequently brings about an early thaw in the south.

Vegetation

The dominant natural vegetation in the north of Alberta is coniferous forest, which becomes tundra especially in the higher regions bordering the Northwest Territories. In the north conifers such as spruce and larch predominate, while towards the south deciduous trees including beech, birch and maple come more into their own. In the south-east flourishes a form of natural grassland, so that the "short grass prairie" of the north becomes the "long grass prairie" of the south.

History

There is evidence of human settlement in Alberta going back more than 11,000 years. Cypress Hills, protected from the ravages of the Ice Age, were inhabited by aboriginals for over 7000 years. Present-day Alberta was entrusted to the Hudson's Bay Company after it was founded in 1670, with trade being mainly in furs. In 1754 Anthony Henday was the first white man to explore as far as the Rocky Mountains. Between 1792 and 1801 Peter Fidler pushed far south into Alberta and discovered rich coal deposits by the Red Deer River. In the south missionaries founded schools and churches and made the first contacts with the Indians. Trading posts – such as that at Peter Pond Lake on the Athabasa River – began to be set up in 1778, and Fort Edmonton was built as a fur-trading centre in 1795. In the Oregon Border Treaty of 1846 it was laid down that the 49th parallel should be the southern border with the United States. In 1870 the area between Manitoba and the Rockies came under the administrative aegis of the Northwest Territories. In 1880 Father Albert Lacomte helped to negotiate a treaty with the Blackfoot Indians, with whose assistance the Canadian Pacific Railway was able to undertake the construction of the Trans-Canada Railroad, which was completed in 1886. In that same year John "Kootenia" Brown was the first to discover oil, and sold it as lubricating oil for one dollar a gallon. The gold-rush started in 1890 and Edmonton became the chief meeting-place of the gold-diggers. The Province of Alberta was founded in 1905 and joined the Confederation of Canadian States on September 1st of that year. The province was named after the fourth daughter of Queen Victoria, Princess Louise Caroline Alberta, the wife of the Governor General of Canada from 1878–83.

During the period of the great drought between 1931 and 1934 there were signs of widespread erosion leading to increased farm failures and death of livestock. In 1962 the TransCanada Highway was built through Alberta, guaranteeing a quicker link between the Atlantic and Pacific coasts. In 1968 a start was made on exploiting the Athabasca Tar Sands near Fort McMurray.

Drought

Alberta's 2,469,000 inhabitants represent 9·2 per cent of the whole Canadian population, and is equivalent to 3·7 persons per square kilometre or 9·6 per square mile. This compares with the appreciably lower population densities found in Manitoba (1·7 per sq.km/4·4 per sq.mile) and Saskatchewan (1·5 per sq.km/3·9 per sq.mile). The reason for this is to be found mainly in the influx of people following the discovery of crude oil in the 1960s. Some 77 per cent of Alberta's population live in the towns and cities, concentrated on four large conurbations, especially Calgary with 671,000 inhabitants and Edmonton with 785,000. From 1869 onwards most of Alberta's settlers were white, a trend which was fostered still further by the Law of Pioneer Settlement passed in 1875. The development of the province was further assisted by the building of the railroad network by the Canadian Pacific Railway after 1885. 44 per cent of the present population have British roots, followed by Germans with 14 per cent and East Europeans with 11 per cent; as a result it is not surprising that the main religion is Protestant. The largest groups of native inhabitants are to be found at Athabasca in the North and Algonkin in the south-east; both are prairie Indians who used to make a living mainly from hunting bison. Today such Indians live on the edge of society, mainly outside the larger towns. 4·4 per cent of Alberta's population is made up of native Indians, which means that 14·6 per cent of all Canada's Indian population live here. An insight into the Indian way of life can be gleaned from a visit to the Indian Collection at the Glenbow Museum in Calgary.

Population

Mention should also be made of the fact that for years Alberta has had the highest divorce rate in Canada, and that Calgary is the city with the most divorces per 100,000 couples.

The province of Alberta contributes annually more than ten per cent to the Canadian gross domestic product, even though its population is only 9·2 per cent of the country's total. The two main branches of Alberta's economy are mining (19·3 per cent of Alberta's G.D.P.) and agriculture and farming (although representing only 3·8 per cent of the G.D.P.). 62 per cent of the land is covered in forests, with only ten per cent under the plough. The forests are mainly state-owned, being leased out to private firms. More than 9000 people are employed in forestry itself, with a further 20,000 in allied industries, and this branch of the economy contributes more than 900 million dollars per annum to the gross domestic product.

Economy

Gigantic excavators dig out the oil-bearing sand

Wheat is the most important crop grown in Alberta. The first large ranch in the West, Cochrane Ranch, was built in 1878, and many other farms and mills followed. The wheat crop is mainly summer wheat and it has been found possible to reduce the growing period to between 100 and 110 days, so that it can now be grown even further north than before. The size of the farms which average some 354ha/874 acres, has resulted in a high degree of mechanisation. Although Alberta covers only 6·6 per cent of Canada's total land area nearly twenty per cent of the country's farms are to be found here. In recent years farmers have diversified and broken away from the tradition of growing only wheat; in particular they now grow more forage cereals to provide food for cattle. Whereas in 1926 56 per cent of farm income evolved from wheat, today 60 per cent is derived from cattle rearing. In the south-east, with the assistance of improved irrigation systems, 4000sq.km/1550sq.miles of new useable land has been opened up. The problems of agriculture, made public in particular in the "Dirty Thirties", are mainly those arising from soil erosion. Drought, pests and acid soil also play a major part.

In the field of mineral resources Alberta also plays an important role, as it is here that 70 per cent of the country's coal stocks, 80 per cent of its crude oil and 68 per cent of its natural gas are to be found, with only comparatively small amounts being used within the province itself. Coal deposits are estimated at 48,000,000,000 tonnes, with about five-sixths thereof under the plains and one-sixth in the Rocky Mountains. In Alberta coal is utilised mainly in the generation of electricity, 91·6 per cent of all electricity being produced with coal as the fuel. Damage to the environment is nevertheless relatively small, as the coal contains only small amounts of sulphur. The remaining electricity needs are met by means of giant hydro-electric power stations.

Crude oil has been extracted in Alberta since 1886, and has increased more and more in importance during the present century. Today there are 17,000 oil-wells in Alberta and a pipeline network stretching more than

100,000km/63,000 miles. While most of the oil-storage sites are in the south, giant deposits of oil in sand have been found in the north (Fort McMurray), estimated at about one-third of the total world supply. Because of the difficult processes involved in separating the oil from the sand it has only recently – since 1967 – been found viable to exploit these resources. All the processes cause some environmental problems since – as well as causing damage to the earth's surface – 22 tonnes of water are required to extract one tonne of crude oil. All Canadian oil companies now have their headquarters in Calgary.

Alberta offers ideal leisure facilities throughout the year. As regards winter sports, there are five well-equipped skiing areas available from November to May, with plenty of ski-runs in the south-west of the province. A lot of ice-hockey is also played in Alberta. In summer 59 provincial parks and five national parks are open – especially Jasper National Park, covering 10,878sq.km/4200sq.miles, and Banff National Park, 6642sq.km/2565sq.miles. Leisure pursuits range from trekking along well-maintained paths to water-sports and riding. Outside the parks there are ideal opportunities for hunting, especially in the north. As well as shooting water-fowl the hunting of large wild animals, including bear and elk, could well prove an attractive proposition. Those who prefer more leisurely pursuits may like to indulge in a little fishing. The towns of Edmonton and Calgary have some unique attractions for visitors. Every July since 1912 the "Stampede" has been held in Calgary, a sort of world championship in rodeo skills. The town's attractions have increased even further since the Winter Olympics were held here in 1988. Edmonton can boast, by way of example, the West Edmonton Mall, the world's largest shopping and leisure complex, where it is quite possible to spend hours or even days without becoming bored. However, tourists from Europe will no doubt wish to concentrate on the natural beauties to be found in the south-western corner of the province, and perhaps not concern themselves with Alberta's other attractions. The Tourist Offices to be found everywhere in Alberta will be more than happy to provide up-to-date information on all manner of sights and facilities.

Leisure, sport, tourism

Algonquin Provincial Park

O 8/9

Province: Ontario
Area: 7600sq.km/2935sq.miles. Founded: 1893

Almaguin Nipissing Travel Association, Box 361, North Bay, Ontario, P1B 8H5; tel. (705) 474–6634
Tourism Ontario, 77 Bloor St. W., Toronto, Ontario, M7A 2R9

Information

Along Highway 60, which cuts through the south-western part of the park.

Access

In Algonquin Provincial Park there are eight camping sites and numerous picnic areas. In addition there are three lodges for anglers and hunters as well as some outfitters.

    Algonquin Provincial Park, the second largest of its kind in Canada, stretches to the south-east of North Bay (see entry) and south of the upper reaches of the Ottawa River. This forest area, studded with more than 2,400 lakes, gets its name from the Algonquin Indian tribe who lived here and indeed still do.

    A start was made on developing this vast area in the 19th c., when it was extensively cultivated. From time to time there have been catastrophic forest fires, and since 1893 continuous attempts have been made to safeguard the threatened forests.

Facilities

The subsoil of the park is of granite. The forest itself is a mixture of deciduous and coniferous trees, with spruce, Scots pine and maple predominating. It is especially beautiful here in the "Indian summer", in early

★ Forest

autumn when the leaves are changing colour. It is here that the artist Tom Thomson and his "Group of Seven" are said to have been particularly inspired.

Fauna

A large variety of fauna inhabit Algonquin Provincial Park: bears, deer, wolves, otters and musk rats are only a few of the many mammals found here. In the rivers and lakes numerous fish are at play, including various species of salmon and trout. The banks of the lakes and brooks as well as many other areas are home to numerous kinds of birds.

Algonquin Indians

Originally the Algonquin lived in the region between the sources of the Mississipi and the St Lawrence River in enclosed villages with houses roofed with thatch and bark. As skilled gatherers, fishers and hunters they were able to exploit to the full the potential of the woodlands. They also knew how to clear the land and grow crops of maize.

Their lives were shattered from the 17th c. onwards when the white man arrived in the forests of eastern Canada, as well as through increasing conflicts with the neighbouring Mic-Mac tribe, who had been driven from the lowlands of the St Lawrence by European colonists from the Atlantic coast. Nowadays the Algonquin barter furs for tools, alcohol and cheap knick-knacks from Europe.

Entrance to the park near Whitney, Pioneer Logging Museum

The Pioneer Logging Museum stands near the Whitney entrance gate to the park. Here stands an old steam locomotive as a reminder of the times when the present nature reserve was the scene of much timber-felling. An old log-cabin gives an idea of the way in which the lumberjacks used to live. Open: mid-June–early Sept., daily 9am–6pm (Sat. and Sun. only in spring and autumn).

★Canoeing

Because of its many waterways Algonquin Provincial Park is very popular with canoeists. There are more than 1600km/1000 miles of rivers and lakes marked out for those keen on this sport.

Park Museum

Some 20km/13 miles from the east entrance to the park will be found the very informative Park Museum, which is open mid-June–mid-Oct. daily 9am–5pm, mid-May–mid-June at weekends only. It portrays in great detail the flora and fauna to be found in the Algoquin Provincial Park.

Kiosk

The village of Kiosk forms the northern entrance to the park. It is a favourite spot for anglers looking for trout.

On the far side of Highway 630 is the Eau Claire Gorge Conservation Area with a wild and romantic stretch of water.

Bancroft

In the Madawaska Valley on the southern edge of the park lies the busy little town of Bancroft, with 3000 inhabitants. In recent years Bancroft has developed into a popular holiday resort. Experts have found some beautiful minerals in the surrounding countryside, which geologically forms part of the Canadian Shield. In August every year a mineral exhibition is held in Bancroft, attended by many people interested in precious stones.

Annapolis Royal · Habitation Port-Royal   Q 8

Province: Nova Scotia. Population: 700

Information

See Nova Scotia

History

The oldest permanent French settlement in Canada, the "Habitation Port-Royal", lies on the estuary of a small river which here enters the Bay of Fundy (see entry). The settlement was founded in 1605 by Sieur de Monts who had emigrated to North America with Samuel de Champlain (see Famous People) and – with the permission of the French King Henry IV –

founded the colony of Acadia (see entry). Thanks mainly to the rich agricultural soil the little colony quickly prospered, and trading links were established with the native Indians. In 1613 Port-Royal was destroyed by a British expeditionary force, and after that it found itself alternately under English/Scottish and French rule.

In 1629 a Scottish fort was built a little way from the French settlement. This Scottish settlement – named after Queen Anna Stuart – is considered to have been the nucleus of the present province of Nova Scotia. After the region had been handed back to France in 1632 the fortified settlement was destroyed by its inhabitants.

The colony was rebuilt by Seigneur d'Aulnay around 1636, and quickly prospered. After quarrels among the French ruling classes Port-Royal again became an English possession in 1654, but under the Treaty of Breda 1667 it was once more returned to France.

In 1710 the settlement was finally captured by the British and Annapolis Royal became the first capital of Nova Scotia.

Sights in Annapolis Royal

Along Lower St George Street some buildings dating from the early period of this old French and later English/Scottish colony have recently been restored, and there are some interesting exhibitions to be viewed.

Lower St George Street

The French dykes around the harbour basin have been preserved, and there is a fine view to be had from there.

Dykes

The 18th c. McNamara House, together with some furniture and fittings from the same period, has been prettily restored.

McNamara House

The Victorian period has been brought back to life in the well-restored O'Dell Inn.

O'Dell Inn

Fort Anne, the scene of so many battles in the past, is today classified as a historical monument. The old fortifications, the powder magazine and the ramparts are all open to visitors. Tall chimneys mark the officers' quarters. There are memorials to Sieur de Monts (see above), Samuel Vetch, Acadia's first governor, and Jean Paul Mascarene. On the fort flies the flag showing the English St George's Cross and the Scottish St Andrew's Cross.

★★Fort Anne

There is also a museum depicting in detail the history of the town and that of Acadia and Nova Scotia, as well as the natural history of the region. Some Indian canoes and various other artifacts complete the exhibition. Open: mid-May–mid-Oct. daily; at other times of the year Mon.–Fri. only, 10am–5pm – guided tours.

To the south of Fort Anne lie some very well-tended gardens, including the Governor's Garden from the early 18th c., a Victorian Garden and a very pretty Rose Garden.

Gardens

The tidal power station at Annapolis is the first of its kind in North America. It started up in 1985 and utilises the hydro-energy released by the tidal rise, which is the highest in the world. It is also a pilot scheme for a much larger power station based on the same principle, which is expected to produce 6000 megawatts of electricity. The information centre is open mid-May–mid-June and early Sept.–mid-Oct. daily 9am–5pm; mid-June–early Sept. 9am–8pm.

★Tidal power station

Surroundings of Annapolis

The North Hills Museum in Granville Ferry is worth a visit. This little half-timbered building is furnished in 18th c. style. (Open: mid-May–mid-Oct. Mon.–Sat. 9.30am–5.30pm, Sun. 1–5.30pm.)

North Hills Museum

★★Habitation
Port-Royal

Outside Annapolis Royal, about 10km/6 miles to the north on the north bank of the Annapolis River, stands the Habitation Port-Royal settlement of Sieur des Monts (see above), which has been faithfully restored. The whole complex is now an historic monument.

The plain wooden buildings are in early 17th c. style. There is a Governor's Residence, a Priest's House, a smithy and a room in which the Indians used to barter their furs for European goods. Most interesting is the house of the apothecary Louis Hébert, the first European farmer in North America who later settled in Québec (see entry).

In the "Habitation" in 1606 Samuel de Champlain (see Famous People) founded "L'Ordre de Bon Temps", the first society in North America based on the doctrine of love for one's fellow man.

Annapolis Valley   Q/R 8/9

Province: Nova Scotia

Information

See Nova Scotia

Annapolis Valley, situated in charmingly landscaped countryside in Nova Scotia, stretches northward from Digby and Annapolis Royal and runs parallel to the coastline of the Bay of Fundy. The valley with its fertile soil is protected on both sides from cold and unfavourable winds by mountains over 200m/650ft high, in the north by the North Range and in the south by the South Range. Being thus protected from the weather various kinds of fruit and vegetable can flourish. A lot of maize (Indian corn) is also grown here. In May, when the fruit trees are in blossom, the valley is a wonderful sight.

★★Drive through the Annapolis Valley

Tip

The best place to set out from on a drive through the Annapolis Valley is Digby or Annapolis Royal (see entry).

Digby

The little fishing village of Digby, famous for its mussels and with a population of 3000, lies by the link road between the Annapolis Valley and the Bay of Fundy. From Digby it is possible to take a boat trip across the Bay of Fundy to St Jean in New Brunswick.

Annapolis Royal

See entry

Beyond Annapolis Royal the road crosses the Annapolis River, lined with well-tilled fields and apple trees as far as the eye can see. The road passes through the pretty townships of Bridgetown, Lawrencetown and Middletown, where a number of neat little Loyalist houses can still be seen.

Greenwich
Prescott House

Then comes Greenwich, about 5km/3 miles beyond which, on the 358, stands Prescott House (open mid-May–Oct. daily 9.30am–5.30pm, Sun. 1–5.30pm), a very beautiful brick house in the Georgian style built by the business man and inspired amateur gardener Charles Prescott in the 19th c. Prescott specialised in producing new varieties of fruit, especially apples, pears and cherries, and the farmers in the region were glad to profit from his experiments. Prescott is renowned far and wide as the father of the Annapolis Valley fruit garden.

Wolfville
★ Grand-Pré
National Historic
Site

The road from Greenwich next passes through the village of Wolfville, and 4km/2½ miles east lies the "Grand-Pré" (Great Meadow), an historical site under a preservation order.

Grand-Pré was one of the main Acadian settlements in the early 18th c. By means of an ingenious system of dams and canals the Acadians succeeded in reclaiming fertile land from the sea and laid out large and

Apple blossom in the Annapolis Valley

productive fields. In its heyday there were more than 200 farms here. However, in 1755 the Acadians were driven out, their homes destroyed and their cattle taken, and the land parcelled out to colonists from New England. After the American Declaration of Independence American Loyalists were also similarly rewarded.

The Grand Pré National Historic Site is mainly in memory of the Acadian settlers and the problems they had with the English and Scottish forces. In the gardens stands a memorial to Henry Longfellow, who in 1847 immortalised the tragic fate of the Acadians in his poem "Evangéline". There is also a statue of his heroine Evangéline. Both memorials were sculpted by the Acadian artist Philippe Hébert.

Open: the gardens are open daily, but the actual buildings are open only from mid-May–mid-Oct, daily 9am–6pm. There are "Living History" presentations.

At the confluence of the Avon and Ste Croix rivers lies the little Nova Scotian port of Windsor (pop. 4000), on the spot where the Acadian settlement of Piziquid stood in the 18th c.

Windsor

Today Windsor is important as a port from which wood and building materials, including plaster, are exported.

The Museum of Nova Scotia on Clifton Avenue is worth a visit. The buildings were constructed in 1833, and the writer and humorist Thomas Chandler Haliburton lived here and wrote his famous "Sam Slick", which tells the story of an American clockmaker who offered his wares to the good people of Nova Scotia.

Clifton, Museum of Nova Scotia

The most impressive parts of the building are the tastefully furnished entrance hall, the dining room and the living room. There are guided tours each day mid-May–Oct.

L'Anse aux Meadows National Historic Park

★Fort Edward
National Historic
Site

Near the dyke stands Fort Edward, built in the mid-18th c. by the English to defend the route from Halifax to the Bay of Fundy. It was here, too, that the sad deportation of the French-speaking Acadians was organised. This wooden fort is one of the oldest existing buildings of its kind in Canada.

From the earth-wall which surrounds the fort there is a beautiful view of the valley of the Avon River and over the Bay of Fundy.

L'Anse aux Meadows National Historic Park   S 7

Province: Newfoundland. Founded: 1962

Access

Roads 430 and 436 from the TransCanada Highway, Deer Lake turn-off, about 400km/250 miles north of Corner Brook, Newfoundland.

Information

L'Anse aux Meadows National Historic Park; tel. (709) 623–2608.
Parks Canada, P.O. Box 70, St Lunaire-Griquet, Newfoundland, A0K 2X0.
  Tel. (709) 623–5151.

L'Anse aux Meadows National Historic Park, a green plain with some moorland, lies at the northern tip of the Newfoundland Great Northern Peninsula. Here were discovered six houses made of grass sods, probably built by the Vikings around the year 1000. Since 1978 it has been the first of its kind to be included in the UNESCO World List of Protected Cultural Monuments.

History

Back in 1962 a small Viking settlement dating from around A.D. 1000 was discovered here. It is the oldest known European settlement in North America and to date is the only authentic trace of Viking settlements in the New World. Probably L'Anse aux Meadows is the "Vinland" discovered by Leif Erikson.

The oldest known European settlement in North America

In the excavations carried out by the Norwegian Helge Ingstad between 1961 and 1968 at least six houses made of turves were discovered, including a smithy of the kind built by the Norwegians in Iceland. Iron relics, various kinds of artefacts clearly of Norwegian origin, as well as bones, peat and charcoal all came to light. Three reconstructed houses are open to visitors; a long-house, a workshop and a stable. The finds unearthed here are on display in the Visitors' Centre.

★★Exhibitions

Open: park open all the year round; Visitors' Centre mid-June–Labour Day daily 9am–8pm or 9am–4pm.

Ashcroft · Cache Creek   E 7

Province: British Columbia
Population: 3000. Altitude: 335–460m/1100–1510ft

See British Columbia

Information

Ashcroft lies almost 470km/292 miles north-east of Vancouver, on the far side of the TransCanada Highway on the eastern bank of the Thompson River where the Cascade Mountains fall away to the east. When the railroad link was completed in 1856 it replaced Yale as the main trade centre for the Cariboo Road. Rainfall here is a mere 180mm/7in. per annum, making Ashcroft one of the driest regions in British Columbia.

Ashcroft

In the Ashcroft Museum at 404 Brink St., which is open 10am–7pm daily from Victoria Day to Labour Day, numerous photographs, slide shows, etc. illustrate the town's glorious history.

Ashcroft Museum

The Ashcroft Manor estate was laid out in 1862 by two brothers from Cornwall. For many years it was a famous resting-place on the Cariboo Waggon Road. The owners lived here in the style of landed gentry, complete with horse-racing and fox-hunting. When post and freight were carried by stage coach the estate served as the first court and post office in the region. Today Ashcroft Manor, lying in the shade of two hundred year-old elm trees, is a museum with two craft and antique shops and a charming tea-room.

Ashcroft Manor

In summer the Travel InfoCentre arranges visits to Highland Valley Copper (Cominco), one of the largest open copper mines in the world, and situated amid the charming scenery of the Highland Valley (in the direction of Logan Lake).

Cominco

In Cache Creek, which exists mainly on income from through traffic and tourism, the Cariboo Highway 97 (see entry) branches off to the north. This road then enters truly unspoilt regions of territory, providing relatively quick access to the Yellowhead region and to Alaska. In Ashcroft-Cache Creek there is much that is reminiscent of the old west of Canada. Many cattle farms in the region take in paying guests. The barren hills nearby are becoming increasingly popular with hang-gliders.

Cache Creek

The little township of Spences Bridge (pop. 300) lies about 30 minutes by car down the valley by a bridge over the Thompson River built by Thomas Spence in 1864. This is where Highway 8 turns south-east and follows the valley of the Nicola River, with its cattle-rearing and fruit growing, to Merritt 65km/40 miles away by the new Coquila Highway. Farmers offer their seasonal produce for sale at roadside stalls. In 1905 there was a powerful landslide, the scars of which can still be seen today, which claimed the lives of eighteen people. An Indian village was destroyed and the Thompson River blocked for several hours.

Spences Bridge

Athabasca River　　　　　　　　　　　　　　　　　　　　　　F/G 6/7

Province: Alberta

Course

The Athabasca River (Indian for "where reeds grow") rises in the Rocky Mountains near the Columbia Icefield (see Icefields Parkway) at about 2200m/7220ft above sea-level. It runs through Jasper National Park (see entry), plunges down on to a shelf some 150km/90 miles above the Grand Rapids and after a further 1225km/760 miles flows into Lake Athabaska in the North-east of Alberta; this lake covers an area of some 8000sq.km/ 3100sq.miles and is 320km/200 miles long and up to 60m/200ft deep. Above it, where the Peace River and Stone River also enter the lake, stands Fort Chipewyan, built in 1788 and one of the oldest fur-trading posts in the whole of Canada.

Along the Athabasca, between the settlement of the same name and the town of Fort McMurray, rich deposits of crude oil and oil-sands were discovered and eventually exploited at great expense.

Means of transport

The Athabasca was an important trade route in the past, used to transport not only furs but also seed and corn.

Sport and leisure

The Athabasca River, over 1200km/745 miles in length, is one of the few rivers in North America to remain clean and it therefore attracts anglers and canoeists in particular.

Athabasca (Town)

Province: Alberta. Population: 2000

Information

See Alberta

Oil-bearing sands
on the Athabasca

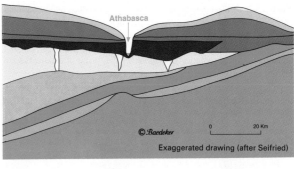

West　　　　　　　　　　　　　　　　　　　　　　　　　　East

Athabasca

© Baedeker

0　　　　20 Km

Exaggerated drawing (after Seifried)

Ice-Age strata	Oil sand (Devon)	Dolomite (Devon)
Clay (chalk)	Chalk, Karst (Devon)	Sand (Devon)
Salt (chalk)	Sand (Devon)	Granite

The rural township of Athabasca lies some 150km/90 miles north of Edmonton (see entry). It is the seat of an Open University. Known until 1926 as Athabasca's Landing, it was the main trading centre for the Hudson's Bay Company in northern Canada. The Athabsaca, most of which is navigable, offered good access upstream via Little Slave Lake to the Peace River region, and downstream by way of Fort McMurray to the Mackenzie River and thence to Alaska. In 1887 the first steamship to be built here was launched. In 1912 the railroad ceased transporting freight along the troublesome 150km/90 mile long Athabasca Landing Trail from Fort Edmonton. For more than 40 years – until the Northern Alberta Railroad to Waterways and Fort McMurray was completed – steamships on the river were the very life-blood of the town.

Today the townscape is dominated by the corn warehouses so typical of the Canadian prairies. Athabasca is also a favourite point from which to set out on tours and excursions into the largely undeveloped forest and lake regions of Northern Alberta.

Baffin Island   M–P 3–5

Administrative Unit: Northwest Territories, District of Franklin
Population: 10,000

Baffin Tourism Association, Box 820, Iqaluit, NWT, X0A 0H0   Information
    Tel. (819) 979–6551
Regional Tourism Office, Iqaluit, NWT, X0A 0H0
TravelArctic, Yellowknife, NWT, X1A 2L9
    Tel. (403) 873–7200 or Arctic Hotline 1–800–661–0788

There are direct flights to Iqaluit from Ottawa and Montréal which take   Flight connections
about three hours. From Iqaluit there are scheduled flights to Baffin Island:
Cape Dorset (1¼ hours), Lake Harbour (¾ hour), Pangnirtung (1 hour),
Broughton Island (1½ hours), Clyde River (3 hours), Pond Inlet (4½ hours),
Nanisvik (2 hours). Considerable savings can often be made if the connecting flight is booked together with the main translatlantic flight; a travel agent can provide up-to-date details.

Baffin Island, the most south-easterly and the largest on the Canadian archipelago, with its breathtaking landscape, the hospitality of the Inuit people and the numerous opportunities for an unusual holiday ("Baffin has adventure for every taste"), is clearly doing all it can to attract tourists. Nevertheless – some might say fortunately – it can hardly be said that it suffers from invasions of visitors. The only way to get to it is by air, and that is rather expensive, the cost of living is high and the climate very "unfriendly", not to mention the hordes of insects which descend on the unfortunate traveller in summer; all in all, perhaps somewhere for the specialist.

Baffin Island forms part of the Franklin District of the Northwest Territories; it covers an area of 507,451sq.km/195,930sq.miles, making it the fifth largest island in the world (Spain, for example, is 497,500sq.km/ 192,085sq.miles). In the east it is separated from Greenland by Baffin Bay and Davis Strait, to the south lies the Hudson Strait and to the west Foxe Basin. The coastline and land surface varies considerably: on the eastern coast, very similar to Norway with its steep fiords and small offshore islands, lies a long, narrow Alpine-like mountainous zone which reaches a height of 2591m/8504ft in the Auyuittuq National Park on the Cumberland peninsula. The southern foothills form highlands, while to the west lie flat lowlands.

In the east of the Northwest Territories the Canadian Arctic extends as far as   Climate
St James' Bay in the south of Hudson Bay; as a result Baffin Island lies in the permafrost region with a summer lasting from early June to the end of August with temperatures above 0°C/32°F. As the distance North to South

111

On Baffin Island

measures some 1300km/800 miles between latitudes 73° 30′ and 61° 30′ and extends beyond the Arctic Circle, there are marked climatic differences; while in Lake Harbour the average temperature in March does not fall below −22°C/8°F, this is the maximum in Arctic Bay. All in all the climate is High Arctic; even Frobisher Bay, situated 230km/143 miles south of the Arctic Circle, is free of ice only in July and August, and Iqaluit has an annual average of −9°C/16°F (July average min. 2·5°C/36°F, max. 9°C/48°F).

History

People of the Dorset culture came to the Cumberland Peninsula around 1500 B.C., and in the 12th–13th c. the Thule culture spread to Baffin Island. It is possible that Vikings came here in the 10th–11th c.; the "Helluland" of Viking legend could be Baffin Island. Baffin Island got its name from the English seafarer William Baffin, but it was "discovered" by Martin Frobisher (1539–94) who landed in Frobisher Bay in 1567 when searching for the North West Passage. He brought back to England from the Meta Incognita Peninsula some ore which he thought to be gold, but it turned out to be iron pyrites, or "fools' gold". The first permanent settlements here were those of whale-catchers, pursuing a trade which prospered until early in the 20th c. The first mission stations were set up by Anglicans on Cumberland Sound. The Hudson's Bay Company first came here to Lake Harbour in 1911, and ten years later the first police station was built.

Settlements on Baffin Island

About 1000 people live permanently on Baffin Island, a quarter of whom are white and three-quarters Inuits, who have given up their nomadic existence and settled along the coast. The main administrative town is Iqaluit on Frobisher Bay; mention should also be made of Cape Dorset, Lake Harbour, Pangnirtung, Clyde River, Pond Inlet, Nanisivik and Arctic Bay.

Cape Dorset

Cape Dorset, pop. 1000, is well-known as a place where many finds have been made relating to the Dorset culture, which flourished roughly between 1000 B.C. and A.D. 1100 and was replaced by the Thule culture, as well as for its outstanding Inuit artists (lithographs, sculptures). At the end of July the Baffin Summer Games, contests in traditional Inuit sports, are held here.

Pangnirtung (Pangniqtuuq in the Inuktitut language, meaning "where there are a lot of caribou bulls"), with a population of 1000, lies in some superb countryside – "Arctic Switzerland" – and is important as a setting-out point to Kekerten Historic Park 50km/30 miles away with an open-air museum of the history of whaling, and to Auyuittuq National Park (see below). The town is also associated with Franz Boa, a German linguist and founder of modern American ethnology, who carried out research here in 1883 and 1884.

Pangnirtung

The mining settlement of Nanisivik, on the north coast, was founded in 1974. Lead, zinc, silver and cadmium are mined here, but there are only eight weeks in the year when the harbour is free of ice and the ores can be shipped away. At the time of the summer solstice the Midnight Sun Marathon is held here, with participants from the whole of North America. Nanisivik can be reached by taxi from Arctic Bay (pop. 550) on Admiralty Inlet, which was founded by the Hudson's Bay Company in the 1920s and can be used as a base for tours.

Nanisivik

For many years the gateway to Baffin Island at the end of Frobisher Bay was frequented by whalers, scientists, traders and missionaries, but only in 1942, when it was a US military airfield, did it grow in size. In the years 1955–58 Frobisher Bay was extended as part of the "Distant Early Warning Line". In 1986 the Inuit name of Iqaluit – meaning "many fish" – was again made official.

Iqaluit
(Frobisher Bay)

Now the service and administrative centre of the Baffin Region, Iqaluit is a modern town with a complete infrastructure of hotels, schools, hospital, weather and radio station and camping-site, and a population of 3200. The tourist will find all he needs in the way of equipment and guides, etc., while the range of goods available, such as jewellery, carvings, parkas, is excellent. No. 212 near the beach, a restored Hudson's Bay Company building, contains the local museum known as Nunatta Sunaqutangit ("Things of the Country").

The most important event held here is Toonik Tyme in the third week in April, a festival with competitions and entertainment, such as beard-growing competitions, igloo-building, dog and snowmobile races, tea-making, traditional singing and dancing. This event celebrates the end of winter and is in honour of the Tooniks, the legendary strong little ancestors of the Inuit. The culmination is the "coronation" of Mr Toonik, who arrives on a dog-sleigh to open the festivities.

Interesting places in the vicinity include Sylvia Grinnell River, with kayaks and raft-races, and Qaummaarviit Historic Park, an island some 12km/7 miles away, taking about 30 minutes by boat. It has relics of the settlement's 2500-year history, including winter dwellings from the Thule culture, c. A.D. 1000–1700.

Surroundings of
Iqaluit

Auyuittuq National Park

Founded: 1972
Area: 21,470sq.km/8290sq.miles

Superintendent, Auyuittuq National Park Reserve, Pangnirtung, N.W.T. X0A 0R0; tel. (819) 473–8828
Director, Prairie Region, Parks Canada, 400–391 Avenue York, Winnipeg R3C 4B7.

Information

Auyuittuq National Park lies in the south-east of Baffin Island, on the Cumberland Peninsula, just north of the Arctic Circle, and extends about

Location and
topography

200km/125 miles to the north. A large part is taken up by the Penny Ice Cap, remains of the Ice Age glaciation of eastern Canada; it is described by the Inuit word Auyuittuq, "land where it never thaws". This landscape of primitive rocks on the edge of the Canadian continent is characterised by broad glaciated valleys and rugged mountains with vertical walls rising up to 1200m/4000ft in height and typical flat-topped peaks, that of Mount Asgard being particularly impressive.

| Pangnirtung Pass | The preferred route through the National Park leads diagonally across the peninsula to a point about 100km/63 miles from Overlord at the end of the Pangnirtung Fiord. Although it is possible to cover the whole stretch, this would take some ten to fourteen days, and the connection to Broughton Island is fraught with problems. Therefore most people prefer to make round trips of varying length from Overlord, the longest one being to Summit Lake or Glacier Lake. This "great" route is 103km/65 miles and takes about 48 hours actual walking time. The only camping site is in Overlord; it is about 31km/19 miles from Pangnirtung and can be reached on foot, by snowmobile or – in summer – by boat ("canoe-taxi"). However, attempting it on foot is not recommended, as it takes considerably longer – about three days – and is unattractive. To undertake such a trek lasting several days in the uninhabited Arctic requires a high degree of fitness and experience as well as very careful preparation; the walker must be equipped so as to be completely self-sufficient and be prepared for the worst of weather – such as rainstorms in summer lasting several days – and for crossing rivers and other watercourses. |

Baie James · James Bay

Province: Quebec

| Information | Tourisme Québec, B. P. 20000, Québec, Canada, G1K 7X2
Société de Développement de la Baie James, Matagami, Québec.
  Tel. (819) 762–81 81
Hydro-Québec, Chantier de la Grande 2A, Radisson, Québec.
  Tel. (819) 638–68 70
Bureau de Tourisme, Matagami-Radisson, Québec; tel. (819) 739–20 30. |

| History | Baie James is the flat southern part of Hudson Bay. It was discovered in 1610 by the English seafarer Henry Hudson and explored by Thomas James in 1631. From 1663 onwards the French adventurers Radisson and Chouart des Groseilliers traded here in furs. In 1671 Father Charles Albanel and Paul Deys de Saint-Simon discovered the region to the east of James Bay. One of the places they passed was Lake Mistassini, the largest lake in the province of Québec.
Between 1930 and 1935 lay brothers from the settlements at Wasganish (Fort Rupert) set out for Chisasibi (Fort George), where they tilled the land and reared cattle. This satisfied the needs of the Cris Indians living there. |

| Settlements | The few villages are scattered along the coast, the main one, Chisasibi (Fort George) being at the mouth of Big River. |

| Note | "La Grande" is the name that has been given to a huge energy-producing project utilising the rivers on the east coast of Baie James, about 1200km/750 miles north of Montréal as the crow flies. The project is to be carried out by Hydro-Québec and is already under way. |

| Importance of the project | Scarcely had the Prime Minister of Québec, Robert Bourassa, made known his intention of carrying out a giant building programme in the region of James Bay than the whole of the population of Québec fervently declared itself either for or against the plan. The ecologists were against it on environmental grounds, fearing for the Indian way of life and culture, while |

others feared extreme climatic conditions would result. Political parties and financial circles considered it to be financially intolerable. The problem came even more to a head when the F.T.Q. (Fédération des Travailleurs du Québec) monopolised the start of work on the project.

After a long and furious parliamentary debate the vote was in favour of the project. The Baie James Energy Company – a branch of Hydro-Québec – emphasised the value of the hydro-energy potential of the region, while the Baie James Development Company pointed to the possible dangers to nature on this 350,000sq.km/135,000sq.mile area.

From the various alternative programmes it was decided for a number of reasons to go ahead with Grande Rivière project. The granite and gneiss stone found on this fairly high plateau behind the coastal strip was well-suited to the construction of a complex of this kind. Other points in its favour were the many Ice Age lakes and moraines, the 800km/500 mile long Grande Rivière river with its tributaries and the other waterways in the region such as Eastmain, Opinaca Rupert, Broadback and so on. There are frequent floods, but as far as the "La Grande" and NBR (Nottaway-Broadback-Rupert, the names of the three rivers) project are concerned the rivers are under control. Weather conditions are extreme: on average, temperatures range between −23°C/−9°F to +20°C/68°F in summer and in winter the dry cold can take temperatures down to as low as −50°C/−58°F.

The Inuit and Cris Indians who lived there presented a further problem. Controversy ranged and in December 1972 work was postponed. In 1975 a contract was signed agreeing on a compensation payment and a change in the way the project was to be carried out.

Among other things this project includes the construction of three giant power stations along the Grande Rivière and the diversion of the Eastmain, Opinaca and Caniapiscau rivers. About 1600km/1000 miles of roads will have to be built, as well as five airports, five villages and seven camps for the 17,000 or more workers. Ultimately the hydro-electric output will be in the region of 16 million kilowatts.

The building programme is in two phases: the first, already completed, embraced the construction of three power stations between 1972 and 1985, a power grid of 5000km/3100 miles with cables carrying some 740kV and two river diversions. The cost was about 15,000,000,000 dollars, with European – especially French – shareholders.

The second phase includes the Grande Rivière, Grande Baleine and Mattaway-Broadback-Rupert projects. Estimated cost: 55,000,000,000 dollars. It appears, however, that this will not proceed unless the USA guarantees that it will buy some of the electricity produced.

While building work is going on the highway from Matagami to Radisson is closed to private traffic.

The Baie James Energy Company (SEBJ) will allow groups of at least fifteen people to visit its building sites between April 15th and October 15th. Access is by aircraft, but there are no overnight facilities. Because of the large distances involved only one site can be visited on any one day. Information: Bureau de Tourisme, km 6, Route Matagami-Radisson; tel. (819) 638–84 86.

In days gone by this town was an outpost of the Hudson's Bay Company, and today has a population of 2000, mostly Indians. About 200km/125 miles further south lies Fort Eastmain, which also used to be a Hudson's Bay Company outpost. Quite a number of descendants of the original inhabitants still live here. | Chisasibi

Waskaganish is the oldest settlement in this inhospitable region. | Waskaganish

The Nouveau Québec region in the north of Québec Province extends to the 62nd degree of latitude. This vast area has only the occasional settlement. North of Chisasibi a few small settlements can be found along the coast of Hudson Bay (see entry), and a few people live by the Baie d'Ungava. | **Nouveau Québec** Location

At the mouth of the Grande Rivière lies the Indian settlement of Poste de la Baleine. | Poste de la Baleine

Banff National Park

Belcher Islands	Off the Hudson Bay coast lie the barren Belcher Islands.
Povungnituk	The Inuit village of Povungnituk consists of about 100 buildings, including a mission station. More recently it has become well-known as a port, fishing-village and handicraft centre producing among other things stone sculptures and decorated textiles.
Sulluk	Sulluk, some 300km/190 miles further north, a mission station since 1947, lies in the Perpetual Ice by the Hudson Waterway. For three hundred years ships have passed by here as they entered Hudson Bay from the Atlantic looking, for example, for the port of Churchill in the south-west of Hudson Bay.

Banff National Park   F 7

Province: Alberta. Area: 6641sq.km/2564sq.miles

Information	Superintendent, Banff National Park, P.O. Box 900, Banff, Alberta T0C 0C0; tel. (403) 762–33 24
Access	Road: TransCanada Highway 1, Calgary–Banff–Lake Louise–Golden–Hwy. 93, Banff–Windemere Hwy., Icefields Parkway (Hwy. 93 N.), Lake Louise–Jasper; Hwy. 11, David Thompson Hwy., Saskatchewan Crossing–Rocky Mountain House.
	Coach: Greyhound
	Railway: VIA-Rail Vancouver–Banff–Calgary.
Location	Banff National Park lies on the TransCanada Highway 1 in the region of the glaciated Rocky Mountain ridge east of the continental watershed and about 130km/80 miles west of Calgary. In the north it adjoins Jasper National Park (see entry), with which it is linked by the unique Icefields Parkway (see entry), and in the west it runs into the Yoho and Kootenay National Park (see entries).

★★ Topography	Banff National Park is one of Canada's greatest tourist attractions. Together with its three neighbouring parks it has been included since 1985 in UNESCO's list of protected natural and cultural monuments. Banff National Park forms part of the main Rocky Mountain ridge east of the continental watershed and the Front Range which falls away steeply to the Great Plain, and in this park alone there are two dozen peaks of more than 3000m/9850ft. More than three million visitors a year are fascinated by the picturesque turquoise mountain lakes mirroring the snow-covered peaks, glaciers and mountain forests, by the luxuriant mountain meadows in early summer and the impressive waterfalls, charming streams, lonely highland valleys and areas of quiet and untamed natural scenery only a few hundred metres from the main roads.
	    The health resort of Banff, with its hot springs, is the only township in the park. Highway 93 (see Icefields Parkway), which winds for 230km/143 miles through the 3000–4000m/10,000–13,000ft high mountains, connects Banff with the numerous sights and Jasper National Park to the north. The highlights of this impressive journey along Highway 93 are the world-famous Lake Louise, in whose ice-cold waters under a deep-blue sky are reflected the surrounding mountains, the aristocratic-looking Canadian Pacific Hotel "Château Lake Louise", and the Columbia Icefield, covering 325sq.km/125sq.miles, the largest glacier in the Rocky Mountains.
	    At any time of the year this national park offers good facilities for sport and leisure: there are mountain tours on foot and on horseback, "back-

Mountain scenery in Banff National Park ▶

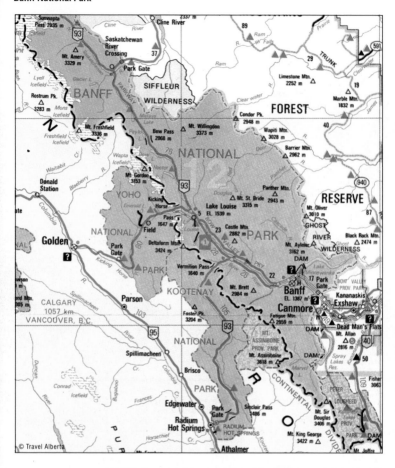

© Travel Alberta

packing'' (a licence being required for trips lasting several days), golf courses and tennis courts, ''river rafting'' on the Bow River or peaceful canoe trips on one of the beautiful lakes.

Climate

Typical of this section of the Rocky Mountains, there are marked seasonal differences depending on the height. The town of Banff itself, one of the lowest places in the national park, lies about 1400m/4600ft above sea-level.

Winters are generally long and minimum temperatures below −30°C/ −22°F are not uncommon. In January the average maximum temperatures are −7°C/19°F, the minima being −16°C/3°F. The relatively cool summers are short, although brief periods when the temperature rises as high as 30°C/86°F are not unknown. In July and August average daily maxima of more than 20°C/68°F and minima of some 7°C/45°F are attained.

In the long valleys in the lee of the high mountain chains annual rainfall amounts are very small, being only 380mm/15in., while in the continental water-shed region they may measure more than 1250mm/50in. The best months for travelling are July and August, but in view of the crowds of tourists at that time it may be better to go earlier in the year or in September.

Man settled in the great valleys 11,000 years ago, as is shown by excavations made at Vermilion Lakes near Banff. When the first Europeans arrived Stoney and Kootenay Indians as well as members of the Blackfoot tribes already lived and hunted here.

History

Banff's first "tourist" was undoubtedly Sir George Simpson who in 1841, when Governor of the Hudson's Bay Company, accompanied by an Indian guide on one of his inspection trips crossed the Bow River to what is now the town of Banff and passed over the Rocky Mountains along a pass since named after him. After that fur-hunters roved through the present national park.

In 1883 the Canadian Pacific Railway reached Banff, then prosaically known simply as "Siding 29", and Lake Louise. In the same year railroad workers seeking minerals stumbled across the hot sulphur springs at Cave & Basin Springs, where initially the railroad workers and subsequently rheumatism sufferers from all over the world came to seek relief. Disputes as to ownership of the springs led in 1885 to the establishment of the Hot Springs Reserve at the foot of Sulphur Mountain. Two years later Rocky Mountains Park was laid out, from which sprang the Banff National Park in 1930.

The opening of the railroad brought settlers and tourists to the mountain valley. In 1888 the Canadian Pacific Railway (CPR) opened the Banff Springs Hotel, followed by the Château Lake Louise in 1890. In 1899 the CPR hired Swiss mountain guides to take tourists up the peaks in the park. By the turn of the century Banff was able to boast more than eight luxury hotels.

As the CPR had a monopoly of entrance to the park it was 1911 before the increasingly popular motor car could bring people in. Then from 1920 until 1940, roads were built to Lake Louise, Radium Hot Springs and Jasper. Around 1930 a start was made on building the first ski huts. Today there are excellent ski slopes to be found on Mount Norquay in Banff, in Sunshine Village 17km/10½ miles west of Banff and on the slopes of Mount Whitehorn near Lake Louise.

Finds of minerals – copper, coal, zinc and lead – in Bow River Valley led to the establishment, albeit short-lived, of mining camps. From 1881 to 1886 the mining town of Silver City existed at the foot of Castle Mountain, but when the copper supply became exhausted it quickly disappeared. Then coal was found 6km/4 miles east of Banff, but the mine closed down around the turn of the century. A further example of a short-lived coal town is Bankhead 6km/4miles north of Banff. Coal was mined here for a few years after 1905; the remains of the settlement can still be seen today.

In the 1930s the authorities put a stop to the mining of minerals and commercial tree-felling in the park. Up to 1915 railroad workers and at times more than 10,000 miners seriously decimated the original giant herds of wild animals, including elk, mountain sheep, caribou and mountain goats, so hunting was banned and rangers employed. Today, however, the authorities try to interfere as little as possible in the natural way of things.

The folding and lifting of the Rocky Mountains took place about 70–75 million years ago during the Miocene period. Under intense pressure from the west the massive layers of sediment, several thousand metres deep in places, were broken up and folded. Several parallel fractures occurred, whole strata were forced eastwards and semi-vertical layers of chalk and sandstone were formed. The main ridge of the mountains which form the western part of the National Park are made up of such layers of sediment which had been forced up and distorted; however, this region is only slightly folded compared with the Front Range which breaks off steeply to the east. The formation of the surfaces as seen today occurred mainly

Geology

during the Ice Ages, the last push ending about 10,000 years ago. At that time great masses of ice filled the valleys, creating wide valley-floors, slopes, passes and sharp ridges. Wind, water, frost and ice still continue the work of the Ice Age glaciers.

Vegetation zones

The broad valleys and lower mountain slopes up to about 1500m/5000ft display typical montane vegetation consisting of open forest – studded with grassy areas – of Douglas pine, silver fir, lodgepole pine and the aspen trees which turn such a beautiful gold in autumn. Steep, dry southern slopes are often carpeted with grass. Above this and up as far as the tree line at about 2200m/7200ft is the sub-Alpine zone. No aspen trees will be found there. Characteristic of the lower slopes are self-contained coniferous forests of spruce and lodgepole pine. In the lower regions where there is considerable snowfall and a vegetation period of one to three months the pine trees gradually disappear. In summer the sub-Alpine mountain meadows are covered with carpets of flowers. The area of bent and distorted trees near the tree line is followed by the Alpine zone. Typical of the vegetation here, reminiscent of the Arctic tundra, are the shrubland, small bushes, heather, mountain flowers and grass, gradually to be replaced in the extreme environmental conditions by the well-suited mosses and lichens before naked rock, rubble and ice finally take over.

Animal kingdom

There are still more than fifty species of mammals to be found in the national parks of this rocky region. Large wild animals are most likely to be spotted in the early morning and the evening. Elk predominate in the damp meadows of the valleys, while forest caribou, roe-deer, wapiti deer and mule deer frequent the thicker woods and meadows. Mountain goats and thick-horned sheep are found on the higher mountain slopes.

Grizzly bear
Black bear

Based on estimates made by the park authorities there are still about 200 grizzly bears in the four national parks. Normally they do not come near roads and towns. When walking in the "backcountry", however, it is wise to keep an eye open for them and for the more common black bear. The latter prefer wooded areas and thick undergrowth on the flat valley floors and sunny south-facing slopes, while grizzlies keep to the Alpine regions in summer but seek food lower down in spring and autumn. Under normal circumstances there is little likelihood of meeting a bear face to face. These animals have poor sight but can smell or hear approaching humans long before they see them. Bears can be surprisingly quick, so on no account approach one. The park administration offices have leaflets on correct behaviour in "bearland". Feeding the bears is strictly prohibited, as this can spoil their natural way of life and make them less shy of people. During long walks and at camp sites, therefore, a close watch should be kept on foodstuffs and cosmetics, and they should be kept either in special bear-proof containers or securely packed in air-tight boxes in the boot of the car. For waste extra bear-proof rubbish-bins are provided. Scratch marks clearly caused by bears' claws should be a warning to take due care. For their own protection, bears found begging or looking for scraps in the vicinity of human habitation are taken into custody.

★Banff (Townsite)

Location

Banff or Banff Townsite, lying in a charming valley in the south of Banff National Park and dominated by high mountains, has a permanent population of some 4200 and ample accommodation makes it the tourist centre of the park. During the summer months its broad main street, Banff Avenue, is crammed with visitors, and it is almost as busy as a city. Between Wolf Street and Bow River will be found row upon row of shopping streets. Here, too, is the Parks Canada Information Centre at 224 Banff Ave., open: mid-June–Sept. 8am–10pm; at other times 10am–6pm; here can be obtained information about events, "backcountry permits", and maps and guides for excursions and tours.

In summer there are pleasant excursions available by horse-driven coaches around Banff and the surrounding countryside. On Banff Avenue –

A grizzly bear on the prowl

between Rocky Mountains Resort Avenue and the Banff Springs Hotel – runs a tram or trolleybus line constructed in early 20th c. style.

It is worth paying a visit to the Natural History Museum at 112 Banff Avenue, on the first floor of the Clock Tower Village Mall, which is open May–June 10am–8pm; July–Aug. 10am–10pm; at other times 10am–6pm. Exhibits explain the formation of the Rocky Mountains and the topography of the region.

Natural History Museum

Banff Park Museum (93 Banff Ave.; open: 10am–6pm) is housed in a building dating from 1903, which used to be the park administration offices. The very instructive exhibition provides information mainly about the animal life of the park.

Banff Park Museum

Banff has the artists Catherine and Peter Whyte to thank for the Whyte Museum of the Canadian Rockies. Situated at 111 Bear St., it is open daily in summer 10am–6pm, at other times by arrangement; concerts on Sun. afternoons. The museum houses the archives of the Canadian Rocky Mountains as well as art exhibitions and some interesting material on the history of Banff. Adjoining it are the "Heritage Homes". Guided tours show what life was like in Banff in the 1920s.

Whyte Museum of the Canadian Rockies

To the south Banff Avenue ends on the far side of Bow River in Cascade Gardens; these are laid out in terrace fashion, and this is where the park administration buildings can be found.

Cascade Gardens

Luxton Museum (1 Birch Ave.; open: daily 10am–5pm) stands on the far side of Bow River.
Sundry scenes from the life of the plains Indians before the Europeans arrived are depicted in a reconstructed fur-trading station.

Luxton Museum

Banff Springs Hotel at Spray Ave. (guided tours) was built in 1888 and is today the emblem of Banff. Once planned to be the largest hotel complex in

★Banff Springs Hotel

the world this traditionally-designed, castle-like Grand Hotel still preserves much of the glamour of the early days of railway tourism, when only very well-to-do travellers could afford to make the journey into the then still remote region of the Canadian Rocky Mountains.

★ Bow Falls

Below the Banff Springs Hotel the Bow River tumbles over a cliff-like rise formed from sloping layers of limestone. In pre-glacial times Bow River initially flowed north of Tunnel Mountain through Cascade Valley and Lake Minnewanka; later the valley became cut off by retrograde erosion, causing the river to flow between Fairholme Range and Tunnel Mountain. Massive moraines of Ice Age glaciers then blocked the original course and probably formed a lake until such time as the river was able to burst through between Mount Rundle and Tunnel Mountain.

Cave & Basin
Centennial Centre,
Sundance Canyon

The Cave & Basin Centennial Centre (Cave Ave.; open: mid-June–Sept. 10am–8pm, at other times 10am–5pm) grew up around the hot sulphur springs discovered in 1883. The Canadian National Park system developed here, based on the US model. Exhibitions, slide-shows and computer games provide information on the national parks, two short instructive walks provide a key to the geology and the history of the hot springs which issue forth from a cave and to the specific ecological system linked thereto.

On the occasion of its centenary the historical buildings around the public swimming pool (open: mid-June–Sept.) were restored. The swimming bath built in 1887 is a most imposing building.

From the Cave & Basin Centennial Centre a charming walkway and cycle path leads along Bow River and past some flat marshland – formed by beaver dams! – to Sundance Canyon.

Marsh Loop

A 2km/1¼ mile long instructive path adjoins this. Marsh Loop, almost 3km/2 miles long, is another way round, leading to beaver dams and lodges. In these marshy surroundings some rare species of birds can be observed.

Upper Hot Springs

Some 4km/2½ miles from Banff Townsite, 1600m/5250ft up on Sulphur Mountain, is the hottest of the five hot sulphur springs. In summer its water temperature is 42°C/107°F, in winter 29°C/84°F.

The baths are open as follows: mid-June–mid-Oct. daily 8.30am–10.30pm, at other times of the year Mon.–Thur. 2.30–8.30pm, Fri., Sat., Sun 8.30am–10.30pm.

Sulphur Mountain
Gondola

From the lower station of the Sulphur Mountain Gondola cable railway, opposite (in use all the year round, but at varying times) it is an eight minute trip to the upper station at 2270m/7450ft above sea-level. On a clear day there a splendid panoramic view from the three terrace decks and the mountain-top restaurant. The mountain walk known as the Vista Trail leads to the nearby Samson Peak.

Mount Norquay
Drive, Mount,
Norquay Scenic
Lift

After travelling for 6½km/4 miles along Mount Norquay Road, with its many hairpin bends, we come to the lower station of the chairlift, which goes up to Mount Norquay, 2135m/7007ft. There is a superb panoramic view to be had from the Cliffhouses Restaurant. Skiers enjoy themselves here in winter.

Vermilion Lakes

A road 11km/7 miles long leads to the three Vermilion Lakes west of the town. They lie in the floodplain of the Bow River and are a refuge for numerous waterfowl. Ornithologists come here to observe bald eagles, osprey and Canadian geese. With a little luck beavers and elk may also be spotted.

Buffalo Paddocks

North of the town – about 1km/½ mile west of the junction of Banff Ave. and the TransCanada Highway – it is possible to drive through Buffalo Paddocks, an area of some 40ha/100 acres where bison graze between May and October.

The impressive mountain country around Banff can also be explored on horseback. Guided tours lasting one or more days are also available.

Horse-riding

It is also worthwhile climbing Tunnel Mountain where hoodoos, or pictures formed in the rock by erosion, can be seen and from where there is a breathtaking view.

Tunnel Mountain

From June to the end of September a number of firms offer trips by rubber dinghy or raft on the Bow, Kootenay and Kicking Horse rivers.

River-rafting

Banff Heli Sports offers sightseeing trips by helicopter and will also take walkers to the more remote valleys or skiers to regions where they can be sure of snow.

Helicopter flights

About 7km/4½ miles north-east of Banff Townsite, on the narrow bending road to Lake Minnewanka, can be found the remains of the old coal-mining town of Bankhead, which enjoyed its heyday in the first half of this century. An instructive footpath – with boards displaying old photographs and explanatory notes – helps give an idea of what this ghost town was like.

Bankhead

Lake Minnewanka ("Devil's Lake" in the Indian language), 11km/7 miles north-east of Banff, is now the largest lake within the national park. Simpson, the Governor of Hudson's Bay Company, rested here in 1841. Along the banks of the lake an old Indian path leads by the edge of the rocky mountain range. Around the turn of the century a small health resort grew up here, but it was not until 1912 that the first dam was built which raised the level of the lake by three metres. When the mines at Bankhead closed the government decided to build a power station here to provide electricity for Banff. Then, in 1941, a further dam was built below the lake on Cascade River, which raised the water level of Lake Minnewanka by a further 25m/82ft. The lake became 8km/5 miles longer, sinking the holiday resort, forests and all traces of the old trail. Now, between May and September, there are trips lasting two hours round the charmingly situated lake which is now some 20km/13 miles long. On the trip it is often possible to spot thick-horned sheep, deer and black bear.

Lake Minnewanka

Lake Minnewanka is the only lake in the park on which motor-boats are allowed. It is worthwhile going on to Two Jack Lake – where canoes can be hired – and Johnson Lake. Swimming is possible in summer in the relatively calm lake. A fairly easy path leads round the lake.

9km/5½ miles west of Banff Sunshine Road branches south off the Trans-Canada Highway. A further 10km/6 miles brings visitors to the lower station of the longest cable railway – about 5000m/16,400ft – in the Canadian Rockies (NB. Winter operation only). A twenty-minute ride takes them up to Sunshine Meadows, a very inviting mountain region where some beautiful hill-walks can be enjoyed, such as that to Rock Isle Lake. This region is particularly magnificent in summer, when the mountain flora is in full splendour. In winter the Sunshine Region is a favourite skiing area. A small Interpretive Centre provides information about the topography, and nature walks start from here. A chair-lift goes up to Standish Peak on the continental watershed, which here forms the boundary with British Columbia. From the end of June to early September the Sunshine Inn guesthouse offers food and lodging.

Sunshine Road, Sunshine Meadows, Sunshine Village

The 48km/30 mile long Bow Valley Parkway to Lake Louise offers an alternative to the busy TransCanada Highway. Viewing points, camping and picnic sites as well as stopping-places with information boards make it possible to get to know the charming countryside of Bow Valley and to learn more about its geology and topography. Towering above it all is Castle Mountain, whose Eisenhower Peak is 2728m/8950ft high.

★ **Bow Valley Parkway**

Highway 1A

Castle Mountain

26km/16 miles along the road sees the start of a favourite path through Johnston Canyon with its two waterfalls. Some 6km/4 miles on the far side

Johnston Canyon

Banff National Park

Ink Pots

of the canyon are the Ink Pots, a group of springs of which two basins are particularly striking because of the bluish-green colour of the water.

Silver City

The only remnants of the old mining settlement of Silver City, 27km/17 miles west of Banff, are a meadow and a sign.

★★Lake Louise

The main attraction in Banff National Park is Lake Louise in its delightful setting 1731m/5680ft above sea-level and 60km/37 miles north-west of Banff. Its shimmering waters are mainly turquoise to dark green in colour, and it is about 2km/1¼ miles long, up to 600m/1970ft wide and 69m/230ft deep and surrounded by glacial mountains up to 3000m/9850ft in height. The Victoria Glacier reaches right down almost to the shores of the lake. Although the water is too cold for bathing it is ideal for canoeing. At the western end of Lake Louise Mount Victoria, 3469m/11,385ft in height, rises in majestic splendour. A breathtaking view can be had from the famous Grand Hotel Château Lake which stands in beautifully tended gardens.

The Stoney Indians named Lake Louise "Lake of the Little Fishes". This "Jewel of the Rocky Mountains" was discovered in 1882 when the Pacific Railroad was being laid. Tom Wilson, survey packer of the CPR, named it Emerald Lake. However, in honour of Princess Louise, the daughter of Queen Victoria and wife of the Governor-General of Canada, the name was soon changed to Lake Louise.

In 1890 the CPR built the first Château Lake Louise on the moraine at the end of the lake. Easily accessible by rail, Lake Louise and the surrounding countryside soon developed into a tourist centre. From here expeditions started out to explore the rocky region on horseback. Mountaineers from England and the United States scaled the as yet unknown peaks. The present massive hotel was built in 1924 after a fire had destroyed its smaller wooden predecessor. In the early days horse-driven coaches – later to be superseded by trams – transported guests from the rail station down in the valley to the hotel 6km/4 miles away

Lake Louise

In the 1920s a road was built from Banff to Lake Louise. In the Bow River Valley the holiday village of Lake Louise developed, with nearly 400 permanent inhabitants.

Well-known from many picture postcards, Lake Louise is a starting point for some rewarding walks, the best of which perhaps being that to the Plain of Six Glaciers, which will take a total of some five hours. First follow the tarred and even road along the north-west shore of the lake as far as the river mouth, then climb up 360m/1180ft to the travellers' rest, where food and drink can be purchased in summer, below the Victoria Glacier. A further 6km/4 miles brings the walker to a good viewing-point.

Plain of
Six Glaciers

Another very popular walk is that to Lake Agnes (difference in altitude 365m/1200ft) picturesquely situated between the two round hills known as the Bee Hives. The strenuous climb to the top of one of the Bee Hives will be rewarded by a superb view. In summer the restaurant supplies food and refreshing drinks.

Lake Agnes

On the far side of the Bow River Valley a chair-lift provides access to Mount Whitehorn and the Lake Louise ski-slopes. This chair-lift operates mid-June–mid-Sept. daily 8am–6pm. The viewing platform at 2034m/6675ft – with restaurant and terrace – offers a magnificent view of Lake Louise, the Victoria Glacier and the glaciated ridges and peaks of the Bow Range. There is skiing from mid-Nov.–mid-May, with ski-school, ski hire and cafeteria.

★Lake Louise
Gondola Lift

Pictured on the reverse of the Canadian twenty dollar note, Moraine Lake in the Valley of the Ten Peaks is just as beautiful as Lake Louise but seems to attract fewer visitors. One charming view after another is revealed along the 13km/8 mile approach road, which soon comes to a lake formed as a result of a landslide (not by a moraine, as Walter Wilcox wrongly assumed). This picturesque lake in a mountain valley, often a shimmering turquoise in colour, is overshadowed by ten peaks each over 3000m/10,000ft high, forming the Wenckchema Glacier. In the distance the thundering of falling glaciers or landslides can be heard. Accommodation, provisions and canoe-hire are available at the rustic Moraine Lake Lodge.

★★**Moraine Lake**

A path 1½km/1 mile long runs along the north-west shore. The short climb up the Rockpile Trail is very worthwhile; from this hill formed as the result of a landslide there is the best view of the lake. The walk into Larch Valley and to Sentinel Pass, one of the highest mountain passes in the national park, is somewhat exhausting, but from this mountain valley some 300m/1000ft up there is another superb view. The tour is particularly charming in autumn (fall), when the larches are changing colour. After climbing a total of 6km/4 miles and ascending 520m/1700ft the Sentinel Pass (2611m/8570ft) is reached.

Banks Island

D–F 3

Administrative Unit: Northwest Territories, District of Franklin

Western Arctic Visitors Association
Box 1525, Inuvik, NWT, X0E 0T0,
Tel. (403) 979–37 56 or Arctic Hotline 1–800–661–07 88.

Information

This, the most westerly island of the Canadian archipelago, covers an area of 70,028sq.km/27,038sq.miles, somewhat less than the Republic of Ireland. North to south it measures about 400km/250 miles between latitudes 71° and 74° 30′ north. Its coasts other than the north are free of ice in summer. In contrast to most islands on the archipelago there are very few fiords along its coastline, and the interior is not boldly formed, the landscape being in the main gently undulating with broad river valleys. Banks

Island possesses rich tundra vegetation, home to many animals, especially 25,000 musk-oxen (*ovibus moschatus*), the largest population of these all together anywhere in the world. The south-western part of Banks Island, equal to about one-third of the whole, is a bird sanctuary. About 100km/ 60 miles of the Thomsen River can be navigated by raft.

Sachs Harbour

Although it had been used for hunting for perhaps 3500 years it was not until 1929 that Banks Island had a permanent settlement, when three Inuit families put down roots in Sachs Harbour on the north-western tip of the island. Its "European" name derives from the Canadian Arctic expedition of 1913–15 led by Viilhjalmur Stefansson, whose ship was called "Mary Sachs". Ikkakuk, the little town on Inuvialktun, with a population of about 160, is a starting point for excursions. Banks Island Museum provides information on the history and archaeology of the island. There are flights to Sachs Harbour from Inuvik.

Archaeological digs

Since 1970 an archaeological institute from Tübingen in Germany has been carrying out digs on Banks Island. In the region around Umingmak ("musk-oxen") by Shoran Lake stone tools and weapons as well as bones from the Pre-Dorset culture *c.* 2000–1500 B.C. were found, some of them decorated with cult and mythological scratch-drawings. From rubbish heaps, some containing skeletons of captured musk-oxen, and the number of fire-places it has been possible to estimate that at that time – with some variations from year to year – the average population was about 80. They were also able to show how the arrival of the Europeans in the 19th c. – particularly Parry's expedition in 1853, when he had to abandon his ship north of Banks – led to the beginning of the new "Iron Age" among the Inuit; the same Inuit who led their traditional, self-sufficient lives right up to the time of the First World War, and integrated the usable materials into their archaic tools.

Barkerville   E 7

Province: British Columbia

Access

Highway 26 (about 100km/62 miles east of Quesnel).

Location

The township of Barkerville, once the centre of the Cariboo gold-rush, is picturesquely situated surrounded by mountains in the valley of William Creek. It is the oldest remaining historic settlement in British Columbia.

★★Barkerville Historic Park

When the news spread in 1858 that gold had been found in the fluvial sand of the Fraser River there were soon thousands of men panning for gold all along the river and its tributaries. When in the summer of 1862 Billy Barker made his sensational find here at Williams Creek a typical gold-digging town of simple wooden huts, tents, saloons and shops sprang up almost overnight.

Until it burned down in 1868 Barkerville was the "largest town west of Chicago and north of San Francisco". Although it was immediately rebuilt to a high standard the end of the gold boom was already apparent. The introduction of machinery meant there was a need for fewer men but more capital. Chinese coolies worked longer hours for less pay and Chinese dealers began to monopolise the market. A marked social regrouping took place in the new Barkerville.

Following the end of the gold-rush Barkerville continued to fulfil the function of the centre of a region which was now inhabited by settlers and lumberjacks. so that the old gold-digging metropolis was saved from becoming just a ghost town.

Today the tourist will find a restored gold-digging town with about 75 historic buildings. When employees dressed in the fashions of the period act out "living history" in summer it is possible to visit a printing-works or smithy, a typical general store, the "Wellington Moses Barbershop" or the

"Barkerville Hotel" and feel completely transported back to the times of the gold-rush. The music-hall tradition is continued in the "Theatre Royal", and in the "Eldorado Mine" visitors can try their luck at panning for gold.

The Barkerville open-air museum is open daily from the end of June to early Sept. 8am–7pm.

About 2km/1¼ miles uphill from Williams Creek, in the historic Richfield Courthouse, lives the ghost of the famous Judge Begbie, remembered for a number of episodes in his colourful career.

Richfield
Courthouse

Bas St-Laurent

P/Q 8

Province: Québec

Tourisme Québec, C. P. 20000, Québec-Cité, Québec, G1K 7X2.

Information

From the city of Québec or Lévis on Highway 20 along the south coast of the St Lawrence River.

Access

"Bas St-Laurent" is the name given to that stretch of gently undulating countryside to the south of the St Lawrence River with a number of impressive agricultural estates. Further south the natural border is formed by the foothills of the Appalachians. A few rocky ridges and sandy plateaux protrude into this intensively cultivated region.

Location and
importance

Immigrants from Europe settled on the southern shores of the St Lawrence many years ago.

Close to the river – alongside which the main road also winds – fishing villages nudge each other like pearls in a necklace. Cod, mackerel, lobsters and shrimps are here in abundance, and everywhere tourists are tempted to stay and watch fish being smoked in little huts.

Pretty villages and industrious towns with woodworking and textile factories and the like bear witness to the prosperity of this stretch of country.

★ Drive to Rimouski from Québec (city) or Lévis (about 300km/190 miles)

The city of Québec (see entry) lies opposite the industrialised suburb of Lévis (pop. 20,000), from where there is a fine view to be had of the silhouette of the provincial capital with such a colourful past.

Lévis

St-Jean-Port-Joli (pop. 4000) is the handicraft centre of Québec province, where dozens of boutiques rub shoulders with one another.

St-Jean-Port-Joli

In the centre of the little town stands the pleasing 18th c. church with its two bell-towers. Also worth a visit is the Musée des Anciens Canadiens (open daily 10am–6pm), exhibiting some outstanding work by native artists, including some Bougault sculptures.

St-Roch-des-Aulnaies (pop. 1200) belongs to the "Siegneurie des Aulnaies", an imposing estate bearing the street number 132, the castle-like main building of which dates from the middle of the 19th c. A guided tour gives an insight into the way the upper classes lived.

St-Roch-des-
Aulnaies

It is possible to visit the 19th c. corn-mill which is still in working order.

The little town of La Pocatière (pop. 5000) lies on a terrace above the St Lawrence coastal plain. It is an important centre of rural education.

La Pocatière

A visit to the Musée François Pilote at the rear of the Collège Ste-Anne is worthwhile. This collection of regional studies (open: Mon.–Sat. 9am–6pm) provides information on the production of maple syrup and on the history of the local woodworking industry. There is also an interesting exhibition of horse-drawn carriages and carts.

Kamouraska	Kamouraska (pop. 500), with its picturesque little houses, is a typical small fishing-village.
	From this side of the St Lawrence River on a fine day there is a beautiful view over towards Charlevoix (see entry), the wild and rugged coastal band opposite and to the north.
Rivière-du-Loup	The busy industrial town of Rivière-du-Loup, with a population of 15,000, is also an important traffic junction, as it is here that the main road branches off southwards to the neighbouring province of New Brunswick. The town has a marina, beautifully laid-out places for bathing and a camp-site. Popular with visitors is the waterfall, which plunges down from a ledge 30m/100ft high.
★Bic	Completely charming in every respect, the end of 18th c. town of Bic (pop. 4000) on the St Lawrence River lies in a "hunchback world" of wooded hills. This has been declared a protected area, with the aim of allowing the marine life to become re-established.
Rimouski	Rimouski (pop. 31,000) is the administrative, economic and cultural centre of the region along the lower reaches of the St Lawrence River. It has a high school and is an important port serving a wider area.
	The Musée de la Mer is open daily 9am–6pm and houses exhibitions on marine studies.
	To the west of the town the waters of the Rivière Rimouski plunge through a wild gorge. Some 5km/3 miles further west a pretty lake for bathing has been constructed.
Ste-Flavie	North-east of Rimouski lies the town of Ste-Flavie, the entrance gate to the Gaspésie peninsula (see entry).

Bathurst · Q 8

	Province: New Brunswick. Population: 15,000
Information	Bathurst Chamber of Commerce, 498 King Ave., Bathurst, New Brunswick. Tel. (506) 84 98
Access	Highway 11; Route 134
Location and history	The very busy little town of Bathurst lies on Baie Nepisguit, a cove at the south of Baie des Chaleurs, into which the Nepisguit River flows.
	The town was founded in the 17th c. by French-speaking Acadians led by Governor Nicholas Denys.
Its importance today	Today Bathurst is an important industrial town and business centre for an extensive area. One of the world's largest zinc mines is worked near here. In the town centre will be found more than 80 different shops and service industries, with a further 50 shops, boutiques, etc. in the modern Centre Chaleur.

Sights

Harbour	Bathurst has a small sheltered harbour used by fishermen and with a marina enjoyed by spare-time sailors.
Farmers Market	The Farmers Market is held in Main Street every Saturday from 9am to 1pm.
Military Museum	There is a Museum of Military History in St Pierre Avenue.
Youghall Provincial Park	The well-tended Youghall Provincial Park extends along the north side of Bathurst harbour bay. There are some fine spots for bathing and a marina. Not far away is an interesting bird-sanctuary.

Surroundings

20km/13 miles south-west of Bathurst is one of the world's most productive zinc mines. The production plant can be visited by prior arrangement with the Chamber of Commerce (see Information above).

★Zinc Mine

Tetagouche, to the south-west of Bathurst, and Pabineau Falls to the south, are two most impressive waterfalls.

Tetagouche Falls
Pabineau Falls

To the north of Bathurst, near Petit-Rocher (see Campbellton) the New Brunswick Mining & Mineral Interpretation Centre is open to visitors. A mining shaft gives an idea of what working underground is like. Visitors can look into caverns and see how an actual subterranean road network is laid out to enable the valuable minerals to be extracted.

New Brunswick
Mining & Mineral
Interpretation
Centre

Batoche National Historic Park   H 7

Province: Saskatchewan

Batoche, the stronghold of the Métis people (the offspring of a white person and a Canadian Indian) on the Saskatchewan River, was the headquarters of their ringleader Louis Riel during the North West Rebellion in 1885. This is where the decisive battle took place between the insurgents under Riel and Gabriel Dumont and General Middleton with his troops from the North West Mounted Police; this marked the end of the rebellion.

History

The village of Batoche was founded in the early 1870s, when Xavier Letendre, also known as "Batoche", constructed a ferry, a shop and a storehouse on the spot where the Carlton Trail crossed the river. It soon grew into a trade centre for the growing number of Métis settlers along the river. In 1883 a presbytery was built, and in the following year the Church of St Antoine de Padoue.

Batoche settlement

Village

Near the river bank lies East Village, the original village, of which foundations and cellars still remain. This is where the Batoche ferry crossed the South Saskatchewan River.

In the Visitor Reception Centre are displays illustrating the way of life of the Métis, the events which led up to the rebellion and the battle of May 1885. Dioramas portray such scenes as a buffalo-hunt, the Métis digging defensive ditches such as those used in the Battle of Batoche, and Middleton's troops using a nine-pounder field-gun. Among the numerous exhibits are Louis Riel's writing-case, his bridle and stirrups.

★**National Historic Park**

Visitor Reception Centre

The presbytery, where shell and bullet-holes suffered in the battle can still be seen, and the Church of St Antoine de Padoue (1883–84) are now excellent museums, displaying photographs and other memorabilia of the battle and of the earlier Métis culture. The Gothic church still contains some of the original pews as well as the harmonium and stove.

St Antoine de
Padoue

The graves of Dumont and Letendre and a mass-grave of fallen Métis can be seen in the churchyard. There is also a memorial to the Métis and Indians who died during the conflict.

Nearby stands a fenced-in store, the "zareba", built by the military. By day it served as a point from which attacks were directed and by night as a defensive post.

Hollows along the river bank mark the position of the trenches from which Middleton's soldiers fired on the Métis. Nearby stands a farmhouse which was rebuilt in 1895 after having been destroyed by the army. From the other side of the road there is a superb view of the South Saskatchewan River. From the presbytery a path leads across the prairie to a defensive trench which has been opened up. These trenches were marked with tree-trunks and cleverly camouflaged with rows of trees.

Battleford

Fish Creek	In Fish Creek, south of Batoche, the first clash between Riel's troops and the military took place. Markings show the way to the field where the battle was fought, Middleton's troops camped and the dead were buried.
Opening times	May, June, Sept. 9am–5pm; July, Aug. 10am–6pm.

Battleford   H 7

Province: Saskatchewan. Population: 20,000

Information	See Saskatchewan
North Battleford Location	The towns of North Battleford (pop. 15,000) and Battleford, linked by the longest bridge over the North Saskatchewan River, lie in the centre of the province of Saskatchewan which is so steeped in history.
★ Western Development Museum	Tourists are recommended to visit the historic Western Development Museum–Heritage Farm & Village (open: May 1st–Oct. 31st 9am–6pm), which illustrates the history of agriculture. The exhibition of agricultural equipment and tools is supplemented in summer by demonstrations of farming techniques from before the 1920s. In addition a small 1925 town has been built incorporating many original buildings from surrounding places. It includes houses built in the style of Ukranian and French-Canadian settlers, a railway station, a barber's shop and a school.
Allen Sapp Gallery	The Allen Sapp Gallery in 100th St. is open Tues.–Sun. 1–5pm. It houses the "Gonor Collection" of pictures by the Cree artist Allen Sapp, one of the leading contemporary Canadian artists. His art gives a rare insight into the lives of the Cree people.
George Hooey Wildlife Exhibit	The George Hooey Wildlife Exhibit, housed in Battleford's Wildlife Federation Building, opens by prior arrangement June 1st–Aug. 31st and displays over 400 preserved specimens of animals, including fishes and birds, some of which date back as far as 1890.
Battleford Importance	Battleford (pop. 5000) was the first seat of government in the Northwest Territories (see entry) and an important Mounted Police post.
★ Fort Battleford	In Fort Battleford National Historic Park the rich and varied pattern of Battleford's history is brought to life. The Fort was the seat of government of the Northwest Territories between 1876 and 1882.
Station	The Canadian Northern Railway Station, built in 1908 at the corner of 22nd St. and 1st. Ave., and which marked Battleford's link-up with the railway, was converted into a restaurant in 1976.
Fred Light Museum	The Fred Light Museum, which is open daily May 5th.–Sept. 10th 10am–6pm, is a reproduction of a shop, a class-room and an armoury with a fine collection of weapons. In addition many utensils are exhibited, such as shaving mugs and lamps, which were in use at the turn of the century. Other departments are devoted to the history of the military and the Mounted Police.
Surroundings ★ Battleford National Historic Park	Nearly 5km/3 miles south-east of Battleford lies Battleford National Historic Park. (Open: May 1st–Oct. 10th, Mon.–Sat. 9am–5pm, Sun. 10am–6pm; July, Aug. daily 10am–6pm.) This clearly explains the role played by the North West Mounted Police (the "Mounties") in the development of Western Canada. For example, on display is their base established in 1876, as well as five buildings, four furnished in the style of the time, and reconstructed ramparts. The 1886 barracks house some informative exhibitions.

16km/10 miles to the north the Cut Knife National Historic Site overlooks Battle River Valley. This is another important arena depicting the North West Rebellion, as it was here that the battle took place in 1885 between the Canadian troops under Colonel Otter and the Indians under Chief Poundmaker. Otter thought the Indians had been responsible for plundering Battleford and burning it to the ground. The natives were victorious in this battle. Chief Poundmaker was convicted of treason, imprisoned, died a year later and was buried up on the hill.

★Cut Knife National Historic Site

The Clayton McLain Memorial Museum (open June 1st–Aug. 31st 9am–8pm, at other times by arrangement) displays articles used by the combatants in the Battle of Cut Knife. In addition, the following restored and furnished buildings are open to visitors: school (1908), railway station (1912), shop (1920), village church (1925) and a log-cabin (1930). Items on display include objects used by the Indians and the pioneers, machines, antiques, shotguns, archive material, etc.

Cut Knife

Hanging near the museum in Tomahawk Park is the biggest tomahawk in the world, nearly 12m/39ft tall and weighing 8 tonnes. This remarkable architectural feat is a symbol of the public-spiritedness and friendship exisiting between the good people of Cut Knife.

Some 40km/25 miles further north Battlefords Provincial Park spans an area alongside Jackfish Lake, a favourite spot with anglers. The park offers the following attractions: camping, picnicking, a golf-course, minigolf, hire of boats and bicycles, a nature path and an excellent sandy beach.

Battlefords Provincial Park

Bonavista Peninsula   T 8

Province: Newfoundland

See Newfoundland

Information

The best-known peninsula in Newfoundland is Bonavista, where John Cabot is thought to have sighted the "New World" for the first time in 1497.

One of the most impressive pieces of scenery on this peninsula so rich in forests and waterways and with its rugged coastline is to be found by turning off Road 230 onto the 235. The beautiful smaller places should also not be missed; these include Plate Cove and King's Cove, one of the oldest settlements here and founded by fishermen from Bonavista in the middle of the 18th c.

The fishing-town of Bonavista with its population of 5000 is one of the main towns on the peninsula. Its port was used by European fishing fleets back in the 16th c. Around 1600 Bonavista was a British settlement and remained so in spite of attempts by the French to take it in the 18th c.

Bonavista

Bonavista Museum in Church Street is open in summer and in winter by prior arrangement. It explains the history of the area by means of exhibits collected by the inhabitants.

The Mockbeggar Property (open: daily in summer) is made up of a number of buildings which reflect various aspects of the traditional Newfoundland life-style.

A very beautiful 5km/3 mile stretch leads from here to the cape which is probably that sighted by John Cabot in 1497 and which he named Bonavista, or "beautiful view". The cape is quite magnificent with its breakers, clear blue sea and interesting rock formations. Here stands a statue of Cabot in memory of the first man to discover North America, although more recent research throws doubt on the authenticity of his claim.

★★Cape Bonavista

The old lighthouse, a Provincial Historic Site, dates from 1843 and was restored about 1870; it is open daily in July and Aug.; guides wear historical costume.

Bonavista Bay

Port Union

Port Union is named after the first Newfoundland fishermen's union. Here will be found an impressive memorial to William Coaker, the organiser of the union and founder of the town.

The old railway station now houses the Port Union Museum with maritime exhibits.

Campers can spend the night in Lockston Path Provincial Park on Route 236. From the view-point above the lake there is a spectacular panorama of the surrounding countryside.

★ Trinity

Picturesque Trinity, from which the offshore bay gets its name, is an old fishing and trading town which still has its wharves. The historical character of the town has been well preserved. Ryan Premises, which are privately owned but may be visited on request, The Society of Fishermen's Hall and other 19th c. buildings have remained almost unchanged in appearance. Trinity is one of Newfoundland's oldest settlements, having been founded in 1615 as the seat of the first maritime court.

Trinity Museum

Over 1000 items are on display in the historical little Trinity Museum and Archives, built in 1880 and open every day in summer; these include models of ships and items connected with whale-catching and with handicrafts such as shoe-making and barrel-making.

Hiscock House – renovated in 1910 and open daily in July and Aug. – is also a Provincial Historic Site; guides in contemporary dress explain how life was in a typical local household in the early 20th c.

Above the marina can be seen the remains of the Battery at Admiral's Point, which was destroyed by the French in 1762. It had been surrendered by the British garrison in the middle of the 18th c.

Brandon   K 8

Province: Manitoba. Population: 40,000

The "wheat town" of Brandon, with the Assiniboine River flowing through it, lies in the Pembina Valley, surrounded by blue hills. Brandon, the central terminal for the shipping of corn, is Manitoba's second largest town and a booming tourist centre, in spite of the fact that it is somewhat spoiled by the presence of dairies, packing industry and even oil refineries.

Location and importance

Paterson/Matheson House in Louise Ave. was built in 1893. It is a very good example of what has become known as the East Lake Style of building.

Sights
Paterson/Matheson House

Daly House, open daily 10am–noon and 1pm–5pm, was the residence of the town's first mayor, Thomas Mayne Daly (1882). The historical furniture and fittings are much to be admired.

Daly House

Also worth a visit is the B. J. Hales Museum of Natural History in Brandon University on 18th St., which is open daily Apr.–Sept. 1.30pm–4.30pm, Oct.–Mar. Mon.–Sat. 1.30pm–4.30pm. On exhibition here are items which belonged to the Sioux and Plains Indians, such as pipes, ceramics, arrowheads and tools. There are also 250 stuffed specimens of local birds in models of their natural habitat. The exhibition is completed by a collection of mammals, such as animals from the North in their "icy" surroundings. Jack Lane was curator of the museum for many years. The legendary "Bluebird Man" saved many species of birds from extinction, such as the American Robin. In the 1930s the number of those birds had reduced to a few dozen. With children's help Lane set up nests around the town and the number of birds increased to 15,000.

★★B. J. Hales Museum of Natural History

Every year there are temporary exhibitions and displays of handicraft and painting to be seen in the Brandon Allied Arts Centre on Princess Ave.

Allied Arts Centre

The Agriculture Canada Station (open Mon.–Fri. 8am–4.30pm, guided tours by arrangement) does research into plant-foods, herbicides and fodder, the genetics of barley and the breeding and feeding of cattle, pigs and poultry. Two-thirds of the total area of corn grown in Western Canada is planted with varieties developed here.

Agriculture Canada Station

At Brandon University, where there are guided tours available, the Administration Building, built in 1901, the 1906 School of Music and the J. R. Brodie Science Building are of interest.

University

The Commonwealth Air Training Plan Museum (No. 1 Hangar, McGill Field; open May–Sept. daily 9am–4.30pm. Oct.–Apr. Mon.–Fri. 9am–4.30pm) restores and exhibits aircraft and training equipment.

Commonwealth Air Training Plan Museum

The 26th Field Artillery Regiment Museum (open: Sun. 2–4.30pm and by arrangement) displays military equipment, uniforms and memorabilia. A library adjoins it.

Artillery Museum

The Keystone Sports Complex, covering some 34ha/85 acres will be of interest to sports enthusiasts. It was built in 1979 as a venue for the Canadian Winter Games.

Keystone Sports

Surroundings

In the Grand Valley Provincial Recreation Park 10km/6 miles west of the town lies Stott Site. In this archaeologically important region where bison were once hunted bones and objects at least 1200 years old have been found.

★Grand Valley Provincial Recreation Park

Brantford

Province: Ontario. Population: 75,000

Information

Tourist Office, Brantford; tel. (519) 753–26 17

Brantford, the main town in Brant Country, lies on the Grant River about 100km/60 miles south-west of Toronto. In the American War of Independence the Six Nations Indians, under their leader Joseph Brant, fought on the side of Britain. When they fled from the USA they founded this settlement in 1784. In 1830 white settlers came here and acquired the area where the town now stands. Economic prosperity came with the railroad. Alexander Graham Bell (see Famous People) also contributed in no small measure to the fame of the town; he solved the problem of passing sound waves along cables and so discovered the telephone, which made him a rich man.

Sights
★ Her Majesty's Chapel of the Mohawk

This chapel stands at the junction of Mohawk St. and Greenwich St. King George II donated the money to the town to build a church in return for its assistance during the American Revolution. This, the oldest Protestant church in Ontario, soon made Brantfort the religious centre of the region.

★ Museum of the Woodland Indian

This museum at 184 Mohawk St. displays an impressive collection of Indian artefacts portraying the everyday life of the Indians of the eastern forests. Naturally, the emphasis is on the Six Nations Indians, who are a part of these ethnic groups.

Bell Homestead

The Bell Homestead estate at 94 Tutela Heights Road is a large and inviting house with period furniture and containing some original memorabilia from the life of Alexander Graham Bell (see Famous People).

British Columbia (Province)

Geographical location: latitude 49°–60° north/longitude 118°–130° west
Area: 948,000sq.km/366,023sq.miles
Population: 3,132,000. Capital: Victoria

Information

Tourism British Columbia,
   Parliament Buildings, Victoria, B. C., V8W 2Z2.

Location and topography

British Columbia covers 9·4 per cent of the total area of Canada, making it the third largest province. The province is characterised mainly by the two mountain chains of the Canadian Cordilleras and the geologically deposited plateau. The Coast Range Mountains are very rugged and carved up by fiords. The offshore islands, including Vancouver Island, are remains of another mountain chain, the Insular Mountains, and provide a unique form of landscape. Mount Waddington, at 4016m/13,180ft, is the highest in the Coast Range Mountains and indeed in the whole of British Columbia. The plateaux are 800–1200m/2600–4000ft high, composed of Tertiary lava, ashes and freshwater deposits. The Rocky Mountains, forming the eastern border of the province of Alberta, are relatively young mountains, having folded in the Tertiary period, and based on sediment from the Triassic and Jurassic periods. During the Pleistocene Age British Columbia, like North and Central Europe, was completely covered in ice. Traces of the four Ice Ages can still be seen in the shape of numerous glaciers, for example in the Columbia Icefield near the border with Alberta, which covers an area of 389sq.km/150sq.miles and is still 1000m/3300ft thick. The main ridge of the Rockies also forms the water-shed of Canada. Thus British Columbia is the only province which drains into the Pacific Ocean; by comparison, 66 per cent of Canada's land surface drains into the Arctic Ocean. The highest mountain in the Rockies is Mount Robson, 3954m/12,977ft high. As a result of the mountain structure the river network is very ramified. The Fraser River is 1360km/845 miles long and the Columbia 1840km/1143 miles.

The individual mountain chains which make up the Canadian Cordilleras have a marked influence on the climate of British Columbia. On the western sides the rainfall is generally very heavy; for example, Prince Rupert has 2330mm/91·7in. per annum, Vancouver 1460mm/57·5in. In the lee of the mountains, on the other hand, there are some very dry pockets, such as Kamloops with 268mm/10·5in. per annum and Penticton with 300mm/11·8in. Winters generally mean a lot of snow, up to 5m/16½ft, although there are some valleys which see very little in the way of snow. In the interior of British Columbia, shielded by the mountains, the climate is quite continental, with short, very hot summers and long, extremely cold winters; Kamloops, for example, has an average January minimum of −10°C/14°F, and an average maximum in July of 29°C/83°F. The coast is blessed with the Kuro Schio, a warm ocean current producing really mild temperatures; Vancouver, for instance, has an average January minimum of 0°C/32°F and an average maximum of 24°C/74°F in July, while Prince Rupert's average January minimum is −1°C/31°F, July maximum 17°C/62°F.

Climate

British Columbia's natural vegetation is determined largely by the high mountains. Coniferous forest predominates, changing to tundra and glaciated regions as one goes higher. The offshore islands, like the whole of the Pacific coast, are heavily wooded, mainly with coniferous trees. Here are still found large expanses of temperate coastal rain forest harbouring some of the oldest and largest fir trees in the world. These primeval woodlands, exceptionally valuable not only in resource terms but also from an ecological point of view, are today under threat from Canada's profit-orientated timber industry (see Baedeker Special p. 000).The hot summers in the valleys and the low rainfall result in steppe-like vegetation where – with adequate irrigation (see The Okanagan) – even fruit such as peaches and apricots can be grown.

Vegetation

In the 17th c. Spanish mariners sailed northwards up the Pacific coast and discovered British Columbia, which until then had for thousands of years been inhabited only by native Indians. In 1778 James Cook was the first white man to set foot on Vancouver Island. In that same year Capt. John Meares founded the first English settlement of Nootka, but this had to be ceded to Spain on the grounds of old claims held by the latter. In 1790 the Spaniards renounced their claims, however, and Capt. George Vancouver was able to take possession of the island for Great Britain. Alexander Mackenzie was the first white man to reach the Pacific by the land route in 1793, to be followed by Simon Fraser and David Thompson, after whom the largest rivers in the province are named.

History

In British Columbia too the "49th parallel" was made the border between Canada and the United States, in accordance with the terms of the Oregon Treaty. In 1849 Vancouver Island was declared a Crown Colony. Seven years later important gold finds attracted large numbers of adventurers and settlers to Fraser Valley and Barkerville. In 1886 the mainland of British Columbia and Vancouver Island off the coast were merged and joined the Canadian Confederation in 1871. Victoria was made the capital of this new province. Between 1923 and 1926 organised immigration from Europe led to further settlements being established in the province. Following the Japanese occupation of the Aleutians during the Second World War the United States decided in 1942 to build a land route to Alaska, the present Alaskan Highway (see entry), which runs from Dawson Creek B.C. to Fairbanks, Alaska. The east–west link was improved in 1962 by the completion of the TransCanada Highway. In 1986 the World Exhibition was held in Vancouver.

With a population density of 3·2 persons to the square kilometre/8·3 to the square mile British Columbia can be compared with Alberta in this respect.

Population

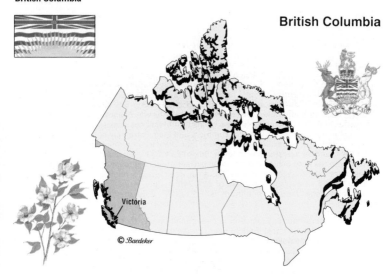

British Columbia

Victoria

© Baedeker

However, there is a marked fall in population as one moves from north to south, and the inhabitants are concentrated in fewer and fewer towns and centres, with Vancouver alone having a population of 1,400,000. The original native inhabitants were basically of two types, the Salish and the Kutenai, who lived mainly from hunting in the interior. In contrast to the Indians in the north-west of British Columbia they are nomads. Those living on the coast – including the Tlingits and the Wakashans – rely mainly on the resources of the sea and live in permanent settlements. 4·4 per cent of the population of British Columbia are the original native Indians, making up 17·8 per cent of the total Canadian native population. While almost 80 per cent of the white population live in towns and cities only 40 per cent of the Indians do so, mainly as a result of the fact that their small settlements are well organised and are almost urban in character. Naturally the British constitute the largest group of immigrants in British Columbia (60 per cent), as can be clearly seen in Victoria, the provincial capital. As Vancouver is an important trading centre with Asia it is not surprising to find a large Asian minority in British Columbia, especially in Vancouver itself.

Economy

British Columbia is one of Canada's richest provinces. The main branches of its economy are forestry, fishing, mining and tourism. About 60 per cent of Canada's utilisable timber comes from British Columbia. The province provides 30 per cent of the needs of the newspaper industry, making it the largest timber-producer in Canada, with 45 per cent of the net product and 45 per cent of the total workers employed in the timber industry. Timber is exported mainly to the United States (42·9 per cent), Japan (19·0 per cent) and to EU countries (22·3 per cent). As in Alberta, the forests are given over to private firms who are allowed to cut down trees on a quota system in line with the reforesting programme. State politics incline towards localised wood-working, thus guaranteeing a balanced sharing. The main difficulties encountered by the timber industry result from many factories being out-of-date and excessive energy requirements compared with its competitors, such as Sweden. Pests and forest fires are natural obstacles which cannot readily be legislated for. Views have changed on the subject of establishing

A gold-washing site

new forests, and in the 1980s 110,000ha/275,000 acres of trees were planted.

In addition to the lumber industry, fishing is also of great importance. 95 per cent of the Canadian salmon industry is in British Columbia. As well as five different species of salmon there is also herring, 95 per cent of which is exported to Japan. Sales of herring alone total $85,000,000 per annum. Together with traditional forms of fishing aquaculture is gaining in importance, breeding mainly salmon, but also trout, prawns and mussels. 22,000 people are directly employed in the fishing industry and 25,000 in allied processing trades.

In contrast to the "prairie states", agriculture plays only a minor role. A small amount of corn is grown in the north-east near Peace River, and fruit and vine cultivation plays is quite important in the valleys to the south. The main mines are those producing coal, stretching from the south-east to the north-west of Alberta across British Columbia to the Yukon Territory. In addition lead, zinc and asbestos is mined, and the copper stocks equal 50 per cent of Canada's total copper resources. Hydro-electric power and natural gas provide the bulk of energy requirements, while crude oil has to be imported from Alberta. Its position on the Pacific means that British Columbia is ideally situated to trade with Asia and Australia. Alberta markets its giant coal and crude oil deposits via the trade centres of British Columbia. The varied leisure facilities make tourism an important economic factor for British Columbia. Most European tourists chose this province for their holiday.

Its unspoiled mountains, extensive forests and numerous lakes make British Columbia a paradise for sports lovers of every ilk. Those keen on water-sports are catered for by numerous lakes and charming rivers, with paddling on lonely lakes to rafting on the rivers. The unique fiord-like coastline is ideal for sailing, while swimming in the Pacific is a question of taste, in spite of the warm ocean currents. In contrast, the hot sun raises the

Leisure, sport, tourism

temperatures of the lakes further inland almost to those of a swimming-pool.

For fishermen the salmon spawning season in August and September offers fantastic sport. Every conceivable variety of fish can be caught in the many lakes and rivers.

The varied nature of the countryside makes British Columbia an ideal place for walking, especially in the national and provincial parks where North America's natural charms are there to be enjoyed. Hunting is forbidden in these parks, but elsewhere there are plenty of opportunities to hunt black and brown bear, mink, beaver and varities of duck. After a tiring day it is so refreshing to relax in a hot spring. For horse-lovers there are wonderful opportunities to hire a horse on a ranch. For anyone wishing to try their hand at golf Canada is the place, because equipment can be hired at any golf-club. In winter thousands of sports are available. Mount Whistler, 125km/76 miles from Vancouver, offers ski-runs of varying degrees of difficulty. There are ample sports opportunities for visitors from Europe to enjoy, and the numerous tourist bureaux scattered throughout the province will be glad to assist in all matters relating to leisure pursuits.

Burin Peninsula   S/T 8

Province: Newfoundland

Information

See Newfoundland

Access

Route 210 to the Burin Peninsula leaves the TransCanada Highway near Goobies. The greater part of this stretch runs inland with short side-roads branching off to some pretty little coastal towns.

The countryside here is hilly and rather barren moorland.

History

The peninsula has a rich history linked to fishing in Grand Banks. From about the 15th c. onwards it became a European fishing ground, when French, British and Portuguese came here in summer to fish. After people began to settle permanently it still remained important from a fishing point of view, and even today the inhabitants depend almost completely on the fishing industry for their living.

Swift Current

Mention should be made of Swift Current, situated 24km/15 miles past the turn-off, because of its magnificent beaches and its beautiful river, Piper's Hole in Provincial Park. There is a stretch of heathland below the town.

Bay l'Argent,
Little Bay East

Route 212 leads off right to Bay l'Argent and Little Bay East, two places of lasting beauty. Bay l'Argent has some long beaches of silvery rocks.

Baine Harbour,
Rushoon

Baine Harbour and Rushoon on the opposite side of the peninsula are also worth a visit. Further south lie the loveliest spots, John the Bay, Little Bay and Beau Bois, known worldwide for its beauty.

Further along Route 210 lie:

Marystown

The shipyard port of Marystown (pop. 6700), beautifully situated on Little Bay, is the largest town in the province. This is where the mainly large fishing-boats are built.

Mortier Bay

Nearby Mortier Bay is both picturesque and tranquil.

From Marystown the 210 and 220 roads lead round the "boot" of the peninsula, with stops in Burin, St Lawrence, Fortune and Grand Bank. A large part of this 159km/99 mile stretch passes through barren and windlashed countryside.

Golden Sands
Resort

At Golden Sands Resort, near Salt Pond, will be found huts and camping-sites and a lovely beach suitable for bathing.

Route 221 leads to an entrancing piece of coast with hundreds of islands and projecting rock formations.

Burin, which developed as a result of the fishing industry, consists of a collection of villages dating back to the 18th c. and scattered between small bays and inlets.

Burin

The 220 leads you to Freshwater Pond Provincial Park, a good place at which to learn more about the island.

Not only is this place a centre of ship-building, it also has large fleets of fishing-steamers and some of the largest fish-production plants on the island. Huge quantities are brought here for processing every year from the towns at the southern tip.

St Lawrence, surrounded by pretty towns and villages, was at one time one of the world's largest producers of the mineral fluorite (fluorspar). Miner's Museum, open daily in summer, documents the history of the local mining industry and the lives of the miners.

St Lawrence

The breakers off the south coast at Allan Island, High Beach and Point au Gaul can be very spectacular.

Just before reaching Grand Bank there is a beautiful view of the south coast, Brunette Island and Miquelon Island.

Grand Bank is the largest and most varied of the "banks" in the south and east, shallow waterways with large stocks of fish which have attracted fishermen for centuries and still continue to do so. Grand Bank is where the Labrador current and the Gulf Stream meet, causing the colder stream to sink below the warmer, thus churning up plankton from the sea-bed. The plankton then rises to the surface and attracts great shoals of fish. Traditionally mainly fish of the cod group are caught, together with some herring. The fishing-boats used to be known as "bankers".

Grand Bank (topography)

Oil and gas are also drilled for on Grand Bank.

The beautifully situated town of Grand Bank is an important fishing centre. It has some attractive houses with "widow-walks", small open galleries on the roof from which the women could watch for the return of their menfolk from the sea.

Grand Bank (town)

In the Southern Newfoundland Seamen's Museum, built in triangular blocks to imitate sails, will be found some interesting exhibits illustrating the history of fishing on the "banks" and the lives of the fisherfolk; it is open every day. Of special interest are photographs of ships and fish, as well as models of the ships which were used.

Cabano

Province: Québec. Population: 4000

Tourisme Québec, C. P. 20,000 Québec, G1K 7X2.

Information

Cabano, the centre of the timber industry, lies in the far south of Québec Province near its border with New Brunswick and the US state of Maine on the TransCanada Highway.

Situated in some most charming countryside nearby is Lake Témiscouta, once an important staging-post in the transport of timber between the St Lawrence and the St John River catchment area.

In the past, especially in the 19th c., there were constant disputes between the owners of land belonging to Québec and New Brunswick on the one hand and their US neighbours on the other.

⋆Fort Ingall

Some 2km/1¼ miles out of Cabano on Route 232 lies Fort Ingall, built of wood in 1839 and which at one time housed 200 soldiers. The fort was lovingly restored a few years ago. A small museum explains how the officers and men lived here and what disputes and clashes they were faced with. From the terrace of the fort surrounded with stout palisades there is a lovely view over Lake Témiscouata. There is also a beautiful picnic site here.

Cabot Trail

See Cape Breton Island

Cache Creek

See Ashcroft · Cache Creek

Calgary   G 7

Province: Alberta
Altitude: 1049m/3443ft. Population: 692,000

| Information | Tourist & Convention Bureau, 237 8th Ave., Calgary, Alberta. Tel. (403) 263–85 10 |

Information Tourist & Convention Bureau, 237 8th Ave., Calgary, Alberta.
  Tel. (403) 263–85 10

Access By air:
Calgary International Airport (12km/7½ miles north-east of the city centre). "The Airporter" airport bus to the Westin Hotel.

By rail:
VIA Rail, station in CN Tower (9th Ave. S. W./Centre St.), daily connections to Banff/Vancouver and to Regina and Winnipeg.

By bus:
Greyhound (Terminal 850–16th St. S. W.), regular connections to Banff, Medicine Hat, Lethbridge, Drumheller, Fort McLeod and most of the large Canadian towns and cities.
Red Arrow Express (Westward Inn, 119–12 Ave. S. W.), several times a day to Red Deer and Edmonton.

City buses Calgary Transit buses cover most parts of the city.

Light Rail Transit Since 1987 the suburban railway system known as "LRT" (Light Rail Transit; called "C" Train) has been in operation. From the city centre three lines run south as far as Anderson Road, north-east as far as Whitehorn Station (44 Ave., N. E.) and north-west to the University. Between Downtown Mall (10th St. S. W.) and City Hall transport is free.

Location and climate The present city of Calgary lies on the western edge of the Canadian prairie where Elbow River enters Bow River, about 250km/155 miles north of the Canada–USA border. Particularly on days when the chinook, a dry warm fall wind, blows over the Rocky Mountains less than 100km/60 miles away, the glaciated mountain peaks on the western horizon appear like an insurmountable barrier rising from the plain. In winter this west wind, related to the föhn of Alpine countries, sometimes causes temperatures rapidly to rise by over 30°C/90°F and the snows to melt. Lying as it does in the lee of the Rockies Calgary has little rainfall; summer days are mostly dry, sunny and warm, the nights refreshingly cool.

★★Stampede Calgary, the city lying between the wilderness and the wheat-fields and ever since its foundation in competition with its sister city to the north,

Calgary Stampede

Edmonton, justifies its reputation as a "cowboy town" only once in the year, when the ten-day "stampede" is held. Then the population seems to feel obliged to dress accordingly, and blue jeans and brightly-coloured stetsons become the order of the day. Calgary becomes the centre of attraction for all Wild West fans; rodeos and wagon-racing teams, an authentic Indian camp of wigwams and traditional Indian dances, as well as agricultural shows all contribute to this great outdoor event.

On the occasion of the Winter Olympics in 1988 Calgary showed that today it is more than just an agricultural arena, a chamber of commerce for the Alberta wheat trade or a trans-shipment centre for cattle. In that year visitors from all over the world found a welcome in the city.

Economy and transport

Calgary can thank the oil being extracted from nearby for its dramatic development during the last 40 years from a provincial town to a modern metropolis, to a veritable "Manhattan of the prairies". In the busy city centre the glittering office buildings belonging to oil companies, banks and insurance companies tower 30 floors or more up into the sky. Around them stretch more than 527sq.km/204sq.miles of suburbs laid out in strict chess-board fashion, making Calgary Canada's third largest city.

Calgary boasts one of the most modern high-speed railway systems in Canada and the unique, mainly covered-in pedestrian street network known as the "Plus 15" Walkway System. Most of the office buildings, department stores, hotels and multi-storey car parks in the city are linked to one another by a system of footbridges totalling some 30km/20 miles in length. A pedestrian zone in the city centre with trees and street cafés is a very pleasant place in which to stroll.

The city's emblem and a useful guide for those who lose their bearings is the 191m/627ft high Calgary Tower, with a superb panorama to be seen from its viewing platform. As the Rocky Mountains with their well-known national parks are relatively near the city is an excellent choice for a holiday stay. The popular skiing and walking regions in the mountains or the unspoilt wilderness can be reached in one or two hours. Fast-water canoeing, more leisurely canoe or cycle trips and excursions into the interesting countryside round about make Calgary a good starting-out point for trips into western Canada.

History

The city developed from a North West Mounted Police (now the RCMP) post which was set up here on Bow River in 1875, with orders to put an end to the smuggling of whisky across the American border. The commandant, named MacLeod and of Scottish extraction, gave this first camp the name of Calgary, which in Gaelic means "quickly-flowing clear water".

Even before the first fur-hunters arrived here in the 19th c. this confluence of two rivers was a favourite camping place for the Indians. After the Blackfoot Indians had obtained horses and weapons from the white man they became the dominant tribe. The increasing influx of white fur-traders and settlers into their tribal territories resulted in a number of conflicts, however, but these were finally largely settled under the terms of a treaty signed in 1877. Today the one-time proud rulers of the prairie live in a number of reservations south of Calgary.

The relatively favourable natural conditions persuaded an increasing number of American cattle breeders to leave their over-grazed ranches and settle north of the border. Soon giant herds of cattle were grazing around Calgary, to be followed by large concerns dealing in meat and foodstuffs.

When the Canadian Pacific Railway reached Calgary in 1883 the little police post rapidly began to develop. By the end of that year it boasted a population of 600. More and more settlers came to the Calgary region, and by 1891 it had its own power and water supplies. In 1893 the town was granted its charter.

Since the turn of the century prospectors have dug for oil in and around Calgary. Finally, in 1914, oil was found in Turner Valley 61km/38 miles to the south-west, resulting in enormous development of the area. Today Calgary is an important centre of the Canadian petro-chemical industry; four-fifths of all the firms engaged in the crude oil and natural gas business in Canada have their head offices in Calgary. The city is also the financial centre of the province of Alberta.

Development has slowed somewhat since oil prices started to fall in the 1980s. Many ambitious city development projects came to grief and unemployment – previously well below the Canadian average – increased enormously. Commercial firms, restaurants and the entertainment industry all felt the effect of the reduced spending power of the workers employed in the petro-chemical industry.

To a certain extent this was offset by the building boom which accompanied the preparations for the XV Winter Olympics in 1988.

Sights in the city centre

★Calgary Tower

The place from which to set out on a tour of the relatively small inner city of Calgary is Calgary Tower on 9th Ave./Centre St., which is open daily 7.30am–midnight. It has a viewing platform and revolving restaurant and being 191m/627ft high it is the city's landmark and was, until 1985, its tallest building. In 1988 a giant torch on the tower bore witness to the spirit of the Olympics.

Stephen Avenue Mall, Toronto Dominion Square, Scotia Centre

Stephen Avenue, Calgary's main shopping street, is a pedestrian zone between 1st. St. S. E. and 4th St. S. W. Here still stand a large number of old buildings built in a variety of styles from local sandstone. In the former Imperial Bank of Canada at 102–8th Ave. the Alberta Historical Resources Foundation has its headquarters; this foundation dedicated to preserving the history and monuments of the province of Alberta is open Mon.–Fri. 8.30am–4.30pm. An informative brochure entitled "Stephen Avenue Mall Walking Tour" can be obtained here.

From Lancaster Building (304–8th Ave.) opposite the Royal Bank building the "Plus 15' Walkway System" (look for the blue and white sign) leads to Toronto Dominion Square and the Scotia Centre, two sizeable shopping centres on 7th Avenue.

.... LRT (Straßenbahn)

On the third floor (4th level) of Toronto Dominion Square at 2nd/3rd St. the visitor will come somewhat unexpectedly upon the Devonian Gardens, a floral paradise covering about one hectare/two and a half acres with ponds, fountains and a small waterfall. 20,000 tropical, sub-tropical and native plants thrive here under glass. Open: daily 9am–9pm.

Devonian Gardens

In 7th Ave, the best way to get about is by using the "C" Train, which is free in this inner city area. By this means the City Hall is reached in a few minutes (two stops).

"C" Train

The historical old sandstone town hall built in 1911 had become too small, so in 1986 a triangular and highly modern office complex was built; its glass front is visible from a long way off. The City Council meets here.

City Hall

In front of the City Hall lies the Olympic Plaza, where medal award ceremonies were held every evening during the 1988 Winter Olympics. It is now a popular meeting-place in summer, and various events, such as open-air concerts, cabarets, firework displays and laser shows, are held here.

Olympic Plaza

South-west of Glenmore Reservoir lies the reservation of the Sarcee (Sarsi) Indians, a tribe which once was linked with the Blackfeet Indians, and now forms part of the Athabask tribe. In 1983, to mark the occasion of the

★Sarcee People's Museum

143

Calgary

century of its written history, the tribe furnished a small museum at 3700 Anderson Rd. S. W., which is open Mon.–Fri. 8am–4pm.

★Canada Olympic Park

In the foothills of the mountains to the west of the city rise the strange-looking towers of the Olympic ski-slopes. The bob-sleigh run and tobog-gan-run are also here. Guided tours take place every day 9am–5pm, when a panoramic view of the Calgary skyline can be enjoyed from the top of the 90m/295ft ski-slope.

Olympic Hall of Fame

Memories of the Olympic Games are provided by means of documents and films in the Olympic Hall of Fame, which is open daily 10am–5pm, to 8pm in high summer.

Calaway Park

About 10km/6 miles west of the city – take the TransCanada Highway and then the Springbank exit – lies the largest adventure park in the whole of south-west Canada. It is open mid-May–mid-Oct., but opening times vary. Coach-loads of visitors come to enjoy the numerous attractions, including roller coasters and an artificial watercourse, as well as colourful evening entertainment programmes. From the Terrace Garden Restaurant there is a good view of the Rocky Mountains.

University of Calgary, Olympic Oval

On the campus of Calgary University (15,000 students) in the west of the city is the Olympic Oval, the first covered 400m speed-skating rink. It is open daily 7am–11pm.

McMahon Stadium

The McMahon Stadium on University Drive, mainly used for football, is where the opening and closing ceremonies for the 1988 Winter Olympics took place.

Nickle Arts Museum

Also on the campus will be found the Nickle Arts Museum containing a large coin collection as well as ancient European exhibits. Temporary exhibitions are also held here.

Alberta Science Centre, Centennial Planetarium

In the Alberta Science Centre at 701–11th St./7th Ave., which is open Wed.–Sun. 1.30pm–9pm, daily in summer, there is the opportunity to enjoy a "hands-on" experience of the natural sciences. There are some three dozen themes of popular interest with which the visitor can himself experiment. The Centennial Planetarium – with laser-astro-shows among other things – also attracts a lot of interest.

Pleiades Theatre

In the neighbouring Pleiades Theatre modern as well as more traditional plays are performed.

Canadian Western Natural Gas Museum

The little museum in the main office buildings of the West Canadian Gas Company at 909–1th Ave. S. W., open Mon.–Fri. 8am–4pm, illustrates the development of the gas industry from July 17th 1912, when Calgary was first provided with natural gas.

Fort Calgary

The first outpost of the North West Mounted Police was set up in 1875 at the confluence of the Elbow and Bow Rivers. The foundations of the original fort can still be seen. The history of the city of Calgary is illustrated in the Visitors' Centre on 750–9th Ave. S. E. (open: May–late Oct., late Oct.–Apr., Wed.–Sun. daily 10am–6pm).

On the other side of the bridge stands Deane House, built in 1906 for the commandant of the outpost, which is now a tea-room.

Calgary Zoo & Prehistoric Park

On St George's Island in Bow River, at 1300 Zoo Rd. N. E., lies Calgary Zoo, founded in 1912. Open: daily 9am–dusk. The owners are particularly proud of their 388 examples of rare and threatened species of animals as well as of the adjoining botanical gardens. In a prehistoric theme park stand numerous replicas of animals which lived in south-western Canada millions of years ago.

Aerospace Museum

In the Aerospace Museum at 64 McTavish Ave. (open: Mon.–Fri. 9am–4pm, Sat. and Sun. noon–4pm) can be seen Second World War aviation equipment and military aircraft supplemented by documents from the period.

Olympic Saddledome

The "Plus 15' System", linked to the Municipal Building, provides access to the modern 1985-built Calgary centre for Performing Arts on the south side of the square at 205–8th Ave. S. E. Comprising three stages and the John Singer Concert Hall, this impressive city theatre is connected to two older buildings, Calgary Public Building (1930) and Burns Building (1913), which is the information centre of the Calgary Tourist & Convention Bureau.

Calgary Centre for Performing Arts

A further footbridge leads from the municipal theatre to the Calgary Convention Centre and to the Glenbow Museum on 130–9th Ave./1st St. S. E., open: Tues.–Sun. 10am–6pm. In the museum can be seen some rare exhibits illustrating the historical development of western Canada., covering the time of the early fur-hunters and the arrival of the North West Mounted Police, as well as the Métis uprising under Louis Riel. The development of the oil industry is also catered for. As well as personal effects belonging to the pioneers who came here from all over the world there are artistic and everyday items left by the Indians, including the Ojibwa, the Cree and some prairie tribes and the Inuit. Particularly impressive is the leather tepee of the Blackfoot tribe.

Convention Centre, ★Glenbow Museum

Another footbridge leads to Palliser Square. At the foot of the lofty CN Tower lies Calgary's main railway station.

Palliser Square, CN Tower

In the south-east of the city, by Elbow River at 14th Ave./4th St., Stampede Park extends over 24ha/60 acres. Every year since 1912 the Calgary Exhibition and the Stampede have been held here. In the month of July the Wild West lives again. In the world's biggest and wildest rodeo cowboys compete to be the "best of the bunch". Prizes are awarded for the best breed of animal and neck-breaking chuckwagon races are held. Spectacular shows are also put on for the public. During the rest of the year fairs and exhibitions of all kinds are held here, and there are horse races in the Grand Stand.

Stampede Park

Calgary

★Olympic
Saddledome

Near the Stampede Buildings is the Olympic Saddledome, probably one of the most beautiful ice-arenas in the world. This giant hall, built in the shape of a saddle, reflects the spirit of the Wild West. In 1988 the Olympic ice-skating competitions were held here. Built in 1983, the Saddledome holds 20,000 spectators and is the home of the world-famous ice-hockey team "Calgary Flames".

Grain Academy

The "Grain Academy" of the Alberta Wheat Pool is also situated in Stampede Park. Linked to it is an exhibition – situated at 17th Ave./2nd St, open: Apr.–Sept., Mon.–Fri. 10am–4pm, Sat. noon–4pm – with a model of a railway which brought the grain from the prairies over the Rocky Mountains to Vancouver Harbour, as well as a functioning granary. There are also films and explanatory documents giving information about the production and importance of various types of grain.

Glenmore
Reservoir

Glenmore reservoir in the south-west of the city is very popular with water-sports enthusiasts, who can sail, canoe and row here.

Heritage Park

A typical village from the pioneering period consisting of more than 100 historical buildings has been reconstructed near the reservoir. Heritage Park is at 1900 Heritage Park Drive/14th St. S. W., and is open July–Labour Day, daily 10am–6pm, and at limited times during the remainder of the year. An old steam engine provides transport to it. There is also a paddle-steamer such as was used years ago on the rivers of western Canada which is available for trips round the reservoir. In addition there are nostalgic ferries operating, an historic bakery and the Wainwright Hotel.

Kananaskis Tour

Note

After leaving Calgary and travelling about 80km/50 miles west along the four-lane TransCanada Highway 1, there is a turn-off south on Highway 40 into some most charming countryside and to the unspoiled Kananaskis Valley, a favourite spot for walkers in summer. A short way from the junction is the Alberta Centre, which provides information and maps.

Some 8km/5 miles further on lies "Colonel's Cabin", a Second World War prisoner-of-war camp, with a watch-tower and the commandant's hut still preserved. Historical photographs may be seen. The dam across Barrier Lake was also constructed by German prisoners-of-war.

★Nakiska
Mt Allan

As the tour continues a fine view opens up of Mt Allan, more than 2800m/9200ft high, on the side of which can be seen the ski-slope laid down for the Alpine competitions. In only two years an international skiing region was created from a veritable wilderness; at the foot was built "Nakiska" (Indian for "meeting-point"), with lift-stations, a ski-school and ski-hire, a cafeteria and a bar.

Some 22km/14 miles south of the TransCanada Highway and by Ribbon Creek 4km/2½ miles away stretches the holiday resort of Kananaskis Village comprising a number of hotel and apartment buildings.

A rather special kind of attraction is the Kananaskis Country Golf Course, laid out almost 1500m/4900ft above sea-level; it is Alberta's only golf-course and has 36 holes.

Fortress Mountain

23km/14 miles further south there is another ski-region on Fortress Mountain, with lifts, ski-school, ski-hire, restaurant and bar.

★Peter Lougheed
Provincial Park

After 136km/85 miles the tour reaches the Peter Lougheed Provincial Park – known as Kananaskis Provincial Park until 1985 – which forms the very heart of the Kananaskis region and where elk, Wapiti deer, thick-horned sheep, mountain-goats, beaver, grizzly and black bears, pumas and wolves may all be encountered. It covers 508sq.km/196sq.miles, which makes it the largest provincial park in Alberta. In summer especially many adventurous holiday-makers are attracted here by the superb mountain scenery, traversed by various trails and dotted with numerous high lakes. Well worthwhile is the detour to the Park Visitor Centre at the northern end of

Lower Kananaskis Lake, which is open end of June–Sept. 9.30am–5pm, Thur., Fri., Sat. to 8pm. Various exhibitions and slide-shows give an insight into the geography and history of the Kananaskis region. Board and lodging is available in nearby William Watson Lodge. A number of interesting trails and instructional paths start from here, including Boulton Creek Trail, Kananaskis Canyon Trail and Rock Wall Trail. The road leading to the park ends at Upper Kananaskis Lake.

This tour starts from Calgary city centre on the TransCanada Highway 1, branching off after 30km/19 miles on to Highway 9 to the north. Passing through rich, partly irrigated arable and pasture land with flat hills it arrives at Drumheller in the valley of the Red Deer River. Some 25km/15½ miles west of the town, in the deeply-slashed Horseshoe Canyon, can be seen for the first time the erosion forms so typical of this part of the Red Deer River and known as the "Badlands"; the complete lack of vegetation makes a lasting impression. It is wise to obtain brochures about the various tours on offer from the Tourist Information Office when arriving in the town.

★**Badlands Tour**

Note

After covering 142km/88 miles the tour reaches Drumheller, a town of scarcely 7000 inhabitants which proudly calls itself the Town of the Dinosaurs. 75 million years ago, in the Upper Cretaceous Period, various species of dinosaurs roamed this region. Some remains of this life form have been preserved in the sedimentary strata.
   From 1910 to the 1940s Drumheller depended on coal-mining. Then oil and natural gas largely took over from coal as energy sources so that today the little town is mainly a commercial centre for the farmers of the region. The very dry Badlands, quite unsuitable for agriculture, have long attracted numbers of tourists.

Drumheller

The Drumheller Dinosaur & Fossil Museum at 335–1st St. E. is open Apr.–Oct. daily 9am–8pm, July–Sept. to 6pm only. In addition to a collection of minerals and some Indian exhibits the main emphasis is on bones and skeletons of dinosaurs and other prehistoric animals.

★Drumheller
Dinosaur & Fossil
Museum

The Dinosaur Trail along Highway 838, a tour 48km/30 miles long to the west of the town along Red Deer River which cuts its way more than 120m/400ft deep into the prairie, takes in the area of steep and barren rocky slopes, from which wind and rain have carved the mushroom-shaped pillars known as "hoodoos" and revealed whole dinosaur skeletons. Ancient river-courses have carved up the prairie here into rocky tablelands on which grass struggles to grow where the soil has not been completely eroded. In the Badlands will be found sagebrush and greasewood bushes, so typical of arid regions in America, as well as cacti. At the bridge where Highway 9 crosses Red Deer River *tyrannosaurus rex*, a much photographed replica of a mighty dinosaur, greets the passer-by.

★Dinosaur Trail

The Homestead Antique Museum (open: May–Oct. daily 10am–5pm, July–Sept. 9am–9pm), will be found about 1km/⅔ mile north-west of the town. In the grounds of the museum can be seen different pieces of farming equipment and machinery from the pioneering period.

Homestead
Antique Museum

The Tyrell Museum of Palaeontology, on the north bank of the Red Deer River, was opened in 1985. It lies 6km/4 miles to the north-west on the western edge of Midland Provincial Park. Open: Apr.–mid-Oct. daily 9am–9pm, at other times of the year Tues.–Sun. and public holidays 10am–5pm. This most interesting museum has earned a worldwide reputation.
   The most modern museum techniques have brought millions of years of the earth's history back to life. 800 fossils, including 35 dinosaur skeletons, films and – last but not least – twenty easy to use computer terminals, provide the visitor with an insight into the fascinating evolution of life on earth. A primeval garden shows tropical and subtropical plant species and

★★Tyrell
Museum
of Palaeontology

A dinosaur in the Tyrell Museum of Palaeontology

their descendants as they were 350 million years ago, at the start of the Carbonaceous Period.

The museum also provides information on the genesis and geology of the region and on the history of discovery.

In 1884, by sheer chance, the geologist J. B. Tyrell happened to stumble across some dinosaur bones lying among the cacti and stones of the Badlands. Quite unwittingly he started the "great Canadian dinosaur-rush": palaentologists and collectors from all over the world streamed into the Badlands in their horse-drawn wagons and dug up many of the skeletons which can today be seen in numerous museums, including some outside Canada.

During the transition to the Tertiary Period Alberta as we know it today was one vast inland lake. The climate was tropical and the vegetation very lush, ideal living conditions for dinosaurs. When these conditions changed within a relatively short period, however, the coast became one giant dinosaur cemetery.

Horsethief Canyon Viewpoint

After a small chapel built in 1957 had collapsed the Horsethief Canyon Viewpoint was constructed, from where there is a good view of the various sedimentary layers in the canyon. Footpaths lead down to fossilised oyster-beds.

Bleriot Ferry

The Bleriot Ferry is in operation from early Apr.–early Nov. daily 7am–11pm. It embarks from the little township of Munson 8km/5 miles to the west and carries passengers across the Red Deer River. This ferry, which has been in operation since 1913, is one of the last sailing-ferries still used in Canada.

From the western bank of the river the tour returns to Drumheller.

Dinosaur Park

1km/⅔ miles west of the town centre lies the Dinosaur Park. Situated on South Railroad Ave. it displays twenty giant dinosaurs made of cement (open: Apr.–mid-Oct. from 9am).

Another charming tour takes in the 60km/37 mile long Hoodoo Drive and starts from Drumheller on Highway 10 to the east. After about 10km/6 miles the route passes the Rosedale Swinging Suspension Bridge, originally built by the workers of the Old Star Coal Mine and which leads across to a now unused coal-mine.

★**Hoodoo Drive**

Note

The actual Hoodoo region, west of East Coulee, is 18km/11 miles further on. Most of these bizarre rock-columns, so typical of the Red Deer River Badlands, are topped with a "bonnet" of hard rock which protects them from erosion.

Hoodoos

23km/14 miles: when coal-mining flourished and there were 34 mines in the valley East Coulee was a lively little town with a population of 4000. Today only some 200 still live here. The schoolhouse built in 1930 today houses a School Museum, which is open July–Aug. daily 9am–9pm, rest of the year 8.30am–4.30pm.

East Coulee

The return trip to Drumheller can be either along Highway 10 or roads 569 and 56.

The tour then continues along Highway 56 to the north initially, and then on Highway 9 eastwards towards Hanna. After some 50km/30 miles the Handhills rise out of the prairie to heights approaching 185m/607ft; these are some of the highest points between the Rockies and the east coast.

224km/140 miles: at the entrance to the township of Hanna (pop. 3000) a picture of a grey goose underlines the good hunting to be had around here. A reconstructed village illustrating the lives of the 19th c. pioneers can be seen in the Pioneer Museum on E. Municipal Rd./4th. St., which is open mid-May–Sept. daily 10am–7pm or other times by prior arrangement.

Hanna

Now turning south on Highway 36 – where some stretches of bad road can be encountered – carry on for about 105km/65 miles and then turn off east to the Dinosaur Provincial Park (about 40km/25 miles).

Typical "Hoodoos"

Campbell Highway

★ Dinosaur
Provincial Park

380km/236 miles: The Dinosaur Provincial Park, covering 6039ha/14,920 acres, is a unique palaeontological site which was declared a World Heritage Site by UNESCO in 1979. The remains of more than 35 species of dinosaurs and other saurians were found here.

In the vicinity of this park the Red Deer River has cut its way more than 100m/330ft deep into the valley floor. Annual rainfalls of 300 to 400mm/ 12 to 16in. have produced what must be the most spectacular Badlands in Canada, with fascinating hoodoos, rock-needles, gorges and mesas. The slopes, devoid of any vegetation, shimmer in shades of reddish-black and greyish-green. This barren moonscape-like region forms the bulk of the park; beyond it the Badland spreads relatively fast and devours about 1cm/½in. more land and loose material every year.

Discovery of
fossil deposits

T. C. Weston discovered these superb fossil deposits in 1889, and by the turn of the century the Canadian Geological Society has carried out extensive digs. The Badlands and the archaeological sites, including a dinosaur skeleton left "in situ", can be seen on a circular tour of 3½km/2 miles. However, most of the park can be seen only on a guided tour led by a park ranger or on a coach trip. Early reservation for these tours is essential; write to P.O. Box 60, Patricia, Alta. T0J 2K0 or tel. (403) 378–45 87.

The Tyrell Museum of Palaeontology maintains a field station here. Palaeontologists can also be watched as they prepare finds.

★ Brooks

430km/267 miles: Brooks (pop. 10,000) lies 48km/30 miles further south in the middle of irrigated farmland and meadows. Brooks Aqueduct was hailed as a brilliant technical achievement when it was built in 1913.

The importance of irrigation is illustrated in the Brooks & District Museum, consisting of several restored buildings and situated at Sutherland Drive; it is open: May–Oct. daily 10am–5pm. Some well-chosen exhibits depict the culture of the Indians and describe the lives of the early settlers, ranchers and railroad pioneers. There is also some Royal Canadian Mounted Police memorabilia.

From Brooks there is an interesting detour of 78km/48 miles into the Badlands of the Red Deer River to the Dinosaur Provincial Park.

Lake Newell,
Kinbrook Island
Provincial Park

13km/8 miles south of Brooks Kinbrook Island Provincial Park lies on the east bank of Lake Newell, a 65km/40 mile long reservoir formed by the Bassano Dam built in 1909. Bathing can be enjoyed here, and there are colonies of cormorants, white pelicans and Californian seagulls, as well as Canadian geese, to be seen. Lake Newell forms part of an extensive irrigation project which was begun early in this century in south-eastern Alberta.

The return route to Calgary from Brooks – 185km/115 miles – is along TransCanada Highway 1.

Campbell Highway   B–D 5

Administrative Unit: Yukon Territory

Information

See Yukon

In the south-east of the Yukon Territory, near Watson Lake, Campbell Highway No. 4 (573km/356 miles in length in all) branches off to the north from the Alaska Highway (see entry) and after some 356km/220 miles passes through the township of Ross River, then after a further 60km/ 37 miles reaches the town of Faro and finally joins up with the Klondike Highway (see Klondike) near Carmacks by the Yukon River.

Robert Campbell

Campbell Highway follows the trail of the Scotsman Robert Campbell who in the 19th c. crossed rivers and passes and pushed forward into the very centre of the Yukon Territory in order to set up trading posts for the Hudson's Bay Company.

Route followed by the Campbell Highway

Watson Lake (see Alaska Highway), the "Gateway to the Yukon", with its 1200 inhabitants, is the point at the junction of Alaska and Campbell where the highway starts.

Watson Lake

For many people the first stop is Simpson Lake, 80km/50 miles away. This lake, nowadays so popular with anglers, was named by Campbell after Sir George Simpson, the general manager of the Hudson's Bay Company.

Simpson Lake

After a further 30km/19 miles or so the road reaches Miner's Junction, named after a jade mine; jade jewellery is on sale in a small shop.

Miner's Junction

To the east of Miner's Junction Nahanni Range Road provides the link with the Northwest Territories (see entry).

At the 268 kilometre point, and at 167m/550ft above sea-level, stands the trading post known as Fort Pelly Banks which was set up by Campbell in 1844, but has been unused for many years.

Fort Pelly Banks

After 360km/224 miles the highway arrives in Ross River on the south bank of the Pelly River. Ross River lies at the junction of Campbell Highway and Canol Road, the latter providing the link between Whitehorse (see entry) via Ross River to the Selwyn and Mackenzie Mountains in the adjoining Northwest Territories (see entry). North of Watson Lake the town of Ross River is the nearest tourist centre and place where anglers and hunters can obtain supplies and provisions. Most of the 400 inhabitants are Kaska Indians. Its convenient situation at the mouth of the river of the same name has meant that Pelly River has grown in importance as a point from which to explore for minerals and other natural resources in the central Yukon.

Ross River

Tours in the unspoilt mountains and flights – such as those offered by Flying Service Ross River, tel. (403) 969–25 47 – over the scenically charming valleys of Ross and Pelly River are much to be recommended.

Campbell Highway now follows the Pelly River until, after covering a total of 415km/258 miles from the start, a road branches off to Faro 6km/4 miles to the north. This mining village, with a population of 1700, grew up in 1968 with the mining of nearby stocks of lead and zinc. After the mines had to be shut down in 1982 because they proved unprofitable Faro threatened to become a ghost town, but early in 1986 a further area was discovered and mined with the aid of new methods of exploration. Between 1986 and 1990 production amounted to some 5 million tonnes per annum; the lead and zinc mines at Faro belonging to Curragh Resources Inc. are now the largest in Canada.

Faro,
Lead and zinc
mines

Campbellton

Q 8

Province: New Brunswick. Population: 9000

Route 11, Route 134

Acess

Tourism New Brunswick, P.O. Box 12345, Fredericton, New Brunswick, E3B 5C3; tel. (506) 453–23 77.

Information

The little harbour town of Campbellton lies at the foot of the Pain de Sucre mountain on the narrow estuary of the Restigouche River and at the western end of the Baie des Chaleurs, quite near the border with the province of Québec. It is an important trade centre for the Gaspésie Peninsula (see entry). Timber and timber products are also shipped from here. Salmon-fishing plays an important role in the town's economy, as is underlined by the "Festival du Saumon/Salmon Festival" which takes place every year in the first week of July.

History   Campbellton was founded in the 17th c. by French-speaking Acadians, but they left in 1760. In that same year the last North American battle of the Seven Years' War betwen France and England took place in the waters off Campbellton.

A few years later the Scots settled here, and the town was named after the governor of the province, Sir Archibald Campbell.

Sights

Restigouche Gallery

In the Restigouche Gallery can be seen works by local artists as well as various temporary exhibitions.

Sugarloaf Provincial Park

A steep path leads up to the peak of the towering mountain known as Pain de Sucre/Sugarloaf. It is 283m/930ft high and there are impressive views.

At the bottom of the mountain a provincial park has been laid out, with sporting and leisure facilities, including bathing in the lake, tennis, camping and picnic-sites. In the Visitor Centre there is much to be learned about Campbellton and its environs.

Surroundings of Campbellton: ★Baie des Chaleurs

Dalhousie

20km/13 miles north-east of Campbellton the pretty little town of Dalhousie nestles by the Baie des Chaleurs. Today it is an important centre of the New Brunswick woodworking industry.

A visit is recommended to the Restigouche Regional Museum with its exhibits covering the pioneering period, development of fishing and agriculture in the region.

In Inch Arran Park there is bathing and tennis. The coastline is impressive, especially the Bon Ami Rocks eroded by the surf.

★Chaleur Bay Provincial Park

The prettily situated Chaleur Bay Provincial Park attracts many holidaymakers, especially in summer. It is also a pleasant place to bathe when water temperatures allow.

Boat excursions to Québec

A boat trip from Dalhousie along the charming Gaspésie (see entry) coast in the province of Québec is a memorable experience.

Charlo

Nearly 30km/19 miles east of Campbellton lies the holiday resort of Charlo on the Baie des Chaleurs.

Route 134

From Charlo Route 134 winds south-eastward along the Baie des Chaleurs to Bathurst (see entry) on Baie Nepisguit. Along the coast beautiful stretches of beach rub shoulders with impressive rock formations. There are pretty bathing places in Jacquet River, Belledune (the largest strawberry market in the world), Petit-Rocher, Nigado, Beresford and Bathurst.

Between Pointe-Verte and Petit-Rocher the New Brunswick Mining & Mineral Interpretation Center, which illustrates the history of mining in eastern Canada (see Bathurst) is well worth a visit.

Canmore   F 7

Province: Alberta. Population: 4000

Information   See Alberta

The now famous winter-sports resort of Canmore, only 3km/2 miles east of the boundary of the Banff National Park (see entry) by the TransCanada Highway and in the Bow River valley, lies under the shadow of the majestic Three Sisters Peaks. During the 1988 Winter Olympics the cross-country and biathlon skiing events were held here. Now the 60km/40 miles or so of ski-runs along the Smith-Dorrien Highway and the Nordic Centre on Mount Rundle, about 2km/1¼ miles south of the town and at a height of 1500m/4920ft above sea-level, are open to serious and amateur sportsmen alike. Heritage Walk, an instructive path with information boards, provides details of the history of the region.

The town of Canmore grew up in 1883 when coal was discovered and mined around here. Now the coal-mines are closed and the town, the local centre of the Kananaskis region (see Calgary, Surroundings), relies mainly on tourism although it is quieter and less overcrowded during the season than Banff.

Canmore, framed by snow-covered mountain peaks, is a starting point for tours of the Rocky Mountains lasting one or several days. Other leisure activities are mountain climbing, cycling, horse-riding, fast-water and other canoeing, fishing, golf and helicopter flights.

A "Winter Carnival", with dog sleigh races, etc., is held here every year in January.

Winter Carnival

The unmade-up road known as the Smith-Dorrien Trail leads southwards through magnificent and wild mountain country to Spray Lake Reservoir and to Highway 40 in the Peter Lougheed Provincial Park (see Calgary).

Smith-Dorrien Spray Trail

Cape Breton Island

R/S 8

Province: Nova Scotia

See Nova Scotia

Information

Cape Breton Island is actually the north-eastern part of the province of Nova Scotia, separated from it by the Strait of Canso and linked by a dam, to cross which a toll is charged.

A charming blend of sea and land is the hallmark of this island, so rich in stocks of coal and at the same time boasting the highest mountains in Nova Scotia.

★Topography

Surroundings of Lac Bras d'Or

Port Hawkesbury is a small industrial town with oil refineries; the three main link-roads on the island fan out from here.

Port Hawkesbury

The village of Whycocomagh nestles enchantingly in a bay on the west bank of a lake. In the old church for many years the first part of the services used to be held in Gaelic and the second half in English.

Nearby is an Indian reserve where wooden sculptures and baskets are made.

Whycocomagh

6km/4 miles north of Whycocomagh in the Baddeck direction lies this charmingly landscaped provincial park with numerous Norwegian spruce, pine, beech and maple trees. A beautiful view can be enjoyed from the 300m/980ft high Mount Salt.

★Whycocomagh Provincial Park

Baddeck is one of the most beautiful villages in Nova Scotia. Its name means "where an island is nearby". Alexander Graham Bell (see Famous People), the inventor of the telephone, had a summer residence here.

★Baddeck

In the Alexander Graham Bell National Historic Site can be seen personal effects and documents belonging to the inventor, as well as parts of two hydroplanes made by Bell and powered by aircraft engines.

Alexander Graham Bell National Historic Site

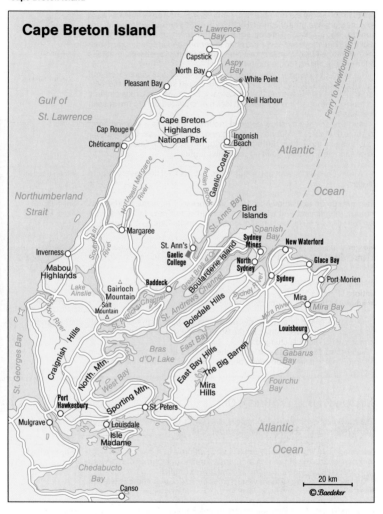

Cape Breton Island

St. Lawrence Bay

Capstick

North Bay

White Point

Pleasant Bay

Neil Harbour

Gulf of St. Lawrence

Cap Rouge

Chéticamp

Cape Breton Highlands National Park

Ingonish Beach

Atlantic

Gaelic Coast

Ocean

Northeast Margaree River

Indian Brook

Northumberland Strait

Margaree

Southwest River

St. Anns Bay

Bird Islands

Spanish Bay

St. Ann's Gaelic College

Sydney Mines

New Waterford

Inverness

Great Bras d'Or

North Sydney

Glace Bay

Mabou Highlands

Lake Ainslie

Gairloch Mountain

Baddeck

Boularderie Island

Barra Channel

Sydney

Port Morien

Salt Mountain

St. Patricks Channel

St. Andrews Channel

Sydney R.

Mira

Mira River

Mira Bay

Mabou River

Craignish Hills

Boisdale Hills

Louisbourg

Bras d'Or Lake

East Bay

East Bay Hills

The Big Barren

Gabarus Bay

North. Mtn.

West Bay

Sporting Mtn.

Mira Hills

Fourchu Bay

Port Hawkesbury

St. Peters

Atlantic

Mulgrave

Louisdale

Isle Madame

Ocean

St. Georges Bay

Chedabucto Bay

Canso

20 km

© Baedeker

Ferry to Newfoundland

Open: July 1st–Sept. 30th daily 9am–9pm, Oct. 1st–June 30th daily 9am–5pm.

North Sydney

From this busy harbour ships sail to Newfoundland. North Sydney is also the eastern terminus of the continental railway network.

Sydney

Sydney is the largest town on the island. Sydney harbour was used from the 16th c. initially by European fishermen and then frequently by English and Scottish fleets. Between 1830 and 1870 the town enjoyed an enormous boost through the ironworking industry, and iron ore from Newfoundland is still processed here today.

St Peters is one of the oldest villages on the island. The restored fortified trading post set up by Nicolas Denis, a 17th c. French colonist, is worth a visit; open: June–Sept. daily 9am–5pm. St Peters

Île Madame was colonised by Acadians after their flight from Louisburg from the English in 1758, and French is still spoken here today. Île Madame

A visit is recommended to the Lenoir Museum in Arichat; this is a reconstruction of an early 19th c. smithy. Lenoir Museum

★★ Cabot Trail

The Cabot Trail is a 300km/190 mile stretch in the north-west of the island, starting from Baddeck. It got its name from the Italian seafarer Giovanni Caboto (John Cabot, see Famous People), who is thought to have been the first to land in North America in 1497.

The enchanting combination of prairieland, hills and forests together with the proximity of the sea must make the Cabot Trail one of the most beautiful scenic stretches in the whole of North America. Scenic stretch

Sights along the Cabot Trail

Margaree Harbour is a small fishing hamlet opposite the Île Margaree, an island which is home to numerous species of birds, such as cormorants and seagulls. Margaree Harbour

Chéticamp is a little Acadian fishing village on the edge of Highlands National Park, with many craft workshops. A visit is recommended to the Acadian Museum and to the prettily decorated Church of St-Pierre built in 1893. Chéticamp

Scottish folklore on the Cabot Trail

★★Cape Breton Highlands National Park

Location	This national park with numerous footpaths extends over 985sq.km/380sq. miles in the north of the island between the St Lawrence River and the Atlantic. The varied animal life is particularly impressive and includes beaver, deer, wild-cats, parrots, wild duck and eagles.
Information	The Information Offices in this park are to be found near Chéticamp and Igonish on the Cabot Trail, They are open in summer daily 8am–9pm, late spring and autumn daily 9am–5pm; during the remainder of the year information can be obtained from the offices in Ingonish which are open every day.
Ingonish	The little fishing village of Ingonish with its picturesque harbour is a favourite place for outings both in summer and winter on account of its sporting attractions which include fishing, golf, tennis and swimming.
Cape Smoky	12km/8 miles south of Ingonish lies Cape Smoky, 365m/1200ft high, with a chair-lift to the top. On clear days there is a fantastic view of the surrounding countryside.

Caraquet · Côte Acadienne   Q/R 8

	Province: New Brunswick. Population: 7000
Information	Office de Tourisme de la Ville de Caraquet
Access	Highway 11 (Campbellton–Bathurst–Chatham–Moncton).
	The little town of Caraquet lies on the Côte Acadienne (Acadian Coast) which forms the southern border of the Baie des Chaleurs, that is to say, on the Acadian Peninsula about 65km/40 miles north-east of Bathurst (see entry).
History	Caraquet was founded in 1758 and now forms the cultural centre of Acadia. Every summer a large-scale Acadian Festival is held here, the highlight of which is August 15th, National Acadian Festival Day.
Fishing port	Caraquet is also the home port of New Brunswick's largest fishing fleet, together with a school for fishermen and a very busy fish-market.
Sights ★Port	Caraquet's picturesque fishing harbour will delight the eye and the palate. It will illustrate how hard the fisherman's life is, while the many harbour bars and smart restaurants all offer a fine selection of speciality fish dishes.
★Musée Acadian	The Acadian Museum in Caraquet, near the wharf and school of fishing, provides detailed information about the history of the Acadian culture and the first French-speaking pioneers in this region. There are also exhibits dealing with the unfortunate disputes with the English, Scottish and Irish.
★★**Village Historique Acadien** Location	To the south-east of Caraquet, near Bertrand on Road 11, lies the "Village Historique Acadien" open-air museum, one of New Brunswick's main attractions.
Old crafts	In this "living visual workshop" visitors can see how Acadians lived between 1780 and 1890. Museum staff dressed in the original costumes of the period perform old crafts, such as spinning wool, weaving cloth and making clothes, forging iron, making furniture and wagons, printing books and posters, making soap, drying fish, and preserving vegetables and meats.
Aboiteaux	A system of dykes and sluices laid out as it was shows how land used to be reclaimed and made into fertile soil for corn and vegetables.

Fishing village in Côte Acadienne

Old handicraft in Village Acadian

In recent years some valuable old Acadian buildings of considerable historical significance have been moved and re-erected here, including the mill known as "Moulin Riordin", "Maison Thériault" and a restaurant where patrons can sample food prepared from old Acadian recipes.

Other buildings

Early June–early Sept. daily 10am–6pm.

Opening times

From the Grand Anse west of Caraquet there is a breathtaking view over the Baie des Chaleurs, with its amalgam of quiet bays and dramatic rock formations. Nearby is a newly laid-out park with a beautiful bathing beach. In the town of Grand Anse, founded in 1810, the "Pope Museum", with a model of St Peter's in Rome and portraits of all the popes, warrants a visit.

Surroundings

★ Grande-Anse

Cariboo Highway (Highway 97)

E 7

Province: British Columbia

See British Columbia

Information

The Cariboo Highway largely follows the route of the Cariboo Trail and Cariboo Waggon Road, which led from Lillooet (see Vancouver) to the gold-rush regions in the Cariboo Mountains. However, the present Cariboo Highway 97 begins at the TransCanada Highway (see entry) near Cache Creek and connects the latter with Yellowhead Highway (see entry) further to the north near Prince George, a distance of 445km/276 miles. From there it is known as the "John Hart Highway" and continues further north to create a link between the TransCanada Highway and Vancouver and Dawson Creek, where the Alaska Highway begins. In a southerly direction the Highway initially follows the TransCanada Highway eastwards, then turns off with three alternative routes into Okanagan Valley (see entry) and links up with the east–west link road, Crowsnest Highway (Highway 3; see entry), which runs near to the USA–Canadian border.

Cariboo Highway

History

The first gold-seekers, on hearing news of great finds of gold in the interior of British Columbia, came north from California, initially following the rocky Cariboo Trail along the Fraser River. In 1862 the governor of the province, Sir James Douglas, had a road 6m/20ft wide and 640km/400 miles long laid into the interior to take wagons and ox-carts; by 1865 it was completed as far as the Barkerville goldfields. Several travellers' rests were built along the way; names such as "100 Mile House" or "150 Mile House" still remind us of these mainly modest stations which have long since disappeared.

Although the new Waggon Road actually started in Yale, skirted Lillooet and did not meet the old Cariboo Trail until it reached Clinton, for some curious reason the miles were counted starting from Lillooet which, following the boom period in the early 1860s, had lost much of its importance. In Lillooet, which today lies 75km/47 miles west of Highway 97, there is a tablet recalling the "0" miles mark of the old Cariboo Waggon Road.

Cache Creek

Cache Creek, lying 670m/2200ft above sea-level and with a population of 1000, was at one time a busy centre for freight going north or east. From here "Bernard's Express", a stage-coach service, ran for 50 years; it could reach Barkerville in four days.

Clinton

40km/25 miles: Clinton (pop. 800; 887m/2912ft), originally called "47 Mile House", was an important traffic junction during the Cariboo gold-rush. In 1861 a road led from here via Pavilion Mountain to Lillooet; today it is a gravel road usable only in summer. Clinton has so far retained the atmosphere of a pionering town, and a number of the "19th c.-type" ranches take in paying guests.

At 1419 Cariboo Highway stands the old brick-built schoolhouse dating from 1892; today it houses the South Cariboo Historical Museum; open: July–Aug. daily 10am–8pm. Its exhibits reflect the pioneering period and the old Waggon Road. The many lakes in the vicinity are very popular with anglers.

Winter on Cariboo Highway

116km/72 miles: 100 Mile House (pop. 2000; 930m/3052ft), a centre for the remote ranches round about and the site of two modern saw-mills, gets its name from the old Cariboo Waggon Road. This is where the "100 Mile Roadhouse" was opened in 1862. One of the original red Bernard's Express mail coaches stands in front of the Red Coach Inn as a reminder of the past. In 1912 the Marquess of Exeter purchased more than 6000ha/15,000 acres of land around here for his extensive Bridge Creek Ranch, which the family still owns.

100 Mile House

The historical 108 Mile House, 13km/8 miles north of here, is currently a Heritage Site Museum.

11km/7 miles south of the town is the turn-off to Highway 24. This winds through some charming countryside to Little Fort 110km/68 miles away on Highway 5 (Yellowhead Highway, South). A few miles further north is the township of Clearwater and the approach road through Clearwater Valley to Wells Gray Provincial Park.

Little Fort, Clearwater, Wells Gray

Access to the western part of Wells Gray Provincial Park is by way of an 88km/55 mile long approach road. The 35km/22 mile long Canim Lake, charmingly situated in the mountains, and Mahood Lake – which is 19km/12 miles long, with a camp site at its western end, and forms part of the provincial park – are very popular with canoeing enthusiasts.

★Canim Lake, ★Mahood Lake

Mahood and Canim River Falls, together with Deception Falls, are favourites with walkers.

140km/87 miles: in recent years tourist facilities (including boat-hire) have sprung up along the 19km/12 mile long Lac La Hache with its beautiful bathing beaches.

★Lac La Hache

204km/127 miles: Williams Lake (pop. 10,000; 586m/1923ft) lies in the centre of the Cariboo region. As well as the timber industry, cattle-rearing and mining of copper molybdenum, tourism – with the attractions of fishing and hunting for wild animals – plays an ever more important role.

Williams Lake

In the vicinity can be found numerous traces of the gold-rush period and the William Lake Museum at 1148 Broadway, open: May–Sept. daily 9am–6pm, provides information about this. A special attraction is a small reactivated gold-mine.

Each year, on the first week-end in July, one of Canada's larger rodeos, the Williams Lake Stampede, takes place here.

There is a detour from Williams Lake to Highway 20 – a gravel road usually suitable for driving in summer – which leads through some charming countryside and for 480km/300 miles west through the sparsely inhabitated Chilcotin or Fraser Plateau with its huge ranches, an area which is reasonably dry because it lies in the rain shadow of the glaciated coastal mountain range. The route then continues via the coastal range of mountains to Bella Coola, the only port on the Pacific coast between Prince Rupert and Lake Powell which has a road-link.

Highway 20 West

Chilcotin Plateau

Highway 20 – only the first 113km/70 miles as far as Alexis Creek and the last 60km/37 miles or so in the Bella Coola Valley are made-up – links the few remote settlements along the frontier with the still largely undeveloped wilderness and opens up some really unspoiled and original hunting and fishing grounds. Several ranches will take in paying guests for riding holidays. Alexis Creek, with a population of about 100, provides supplies and provisions to the 1000 or so people who live by the Chilcotin River.

In Tatla Lake, a small township 69km/43 miles further west with a restaurant, school, shop, post-office and medical station, a road branches off to the Coastal Mountains. The shimmering turquoise waters of Tatlayoko Lake are highly attractive; here visitors can enjoy Alpine Wilderness Adventures, ranch holidays, treks with pack-horses in the Coast Mountains and fishing. A few miles further west rises British Columbia's highest mountain peak, Mount Waddington, which is 4016m/13,180ft high.

Tatla Lake

Cariboo Highway

Anahim Lake

Anahim Lake (142km/88 miles), at the western end of the Chilcotin Plateau and a westerly provisions centre, is a starting-out point for wilderness tours. A certain degree of "outdoor experience" and a locally knowledgeable guide are recommended.

Tweedsmuir Prov. Park (South)

From here the road climbs up to Heckman Pass (1524m/5060ft) in Tweedsmuir Provincial Park, which covers an area of 9810sq.km/3787sq.miles, making it the largest such park in British Columbia. The road then zigzags its way down to Bella Coola Valley, surrounded by snow and ice-capped peaks.

Rainbow National Conservation Area

The southern part of the park, better reached along Highway 20 (for the northern part see Yellowhead Highway), is an undeveloped wilderness. In the east, in the Rainbow Nature Conservancy Area, the Rainbow Range – including Tsitsutl Peak 2478m/8133ft – protrudes sharply up from the plateau which itself is some 1350m/4430ft above sea-level at its centre. This mountain range resembles a massive cathedral of volcanic origin and unusual coloration. In the west tower the glaciated peaks of the rugged Coastal Mountains.

★Hunlen Falls

The spectacular Hunlen Falls at the northern end of Turner Lake are an outstanding sight. The water plunges down from a height of 260m/853ft, making them the highest waterfalls in the whole of Canada. It takes a day's trek to reach them; there is a primitive tent-site by Turner Lake. During the autumn salmon season large numbers of grizzly and black bear find their way to the Atnarko River (visitors should exercise caution). There is limited basic accommodation to be had in Tweedsmir Lodge by the Atnarko River and in Tweedsmuir Wilderness Centre.

Alexander Mackenzie Heritage Trail

This exhausting trek through wild country takes at least three weeks and follows in the footsteps of Alexander Mackenzie in 1793. The path leads from West Road (Blackwater) River – between Quesnel and Prince George – to Burnt Bridge Creek on Highway 20, and has become well-known even outside Canada. After covering about 80km/50 miles the road passes through an extremely charming part of Tweedsmuir Provincial Park; information and a trail guide can be obtained from The Alexander Mackenzie Trail Association, P.O. Box 425, Kelowna, B.C. V1Y 1Y1.

Bella Coola

The little Indian fishing village of Bella Coola (pop. 2000) at the end of Highway 20 lies in a protected spot on North Bentinck Arm, a fiord which reaches far inland. On the northern shore of Dean Channel west of Bella Coola there is a plaque on "Mackenzie's Rock" in memory of Alexander Mackenzie, who in 1793 became the first European to cross the whole of the North American continent. He and his Indian guide followed the Indian "Grease Trail", an old trade route along which the coastal Indians transported fish-oil, dried fish, berries or cedar-bark far into the interior in order to barter them for elk and buffalo hides, beaver-fur and obsidian. When he reached the western end of his journey Mackenzie inscribed on a rock the words "Alex Mackenzie, from Canada, by Land, the 22nd day of July 1793". This rock now stands in the Sir Alexander Mackenzie Provincial Park and can be reached only by boat or seaplane from Bella Coola.

From 1869 onwards the Hudson's Bay Company had an outpost here for thirteen years, but it was not until 1894 that some 90 or so Norwegian settlers and fishermen established a colony here. The little museum in the town centre (open: June–Sept. Mon.–Fri. 10am–4pm) includes in its exhibits some items which these settlers from Norway brought with them.

Quesnel

325km/200 miles: The town of Quesnel, 545m/1790ft above sea-level and with a population of 9000, lies at the confluence of the Quesnel and Fraser Rivers. It is the centre of the northern Cariboo region and proudly calls itself "Gold Pan City" in memory of the 1860 gold-rush. Various old buildings have been restored, such as the Hudson's Bay Company Trading Post of 1867, the Cornish Wheel, a giant water-wheel used at the time of the gold-rush, and Bohanon House, a lovingly restored dwelling.

The Quesnel & District Museum at 707 Carson Ave./Highway 97 (open: May–Sept. Tues.–Sun. 10am–5pm) documents the history of settlers in the region, including gold-diggers, farmers, lumberjacks and ranchers as well as Indians and Chinese.

Billy Barker Days are held every July as a reminder of the gold-rush period.

33km/20 miles east of Wells along a gravel road brings the visitor to Bowron Lake Provincial Park. This magnificent region, mainly an untamed wilderness, covers an area of 1231sq.km/475sq.miles. Ever popular are canoe tours on the eleven lakes in the park covering a total of 116km/72 miles and lasting eight to ten days; linked one with the other by five rivers, these lakes are surrounded by the massive peaks of the Cariboo Mountains rising to heights of up to 2530m/8300ft. There are only seven occasions when the pleasure of canoeing has to be interrupted by the need to convey the canoe to the next stretch of water, the maximum length to carry it being 3km/2 miles; mosquitoes can be a nuisance.

★Bowron Lake Provincial Park

Most of the time is spent paddling along still or gently flowing waters. There are 45 places where overnight stays can be made in small tents equipped with bear-proof platforms in order to keep food stocks safe, simple toilet facilities and some with cooking shelters. Canoes can be hired at two lodges at the park entrance; information and maps can be obtained from the Nature House at the northern end of Bowron Lake, where those going on a canoe tour must sign themselves in and out. Outward-bound experience, physical fitness and suitable equipment are essential.

In summer the number of permits issued for the total round trip is limited to 50 canoeists per day. Bowron Lake and the straggling Spectacle Lakes are suitable for shorter boat trips – without the need to carry the boat across land.

Information: Ministry of Environment & Parks, District Manager, Parks and Outdoor Recreation Division, RR1, Dunsmuir Road, Lac La Hache, B.C. V0K 1T0; tel. (604) 396–72 25.

Charlevoix

Province: Québec

Charlevoix is the name given to the stretch of country along the left bank of the St Lawrence River, from Côte de Beaupré as far as Saguenay. It gets its name from the Jesuit François Xavier De-Charlevoix (1682–1761), who published the first historical record of Canada in 1744. Extensive forests, mountains and the St Lawrence give Charlevoix its charm.

Location

The first settlers arrived in Charlevoix early in the 18th c., when farmers, hunters and lumberjacks began to put down roots here in small numbers, at first in Petite-Rivière-St-François, then in Baie-St-Paul and on the Île aux Coudres.

History and economy

After 1760 many Scottish Highlanders emigrated to Charlevoix. The Scottish ancestry of their descendants is still to be found in the names commonly met in this area, such as Warren, Harvey or Blackburn.

Before the first road was built in 1824 the St Lawrence River provided the only means of access. As a result professions linked with sea-faring continued to dominate here into the 20th c. Today the woodworking industry, with giant resources at its command, still plays an important role

Sights along the Charlevoix

From St-Joseph-de-la-Rive boats ply to Île aux Coudres, which lies in the Baie-St-Paul, about 3km/2 miles off the bank of the St Lawrence. Jacques Cartier was the first to land here on September 6th 1535 and gave it its

Île aux Coudres

present name because of the large number of hazelnut bushes he found growing on the island.

With its many stone houses and windmills the Île aux Coudres must be one of the most idyllic regions of Québec province.

On September 7th 1535 the famous Guillaume le Breton, one of the two priests who had accompanied Cartier on his expedition, celebrated the first mass to be held in the new French colony. There is a memorial to this event in St-Bernard. In St-Louis visitors can explore the interior of one of the many ships which have run aground here. The schooner "Mont-St-Louis" today houses the "Musée des voitures d'eau", which is open daily in summer, and provides background on the history of sea-faring in this area. Also worth a visit are the two 18th c. Desgagné windmills and Maison Leclerc in La Baleine which contains some old Québec furniture; the latter is open daily in summer 10am–6pm.

Pointe-au-Pic

In the upper-class villa district of Pointe-au-Pic can be found one of the oldest hotels in Canada, the luxury Manoir Richelieu.

La Malbaie

The name of this little industrial town, which translates into English as "Bad Bay", is attributed to Samuel de Champlain, whose ship ran aground here in 1608.

Port-au-Persil

From the enchanting hamlet of Port-au-Persil there is a wonderful view of the Île aux Lièvres.

Charlottetown R 8

Province: Prince Edward Island · Île Prince Edouard
Population: 16,000

Charlottetown, the smallest of all Canadian provincial capitals, lies in the middle of a fertile agricultural region, the produce of which is shipped from its harbour. It is a quiet old country town with pretty Colonial and Victorian buildings, and although new parts are being added the centre of Charlottetown remains unaltered, and the restored harbour district makes it particularly interesting. The red stone fronts of the old buildings and the "gingerbread" architecture of the wooden houses in the side-streets are all so reminiscent of the past. In Great George Street a whole block of houses has been renovated.

The town centre is very compact and it is easy to see everything on foot.

History

After Prince Edward Island had been conquered by the British Charlottetown was founded in 1764 and named after the wife of King George III. It was elevated to town status in 1855. It has been named "The Cradle of the Federation" because of the conference held here in 1864 which led to the unification of Canada.

Sights

★ Confederation Centre of the Arts

The ultra-modern Confederation Centre of Arts on the corner of Grafton Street and Queen Street was opened in 1964 as Canada's national monument to the Confederation. Every Canadian citizen paid fifteen cents towards the cost of the building and continues to pay towards its maintenance. Inside will be found an art gallery, a museum, a provincial library, a memorial hall, two theatres and a restaurant.

The museum is on the ground floor, the entrance being on the side opposite Province House (open: July–Aug. daily 10am–8pm; other times of the year daily except Mon. 10am–5pm).

In the foyer stands a very beautiful sculpture in chrome and crystal decorated with the coats-of-arms of each Canadian province; it was a gift from the USA to mark the centenary of the Confederation of Canada.

In the art gallery on the third floor some magnificent works by modern Canadian artists are on display. One room is devoted to Robert Harris, one

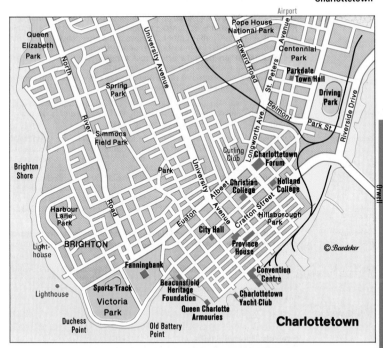

Airport

Queen
Elizabeth
Park

Pope House
National Park

Centennial
Park

Parkdale
Town Hall

Driving
Park

Spring
Park

Simmons
Field Park

Brighton
Shore

Curling
Club

Charlottetown
Forum

Park

Christian
College

Holland
College

Harbour
Lane
Park

Hillsborough
Park

Light-
house

BRIGHTON

City Hall

Province
House

© *Baedeker*

Lighthouse

Fanningbank

Sports Track

Victoria
Park

Beaconsfield
Heritage
Foundation

Convention
Centre

Charlottetown
Yacht Club

Charlottetown

Duchess
Point

Old Battery
Point

Queen Charlotte
Armouries

Orwell

of Canada's most renowned painters from the turn of the century. Also well
worth seeing is the soapstone sculpture of Mother and Child by Inukpuk, a
master of Inuit art.

The Charlotte Town Festival, held in the Confederation Centre from June
to September, offers excellent entertainment; The highlights are visits by
guest stars with shows and musical performances, including the annually
performed musical version of the successful play "Anne of Green Gables".

Near the Confederation Centre stands Province House, the "Birthplace of
Canada". This three-storey sandstone building was constructed as the
colonial government building in 1843–47. Other buildings were pulled
down in 1963 to make room for the Confederation Centre. Today Province
House is the seat of the Parliament of Prince Edward Island; open: June–
Sept. daily 9am–8pm; at other times of the year 9am–5pm.

The Confederation Chamber, where discussions were held in 1864 on the
Confederation of Canada, has been returned to its original condition.
Photographs and documents of this historic event are also on display. The
parliamentary rooms are also open to visitors.

★Province House
National Historic
Site

Standing to the east of Province House, St Paul's Anglican Church of red
sandstone was built in 1747 and is the island's oldest Protestant church.

St Paul's Anglican
Church

St James Presbyterian Church, better known as simply "The Kirk", has
some impressive stained glass windows and old relics from the island of
Iona, the first part of Scotland to become converted to Christianity. A
granite block standing on a marble slab in the north wall comes from St
Mary's Cathedral on Iona.

St James
Presbyterian
Church,
"The Kirk"

163

Chilliwack

St Dunstan's Basilica	To the south of Province House on the corner of Great George Street and Richmond Street stands St Dunstan's Basilica, built in 1898 in the Gothic style, the seat of the Roman Catholic diocese of the province. It is one of the largest buildings of its kind in eastern Canada and famed for its altar with its beautiful Italian carving and a superb rose window. A walk along Richmond Street and Kent Street to its north with their gabled houses and extensive parks and gardens provides an impressive reminder of Charlottetown's Victorian heritage.
St Peter's Cathedral	St Peter's Cathedral in the north-west corner of Rochford Square was built in 1879. The 1888 chapel was designed by W. C. Harris and is decorated with murals by his famous brother Robert Harris.
Beaconsfield	At the beginning of Kent Street stands Beaconsfield, a villa designed by W. C. Harris and built in 1877, with lace-like wooden decoration, a mansard roof and a graceful dome – a prime example of Victorian architecture. It now houses the Prince Edward Island Museum, the offices of the Heritage Foundation, the Centre for Genealogical Research and a bookshop which specialises in publications relating to the island. From time to time exhibitions of local history are held here, and the interior design of this lovely old house itself makes a visit well worthwhile. Admission is free; open: Mon.–Fri. 10am–4pm.
Government House	The white edifice of Government House built in Colonial style on the top of a hill, can still be seen. After 1835 it became the official seat of the Governor of the island.
Fort Edward	Also in Victoria Park and looking down on the harbour stands Fort Edward, built in 1805. It is one of the fortifications along the harbour entrance and from it there is a view over the said entrance to Fort Amherst.

Chilliwack   E 8

	Province: British Columbia Population: 42,000. Altitude: 10m/33ft
Information	See British Columbia
	240km/150 miles east of Vancouver lies Chillawack, a striving rural town which proudly calls itself the "Green Heart" of British Columbia. Yale Road, the old meandering road to Rosedale, passes through fields of hops and vegetables and pastureland. Farmers offer their produce for sale at the roadside. Chilliwack – its name comes from the Indian word meaning "valley of many rivers" – dates from 1858, when Volker Vedder settled here. He had crossed the continent in an ox-wagon and was the first settler in this fertile valley.
Museum	Chilliwack Museum is devoted to the culture of the Salish Indians and of the pioneering period. It is situated at Evergreen Hall, 9291 Corbould St. (open: Mon.–Fri. 9am–4.30pm, Sat. 10am–4pm). The Canadian Military Engineers Museum is to be found at Canadian Forces Base Chilliwack, Vedder Crossing (open: Sun. 1–4pm, and in summer also on Tues.–Fri. 10am–4pm). On display are weapons and militaria collected since 1815, together with a diorama of the Battle of Waterloo.
Cultus lake	14km/8¾ miles south-west of Chilliwack in the midst of wooded hills lies Cultus Lake, 5km/3 miles long. It is one of the most popular lakeside leisure resorts in the south of the province, with a park and recreational area. In the north on Cultus Lake Waterpark there are water-chutes and a go-cart track.
Chilliwack Lake	Near Vedder Crossing Chilliwack Lake Road branches off into the charming mountain landscape by the USA border north of the Cascade Mountain Range. For the most part the road follows the enchanting valley of the Chilliwach River, where there are opportunities for white-water canoeing and rafting as well as fishing.

After a further 64km/40 miles, the last 15km/9 miles of which are gravel, the road comes to Chilliwack Lake, a beautiful lake surrounded by mountains over 2000m/6600ft high and very popular with water-sports enthusiasts and anglers alike. Canoes can be hired from Western Canoeing in Abbotsford.

250km/155 miles: Here, at the junction with Highway 9, a number of tourist attractions have grown up in recent years.

Bridal Falls
Tourist Area

Flintstone Bedrock City is a leisure park with themes and figures from the animated cartoon film of the Flintstone family. Life-sized figures of Wilma and Fred Flintstone, Barney Rubble and Dino greet the visitors. Open: May and Sept. Sat. and Sun. only; mid-June–beginning Sept. daily, 9am–8pm.

Flintstone Bedrock
City

Between April and October the 10ha/25 acres of Minter Gardens offer lavish displays and charming gardens and open areas divided into ten different theme parks. Open: Apr.–Oct. daily from 9am.

Minter Gardens

Open from the end of May, the Trans-Canada Waterslides offer five swimming-pools with water-chutes. A mini-golf course adjoins.

Trans-Canada
Waterslides

From the rest-area it is a three-quarters of an hour walk through a forest of spruce and cedar to the impressive 60m/200ft high Bridal Veil Falls.

Bridal Veil Falls
Provincial Park

Churchill

Province: Manitoba
Population: 1500. Altitude: 30m/99ft

Parks Canada, Bayfront Plaza

Informaton

By air: from Winnipeg, The Pas or Thompson
By rail: from Winnipeg.

Access

Inuits or aboriginals lived in the Churchill region at least as long ago as 1700 B.C. The first European settlers arrived when the Danish seafarer Jens Munck spent the winter of 1619–20 here during his unsuccessful search for the Northwest Passage. Of his original crew of 65 only Munck and two sailors survived the winter to return to Denmark. In 1717 the Hudson's Bay Company built a trading-post in Churchill. Between 1731 and 1771 Fort Prince of Wales was built.
    Churchill, popularly known as the "Polar Bear Capital of the World" and an important corn transporting centre, lies on the harsh rocky coast of Hudson Bay. It is the terminus of the Hudson Bay Railway which was completed in 1929 by 3000 men who had to struggle through freezing conditions and bogs.
    The spectacular aurora borealis lights up the long sub-arctic nights.

History

In and around the town there is a thriving animal kingdom, including some species not found anywhere else in the world. It is a paradise for bird-lovers. Countless geese, cranes and 200 other species of birds pass along the coast of Hudson's Bay and through the town on their way to their nesting sites in the Arctic. For a number of years now even the rare and beautiful Ross gull, which originates from Siberia, has been nesting here.
    Various kinds of seals surface in the harbour, and the protected beluga whales frolic in the waters between June and early September. Caribou can also be spotted along the coast at that time of year.
    In autumn polar bears wander onto the ice-floes in the bay to hunt seals. The visitors who come here every year can go on tours in tundra-buggies – giant large-wheeled vehicles – of the places where the bears collect.

Fauna and flora

Along the harsh coast trees have been lashed by the wind and withered away. In spring – which starts in the middle of June – and autumn the Arctic flora, lichen and miniature bushes present a marvellously colourful scene.

Visitor Reception Centre

In the Visitor Reception centre at Bayport Plaza, which is open June–mid-Sept. daily 9am–6pm, films are shown on various subjects, such as polar bears, the construction of the railroad and the Arctic landscape, and furs, muskets and trade goods used by the Hudson's Bay Company in the 18th and 19th c. are also on display.

★★ Inuit Museum

The excellent Inuit Museum in Vérendrye St. is open: Mon. 1–5pm, Tues.–Sat. 9am–noon and 1–5pm. Its exhibits include Inuit works of art and tools dating from the Pre-Dorset (1700 B.C.) through the Dorset and Thule cultures to the present day, and information is also provided on the fauna of the North.

★ Fort Prince of Wales

The large and partly restored Fort Prince of Wales, a National Historic Park accessible by boat and open in July and August, lies on the other side of the river. It was built by the Hudson's Bay Company in the 18th c. in order to defend the interests of the English fur trade in the New World. A start was made on its construction in 1732, with workers, horses and oxen shipped over from England. Forty years later this outstanding building with its extremely beautiful masonry was finally finished. In 1782 the fort, its garrison led by Samuel Hearne, fell without a struggle into the hands of the French, who then destroyed it.

At each corner stands a lozenge-shaped bulwark; one was a storehouse, the second a carpenter's workshop, the third a stable and the fourth a powder magazine. Inside the walls is a gallery for cannon. On the ground floor can be seen the remains of the commandant's quarters, the provisions store and barracks.

Cape Merry

On the Cape Merry coast on the eastern side of the river mouth, 3km/2 miles from the town, stand heaps of giant grey blocks of quarzite, which were smoothed and rounded by retreating glaciers. On the soft tundra grass between the rocks grows a magnificent plethora of plants, including willow, dwarf cranberries, bear-berries and crowberries.

Here stood a stone bastion which was supposed to protect the fort. One of the six original cannon and a part of the powder magazine can still be seen. A mound of stones is in memory of the Danish Captain Jens Munk who landed here in 1619 with two ships. There is also a tablet here in honour of Thomas Button; in 1612 he became the first European to reach the mouth of the Churchill River.

Cochrane   N 8

Province: Ontario Population: 5000

Information

Cochrane Timiskaming Travel Association, P.O. Box 1162, Timmins, Ontario, P4N 7H9; tel. (705) 264–95 89.

Access

From North Bay (see entry) about 370km/230 miles north on the Trans-Canada Highway.

This little mining and industrial town situated in the district of the same name in north-eastern Ontario grew up early in the 20th c. as a result of the legendary finds of gold. Its own iron and steel industries combined with its location at the rail junction of the Ontario Northland Railway linking it to the north and the east–west line of the Canadian Pacific Railway made it an important loading and transportation centre for the minerals mined throughout the region. As a gateway to the as yet undeveloped hinterland south of James Bay the town is now a valued and busy place where trappers, outfitters and those in search of adventure meet and set out on their journeys.

A locomotive with four wagons, reconstructed interiors, historical imple- **Railway & Pioneer**
ments and photographs from the pioneering period provide the visitor with **Museum**
a vivid picture of the history of the James Bay frontier. The museum is open
daily mid-June–Labour Day.

This nature park near Cochrane is ideal for walks, camping and fishing. **Greenwater**
Provincial Park

The 300km/190 mile stretch of railway between Cochrane and Moosonee **★Polar Bear**
was built in 1932 and for a long time thereafter remained the only link with **Express**
the region at the mouth of the Moose River. A one-day excursion from
Cochrane involves a five and a half hour journey on the legendary Polar
Bear Express through the untamed wilderness. In the summer months the
train travels each way every day except Fridays, and three days a week in
winter. Anyone with more time to spend and who wants to get a genuine
feel of the hunting and trapping atmosphere should take the slower train
which stops at all stations on the way.
   More detailed information available from Ontario Northland Railway,
Passenger Service Department, North Bay, Ontario, P1B 8L3.
Tel. (705) 472–45 00.

See entry **Moosonee**

Columbia River   F 7/8

Province: British Columbia

See British Columbia **Information**

The Columbia River rises in the Kootenay District, in the south-east of **Course**
British Columbia at the foot of the Kootenay National Park (see entry), a part
of the western edge of the Rocky Mountains. First it flows north along a
deeply slashed valley – known as the Rocky Mountains Trench – which was
formed as the result of tectonic folding of the earth's crust. As these
geological deformations were accompanied by strong volcanic activity
many places with hot springs were formed on the edge of the valley, such
as Fairmont Hot Springs and Radium Hot Spring.
   Initially the Columbia River flows round the Columbia Mountain ranges,
which consist of several chains – the Purcell, Selkirk, Cariboo and
Monashee Mountains – rising to more than 3000m/9850ft. In Glacier
National Park (see entry) they reach heights of 3390m/11,125ft. Rogers
Pass, 1327m/4355ft up, was an ideal route for the TransCanada Railway and
the TransCanada Highway to wind its way over the Columbia Mountains.
   South of the Cariboo Mountains – which extend as far as the Fraser River,
another important river system in British Columbia –the Columbia River is
diverted southwards. The Mica Dam blocks off the river for the production
of hydro-electric power. The Columbia now flows southward along the
Monashee Mountains. Numerous dams have been built in this wide
canyon in order to provide water-power, including the Revelstoke Dam,
Whatshany Dam and others, forming elongated lakes, such as Revelstoke
Lake and Upper Arrow Lake. Numerous tributaries flowing down from the
adjoining mountain chains and often fed by melting glaciers provide the
Columbia with ample supplies of water. In spring, when snow melts in
Canada's most snowy regions, the water level can be too high.
   After passing the USA border the Columbia is again frequently dammed
and now flows along the Columbia Plateau, the northernmost of the three
great intermontane highlands of the USA, where flat tertiary layers of
basalt lava are frequently found.
   After 1840km/1150 miles the Columbia reaches the Pacific in Oregon. Its
delta is about 56km/35 miles long and 11km/7 miles wide. In all the Columbia has a catchment area of 775,000sq.km/300,000sq.miles. Only parts of it

Valley of the Columbia River

are fully navigable, however; smallish ships can sail as far as 250km/150 miles inland.

Côte Nord

Q–S 7/8

Province: Québec

Information

See Québec

The Côte Nord stretches along the left bank of the St Lawrence River between Saguenay and the Belle-Île Straits. Because of its relatively un-spoiled hinterland with extensive coniferous forests and numerous rivers North Shore – especially Sept-Îles – is an ideal setting-out point for walkers, anglers and hunters.

Blanc-Sablon

The road for vehicular traffic ends in Havre-St-Pierre, the region further north being accessible by ferry. The firm of Relais Nordik provides a ferry-service from Rimouski, Sept-Îles, Port-Menier and Havre-St-Pierre between early April and the end of September.

Port-Cartier

Founded in 1958, the fast-expanding town of Port-Cartier has the second most important harbour, after that of Sept-Îles, for the export of the iron-ore mined in Nouveau Québec and Labrador.

Sept-Îles

Sept-Îles, the largest town on the North Shore, lies at the entrance to Sept-Îles Bay. It was given its name by Jacques Cartier, who discovered this bay with its seven islands in 1535. In 1650 Father Jean Dequen founded a mission here. Following colonisation in the middle of the 19th c., mainly fishermen and lumberjacks settled here.

On the Côte Nord

Mingan is a little fishing port on the Détroit Jacques Cartier (Jacques Cartier Strait). In Ste-Geneviève Bay, near the coast between Mingan and Havre-St-Pierre, lies a string of forty islands, the Îles de Mingan. This archipelago is a National Park and a paradise for birds.

★★Mingan
National Park

Since 1975 the Île d'Anticosti has been under the control of the Ministry of Tourism, Hunting and Fishing in Québec. Discovered by Jacques Cartier in 1534, the island has a population of only 300 or so. The climate is damp and cold and the island often disappears under a mantle of thick fog.

Île d'Anticosti

Anyone wishing to wander on the island needs a permit from the above-mentioned ministry.

Note

Crowsnest Highway (Highway 3: Dewdney Trail)

E–G 7/8

Province: British Columbia, Alberta

Crowsnest Highway is the scenic and, in parts, quite charming south-lying road in Western Canada which provides the east–west link via Crowsnest Pass (1396m/4581ft). Near Hope (see entry), 154km/96 miles east of Vancouver, this less busy highway branches off from the TransCanada Highway and passes close to the USA border through the south-east of British Columbia and over the Rocky Mountains into southern Alberta. After nearly 2000km/1240 miles it again meets up with TransCanada Highway 1 in Medicine Hat near the Saskatchewan border. It then continues in the shape of the "Red Coat Trail", a tourist route consisting mainly of by-roads through unspoilt rural countryside in the south of Saskatchewan and Manitoba as far as Winnipeg; to a large extent this is the route taken in 1874 by the men of the North West Mounted Police when they came West to restore law and order. After the Oregon treaty of 1846 had decreed that the lower

Historical origin

reaches of the Columbia River south of the 49th Parallel should belong to the USA the Hudson's Bay Company was obliged to find new routes along which to transport their goods into the interior of British Columbia. In the middle of the 19th c. they built a trading post in Hope. In 1859 gold was discovered by the Kettle and Similkameen Rivers, whereupon the governor, James Douglas, appointed two young British engineers, E. Dewdney and W. Moberly, to construct the first "mule-track" along the 120km/75 mile stretch between Hope and Vermilion Forks, now Princetown. Further discoveries of gold in the Kootenay region persuaded his successor Seymour to build a 480km/300 mile extension of the road through the wilderness to Wild Horse Creek in the Rocky Mountains, so that gold being found would not be lost to the United States simply because of a lack of an adequate road link with Vancouver. At that time it took at least three weeks to travel from the Okanagan Valley to Wild Horse Creek in the Rockies. Today long stretches of the modern Crowsnest Highway 3 follow the route chosen by Dewdney.

The Crowsnest Highway crosses five massive mountain chains, the Cascade, Monashee, Selkirk, Purcell and Rocky Mountains, winding through passes up to 1774m/5822ft high and sampling almost all British Columbia's varied scenery, from the rain-forests of the Pacific Coast through the fruit plantations of the climatically-favoured Okanagan valley (see entry), the green farmlands around Creston to the snow and ice-covered Rocky Mountains and the gently undulating prairies of southern Alberta.

Between Princetown and Keremeos there is good wild-water canoeing on the Similkameen River. In Princetown Highway 5A branches off to the north to Merritt and Kamloops (see entry).

★★Drive on Crowsnest Highway from Hope to Medicine Hat

Keremeos

204km/127 miles: Keremeos (pop. 1000; 413m/1355ft), the fruit-growing centre situated in the middle of the fertile Simikameen valley, a protected

An old mill near Keremeos

area, boasts that it has more fruit-stalls per inhabitant than any other town in Canada. During the harvest season the roadside is littered with stalls set up by the farmers and fruit-growers.

In the first half of the 19th c. the Hudson's Bay Company ran a ranch in Keremeos, and in the 1860s the first settlers came to the warm valley, a Mexican built the first and for a long time the only corn-mill, great herds of cattle spent the winter on the wide valley floor and in spring were driven along the Dewdney Trail to Hope. In 1897 F. X. Richter, an immigrant from Bohemia, planted the first fruit plantation. After the introduction of artificial irrigation meadows gave way to fields of vegetables and fruit plantations. In 1907 the first canning factory was built.

What was once the prison cell in the court building on 6th Ave. and 6th St. today houses the little Keremeos Museum (open: June–Aug. 9am–5pm).

On Upper Bench Road, 3km/2 miles north via Highway 3, will be found Price's Grist Mill, a corn-mill with a water-wheel, built in 1876. The mill, together with a small historical museum in the former general store, is open to visitors May–Sept. Wed.–Sun. 9am–5pm.

Highway 3 leads from Keremeos direct into the Okanagan Valley (see entry) at Penedicton, 50km/30 miles north.

5km/3 miles before it reaches Keremeos the 24km/15 mile approach road turns off along the Ashnola River to the Cathedral Provincial Park. This untamed mountain wilderness on the border with Washington USA, with its deep-blue lakes, steep peaks more than 2000m/6600ft high, imposing rock formations and Alpine-like meadows is particularly attractive to those keen on "the great outdoors".

Cathedral Provincial Park

This park in the Okanagan Mountain Range, covering some 330sq.km/ 205sq.miles, is the area between the thick, damp forests of the Cascade Mountains and the arid Okanagan Valley. When walking through it the visitor can observe deer, mountain-goats or Californian thick-horned sheep, as well as marmot. The centre of the park is the area surrounding the charming Cathedral Lakes; note, however, that it is not accessible by private car – only all-wheel drive vehicles can cope with the rough road, and walkers and guests of the Cathedral Lakes Resort by Quiniscoe Lake, which is not run by the parks authority, will be collected and driven there.

There is a walk lasting several hours from Quiniscoe Lake and by way of Glacier Lake to Stone City, a group of huge granite blocks, and to Giant Cleft. This great cleft was left after the removal of the geomorphologically softer volcanic materials that had been forced into the granite. Other interesting geological formations along the way are Devil's Woodpile, a group of basalt columns so named because they are thought to resemble a pile of wood gathered by the Devil for his fires in Hell, as well as "Smokey the Bear", a prominent rock overhang which looks very much like the figure of a bear which is used by the Forestry Commission in their campaign to prevent forest fires.

On clear days there is a magnificent view from the crest of the Cathedral Range as far as Mount Rainier 290km/180 miles to the south-west which, being 4392m/14,415ft high, is the fifth highest peak in the USA, or of the snow-capped peak of Mount Baker (3285m/10,781ft) to the west.

Crowsnest Highway 3 now continues southward for 30km/19 miles along the winding Simikameen Valley and then by way of the Richter Pass (682m/2238ft) into the lower Okanagan Valley.

252km/156 miles: Osoyoos (pop. 3000; 277m/909ft), only 6km/3¾ miles from the US frontier, lies at the southern end of the "Canadian Desert". From here as far as Okanagan Falls, some 43km/27 miles to the north, stretches a northern outcrop of the semi-desert region which extends from Mexico and Arizona as far as Montana and Washington. The average annual rainfall is less than 200mm/8in., and summer temperatures between 40°C and 50°C/104°F and 122°F are not uncommon. Keep an eye open for rattlesnakes when walking in this region.

Osoyoos

This sandy tongue of land, known since 1811 and extending through almost the whole of Osoyoos Lake, was favoured as a storage place by the

Indians and fur-hunters. The first ranch was built here more than 50 years later. Around 1890 more than 20,000 cattle grazed between Keremeos and Osoyoos.

Since the early 20th c., however, intensive fruit and vegetable cultivation has formed the basis of the life of the region, aided by between 120 and 180 frost-free days each year. From March to May thousand of apricot, cherry, peach and apple trees transform the valley into a sea of blossom. The "Cherry Festival" is held every year. In summer Osoyoos Lake, with its sandy beaches and water temperatures of 24°C/75°F, is a favourite place for bathers.

This region resembles the dry areas of southern California and is also reminiscent of parts of the Iberian Peninsula; to give the place a unique appearance it was decided in 1975 to introduce a Spanish style of building. Since then the main street has been dominated by whitewashed buildings with gleaming red roofs and wrought-iron grilles.

In Community Park there is a small museum (open: July–Sept. 10am–5.30pm), which provides details of the town's history and of the methods of artificial irrigation and cultivation of fruit in the region. Works of art and utensils produced by Okanagan Indians can also be purchased here, and tourist information is available.

Greenwood   335km/208 miles: (pop. 1000; 750m/2461ft). Evidence of the wealth formerly enjoyed by this once flourishing mining town is provided by the magnificent buildings in the town centre, such as Greenwood Inn (1899), Sacred Heart Catholic Church (1900), the vicarage (1906), the court buildings (1902) and the post-office built in 1915. In the 1880s ore deposits were discovered in the mountains. In the town's heyday more than 2000 people lived here. Of the smelting works set up in 1901 by the B. C. Copper Co., which once employed 400 men, only the ruins of the 37m/121ft high chimney in the Lotzgar Memorial Park and the slag-heaps still remain. As early as 1918 the fall in copper prices after the end of the First World War led

Fruit for sale on the Crowsnest Highway

to the closure of this and of the two other plants in the vicinity. Greenwood was on the way to becoming a ghost town when in 1942 some 1200 Japanese living in western Canada were interned here and some remained when the war ended.

In the new Greenwood Museum and Tourist Information Centre at Copper St./Highway 3 (open: mid-May–mid-Sept. daily 9am–6pm), the history of mining in this region is illustrated.

In Phoenix 8km/5 miles away, which for twenty years was one of the richest mining towns in Boundary Country, only two graveyards and a memorial remain. In 1919 Granby Consolidated Mining closed down its copper mine and the people left. When mining was resumed in 1955 the remains of the town disappeared under a giant open-cast mine which was itself closed down in 1978.

378km/235 miles: From the top of Phoenix Mountain (1105m/3627ft) there is a fine view to be had of Grand Forks (pop. 3000; 516m/1693ft) situated in the broad and sunny Sunshine Valley at the confluence of Kettle River and Granby River. The first cattle-breeders settled here at the end of the 19th c., and in 1894 the little town of Grand Forks was founded. During the mining boom three smelting plants were built in the town, and dark slag-heaps remain as a reminder. Granby Mine ran one of the largest of such plants in the British Empire here, with a daily capacity of up to 5000 tonnes. | Grand Forks

Together with fruit and vegetable growing, the paper factories and slag-processing plants today constitute the main industries, and modern Grand Forks boasts excellent potato crops. A large number of wooden buildings in the Victorian style bear witness to the former wealth of this little town; for example, various buildings at "Golden Heights" can be visited in the course of the Heritage Home Tour. In the charming Grand Forks Boundary Museum & Tourist Information Centre at 7370 5th St./Highway 3 (open: mid-May–mid-Oct. daily 9am–5pm, to 8pm in summer) the brief but highly varied history of Boundary Country is documented.

Conspicuous in the townscape and surounding countryside are several sizeable dwelling-houses. They were built early in the 20th c. by the Doukhobors, members of a spiritualist sect formed in Russia in the 18th c. under the influence of the Quakers. After suffering persecution in Russia they came to Canada in 1898 and to Grand Forks in 1909. About one thousand of them lived in large communal dwellings each housing up to 35 or 40 people, built a saw-mill and began to irrigate the land and plant fruit trees.

Mountain View Doukhobor Museum on Hardy Road, 5km/3 miles to the north-west, which is open June–Sept. daily 9am–7pm, gives an insight into the beliefs and lives of this group of people, whose influence can still be felt in the town's restaurants. On the first week-end in August each year the "Sunshine & Borschtsch Festival" is celebrated.

20km/12½ miles further east Highway 3 crosses the US 395; 207km/129 miles down the latter road lies the town of Spokane in the US state of Washington.

400km/250 miles: Christina Lake (pop. 2000; 600m/1969ft) lies by the lake of the same name 20km/12½ miles long but at the most 1½km/1 mile wide, which is very popular with water sports enthusiasts because of its clear warm water and sandy banks, and with anglers because of its abundance of fish. | Christina Lake

36km/22 miles of the historic Dewdney trail across the mountains have been reconstructed between Christina Lake and Rossland. The present Highway 3, laid down in 1962, deviates from this old road and now climbs up to the 1535m/5038ft high Bonanza Pass. This mountain area marks the beginning of the Kootenay Region with its chain of mountains running north to south and the deeply-slashed valleys and lakes, earning it its familiar name of the "Switzerland of North America".

473km/294 miles: Castlegar (pop. 7000; 610m/2000ft), at the confluence of the Kootenay and Columbia Rivers, was for many years an important traffic | Castlegar junction in the Kootenay region. Today the main employment is in the timber industry and the sawmill, while the CanCel cellulose factory has 750 workers.

North of the town the 51m/167ft high Hugh Keenleyside Dam controls the flow of the Columbia from Arrow Lake, providing electric power and guarding against flooding. There is a lock for small boats. Boats can be chartered or rented, cycles rented and there are sightseeing flights available.

★ Doukhobor
Historic Village

Doukhobor Historic Village near the airport off Highway 3 (open: May–Sept. 9am–5pm). It provides an insight into the way of life of the Russian Doukhobors who emigrated here around the turn of the century and lived here from 1908 until the 1930s (see also Grand Forks p. 173). Typical of the settlements of the "Christian Community of Universal Brotherhood", as they called themselves, were their brick-built communal houses surrounded by working quarters. The nearby "Doukhobor Restaurant" specialises in Russian food.

Difficulties with their Canadian neighbours arose mainly with the members of a fanatical Doukhobor sect who settled in Krestova, the "Sons of Freedom" who – like almost all Doukhobors – refused to register births and deaths and rejected the state educational system as being an intrusion into their pacifist and secluded ways. They set fire to schools and protested naked in the streets against government ordinances. Time and again they threw home-made bombs on the grave in Robson Rd/Highway 3 of the founder of the settlement, Pjotr Verigin, who was killed in 1926 during an attack on a train. Today all has quietened down and most of the Doukhobors have become farmers and adjusted to the Canadian way of life. Only a few of the typical Doukhobor villages are still inhabitated.

Zuckerberg Island
Heritage Park

From 7th Ave in the town centre a suspension bridge leads to an island at the mouth of the Kootenay River, on which will be found Zuckerberg Island Heritage Park. In this park lies Chapel House, erected in the style of a Russian church and the house and studio of the Russian emigré mathematics teacher, engineer and sculptor Alexander F. Zuckerberg, who came to Castlegar to teach in 1931 at the request of the then leader of the Doukhobors, Pjotr Verigin II. Zuckerberg died in 1961 and the island started to become overgrown. However, the town council took it over in the early 1980s and the buildings were restored. Today walkways lead through the sparse woods along the river bank. Traces of Indian mud-huts and a small reconstruction serve as a reminder that for at least 3500 years the island served as winter quarters for Salish Indians living in the Kootenay region. It is thought that they built a sort of weir or dyke out of large stones from the river in order to catch salmon as they swam upstream. However, since the first dam was built across the Columbia in 1934 there have been no more salmon in the river.

A car-ferry runs from Castlegar across the Columbia River, which is not very wide here, to Robson Trail – there are Trail Rides to be had at Dry Creek Ranch – and further to the Syringa Creek Provincial Park 19km/12 miles north of Castlegar on the eastern shores of Arrow Lake. The park offers a beach, windsurfing and fishing, and there are guided natural history tours from mid-June to Labour Day.

Nelson
★ Kootenay Lake

43km/26¾ miles: Nelson (pop. 10,000; 543m/1782ft) lies in a beautiful spot on the western arm of the long and charmingly situated Kootenay Lake, surrounded by the snow and ice-covered peaks, some as high as 2000m/6500ft, of the Selkirk Mountains. This mining town which grew up at the end of the 19th c. quickly developed into a tourist centre. There are skiing regions in the surrounding area, such as the "Wild Water Ski Area", 20km/12½ miles to the south on Mount Ymir which is 2585m/8484ft high; there are chair-lifts and a ski-tow, and the top of the ski-slope is 400m/1300ft from the bottom.

Its many carefully preserved Victorian buildings give Nelson a charm all of its own, and it proudly calls itself the "Heritage Capital of the Kootenays".

63km/39 miles: Kokanee Creek Provincial Park by Kootenay Lake covers 260ha/642 acres and lies in the delta of Kokanee Creek at the foot of the Slocan Range which forms part of the Selkirk Mountains. There are sandy beaches, a camp-site, a visitors' centre and an office providing information on tours in Kokanee Glacier Provincial Park and various walks through sparse deciduous forests of alder and cottonwood-poplar and through mixed and coniferous forest higher up. The name Kokanee, which is Indian for "red fish", refers to the Kokanee salmon which spawns in Kokanee Creek and is a species of salmon which lives only in inland waters; during the spawning season in August and September there are guided explanatory tours and informative events.

Kokanee Creek
Provincial Park

Archaeologists have found signs of two seasonal Indian storage sites in the park as well as remains of settlements from the pioneering period.

West Kootenay Visitor Centre provides information on the history of the region, mining, the Kootenay (Kutenai) Indians as well as about the paddle-steamer with its paddle-wheel at the stern which used to ply on the lake. Open: July–Aug. daily 11am–9pm; other times of the year Sun. only 1–4pm.

A gravel road some 16km/10 miles long winds alongside the deeply slashed Kokanee Creek to Gibson Lake and provides access to a magnificent area of wild country in the Slocan Range of the Selkirk Mountains. Kokanee Glacier Provincial Park, covering almost 260sq.km/100sq.miles, are numerous picturesque mountain lakes as well as snow and ice-capped peaks. Most of this unspoilt mountain region lies at a height of more than 2100m/6900ft above sea-level. Kokanee Peak, 2774m/9100ft high, towers majestically above the rest. This is a splendid spot for mountain walks and climbs.

Kokanee Glacier
Provincial Park

512km/318 miles: Near Salmo (pop. 1000; 663m/2176ft) Crowsnest Highway 3 crosses Highway No. 6 which runs from Nelson to the US frontier.

Salmo

15km/9 miles to the south is the beginning of the new "Kootenay Skyway" across the southern part of the Selkirk Mountains, which winds its way up over a distance of 23km/14 miles to Kootenay Pass, 1774m/5822ft above sea-level. All along this stretch of 70km/43 miles in total the traveller will keep coming across tower-like huts from which, when there is a threat of avalanches in winter, action can be taken in good time to avoid them.

550km/342 miles: Along the pass lies Stagleap Provincial Park, named after the mountain caribou which pass through here during the short summer. At present there exists only a small herd of less than two dozen animals which, in the course of their annual wanderings, also pass through the north-eastern part of the US state of Washington and north Idaho. At the western end of Bridal Lake – which is often frozen over until June – at the foot of the 2393m/7854ft high Riddle Mountain a small visitors' centre provides information on the flora and fauna, especially about this rare species of caribou now threatened with extinction and which the American and Canadian authorities are co-operating closely to try and save.

Stagleap
Provincial Park

596km/370 miles: Creston (pop. 4000; 611m/2005ft) in the broad Kootenay Valley, surrounded by long snow-covered peaks, lies in the midst of fields of corn, strawberries and vegetables as well as fruit plantations. This land, once swamps and damp meadows, was dyked and drained at the end of the last century. Every year prior to this the untamed Kootenay River had flooded wide expanses of the fertile valley floor. By 1930 80km/50 miles of dams had been thrown up and 10,000ha/250,000 acres of arable land reclaimed. Today the town proudly calls itself the "Fruit-basket of the Kootenays" and boasts its own corn warehouses in the south of British Columbia just like those of the Canadian prairie regions.

Creston

For more than forty years the four-day "Blossom Festival" has been celebrated every May.

The dams are now a favourite spot for walks and strolls.

175

Crowsnest Highway

Creston Valley Museum

Creston Valley Museum at 219 Devon Rd./Highway 3 North (open: in summer daily 9am–5pm at other times by arrangement), is built of local stone and contains relics from the pioneering period as well as numerous works of art and everyday utensils of the Kootenay (Kutenai) Indians, including reproduction of a canoe such as was used by that tribe. Life-sized speaking dolls give information about life in the times of the early pioneers.

Creston Valley Wildlife Management Area, Creston Valley Wildlife Interpretation Centre

10km/6 miles north-west of the town, on Highway 3, in a nature reserve covering 6½sq.km/2½sq.miles, which preserves a part of the typically swampy areas of the Kootenay River delta. It has become a refuge for more than 240 species of birds – such as osprey, blue heron and countless migratory birds including "whistling swans" – as well as for elk, beaver, bears, coyotes and deer. An insight into the flora and fauna of the region is given by means of instructive nature walks, guided treks and canoe-tours, an observation tower with telescopes, and an Interpretation Centre (open: May–Oct. 9am–5pm, Mar.–Apr. restricted opening times).

From Summit Creek Recreation Area there is access to a reconstructed section of the 1865 Dewdney Trail along the south-western shores of Leach Lake.

From Creston Highway 21 leads southwards into "Panhandle", the name given to the northern extremity of the US state of Idaho.

42km/26 miles further east Highway 95 turns off to the state frontier and continues in the USA as US 95.

Crowsnest Highway 3 now winds for the next 60km/37 miles through the sparsely inhabited Purcell Mountains and, at the 653km/406 mile point on the journey, crosses from the Pacific to the Mountain Time Zone.

Cranbrook

703km/437 miles: Cranbrook (pop. 16,000; 921m/3023ft), lying in the valley between the Purcell Mountains and the Rockies, is the largest town in the south-east of British Columbia. Sheltered from the rains by the Purcell Mountains Cranbrook enjoys a dry climate with plenty of sunshine and there are some excellent excursions to be made into the charming country-side surrounding it.

In addition to tourism, the town's economy is nowadays based mainly on the timber industry, mining, cattle-rearing and service industries for the region's 70,000 or so inhabitants.

In the mid-1880s, a time of great tension between the settlers who streamed here across the Rockies when the Canadian Pacific Railway was completed and the native Kootenay Indians who feared for their traditional way of life. Colonel James Baker built a ranch here on Joseph's Prairie and fenced in grazing land. From this modest beginning the township of Cranbrook gradually grew. Later Colonel Baker became a partner in the Crowsnest Coal and Mineral Company, which won the contract to build a railway line for the CPR from Lethbridge in Alberta over Crowsnest Pass to Kootenay Lake, thus running across Baker's land. The line was completed in 1898, Baker's ranch had a link to the main line and he was able to set up a small township here.

Fort Steele 16km/10 miles away, at the time a booming mining town and provision centre for the region, was by-passed by this rail route and gradually surrendered its importance to the new town.

In the old town centre, at 10th–13th Ave. and 1st–4th St. South, a number of stately buildings from the turn of the century have been preserved; these include the City Hall, Fire Hall, Mount Baker Hotel, Tudor House Hotel (1900), the old Freemasons' Lodge and the 1902 Imperial Bank Building. "Baker's House" at 1st. St./Baker Park, the residence of the founder of the town and built in 1889, today houses some offices and also a small museum displaying some historic photographs (open: Mon.–Fri. 9am–5pm).

St Eugene Mission Church – at St Mary's Reserve, between Cranbrook and Kimberley (open: Mon.–Fri. 9am–4.30pm) was built in the 1890s for the Kootenay Indians. It is a good example of a typical Victorian wooden church.

Cranbrook Railway Museum is at 1 Van Horne St. North (open: June–Aug. daily 9am–8pm; at other times of the year Sun.–Thur. noon–5pm) has on exhibition some restored carriages dated 1929 of TransCanada Limited, the legendary train belonging to the Canadian Pacific Railway. Sleeping-cars, dining and saloon cars have been refitted with their original furnishings and show the luxurious standards enjoyed by the rail-travellers of the 1930s.

★Cranbrook
Railway
Museum

Since the 1960s, as a reminder of the pioneering days, Cranbrook has been holding "Sam Steele Days", a week-long celebration with numerous events and a procession.

A few miles beyond Cranbrook Highway 95A turns off to Kimberley; Fort Steele and Highway 3 can be reached by means of a detour of some 70km/43 miles.

Highway 95A,
Kimberley

30km/19 miles: Kimberley (pop. 7000; 1113m/3653ft) promotes itself as the "Bavarian City". A start was made in 1972 to change the appearance of this old highland mining town to a tourist resort in the Bavarian style. A "Bavarian Platzl" (square) was built in the town centre, and a pedestrian zone laid out with a small stream, flower-tubs, seats and benches, street-cafés and buskers. It also boasts what is said to be the biggest cuckoo-clock in the world. The houses are decorated with Alpine façades or are half-timbered, and the "Bavarian atmosphere" is further emphasised by the wearing of "lederhosen" and "dirndl" (Alpine dress with bodice and full skirt) by assistants in shops and bars. At the end of the square, in the library building, is the Kimberley Heritage Museum (open: July–Aug. Mon.–Sat. 9am–4.30pm, at other times of the year 1–4pm) with exhibits from Kimberley's mining past and some minerals.

Kimberley

Further attractions are the Bavarian City Mining Railway, a narrow-gauge railway at Gerry Sorenson Way (open: July–Aug. 11am–7.30pm), a guided tour through Sullivan Mine belonging to Cominco Ltd. (meeting point at Travel Infocentre, "The Hut", 255 Walinger Ave.; July–Aug. Mon.–Fri. 9am), a functioning lead and zinc mine, one of the largest of its kind, as well as the Alpine Slide and Chairlift in the Kimberley Ski and Summer Resort, 3km/2 miles from the town centre.

A charming skiing area has developed here on North Star Mountain. The distance from top to bottom is 700m/2300ft, and there are 34 descents, a chair-lift and ski-tows. In summer the chair-lift and the 800m/2625ft long summer chute are in use. From the upper station there is a magnificent view over the wide valley to the distant Rocky Mountain chain, a part of the Rocky Mountains Trench, a tectonic rift valley zone almost 1500km/930 miles long and 3 to 16km/2 to 10 miles wide running parallel to the Rockies.

North Star
Mountain

A Winter Festival is held on the second week-end in February, and later in the year there is the "July Festival" when beer is consumed by the gallon! After 55km/34 miles Highway 95 joins Highway 95/93, which leads southwards to Fort Steele, a journey of 33km/20 miles.

To the north is a scenically charming route by way of Fairmont Hot Springs (pop. 200; 800m/2625ft). Here there is a bathing centre, opened in 1922, with four thermal pools with temperatures of up 42°C/108°F (open: daily 8am–10pm). More than 750,000 visitors come here every year. There are helicopter flights and flights over the glaciers, trail riding June–Sept. and an 18-hole golf course.

The town of Invermere (pop. 2000; 859m/2820ft) lies by Lake Windermere which is drained by the Columbia River; here windsurfing, trail riding and hang-gliding can be enjoyed. Windermere Valley Pioneer Museum at 622 3rd. St. (open: June–Aug. daily 10am–4.30pm), is an historical museum built round the old Canadian Pacific Railway station.

Invermere

In a nearby mountain valley lies Panorama Resort in the middle of a large skiing area where snow is assured. The slopes are 1156m/3794ft from top

177

to bottom, with 33 descents, four chair-lifts and a ski-tow. This was used for skiing races in the World Cup Competition. After Radium Hot Springs the route continues to Kootenay National Park – 74km/46 miles in all – or further on Highway 95 downstream by the Columbia River to Golden (see entry) by the TransCanada Highway 1 (180km/112 miles).

Fort Steele 720km/447 miles: see Fort Steele Provincial Park

Fernie 812km/505 miles: Fernie (pop. 6000; 1009m/3312ft), a small mining township at the foot of Trinity Mountain, lies in the middle of the Rocky Mountains and in recent years has developed into an all-the-year-round holiday centre. In winter Fernie Snow Holiday Resport offers excellent winter sports facilities, especially for families. The slopes are 640m/2100ft, with 34 descents, three chair-lifts and three ski-tows.

Fernie and District Museum was opened in 1979 in the old vicarage of the 1905 church at 502–5th Ave. (open: July–Aug. daily 1.30–5pm), and its exhibits illustrate the lives of the early pioneers in this region as well as coal-mining at the turn of the century.

In 1908 a catastrophic fire devastated this young mining town. When it was rebuilt many of the typical wooden houses were replaced by sturdier brick and tile buildings, some of which still remain. The Court Building and Leroux Mansion are fine examples of this style of building.

During working hours Weststar Mining Ltd. and Fording Coal Ltd. offer guided tours through their large open-cast coal-mines; information is obtainable from Travel Info Centre, Rotary Park.

★Crowsnest Pass From Sparwood Crowsnest Highway 3 turns south-east and after 18km/11 miles at Crowsnest Pass it crosses the border into Alberta.

Crowsnest To the east of the pass, in Crowsnest Valley, sprawls the parish of Crowsnest (pop. 8000), formed from the mining settlements of Blairmore, Coleman, Frank, Bellevue and Hillcrest Mines.

When the Canadian Pacific Railway line was laid across the pass in 1897–98 conditions improved for mining the rich coal deposits in the region, and settlers and miners flocked here from all over the world.

Lundbreck Falls Some 50km/31 miles east of the border the Crowsnest River plunges down 12m/40ft into a gorge.

Pincher Creek 923km/573 miles: Highway 6 turn-off to the south leads to the Waterton Glacier International Peace Park (see entry) and to the US frontier. The township of Pincher Creek (pop. 4000) lies a few miles to the south in the midst of the gently undulating foothills. It is the gateway to the Rocky Mountains and the already mentioned National Park 48km/30 miles further south. Summer activities here include trail riding, walking in the charming countryside, water-sports and fishing. In winter Westcastle Park, 47km/29 miles south-west on Highway 507/744, is a popular ski resort, with slopes measuring 520m/1700ft and three ski-tows.

In 1875 the North West Mounted Police built a stud-farm here in the wide grasslands on the eastern edge of the Rockies for the troops stationed in Fort MacLeod. At the end of the 18th c. the first cattle-breeders and settlers followed their example. In the Pincher Creek Museum and Kootenay (kutenai) Brown Historical Park at James Ave./Grove St. (open: daily in summer 10am–8pm, 1–4pm at other times of the year) the history of the region is depicted. Several buildings and log cabins built true to the originals, including that of Kootenay (kutenai) Brown, an Irishman who was the first man to settle here in 1889, are open to visitors.

Cypress Hills Provincial Park G/H 8

Provinces: Alberta, Saskatchewan
Area: 200sq.km/77sq.miles

Travel Alberta, 3rd Floor, 10155 102nd St., Edmonton, Alta., T5J 4L6.   Information
   Tel. (403) 427–43 21
Travel Saskatchewan, Information Centre, 1919 Saskatchewan Dr., Regina,
   Saska., S4P 3V7; tel. 1–800–667–75 38 (no charge).

Cypress Hills Provincial Park – access to which is by way of the Buffalo Trail   ★★ Topography
(Highway 40) – lies about 60km/37 miles south-east of Medicine Hat by the
TransCanada Highway. This impressive piece of countryside extends into
the neighbouring province of Saskatchewan. The plateaux are covered
with rich forests in the midst of a flat, dry prairie. Scientists assume that
about 30 million years ago a river running westwards deposited both
coarse and fine sediment over an area which thus gradually became higher
and was then shaped by the forces of erosion.
   In the middle of the prairie wooded mountainous country rises to as high
as 1462m/4800ft above sea-level. During the last Ice Age this region was
not covered by glaciers. When John Palliser arrived here in 1859 when on
an expedition he described it as a green oasis in the middle of the dry
prairies he had spent weeks in crossing. The hills rising 500m/1640ft above
the flat surrounding countryside represent an eco-system which is unusual
for this part of Canada, and the vegetation is somewhat reminiscent of
Alpine regions. Until the early 20th c. these hills provided a refuge for many
species of animals threatened by the increasing numbers of settlers on the
plains; the last bison was shot here in 1882, the last puma in 1912 and the
last wolf in 1925. Today only a few wild turkeys still live here.
   For more than 7000 years the Indians came to Cypress Hills and its
sheltered valleys abounding in water. In the 1870s the hills provided hide-
outs for American traders selling illegal whisky to the Indians.
   Being 1392m/4568 high, the Cypress Hills are the highest in Saskatchewan. The region has pine forests and rare wild flowers and animals such as
the wapiti and the endangered trumpet-swan. In many areas prairie falcons, some rare species of song-birds and elk can be seen. The park has
some very instructive walks – that to Bald Butte being particularly picturesque – and also contains an artificial lake. Its main attractions include the
Conglomerate Cliffs as well as a swimming-pool, beach, golf-course, riding
stables, camp sites and tennis courts. In winter cross-country skiing and
rides on snowmobiles are possible.

Fort Walsh (open: May–Sept. 9am–6pm) was one of the most important   ★★ **Fort Walsh**
posts set up by the North West Mounted Police in western Canada in the   **National Historic**
19th c. It was built in 1875 under the leadership of James Walsh in order to   **Park**
put an end to the illegal whisky trade, and was in use for eight years. During
that time the troops fought for law and order and negotiated with the
whisky traders, the native Indians and the thousands of Sioux warriors who
sought refuge in Canada after clashes with the US cavalry. Following the
building of the railway and the return of the Sioux people to the USA the
fort was dismantled and left. For many years after that the area was used
privately for cattle-rearing. In 1942 the Royal Canadian Mounted Police
acquired the land and built a ranch on which to breed horses for the army.
When the RCMP were transferred to Ontario the estate became a National
Park. Since then extensive historical and archaeological research has been
carried out, being the first stage in a comprehensive reconstruction programme for the fort. This reconstruction, which will include the still existing ranch buildings, will give an idea of what Fort Walsh looked like during
its heyday in 1880.
   The first thing to do on arriving in the park is to call at the Visitor
Reception Centre. Here in the large gallery an exhibition illustrates the
highlights of the region's rich history, such as the Mounted Police, the
people of the plains, the fur and whisky traders, government expeditions
and the town of Fort Walsh.
   The fort buildings are made of whitewashed tree-trunks, one with a roof
of turfs, the others with pointed roofs to keep out the damp.

The Royal Canadian Mounted Police in action

Sitting Bull	In 1877 an important meeting was held in the officers' mess, attended by Chief Sitting Bull and other Sioux chiefs as well as representatives of an American commission. The aim was to persuade the Sioux to return to the USA.
Other buildings	Other buildings of interest are the police commissioner's house, the smithy, a carpenter's shop, stables, the guard-room as well as arms and goods stores.
Cemetery	Near the fort lies the North West Mounted Police and civilian cemetery.
Salomon's Trading Post, Farewell's Trading Post	Some 3km/2 miles further south will be found Salomon's Post (not open to visitors) and Farewell's Trading Post (open: daily 9am–5.30pm) furnished with items used by the American traders who crossed the border and sold whisky illegally to the Indians. In the 1870s rifles and furs were the most important commodity. The present-day posts are reconstructions built on the site of the original buildings which were burnt down in 1873.

Farewell's Trading Post consists of four buildings, namely, the shop containing brightly-coloured clothing, pearls, furs, blankets and canned goods, the barrack dormitories, Farewell's house and that of his assistant.

Near Fort Walsh a flourishing town grew up, which in its heyday had several hundred inhabitants. Embankments and cellars are all that remain.

Dawson   B 5

Administrative unit: Yukon Territory
Population: 1900

Information	Visitor Reception Centre, Front St.; tel. (403) 993–55 66

Dawson, formerly known as Dawson City, lies in the west of the Yukon Territory (see entry), roughly 100km/60 miles from the Canadian frontier at the confluence of the Klondike and Yukon Rivers.

Dawson was founded and flourished during the time of the gold-rush along the Klondike and Yukon Rivers (see Yukon Territory). A few months after George Washington Carmack found gold-nuggets the size of his fist in Bonanza Creek in 1896 thousands of gold-seekers streamed into the Yukon and Klondike region hoping to stumble on equally rich veins. Dawson City grew up in the middle of it all.

History

Most of the early gold-seekers came ill-equipped with provisions. Later Canada did pass a law making it a rule that every person had to bring with him clothing and food for at least one year, but at the end of 1897 Dawson already had 3500 inhabitants who were not adequately provided for. When ships were unable to get through with stocks of provisions before the onset of winter a large proportion of the townspeople were evacuated to an outpost 350 miles away, but in spite of these measures many did not live to see the spring, when the longed-for wagons finally got through with supplies. A number of traders were then able to make their fortune selling food on Dawson market.

Gold-seekers arriving in the summer of 1898 soon realised that all the profitable claims had been staked long before. The uncrowned "Kings of the Klondike" subsequently turned the town into the "San Francisco of the North" and used their gold to finance the building of luxurious albeit dubious hotels, saloons, dance-halls and casinos and acquired a number of shipping companies. The ships brought in the finest Paris fashions, Persian carpets, expensive furniture and delicacies to Dawson; and the French can-can took the saloons and dance-halls by storm the theatre built by Arizona Charlie Meadows, saw the appearance of the legendary Kitty Rockwell alias Klondike Kate. One of the Klondike's best-known adventurers was "Big Alex" McDonald, owner of numerous claims to gold and who at one time made 5500 dollars a day and amassed a fortune of seven million dollars. "Big Alex" became so famous that he even earned a private audience with the Pope in Rome. For most of the gold-seekers however Dawson meant a daily struggle for survival with only very faint hopes of stumbling on a rich find, and many ended up working in the large mines for men like Big Alex. No sooner were gold nuggets found or wages earned than they were spent in the saloons, and it was not uncommon for hundreds of thousands of dollars to change hands in one night at the gaming tables. After an initial "Wild West" era posts of the North West Mounted Police were set up to guarantee law and order and to control the border with Alaska. When new gold finds were reported near Nome in Alaska in August 1899 the first 8000 gold-seekers returned west, soon to be followed by further people from Dawson, so that by the 1930s the town had a population of only about 4000. Dawson retained its position as capital of the Yukon Territory until 1953, when it had to cede it to the up-and-coming Whitehorse (see entry).

Today Dawson has the appearance of a Wild West scene from a Hollywood film, the only difference being that here everything is genuine. Since the 1960s over thirty buildings have been restored by the Canadian Office for the Preservation of Historical Monuments and more wooden houses have been built in the style of the turn of the century. In the early 1980s the whole town was declared an historical area and is now visited every summer by more than 17,000 tourists wishing to see can-can shows, visit the old goldfields and savour the atmosphere of days gone by, when the glamour and the misery of the gold-rush left their stamp on the town.

One of the most impressive reminders of the past is Palace Grand Theatre in King Street, built in 1899 by the American Arizona Charlie Meadows and restored in 1962 by order of the Canadian Government. During the day visitors can inspect the theatre, and in the evening (except Thursdays)

Sights

★Palace Grand Theatre

Dawson

Winter 1899 in Dawson City

Can-can girls, as in the time of the Gold Rush

"Gaslight Follies" present an authentic 1898 vaudeville show with songs, can-can dancers and cabaret.

Canada's only legalised casino is Diamond Tooth Gertie's Gambling Hall on Fourth Avenue at the corner of Queen Street, which has been faithfully restored. It owes its name to one of the "Queens of the Dance Halls" of 1898. As well as blackjack, roulette and poker there are also can-can shows.

★ Diamond Tooth Gertie's Gambling Hall

Dawson City Museum on 5th Avenue gives an insight into the town's history as well as that of the Klondike (see entry) from the start of the gold-rush to the present day. A slide show about Dempster Highway (see entry) gives a good impression of the only highway in Canada to cross the polar circle.

Municipal museum

In the wooden cabin where the American writer Jack London (actually John Griffith London, 1876–1916) lived in 1897 readings are given daily from his novels, such as "Call of the Wild" (1903), "The Sea Wolf" (1904) and "The Lure of Gold" (1910).

Jack London's Cabin

In 8th Avenue stands the log-cabin built in 1898 by Robert Service, known as the "Bard of the Yukon" and who around the turn of the century composed numerous poems and ballads, including "The Funeral of Sam McGee" and "The Shooting of Dan McGrew".

Robert Service's Cabin

Along Front Street several buildings dating from the time of the gold-rush are still standing. The most notable are the Federal Building, once the seat of government before it was moved to Whitehorse (see entry), the Old Post Office of 1901, Madame Tremblay's shop complete with articles of clothing like those worn by the gold-seekers, the Canadian Bank of Commerce, where gold was once melted down, and the 1922 paddle-steamer S.S. "Keno" – now a museum – the last of over 200 "sternwheelers" which plied on the Yukon between Dawson and Whitehorse (see entry) until the end of the 1850s.

Front Street

★ S.S. "Keno"

A favourite outing, usually combined with a visit to the theatre, is the trip to the hill known as Midnight Dome, about 7km/5 miles south-east of the town, from where a fantastic panoramic view of Dawson and the Yukon River, the Klondike Valley and the surrounding Ogilvie Mountains can be enjoyed. Many of the gold-seekers found their last resting-place in the cemetery on the side of the hill.

★ Midnight Dome

A trip along the Yukon River on the "Yukon Lou" miniature steamer or the luxury catamaran, the M.V. "Klondike", will be found most rewarding. These trips take in the "cemetery" of the old paddle-steamers.

Surroundings

Trips on the Yukon

All around the town are many sites where prospectors used to sift and pan for gold. Anyone wishing to follow in the footsteps of George Carmack can visit the spot by Bonanza Creek where he made his discovery claim. The Visitor Reception Centre in Dawson will provide information about tours to the gold-fields and mines in Bonanza Creek and Guggieville as well as in Bear Creek Complex 13km/8 miles to the south, the massive machines of which were still being used to quarry gold deposits until 1966.

Search for gold

The Top of the World Highway owes its name to the many plateaux and ranges of hills – mainly above the tree-line – over which it runs on its route between Dawson and then westwards to Alaska. The border is passed after covering a 107km/66 mile stretch of road with some of the most impressive panoramic views imaginable. From the border it is a further 181km/112 miles to Tetlin Junction, where the Alaska Highway is reached.

★Top of the World Highway

Southwards from Dawson the Klondike Highway (see Klondike) provides the link with Whitehorse (see entry).

★Klondike Highway

Dempster Highway   B/C 4/5

Administrative Units: Yukon Territory/Northwest Territories

Information   See Yukon, Northwest Territories

The only public road in North America which actually extends beyond the Arctic Circle starts 40km/25 miles south of Dawson City in the Yukon Territory and ends some 740km/460 miles further north in Inuvik in the Mackenzie Delta (Northwest Territories) on the Arctic coast.

This largely untarred road threads its way through a mainly untamed wilderness with areas of varying vegetation and marked variations in climate, temperatures ranging from 35°C/95°F in summer to −45°C/−49°F in winter.

As early as the beginning of this century a trail, following an old Indian trade route, led from Dawson to Fort McPherson and was patrolled by the Northwest Mounted Police. This path received sad notoriety in the winter of 1911 when a police patrol strayed from the route and were later found dead. The present highway is named after the leader of search party which found them, Corporal W. D. Dempster. When, in the 1950s, a start was made on searching for raw materials in this largely unexplored region the first few miles of the rough road were made up. Oil and gas exploration in the Beaufort Sea speeded up work on the road – necessary to provide a link and transport provisions to the sites – as far as the mouth of Mackenzie River (see entry) and this was completed in 1979.

Note   A thorough servicing of the car is strongly recommended before setting off along this highway. Petrol stations with repair facilities will be found only in Eagle Plains, Fort McPherson and Inuvik.

Route followed by the Dempster Highway

Ogilvie Mountains   The highway begins on the southern slopes of the Ogilvie Mountains some 40km/25 miles south of Dawson (see entry). After about 70km/44 miles, just before North Fork Pass (1290m/4234ft) it reaches the timber line. From the pass can be seen the wedge-shaped Tombstone Mountain standing out against the background of hills.

The Blackstone Highlands on the far side of the pass are home to several species of birds and dall sheep.

Eagle Plains   Eagle Plains Hotel, one of the few places on the edge of the Highlands which offer accommodation, lies about halfway between Dawson and Inuvik and offers the only opportunity of enjoying a restaurant meal and sleeping in a hotel bed instead of a tent.

Arctic Circle   After travelling a further 403km/250 miles the Arctic Circle is reached. The highway climbs up the slopes of the Richardson Mountains, almost bare of trees and covered in detritus and boulders. After crossing the high land of the Peel Plateau the road descends gradually to the plains of the Mackenzie Delta.

Peel River   Peel River, crossed by a ferry, is one of the longest tributaries of the Mackenzie River (see entry).

Fort McPherson   On the east bank of the Peel River lies Fort McPherson an old fur-trading station, like most of the settlements near the Mackenzie River. Today it is home to about 820 Dene Indians. The highway then threads its way through a forest region rich in lakes to the Arctic Red River (see Mackenzie River, Arctic Red River), where the ferry crosses the Mackenzie.

Inuvik   See entry.

Edmonton   G 7

Province: Alberta. Altitude: 668m/2192ft
Population: 572,000 (Metropolitan Area: 756,000)

Edmonton Convention & Tourism Authority, 9597 Jasper Ave., No. 104,
   Edmonton, Alberta, T5J 1N9; tel. (403) 422–55 05, 988–54 55 (near the
   Convention Centre).
Travel Alberta, 15th Floor, 10025 Jasper Ave., Edmonton, Alberta T5J 3Z3.
Tel. (403) 427–43 21, in Alberta 1–800–222–65 01, in Canada and USA
   1–800–661–88 88.

Access

By air:
Edmonton International Airport, 29km/18 miles south; national and in-
   ternational flights.
Edmonton Municipal Airport, north-west of the town centre; regional
   flights.
Coach shuttle-services between the town centre and the two airports.

By rail:
VIA Rail (10004–104 Ave.). Routes: Edmonton–Jasper–Vancouver;
Edmonton–Prince George/Prince Rupert; Edmonton–Saskatoon–
Winnipeg.

By coach;
Greyhound Bus Lines (Depot 10324 103 ST.); Red Arrow Express between
Edmonton–Calgary, Edmonton–Fort McMurray.

Edmonton Transit; bus routes to all parts of the city and its suburbs.   City buses

Light Rail Transit (LRT); underground and suburban lines between Corona   LRT
Station (city centre, Jasper Ave./108 St.) and the north-eastern suburb of
Clareview.

Edmonton, the capital of Alberta, stretches along both banks of North
Saskatchewan River in roughly the centre of the province. This dynamic
and rapidly growing metropolis is the fifth largest and most northerly city
in Canada. Edmonton lies in the northern extremities of the great Canadian
prairies and is the centre of the wheat-growing region which extends to the
north and to the east but soon changes to vast expanses of forest and lakes.
Since its very beginnings the city has been the gateway to the north and an
important communications centre.
   Edmonton competes with Calgary – only 300km/190 miles to the south –
for the title of "oil capital of Canada". More than ten per cent of Canada's
total crude oil is produced from fewer than 2300 boreholes within a radius
of 40km/25 miles. Giant refineries and petro-chemical works have sprung
up in the south-eastern part of the city.
   During the last twenty years whole streets in the inner city have had to be
sacrificed to make way for hyper-modern high-rise buildings, side by side
with congress halls, leisure facilities and large shopping centres. The West
Edmonton Mall is the largest leisure and shopping centre in the world,
where even during the long cold winters, when temperatures average
−15°C/5°F, shoppers are still enticed to linger.
   In the mainly dry and warm summers many people are attracted by the
various charmingly laid-out squares, the parks along both sides of the
North Saskatchewan River and the numerous lakes around the city.
   The city has also invested in art and culture and built theatres and
museums. A start has also been made on cleaning and restoring the older
parts and buildings.
   In spite of the oil and construction boom of the 1970s and 1980s something of the typical West Canadian atmosphere can still be detected in
Edmonton.

Edmonton

The skyline of Edmonton

★★ Klondike Days

The greatest event in Edmonton's calendar is the ten-day festival known as the "Klondike Days", held every year at the end of July. The wild days of the Klondike Gold-rush of 1890 come to life once more. The citizens act out the pioneer period and don the clothes of the late 1890s. Street-parties, dancing, parades, gold-panning competitions liven up the whole city. The highlight, however, is the "World Championship Sourdough Raft Race" on the North Saskatchewan River.

History

Edmonton was founded on the fur trade. Back in the 17th c. hunters from the two rival fur companies made their way through the fur-rich region of Northern Alberta. In 1795 both the North West Company (Fort Augustus) and the Hudson's Bay Company (Edmonton House) set up trading posts along the North Saskatchewan River for the Cree and Blackfoot Indians living there. The two posts were protected by a common wooden palisade almost 5m/16ft high, and soon developed into the chief administrative and supply centres for the whole of the Saskatchewan Basin. Almost everyone travelling north or to the Pacific stopped off in Edmonton.

In the 1870s the first settlers came to the region and in 1874 a base for the Royal Canadian Mounted Police was set up. The timber industry gradually began to oust the fur-trade and river traffic on the North Saskatchewan became more and more important. Initially the town's development was hampered by the decision of the Canadian Pacific Railway to build the transcontinental line through the more southerly town of Calgary, and it was not until 1891 that the railway age started in earnest for Edmonton. When in 1897/1898 the rush for gold in the Klondike (Yukon) began the town became the chief maintenance centre. Within a short time its population sextupled, and so there was no question that Edmonton would be chosen as the capital when the province of Alberta was founded in 1905.

Two new railway lines were built, and from 1915 onwards Edmonton quickly developed into the main western rail junction. More and more European immigrants settled here and in the area around. In the 1930s

VIA Station

Edmonton Downtown

103rd A

Law Courts Bldg.

Oxford Bldg. Centennial Bldg. City Hall

Greyhound Terminal

Commercial Bank Tower

Art Gallery Century Place

103rd Avenue

Four Seasons Hotel YMCA

Land Titles

Continental Bank Bldg. Trust Tower Royal Civic Centre

Sir Winston Chancery Churchill Hall Square

Eatons

TD Tower

102nd Avenue

102nd

Chancery Hall

Public Library Citadel Theatre

AGT Toll Bldg.

Beaver House Gallery

Manulife Bldg. Phipps-McKinnon Bldg.

Sun Life Place

101st A

Hudson's Bay

McLeod Bldg.

Jasper Avenue

Royal Bank Bldg. Capital Square Bldg.

Jasper

Imperial Oil Bldg. Convention Centre

IPL Tower

One Thornion Court

Standard Life Centre

Principal Plaza

Alberta College

AGT Tower

Edmonton Journal

Château Lacombe McDougall Hill

YWCA Avenue

200 m

© Baedeker

North Sask. River

Muttart Conservatory

bush-pilots began to take provisions to the remote settlements in the north. The building of the Alaska Highway in 1941 brought a new upturn in economic fortunes and the discovery of rich oil deposits in 1947 in Leduc 40km/25 miles to the south-west was the start of the transformation of the western provincial town into a modern industrial city.

Sights

It is suggested that a tour of the relatively small city centre should begin with a visit to the modern Congress Centre, built in 1983 at 9797 Jasper Ave., which is constructed in the form of terraces on the steep northern bank of the North Saskatchewan River.

★Edmonton Convention Centre

Opposite stands "Canada Place", an impressive post-modern skyscraper accommodating shops, business premises and some Alberta government offices.

Canada Place

A few blocks to the north the new Civic Centre has gone up in the last few years on 100th Street and around Sir Winston Churchill Square which itself takes up a whole block. The City Hall, the Court Buildings, the impressive Citadel Theatre of glass, comprising several theatres and a charming Winter Garden, the 1924 Art Gallery (open: Mon.–Wed. 10.30am–5pm, Thur., Fri. 10.30am–8pm, Sat., Sun. 11am–5pm) and the Centennial Library all form one urban development unit. To the north it adjoins the railway station built in 1966 and the CN Tower.

Civic Centre, Sir Winston Churchill Square, Citadel Theatre, Edmonton Art Gallery

To the west of the square towers Manulife Place, a new glass-built landmark. Like the neighbouring 40-storied Eaton Centre it houses shopping arcades and large businesses on several levels.

Manulife Place, Eaton Centre

A fine panoramic view of the city can be enjoyed from the 33rd floor (118m/387ft high) of the Alberta Government Telephone Tower, 10020 100 St. (open: daily in summer 10am–8pm),which was built in 1971 and houses the administrative offices of AGT.

Alberta Government Telephone Tower, Vista 33

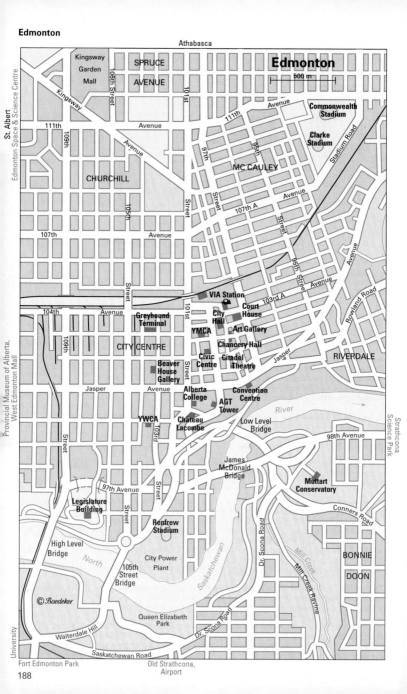

Edmonton

Provincial Museum of Alberta
Edmonton

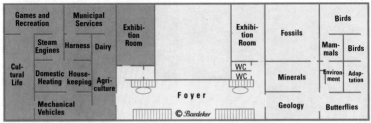

FIRST FLOOR

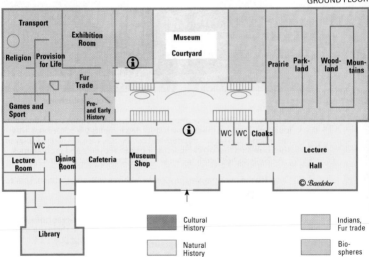

GROUND FLOOR

The small exhibition entitled "Man and Communications" provides information about historical and modern news techniques.

In the midst of a park-like garden high above the North Saskatchewan River where the last Fort Edmonton once stood, is today the site of the Government Centre together with the Legislature Building constructed in 1911/1912 (109 St./97 Ave., it is open to the public Mon.–Fri. 9am–8.30pm and Sat., Sun. 9am–4.30pm). From the terrace there is a beautiful view across the river. In the basement is the Exhibition Hall with exhibits illustrating the history, art and culture of Alberta Province.

Legislature Building

The Centennial Carillon can often be heard in the 13ha/32 acre park with its music pavilion and hothouses.

The Provincial Museum of Alberta is to be found at 12845–102 Ave. and is open daily 10am–8pm. Its four main departments provide information about the varying topography and the fauna, geology and paleontology of

★Provincial Museum of Alberta

189

Edmonton

Downtown Edmonton

Aviation Hall of Fame, Wetaskiwin

the province. Particularly impressive are the life-size models of dinosaurs found in Alberta. In the cultural history departments the culture and lives of the Indians, fur-traders, trappers and early settlers are all vividly displayed. There are also touring exhibitions and special events and programmes.

All kinds of handicraft techniques are demonstrated on Sundays.

Alberta Archives
Linked to the museum are the Alberta Archives with an exceptional collection of historical photographs.

Government House
High above the river near the museum stands Government House, built in 1912. Until 1938 it was the seat of the Lieutenant Governor of Alberta. Today it is used for official receptions and conferences; there are guided tours on Sundays.

Carriage House
Nearby stands the charming Carriage House, where the Lieutenant Governor's staff once lived and the state coach was housed.

In the surrounding parkland will be found some excellent sculptures by Canadian artists. Also worthy of note are the totem-pole erected here in 1983 and a massive fossilised tree-trunk.

Other historical buildings have been preserved to the east of the Provincial Museum.

Edmonton Space Science Centre
A few street blocks further north at Coronation Park, 142 St./111 Ave. stands the impressive modern white building of the Edmonton Space Science Museum. It is open daily 10am–10pm. Sat., Sun to 10.30pm. In the IMAX Theatre fascinating films from all over the world are shown. Adjoining is an excellent planetarium. Laser shows and sundry exhibitions are given.

★★West Edmonton Mall
West Edmonton Mall at 8770 – 170 St. on the western edge of the city (open: Mon.–Sat. 10am–10pm, Sun. 10am–8pm). At present it is the third largest covered shopping and leisure centre in the world, and was completed in

West Edmonton Mall: World Water Park

1986. The Perso-Armenian family clan of Germesian amassed 1·1 billion Canadian dollars to pay for the project and also intends to build similar centres elsewhere in the world.

Within a year from opening West Edmonton Mall became a top tourist attraction, and now has some six million visitors every year!

Mall

West Edmonton Mall with its many and varied attractions has already appeared three times in the Guiness Book of Records. Over an area the size of more than 100 football pitches there are more than 830 shops and branches of large departmental stores, over 110 restaurants, about twenty cinemas and the twelve-storied "Fantasyland Hotel". In Europa Boulevard many of the shops have European-style fronts and carry the names of international fashion designers, and in Bourbon Street, a copy of the famous street in New York, the tourist will find restaurants serving Creole food and bars serving up jazz. Among other major attractions are the very popular "Ice Palace" which hosts top quality ice-hockey matches, and the highly impressive "World Water Park" boasting an exciting range of water chutes as well as several temperate aquaria with sharks, tropical fish and penguins. There are also animal enclosures.

Canada Fantasyland

Canada Fantasyland, a large covered amusement park, offers 25 different sorts of rides. The main attraction is a roller coaster with three "loop the loops", the "Deep Sea Adventure", a real lake with four submarines, a full-scale replica of Christopher Columbus' ship, the "Santa Maria" (marriage services are conducted in the captain's cabin), and a dolphinarium.

World Water Park

The World Water Park covers 2ha/5 acres and is the world's largest indoor swimming-pool. Covered by a glass dome this giant leisure pool with artificially-induced waves has no less than 22 water-chutes.

Valley Zoo

Opened in 1959, Edmonton's Valley Zoo is at 134 St./Buena Vista Road. Open May–Sept. 10am–6pm, its main object is research into threatened animal species and keeping them for breeding.

Edmonton

River Valley

In the valley pastures of the North Saskatchewan River extends a 16km/10 mile long leisure area consisting of several parks linked one with the other; here there are excellent opportunities for long walks and cycle tours. Cycles can be rented Apr.–Sept. from River Valley Cycle Tours, 9701 100 A St.

★Fort Edmonton Park

A little way outside the city, on the south bank of the river on Whitemud Drive/Fox Drive, lies Fort Edmonton Park, open mid-May–early Sept. daily 10am–6pm, Sept.–Oct. Sat., Sun. only 1–5pm. In this open-air museum, with old buildings faithfully reconstructed and staff dressed in contemporary costume, a successful attempt has been made to reflect Edmonton's historical development. The buildings include a typical 1846 fort belonging to the Hudson's Bay Company, a street from a pioneer town of 1885 and the up-and-coming provincial capital in 1905, as well as buildings from the 1920s. Among the different forms of old transport displayed in the extensive grounds are an historic mail coach and horse-drawn wagon as well as an old tram and a steam train.

John Jantzen Nature Centre

Near Fort Edmonton Park will be found an interesting Nature Centre covering various aspects of the geology and ecology of Alberta. The rich and varied programme of events includes nature walks. The centre is open Victoria Day–Labour Day daily 10am–6pm, otherwise Mon.–Fri. 9am–4pm, Sat., Sun. 1–4pm.

Old Strathcona

Strathcona, also on the south bank of the North Saskatchewan River, was a separate town until 1912. It grew up in 1899 by the railway line to Calgary. In the former town centre, about ten blocks between Saskatchewan Drive and Whyte Avenue, some of the original buildings still remain, and restoration work has been going on since the 1970s.

Main Street

In recent years traders have been moving back into Main Street (104 St.) and those running parallel to it. Here the visitor can stroll and shop among souvenir and speciality goods shops, booksellers, boutiques and art galleries, natural food shops, European-style bistros and restaurants. Special events are held throughout the year, such as theatre festivals, jazz concerts, street parties, markets and art exhibitions.

A short walk through the historic quarter, armed with a brochure obtainable from the Old Strathcona Foundation at 8331–104 St., 2nd floor, or from the Information Centre, will enable the visitor to enjoy a number of renovated old buildings.

★University of Alberta

Further west sprawls the campus of the University of Alberta. This educational site is the second largest and the oldest of the four such colleges in the province of Alberta.

Rutherford House

At 11153 Saskatchewan Drive stands historical Rutherford House, open Victoria Day–Labour Day daily 10am–6pm, at other times of the year Sat., Sun. noon–5pm. Built in 1911, it was for a long time the residence of A. C. Rutherford, Alberta's first prime minister. The building has now been refurnished in the 1915 style and gives a good idea of the urban lifestyle enjoyed in Alberta at that time.

Staff in contemporary dress busy themselves in the house, and the programme of events is extremely varied.

★Muttart Conservatory

On the south bank, at 98 Ave./96A St. will be found four hothouses built in a most unusual pyramidal shape. They are open daily 11am–9pm during the summer months, with restricted opening times during the rest of the year. In the Tropical Pavilion a study can be made of plants native to Burma and the Fiji Islands. In the Temperate Pavilion the visitor can see American Redwood, Australian eucalyptus and magnificent magnolias, while in the Arid Pavilion plants from various desert regions of the world are displayed. There is a Show Pavilion for special exhibitions.

Muttart Conservatory

From the high ground above the river there is a beautiful view of the gleaming pyramids against the skyline of Edmonton city centre.

In the east of the city, also on the south bank of the river and on the edge of the industrial zone, Strathcona Science Park has been constructed on the site of an abandoned coal-mine. Adjoining it is the Alberta Natural Resources Science Centre, at 17th St., between Highway 16 and 16A East (open: Victoria Day–Labour Day daily 10am–6pm; other times of the year Sun. only 11am–5pm). These centres are concerned with mineral and raw material deposits in Alberta, and displays and sundry exhibits seek to explain how minerals are discovered and mined. The Energy Department, providing information about the way oil is obtained from Edmonton's sub-soil, is particulary interesting.

Strathcona
Science Park
Alberta Natural
Resources
Science Centre

Nearby, at 17th St. in Strathconal Science Park West, lies Strathcona Archaeological Centre (open: Victoria Day–Labour Day daily 10am–6pm; closed in winter). This park was constructed on the excavated site of a 5000 year-old Indian settlement. In the course of a walk through the 1·6ha/4 acre site and the archaeological laboratory scientists can be observed as they work.

Strathcona
Archaeological
Centre

Ample informative material about the history of Indian settlements can be obtained from the Archaeological Pavilion.

Archaeological
Pavilion

North of the city centre, at 9543–110 Ave., will be found the institute known as the Ukrainian Canadian Archives & Museum of Alberta (open: Mon.–Sat. 1–5pm, Sun. 2–5pm). This building houses a collection of documents relating to numerous Ukrainian pioneers who laboured under the harshest of conditions to contribute in no small degree to the opening up of the prairies of Alberta. Typical dress and traditional musical instruments are on display in the adjoining museum. Further exhibits bear witness to the rich religious and cultural customs of this ethnic group.

★Ukrainian
Canadian Archives
& Museum of
Alberta

Sights around Edmonton

★ **Elk Island National Park**

About 35km/22 miles east of Edmonton, surrounded by cornfields, meadows and townships and covering an area of almost 200sq.km/77sq.miles, lies an oasis of natural countryside, mainly hills, lakes, beaver dams, aspen forests and grassland. The main entrance to this park is on Yellowhead Highway No. 16 East or Highway 15 North. The Information Centre, about 1km/110yd north of the entrance, is open from Victoria Day–Labour Day Mon.–Sat. 10am–6pm, Sun. 8am–8pm. The Astonon Interpretative Centre by Astontin Lake, 23km/14 miles north of the main entrance, is open all the year round, viz. mid-June–Labour Day Mon.–Fri. noon–4pm, Sun. noon–5pm, at other times of the year Sat., Sun. 11am–4pm. Here the visitor will find varied leisure facilities available, including a camp-site, golf-course, bathing beach, canoes and boats for hire. There are also delightful round walks through some fascinating sections of the park.

Bison

The main attraction nowadays however is the herd of some 450 prairie bison which graze here. If one or more of these massive, shaggy beasts are not met while strolling through the park there are usually some to be found in the Buffalo Paddock. The latter should be passed quietly and at walking pace only, and visitors are warned to take care when encountering these beasts.

South of Yellowhead Highways a herd of rarer and somewhat smaller forest bison lives in a fenced-in area. Almost all the forest bison kept in zoos the world over stem from this herd.

★★ **Beaver Pond National Park**

The short walk to Beaver Pond can also be very rewarding; by keeping still and quiet observers may be fortunate enough to see the shy beavers at work on their dams or lodges.

Beaver Hills was originally the tribal home of the Sarcee Indians, who were later driven out by the Crees when they came hunting beaver for the fur-traders. By the end of the 19th c. both beaver and buffalo had been almost wiped out in this region. The Indians were followed by settlers, whose names are now remembered only by their having had lakes named after them. Fires got out of control and destroyed large areas of the original parkland and threatened the remaining herds of wild beasts. Following pressure from alarmed conservationists the remainder of the forest land was first placed under a protection order in 1899. In 1906 a federal reserve, the first of its kind for wild animals in Canada, was set up for the remaining elks (wapitis).

The bison came here a year later quite by chance. When in 1909 an attempt was made to round them all up in order to house them in their own reserve near Wainwright, about 180km/112 miles to the south-east, about 50 animals could not be found. They are the ancestors of the present herd.

In 1913 Elk Island was declared a Dominion Park and after various extensions it was made completely independent and renamed Elk Island National Park. When some almost pure forest bison were found in the 1960s in Wood Buffalo National Park 25 of them were sent here and housed in an isolated reserve in order to breed and help preserve the species.

Information: The Superintendent, Elk Island National Park, Site 4 R.R.1, Fort Saskatchewan, Alberta, T8L 2N7; tel. 9998–3781.

★ **Ukrainian Cultural Heritage Village**

A few miles further along Yellowhead Highway 16, about 50km/30 miles east of Edmonton, the Ukrainian Cultural Heritage Village grew up in the 1970s. This fascinating open-air museum (open: Victoria Day–Labour Day daily 10am–6pm; Labour Day–Thanksgiving Day daily 10am–4pm, at other times of the year Mon.–Fri. 10am–4pm) commemorates the large numbers of immigrants who came to the eastern part of central Alberta from the Ukraine and Bukovina. The Visitor Centre provides information on the reasons behind these migrations, which continued from 1891 right up to the 1920s, and about the extreme conditions under which most of them had to exist during their early years in the New World as well as about the way the Ukrainian settlements developed. Various historical buildings, including an old railway station, a church, a shop, a smithy, a schoolhouse and some typical farmsteads have all been reconstructed. This is also aided by means of "living history", with people in old costumes or historical dress "living in" the houses and displaying old crafts. Folk-dance performances and horse and cart rides are particularly popular.

Polar Park lies 22km/14 miles east of Edmonton at Sherwood Park, Highway 14, and is open daily from 8am–sunset. The owners are striving to keep, in surroundings which are as natural as possible, about 100 species of animals typical of the northern latitudes, such as snow-leopards, Siberian tigers, polar bears, wolves and caribou.

Polar Park

The town of St Albert (pop. 30,000) on the Sturgeon River about 17km/11 miles north-west of Edmonton, was founded in 1861 by Father Albert Lacombe (1827–1916). For 60 long years this missionary applied himself tirelessly to helping the prairie Indians and the Métis, all in the name of Christ. His mission station quickly became the largest Métis community in the Canadian west.

St Albert

Father Lacombe Chapel

Between 1870 and 1900 large numbers of French-Canadian settlers came to the region around St Albert, and the old Métis and Indian mission became a town and was an episcopal seat until 1912 (cathedral built 1871). Father Lacombe's modest wooden chapel at 7 St Vital Ave. has been lovingly restored and is open from Victoria Day–Labour Day daily 10am–6pm.

Granit House, built in 1882 as a hospital, was later the bishop's residence. It also is open to visitors.

Granit House

Of considerable interest is the St Albert Heritage Museum at 5 St Anne St. (open: Mon.–Fri. 10am–6pm, Sat., Sun. noon–5pm) which gives a good insight into the history of the mission station.

St Albert Heritage Museum

The principal focus of interest in the small town of Wetaskiwin, about 65km/40 miles south of Edmonton, is Canada's Aviation Hall of Fame (open daily 10am–5pm). Old aircraft and a variety of other exhibits recall numerous of the country's aeronautical pioneers.

Wetaskiwin
★Canada's Aviation Hall of Fame

Ellesmere Island

L–R 1/2

Administrative Unit: Northwest Territories, District of Franklin

TravelArctic, Yellowknife, NWT, X1A 2L9; tel. (403) 873–72 00.

Information

Ellesmere Island lies in the extreme north of Canada. Measuring 800km/500 miles from north to south between latitudes 76° and 83°N, it covers an area of 212,000sq.km/81,850sq.miles, making it the second largest island – after Baffin Island (see entry) – on the Canadian archipelago; the United Kingdom, by comparison, covers 242,496sq.km/93,629sq.miles. William Baffin had reached the south-east of the island as early as 1616, and in the second half of the 19th c. attempts were made to explore even further north by way of the narrow Smith Sound, which separates Ellesmere Island from Greenland. It was from Cape Columbia that Peary set out in 1909 to walk to the North Pole.

Location

Traces of prehistoric settlements have been found on the south coast of Ellesmere Island, and there is also evidence of Thule culture. The "recent" history of Grise Fiord, the northernmost Canadian Inuit community, began in 1953 when the Canadian government moved four Inuit families from the east coast of Hudson Bay to the south-east of Ellesmere Island, without taking account of the fact that these people were accustomed to quite different living conditions. Here, only 1500km/930 miles from the North

Grise Fiord Project

Pole, average temperatures in March lie between −35°C and −25°C/−31°F and −13°F, and in July between 0°C and 6°C/32°F and 43°F, and winter is spent in total darkness, making the climate even more inhospitable to man than Labrador; to make matters worse, while on Hudson Bay rivers and lakes provide drinking water all the year round, on Ellesmere drift ice has to be melted down for this purpose, and only an expert can tell which is freshwater ice. The reasons behind the move were a certain colonialist attitude on the part of the government linked with a growing unfavourable situation in the Hudson Bay region brought about by increases in population and a resultant strain on resources. After the Québec Indians had spent a winter under very difficult conditions a family from Pond Inlet on Baffin Island who were familiar with the conditions was sent to help them. In spite of the good conditions for hunting – the "Northwest Territories Explorer's Guide" for 1986 stated "Inuit families moved here to settle because of the rich stocks of animals to hunt . . ." – the Inuits never felt at home here and after nearly forty years many considered leaving. The two Inuit groups have failed to integrate and have retained their separate languages and customs; even as late as 1962, when Grise Fiord was founded as a settlement, their houses were kept separate. In spite of Grise Fjord being a show-piece settlement with a number of advantages – relatively well provided with the benefits of "civilisation" – these are more than offset by the disadvantages of a small, still somewhat "artificial" settlement with a number of social problems, not the least of which is finding a suitable spouse.

At present Grise Fiord (Ausuittuq, or "place where it never thaws") has rather more than one hundred inhabitants and is trying to share in the benefits of Arctic tourism; again in the words of the "Explorer's Guide" it offers "the most beautiful landscape in the NWT" and tours by canoe and snowmobile to view Arctic birds and polar bears! Grise Fiord can be reached by air from Yellowknife and Iqaluit via Resolute Bay.

Eureka	The Eureka Radio and Weather Station, run by the USA and Canada since 1948, lies at latitude 80°N on the west coast, separated from Axel Heiberg Island only by a narrow strait. Eureka became known for the fossilised forests from the Eocene Period, approximately 35–60 million years ago, which were discovered on Eureka Sound and Hot Weather Creek in the Remus Basin. In the cold, dry Arctic climate tree-stumps, covered in sand, remained almost unchanged and – together with fossils of turtles and lizards – are evidence of a former much warmer climate.
Alert	The most northerly and permanently inhabited settlement in the world is Alert, a radio and weather station set up by the Canadian army in 1950 on the north coast at 82° 30′N and 700km/435 miles from the North Pole. Alert was the name of the flagship of a British marine expedition under Captain Nares which spent the winter here in 1875. Being a military station, Alert is not open to tourists.
Ellesmere Island National Park Reserve	In the extreme north of the island, in mountainous and glaciated country rising to some 2600m/8500ft, an area of about 40,000sq.km/15,500sq.miles has been designated a National Park. In this predominantly dry Arctic waste there are pockets which are warm and moist enough to enable plants to grow and animals to exist, such as in the area around Lake Hazen – a large lake north of the Arctic Circle – which enjoys a surprisingly long and warm summer. Here can be found musk-ox, Peary caribou, arctic foxes and wolves, lemmings, and over thirty species of birds have been counted. The flora is made up of over 130 kinds of plants. It is hoped that the National Park will serve to safeguard these sensitive forms of animal and plant life.

Estrie

	Province: Québec
Information	See Québec

The Estrie region – also known as "Cantons de l'Est" or "Eastern Town-ships" – covers an area of more than 13,000sq.km/5000sq.miles east of Montréal, and is one of the most varied regions of Québec province. Large uninhabited areas mingle with picturesque little towns. The hilly and wooded stretches are the most charming. At the feet of Mont Sutton and Mont Orford some of the province's major winter sports centres have sprung up.

Location

People began to populate Estrie at the end of the 18th c. when many Americans and British fled there in the confusion of the American War of Independence 1776–83. It was they who chose the best places for their rich towns surrounded by parkland. After 1850 more and more French-speaking people settled in the area, and since 1950 they have dominated the entire Estrie region.

History

The little industrial town of Granby, the "Princess of Estrie", was founded in 1842. It owes its name to John Manners, the margrave of Granby, and is today the gastronomic capital of Estrie. Particularly charming are the open spaces such as Parc Pelletier. Also worth a visit is the Zoological Garden at 347 Avenue Bourget (open: May–Oct. daily 10am–5pm; in July 10am–6pm).

Granby

Parc du Mont-Orford covers an area of almost 40sq.km/15½sq.miles at the foot of the 793m/2602ft high Mont-Orford. This mountain is very popular with skiers in winter, and from its peak – accessible by means of a chair-lift – there is a wonderful view of Estrie, Lac Memphremagog and the Vermont heights.

Parc du Mont-Orford

The industrial town of Magog, also known as the "Jewel of Estrie", was founded by Loyalists in 1799. Because of its charming position on the north bank of Lac Memphremagog is popular with tourists. The green sheen of Lac Memphremagog, 52km/32 miles long and 3–6km/2–4 miles wide, a fifth of which forms part of the US state of Vermont, is an ideal spot for quiet boat trips in summer.

Magog

About 20km/13 miles south of Magog stands the Benedictine abbey of St-Benoît-du-Lac. This imposing Neo-Gothic building was consecrated by Paul Vannier in 1912. Some 60 monks live here today. Visitors are welcome to join in morning mass, held daily at 11am, and vespers each evening at 5pm.

★St-Benoît-du-Lac

Sherbrooke, the chief town in Estrie, lies surrounded by hills at the confluence of the Magog and St-François Rivers. The town owes its name to Lord Sherbrooke who was Governor of Canada from 1816 to 1818.

Sherbrooke

The rock in the town centre known as "Pin Solitaire" is a reminder of the time when the Iroquois and Abenaqui Indians lived in the area. In February 1592 the two tribes were unable to agree on the outcome of a battle, so a curious competition was held at this spot. One Iroquois and one Abenaqui had to run round and round a pine tree until one dropped from exhaustion. The Abenaqui lasted the better and so won the right to kill the Iroquois.

Pin Solitaire

A visit is recommended to the Musée des Sciences Naturelles du Séminaire, one of the oldest museums in Québec province (195 Rue Marquette; open: Tues.–Thur. and Sun. 12.30–7.30pm).

Musée des Sciences naturelles

The important industrial town of Drummondville is Estrie's second largest town. It was founded in 1816 by the Scottish General Heriot.

Drummondville

The "Village québécois d'antan" (open: daily June 1st–Labour Day) is well worth a visit. Reconstructed in the style of the pioneering period, staff dressed in period costume describe everyday life between the years 1840 and 1910.

★Village québécois

Surroundings of Drummondville

Arthabaska

6km/4 miles east of the neighbouring town of Victoriaville lies the little township of Arthabaska. Canada's first Prime Minister, Wilfred Laurier, had a house built here in 1877; situated at 16, Rue Laurier Ouest, it today houses the Musée Laurier (open: June–Aug. daily, 9am–noon and 1.30–7pm; Sept.–May closed on Mon. and public holidays).

Flin Flon   J 7

Province: Manitoba. Population: 8000

Information

See Manitoba

Flin Flon lies in the middle of mountainous and very wooded country, marked by steep rocky slopes. All round the town are stores of ore and raw materials, including gold, copper, zinc and silver, so it will come as no surprise to learn that mining is the dominant industry, the main mines being those belonging to Flin Flon Mines and the Hudson Bay Mining and Smelting Company.

The town's second most important source of income is the timber industry.

The town's name

In 1915 gold-seekers found a tattered copy of a penny novel about Josiah Flintabbatey Flonatin who discovered a gold-town. They named the place after this fictional character, and the name soon became shortened to "Flin Flon".

Sights
Flonatin statue

In the town centre stands a 7½m/24½ft tall statue of the legendary Mr Flonatin, designed by the caricaturist Al Capp.

Museum

The Flin Flon Museum near Highway 10A is open: May–mid-Sept. daily 10am–6pm. It exhibits items from the pioneering period as well as tools and impressive minerals belonging to the Hudson Bay Mining & Smelting Company.

Many Mine

At the junction of Highways 10 and 10A lies Many Mine, Manitoba's first copper mine.

Hudson Bay Mining & Smelting Company

In addition to gold the Hudson Bay Mining & Smelting Co. mines copper, zinc and silver. Visitors can watch the above-ground workers between June and August. There are guided tours.

Forestry Trunk Road   F/G 7/8

Province: Alberta

Information

See Alberta

Route

Eastern slopes of the Rocky Mountains.

★★Topography

Forestry Trunk Road (Highway 940) in Alberta, parts of which are well surfaced, threads its way for some 1000km/620 miles along the eastern slopes of the Rockies in Alberta. It was initially laid to make it easier to fight the forest fires which are a frequent feature of this region. This route, so far known to only few tourists, covers some scenically spectacular parts of the country. There are magnificent views to be had from Plateau Mountain, and many visitors are particularly impressed by the rushing waters of the Oldman River.

Kananaskis Provincial Park (see Calgary) is also very beautiful.

Highway 940 starts in Hinton, 250km/155 miles west of Edmonton. It can also be joined near Nordegg (Highway 11), Ghost Lake (TransCanada

Highway 1a), Seebe Highway (the 541 from High River onwards) or Crowsnest Pass.

See Calgary, Surroundings.

Fort Carlton

Province: Saskatchewan

See Saskatchewan

Information

Fort Carlton, in the Historic Park of the same name (open: mid-May–early Sept. daily 10am–6pm) was built in 1820 at the bottom of a valley by a natural ford of the North Saskatchewan River.

Location and history

For 75 years it was an important outpost, lying as it did at the junction of a main waterway, the North Saskatchewan River, with an important overland route – the Carlton Trail – which linked Winnipeg with Fort Edmonton (see entries).

In its early years the fort's main task was to provide the river patrols and other posts of the Hudson's Bay Company with supplies. It obtained meat, lard, furs and skins from the Indians and other traders, in exchange for rifles, tobacco, clothing, blankets, pearls and metal goods such as cooking utensils, axes, knives and traps.

Even when canoe patrols, York boats and steamships came west the fort remained an important trading centre and continued to look after the settlers who arrived in the 1870s.

Officers of the Northwest Mounted Police were sent to the fort to negotiate with the Indians.

East of the fort a stone pyramid marks the spot where a treaty was signed under the terms of which the Cree Indians renounced their claim to 320,000sq,km/123,500sq.miles of land.

Using the fort as a base Commander Crozier of Battleford first led his troops into battle near Duck Lake against the insurgents in the Northwest Rebellion in 1885. The police troops suffered heavy losses and retreated to the fort. As they were unable to defend it the post was surrendered and the troops withdrew to Prince Albert. During the hastily organised evacuation fire broke out and destroyed large parts of the fort.

Earlier this century archaeologists examined the site and as a result it has been possible to carry out a partial reconstruction of Fort Carlton as it once was. In 1967 the historical provincial park was opened.

★Reconstructed buildings

The period around 1860 is also reflected in the rebuilt wooden houses and stockade fences. At one end stands the largest building, a Hudson's Bay Company store, equipped with the type of goods needed in those days, such as blankets, rifles, pearls, pipes and snowshoes. Also displayed here are agricultural products, dried meat and lard which formed the basis of the fur-traders' diet.

Store

Another wooden shack, fitted out with old furniture, gives a good idea of how the Hudson's Bay Company's employees lived in the late 19th c.

Dwelling

A press has also been installed, such as was used to press skins and hides into compact bundles.

Press

Various kinds of furs are exhibited in another wooden shack, together with information about the fur trade.

Exhibition of furs

A short path leads to the river where the fur-traders tied up their boats and stored goods and provisions.

Canoe landing

The Carlton Trail starts behind the picnic site and threads its way over hills and through woods, where the old trappers' path can still be seen.

★Carlton Trail

Fort Langley

E 8

Province: British Columbia. Population: 16,000

Information

See British Columbia

Fort Langley, strategically well-placed near the mouth of the Fraser River, was built in 1827 as the first permanent outpost of the Hudson's Bay Company. George Simpson, the then Governor of British Columbia, thought the Fraser would become an important connecting link with the countryside beyond, but in fact this was not to be so, mainly because of the sheer and insurmountable Fraser Canyon. As a result the trading post lost importance, and even the Cariboo gold-rush passed it silently by. In 1839 it was burned down, but was rebuilt in the following year. In 1886 the Hudson's Bay Company closed down this outpost.

After a very quiet period, however, the settlement developed to become the centre of the "Langley prairie", where agriculture and farming, particularly dairy-farming, now predominate.

Renovation of the fort began in 1955 when laying out the Fort Langley National Historic Park (see below) was begun.

Sights

Farm Machinery Museum

In the British Columbia Farm Machinery Museum at 9131 King St. (open: Mar.–Nov. Mon.–Sat. 11am–5pm, Sun. 1–5pm) visitors can view numerous examples of old engines and equipment that were once used in agriculture, forestry and fishing in the Fraser region.

Centennial Museum & National Exhibition Centre

The neighbouring Langley Centennial Museum & National Exhibition Centre at 9135 King St. is open daily in summer 10am–5pm, in winter Tues.–Sat. 10am–5pm, Sun. 1–5pm; on display are objets d'art and everyday articles used by the coastal Salian tribes as well as relics of the pioneer age.

★★Fort Langley National Historic Park

5km/3 miles north of the TransCanada Highway can be found the partially reconstructed old Hudson's Bay Company trading post on the banks of the Fraser River, at 23433 Mavis St. Now accessible to the public it is known as Fort Langley National Historic Park (open: June–Labour Day 10am–7pm, at other times of the year 10am–4.30pm).

4km/2½ miles further downstream is Fort Langley (see above). The only preserved building is the former general store, which still reflects the style of the 19th c. It was in the "Big House" (officers' mess) here that British Columbia was declared a British Crown Colony in 1858. James Douglas was its first governor.

Inside the renovated fort it is possible to get a good idea of how the fur-traders and trappers lived along the Canadian west coast in the mid-19th c.

Employees of Parks Canada enthusiastically act out "Living History", portraying typical scenes from everyday life as it was in this Hudson's Bay Company fort.

Fort MacLeod

G 8

Province: Alberta. Population: 3000

Information

See Alberta

It was the whisky-smuggling trade which led to the founding of the town of Fort MacLeod by the Crowsnest Highway (see entry) in southern Alberta. In the 1870s American smugglers traded extensively with the prairie Indians, especially with the Blackfoot, bartering cheap whisky for buffalo hides.

In 1874, after their famous march through wild country, the Northwest Mounted Police set up their new headquarters here with the aim of putting an end to this illegal trade and restoring peace and order to this frontier region. The "Old West" is remembered in various historical buildings in the town centre.

Built in 1957 at 25 St./3rd Ave., the Fort MacLeod Museum (open: May–mid-Oct. daily 9am–5pm; in summer to 7pm) sets out to portray the Northwest Mounted Police fort built in 1874 and southern Alberta's first outpost; this is achieved by means of some original buildings, Indian tepees made of buffalo hide, exhibitions about the police, the lifestyle and history of the Blackfoot Indians and pioneers, and the story behind the fortifications.

Sights

★Fort MacLeod Museum

A slide-show provides information about the Head-Smashed-In Buffalo Jump (see below).

In July and August a police patrol wearing the 1878 scarlet uniforms rides through the streets four times a day.

Some 16km/10 miles west of Highway 2 North, by the unmade-up Highway 785, lies the area known as Head-Smashed-In Buffalo Jump, declared a World Heritage Site by UNESCO in 1981. A band of rock some 300m/330yd long in the lush, undulating grassland ends in a steep precipice, and for more than 5000 years the prairie Indians in the course of their organised buffalo hunts used to drive the panic-stricken beasts over the precipice to their death. It was not until the Indians obtained horses and firearms from the white man in the 18th c. that they finally gave up this traditional method of hunting.

★★Head-Smashed-In Buffalo Jump

The name of this place is also attributable to a hunting accident in the 18th c. A man watching the hunt from below the cliff was killed when Blackfoot Indians drove some fleeing animals over the precipice on top of him. In 1987 a modern Interpretive Centre (open: May–Labour Day 9am–8pm; other times of the year 9am–6pm) was inaugurated.

Lifts bring visitors up to a viewing point on the edge of the rocks, and down to the site of archaeological digs at the foot of the precipice.

Northwest Mounted Police in Fort MacLeod (Alberta)

In the interesting museum local topography is described, and the life of the prairie Indians and their hunting techniques are explained. Emphasis is also laid on the rapid changes in the lives of the Indians after they came into contact with the white man.

Fort McMurray   G 6

Province: Alberta. Population: 38,000

Information

See Alberta

The town of Fort McMurray lies at the confluence of Clearwater River and Athabasca River (see entry). Its somewhat stormy development since the 1960s is due in no small measure to the existence of giant stocks of oil for many miles around. It is anticipated that more than 700 billion barrels of this valuable form of energy can be brought to the surface.

In 1971 the population of this remote town was only 7000; in 1990 it was almost 40,000. A third of the inhabitants are between 20 and 35 years of age.

History

The history of Fort McMurray begins in the last quarter of the 18th c., when the North West Company set up a trading post here in the fur-rich north of Alberta. In the 19th c. it developed into the main supply centre along the fur-route from the northern Saskatchewan River to Lake Athabasca. In 1883 regular steamship services were extended as far as this, and a start could be made in exploiting the rich natural resources of this vast region. The railroad connection laid in 1925 was an important factor in its continued development; it was now possible to transport timber and mineral resources at an economic cost.

★Extracting oil from sand

The presence of oil beneath the sand was mentioned in reports by the explorers Peter Pond and Alexander Mackenzie back in the 18th c. Indians and fur-hunters were in the habit of mixing the crude tar with resin to caulk their canoes. In the early 20th c. a start was made on using the sand for surfacing Alberta's roads. Attempts to extract crude oil were initially unsuccessful, but during the Second World War the Abasand Oils Project, 8km/5 miles north of Fort McMurray, succeeded in producing about 200 barrels a day. It was not until the 1960s that resources were really tapped to an economic degree, leading finally to an oil-boom in Fort McMurray.

Today the oil is extracted by means of very sophisticated processes, e.g. by the firms of Suncor and Syncrude, 34km/21 miles north of Fort McMurray. Obtained by means of the hot-water process – at present some 180,000 barrels a day – the oil is pumped to Edmonton through a pipeline.

★★Fort McMurray Oil Sands Interpretive Centre

The Fort McMurray Oil Sands Interpretive Centre is worth a visit; it is situated in Mackenzie Building on Highway 63, and is open from Victoria Day–Labour Day daily 10am–6pm, at other times of the year noon–5pm. Models, drawings, films and experiments spread over more than 2300sq.m/2750sq.yd provide information about the development of the extraction of crude oil from the sand, with the emphasis on the highly modern technology now used. Equally impressive are the huge machines used to extract the valuable raw material.

Syncrude Tours (extracting oil)

By prior arrangement during the summer months visitors can join in guided tours of the Syncrude Works at 400 Sakitawaw Trail. The tours commence at 9.15am Tues.–Thur. and at 11.15am Sat.

Heritage Park

Some buildings which formed part of the old Fort McMurray have been restored. Situated at King St./Tolen Drive on the bank of Haningstone River, they are open end of June–end of Aug. daily 10am–6pm. They include a church, the Hill Drugstore Museum and, last but not least, the former posts of the Royal Canadian Mounted Police.

Bulldozer

Fort Providence   F 5

Territory: Northwest Territories
Population: 700

See Northwest Territories   Information

By air or via the Mackenzie Highway   Access

The little town of Fort Providence lies on the Mackenzie River where it flows into the south-western corner of Great Slave Lake, on Highway 3 going towards Rae-Ezdo. The town is known for the wide selection of Indian arts and crafts and handmade anoraks and parkas in the shops. Boats can be rented at the filling stations in the town.

The famous American Arctic explorer Sir John Franklin (1786–1847) chose Fort Providence as the starting point for his journeys of discovery to the Barren Grounds in 1819–22. At the western end of town stands a memorial to the American explorer Sir Alexander Mackenzie (see Famous People), who stopped off in Fort Providence in 1789 in the course of his putative trek to the Pacific Ocean which he hoped would take him to the Arctic Ocean.

The Mackenzie Bison sanctuary lies north of Fort Providence on Highway 3 in the direction of Rae-Edzo. In 1963 the Canadian Government transferred here nineteen forest buffalo, a species threatened with extinction. This, the only herd of these buffalo still in existence in North America, has since grown to about 500. The animals are rarely to be seen from the roadway, as they mostly stay nearer to the shores of the Great Slave Lake.

★**Mackenzie Bison Sanctuary**

Fort St James   E 7

Province: British Columbia. Population: 3000

Information

See British Columbia

History

Fort St James on Stuart Lake is the capital of the historic district of New Caledonia and the second oldest town in British Columbia. As long ago as 1806 Simon Fraser and John Stuart of the North West Company set up a trading post here near an Indian settlement at the eastern end of the over 100km/62 mile long Stuart Lake. This lake actually forms part of a system of lakes and rivers more than 400km/250 miles in length. In 1821, when the two rival fur companies, North West and Hudson's Bay, amalgamated, Fort St James became the administrative and supply centre of the fur hunting teams which operated from here throughout western Canada. In 1843 a Catholic mission was built near the fort.

In 1869 gold was found in the Omineca Region further north. A veritable gold-rush resulted which had its effects on Fort St James as well.

Today Fort St James is a modern township on the northern edge of the old settlement. Four large timber concerns, mining and tourism form the backbone of its economy.

Sights

★★ Fort St James National Historic Park

In 1971, at great expense, the old fort was reconstructed to resemble its appearance in 1896. During the summer months park staff dressed in contemporary costume, employing much enthusiasm and imagination, act out typical everyday situations portraying the hard lives led by the fur-traders. Visitors can look over the somewhat more comfortable administrator's residence, various storehouses, men's quarters, shops and offices. Exhibitions and film-shows in the Visitor Centre provide background on the history of this remote trading post in the "Canadian Siberia".

Fort St James Historic Site

There are guided tours May–Oct. 9am–6pm, at other times of the year Mon.–Fri. 9am–noon and 1–4pm.

Nearby stands the Catholic Church of Our Lady of Good Hope, a pretty wooden church built in 1873, where mass is still celebrated in summer.

Our Lady of Good Hope

Fort St John

E 6

Province: British Columbia. Population: 14,000

See British Columbia

Information

Fort St John, standing 693m/2275ft above sea-level and situated about 80km/50 miles north-west of Dawson Creek, grew from a fort built in 1806 by the North West Company at the nearby mouth of the Beatton River.

History

However, archaeologists have established that as long ago as 1794 there was already a fort at the mouth of the smaller Peace River 8km/5 miles south of the present town centre, thus making the town one of the oldest Euro-Canadian settlements on the mainland of British Columbia.

Back in 1793, when he became acquainted with this region during his voyage to the Pacific, Alexander Mackenzie (see Famous People) recognised how suitable this spot was for a settlement. When, in 1821, five men from the trading post since set up by the Hudson's Bay Company were killed by Indians the company decided to close the outpost down.

It was not until 1860 that a new fort was built on the banks of Peace River; this was moved several times in the years that followed. In the 1890s a Catholic mission station was attached to the Hudson's Bay Company fort.

During the Klondike gold-rush Fort St John lay on the route taken by the gold-diggers. Around the turn of the century the first settlers also came north to Peace River (see entry) and realised the agricultural potential of the region. Gradually Fort St John became an important rural centre.

Gold-rush

During the Second World War an airport and the Alaksa Highway were built, resulting in an economic upturn for Fort St John.

In 1952 the John Hart Highway was completed, and for the first time in its history Fort St John had road links with the other major centres in British Columbia.

In the 1950s deposits of oil and natural gas were discovered in the countryside around Fort St John. A large refinery was built in the neighbouring town of Taylor. In addition to agriculture and forestry, the petro-chemical industry developed into an important branch of industry. Furthermore, new coal deposits were found to the south and west of the town.

Economy

Built in 1983, this museum (open: daily in summer 8am–8pm; other times of the year Mon.–Fri. 11am–4pm). The exhibits vividly portray the history of the region, the lives of the Indians and trappers and first settlers, the construction of the Alaska Highway and the development of the oil industry. The 40m/130ft high derrick was constructed by the museum in 1982.

Sights

North Peace Museum

Fort Steele

F 8

Province: British Columbia

See Crowsnest Highway

Access

See British Columbia

Information

In 1864 gold was discovered by three American gold-diggers at Wild Horse Creek, in country which until then had been penetrated only by the Koote-

Location and History

Fort Steele

nay Indians. Within a few weeks a gold-rush town had grown up, most of the inhabitants having come from the USA, since getting here from the west across the high mountain chains was too difficult. So the first politicians in Victoria heard about the finds of gold in the remote south-west of their territory was when they read about it in the American newspapers. Even before the completion of the Dewdney Trail the gold-boom at Wild Horse Creek reached its peak in 1865, when more than 5000 gold-diggers were at work, some even digging out deposits from under the very town itself.

A new town grew up on the Kootenay River near Galbraith's Ferry, the present-day Fort Steele. Galbraith had soon realised the need for a ferry over the Kootenay and operated such a service until the first bridge was built in 1888.

After the gold-rush
Around 1880, after the gold-rush, farmers and ranchers settled here in increasing numbers. There were the inevitable conflicts with the original owners of the land, the Kootenay Indians. Chief Isadore and his warriors declined to enter the Indian reserve that was quickly set up and there continued to be many battles with the white settlers who refused to entertain the Indians' claims to ownership of land. There were fears of a new uprising only a few years after the Riel uprising had been quelled. In 1887 a unit of the Northwest Mounted Police was sent from Fort MacLeod to the Kootenay River with instructions to arbitrate. Only a year later this first troop of "Redcoats" to come west of the Rocky Mountains was able to withdraw, its task successfully accomplished, and the grateful settlers re-named the place Fort Steele, after Samuel Steele, the superintendent in charge of this troop of 75 policemen.

Mining boom
The discovery of rich silver deposits in eastern Kootenay in the 1890s resulted in a fresh mining boom. Ore and supplies were transported by steamer along the Kootenay River between Fort Steele and Jennings in Montana, where there was a link with the Great Northern Railway to Seattle. Fort Steele became the region's administrative and supply centre and following the boom there was strong speculation about a rail link. The inhabitants were bitterly disappointed therefore when, contrary to all expectations, it was the neighbouring town of Cranbrook which was in fact connected to the railway.

"Ghost town"
As early as 1910 Fort Steele had become a ghost town, and by 1945 only 50 people still lived there.

Present importance
The decision taken some thirty or so years ago by the provincial government to build an open-air museum breathed fresh life into Fort Steele and the surrounding countryside. Today several hundred people earn their living here.

Sights

★★ Fort Steele Provincial Historic Park
Fort Steele Provincial Park was built in the 1960s on Highway 95/93, a few miles after Crowsnest Highway 3 turns off south-east. Open: May–Oct. daily 10am–5pm, in summer 9am–8pm, it is laid out in the form of a typical town from the turn of the century, complete with a Northwest Mounted Police post. Many visitors are attracted every year to the open-air museum with four dozen buildings, either restored, reconstructed from historical records or moved here from other parts of the Kootenay (see entry) region. Staff and volunteers dressed in contemporary costume act out "living history" in the houses, most of which are furnished in Victorian style, and demonstrate old crafts and perform household tasks in the manner of the pioneering period.

Wild Horse Theatre
Musicals, drama and comedies from that period can be watched in the Wild Horse Theatre.

Wasa Hotel
The region's varied history is portrayed in a building constructed on the lines of the old Wasa Hotel.

In the Kershaw General Store the visitor can purchase goods such as were bought in the early 19th c.

There are horse-rides with guides, coach drives, and special trips in an old steam train, covering a distance of 4½km/2¾ miles.

Fraser Valley

E/F 7/8

Province: British Columbia

See British Columbia

Information

TransCanada Highway, eastwards from Vancouver (see entry).

Access

The Fraser, or Frazer River, 1368km/850 miles long, is one of the major rivers in North America. It rises in the Rocky Mountains near Jasper National Park (see entry), flows north for 440km/275 miles through the Rocky Mountain Trench and then turns south near Prince George (see entry). On its path southwards of some 660km/410 miles it cuts through the Fraser Plateau, 1200–1500m/4000–5000ft above sea-level, and then flows along the eastern slopes of the Coast Mountains.

Near Hope (see entry) it turns west and bursts through the Coast Mountains walled by a magnificent, deeply-slashed canyon.

Finally the Fraser River enters the Pacific Ocean in the Strait of Georgia near Vancouver (see entry).

Course

The most generously watered tributaries of the Fraser are the North Thompson River (340km/212 miles long), the South Thompson (330km/205 miles), the Nechako (460km/286 miles) and the Stuart (410km/255 miles).

Important tributaries

View of Fraser Valley

Fish Ladder on Fraser River

Fraser Valley

Economy

Profitable agricultural and horticultural businesses flourish in the wide southern valleys and the river delta. A number of sizeable industrial firms have also become established in the delta region.

Hydro-electric power

As salmon fishing remains of paramount importance it has not been possible to utilise to the full the water-power potential of the Fraser River. The only high-performance power-stations belonging to the B. C. Electric Co. are those installed on the two small tributaries, Bridge River and Stave River.

History of discovery

The important contribution that the Fraser Valley could make to the opening-up of the mainland of western Canada was realised by Alexander Mackenzie (see Famous People) in 1793. From 1808 onwards the legendary adventurer explored the course of the river; fifty years later huge numbers of gold-seekers settled on its banks.

Around 1886 a new communications centre grew up near Ashcroft, and the old Cariboo Waggon Road through the canyon was no longer used. Until 1915, when a start was made on building the Canadian National Railway, the Canadian Pacific Railway line was the only traffic route through the Fraser Canyon.

In the 1920s the authorities realised the need for a road link, but there was little room for this, because the railway lines already took up the narrow space available along both river banks. In 1926, however, the road to Lytton was completed and in the 1950s, at great expense, this was extended to become the TransCanada Highway as we know it today.

Yale

Location and history

The little town of Yale (76m/249ft; pop. 500) lies at the southern entrance to the Fraser Canyon. It was here that Simon Fraser once camped after his famous trek through the canyon, aided by Indians who for centuries had roamed through it and scaled its semi-vertical walls with the aid of ladders. In 1848 the Hudson's Bay Company set up a small trading-post here, which developed within ten years – as a direct result of the gold-rush – into a wild gold-diggers' town. Yale, the terminus of all river traffic, remained until the 1880s the main trade centre for all goods passing through deeper into British Columbia and to the gold-fields. Until the Cariboo Waggon Road was built in 1861–63 all goods being transported to Kamloops (see entry) had to be transferred to the backs of mules. A number of historic buildings still remain as a reminder of the times when Yale was such an important trading centre.

Yale Museum

Nearby, in an 1880 building at 31179 Douglas St., stands the historic little Yale Museum (open: June–Sept. daily 10am–5pm). In front of the museum there is a memorial stone to the Chinese workers employed in the building of the Canadian Pacific Railway. About three quarters of all the workers came from China; they were paid only half the wages of the white workers, and hundreds died in accidents or from sickness. The route taken by the railroad followed in the main the Cariboo Waggon Road. Parts had to be detonated through the Fraser Canyon. With the completion of the railway line as far as Kamloops the setting-out point for mail-coaches and freight wagons was moved further upstream.

★★Hell's Gate · ★★Fraser Canyon

The wild Fraser Canyon, about 350km/220 miles east of Vancouver, is one of Canada's most impressive gorges. Here the raging torrents of the Fraser force their way through a narrow pass between rocky walls towering almost vertically above the river. In days gone by the Indians found a perilous way across by using ladders. The first things to take the eye are the narrowness and rough-hewn walls of the Fraser Canyon and the difficulties involved in laying a road at the narrowest spot, known as Hell's Gate. A funicular railway, giving a view of the wild gorge below, leads down to the other bank which is 150m/490ft lower. Down here the tourist will find

Hell's Gate ▶

souvenir shops, a restaurant and a small centre providing information, by means of films, models of the "fish-ladders" (see below), etc., about the four-yearly migration cycle of the salmon. It is a climb of a few minutes down a reasonable path to the white, foaming river below. The opposite bank can be reached by means of a swaying suspension bridge.

On average, 900 million litres/200 gallons (British) or 240 gallons (American) of water per minute shoot through the canyon which is only 34m/112ft wide at this point. Normally the river here is about 40m/130ft deep, but when the snow thaws it can rise by more than 20m/65ft within a very short time.

When dynamite was used to provide a way through for the railroad in 1914 a massive rock-fall resulted, thus narrowing the river-bed still further. The estimated 5 million salmon swimming upstream were now no longer able to battle against a river flowing at 37kmph/23mph and so found themselves cut off from their spawning grounds. This resulted in a catastrophic reduction in the numbers of salmon caught in the Fraser River. Therefore from 1944 "fish-ladders" were built, long stepped concrete tunnels through which the water flows comparatively slowly, thus enabling the salmon to pass through Hell's Gate once again. Today more than two million salmon a year successfully negotiate the canyon.

The tourist facilities near Hell's Gate are open Mar.–Oct. daily 9am–4.30pm, June–Aug. daily 8am–8pm.

Lytton

The town of Lytton (171m/561ft; pop. 400) lies about 400km/250 miles upstream from Vancouver along the TransCanada Highway. Before the gold-rush and the building of the Canadian Pacific Railway there was an Indian village here at the confluence of the Fraser and Thompson Rivers. Named Cumchin, meaning "fork in the river", it lived mainly from salmon-fishing.

Rafting Capital

Lytton, lying in the rain shadow of the Coastal Mountains, is known for its hot, dry summers and proudly calls itself the "Rafting Capital of Canada". Kumasheen Raft Adventures, of 281 Main Street, P.O. Box 339, Lytton B.C. V0K 1Z0; tel. (604) 455–22 96, are one of the largest organisers of raft trips in British Columbia; they offer half to five-day "whitewater rafting" trips between May and September on the Fraser, Thompson, Chilko and Chilcotin Rivers, as well as through the raging rapids at Hell's Gate.

In Lytton Highway 12, following the old Cariboo Waggon Road, branches off to Lillooet 70km/44 miles north on the Fraser River (see Vancouver, Nugget Route).

Thompson River

From Lytton the TransCanada Highway follows the Thompson River. As a result of the dry conditions the rocky slopes are relatively devoid of vegetation. The main trees found here are Ponderosa pine or the "sagebrush" so typical of the arid regions of America and cacti which, of course, also thrive in relatively dry conditions. For the most part, crops can be grown only with the aid of artificial irrigation.

Narrow defile

In the narrow river-valley between Lytton and Spences Bridge there was often scarcely sufficient room for the modern highway to be built by the side of the railway lines, so frequently the road was constructed on steel girders directly above the river.

Fredericton

Province: New Brunswick. Population: 45,000

Information

Fredericton Tourism Department, corner of Queen St. and York St., P.O. Box 130, Fredericton, New Brunswick, E3B 4Y7; tel. (506) 452–95 00.

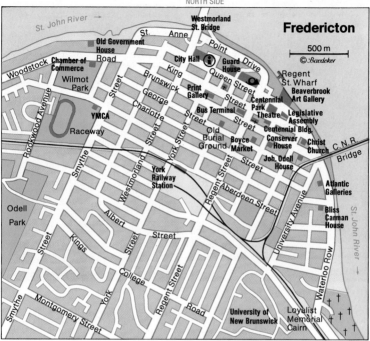

Fredericton, the capital of the east Canadian province of New Brunswick, is charmingly situated on the lower reaches of the St John's River. It is home to a university and the seat of an Anglican bishop. Although, in comparison with other Canadian cities, it is quite small it boasts an active cultural scene.

Fredericton, originally limited to administrative and educational establishments, has developed in recent years into a commercial and service centre for a wide area around. In addition a number of industrial firms, including a leather manufacturer, have set up here.

The capital of New Brunswick grew out of a small Acadian settlement named Pointe Ste-Anne, founded by French-speaking immigrants around 1732. In subsequent years the new settlement suffered as a result of civil war-like disputes among the Acadians themselves as well as from attacks by the British and by the native Micmac Indians who refused to tolerate the settlement.

From 1768 onwards American loyalists settled here. They named the colony after the second son of King George III of England, and this received the blessing of Queen Victoria in 1845. From then onwards it developed into a prosperous garrison and residential town.

History

Christ Church Cathedral, an Anglican diocesan church, is a remarkable building. It was built in the Neo-Gothic style in the middle of the 19th c. The stained glass and the wooden interior are true works of art. The visitor's attention is also drawn to the gravestone of the first Anglican bishop of Fredericton, constructed in a form not usually found in North America.

Sights

★Christ Church Cathedral

211

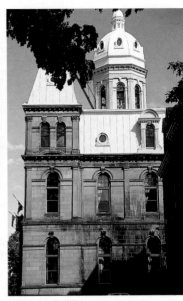

Fredericton: Christchurch Cathedral   *Legislative Building*

Legislative Building

The venerable building occupied by the New Brunswick legislative assembly was built in the 1880s. The high conference chamber is very beautiful; here visitors can admire portraits of King George III and Queen Charlotte by the famous artist Joshua Reynolds.

★ Birds of America

The parliamentary library owns a complete set of copper-plate engravings of the famous "Birds of America" by the Haiti-born American artist John James Audubon (1785–1851).

There are guided tours of the parliamentary buildings mid-June–early Sept. daily by prior arrangement at the entrance door.

★★ Beaverbrook Art Gallery

Opposite the Legislative Building, at the north end of "The Green" by St John River, stands the Beaverbrook Art Gallery, opened in 1959.

The gallery is named after Lord Beaverbrook (1879–1964), who was raised in Newcastle, New Brunswick, settled in England in 1910 and built up a giant newspaper empire there. During the Second World War he was a very influential member of Sir Winston Churchill's cabinet. Lord Beaverbrook first came to the fore as a great patron of the cultural life of New Brunswick. His collection of paintings forms the basis of the gallery's exhibits. He also financed the local playhouse and several of the buildings of New Brunswick University.

Resplendent in the entrance hall hangs the giant work by Salvador Dali, "Santiago el Grande". Other magnificent paintings include Botticelli's "Resurrection", a portrait of Lord Beaverbrook by Graham Sutherland, Krieghoff's "Merrymaking" and a number of works by the British painters Gainsborough, Hogarth, Reynolds and Turner as well as some by Corneille, Lukas Cranach and Delacroix. Outstanding, too, is the collection of works by Canadian painters, including Cornelius Krieghoff (see above), Paul Kane, the Group of Seven and Emily Carr. Also on display are some fine works by Inuit artists. The gallery is open daily 9am–6pm, except Sun. and Mon. mornings.

The neighbouring playhouse in St John Street also owes its existence to the town's great patron, Lord Beaverbrook. He also financed the first theatrical troupe in the province.

Playhouse

The park-like area known as the Military Compound lies in the town centre between Queen Street and the river. At one time the British garrison was stationed here. In more recent years the trappings and equipment of the Canadian army have been moved to a site out of town.
    The Guard House on Carleton Street, between Queen Street and the bridge, has been reconstructed in the style of the 19th c. It contains quarters for officers and other ranks. Uniforms and military equipment are also on display. Open: June–early Sept. Mon.–Sat. 10am–4pm.

Military Compound, Guard House

The York-Sunbury Museum with its comprehensive collections is housed in an extension to the officers' mess and provides background information on the history of the region. Of particular interest are the exhibitions dealing with the Indian aboriginals, as well as those collections covering the Victorian period and the story of Fredericton as a garrison town up to and including the First World War.

★ York-Sunbury Museum

The New Brunswick Craft School is also housed in the Military Compound. Here the artists and craftsmen can be watched as they work and examples of their work can be purchased.

Craft School

Daily in the high season the paddle-steamer "Pioneer Princess III" leaves from Regent Street Wharf for trips on the river.

Regent Street Wharf, "Pioneer Princess III"

The University was built in 1785, making it the third oldest in Canada. It stands southwest of the St John River on a hill from which there are excellent views. The library and the provincial archives it houses include a number of first editions donated by Lord Beaverbrook, including works by V. Bennett, Charles Dickens and H. G. Wells.

University of New Brunswick

Access to the picturesque town of Oromocto is by Route 102. It lies at the confluence of the Oromocto and St John Rivers, and its history of the place goes back to the times of the Micmac and Malecit Indians. A reconstructed log-cabin is reminiscent of the Canadian Revolution of 1777. Near Oromocto is one of the largest military academies in the British Commonwealth.
    In the Canadian army base at Gagetown there is an interesting military museum.
    Scottish Highland Games are held every summer in Oromocto. It also has a popular golf-course.

Surroundings

Oromocto

In the nearby Sunbury-Oromocto Provincial Park there are facilities for cycling, bathing and horse-riding excursions, together with a camp-site and several picnic areas.

Sunbury-Oromocto Provincial Park

In the picturesque old town of Gagetown, wonderfully situated by the river, time seems to have stood still. Numbers of craftsmen, especially weavers, have come here to live and work. The Queen's County Museum can be found in the house which belonged to Sir Leonard Tilley, one of the co-founders of the Canadian Confederation.
    During the summer months Gagetown boasts a very popular marina, where amateur sailors from all over the world can feel at home.

Gagetown

Route 102 winds along through the charming countryside at the mouth of the St John River, which is here strongly influenced by the marked variations in tide levels in the Bay of Fundy. There are ample opportunities to cross to the other side of the river by ferry. Also along the road the visitor will obtain a good impression of the land as developed and cultivated by man. There are also opportunities for bird-watching.

★ Route 102

St John River Valley. See entry.

Provinces: New Brunswick/Nova Scotia

Information	See New Brunswick
	See Nova Scotia

★★ Topography | Measuring up to 80km/50 miles wide at its mouth, Fundy Bay (Bay of Fundy) is a delta-shaped bay in the Atlantic Ocean, almost 300km/190 miles deep and penetrating the North American mainland between the Canadian provinces of New Brunswick and Nova Scotia.

★★ Tides | Fundy Bay is neither the largest nor the deepest in the world, but its maximum tidal flow between low and high of 19m/10 fathoms in the extreme north of the bay at Moncton and Truro (see entries) is not exceeded anywhere else. Its average tidal flow is about 9m/30ft, but during the spring tides 13m/43ft can easily be exceeded. Ebb and flow, brought about by the gravitational pull of the sun and the moon, occur when waves in the ocean are stationary. As a result of the earth's rotation, or coriolis power, and the shape of the oceanic basin the tidal waves revolve around a central point, or amphidrom. The determinant amphidrom in the North Atlantic revolves anti-clockwise once every 12½ hours, producing a complete tidal change. The extended delta-like shape of the Bay of Fundy has an intensifying effect on the tides which are a mere 80cm/32in. (!) high out in the open sea. The relative rise in the sea-level about 6000 years ago resulted in Fundy Bay being joined to the Atlantic, and from then onwards the tides were high. Since then the average tidal flow has continually increased, so that now during the spring tides it reaches up to 16m/53ft in the furthermost corner of Fundy Bay. If in the future either man – by, for example, building giant tidal power-stations – or Mother Nature herself brings about marked changes in the shape of the bay that will almost certainly put an end to this fascinating natural spectacle.

Places and islands of interest around Fundy Bay

St Stephen | The small industrial town of St Stephen lies on the little St Croix River where it enters Fundy Bay. Founded in the 17th c., St Stephen did not really develop until one hundred years later, when American loyalists settled here. It is now home to the woodworking, paper and textile industries. The bridge over the river leads to Calais, in the US state of Maine.

St Andrews | In the far south of New Brunswick and close to the border with Maine the pretty little fishing-port of St Andrews (pop. 2000) lies on the "appendix" of the Bay of Fundy known as Passamaquoddy Bay. Its typical New England-type houses are very pretty. Twice daily between mid-May and October boats leave St Andrews for trips around Fundy Bay.

Deer Island | On little Deer Island off the coast live some 1000 descendants of American loyalists who settled here in 1784. The island is best known for the large numbers of lobsters which breed on the giant lobster-banks.

★ Campobello Island | On the island of Campobello further offshore to the south lies the spacious country seat of the Roosevelt family. Until 1921 the US President often stayed here, but his visits became less frequent in the 1930s.

At one time Campobello was named "Port-aux-Coquilles" by the French colonists because of the abundance of mussels to be found here.

Black's Harbour | The fishing port of Black's Harbour is the home of Canada's largest canning factory, where sardines are processed. There is a ferry service across to Grand Manan Island.

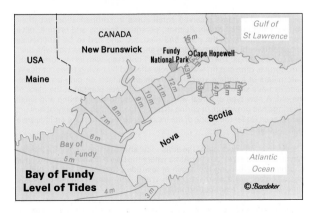

Grand Manan Island lies at the south-western entrance to the Bay of Fundy. Barely 3000 people live on the island, which is about 35km/22 miles long and up to 10km/6 miles wide. The marshlands interspersed with rocky ridges make it a favourite resting place for numerous species of birds – more than 300 different kinds have been spotted. The Ornithological Museum in the town of Grand Harbour is worth a visit.

 Mineral-hunters will be attracted to the north-western part of the island near Dark Harbour, shaped by volcanic activity. Here semi-precious stones such as amethysts, jasper and agate can be found.

★Grand Manan Island

★★Fundy National Park

Area: 206sq.km/80sq.miles. Established: 1948

The Superintendent, Fundy National Park, P.O. Box 40, Alma N.B., E0A 1B0; tel. (506)–887–20 00.

Information

From the TransCanada Highway, turn off on to Route 114 near Sussex/Moncton.

Access

There are four camp sites with a total of 660 places, a motel and holiday-homes in the park, and bed and breakfast is available in Alma and the surrounding villages.

Accommodation

This park on the steep south coast of New Brunswick includes a 13km/8 mile strip of the wild coast on the Bay of Fundy. Cliffs rise steeply up from the shore and the otherwise slightly hilly landscape is slashed here and there by deep gorges.

 The strong influence exerted by the bay means that two quite different climatic regions are to be found within the comparatively small National Park. That on the coast is characterised by cool summers with frequent mist and mild winters. On the higher land the summers are warmer, with no mist, and the winters colder. When the wind comes off the sea in summer the temperature on the coast can differ by as much as 6°C/11°F from that inland.

 The arrival of European settlers had an adverse effect on the eco-system of Fundy National Park. In the 19th c. the developing timber industry meant that large areas of trees were cut down for ship-building. When the timber industry declined in the early years of this century the land was deserted. Attempts to mine ore failed, and only very few mines – which are now open to visitors – proved profitable. The topsoil was not deep enough to be properly cultivated, although a few farmers managed to scrape a living by diversifying. When the region was declared a National Park in 1948 the few remaining inhabitants received small sums in compensation and their houses were pulled down. Salmon, peregrine falcons and ermine, once frequent denizens of the park, had died out, and had to be laboriously imported over the last forty years or so and gradually familiarised with their new surroundings. The natural Arcadian Forest too, with its mixture of ash, elm, spruce, pine and fir, was severely affected by having trees cut down. Caterpillars of a certain species of moth which feed on pine and spruce-needles have seriously decimated the young trees planted in the place of the old. A new type of forest with a higher proportion of birch and small clearings has grown up. In spring in particular a brilliant display of flowers can be seen under the shade of the trees. Large ferns and rare orchids are a sight to behold.

★★ The Edge of the Tide

The fascinating spectacle of the tides – low and high tides every 6¼ hours – can best be experienced near Alma where the beach is about a mile long at ebb tide. A walk along the beach at low tide provides an insight into an unsuspected world of theatre with crabs, shrimps, sea-anemones and sand-fleas as the main performers.

★ Devil's Half Acre Trail

In 1852 a surveyor wrote thus about this strip of land: "The land is stony, rough and littered with fallen trees, is known as the Devil's Half Acre and is as full of holes as a piece of Swiss cheese". Even though geologists can explain the curious natural phenomena as being the result of erosion by water and unstable stone strata, anyone walking through here is more likely to be reminded of the local legend which says that these strange hollows and holes are the work of the very Devil himself. On a foggy day or after a shower of rain the inhospitable trail takes on a most eerie atmosphere. At the end, however, the rambler is rewarded with a superb view over the bay. It takes about 30 minutes to cover the 2km/1¼ miles stretch.

★ Coastal Trail

From the main offices a single path 9km/5½ miles long leads up onto a mountain ridge and past deep, moss-covered crevices to a viewing place with a protective fence by the beach in Herring Cove, from where a tele-scope can be used to view the cove. The walk takes about four and a half hours. The path then continues up through the coastal forest which is often heavy with mist, along the cliffs and ending in Pointe Wolfe.

Pointe Wolfe Gorge

The rambler will soon come to a waterfall in a narrow ravine below the wooden bridge. In 1826 a sawmill was built near the dam and a small village grew up around it. Much of the sawn wood was sent to the USA or to St John for building sailing ships.

The dam, like those in most rivers in the bay, cuts off the upper reaches from the lower, resulting in a drastic reduction in fishing. Salmon, smelt and Canadian herring could no longer swim upstream to spawn. From the dam the trail leads to a viewing platform overlooking the "fiord"; distance 1km/⅔ mile, time required about 30 minutes.

Caribou Plain Trail

This trail is 3½km/2 miles in length and takes about 1–1½ hours to cover. The vegetation along the edge is typical of that in the National Park; passing by evergreen bracken and through dark deciduous forests and rivulets lined with alder trees it finally reaches a lowland moor. Near the two moorland lakes the visitor can observe some rare plants as well as snakes, beaver and elk.

Information boards give details of the origin and the inhabitants of the moors.

Upper Salmon River

This river, quiet in its upper reaches, wild and spectacular in the middle and flat and stony lower down its course, is typical of the park. Situated in the north-east, the river is pleasantly situated off the main tourist track. Being so quiet it is a good place to visit in the high season, and deep pools and small waterfalls make it a bathing paradise for dedicated walkers. However, the water temperature rarely exceeds 18°C/65°F. In late summer Atlantic salmon can often be observed resting in certain pools at the bottom of waterfalls. The distance to be covered is between 10–20km/6–12 miles, depending on the trail chosen.

Gaspésie

Province: Québec

See Québec
Office de Tourisme de Percé; tel. (418) 782–5448

Information

The Gaspé Peninsula (250km/155 miles long and 100–140km/62–87 miles across), on the Gulf of St Lawrence, is more or less cut off from the rest of Québec Province by Lake Matapédia and the Matapédia River. Inland, Gaspésie is a mountainous, wooded wilderness, and the only sizeable settlement has grown up around the copper mine at Murdochville.

The highest point on the peninsula is Mont Jacques-Cartier (1268m/5162ft), part of the Schickshock Mountains, geologically the northern terminal of the Appalachians.

The peninsula has a wild and rugged north coast, where the people live in small villages and depend partly on fishing for their livelihood.

The south coast, on the other hand, is gentler and not so steep, and has some farmland as well as the usual timber. Tourism plays a role too, with arts and crafts such as weaving, wood-carving, and making model ships providing another source of income.

South Coast

Not least of Gaspé's attractions is its excellent cuisine, which is in the best French tradition, especially the game and fish (including trout, Atlantic salmon, lobster and other seafood).

The Parc de Métis extends from Ste-Flavie to Matane, below Lake Matapédia, and is notable for its great variety of vegetation. The climate means that most plants flower two months later than elsewhere, so spring does not start until June.

North Coast

★Parc de Métis

The Parc de Métis was the work of Elsie Reford, niece of Canadian railway tycoon Lord George Stephen. She transformed the area, originally used for salmon fishing, into magnificent English-style gardens.

The Stephen mansion and the Reford Apartments are well worth visiting for the glimpses they afford of life here at the turn of the century.

The small industrial centre of Matane lies on the Matane River, famous for its salmon. Between mid-June and October a nearby path around a dam is a good viewpoint for watching the salmon on migration.

Matane River

The road from Matane to de la Gaspésie Park leads up into a hilly, wooded area before the park gives way to the broad valley of the Ste-Anne River. This area contains the highest points in the Shickshocks, including Mont Jacques-Cartier, Mont Richardson and Mont Albert, with, between them, spacious valleys, while, around Gîte du Mont Albert, the proportions are postively alpine. The trails here include one to Mont Cartier, and a Nature Interpretation Centre for the Gaspésie area.

Parc de la Gaspésie

The road to Ste-Anne-des-Monts is typical of the rocky coast, running through impenetrable terrain, either at the water's edge or along the clifftops, and passing through many little fishing villages with relatively large churches, and nothing but waves, white horses and seagulls as far as the eye can see.

Ste-Anne-des-Monts

The slate cliffs surrounding Mont-St-Pierre Bay are particularly spectacular.

Mont-St-Pierre

Gaspésie

Grande-Vallée
The village of Grande-Vallée still has a covered wooden bridge, dating from 1923.

Rivière-au-Renard
The road also leads through Gaspésie's most important fishing centre, Rivière-au-Renard, before circling round the Forillon Peninsula where the land is highly cultivated.

★★Parc National de Forillon
At the tip of the Gaspé Peninsula, this scenic park extends into the Gulf of St Lawrence. Its northern coast is wild and rugged, with mostly limestone cliffs. The southern coastal strip is less grand, but just as impressive, with opportunities for birdwatching and for whalewatching trips by boat. For anyone wanting to know more about the wildlife of the area there is an information centre at Cap des Rosiers.
Further on, at Cap Bon-Ami, a narrow path leads down to the beach and there is a magnificent view of the cape and the cliffs.

Anse-aux-Sauvages
A road on the south side of the peninsula leads to Anse-aux-Sauvages, from where a path goes to Cap Gaspé, the eastern tip of the national park.

Gaspé (town)
Gaspé, the main town of the peninsula and the administrative and commercial centre, is on a hillside overlooking the York Rivière, which runs into Gaspé Bay. The town owes its fame to Jacques Cartier (see Famous People), since it was here that he first set foot on the continent of North America in July 1534, fashioned a wooden cross under the gaze of the local settlers and took possession of the land "in the name of the King of France".
Nowadays Gaspé has a population of over 17,000, earning their living from fishing and the fishing industry. It is the see of a Catholic bishop.

Cathedral
The modern cathedral, built almost entirely of wood and containing beautiful stained-glass, is well worth a visit.

★Croix de Gaspé
The legendary wooden cross was replaced in 1934 by the stone cross near the city hall.

Musée
The local museum tells of Jacques Cartier's voyages. It also gives an account of the Anglo-French struggle for power over this region, and depicts the lives of those early settlers.

Percé
Formerly a remote fishing village, its wonderful setting has made Percé a great attraction for visitors, especially in the summer months. It has plenty of good restaurants and cafés, and there is even an open-air theatre.
The town gets its name from a heavily eroded rock, which is pierced (percé in French) by a large hole at one end.
All the natural beauties of the Gaspé Peninsula are to be found in and around Percé within a very small area, and it is a good place to see the effects of the forces that have shaped the landscape (the rising and falling in geological periods, erosion).

Percé coast
The whole of the coast around Percé is a magnificent natural spectacle, providing many opportunities for photography, with rocky outcrops, and towering cliffs, often bare, or only sparsely covered with turf.

Belvédère, ★★Pic de l'Aurore
From the "Belvédère" there is a good view of the Pic de l'Aurore, looking like a giant tooth, and of the Grande-Coupe range of hills.

Cap Barré Trois Sœurs
Cap Barré has a view of the offshore rocks known as the "Three Sisters", the Trois Sœurs.

★★Mont-Joli
From Mont-Joli there is a view of the Trois Sœurs, Cap Barré and, inland, the red cliffs of Mont Ste-Anne and a sculpture-like block of limestone which resembles a ship at anchor. The rock has meanwhile has broken up, the remains forming a kind of obelisk joined to Mont-Joli by a sandy spit.

The coast of Percé

This island is a bird sanctuary, and its about 4sq.km/1½sq.miles is North America's largest gannetry, with about 50,000 birds here in summer. The eastern side of the island is an ideal nesting site with rocky clefts and ledges. Besides the gannets, there are cormorants and other seabirds, with a nature trail so that visitors can see them better. — **Île Bonaventure**

From the top (320m/1050ft) of this gleaming redrock mountain there is a magnificent view of Percé and the surrounding region. — **★Mont Ste-Anne** ★★View

A path from the Gîte de Gargantua along the western slope of the 426m/1398ft Mont-Blanc leads to a precipitous chasm known as ''Grande Crevasse'', although this is a walk for experienced ramblers only! — ★Grande Crevasse

The interpretive centre above Percé to the south gives an account of Percé's wildlife, heritage and local history. — Centre d'Interpretation

Gaspé's south coast has a considerably less rugged landscape than the north, much of it farmland but there is also all kinds of economic activity. Each small bay has its fishing village. On a clear day it is possible from many observation points to see Acadia (see entry) over the other side of the Baie des Chaleurs. — **South Coast**

This little holiday place is on a bay, and was founded by Acadians fleeing here to escape deportation. — Bonaventura

Carleton is on a bay with an offshore sandbank. The scenery here is dominated by Mont St-Joseph, which is just under 600m/197ft. From Carleton a small road leads up to the top from where there is a magnificent view over the Baie des Chaleurs. — Carleton

This peninsula marks the beginning of the Baie des Chaleurs, or the end of the estuary of the Restigouche River (see Campbellton). — **Miguasha Peninsula**

Gaspésie

Musée de
Miguasha

This museum of palaeontology provides an introduction to petrology and helps with the identification of the many kinds of fossils that can be found in the local rock formations.

Matapédia

This little village is in a lovely setting amidst green hills between famous salmon rivers.

Georgian Bay

Province: Ontario

Information

Georgian Lakelands Travel Association, P.O. Box 39, 66 Coldwater St. E., Orilla, Ontario L3V 6H9; tel. (705) 325–7160.

Access

Highways 400 and 93 from Toronto (see entry).

A large bay, so cut off it is almost a lake, Georgian Bay is part of Lake Huron, and was named after George IV. In the north, with its wild, rocky shoreline, it has an atmosphere all its own, dotted with small islands, some no more than a big, bare rock, others with a couple of crooked pine trees. The bay shore in the west and in parts of the south has the high limestone cliffs of the Niagara Escarpment, which, together with the long, sandy beaches on the southern shore and the Midland Peninsula, help to make Georgian Bay the ideal place for anyone who enjoys spending time on, in, or around the water.

Owen Sound, Penetanguishene, Washaga Beach, Midland, Parry Sound and Collingwood are all popular holiday resorts on the bay's shores, rich in history and atmosphere.

Huronia

In the early 17th c., Georgian Bay, home to the Huron Indians, was where the Jesuit missions first set out to convert the Indians, starting with Etienne Brulé in 1610. He was followed by trappers and Jesuit missionaries from Québec, who established their first station here in 1639. Weakened by disease introduced by the new settlers, and under constant threat of attack from the Iroquois to the south, the Huron eventually succumbed, but when several of the Jesuits were tortured to death in 1649, the Ste-Marie mission station was abandoned.

Sights on Georgian Bay

The resorts on the southern shores of Georgian Bay are very popular at weekends and in the summer, and can become just as crowded as any European holiday playground.

Midland

The little port of Midland (population: 13,000), on the southern side of the Bay, is the centre for a fairly large surrounding area, and a considerable amount of grain passes through it every year. It is also a good base for visiting several nearby historical sites.

Huron Indian
Village

The replica of an Indian village in Little Lake Park (King St.) shows what life was like for the Huron. It includes the big longhouses that a large family would have lived in, a medicine man's house, store-rooms, etc., plus demonstrations of how canoes were made.

Huronia Museum, nearby, holds an interesting collection of Indian utensils and artefacts.

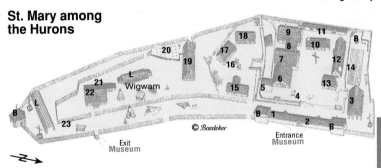

Georgian Bay

St. Mary among the Hurons

© Baedeker

Entrance
Museum

Exit
Museum

1 Tannery	7 Chapel	14 Herb Garden	20 Cemetery
2 Timber store	8 Recreation room	15 "En Columbage"	21 Pharmacy
Huts	9 Jesuits' quarters	16 Sawhorse	22 Sick quarters
3 Grain store	10 Kitchen building	17 Tailoring	23 Well
4 Stonemasonry	11 Stables	Shoemaking	
5 Smithy	12 Farmhouse	18 "En Pilier"	B Bastion
6 Carpentry	13 Bolvin House	19 St Joseph's Church	L Nave

The reconstruction of the mission station of St Mary among the Hurons is about 5km/3 miles east of Midland on the Wye River. Founded by the Jesuits in 1639, for a decade the mission served as the mainstay for Europeans in "Wendat", the land of the Huron – in 1648 about 20% of the Europeans living in New France were probably in Ste-Marie. The fortified mission station, which was organised along the lines of a European monastery, was divided into three parts.

The northern section was where the Europeans and the priests lived. They also had a chapel, the mission kitchen and a few workshops.

Next came some more workshops to the south, while the rest of the southern section was where the Indian converts lived. Here there was a longhouse, the Indians' own church, an infirmary and a vegetable garden. In front of a palisade, but still within the confines of the station, Indians who had yet to be fully converted could live in a longhouse or wigwams.

As time went on there was constant conflict with the Indians. The Huron (Wendat) were decimated by diseases imported by the Europeans. Several Indian tribes fought each other and occasionally there were attacks by the Iroquois in which not only Christians and Hurons but even European priests were killed. In 1649 the Jesuits abandoned their settlement and returned to Québec.

Reconstructed between 1964 and 1967, the mission is also the final resting place of Jean de Brébeuf and Gabriel Lalement who were tortured to death and are now venerated as martyrs.

Designated a national monument in May 1989, the station also has a museum dealing with its history and showing a documentary film on the subject, as well as putting on occasional "Living History" shows in which amateurs portray life in the mission station as it was in the 17th century.

Across Highway 12, the massive church built in 1926 serves as a memorial to eight French Jesuit priests from the first mission station, who were murdered and are commemorated in its Martyrs' Shrine, consecrated in 1926. This shrine to René Goupil, Isaac Jogues, Jean de la Lande, Antoine Daniel, Jean de Brébeuf, Gabriel Lalement, Charles Garnier and Noël Chabanel is visited by thousands of pilgrims every year. Pope John Paul II celebrated mass here a few years ago. Inside the church, which is almost entirely wood-panelled, the sandalwood canoe-shaped vault is particularly impressive. A small lookout tower in front of the church affords a splendid view of the surrounding area.

★★ **St Mary among the Hurons**

Open:
End of May to Oct.
10am–6pm

★ **Martyrs' Shrine**

Georgian Bay

★**Wye Marsh Wildlife Centre**
Situation
6km/3½ miles east of Midland

Nature lovers, and birdwatchers in particular, should be sure to visit the Wye Marsh Wildlife Centre, a marshland area by the Wye River, with board-walks and a tower hide where many kinds of flora and fauna can be seen.

Penetanguishene

Penetanguishene is a former garrison town, a few miles northwest of Midland, in a scenic setting on Georgian Bay. A large hospital has been established here. To symbolise Anglo-French harmony, the French-Canadians, who are in the majority here, have put up two angels at the south entrance to the town.

★**Naval and Military establishments**

In 1812 the war with the Americans forced the British to set up a naval base on Lake Huron. After two garrisons in the area fell to the Americans in 1818 Penetanguishene became a garrison town as well. Some buildings on the harbour have recently been restored, and visitors can see recreations of the officers' quarters, crew rooms, stores, and ships' repair shops.

★**Wasaga Beach**

The busy holiday resort of Wasaga Beach (pop. 6000) lies on a sandy spur of land between Georgian Bay and the Nottawasaga River. Its main attraction is its beach of fine, white sand, stretching for about 14km/8½ miles.

★**Nancy Island Historic Site**

The Schooner "Nancy" was a British supply vessel, and the only ship to survive the naval battle on Lake Erie which the British lost in 1812, but the Americans discovered the "Nancy" hidden away on the Nattawasaga River and subsequently sank her. The hull was salvaged in 1927 and today stands in front of the museum which tells the story of the War of 1812 and the three hundred years of navigation on Lake Superior. There is also a reconstruction of the engine room of a Great Lakes steamer.

Wasaga Provincial Park

Wasaga Provincial Park (140ha/346 acres) is open all year round and has beautiful beaches, picnic areas, tennis courts, cycle tracks and, in the winter, ice rinks, and snowmobile and cross-country skiing trails.

Water Theme Parks

"Wasaga Waterworld" and "Wasaga Landing", two immensely popular water theme parks, are open from mid-June to the beginning of September.

★**Thirty Thousand Islands**

Boat cruises

A boat cruise is a good way to enjoy the "thirty thousand islands" of Georgian Bay. These trips can start from Midland, Penetanguishene or Parry Sound (mid-May–Oct.), and follow roughly the same routes as those chosen by the Frenchmen Brulé, Champlain and La Salle when setting out to explore the North American interior.

Owen Sound

Owen Sound, a friendly town (pop. 20,000) in a delightful setting at the south end of Georgian Bay, is surrounded by limestone hills forming part of the Niagara Escarpment, and has good sailing and fishing.

County of Grey & Owen Sound Museum

This museum (975 6th St. E.), housed in three galleries and five restored old buildings, is the local history museum providing a survey of events from 1815 to 1920. Open: Tues.–Sun. 9am to 6pm.

Harrison Park

This well-kept park (46ha/114 acres) is especially worth visiting in spring for the blossom and in the autumn "Indian Summer". There are picnic areas, campsites, and waterfalls, etc.

★**Tom Thomson Memorial Art Gallery**

The Tom Thomson Memorial Art Gallery (840 1st Ave. W.; open: Tues.–Sun. 9am–6pm) is worth a visit to see a small cross-section of the work of probably Canada's best-known landscape artist, along with works by the "Group of Seven" and several other artists.

Story Book Park

Story Book Park is about 3km/2 miles south of the town beyond Highways 6 and 10, and is aimed at families with children. Open: end-May–beginning Oct. daily 10am to 6pm.

These three lovely waterfalls, hidden away outside Owen Sound, are top favourites with photographers.

Inglis Falls, Jones Falls, Indian Falls

The breathtakingly beautiful Bruce Trail leads up along the Niagara Escarpment, with its great views, and is the main trail in a whole network of paths, opening up one of Ontario's finest areas for hiking and walking.

★ Bruce Trail

The scenic road along the southern shore of Georgian Bay from Collingwood to Meaford – 35km/22 miles on Route 26 – leads to the Blue Mountain Chairlift, 11km/7 miles west of Collingwood. On a clear day the view from the highest part of the escarpment over the Bay and surrounding cliffs is an exceptional experience.

Blue Mountains

Tobermory is a picturesque little fishing village (pop. 600) with half-timbered houses and secluded coves at the northern tip of the Bruce Peninsula – geologically speaking a foothill of the Niagara Escarpment – which separates Georgian Bay from Lake Huron itself. The crystal-clear water also make it very popular with scuba-divers.

★ **Tobermory**

The Peninsula & St Edmunds Museum, about 3km/2 miles south of Tobermory, on Highway 6 (open: Victoria Day to Thanksgiving Day at weekends and in July and Aug. daily) has mementoes from the pioneering days and displays on the natural history of Georgian Bay.

Peninsula & St Edmunds Museum

The northern tip of the Bruce Peninsula, recently designated a National Park, has bizarre limestone formations and eroded rock pillars, very rare orchids and all kinds of wildlife, but especially amphibians. It is accessible from a network of footpaths.

★★ Bruce Island National Park

Fathom Five National Marine Park off Tobermory to the north holds at least twenty shipwrecks, some of them thickly overgrown. Georgian Bay's extraordinarily clear waters make it a real joy to the underwater photographer.

★★ Fathom Five National Marine Park

Flowerpot Island is a vase-shaped rock pillar in the Marine Park, and is visited by Tobermory's glass-bottomed boats.

★ Flowerpot Island

Boat trips in Georgian Bay

These three boats sail from Tobermory to Flowerpot Island and also take divers out to the wrecks in the Fathom Five National Marine Park, especially those in Big Tub Harbour.

M.V. "Seaview III" M.V. "True North II" M.V. "Blue Heron V"

M.S. "Chi-Cheemaun", a car-ferry known as the "Big Canoe" with space for 600 passengers and 115 vehicles, sails between Tobermory and nearby Manitoulin Island to the north twice a day from the beginning of May to mid-October. To book tel. 1–800–265–3163.

Big Canoe

Glace Bay

S 8

Province: Nova Scotia. Population: 22,000

This busy town's stormy history dates from the discovery of coal by French soldiers. It gets its name from the ice ("glace" in French) that the Louisbourg soldiers found in the bay in winter. It was built on a hill with vast coal deposits, mined by the French since 1720. In the 19th c. iron was discovered in nearby Newfoundland, and a rapidly growing steel industry sprang up near Sydney. Glace Bay flourished and many European emigrants arrived in the area. Nor did the town's growth grind to a halt when the coal ran out in the 1950s. A State programme helped to set up new industries, and rising oil prices could make the liquefaction of coal a profitable proposition here also.

★ Cape Breton Miners Museum

The Museum at Quarry Point shows how coal originated, as well as demonstrating old and new coal mining methods. A tour of a mine is particularly impressive. Old miners graphically illustrate life at the coal seams.

Next to the museum is a reconstruction of miners' quarters in the second half of the 19th c. The coal company's shop impressively illustrates how dependent the miners were.

Glacier & Mount Revelstoke National Park   F 7

Province: British Columbia
Area: Glacier National Park 1350sq.km/521sq.miles, Mount Revelstoke
National Park 263sq.km/102sq.miles

Information

The Superintendent, Glacier & Mount Revelstoke National Parks, P.O. Box 350, 301 Campbell Ave., Revelstoke, B.C. V0E 2S0;
tel. (604) 837–5155/837–6274.

Access

Road:
TransCanada Highway 1 (Golden–Rogers Pass–Revelstoke) passes through Glacier National Park and skirts the edge of Mount Revelstoke National Park.

Rail:
VIA Rail: stations at Golden and Revelstoke

Bus: Greyhound

Glacier National Park, very scenic and a great favourite with climbers, and Mount Revelstoke National Park, a few miles further west, lie in one of Canada's most inhospitable mountainous regions, the almost inaccessible northern Selkirk Range of the Columbia Mountains. These run parallel to the Rockies, with lots of jagged peaks, steep descents and narrow valleys cut deep into the rock, to the west of the Rocky Mountain rift valley. The wet west winds from the Pacific result in high levels of precipitation on the western flank of the Columbia Mountains which are over 3,000m/9846ft high. It rains almost every day, even in summer, and snows almost every day in winter – the weather station on Mount Fidelity has in fact measured 23m/75ft of snow in a year. These considerable snows feed more than 400 glaciers in and around Glacier National Park. Over 12½% of the park is permanently covered in ice and snow and the roads are very prone to avalanches. At lower levels, up to about 1300m/4267ft, there are real "Columbia type" rain forests with some enormous old trees – western red cedars, hemlock firs – with groundcover of ferns and the densest of undergrowth.

The eastern flank, on the other hand, starved of rain, has a dry, continental climate.

Both parks are home to mountain goat, caribou, and golden eagle, and the scrub in the wake of avalanches is the haunt of black and grizzly bear.

History

Even the Indians fought shy of the Selkirk mountains, on account of their terrain, climate, avalanches, lack of game and almost impenetrable vegetation, and they were only really explored when the need to build the railway became apparent. It was not until 1881, when Major A. B. Rogers discovered the 1327m/4355ft high pass that bears his name, that the barrier of the Selkirk Mountains could finally be overcome.

When the Canadian Pacific Railway went through the pass in 1885, the first Canadian trans-continental railway line was complete, and tourists

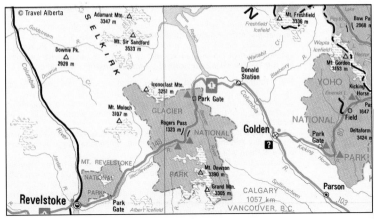

came to see the remote mountain landscape. The railroad company built four hotels along the line.

One of these was Glacier House, on the Illecillewaet Glacier, a Grand Hotel that by 1900 was attracting guests and climbers from all over the world – two Swiss mountain guides had been taken on in 1899 for visitors to the "Canadian Alps".

When, despite avalanche barriers and galleries, 62 railway workers lost their lives in an avalanche in 1910, it was decided to cut the 8km/5 mile-long Connaught Tunnel through Mount MacDonald, thus cutting off the world-famous Glacier House from the railway. Since few guests were prepared to undertake the long journey in horse-drawn carriages, the hotel was closed in 1925 and demolished soon afterwards. Today this elegant establishment is commemorated by a memorial tablet at the Illecillewaet campsite.

Avalanches

In 1962 part of the new TransCanada Highway was built on the old railway route over the Rogers Pass – too late for Glacier House.

The Canadian government made 76sq.km/29sq.miles of this spectacular alpine landscape a national park as early as 1886 and Glacier National Park was opened in 1930. The beauties of Mount Revelstoke's scenery inspired the creation of Mount Revelstoke National Park in 1912, and in 1927 the Prince of Wales opened the Summit Road, leading to the top of Mount Revelstoke, with its breathtaking views.

A 50km/31 mile section of the TransCanada Highway runs through Glacier National Park, providing easy access to trails such as the Loop Brook Interpretive Trail (round trail 6km/3½ miles west of Rogers Pass, 1 hour's walking) with several good views and interpretive panels about the old railway route over the pass. The Illecillewaet campsite also serves as a starting point for the Avalanche Crest Trail (steep climb, 3 hours; magnificent view from the ridge), the Great Glacier Trail (2–3 hours, climb to the head of the Illecillewaet Glacier) or the Glacier Crest Trail (several hours' climb, 800–1000m/2600–3300ft difference in height; good view of the Illecillewaet and Asuikan Glaciers).

★Glacier National Park

TransCanada Highway trails

As the Glacier National Park is "bear country", many walkers fix small bells to their rucksacks to warn the bears of their approach.

The visitors' centre at Rogers Pass (1327m/4355ft) is in a building like the old avalanche galleries (also accommodation, restaurant and filling station; open: June/Oct. daily 8am–8pm; Apr./May daily 9am–4pm, and at other times Mon.–Fri. only 9am–4pm). The centre has models showing the

Rogers Pass

history of the railway as well as maps and information about the national park.

Anyone wishing to hike or climb in the mountains, explore caves, or walk on glaciers, must register with the Ranger Station opposite.

The Abandoned Rails Interpretive Trail is about an hour's walk along a small section of the old railway line to several old avalanche galleries. Interpretive panels with historic photographs provide information.

★**Mount Revelstoke National Park**

★Summit Road

From Revelstoke (435m/1428ft; pop. 9000), the scenic Summit Road, 26km/16 miles long and passable only in summer, winds its way to the summit of Mount Revelstoke (1936m/6354ft). The alpine-like plateau on the western edge of the Selkirk Mountains is especially worth visiting for its wild flowers in summer.

From the summit there is a breathtaking view across the broad Columbia River valley and the mountain peaks of the Monashee Range in the west, some of them still unnamed.

Various trails branch off from the road, leading to the three mountain lakes, Eva Lake, Miller Lake and Upper Jade Lake – several hours of very strenuous hiking. Apart from Mount Revelstoke itself, the rest of the National Park, with the Clachnacudainn Icefield, is not easy to reach. The TransCanada Highway, which follows the Illecillewaet River valley, only skirts its southern edge.

Giant Cedars

The Giant Cedars Interpretive Trail, before the entrance to Revelstoke, is a boardwalk through what is still a well-preserved section of typical "Columbia" rain forest, with giant red cedars.

Golden   F 7

Province: British Columbia
Population: 4000

Information

See British Columbia

Golden (790m/2593ft), the famous holiday and winter-sports resort at the confluence of the Columbia and Kicking Horse rivers, is the gateway to the magnificent National Parks of the Canadian Rocky Mountains. Amid the jagged peaks of the Selkirk Mountains and the Rockies, Golden is the starting point for tours into largely unspoilt wild mountain regions, where visitors can go hiking, mountain-climbing and tour the Mummery Icefield glacier. There is whitewater rafting on the Kicking Horse River and canoeing on the Columbia and Blackberry rivers, as well as golf, riding (several guest ranches), fishing and big-game hunting, plus "Flightseeing" tours, which can also be booked.

The "Golden Triangle" cycling tour is very popular, from Golden, through Radium Hot Springs into Banff National Park, and back through Lake Louise to Golden again (320km/199 miles).

The Rodeo on Labour Day every year is a great attraction.

Ski area

The new Whitetooth Ski Area, on the slopes of the Purcell Mountains southwest of the town, was opened in 1987. With a descent of 526m/1726ft, it has eight ski-runs, ski lifts (usually weekends only), heliskiing and snow-mobiles.

History

Golden, which dates from the building of the railroad, now mainly lives from tourism, but also has a timber industry and a Canadian Pacific Railway repair shop.

The old town centre south of the Kicking Horse River has been made more attractive by the restoration of stores and houses in the early 1980s.

Museum

The small Golden & District Museum in the old schoolhouse (11th Ave./14th St, open: July–Labour Day, daily 9am–5pm) gives the history of the town and tells how the first Swiss mountain guides helped to open up the surrounding mountain areas.

Edelweiss, above Golden to the north, has houses built by the Swiss guides at the turn of the century.

Edelweiss

From Golden, the TransCanada Highway follows the Kicking Horse River into the Rocky Mountains to Kicking Horse Pass (72km/45 miles) passing through Yoho National Park (see entry).

TransCanada Highway

Grasslands National Park

H 7/8

Province: Saskatchewan
Area: 907sq.km/350sq.miles

Grasslands National Park Administration Office, Val Marie, Saskatchewan; tel. (306) 298–2257.

Information

The beauty, grandeur and solitude of the Great Plains is to be found in the recently designated Grasslands National Park between Val Marie and Killdeer. Open all year, this virtually untouched landscape is unique in its wild beauty.

★Natural features

Its harsh climate has helped to preserve this part of the plains. A few people came here in the early days of prairie settlement, but were unable to bear the conditions for long, since when Grasslands has been used for virtually nothing but grazing.

Harsh climate

This area has a history to it, despite its poor climate. Prairie Indians roamed here in search of buffalo, as the rock drawings and tepee rings show. It was

History

In Grasslands National Park (Saskatchewan)

also a favourite hunting-ground of the Métis from the early Red River settlements.

Wildlife

The Grasslands are home to many different creatures. Frenchman River Valley has antelope, hawks, eagles, reptiles (including many rattlesnakes) and packs of prairie dogs.

Prairie Dog Town

South of Val Marie is the Prairie Dog Town Nature Reserve, set up by the Saskatchewan Natural History Society.

Killdeer Badlands, Sinking Hill

Other attractions include the Killdeer Badlands, Sinking Hill and historical trails from the pre-settlement period.

As the park is still being developed, permits are issued by the Administration Office in Val Marie, which is also still quite short of recreational facilities.

Great Bear Lake   E/F 4/5

Administrative Unit: Northwest Territories
Altitude: 156m/512ft. Area: 31,153sq.km/12,025sq.miles

Information

TravelArctic, Government of the Northwest Territories, Yellowknife, Northwest Territories XIA 2L9; tel. (403) 873–7200

The eighth largest lake in the world, Great Bear Lake is 240km/149 miles long and 400km/249 miles across. It is covered with ice for eight months of the year, often as late as July. It has an outflow via the 120km/75 mile Great Bear River to the Mackenzie River (see entry). It has an all-year-round population of only 500 inhabitants, most of them around Fort Franklin.

Wildlife

The shores of Great Bear Lake are rich in wildlife, martens are particularly numerous. The shores are roamed by grizzly bears in summer, and the pinewoods are the haunt of elk in winter.

Great Bear Lake has achieved more angling records than any other lake in North America. It is especially famous for its trout, and the world's biggest trout, weighing up to 65 pounds, have been caught here, as well as the top-weight grayling and whitefish. Arctic char can be found in the nearby Tree River which can be reached from Plummers Great Bear Lodge.

For a fishing tour of Great Bear Lake, hire a guide in Fort Franklin.

Ecology

The waters of Great Bear Lake are ecologically extremely sensitive. Its lake trout take at least 15 years, and in some cases as many as 26 years, to reach sexual maturity, and they also only spawn once every 2 to 3 years. This means that stocks can soon become endangered, as has happened several times in the past. Today, however, strict regulations are in force, applying to anglers as well, in order to conserve this incomparable resource.

Fort Franklin

Most of the 500 permanent population of Great Bear Lake live in Fort Franklin, depending mainly on fishing.

Great Slave Lake   F–H 5

Administrative Unit: Northwest Territories
Altitude: 156m/512ft
Area: 28,570sq.km/11,028sq.miles

Information

TravelArctic, Government of the Northwest Territories, Yellowknife, Northwest Territories XIA 2L9; tel. (403) 873–7200

Access

Mackenzie Highway

Great Slave Lake gets its name from the Slave Indians who used to live on its shores. Part of the Mackenzie river system (see entry), it is in the district of the same name and the fifth largest lake in North America, with a number of tributary lakes to the north-east and the south. The lake is more than 600m/1970ft deep in places, reaching a length of up to 480km/298 miles east to west, and 110km/68 miles across at its widest part.

⋆ Natural features

It is covered with ice for eight months of the year. Its main source is the Slave River and it flows out into the Mackenzie River (see entry).

Most settlement is at the mouths of the tributaries. Lead and zinc are also mined on the southern shore.

Settlement, mining

Great Slave Lake is famous amongst anglers for its excellent trout and pike, while there are plenty of Arctic grayling in the tributaries.

Recreation

Spectacular sailing races are held on the lake, which also has some sandy beaches.

Great Slave Lake was discovered by Samuel Hearne in 1771. He was followed by Alexander Mackenzie (see Famous People) heading for the mouth of the river named after him, and by John Franklin. The gold prospectors who passed here on the way to Klondike in 1896–99 reported on the region's beauty, but nobody wanted to come here. It was not until 1930, when pitchblende was discovered on the lakeshore, that people got more interested in the area. The discovery of gold on Yellowknife Bay four years later led to a boom in Yellowknife (see entry).

History

Fishing has gained in importance since the Second World War.

Places on Great Slave Lake

See entry.

Fort Providence

See Fort Providence.

Mackenzie Bison Sanctuary

Fort Resolution was built by the Hudson's Bay Company on Moose Deer Island in 1819, and transferred to its present site around 1822. It was an important centre, with lighters bringing goods from Fort McMurray up the Slave River. The trading post lies 5km/3 miles south-west of the main estuary of Slave River. The large mission house and the school are no longer used.

Fort Resolution

See entry

Hay River

Gros Morne National Park

S 8

Province: Newfoundland
Area: about 1,943sq.km/750sq.miles

Gros Morne National Park, P.O. Box 130, Rocky Harbour, Newfoundland A0K 4N0; tel. (709) 458–2066

Information

Gros Morne National Park is undoubtedly one of the most impressive natural features in eastern Canada, a magnificent landscape of fiords and mountains, partly covered with dense forest, and with wildlife and plantlife adapted to cold conditions which are found scarcely anywhere else so far south.

⋆⋆ Natural features

The slopes of the Gros Morne (French for "big bleak hill") end in a plateau at about 600m/1970ft, with cliffs dropping down to the deep fiords (750m/2460ft) of the Gulf of St Lawrence.

The park clearly shows the results of 400 million years of continental drift followed by successive ice ages which ended 12,000 years ago. The Long

Geology

In the Gros Morne National Park

Range Mountains are amongst the oldest mountains on earth and have been shaped by advancing ice and the forces of erosion.

Trail

The difficult, 4km/2½ mile rocky ascent to the summit of the Gros Morne Mountain (806m/2645ft) by the James Callaghan Trail is worth making for the breathtaking view over the whole park and coastal towns below. This is a place to see caribou and snow hares.

Leisure pursuits

The park offers rock-climbing, boating, swimming, camping and fishing.

★ Bonne Bay

Route No. 431 from the park entrance at Wiltondale follows the south shore of the delightfully scenic Bonne Bay, alongside a deep fiord enclosed by the peaks of the Long Range Mountains.

Glenburnie,
South Arm

Route 431 runs through a hilly lake district to Glenburnie, from where there is a pleasant trip along the South Arm.

Trout River

It is worth making the detour to Trout River for the wonderful view over the coast and the plateau.

★★ Woody Point

Woody Point, one of the picturesque places on the west coast, is a good place to visit on the way back, since the scenery here is truly beautiful.

Norris Point

From here it is possible to take a 15–minute ferry trip to Norris Point, and return to Route No. 430 in Rocky Harbour by a different route. This was where the Dorset Culture of the Inuit once flourished, and their artefacts, along with those of other pre-European cultures dating back to 2500 B.C., have been found in the coastal regions of the National Park.

Rocky Harbour,
Neddy Harbour

The drive from Norris Point to Rocky Harbour affords splendid views over Bonne Bay. Like its neighbour Neddy Harbour, Rocky Harbour was named after one of the earliest pioneers. It is in a scenic setting at the entrance to the bay, surrounded by cliffs.

Route No. 430 from Wiltondale to Rocky Harbour on East Arm Fiord is another beautiful road. After Baker's Brook there is a lovely stretch along the coast, with views of the mountains around Bonne Bay to the south.

★ East Arm Fiord

The sealife exhibition in the restored lighthouse-keeper's house at nearby Lobster Cove Head is worth seeing. Below the lighthouse, there are sea-water pools full of sea urchins, starfish and sea snails.

Lobster Cove Head

Route 430 now crosses the higher western coastal plain to Green Point campsite, a few miles from Sally's Cove.

Green Point, Sally's Cove

The Western Brook gorge, cutting through the Long Range Mountains, is one of the most spectacular sights in North America. It is 200m/656ft deep, with steep faces towering as high as 600m/197ft on either side, and an 8km/5 mile circular trail on a wooden walk-way leads through magnificent forests and marshy meadows to the edge of the "Pond" the central part of which can only be reached by boat. Along the 14km/8½ mile trail to the end of the pond there are waterfalls plummeting 600m/1970ft from the plateau. (Tours can be booked in the park information centre.)

★★ Western Brook Pond

The road continues along the coast through St Paul's, a fishing village huddled around the entrance to a very impressive deep fiord.

St Paul's

Swimming in the Gulf of St Lawrence is not to be recommended, since the temperatures off the beaches of Shallow Bay (campsite) and Western Brook scarcely rise above 15°C/47°F.

Black bear, moose, otter, beaver, caribou, bald eagles, sea eagles, ospreys, snow grouse, and snow hares can all be seen along the local trails.

The Tête de Vache Museum at Cow Head is worth a visit. It is a local museum illustrating daily life in the early 20th c.

Cow Head

Halifax

Province: Nova Scotia. Population: 300,000

See Nova Scotia

Information

Halifax, the capital of Nova Scotia (New Scotland), is on a bay cut deeply into the Atlantic coastline, and has one of the most beautiful natural harbours in the world, with docks and piers starting at the point where the 7km/4½ mile-long outer bay narrows. The 5×2½km/3×1½ mile inner harbour, known as the Bedford Basin, is very deep and sheltered by the peninsula on which the city is built. Despite the skyscrapers of more recent times, the peninsula is still dominated by a hill topped by a star-shaped citadel. Halifax owes its existence to these two factors – its natural harbour and its citadel.

Halifax was founded in July 1749 when Edward Cornwallis and a number of settlers built a garrison here. The idea of a stronghold on this natural harbour (named "chebucto" or "great harbour" by the Indians) was not new, and the French had considered it after they lost the mainland of Nova Scotia in 1713 before opting for Louisbourg on Cape Breton instead. Louisbourg was the real reason for the building of Halifax, which was intended to act as its strategic counterpoint after the French fortress had been returned to the French following capture by the British in 1744.

History

Halifax was a thus a garrison from the outset, full of soldiers in the citadel and other military buildings, and of British sailors from the naval vessels

Military base

The famous clock-tower of Halifax

always in the harbour. This military presence made its mark on the city – from the balls and assemblies held by the naval and army officers, to the countless brothels round the harbour and below the citadel. Even justice was meted out according to martial law, and it was more than a hundred years before the civilians in Halifax had a say in how their community was run.

The royal princes

Halifax offered a home to two unruly sons of King George III when he more or less banished them from England. The future King William IV celebrated his 21st birthday with a wild party in the port, and passed many a night in the arms of Frances Wentworth, later to become the wife of the Governor.

His brother, Prince Edward, the Duke of Kent and future father of Queen Victoria, lived for six years in Halifax as Commander of the Nova Scotia forces. During that time he spent a fortune on fortifying the city, and made Halifax part of the famous British defensive square – Britain, Gibraltar, Bermuda and now Halifax. He was a strict disciplinarian, and would have his men whipped or even hanged for minor offences. But he also created the first telegraph system in North America, making it possible for him to issue orders to his men from Annapolis Royal (on the other side of the peninsula) or from his love-nest on the Bedford Basin, where his mistress, the beautiful Julie St Laurent, lived.

The Halifax explosion

The history of Halifax was not always so colourful. However, periods of prosperity often coincided with times of war, while peacetime often brought economic depression. The Napoleonic Wars, the American Civil War and, finally, the First and Second World Wars were times of major military activity in Halifax, and of burgeoning wealth as well as great tragedy. During both World Wars Halifax was a collection point for convoys which were supposed to enable shipping to cross the Atlantic in greater safety, and protect themselves against attack from German U-boats. In 1917 the French munition ship "Mont-Blanc", which had arrived to join one

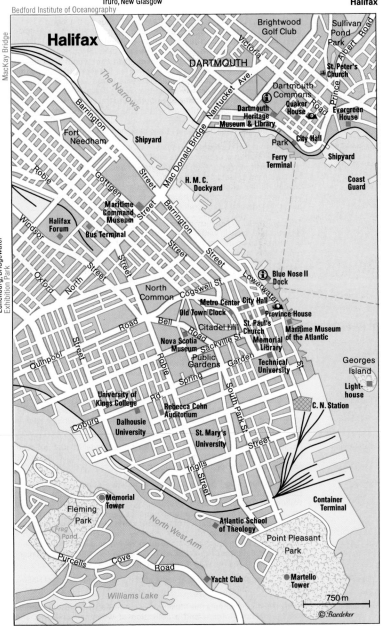

Truro, New Glasgow
Bedford Institute of Oceanography

Brightwood Golf Club

Sullivan Pond Park

Halifax

Halifax

DARTMOUTH

St. Peter's Church

Victoria

MacKay Bridge

The Narrows

Dartmouth Commons

Evergreen House

Quaker House

Barrington

Fort Needham

Shipyard

Dartmouth Heritage Museum & Library

Roble

Gottigen

City Hall

Park

Shipyard

Robie

Street

Mac Donald Bridge

Nantucket Ave.

Ferry Terminal

Coast Guard

H. M. C. Dockyard

Windsor

Halifax Forum

Maritime Command Museum

Street

Barrington

Street

Bus Terminal

Oxford

North

Street

Street

Blue Nose II Dock

Lowerwater

North Common

Cogswell St.

City Hall

Georges Island

Quinpool

Road

Bell

Metro Center

Old Town Clock

Citadel Hill

Province House

St. Paul's Church

Maritime Museum of the Atlantic

Light-house

Road

Nova Scotia Museum

Sackville St.

Memorial Library

Roble

Public Gardens

Garden

Technical University

Street

C. N. Station

University of Kings College

Spring

South Park St.

Coburg

Rd.

Rebecca Cohn Auditorium

Dalhousie University

St. Mary's University

Street

Inglis

Container Terminal

Memorial Tower

Fleming Park

Frag Pond

North West Arm

Atlantic School of Theology

Point Pleasant Park

Purcells

Cove

Road

Yacht Club

Martello Tower

Williams Lake

750 m

© Baedeker

such convoy, collided with the Belgian "Imo", causing the world's worst explosion prior to the dropping of the atom bomb on Hiroshima in 1945. The whole of the northern end of Halifax was razed to the ground, and port and rail installations were destroyed. The casualties included 1400 people killed outright, several hundred more who died later, about 9000 injured and 200 blinded. Windows were shattered as far away as Truro, some 100km/62 miles distant. The explosion was heard within a radius of 160km/100 miles. All that was left of the "Mont-Blanc" was a cannon in Albro Lake behind Dartmouth and a fragment of the anchor, which landed in the forest over 3km/2 miles away (the ship's crew survived, however, having left the ship in good time). There are still people in Halifax today drawing pensions for the injuries they sustained at the time.

Importance today

Halifax is not just the capital of Nova Scotia, it is also the commercial hub of Canada's Maritime provinces, as well as being an important centre for research with no fewer than six universities and colleges. It continues to have a strong military presence, although the soldiers are no longer in the citadel. Halifax is the Atlantic base of the Canadian navy, with large dockyards and a research centre (the latter in Dartmouth, Halifax's twin town on the other side of the bay, connected to it by two bridges).

Port

The port of Halifax can turn around more than 16 million tonnes a year, and is particularly busy in winter when the St Lawrence Seaway is closed. It has an enormous container port and auto-port, as well as shipbuilding and repair dockyards.

Events

Important dates in Halifax's annual calendar of events are July 24th, or Natal Day, when Halifax celebrates its birthday, mid-August, when the Nova Scotia Festival of the Arts takes place, and the end of September, date of the Joseph Howe Festival.

Sights of Halifax

★★Old Town Clock

The Old Town Clock, which has become the symbol of Halifax, was originally commissioned by Prince Edward in 1803. It has four clock-faces and chimes, and is an enduring memorial to the punctuality of that strict disciplinarian. Open: daily 9am to 5pm, and until 8pm in summer. There are guided tours and a snack bar.

★★**Citadel**

Location

The hill on which the citadel stands (National Historic Park) is in downtown Halifax, rather like Mont-Royal in Montréal. The top of what was a precipitous, tree-covered hill was levelled off to build the garrison which has been part of the townscape since the 18th c.

Citadel Road

Easily reached by car from the city centre along Citadel Road, the Citadel has excellent views of the city, the harbour, Dartmouth, little George Island and the Angus McDonald suspension bridge.

History

Three citadels stood here before the foundation stone for the present star-shaped construction was laid in 1828 on the order of the Duke of Wellington. The entrance is by a bridge over a wide, dry moat. Infantry and artillery drills are re-enacted in summer on the parade ground in the centre. Visitors can walk along the top of the earthworks and see the cannons that were the citadel's main means of defence. They can also go through a tunnel under the moat, marvel at the mighty walls, and look at the cannon-proof outer defences. This outer wall also contains a musketeers' gallery for shooting at anyone who managed to get as far as the moat.

"Tides of History"

This is an excellent audio-visual account of the turbulent history of Halifax and its fortifications.

Army Museum

Housed in the casements this museum has a number of interesting models from the Halifax region and a collection of weapons, uniforms and decorations.

There is a exhibition in the old Powder magazine, with exhibits about communication methods and the construction of the Citadel. A replica of the defence casement and a garrison cell can also be seen.

The harbourfront area on either side of Lower Water Street between Duke Street and the Cogswell intersection has been refurbished as "Historic Properties", an attractive pedestrian precinct containing restored 19th c. stone warehouses and old wharf buildings made into bright shops and artists' studios, restaurants and taverns with terraces overlooking the harbour. The roads are closed to normal traffic. The square between two warehouses has been roofed over to make an equally attractive mall; there are sightseeing cruises round the harbour, some of them on sailing ships.

Depart from Privateers' Wharf, daily from June to mid-October (duration: 2 hours).

The best cruise of the harbour and the North West Arm is on the "Haligonian III". An interesting commentary describes such features as the Halifax shipyards, where 7000 ships were repaired during the Second World War, the vast naval docks, with destroyers, submarines, etc., the National Harbour Board's loading station with a gigantic grain-conveyor (busiest in winter when the St Lawrence Seaway is closed to shipping), and the container terminal, where immense cranes are at work, loading and unloading the container vessels.

This cruise also takes in Mount Pleasant and the North West Arm, a beautiful inlet, lined with yacht clubs and the waterfront homes of the rich – a contrast to the dockyards.

The nearby Maritime Museum of the Atlantic (open: daily, except in the winter holidays) has a view over Halifax harbour. It contains a selection of small craft, model ships, photographs and exhibits of maritime history. The restored ship's cabin housed in one of the warehouses, is of particular interest, giving a survey of the tools used by sailors. Other exhibitions are devoted to the age of large sailing ships and to steamships.

The survey vessel "Acadia", berthed at the museum wharf, was built for the Canadian hydrographic service in 1913. It is open to visitors in the summer.

The "Bluenose II" is sometimes here as well. This was the winner of the International Fishing Trophy in 1921, which it held for the whole of its career, before being taken out of service in 1963 to act as a good will ambassador for Nova Scotia. In summer, when not on a visit to foreign ports, it does duty as a harbour sight-seeing schooner (2-hour cruises three times daily except Monday, July/August).

This Georgian sandstone building (main entrance on Hollis Street), completed in 1819, is the seat of Nova Scotia's Parliament, in existence since 1758. The guided tour includes the "Red Chamber" where the Council used to meet. The two portraits are of Caroline von Anspach, wife of King George II, and of her father-in-law, King George I, whose portrait was sent over from England in 1820 in mistake for that of his son. The tour also takes in the parliament chamber and the library which, with its two grand staircases, was once the Supreme Court of Nova Scotia. This is where, in 1835, Joseph Howe defended himself against the charge of defamation. His acquittal is regarded as the beginning of a free press in Nova Scotia. He later went into politics and led the campaign against confederation, but ultimately joined the dominion government in Ottawa.
The last room on the tour has two sculptures of headless hawks. They were beheaded at the height of anti-American feeling in the 1840s because they looked too much like the American eagle! Tours last half an hour and take place daily except Saturdays and Sundays and winter holidays.

Halifax

★Grand Parade

This lovely square, bordered by the City Hall at one end and by St Paul's Anglican Church – a half-timbered building dating back to 1750 and the oldest Protestant church in Canada – at the other, was the centre of Halifax from the very beginning. This was where military drills and parades took place.

★Nova Scotia Museum

This museum, with its entrance on Summer Street, gives a full account of the natural history of the province, including particularly impressive natural history and sealife dioramas (including whales and sharks). The museum also has exhibits about past history and social life.

The first sight to greet the visitor is a restored mail-coach, used on the Yarmouth–Tusket line in the late 19th c. There are also exhibits about the Micmac Indians and furnishings of the first European immigrants. The museum also maintains various historic buildings scattered over the entire province.

Open: daily except Mondays and winter holidays.

★Point Pleasant Park

Point Pleasant Park is closed to vehicles; these can be parked on Point Pleasant Drive, Tower Road, and near the container station.

There are magnificent views from this beautiful park, situated on the southernmost point of the Halifax peninsula, over Halifax harbour and the North West Arm. This is also the best place to watch "Bluenose II" cruising in the harbour under full sail.

There are plenty of footpaths and trails, as well as excellent picnic sites. Intrepid bathers can also take the plunge here.

For a long time this was a military no-go area, full of dugouts and fortifications, some of which can still be seen.

Prince of Wales Martello Tower

This round stone tower was built by Prince Edward in 1796. It was the first of its kind in North America, the prototype "Martello Tower". Prince Edward adapted the shape of a similar structure on the island of Corsica which had proved virtually impregnable. The basic idea was to combine soldiers' accommodation, a store-house and cannon mountings in a unit capable of defending itself, surrounded by immensely thick stone walls, with access only by a retractable ladder to the first floor. Canada subsequently had a great many of these towers which became redundant from about 1870 with the advent of steam engines, metal hulls and improved ship's artillery.

The Prince of Wales Tower, named by Edward after his brother who was to become King George IV, was built to keep guard over Halifax harbour – a fact not immediately obvious today, because of the tall trees that have grown up around it. Visitors can look at the powder magazines and the gun emplacements on the roof. Open: mid-June to Labour Day (first Monday in Sept.) daily.

Public Gardens

This 7ha/17 acre park was opened to the public in 1867, and is a good example of Victorian horticulture, with an ornamental bandstand, fountains, statues and formal flower-beds (open: May to Oct., daily 8am till dusk).

Surroundings

★Uniacke House

About 40km/25 miles to the northwest, on Mt Uniacke, in a beautiful setting in a park near a lake, stands this fine example of colonial architecture with a portico over two storeys high. It was built between 1813 and 1815 by Richard Uniacke, Nova Scotia's Public Prosecutor from 1797 to 1830.

Inside it looks exactly as it did in 1815 when furnished by the Uniacke family. Open: mid-May to mid-October daily 9am to 5pm.

★York Redoubt (National Historic Site)

The first defence works outside Halifax are about 11km/7 miles away at Sandwich Point. They were built in 1793 and substantially reinforced on the orders of Prince Edward, who had a tower built as part of his telegraph signalling system. Edward later named the redoubt after his brother, the Duke of York, and it remained in military use until the Second World War, when it was the centre for co-ordinating defence of the harbour and city against possible German attack.

This command post, a labyrinth of underground passages below the tower, is open to visitors. The tower itself, with displays on Halifax's fortifications, has a splendid view of the harbour on a clear day.

Command post

Along the walls of the redoubt there are 250mm/10 inch front-loader cannons, and the adjoining buildings have such items on show as a furnace for heating up cannon-balls, and transport to take the hot cannon-balls to the cannons (cannon-balls were only heated for smooth-bore cannons).

Open: mid-June to Labour Day 9am to 6pm; park open all year round (picnic area).

Hamilton
O 9

Province: Ontario. Population: 310,000

Hamilton Tourist Board, City Hall.
Niagara & Mid-Western Ontario Travel Association, 38 Darling St, Suite 102, Brantford, Ontario N3T 6A8; tel. (519) 756–3230

Information

Located at the westernmost point of Lake Ontario, Hamilton is the third largest city in the province of Ontario and the main centre of the Canadian steel industry (Hamilton Steel Co., etc.). It owes its importance to its harbour, which lies on the shipping route from the Great Lakes to the Atlantic via the St Lawrence (see entry). Industries include engineering, instrument-making and chemicals. Hamilton has a technical university (with the first Canadian atomic-research reactor) and is the seat of a Catholic and an Anglican bishop. Its pleasant climate also makes it famous for its vineyards and its apricots.

Hamilton is known to have been settled since the 1660s, but the city's foundation was actually in 1812. The modernisation of navigation and the completion of the Welland canal (see entry) meant that Hamilton became much more important, as raw materials from around the Great Lakes could be processed here at low cost. This was particularly true of iron and steel, which became a major industry very early on.

History

Sights in Hamilton city centre

Hess Village, between Hess Street, George Street and Main Street, is the 19th c. quarter, with pretty restaurants, boutiques and some commercial art galleries.

★Hess Village

Whitehern House (Jackson Street) is a Georgian mansion with a small garden that was the home of the McQuestern family (1840–1959), and has its original furnishings. The well-to-do McQuesterns were steel tycoons who lived in Hamilton from the early 19th c. Open: daily 2pm–5pm (guided tours).

Whitehern House

The city centre's main attraction is the ultra-modern cultural centre Hamilton Place, built in the 1970s, with a large auditorium seating 2200, and a studio theatre seating 400. This is home to the Hamilton Philharmonic Orchestra, and a venue for major dance and drama companies.

★Hamilton Place

Hamilton's Art Gallery contains collections of 19th and 20th c. Canadian art, while showing temporary exhibitions as well. Open: Tues.–Sun., 10am–6pm; tel. 527–6610.

Art Gallery

On York Boulevard there is one of the largest market halls in Ontario, selling local produce on Tuesdays and Thursdays.

Market

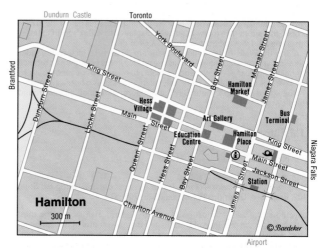

★ Dundurn Castle

Dundurn Castle, the 25–room mansion of Sir Allan Napier MacNab, Prime Minister of Canada from 1854 to 1856, was built between 1832 and 1835 overlooking the harbour. Today it is a museum of military history and has a collection of 19th c. furniture.

Canadian Football Hall of Fame

The Canadian Football Hall of Fame, near the cultural centre (open: Mon.–Fri., 11am–5pm, and Sun. also 11am–5pm in summer, portrays various aspects of this typical Canadian sport.

New City Hall

New City Hall has a mural by artist Franklin Arbuckle on the theme "A City and its People".

Outskirts of Hamilton

★★ Botanical Gardens

The Botanical Gardens (Plains Road) extends up over 1000ha/2500 acres on the western side of Lake Ontario, with an alpine garden, an arboretum, rose and lily gardens and gardening exhibitions and flower shows according to season. There is a garden centre and a cafeteria. Open: daily 9am to sunset (information in visitors' centre; tel. 527–1158).

Technical Museum

A Victorian pumping station (900 Woodward Ave.) still equipped as it was in 1859 is furnished as a technical museum (open: June–Sept. noon–5pm; Oct.–May 11am–4pm).

Surroundings of Hamilton

African Lion Safari

Some 32km/20 miles west of Hamilton, at Rockton, there is a drive-through safari park with African and North American animals (including lions, tigers and elephants) plus, of course, some North American bison. Open: mid-Apr.–mid-Oct., 9am–6pm.

Burlington

Burlington (population 117,000), a few miles north of Hamilton is in a delightful setting on the western shore of Lake Ontario. Places worth seeing include the Cultural Centre (425 Brock Ave.; open: Tues.–Sun.), the

Joseph Brant Museum (1240 N.Shore Blvd. E; open: daily) with mementoes of the Mohawk leaders and other Indian artefacts, and the Village Square with its attractively restored old houses.

Hay River   F 5

Administrative unit: Northwest Territories
Population: 3200

See Northwest Territories   Information

Hay River is one of the largest places in the Mackenzie District. On the southern bank of Great Slave Lake (see entry), it is the southernmost port on the Mackenzie river system (see entry).

Its strategic position earned it the title of "Centre of the North". During the five-month shipping season Hay River is packed with lighters, fishing boats and coastguard launches.

The town is the hub of the Great Slave Lake fishing industry, and the lake's famous whitefish are processed here. At Hay River freight for Arctic settlements is transferred onto barges and then taken almost 2000km/ 1250 miles down the Mackenzie River (see entry) to the far North. The people living along the river and in the Arctic settlements depend on these supplies of food, fuel and building materials.

For thousands of years this was the home of the Slave and Dene Indians.   History
The Hudson's Bay Company built the first trading post here in 1868, but the population only started to grow when the Mackenzie road system was complete and oil and gas began to be taken out. The railroad, which was completed in 1964, brought ore from Pine Point for smelting, making the town an important forwarding depot.

The little wooden houses of the old town lie at the mouth of the Hay River,   **Sights**
where the quays are piled high with supplies for despatch to distant settlements. This is also where the all-year fishermen live, catching trout, white-   ★ Old Town
fish and pike, some of which is exported to France, for example, to make
into pâté.

Devastating floods led to the building of a new town centre on higher   New Town
ground, dominated by a 14–storey tower block awaiting a gas pipeline in
the Mackenzie Valley.

Anyone wanting to find out more about the kind of situation that can arise   Coast Guard
on Great Slave Lake and along the MacKenzie River should arrange to visit
the Hay River Coast Guard station.

The Diamond Jenness School, opposite the tower block, is an outstanding   Diamond Jenness
example of northern architecture. Named after an anthropologist who,   School
around 1910, was the first to study northern native culture, its colour purple
makes it the landmark of Hay River.

Hay River Indian Reserve, a few miles outside the town, centres on the old   Hay River
Hudson's Bay Company's trading post, where there are still a few old   Indian Reserve
buildings, including a church.

Hope   E 8

Province: British Columbia. Population: 4000

See British Columbia   Information

Hope

History
The township of Hope (42m/138ft), amidst the often snowcapped Coastal Mountains, was originally a fort erected there in 1848/49 by the Hudson's Bay Company at the mouth of the Coquihalla River. The territory of the lower reaches of the Columbia River, the old route for the fur traders, was transferred to the USA with the Treaty of Oregon in 1846, and the Hudson's Bay Company was forced to find new ways into the interior. When gold was discovered on the Fraser River in 1858, a new town grew up next to the old trading post, which could now be reached by river steamers from Fort Langley (see entry). The first sawmills appeared, then in the 1870s silver deposits were found nearby and the first Waggon Road to New Westminster was built. The building of the railroad which started in the 1880s also acted as a boost to the whole region.

Road routes
Nowadays the TransCanada Highway runs north from Hope through the Fraser River Canyon (see entry), and the wonderfully scenic Crowsnest Highway 3 (see entry) goes east. A 134km/83 mile stretch of mountain and valley road takes in several mountain ranges, from Hope to the 1352m/4437ft Allison Pass in Manning Provincial Park. Coquihalla Highway 5, opened in 1986/87, also starts here. This new, four-lane highway which provides a 90km/56 mile shortcut to Kamloops (toll road), goes round the Fraser Canyon and acts as a relief road to the TransCanada Highway, taking much of the through traffic. Surrounded by lakes, rivers and mountains, Hope is a great place for outdoor pursuits as well as being the gateway to Manning Provincial Park, the Canadian continuation of the North Cascades National Park in the USA.

Sights of Hope

Hope Museum & Hope Travel InfoCentre
Hope Museum, on the TransCanada Highway (919 Water St; open: May–Sept. daily 9am–5pm), with items from the days of the fur traders and the Cariboo gold-rush, is also where the Tourist Information Centre is located.

Christ Church
Christ Church, a few blocks down the street, is a wooden Anglican church dating from 1861 and one of the oldest churches in British Columbia; services are still held here.

Surroundings of Hope

The Hope Slide
The Hope Slide, just under 20km/12 miles away, is where a landslide caused by an earthquake in 1965 buried a 3km/2 mile stretch of the highway, filling in a lake in the Nicolum River valley as well. There is a plaque commemorating this natural disaster in a lay-by 55m/180ft above the original road level.

★Manning Provincial Park
Manning Provincial Park, about 25km/16 miles from Hope, was opened in 1941, and covers more than 714sq.km/276sq.miles of magnificent mountain scenery. It is characterised by jagged mountain peaks over 2000m/6500ft high, deep valleys, and thickly wooded slopes, making it the northern continuation of the North Cascades National Park in the USA.

Skagit Valley
To the west of the park, in the Cascades, lies the 326sq.km/126sq.mile Skagit Valley Provincial Recreation Area (drive to Ross Lake but from the TransCanada Highway). There are canoe trips on the Skagit River, and good hiking on the Skagit River Trail (30km/19 miles), as well as horseback riding, fishing, hunting and, in winter, skiing.
From the western park entrance, the highway first crosses the "Rhododendron Flats", which are at their best in mid-June when the wild rhododendrons are in bloom (20-minute round trip).

Manning Park Resort
Manning Park Resort, 32km/20 miles beyond the Allison Pass, has a motel, restaurant, riding stables, 190km/118 miles of Wilderness Trails, and is

relatively sure of snow in winter, with more than 30km/19 miles of cross-country skiing trails, downhill skiing around the Gibson Pass, ski-lifts, snow-mobiles, etc. Information about the area can be obtained from the visitors' centre.

It is well worth driving up to Cascade Lookout with its magnificent view of the Similkameen Valley and the surrounding 2000m/6500ft mountain peaks.

★ Cascade Lookout

Hudson Bay

L–O 5–7

Hudson Bay, in north-east Canada, is the world's largest inland sea, extending between 63° and 51° latitude north. 1350km/839 miles from north to south, and 830km/516 miles across, it covers an area of 637,000sq.km/395,830sq.miles and has an average depth of 128m/420ft and a maximum depth of 259m/850ft. Partly within the Arctic Circle, it connects with the Atlantic to the east by the Hudson Strait (60–240km/37–150 miles across and about 800km/500 miles long) and the Sea of Labrador, and with the Arctic Ocean to the north, by the Foxe Channel (150–300km/93–186 miles across, about 300km/186 miles long), the Foxe Basin and the Gulf of Boothia.

Hudson Bay, around it the glacial elevations of the Canadian Shield with Pre-Cambrian gneiss and granite, has a hinterland with the typical, flat ground-moraine landscape of Arctic tundra, stretching to the northern timber line far to the south in the James Bay area. Baffin Island, a remainder of the crystalline mountains of the Canadian Shield, rises to heights of 2000m/6500ft in the north.

Landscape

The harshness of the terrain has so far made it difficult to produce accurate maps.

The climate is subpolar-continental. During the long winter, with temperatures as low as −60°C/−76°F, Hudson Bay is covered with ice 1–2m/3–6½ft thick. When there are strong north-westerly winds, the pack-ice can tower as high as 8m/26ft. During the brief summer, when temperatures can reach 20°C/52°F, the permafrost on land thaws down to depths of 60m/197ft, transforming the landscape into a broad, impassable bog.

Climate

The constant process of freezing then thawing has led to the formation of special phenomena such as pingos, mounds of earth formed through pressure from a layer of water trapped between newly frozen ice and underlying permafrost.

Although the growing season is generally less than five months, there is still an astounding variety of Arctic vegetation. In fact, more than 800 plant species have been identified, including mosses, lichens, ferns, and flowers such as polar poppies, purple saxifrage, arctic campanulas and arctic lupins. However, the harsh climate also means there is less wildlife, although there are plenty of migratory birds and seals, as well as the polar bears that occasionally venture into the settlements in search of food. In summer the marshy landscape swarms with midges and flies. Hudson Bay has vast fish stocks, as yet largely untapped, and the occasional school of white Beluga whales.

Wildlife

Hudson Bay was discovered in 1610 by Henry Hudson (see Famous People) and later named after him. The first European to reach Hudson Bay overland was Pierre Esprit Radisson, in 1662, and the first trading post followed, at the mouth of the Rupert River, in 1668.

History

The area around Hudson Bay is very sparsely populated. The biggest sector of the population is the Inuit, who have largely given up their traditional way of life as hunters, living from fishing and handicrafts in the few small trading posts along the coast.

Population

Hull

Economy

The Hudson Bay region is rich in natural resources, but their exploitation and transport have been so seriously curtailed by the nature of the terrain and the harsh living conditions as to make their extraction uneconomical. The fact that this potentially good waterway freezes over brings shipping to a standstill from October to June. It was 1929 before what is still the only railway line was opened between Winnipeg (see entry) and Churchill (see entry), a newly created port for getting wheat out of the Canadian prairie provinces. There are no roads that are passable all year round. The most important means of transport is currently by plane. The fur trade, and cod and salmon fishing are still of economic importance.

Hudson's Bay Company

The oldest company still trading in North America, the Hudson's Bay Company can look back over a 300-year history. On May 2nd 1670, King Charles II granted a team of Englishmen led by his cousin, Prince Rupert of Bohemia, full mining and trading rights for the territories draining into Hudson Bay. The company thus acquired control of a territory of around 8 million sq.km/5 million sq.miles, or 1/12 of the earth's surface, with rich mineral resources and fabulous fur-hunting grounds. The fur of the beaver, widespread here, was a sought-after luxury in Europe at that time, used for making beaver hats and other articles of clothing. The Hudson's Bay Company established a network of trading posts over the largely unexplored north of Canada, bases for the later settlement and development of the country. The English traders' almost total monopoly of the fur trade did not run into any serious competition until a century later, when the North West Company was founded in 1779. After a bitter struggle however, this new rival was forced into a merger in 1821. Nevertheless the changed technical, political and social circumstances meant the powerful company could no longer maintain its hegemony and, in 1870, it had to sell its land to the Canadian government. Other holdings, including the fur trading company, have been disposed of in recent decades. Nowadays the former fur traders own many big department stores throughout Canada and still employ over 38,000 people.

Baie James
(James Bay)

See entry

Province: Québec. Population: 60,000

Information

See Québec and Ottawa

Hull, which is a French-speaking city, stands on the banks of the Gatineau and Ottawa Rivers on the edge of the Outaouais (see entry), across the river from Ottawa. An important centre for the timber and paper industry, it also has a number of federal government departments, their buildings dominating the landscape, especially La Chaudière and the Place du Portage.

In recent years Hull city centre has been restructured into two core areas, linked by the Promenade de Portage, an ultra-modern administrative complex of six buildings for approximately 19,000 federal and provincial government officials.

View

From Jacques-Cartier Park, there is a fine view over the Ottawa River to the Parliament building, the Rideau slopes and other major features of Ottawa.

History

The Gatineau area was traversed by the Indians long before the first European settlement. The first French explorers, such as Champlain, came here in 1613 and 1615, to be followed by woodsmen and other adventurers in search of furs and engaged in setting up trading posts. Around 1800 the American Philemon Wright began farming here, using the slopes of the Chaudière, and founded a colony which he named Hull after his parents' birthplace in England. In 1806 he sent a consignment of timber by raft to Québec, and thus became the founder of a major industry. Some time later another American, Ezra Butler Eddy, made the town famous throughout the world with the matches he produced here.

This magnificent museum stands on the river bank opposite Ottawa's Parliament buildings. Its architect, Douglas Cardinal, wanted its flowing lines to call to mind the immensity and diversity of the Canadian landscape.

The Pavillon du Bouclier Canadien, to the left of the main entrance, holds the museum's offices, laboratories and storage for about 3,500,000 items. The exhibition rooms of the Pavillon du Glacier (total area 16,500sq.m/ 6369sq.ft) are to the right of the entrance. There are also audio-visual displays illustrating the many different cultures found in Canada.

★★Musée Canadien des Civilisations

Location
Rue Laurier 100
Port Alexandra

Open: Tues–Sun.
10am–5pm

In the Grande Galerie, six wooden longhouses and their totem poles symbolise the culture of six Indian tribes on the Pacific.

Grande Galerie

Here a thousand years of Canada's past history is brought to life in a succession of scenes of costumed figures from the period in question before a magnificent natural backdrop.

Salle de la Histoire

In this children's museum, children can play at discovering the world's remotest corners.

Musée des Enfants

The vast IMAX screen is seven stories high under an enormous dome, and shows special films that provide an unforgettable experience.

Ciné-Plus

Gatineau Park, administered by the federal government, is a woodland and lakeland district in the hills of this part of the Canadian Shield alongside the River Gatineau, large areas of which are still primeval forest. Some places are set aside for outdoor activities such as camping, jogging, walking, riding, swimming, fishing, cycling and downhill and cross-country skiing.

★★Gatineau

The official summer residence of the prime minister of Canada is on Lac Mousseau in the centre of the park.

Lac Mousseau

The footpaths through the southern part of the park are an especially beautiful walk in the autumn, as the leaves change colours.

Autumn colours

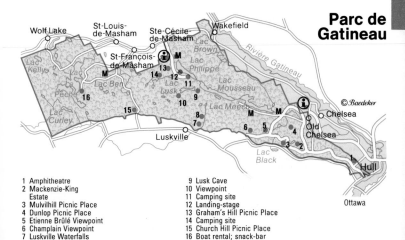

Parc de Gatineau

© Baedeker

1 Amphitheatre
2 Mackenzie-King Estate
3 Mulvilhill Picnic Place
4 Dunlop Picnic Place
5 Etienne Brûlé Viewpoint
6 Champlain Viewpoint
7 Luskville Waterfalls
8 Fire tower

9 Lusk Cave
10 Viewpoint
11 Camping site
12 Landing-stage
13 Graham's Hill Picnic Place
14 Camping site
15 Church Hill Picnic Place
16 Boat rental; snack-bar
M Toll

★Belvédère Champlain	The Belvédère Champlain, about 26km/16 miles from the park entrance, provides a wonderful view over the Gatineau hills, a sharp contrast with the farmland in the Ottawa and Gatineau river valley.
Domaine Mackenzie-King	The country estate of former premier William Mackenzie-King can be found in the heart of the Gatineau mountains on the way to Kingsmere. The estate includes several small homes on a lakeshore, with period settings, and audio-visual aids to take the visitor back to the early years of this century.
Moorside	The main house is Moorside (open: mid-May–mid-Oct. daily 11am–6pm), where the visitor can have tea or a meal in the dining room, and see items from the Mackenzie-King days. The ruins in the park are from the Canadian Parliament building in Ottawa which burned down in 1916, and were put there by MacKenzie-King.
Moulin de Wakefield	The Moulin de Wakefield stands about 40km/25 miles north of Hull (Highway 105) above the River Pêche just before it joins the Gatineau. Built in 1838 to grind corn, it has been restored to working order (guided tours: end of May–mid-Oct.).

Icefields Parkway   F 7

	Provinces: Alberta/British Columbia Length: 230km/143 miles Driving time: at least 4 hours Highest point: Bow Pass, 2068m/6787ft
Information	See Alberta and British Columbia
★★Route	Icefields Parkway is the name given to Highway 93 which connects Lake Louise (TransCanada Highway) with Jasper (Yellowhead Highway 16), passing through Banff and Jasper National Parks in the Rocky Mountains on the way.

Unlike the busy through-route of the TransCanada Highway, Icefields Parkway is purely for sightseeing, winding through 230km/143 miles of magnificent mountain scenery from Lake Louise to Jasper, following a valley north–south between the peaks of the main range of the Rocky Mountains, most of them well over 3000m/9850ft high. Originally built as a project to create work during the Depression, the highway was extended and completed in 1960. It passes first along upper Bow Valley, and winds over Bow Pass (2068m/6787ft) to the Mistaya and Saskatchewan River valley, then over the Sunwapta Pass, only marginally lower at 2035m/6679ft, and close to the Columbia Icefield it reaches the Sunwapta/Athabasca River and Jasper. Frequent lay-bys and parking places provide opportunities to enjoy the breathtaking views and there are interpretive panels to fill in the background about the landscape and local history.

Bighorn sheep and mountain goats – down at the roadside or on the mountain tops – romantic waterfalls, the shimmering turquoise waters of mountain lakes, looming icefields and snowclad mountain peaks all make for a journey of infinite variety.

★Bow Lake · Bow Glacier · Crowfoot Glacier	Bow Lake, 34km/21 miles north of Lake Louise (see Banff), lies below the Crowfoot Glacier (shaped like a crow's foot and clearly visible from the road) and Bow Glacier. The lake's still, clear waters mirror the towering, snow-covered peaks of the continental divide. These glaciers form part of the great Waputik Icefield. Num-ti-jah Lodge, a little hotel on the shore of Bow Lake, built in 1939 by Jimmy Simpson, an early pioneer of mountain tourism, was the setting for many a Nelson Eddy movie in the 1950s. There are lovely walks along the lake to a waterfall at the foot of the Bow Glacier (half a day) or to Helen Lake and Catherine Lake at the Dolomite Pass to the east (whole day).

Angel Glacier

Athabasca Glacier

At 2068m/6787ft Bow Pass is the highest pass in the Banff National Park (see entry), and the watershed between the river systems of the North and South Saskatchewan River. A short branch road leads to the magnificent Peyto Lake viewpoint and there is another superb lookout point that can be reached on foot about a third of a mile further on. This is especially lovely in summer, when Bow Summit's mountain meadows are carpeted with wild flowers.

Bow Pass

A longer and steeper path leads down for 2½km/1½ miles to Peyto Lake, named after the mountain guide Bill Peyto, who began exploring the area in 1894 and took packhorses of supplies north over Bow Summit.

★★Peyto Lake

About 70km/43 miles north of Lake Louise, a short path leads down from the car-park to the narrow, winding Mistaya Canyon ("mistaya" is Indian for "grizzly bear"), with its virtually vertical rockfaces and characteristic "pot-holes".

Mistaya Canyon

After another 6km/3½ miles, the David Thompson Highway branches off towards the east where the North Saskatchewan River cuts north/south through the Rocky Mountains.

David Thompson Highway

About 120km/75 miles north of Lake Louise there is a path leading from the far end of the car park down to Nigel Creek and the awesome Panther Falls. These can be seen from above by taking the footpath from the top end of the car park.

Nigel Creek
★Panther Falls

About 4km/2½ miles further north a winding path climbs 275m/903ft from the car park up to Parker Ridge. From the top there is a magnificent view of the 11km/7 mile-long Saskatchewan Glacier, the longest glacier tongue of the Columbia Icefield. Mountain goats can often be seen on the ridge. This is a particularly attractive area in summer when the wild flowers are in bloom.

Parker Ridge

245

Picturesque Peyto Lake

Sunwapta Pass

The Sunwapta Pass (2035m/6679ft) forms the watershed between the North Saskatchewan River which flows into the Hudson Bay and the Athabasca River which flows into the Beaufort Sea. It is also the borderline between Banff and Jasper National Park (see entries).

★★**Columbia Icefield**

Situation

The Columbia Icefield, the most important of the icefields from which the parkway gets its name, is close on 130km/80 miles north of Lake Louise. Covering a total area of 389sq.km/150sq.miles, with the surrounding glaciers, it is the biggest continuous icefield in the Rockies. On the main field, the ice is 600m to 900m/2000 to 3000ft thick in places.

From the Columbia Icefield, which lies on the continental divide, several hanging glaciers flow down the mountain, their tongues stretching deep into the valleys.

Mount Snowdome (3520m/11,553ft) is the very apex of Canada, from where the melted snow and ice flow into three different oceans, the Pacific to the west, the Beaufort Sea to the north through the Athabasca River and Mackenzie River, and hence the Arctic, and through the Saskatchewan River into Hudson Bay, and thence the Atlantic. The enormous icefield – its size can only be appreciated from the air – is a relic of the immense glaciation in the Rocky Mountains during the ice age which shaped the present topography of the area. Over the last 300 years the individual tongues of the Columbia Icefield glaciers have retreated considerably.

Icefield Centre

In the Icefield Centre (open: end of May–mid-Oct. daily 9am–5pm, and till 7pm in high summer) can be seen a model of the Columbia Icefield and a multi-vision slide show explains the development of the icefield and its individual glaciers.

From the Icefield Centre there is an excellent view of the tongue of the 7km/4½ mile-long Athabasca Glacier and the glaciated north wall of Mount Athabasca (3491m/11,457ft). There is an even better view from the meadows above the Icefield Chalet (overnight accommodation), which is also a good starting point for several hikes in the mountains.

The world-famous Columbia Icefield

The guided tours by Snow Coach onto the surface of the Athabasca Glacier are a memorable experience. These robust coaches with four-wheel drive travel on part of the glacier. Guided walks on the glacier lasting several hours can also be booked (tel. 762–2241), but these chances to walk on ice which is about 400 years old are very popular, so it is necessary to book early.

Early in this century the tongue of the Athabasca Glacier still covered the whole valley, including where the highway runs today, so explorers and early travellers went over the nearby Wilcox Pass to reach Jasper.

After parking at Sunwapta Lake and climbing up to the debris-strewn tongue of the glacier, it is possible to see from the date-posts just how fast the ice has retreated, leaving clearly identifiable moraine deposits in its wake.

Just 180km/112 miles north of Lake Louise, and 60km/37 miles south of Jasper, a side-road leads to the Sunwapta Falls ("sunwapta"=rushing water) where the Sunwapta River abruptly changes course and cascades down into a ravine.

About 200km/125 miles north of Lake Louise (and 33km/20 miles south of Jasper) the Athabasca River plunges down over a solid rock of Pre-Cambrian quartz sandstone. By retrograde erosion the waterfall is steadily retreating leaving a narrow gorge which funnels masses of water into a seething maelstrom, especially when the snow melts in early summer.

A path with a bridge and various lookout points circles around the 22m/72ft waterfalls and the gorge with its precipitous rockfaces.

Highway 93A, which used to be the main road to Jasper, branches off near the waterfalls and serves as an alternative route. It can be used to reach the approach roads to Mount Edith in the Cavell district (see Jasper), with the Angel Glacier and the Marmot Basin, very popular for skiing in winter.

Margin notes:

Snow Coach tours May–Sept. daily 9am–5pm

Athabasca Glacier Sunwapta Lake

Sunwapta Falls

★Athabasca Falls

Highway 93A

Route

Îles de la Madeleine   R 8

Province: Québec

Information   See Québec

Ferries   Car ferries to the Îles de la Madeleine operate daily in summer, except Thursdays, departing from Souris (see Prince Edward Island), and once a week departing from Montréal (see entry).

Flights   There are flights from Charlottetown, Gaspé, Québec and Montréal (see entries).

The Îles de la Madeleine archipelago lies in the Gulf of St Lawrence, close on 300km/186 miles from Gaspé and 120km/75 miles from Prince Edward Island (see entry) and consists of twelve islands and a few small reefs. Their name goes back to Samuel de Champlain (see Famous People), who in 1629 entered "La Magdeleine" on his chart. Of the seven inhabited islands, six are joined together by a road running along a 90km/56-mile strip of dunes.

★Topography   The Îles de la Madeleine are typically grayish-red sandstone, gypsum and other volcanic rock. The cliffs and rocks have been carved into fascinating shapes by erosion, and have disintegrated in parts to form broad, long sandy beaches, washed by the warm Gulf Stream. The contrast between the white houses and the intense colours of the landscapes gives the islands an appeal all their own.

The inhabitants of the Îles de la Madeleine, or the "Madelinots", are mainly descendants of the Acadians who settled here after 1755. About 150,000 people – French, Scottish, English and Irish – live here throughout the year, fishing and farming, and seal-hunting in March and April.

Coast of the Îles de la Madeleine

The islands are ideal for water-sports enthusiasts, birdwatchers and anyone who enjoys long walks in the dunes.

Sport and Leisure

The best time for a visit is in August. Spring is less to be recommended because of the thick fogs.

The Île du Havre aux Maisons, with its gentle, green hills, its winding paths and scattered houses is one of the archipelago's most beautiful islands. In the south of the island the Hydro-Québec Generating Company has set up a windmill park.

Île du Havre aux Maisons

Cap Alrith is noted for its impressive offshore rock formations.

Cap Alrith

Half the people of the archipelago live on Île du Cap aux Meules, the source of all the islands' supplies. There is a wonderful view from the Butte du Vent over the surrounding islands and on a clear day it is possible to see as far as Cape Breton Island (see entry), nearly 100km/62 miles away.

Île du Cap aux Meules

Near Etang-du-Nord the sea has created some particularly bizarre rock shapes.

From Cap-aux-Meules, a ferry crosses to Île d'Entrée, the only inhabited island not connected to the others.

Île du Havre-Albert is the southernmost island in the archipelago and its little town has a Musée de la Mer (open: Mon.–Fri. 9am–6pm, Sat. and Sun. 10am–6pm).

Île du Havre-Albert

Inside Passage

C/D 7

Province: British Columbia
Ferry between Port Hardy (Vancouver Island) and Prince Rupert
Distance: 274 nautical miles (about 507km/315 miles)
Time taken: 15 hours

B.C. Ferries, Reservations Centre, 1112 Fort St, Victoria, B.C.
V8V 4V2; tel. (604) 386–3431 or 669–1211 (Vancouver)

Information

The Inside Passage, a shipping route off the Canadian Pacific coast, in the lee of countless small islands, extends from Puget Sound in the south, near Seattle (Washington), through the Georgia and Queen Charlotte Straits, up towards the "Alaska Panhandle" (about 1500km/930 miles).

★Situation

There are cruises to Alaska, lasting about a week, from Seattle and Vancouver. The best time to go is from July to September, when according to the statistics there should be a greater number of sunny days. In fact the climate on the Canadian Pacific coast is relatively mild all year round, although the mainly westerly winds bring plenty of rain, because of the warm Japanese current.

The best known cruise, and a particularly impressive one in fine weather, is the 15-hour voyage on the M.V. "Queen of the North", a ferry which takes about 750 passengers and 150 vehicles along the Inside Passage from Port Hardy, on the north-east tip of Vancouver Island, to Prince Rupert through a labyrinth of thickly wooded, hilly and virtually uninhabited islands, narrow channels and fiords, a lonely, almost untouched landscape. Only occasionally do slopes devoid of trees bear witness to human activity. With luck the ship will be accompanied part of the way by dolphins or killer whales, sea-lions will be sunning themselves on the rocks, and eagles will be circling above, while on the mainland the snow-capped coastal mountain ranges can be seen looming against the sky.

"Queen of the North"

During the six months of summer, the ferry runs north one day and south the next. Once a week it also calls at Bella Bella a fishing and lumbering settlement on Campbell Island, where most of the population are Indians (Waglisla Indian Village).

Inside Passage: on the M.V. "Queen of the North"

At Prince Rupert passengers can join the Alaska Marine Highway ferries and continue on through Ketchikan (a busy little fishing harbour, with impressive totem poles and historic Creek Street built on stilts), Wrangell, Petersburg, Juneau (capital of Alaska in the USA with excursions to Glacier Bay National Park) and Haines (for the Chilkat Indian Dancers and Chilkat State Park), to Skagway, the "Gateway to the Yukon", and Klondike Goldrush National Historical Park, the road to the Alaska Highway. The whole trip takes about 36 hours.

Alaska Marine Highway

Information and reservations: Alaska Marine Highway, P.O. Box R, Juneau, Alaska 99811, USA; tel. (907) 465–3941, or within the USA 1800–642–0066.

Inuvik

C 4

Territory: Northwest Territories
Population: 4000

Access

By air or the Dempster Highway (see entry)

"Place of Man" is the Inuit meaning of the name for this modern settlement in the Arctic circle on the Mackenzie River delta (see entry). Built between 1955 and 1961, during the oil and gas exploration, it replaced Aklavik, which was badly located and prone to flooding. Today Inuvik is the trading, administrative and supply centre for about 9000 local people, most of them Inuit. It has an airfield, several schools, a hospital and a police station. From here the supply planes set off for the exploration bases in the far north (Mackenzie delta, Beaufort Sea). Sightseeing flights over the Arctic also take off from here.

Since the earth is permanently frozen in this arctic climate to a depth of several hundred feet, all utility supply lines have to be laid above the ground and the houses built on stilts to prevent the melting of the perma-frost, which would result in subsidence.

A famous curling tournament is held here at the end of March, followed a month later by the Top of the World skiing championship.   **Events**
   There are many street parties during June and July in the long daylight hours of midsummer.

Sights of Inuvik

Inuvik's Catholic church, a modern, igloo-shaped building, is very impres-sive and contains a tabernacle which is also igloo-shaped, and a remark-able "Way of the Cross" by Inuit artist Mona Trasher.   ★ Roman Catholic Church

Surroundings of Inuvik

Aklavik, Inuit for "home of the polar bears", is west of Inuvik and has a population of 800. It was founded by the Hudson's Bay Company in 1912 in the middle of the Mackenzie delta, an area prone to flooding.   **Aklavik**
   Aklavik was the main town in the western Arctic until the building of Inuvik.

The Anglican episcopal church with its highly original stained-glass is well worth a visit. Scenes from the life of Christ are set in local conditions, so the Holy Family are depicted with a polar bear, the Adoration of the Magi takes place in the snow, and the Virgin and Child are wrapped in furs.   **Church**

The area surrounding Inuvik, especially the nearby lakes, has good oppor-tunities for fishing and camping, and boats can be hired to explore the lakes.   **Surrounding area**

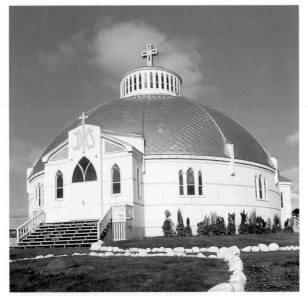

Like an igloo: the Catholic Church of Inuvik

Mackenzie Delta   See Mackenzie River

Jasper National Park   F 7

Province: Alberta. Situation: Rocky Mountains
Area: 10,878sq.km/4199sq.miles

Information
The Superintendent, Jasper National Park, 500 Connaught Ave., P.O. Box
    10, Jasper, Alberta T0E 1E0; tel. (403) 852–6161
Jasper Park Chamber of Commerce, 632 Connaught Ave., P.O. Box 98,
    Jasper, Alberta T0E 1E0; tel. (403) 852–3858

See Alberta

Access
By road
Yellowhead Highway 16, Prince George – Jasper – Edmonton; Icefields
Parkway (see entry; Highway 93 Jasper–Lake Louise)

By rail
VIA-Rail Edmonton–Jasper–Vancouver or Prince George/Prince Rupert

By bus
Brewster Transportation & Tours, connection to Calgary Airport

★★Situation
Jasper National Park, adjoining Banff Park's northern boundary (see entry),
with an area of 10,878sq.km/4,199sq.miles, is the biggest National Park in
Canada's Rocky Mountains, a continuation of magnificent mountain scenery, with majestic mountains, glaciers, crystal-clear lakes, waterfalls and
narrow gorges, pine woods and, in summer, lovely mountain meadows
covered with flowers. Here on the border of British Columbia the snow-
capped pyramid of Mount Columbia peaks at 3747m/12,298ft on the edge
of the Columbia Icefield (see Icefields Parkway). Some tourist roads to
particularly lovely areas also give the motorist easy access to the most
spectacular scenery. However large sections of the National Park are being
kept in their original state, and can only be reached on foot, by canoe or on
horseback.

History
The town of Jasper dates from 1911 when the Grand Trunk Pacific Railway
was built along the Athabasca River to the Yellowhead Pass, although
David Thompson had already established a modest little settlement here a
hundred years earlier for the North West Company when he was looking for
a northern route over the Rocky Mountains in 1811. For fifty years the fur
trappers' main route was to lead over the Athabasca Pass. A little monument near Beauvert Lake commemorates "Henry House" (Old Fort Point), a
hideaway for trappers and the place where they got their supplies.
Jasper House, named after Jasper Hawes who lived here for a long time,
was built in what is now the eastern section of Jasper Park in 1813. In the
second half of the 19th c. the number of travellers here dwindled until
Jasper was visited only by a few adventurers and gold-prospectors, explorers and particular enthusiasts such as the painter Paul Kane or the extraordinary Mary Schäffer, who followed old Indian trails and in 1908 reached
Maligne Lake, hitherto unknown.
By 1907 several thousand square miles of wilderness had been designated the Jasper National Park.

Jasper townsite

History
When the railroad reached Jasper in 1911, the settlement which grew up on
the Athabasca River was initially called Fitzhugh, and this remained its
name until it was changed to Jasper in 1913. The Brewster brothers set up a
small tent city for tourists on Beauvert Lake, which was replaced by Jasper

Jasper National Park: Maligne Lake ▶

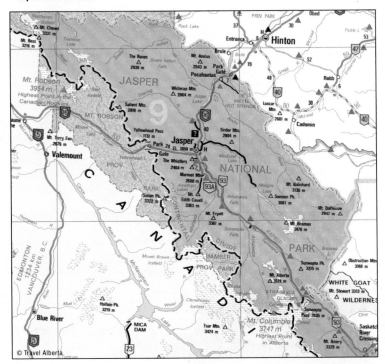

© Travel Alberta

Park Lodge in 1920. Mountaineers climbed the previously unknown peaks, and outfitters took enterprising tourists to remote regions on horseback.

Present importance	Jasper townsite, somewhat less crowded than its sister resort of Banff, has a permanent population of about 3300. It is the tourist centre for Jasper Park, with plenty of accommodation, stores, etc.
Connaught Drive	Connaught Drive is Jasper's main street. The Canada Parks offices are opposite the station where, from late summer onwards, long goods trains, often numbering more than a hundred freightcars, laden with grain from the prairies, are assembled in the vast marshalling yards before going on to Vancouver through Yellowhead Pass.
Beauvert Lake, ★ Jasper Park Lodge	Jasper Park Lodge, about 7km/4½ miles east of Jasper townsite and in a beautiful setting on Beauvert Lake, is a vacation resort open from mid-May to October and dating back to the 1920s. It has excellent facilities, including a golf course, riding stables, boat-hire, etc.
★ Whistlers Mountain, Jasper Tramway	The Jasper Tramway station is about 7km/4½ miles south of the town, near a large campsite. This mountain tramway, which runs from 8am to 6pm, April to October, goes up Whistlers Mountain, named after the whistling of the marmots which run around here in the summer. There is a good view of Jasper from the mountain station (restaurant) at 2277m/7473ft, but it is also well worth walking all the way up to the summit (2464m/8087ft) to take in the magnificent panoramic view.

Half-day raft tours on the lovely Athabasca River, the one-time highway of the furtrappers, operate from the Brewster Bus Depot on Connaught Drive from June to September.

Athabasca River, Jasper Raft Tours

About 7km/4½ miles north of Jasper, Pyramid Lake and Patricia Lake are reached by a winding road. These two attractive mountain lakes below the impressive 2768m/9085ft Pyramid Mountain have good windsurfing, canoeing and boating as well as sailing.
A 5km/3 mile circular trail past Patricia Lake leaves from the Pyramid riding stables.

Pyramid Lake, ★ Pyramid Mountain, Patricia Lake

Moose, deer and beaver can be seen in the Cottonwood Creek area, in the early morning or in the evening.

Cottonwood Creek

Scenic Maligne Lake is a good destination for a day out, reached by taking the Maligne Road, which branches off from the Yellowhead Highway 3km/ 2 miles beyond Jasper. The Maligne Canyon, 11km/7 miles east of Jasper, is one of the most beautiful canyons in the Rockies. It has several waterfalls and a 4km/2½ mile nature trail, starting at the lodge (open in summer) and leading along the Maligne Canyon, its chalky sandstone walls as high as 50m/164ft, with interpretive panels explaining the geomorphological features. The canyon is very narrow in places and spanned by several bridges. Its lower section carries far more water than the upper part since water from Medicine Lake enters the canyon at various places, flowing through subterranean clefts and gushing out of karst hollows.

Maligne Road, ★ Maligne Canyon

Medicine Lake, a few miles further south, is 6km/3½ miles long, and appears to have no outflow to speak of at its northern end, yet the water-level varies greatly during the course of the year. In late autumn the lake is almost empty, with only a trickle of water meandering between the mud banks on the lake bed, to seep away at the north-east side of the basin. This

Medicine Lake

Cordilleras: Medicine Lake in Jasper National Park

255

phenomenon was a mystery to the local Indians, and their medicine men took advantage of it, hence the name.

★★ Maligne Lake

Maligne Lake, 11km/7 miles further on, is the largest glacial lake in North America. At a height of 1673m/5491ft in the beautifully scenic Maligne Valley, the lake, which is surrounded by majestic ice and snow-covered peaks, is about 22km/13½ miles long and just under 2km/1¼ miles across at its widest part. It is well worth taking the boat trip (June–Sept., 10am–4pm) to the southern end of the lake, past the world famous picture postcard views of the Narrows and Spirit Island.

There are also very lovely walks along the lakeside to Schäffer Viewpoint (about 1.5km/1 mile) or up to the Opal Hills. The climb of about 8km/5 miles, taking 3 hours brings the walker 305m/1001ft higher up and is rewarded by a splendid view.

Whitewater rafting

From June to September, visitors can join in whitewater rafting for 11km/7 miles downriver on Maligne River. For information contact Maligne Tours, 626 Connaught Dr., Jasper, or The Chalet, Lake Maligne.

Pocahontas

Just 50km/31 miles north of Jasper, the Miette Hot Springs road branches off the Yellowhead Highway at Pocahontas, a few miles before the eastern entrance to the park. Coal deposits were discovered here in 1908 and mined for about ten years after the railway line was completed in 1911. All that now remains of the Pocahontas mine are a few foundations.

Punchbowl Falls

The Punchbowl Falls, cascading down a narrow crevasse, are a few miles further on.

Miette Hot Springs

From here there is still a drive of 15km/9½ miles to Miette Hot Springs, at 54°C/129°F the hottest springs in the Canadian Rockies. The thermal baths (39°C/102°F; open 8.30am–10.30pm, May to Labour Day) are part of a larger leisure complex with accommodation, restaurants and riding stables. There are also some lovely walks in the vicinity.

★ Mount Cavell Angel Glacier

From Jasper, it is well worth making the trip 30km/18½ miles further south to Mount Cavell (3363m/11,0374ft; approach on Highway 93 A) named after the British nurse who was a First World War heroine. A winding mountain road, about 15km/9½ miles long (open: June–Oct.) twists and turns up to Cavell Lake and a car park at the foot of the impressive north face. The Angel Glacier moves downwards from a saddle. A short footpath leads through the moraine to a little lake below the tongue of the glacier. There is a very pleasant 3 to 4-hour walk up to the Cavell Meadows, from where there is a particularly good view of the Angel Glacier.

Marmot Basin

Marmot Basin, just 20km/12½ miles south of Jasper, on the other side of the Whistler massif, is a popular new ski resort with a restaurant, cafeteria, ski school, ski hire, etc.

John Hart–Peace River Highway   E 6/7

Province: British Columbia
Prince George – Fort St John/Dawson Creek

Information

See British Columbia

★ Route

The John Hart–Peace River Highway (Hwy 97) is the northern continuation of the Cariboo Highway (see entry). It starts at Prince George on the Yellowhead Highway (Hwy 16; see entry), the northernmost of Canada's three east–west routes across the Rockies. The highway then runs north for 412km/256 miles through timberland to join the Alaska Highway at Dawson Creek.

There is an alternative route to the west on Highway 29 which follows the Peace River for 465km/289 miles to Fort St John (see entry) and the Alaska Highway (see entry).

At Summit Lake, a few kilometres beyond Prince George, the road almost imperceptibly crosses the Great Divide, the continental watershed, which is quite flat here.

After 143km/90 miles, at MacLeod Lake, a narrow, winding metalled road branches off westwards to Carp Lake Provincial Park on the Nechako Plateau (32km/20 miles). The lake, full of islands, is very popular with anglers and open-air enthusiasts. In the days of Simon Fraser and the North West Company, the major route connecting Fort St James and Fort MacLeod passed through here, and parts of this have been retained at the northern and western ends of the lake. As yet unrestored ruins of the historic Fort MacLeod (Fort MacLeod Provincial Historic Park), in 1805 the first of Simon Fraser's trading posts west of the Rockies, are near the present-day settlement of McLeod Lake, but can only be reached on foot.

★Carp Lake Provincial Park

After 160km/100 miles, Highway 39 branches off to Mackenzie (30km/18½ miles; 701m/2300ft) at the south end of Lake Williston, an artificial lake which has scarcely been opened up to tourism. Until 1965 the area around the northern Rocky Mountain Trench was still just a wilderness. Since then a town has grown up, its population of 6000 here to work in the sawmills and paper factories of the local economic mainstay, the timber industry, although ore deposits have now also been found in the vicinity. At the entrance to the town stands the huge "tree crusher", an enormous, 175-tonne machine, which, when Lake Williston was created, was used to crush the trees which were of no commercial value. Morfee Lake, a nearby resort, has a hydroplane base and swimming, water sports and fishing.

Mackenzie

190km/118 miles: Highway 97 crosses Pine Pass, at 935m/3069ft, the lowest pass in the Canadian Rockies. Not far from the pass there is Powder King Ski Village, a popular ski resort (640m/2100ft descent, 23 ski runs, 1 chairlift, 2 ski tows), and the Bijoux Falls (about 40m/131ft-high waterfall).

Pine Pass

310km/193 miles: Chetwynd (pop. 3000, 615m/2018ft), already in the foothills of the Rockies, is another young settlement on the northern frontier, on the edge of the untamed wilderness and the starting point for wilderness tours (hiking, canoeing, hunting, fishing).

Chetwynd

From here, Highway 23 leads southwards to Gwillim Lake (56km/35 miles), a beautiful, deep-blue lake in largely untouched surroundings (splendid view of the bare mountain ridges to the northwest of the lake), and to Tumbler Ridge (105km/65 miles), a new mining town, part of the Northeast Coal Project, and currently home to about 2000 workers and their families. There are sightseeing tours from mid-June to mid-September round the mining areas, and the enormous computerised conveyor systems of Quintette Coal Ltd., plus excursions to Monkman Provincial Park with the impressive 70m/230ft Kinuseo Falls (accessible only on foot or by hydroplane).

Gwillim Lake

412km/256 miles: Dawson Creek (pop. 11,000, 666m/2186ft), at the end of the John Hart Highway, is already in the predominantly flat lands of the Peace River Region, Canada's northernmost farming area (grain, oilseed rape, dairy farming).

Dawson Creek

The "0" milepost, 3m/10ft high and decorated with flags, marks the start of the famous Alaska Highway (see entry) built by the US Army between 1942 and 1944. The town first came into being in the 1930s, when a railhead was built here to serve Peace River's wheatlands, but its rapid growth only took off with the construction of the Alaska Highway. The town landmarks are the big grain silos of Alberta Pool Elevators Ltd. at the station.

Nowadays the railroad is freight only; the old Northern Alberta Railway station at 900 Alaska Avenue, built in 1931, houses the Dawson Creek

Station Museum (open: June–Aug. daily 8am–8pm; at other times Mon.–Fri. 9am–5pm) with displays about the local wildlife, the culture of the Cree Indians, pioneer days, historic grain silos from the 1930s, and a small art gallery and tourist information centre.

Walter Wright Pioneer Village

Walter Wright Pioneer Village (open: June–Sept. daily 10.30am–6.30pm) is about 3km/2 miles east of Dawson Creek on Hwy 2 to Edmonton. It is an open-air museum with 14 typical historical buildings that have been moved here. These include an old smithy, grocery store, school-house, two churches and a trapper's log cabin.

Alternative route Highway 29

The beautifully scenic Highway 29 branches off at Chetwynd (310km/193 miles) and follows Peace River to Fort St John.

Hudson's Hope

376km/234 miles: Hudson's Hope (pop. 1000, 520m/1707ft) is one of the oldest settlements in British Columbia. A small trapper post was established here on Peace River as long ago as 1805. Whether it got its name from a hopeful prospector by the name of Hudson, or because the Hudson's Bay Company was trying to steal a march on its rival the North West Company, it is too late to tell. Nowadays most of the people living here on the edge of the wilderness work for the two power stations at the Bennett and Peace Canyon dams. These produce just under 40% of British Columbia's hydro-electric power.

From the highway it is possible to see black bears (often scavenging on the local rubbish tip), white-headed sea-eagles, moose and deer.

The little museum on the north bank of the Peace River (open: Victoria Day to Labour Day daily 9.30am–5.30pm; and Labour Day to Thanksgiving, Sat. and Sun. only) vividly conveys the history of the region, and tells of the dinosaurs whose bones and footprints have been found in the sedimentary rocks of the Peace River Canyon, now flooded. Visitors can obtain pans in the museum to try their luck at panning for gold in the Peace River.

Next to the museum stands St Peter's Church, built in a simple log-cabin style.

★Peace Canyon Dam and Visitor Centre

About 5km/3 miles south of Hudson's Hope, Peace Canyon Dam, 50m/164ft high, and 533m/1749ft long, dams up Peace River for a second time, where it leaves the canyon, 23km/14 miles below Bennett Dam. In the Visitor Centre next to the power station (open: Victoria Day–Labour Day daily 8am–4pm; Mon.–Fri. at other times) more exhibitions tell of the natural history of the region and the history of its settlement. These include life-size models of dinosaurs, a reconstructed stern-wheel steamer, that used to ply on the Peace River, and a model of a dam and power station. The power station can be visited by arrangement.

★W. A. C. Bennett Dam and Visitor Centre

The W. A. C. Bennett Dam, one of the world's biggest earth-filled dams, is 24km/15 miles west of the town and reached via a scenic side-road. This dam, which is 2km/1¼ miles long, 183m/601ft high, and up to 830m/2724ft thick at its base, was completed in 1967 and holds back the 362km/225 mile-long Williston Lake in the Rocky Mountain Trench. Until recently, the 1646sq.km/635sq.mile artificial lake had hardly been opened up for tourism, but more and more water-sports enthusiasts are now making their way here. Anglers can charter boats as well. The Visitor Centre (open: Victoria Day–Labour Day daily 8am–4pm; Mon.–Fri. 8am–4pm at other times) gives information about hydro-electric power generation and the construction of the enormous dam, and on working days there are guided tours of the power station. From May to September there is a good view of it from a lookout point on the west side of the dam.

From Hudson's Hope the highway follows the Peace River northwards, mostly high above the steep banks, and after 76km/47 miles reaches the Alaska Highway 13km/8 miles north of Fort St John.

465km/289 miles: Fort St John (see entry)

The Bennett Dam on Williston Lake

Joliette   P 8

Province: Québec. Population: 17,000

See Québec   Information

This charming little town is at the centre of a region of beautiful scenery, known as Lanaudière. It was founded in 1841 by Barthélemi Joliette, a descendent of Louis Joliette, discoverer of Mississippi.

Joliette's art museum (Wilfrid-Corbeil 145; open: Tues.–Sun. end of June–   Musée d'Art
beginning of Sept.; Wed.–Sun. at other times) provides a complete over-
view of Canadian art, with special emphasis on Québec artists such as
d'Ozias Leduc, along with church art from Québec and Europe.

Kamloops   E 7

Province: British Columbia. Population: 62,000

See British Columbia   Information

Since the time of the trappers, Kamloops has been at the heart of the dry,   History
high country of south-central British Columbia. First settled in 1911 at the
confluence of the North and South Thompson Rivers, which here form the
narrow Kamloops Lake, by the North West Company under the name of
Fort Thompson, the town was later renamed "Kamloops" from the local
Indian dialect for "meeting of the waters".
   In the 1860s this little settlement found itself in the throes of the gold-rush
as the "Overlanders", a group of gold-seekers and pioneers, arrived here in

1862, who, embarking on a dangerous and exhausting three-month journey, crossed the Yellowhead Pass, hitherto virtually unknown, and followed the North Thompson River southwards into the heart of British Columbia.

In the 1880s there were also steamboats on the Thompson River at Kamloops and on the Sushwap Lake, but this came to an end when the Canadian Pacific Railway reached Kamloops in 1885.

Economy

Today Kamloops is an important junction. It is the meeting point for several road and rail routes – the Canadian Pacific Railway, Canadian National Railway, TransCanada Highway, Yellowhead Highway 5 north, Coquihalla Highway and Highway 5 south into the Nicola Valley and to Merritt, and Highway 97 south-eastwards into the Okanagan Valley – as well as being the local capital for the 122,000 people living in what is mainly a rural region, farming sheep and cattle, while sawmills and paper factories exploit the timber from the hinterland. The firm of Wayerhaeuser-Canada provides guided tours through their factory where 700,000 tonnes of timber and wood shaving are processed annually.

Tourism

Tourism is also starting to play an increasingly important part in this lake district setting (fishing, windsurfing, sailing and mountain tours) with its favourable climate – Kamloops has only about 160mm/6½in. of rainfall and more than 2000 hours of sunshine a year. There is also horseracing as an added attraction.

Sights

★Heritage Walking Tour

The Travel InfoCentre has leaflets for a tour of the town centre which still has many of its old buildings (courthouse, St Joseph's Church (1887), Chinese cemetery, reconstruction of Fort Kamloops in McArthur Island Park, and an old Canadian steam loco 2141 in Riverside Park).

Kamloops Museum and Archives

The historic Kamloops Museum (207 Seymour St., open: June–Aug. daily 10am–9pm, at other times Mon.–Sat. 10am–5pm, Sun. 1–5pm) has exhibitions on how the Indians lived, the days of the pioneers and fur trappers, and life in Kamloops at the turn of the century.

"Wanda Sue"

From May to September the paddlewheeler "Wanda Sue" takes people on 2-hour trips on the Thompson River.

★Secwepemc Museum (Indian Band Museum)

The Secwepemc Museum (345 Yellowhead Hwy. 5; open: Mon.–Fri. 8.30am–noon and 1–4.30pm) is primarily an Indian museum, concentrating on the culture of the local Sushwap, and the Salish Indians.

Indian Band Days

Kamloops' famous Indian Band Days take place in August.

Surroundings

Kamloops Wildlife Park

The Kamloops Wildlife Park with its small zoo and leisure pool is another attraction. It has about 100 different species, including many native to Canada (e.g. bear, puma, moose, Wapiti, eagle and buffalo). The miniature railway is also very popular.

Kamloops Waterslide

Kamloops Waterslide & Vacation Land, with waterchutes, whirlpools, etc., is about 20km/12½ miles from the town centre, on the TransCanada Highway, and is a good place for a swim to cool off during the relatively dry, hot summer. It also has a miniature golf course.

Harper Mountain

Harper Mountain, 23km/14 miles northeast of Kamloops, is a popular ski area in winter (425m/1395ft difference in altitude, 13 pistes, ski lifts).

Tod Mountain

Tod Mountain winter sports resort is 53km/33 miles north of Kamloops. It has a difference in altitude of 945m/3101ft, and boasts 42 pistes with chairlifts and ski tows.

Lac Le Jeune Resort

The Lac Le Jeune Resort, 25km/15½ miles further south, has 100km/62 miles of cross-country skiing courses, and a further 130km/80 miles of marked ski trails on a high plateau.

Chase (457m/1500ft; pop. 3000), at the western end of the Little Shuswap Lake, is the western gateway to the Shuswap Lakes. There are more than 1600km/994 miles of banks and a relatively hot, dry climate make these ideal for those who enjoy water sports. They are best explored from a houseboat.

★**Shuswap Lakes**

Chase

Its Rodeo in the autumn provides a real touch of the Wild West.

Rodeo

The Squilax Pow Wow in the nearby Squilax Reserve, where Indian dance groups from all over North America come to take part, attracts thousands of visitors every year.

Squilax Pow Wow

At Squilax the road branches off to the south end of Adams Lake, which is 70km/43 miles long (houseboats), and to the resorts, campsites and bathing beaches on the north shore of Shuswap Lake. Scotch Creek (boat rental) is very pleasant, as is Shuswap Lake Provincial Park (open from May to September; visitor centre with wildlife and cultural exhibits). The reconstruction of a Kekuli pit-house is worth seeing. Shuswap Indians lived in these during the winter until about 1908. Other beauty spots include Magna Bay and Anglemont (houseboats).

Adams Lake

The town of Sorrento (350m/1149ft; pop. 3000) was given its name by J. R. Kinghorn, a pioneer who, seeing Copper Island in the distance, was reminded of the Isle of Capri and the Gulf of Naples. Houseboats can be taken out on the Shuswap Lake, where there is a fine beach for swimming. A popular summer resort, especially with senior citizens, Sorrento owes its growth primarily to the construction of the railroad in 1885 when a rail station and a little settlement were built because of the additional steam locomotives (in use until 1958) that were needed for the steep haul up Notch Hill. Farmers settled in the fertile surroundings.
    Interior White Water Expeditions offer whitewater rafting on the nearby Adams River or on the Clearwater River in Wells Gray Provincial Park (Yellowhead Highway 5 South).
    East of Sorrento the TransCanada Highway turns south.

Sorrento

Salmon Arm (358m/1175ft; pop. 12,000), on the southern arm of Shuswap Lake, is the centre of the Shuswap Region, and grew up when the railroad was built in the 1890s. The moderate, dry climate (1800 hours of sunshine, 140mm/5½in. of rainfall a year) has made Salmon Arm popular as a retirement haven.
    Houseboat rental; day trips on Shuswap Lake on the little paddlewheel boat M.S. "Rockwood"; sailing, wind-surfing. Also Salmon Arm Waterslide, local market (Tues. and Fri. 8am–1pm; farm produce, handicrafts), Salmon Arm Museum (51 3rd St; open May–Aug. Tues.–Sun. noon–5pm), and horseback riding.

Salmon Arm

Sicamous (352m/1155ft; pop. 4000), between Shuswap Lake and Mara Lake, proudly proclaims itself Canada's "Houseboat Capital". It also has golf, hang-gliding, water sports, and fishing, and the "Phoebe Ann" takes people for cruises on the lake (June–Sept. Mon., Wed., Fri.; July and Aug. daily except Sat. 8am).
    Highway 97A branches off towards the south here, past scenic Mara Lake (16km/10 miles) to Vernon in the Okanagan Valley (see entry).

Sicamous

From Sicamous the TransCanada Highway follows the route of the Canadian Pacific Railway, built in the 1880s, over Eagle Pass (discovered in 1865) through the rugged 2500–3000m/8200–9850ft Monashee Mountains, where the road can be blocked at times by heavy snowfalls in winter. After 26km/16 miles, at Craigellachie, the place is reached where in 1885 the last spike was driven into place in the Canadian Pacific Railroad, completing the country's first trans-continental railway. Six months later the first passenger train left Montréal to arrive after six days in Port Moody, near

Craigellachie
CPR Last Spike
Site

Vancouver, making what was then the longest scheduled railway connection in the world, and the monument here commemorates the importance of this event.

Enchanted Forest
The "Enchanted Forest", 13km/8 miles further east, and open from 8.30am May to September, is a fairy-tale theme park beneath gigantic cedars hundreds of years old, with a pseudo medieval castle and populated by about 300 fairy-tale characters – fairies, witches and mermaids – with, of course, a wishing well.

Three Valley Gap
Three Valley Gap, situated in a valley in the Monashee Mountains at the eastern end of Three Valleys Lake, with its inviting little sandy beach, is a recreation of the old Wild West, built here in the 1960s near the 19th c. gold-rush ghost town and lumbering settlement. Open: May–Sept. from 8am. It has old buildings that were moved here from all over the region, trappers' log cabins, Sicamous' historic Bellevue Hotel, and old barns, complete with a few donkeys and other animals in the stables. There is also a motel, restaurant and miniature railway.

Kingston   O 9

Province: Ontario. Population: 61,000

Information
See Ontario

The city of Kingston lies at the northern end of Lake Ontario, where it becomes the St Lawrence River. It attracts many visitors and is the starting point for cruises to enjoy the beautiful scenery of Thousand Islands (see below).

History
Fort Catasaqui, or Fort Frontenac as it was also called, was established here in 1673 to oversee the fur trade, and for a short time was itself an important fur-trading post.

In 1788 the place was resettled by the English who christened it Kingston. Its strategic location soon made it an important naval base, especially during the 1812 war with the Americans.

After the war the English built the Rideau Canal, linking Montréal with the Great Lakes, via the valley of the Ottawa River.

Kingston rapidly expanded between 1841 and 1844 when it was the capital of Upper Canada.

Sights of Kingston

City Hall
City Hall, opposite the harbour, dates from 1844 and its sandstone architecture is indicative of the hopes once cherished by the people of Kingston that their city might become the capital of all Canada.

The Law Courts and the University also date from the 19th century.

★Fort Henry
Fort Henry was built on the river between 1812 and 1837 to defend Kingston and to bar the way to the St Lawrence, but it never came under attack.

Nowadays the fort houses a museum of British-Canadian military history which is open from mid-May to mid-October from 9am to 6pm. In summer students from Kingston's Royal Military College re-enact the 19th c. ceremonial retreat at sunset on Mondays, Wednesdays and at weekends if the weather is fine.

Villa Bellevue
The Villa Bellevue, built in 1840 near the university, is modelled on an Italian Palazzo. Open daily except for winter holidays, it belonged to Sir John MacDonald, Prime Minister from 1867 to 1873, and is furnished as it was at that period.

Steam pump museum
This museum is in a former pumping station which was built in 1849. The two pumps also date from this period. All the machines on display have

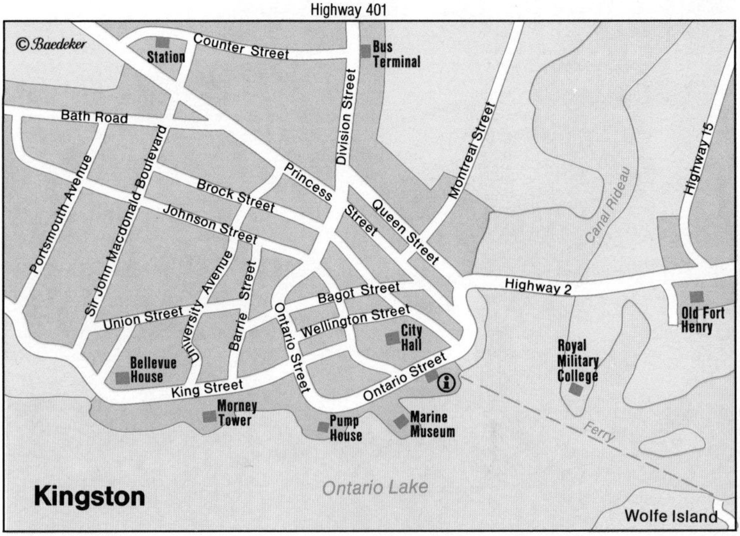

Map labels: Highway 401 · © Baedeker · Station · Counter Street · Bus Terminal · Bath Road · Division Street · Montreal Street · Highway 15 · Portsmouth Avenue · Sir John Macdonald Boulevard · Brock Street · Princess Street · Johnson Street · Queen Street · Canal Rideau · Thousand Islands · Union Street · University Avenue · Barrie Street · Street · Bagot Street · Highway 2 · Old Fort Henry · Ontario Street · Wellington Street · City Hall · Royal Military College · Bellevue House · King Street · Ontario Street · (i) · Morney Tower · Pump House · Marine Museum · Ferry · Kingston · Ontario Lake · Wolfe Island

been restored to full working order. Open: mid-June–Sept. daily except Fridays (technical demonstrations) and mid-Mar.–mid-Nov., but without guided tours.

The shipping museum in a former shipyard on Lake Ontario (open: Apr.–mid-Dec. daily 9am–6pm; closed Mon. in Nov. and Dec.) has various types of steam and sailing ship on display, a reminder that Kingston was at one time important for its shipyards.

Shipping museum

Dotted all over an 80km/50 mile stretch of the St Lawrence are thousands of little islands.
   They are on a granite shelf extending from the Canadian Shield to the Adirondack Mountains in the United States – the boundary actually runs between the islands. It is an area of great scenic beauty, and one of the oldest and best-known holiday venues in North America, particularly for holidays on and around the water.

★★Thousand Islands National Park (St Lawrence Islands National Park)

A cruise in this maze of islands is highly recommended. Operating between mid-May and mid-October; lasting about 3 hours, and the everchanging vistas will include glimpses of holiday homes that range from the plainest of log cabins to the most luxurious of summer villas.

Cruises

Some cruises call at Heart Island to enable passengers to look round Boldt Castle (NB: US formalities), which is well worth a visit. It was built by the wealthy owner of New York's Waldorf Astoria, but was never completed.
   The scenic road along the St Lawrence, between motorway exits 107 and 110A, has many lovely views over the water.

Heart Island, Boldt Castle

Another good view is to be had from the outlook tower of Hill Island-Skydeck (120m/400ft high; open; May–Oct.). From here a whole range of islands can be seen.
   Hill Island Skydeck can be reached over a bridge near Ivy Led.

Hill Island Skydeck

263

Thousand Islands National Park

★Mallorytown
Landing
National Park

The road alongside the St Lawrence leads to Mallorytown Landing and the official entrance to Thousand Islands National Park (open: mid-May–mid-Oct.). From here it is possible to get to several islands which can only be reached by boat, and to see the wreck of an early 19th c. gunboat.

Kitchener-Waterloo   N 9

Province: Ontario. Population: 210,000

Information

See Ontario

The twin cities of Kitchener and Waterloo are about 100km/60 miles west of Toronto on Highway 8.
   Kitchener, known as "Berlin" until the First World War, and renamed after General Lord Kitchener, is Canada's biggest centre of German immigration. It derives most of its income from the food and drink industry.

October festival

Kitchener's special attraction is its annual October festival complete with Bavarian brass bands, beer, sausage and sauerkraut, the second largest in the world after Munich. It attracts visitors from all over North America.

History

The twin cities of Kitchener and Waterloo were founded in the late 18th c. by the Mennonites, originally a German sect and named after its Friesian founder, Menno Simons (1492–1559). Some of its members emigrated straight to Canada, while others came here from Pennsylvania in 1783 during the American War of Independence. Like the Amish – named after their founder Jakob Ammann – the Mennonites are Anabaptists, a sect founded in Zurich in 1525 and persecuted from the outset because of their beliefs in adult baptism and pacifism, who finally found a new homeland

Mennonites on the road

on the North American continent. Today the orthodox Mennonites still speak an old German dialect and wear plain, unadorned dress with no buttons, collars or pockets.

They ride in horse-drawn buggies as they are not allowed to own cars; neither can they own telephones or other such products of modern technology, and live by farming without machinery, as they did 150 years ago. They still sell their produce on local markets in Kitchener and Waterloo. The Mennonites in Canada now number around 100,000.

Buggies

Sights of Kitchener-Waterloo

Joseph Schneider House (466 Queen St S.) is a Mennonite home with original 19th c. furnishings. As "living history" the "inhabitants" of the house, in traditional costumes, offer visitors biscuits baked in the old German manner, and re-enact life as it was lived in the 19th c. (open: daily 10am–5pm in summer; Wed.–Sat. 10am–5pm and Sun. 1–5pm in winter).

★Joseph Schneider House

Doon Heritage Crossroads, on Houmer Watson Boulevard, is an open-air museum showing life in the town in the days of the pioneers. Its thirty or so buildings on a site of 23ha/57 acres provide an insight into what life was like here in the 19th century (open: May–Sept. 10am–4.30pm; end of Sept.– Christmas 1–4.30pm).

★Doon Heritage Crossroads

Seagram Museum, at 57 Erb Street West, provides a wealth of information on the history of the wine and spirits industry. In the old storage rooms of the first Seagram distillery, now extended with a modern wing, it illustrates the various stages of the distillation process with exhibits and film shows (open: Tues.–Sat. noon–6pm; for information tel. 885–1857).

★Seagram Museum

Woodside House, built in 1853 and open daily from 10am to 5pm, was the parental home of Mackenzie King, Prime Minister of Canada from 1921 to 1930 and from 1935 to 1948, and is furnished as it was in the late 19th c.

★Woodside House & Park

Kitchener Market: since 1839; Duke St/Fredrick St; open: Wed. and Sat. mornings. Waterloo Market: Webber St; open: Wed. all day and Sat. morning. St Jacob's Farmers Market: north of Waterloo; open: daily 10am–5pm.

Markets

Besides selling farm produce and such specialities as maple syrup and maple syrup products, these markets also sell Mennonite handicrafts and their home-produced remedies and cosmetics.

Surroundings of Kitchener-Waterloo

Around Kitchener and Waterloo there are still a few Mennonite villages, such as Elmira and Elora. St Jacobs, at the heart of Ontario's Mennonite

Elmira, Elora, St. Jacobs

country, seems like an open-air museum in itself, but has a museum of its own, "The Meeting Place" at 33 King Street, which tells the story of the Anabaptists and how they were driven out of Europe in general and Switzerland in particular.

★Elmira
Provincial Park

This scenic park, along the course of a pretty river, is particularly lovely in the spring and in the autumn, when it attracts many visitors. It has a campsite, picnic areas, footpaths, and an information centre, and there is canoeing on the river.

Elmira Valley

The river valley above Elmira has lovely scenery and is a favourite recreational area for people living around Toronto and Hamilton. There are also designated recreational areas around the artificial lakes created by the damming of the river.

Klondike   A/B 5

Administrative unit: Yukon Territory

Information

Klondike Visitors' Association; tel. (403) 993–5575

Klondike River

The Klondike is a tributary of the Yukon River, and flows for 150km/93 miles from its source in the Tintina, east of the Klondike Highway, into the Yukon at Dawson City (see entry).

Gold-rush

The legendary gold-rush in the Klondike began when George Washington Carmack and his two Indian brothers-in-law, Tagish Charlie and Shookum Jim, registered their first claim which they had made in Bonanza Creek (formerly Rabbit Creek) on August 17th 1896 in Fortymile. News of the gold nuggets – as big as a fist – which Carmack had found on the bed of Bonanza Creek spread like wildfire in the Yukon and neighbouring Alaska. When the largest shipment of gold which had ever been made in the States was loaded in Seattle it triggered a gold-rush, and in a short time more than 100,000 people from all over the world came pouring into the Klondike. The worldwide depression meant that the lure of the gold, so vividly described by Jack London, proved irresistible, although less than half those who hoped to make their fortune in the Yukon probably never actually got there. Many of them who came from the Pacific died trying to get over White Pass or even Chilkoot Pass to Bennett Lake and to the boats in Carcross which would take them down the Yukon to Whitehorse (see entry); as many again suffered the unspeakable hardships of the long trek from the east through Edmonton (see entry) to the Yukon. Dawson City (see entry), the gold-rush's famous capital city of tents and log cabins, sprang up overnight at the confluence of the Klondike and the Yukon, and by 1898 had a population of about 25,000. By 1903 the rivers and creeks of the Klondike had yielded gold worth about 96 million dollars, at an average price of 20 dollars per ounce (28g), but there were very few whose dreams of great riches came true.

When gold was found in August 1899 at Nome, near the mouth of the Yukon, the prospectors moved on to Alaska. The Klondike gold-rush eventually ended ten years after it began, leaving the valley to sink back into obscurity.

The search for gold continued, but the individual gold-panners were replaced by big corporations using industrial machinery. The damage they caused to the environment is still visible, as gold continues to be mined, and more extensive operations are under discussion.

★Klondike
Highway

The 717km/445 mile Klondike Highway, completed 1979, leads from Skagway (Alaska) through Whitehorse (see entry) to Dawson City (see entry) and the Klondike goldfields.

It follows the route taken by the prospectors in 1898, a gruelling and perilous journey from Skagway over White Pass to Carcross, from where

Klondike

they continued by boat, raft and later by sternwheeler through Whitehorse (see entry) to Dawson City (see entry).

Tourists can now travel this legendary stretch by boat, an unforgettable experience and far less harrowing than it was 100 years ago. Information is available from the Visitor Reception Centres in Whitehorse and Dawson (see entries).

Today Skagway (pop. 1000) lives from tourism and its many renovated buildings and boardwalks have the feeling of the gold-rush days. Its name comes from the Tlingit dialect and means "home of the north wind".

Skagway

The road from Skagway to Carcross, 106km/66 miles away, is passable all year round. Situated 40km/25 miles south of Whitehorse (see entry) on Bennett Lake, Carcross, where time seems to stand still, was such an important place at the turn of the century, but now has a population of only 150. The first people to live there were Indians who hunted around this area. They named the place "Caribou Crossing" and the abbreviated version of this was later adopted by the gold-prospectors.

Carcross

The Caribou Hotel, built in 1898 and renovated in 1909 is the oldest hotel still trading in the Yukon. Visitors can see S.S. "Tutsi", an old paddle-steamer, and the "Duchess", a tiny locomotive that travelled the line from Taku to Atlin Lake early this century. Matthew Watson's General Store was built in 1911, and the Watson family still ran it until quite recently.

See entry

Whitehorse

The Klondike Highway crosses the Alaska Highway (see entry) at the 158 kilometre mark (98 miles).

Alaska Highway

Takhini Hot Springs, at the 198 kilometre mark (123 miles), is a good place for a swim, with temperatures of 36°C/97°F.

Takhini Hot Springs

Kluane National Park

Braeburn Lodge	Braeburn Lodge, famous for its food, at 281km/189 miles, is worth making the next stop.
Carmacks	Carmacks, after 357km/222 miles, named after George Washington Carmack one of the three discoverers of the Klondike gold, is a place to stop for services. Most of the 400 people living here are descendants of the original Indian inhabitants.
Campbell Highway	Just north of Carmacks the Campbell Highway (see entry) forks east to Watson Lake on the Alaska Highway (see entry), passing through Faro and Ross River.
Five Finger Rapids	Five Finger Rapids, where the prospectors had to haul their boats through on ropes, are at 381km/237 miles.
Minto	At Minto (431km/268 miles), another trading post set up by Robert Campbell for the Hudson's Bay Company, the Klondike Highway leaves the Yukon River to cross the central Yukon Plateau and the valleys of the Pelly and Steward rivers.
Stewart Crossing, Silver Trail	At Stewart Crossing (538km/334 miles), the last services for 140km/87 miles, the Silver Trail branches north-east to Mayo, Elsa and Keno in the silver-mining territory around the upper Stewart River.
Silver mining	Today most of the silver is mined in the United Keno Hill Mine at Elsa, and the ore shipped to Mayo, an Indian township about 46km/29 miles south. Keno City, in a lovely setting at the foot of the Keno Mountain (1889m/6170ft) is pretty much a ghost town, since mining here has long since been abandoned.
Klondike River Lodge, ★Dempster Highway	Soon after reaching the Klondike Valley, the Klondike River Lodge services come up at the 678 kilometre mark (421 miles). Here the Dempster Highway (see entry) turns off into the Canadian north, eventually reaching to Inuvik in the Mackenzie River delta (see entry) after about 750km/466 miles of magnificent scenery.
Dawson City	See entry

Kluane National Park   B 5

	Administrative unit: Yukon Territory
Information	Visitor Centre, Kluane National Park, Haines Junction, Yukon Y0B 1L0; tel. (403) 634–2251
	Kluane National Park, in the south-west corner of Yukon Territory (see entry) and bordering on Alaska and British Columbia (see entry) extends over an area of 2,2015sq.km/8498sq.miles. Part of the Haines Road (Highway 3) and the Alaska Highway (see entry) run along its eastern edge.
★★National Park	The snowcapped mountains of the Kluane (pronounced Klu-ah-nay), Canada's largest park of its kind, which has the world's most massive icefields outside the polar region, was designated a Mountain Park in 1976, and recognised as a United Nations World Heritage site in 1979. Great glaciers at the edges of the ice – up to 1.6km/1 mile thick in places – have swept over the mountain valleys. Many of the close on 4000 glaciers are more than 10km/6 miles across and up to 100km/60 miles long.
Flora and fauna	The most common conifer in the park's river valleys is white spruce (*picea glauca*), and the most common deciduous trees are birch (*betula*) and poplar (*populus*). The colourful alpine and arctic flora beyond the tree line

Mount Logan, Canada's highest mountain

extend to stunted shrubs, flowers and grasses, whilst on islands in the everlasting ice mosses and lichens defy the harsh winters, forming a vital link in the food chain. The park is rich in wildlife such as grizzly and black bear, moose, caribou, wolf, mountain goat, Dall sheep, beaver, marten, fox, musk rat, and eagle, and has many kinds of fish, including salmon, trout and pike.

Dominating Kluane National Park, the peaks of the St Elias Mountains, traverse it in a south-easterly direction. Mount Logan, Canada's highest mountain peak (6050m/19,856ft) soars above the vast icefields, the highest mountain in North America after Alaska's Mount McKinley (6193m/20,325ft).

★ St Elias
Mountains,
★★ Mount Logan

The ice-covered peaks of the St Elias Mountains can be seen from the Alaska Highway (see entry), almost 160km/100 miles away, beyond the Kluane Range (up to 2500m/8205ft).

★★ Alaska
Highway
Kluane Ranges

Climbers and naturalists from all over the world come here every year to explore this fantastic mountain world. The first of the St Elias peaks to be conquered was Mount St Elias (5498m/18044ft), climbed by the Duke of Abruzzi in 1897. Mount Logan was first climbed in 1925. Trekking tours in the park and around Mount Logan require physical fitness and careful planning. For further information, including details of such facilities as winter camping, contact the Visitor Centre and park headquarters at Haines Junction (tel. (403) 634–2251).

Tourism

Kootenay National Park

E/G 7

Province: British Columbia
Area: 1406sq.km/543sq.miles

Kootenay National Park

Information

The Superintendent, Kootenay National Park, P.O. Box 220, Radium Hot Springs, B.C. V0A 1M0; tel. (604) 347–9615

Access

The Banff-Windermere Parkway (Highway 93) runs through Kootenay National Park. It is at least a 3-hour drive.

★★Landscape

Kootenay National Park ("kootemik" is Indian for "places of hot water") is in the Rocky Mountains, in south-east British Columbia. It adjoins the more famous Banff National Park (see entry) and Yoho National Park (see entry), and takes in the magnificent western flank of the Canadian Rockies.

★Banff-Windermere Highway

Banff-Windermere Highway, 105km/65 miles long, runs south from the TransCanada Highway at Castle Junction, 28km/17 miles north-west of Banff, down to Radium Hot Springs, passing through spectacular mountain scenery west of the continental divide and following the valleys of the Vermilion and Kootenay rivers. These two valleys form the core of Kootenay National Park. There are plenty of parking places along the way so that visitors can explore the virtually untouched hinterland.

Geology

The main mountain range reaches heights of over 3,000m/9846ft, and is predominantly closely packed layers of stratification. The younger sedimentary layers of the western ranges show much more folding and erosion, and such typical features as rugged rocky ridges and sawtooth peaks, snow and ice-covered massifs, cirques, glaciers, hanging valleys and narrow gorges cut deep into marbled limestone, make the drive through the Kootenay National Park quite a unique experience. With any luck, it will be possible to see moose, Wapiti and mountain goat as well.

Unlike the towering mountains of the north, the less rugged uplands in the south of the park get less snow and rain, and have a milder climate that enables many of different creatures to spend the winter in the lower Kootenay valley.

History

Archaeological evidence shows that for thousands of years the valleys and passes of what is now Kootenay National Park served as important trade routes for the Indians. The rock drawings at Radium Hot Springs are an indication of how significant a place this was for the Indians of the Plains as well as those of the mountains.

In the 19th c. the Hudson's Bay Company explorers followed the old Indian trails into the Kootenay area in search of furs and a suitable route to get to the Columbia River and the Pacific. They were followed by settlers, prospectors and mountaineers. Resourceful entrepreneurs soon discovered the value of the hot springs, and Radium Hot Springs got its first spa hotel in 1911. The area was declared a national park in 1920 when the province of British Columbia transferred the land to the Canadian government. The Banff-Windermere Parkway, the first major highway through the central Rockies, was built without delay and subsequently much improved in the 1950s. It now has plenty of parking places and lookout points where visitors can stop to admire the magnificent scenery.

★Vermilion Pass

The Vermilion Pass (summit 1651m/5382ft), only 38km/24 miles north-west of Banff (see entry), is where the Parkway crosses the Continental Divide, and where Alberta meets British Columbia and Banff National Park (see entry) meets the Kootenay National Park.

Here in 1968, a forest fire, started by lightning, raged for four days, and devastated 2440ha/6029 acres; the results are still clearly visible.

★Stanley Glacier

The scenery around Vermilion Pass is reminiscent of the Swiss Alps: the famous Stanley Glacier, on the slopes of Stanley Peak (3155m/10,355ft) to the south, can be reached by a lovely if rather strenuous hike in one day through the Stanley Creek hanging valley.

The Banff-Windermere Highway in the Kootenay National Park ▶

Mount Whymper	Mount Whymper (2844m/9334ft) to the west of Vermilion Pass also has its glacier. It is named after the conqueror of the Matterhorn, who also climbed many of Canada's mountains.
★ Marble Canyon	45km/28 miles: Marble Canyon is a deep narrow gorge, formed by Tokumm Creek, which owes its name to its pale marbled limestone and dolomite walls. An interpretive trail of about a mile circles the canyon to a waterfall. Marble Canyon is spanned by several bridges, and has a small information centre open to visitors in summer.
Paint Pots	48km/30 miles: a little trail of about 1km/⅔ mile leads from the next parking area over the Vermilion River to the "Ochre Beds", and the three small pools known as the "Paint Pots". These are fed by mineral springs with a high iron content, hence the colour. The Indians came here from far afield to get the ochre-coloured clay for their war-paint and for dyeing their clothes and tepees. The Europeans took advantage of the red clay, too, using it to produce dyes in Calgary.
Kootenay Crossing	The Banff/Windermere Highway Exhibit at Kootenay Crossing is worth seeing, particularly for its account of how this part of the Rockies was opened up by the highway, and how the national park was set up.
Crooks Meadow, Dolly Varden, McLeod Meadow	Further south the highway passes by Crooks Meadow, Dolly Varden, and McLeod Meadow, all pretty resorts where campsites should be booked in advance.
Kootenay Viewpoint	There is a wonderful view from Kootenay Viewpoint over the Kootenay River valley to the Mitchell and Stanford mountain ranges.
Sinclair Pass, Sinclair Valley, Iron Gates	120km/75 miles: from the Kootenay Valley the route crosses Sinclair Pass (1486m/4877ft) to get into the lovely high-mountain valley of fast-running Sinclair Creek. After the Iron Gates Tunnel steep limestone and dolomite walls, coloured red by iron oxide form a kind of gateway. In spring and in August big-horn sheep congregate here.
Redwall Fault	Redwall Fault is the site of mineral springs with a high iron content.
★ Radium Hot Springs	Still within the national park, Radium Hot Springs (pop. 1000) was a place prized by the Indians for its hot springs, and these continue to be the source of its fame. Its Aquacourt (open: daily in summer, 8.30am–11pm, otherwise Mon.–Fri. 2–10pm, Sat./Sun. 10am–10pm) has two swimming pools (39°C/102°F and 28°C/82°F), thermal baths, and a restaurant. Radium Hot Springs Lodge, above the springs, also has beautiful views. Whitewater rafting is possible as well.
Sinclair Canyon	Near the Radium Hot Springs Sinclair Canyon forces its way through a wildly romantic defile.

'Ksan   D 6

'Ksan

	Province: British Columbia
Information	See British Columbia
The Hazeltons	The fact that there are three Hazeltons – Hazelton, New Hazelton (306m/1004ft) and South Hazelton – with a total population of about 400, is due to a dispute about the station for the Grand Turk Pacific Railway. Nowadays the trains stop at New Hazelton, at the foot of the impressive, partially glaciated Rocher-Déboulé massif. In 1914, when the railway was being built, this was the scene of a spectacular bank holdup, when five of

'Ksan Indian Village

the gang were gunned down and the sixth escaped with the loot of just 1400 dollars.

Hazelton old town is 8km/5 miles north of Yellowhead Highway and the railroad, on the north bank of the Bulkley River, near where it flows into the Skeena River.

The deep canyon here is spanned by a 76m-/250ft-high suspension bridge. Below it there used to be a rock that formed a kind of natural weir in the rushing river, used to their advantage by the Indians who lived mainly from salmon fishing. The remains of Hagwilget, "the home of the quiet people", where the Indians lived, are to be found below the bridge. This was a Carrier Indian Village used only in summer, and archaeologists have found traces of settlements here dating back to 3000 B.C. When the fishing authorities removed the rock in 1959, the Indians, who fished only with wooden fish traps and harpoons, found that their catches were drastically reduced, and the village was abandoned. As early as the 19th c. the Indians had skilfully constructed a wooden suspension bridge over the canyon.

Hagwilget

'Ksan Indian Village, near Hazelton, is an open-air museum near a traditional Gitksan Indian settlement (open: mid-May–Oct. 9am–6pm, limited opening in winter). In summer there are also film shows and traditional dances. Various aspects of Gitskan culture are on display in seven tribal longhouses, each guarded by their ancient totem pole.

★★'Ksan Indian Village (North Western National Exhibition Centre and Museum)

Three houses can only be viewed as part of a guided tour. This is an opportunity to learn about these people's daily lives and the potlatch ceremony, as well as the symbolism of the carving on the totem poles. A number of Indian carvers have their workshops in the village, and their work is on sale in the Gift Shop together with other Indian books and artefacts.

The North Western National Exhibition Centre and Museum (open: daily in summer 10.30am–4.30pm; at other times closed Tues./Wed.) houses valuable carvings and ritual objects.

Labrador O–S 5–7

Provinces: Québec, Newfoundland

Information

Québec Province, Newfoundland (see entries)

★Natural features

The Labrador Peninsula, an area of 1,560,000sq.km/602,160sq.miles between Hudson Bay and the Atlantic, is the eastern flank of the Canadian Shield, and contains a wealth of mineral deposits in its Pre-Cambrian plutonic rocks. Labrador's central uplands range between 200m/650ft and 500m/1650ft, reaching heights in the north-east of between 800m/2625ft and 1800m/5907ft. The peninsula was the final resting place of the glaciers of the last continental Ice Age, until they too melted about 6000–7000 years ago. The landscape has many clearly glacial features, especially in the north. Countless rivers have carved deep valleys across the face of Labrador, which has deep fiords as well, particularly along the Atlantic coast, also typically glaciated. The hummock-covered pristine wilderness of the interior has broad basins that have been filled with lakes, moraine spoil or sand. The lowlands around Hudson Bay and Ungava Bay were under water when times got warmer.

Climate

The Labrador Peninsula lies between 50° and 60° latitude north, and has a sub-arctic climate that counts as extreme in European terms. This is intensified by the cold Labrador current that swirls around the edge of this land mass. Temperatures in central Labrador can fall to −50°C/−58°F, and they can even get as low as −40°C/−40°F on the coast. Average summer temperatures are between 5°C/41°F and 10°C/50°F, and higher in places. Average precipitation is between 500mm/20in. and 1000mm/40in., depending on the lie of the land, and rather less on the Ungava peninsula, with a quarter to a third falling as snow.

Traces of the Ice-Age: a fiord in Labrador

Most of northern Labrador is in the permafrost, and has the typical tundra vegetation of sparse, sub-arctic pine and birch. The south, on the Gulf of St Lawrence and around Goose Bay, mostly has boreal timber.

Vegetation

The Labrador is a breed of dog native to eastern Canada, and probably related to the Newfoundland, although not as large. Labradors have a short, thick coat, ranging in colour from pure white to black, occasionally with a tinge of brown. Here in Canada they are mainly used for pulling sledges.

Labrador dog

The waters off Labrador are among the world's best fishing grounds, so there is a long fishing tradition. In the past furs also played an important role in the local economy. Timber felling and processing are also of economic importance, mostly concentrated on the Gulf of St Lawrence seaboard.

Resources, economy

Eastern Labrador is among the world's major mining regions, and the vast iron ore reserves between the Churchill and Koksoak rivers yield over 10 million tonnes a year.

Its enormous hydro-electric potential has made Labrador a major supplier of energy to the industries of south-eastern Canada and the United States eastern seaboard.

Labrador was probably discovered by the Vikings in about 986. John Cabot reached the peninsula in 1498, then later came immigrants from the British Isles. Trappers, fur-traders and lumbermen were roaming the territory up until 1900, when the population numbered about 5000, most of them Inuit and Indian.

History

Vast reserves of iron ore were discovered in the late 19th c. and as they came to be mined, particularly after the Second World War, the population grew. By 1950 it had already risen to 18,000, about a third being Inuit or Indian.

Most of Labrador is in Québec Province, but the east coast and part of the hinterland come under Newfoundland, although these boundaries have shifted several times since 1763.

Schefferville (Québec Province) is a young town at the end of the Québec Shore & Labrador Railway, founded in 1950 as a mining settlement when vast iron ore reserves – estimated at four billion tonnes – were discovered at Knob Lake, as the place was then called. Only ten years later there were 4000 people living in what is now Schefferville. It is linked to the port of Sept-Îles by rail, and by occasional flights, which also go to Québec and Montréal.

Schefferville

Sept-Îles (Québec Province, pop. 30,000) is a booming French-Canadian port on the Gulf of St Lawrence, about 600km/373 miles north of Québec City (see entry).

Sept-Îles (Seven Islands)

At the entrance to a fiord, in the lee of seven rocky islands, its site was discovered by Jacques Cartier (see Famous People) in 1535. A mission station was founded here in the 17th c. but the place only appears to have been permanently settled from the mid-19th century. In 1950 Sept-Îles was a sleepy fishing village of a few hundred people.

Since then, the port of Sept-Îles, which also has the regional airport, has become the administrative and supply centre for the entire north shore, due largely to being the terminal for the 575km/357–mile rail line bringing mineral raw materials from such parts of Labrador as Labrador City and Wabush, and above all the iron ore from Schefferville for shipment to the USA, Japan and Europe in the giant freighters operating out of the sheltered, deepwater fiord harbour, with the second highest volume of shipping tonnage in Canada.

The reconstructed fort (open: June–Aug. daily 10am–5pm) on the Vieux-Poste River was originally founded by Louis Jolliet in 1661, but burned down in 1695.

Fort

Labrador

Sept-Îles Musée Régional	The north coast regional museum on Laure Boulevard is open: Mon.–Fri. 9am–noon; and weekends 1–5pm.
Surroundings	Sept-Îles is a good base for hunting and fishing trips in the locality, and particularly for salmon at Moisie, about 12km/7½ miles to the east.
Ungava Bay	Ungava Bay, covering 621,000sq.km/239,700sq.miles and only ice-free in summer, is in the north-east of the Labrador peninsula, opening onto the Hudson Strait. The many large rivers flowing into the bay include the George, Koksoak, Leaf, Payne and Whale. Large iron ore deposits were found around the bay in the 1950s and these are now being mined on a grand scale.
Fort Chimo	Fort Chimo is an Inuit settlement on the Koksoak River, about 50km/30 miles inland from the bay.

Labrador current

The Labrador current is an ocean current that flows along the north-east and east coast of North America southwards from Baffin Bay. It is basically a coldwater current that flows from the Arctic, and is joined off the coast of Labrador by the waters from Hudson Bay off the Labrador coast. Up to 200m/656ft deep, the current flows south over the coastal shelf of Labrador and Newfoundland. Its salt content, at 3.3%, is 0.2–0.3% lower than normal. The temperature of the water in the deeper layers gets close to the freezing mark. On the surface the current moves at a rate of 0.5km/¼ mile–1.5km/1 mile an hour. The intensity of the current varies considerably from year to year and according to the time of year.

These variations can also have a considerable influence on Europe's weather. When it meets the Gulf Stream (west of Newfoundland) the intensity of the current determines whether the Gulf Stream turns north or south. The cooler and therefore denser waters of the Labrador current sink below the warmer, less dense waters of the Gulf Stream. The Labrador current therefore helps to determine whether spring will be late in Europe, or whether it will be very wet. The icebergs that accompany the current also present a considerable danger to shipping when the Gulf Stream carries them eastward into the North Atlantic sea lanes.

The meeting of the ocean currents with their different temperatures and carrying their different nutrients provides good conditions for a whole host of marine creatures.

For centuries, the waters off the Canadian coast have been known for their rich stocks of fish, and their cod, salmon, herring and mackerel have provided catches for fishing vessels from all over the world. In more recent times it has been possible precisely to chart and plot the size and direction of the ocean currents by satellite, and then relay the information to the fishing fleets to direct them to their fishing grounds.

Labrador Straits

The icy-cold Labrador current flows through the 17km/10½ mile-wide Strait of Belle Isle which separates Labrador from Newfoundland (see entry), into the Gulf of St Lawrence. Southern Labrador was traditionally the summer fishing grounds for centuries of fishermen heading here from Newfoundland (see entry).

L'Anse Amour	At L'Anse Amour archaeologists have uncovered an ancient burial site with finds over 7500 years old. The people who originally lived here on the south coast of Labrador almost 9000 years ago, at the end of the ice age, were the ancestors of the primitive caribou-hunters of eastern North America. They

lived in small settlements and were later to become the fishing and whaling tribes of the Belle Isle Strait.

Red Bay is the oldest industrial archaeological site in the New World, with the remains of a 16th c. Basque whaling station and shipwrecked Basque vessels. The Basque Whaling Archaeological Site can be visited in summer by arrangement.

Red Bay

Baie Comeau/Québec · Goose Bay/Newfoundland

Goose Bay can be reached by a 34-hour ferry trip from Lewisporte in Newfoundland, passing through Lake Melville, the "Markland" (woodland) discovered by the Vikings.

Goose Bay

Trip to Goose Bay

Along the shores of Lake Melville between Rigolet and Goose Bay there are a number of smallish but major settlements, where conditions are ideal for trapping, fishing and felling timber. One of the most important is North West River, or Sheshatshui ("narrow place in the river" in the Naskapi language) home to the Naskapi and the descendants of the English, French and Scottish settlers who originally worked here as hunters and trappers. The whole area has undergone considerable change since the Second World War, especially Happy Valley and Goose Bay.

The Goose Bay region – part of Newfoundland – is in eastern Labrador. The Allies built a big military base here during the Second World War, and the area is still used for military purposes, such as NATO training and low-level flying.

Goose Bay Region

The Goose Bay area has a population of over 10,000. Close on 1200 are from the original Indian peoples, but their lives are seriously affected by the military presence.

The town of Goose Bay (pop. 7000) is on an ice-age sandy site on the shore of Lake Melville. Its Labrador Heritage and Culture Centre Museum, in the north of the town, is open daily in summer, and its exhibits telling the story of Labrador and its people include a trapper's tilt, a kind of tarpaulin tent that provided shelter in the wilderness, trappers' tools and some beautiful furs. The items from Wallace Hubbard's ill-fated expeditions into the interior are of particular interest.

Goose Bay town

From Goose Bay the route continues on the Trans-Labrador Highway, to Churchill Falls.

Churchill Falls has what is considered to be the world's greatest hydro-electric power site. The main reservoir, covering an area of 3520sq.km/1359sq.miles, is as big as Sicily, and the water drops 300m/985ft over a distance of about 32km/20 miles. The largely automated power station generates 5,225,000 kW of electricity, serving over 3,500,000 Canadians and exporting the rest to the USA.

Churchill Falls

Travel around this area requires a special permit, but the scenery and the sight of partridges, beavers, caribou and even black bears compensate the visitor for the difficult drive.

The twin towns of Wabush and Labrador City, are in the middle of the wilderness, about 25km/15½ miles from the Québec border. They were constructed in the 1960s in an iron ore area. Ore to the value of about 1 billion Canadian dollars is mined here annually.

Wabush and Labrador City

From Labrador City it is possible to cover the 400km/250 miles to Sept-Îles by rail, a journey that takes six hours.

North Labrador

To get from Goose Bay to Nain it is best to take the ferry that sails along the coast once a week between late June and late November. Anyone wanting to travel further north will have to charter a boat or plane, always allowing for the harshness of the terrain and the changes in the weather.

Hopedale

In 1782 the British Government allowed the Moravian Brethren to set up a mission station in Labrador. This little complex is made up of a church, a grocery store, the minister's house, stores and little log-cabins for the native Indians.

Nain

Founded in 1771 by a group of Moravian Brethren, Nain's population of 1000 are Inuit, who live either from welfare or by the traditional ways of taking shellfish and salmon, and hunting caribou. The interesting little Nain School Museum illustrates the life of the Inuit and the Moravian Brethren, with kayaks and other items from northern Labrador, as well as telling the story of the Moravian mission.

Hebron

Hebron, the northernmost of the Moravian Brethren's Labrador missions, is on the remote shore of Kangershutsoak Bay. Established in 1829, it was abandoned in 1959 but the buildings remain, having been declared a national monument in 1970.

Lac La Biche   G 7

Province: Alberta. Area: 230sq.km/89sq.miles.

Information

See Alberta

Lac La Biche (230sq.km/89sq.miles), about 200km/125 miles north-east of Edmonton, has miles of sandy beaches, plus boat slipways.

Settlement

The settlement of Lac La Biche (pop. 6000), at the south-east end of the lake, dates from the trading post set up by David Thompson for the North West Company in 1798. It lies on a well-trodden route for the fur trappers, who could use a 2km/1 mile portage between Beaver Lake (the route into Hudson Bay through Churchill River) and Lac La Biche (already part of the Athabasca/MacKenzie River system).

Mission station

A mission station was built here in the mid-19th c., and Alberta's first wheat was grown in its fields. It had relatively more comfortable wooden houses, instead of the usual log cabins, and even ran to its own library.

Pow Wow, Blue
Feather Fish Derby

Lac La Biche Pow Wow and Blue Feather Fish Derby every year at the beginning of August provide a good opportunity to find out more about the culture of the Métis.

Sir Winston
Churchill
Provincial Park

On an island about 10km/6 miles north of the town, where farmland meets the northern pine forest, this provincial park is a great place for watching waterfowl and migrant birds. There are nature trails through the dense woodland of conifers, some of them over 140 years old and as tall as 23m/75ft.

Lac Megantic   P 8

Province: Québec (Frontenac County)

Information

See Québec (Province)

Lac Megantic, in Frontenac County, was and continues to be the homeland of the Abnaki Indians, and has good hunting and fishing.
The principal town of the locality, also called Lac Megantic (pop. 10,000), is on the Chaudière River, and has several lumber companies, as well as some farming.

Lac St-Jean

Province: Québec. Area: 1002sq.km/387sq.miles

See Québec (Province)

Information

Lac St-Jean, a former glacial basin, is the source of the Saguenay River that flows out through the scenic cliff-lined Saguenay Fiord (see entry) to the northern shore of the St Lawrence. The fertile plains and forests around the lake are part of the Canadian Shield, and its mountain setting gives Lac St-Jean some of the most beautiful scenery in the Province of Québec.

★★ Scenery

In August large quantities of blueberries are harvested here and the district is also well-known for its cheese.

Every year there is an international marathon swim on the last Sunday in July across the lake from Péribonca to Robertval.

Trans-lake swim

In May every year the "Festival de la Ouananiche" (Indian for freshwater salmon) is held in Desbiens, a little village at the mouth of the Métabetchouane.

★ **Surroundings**

Desbiens

The "Trou de la Fée", or "Fairy Hole", is a cave about 8km/5 miles south of Desbiens, which can be seen on a very steep trail.

Trou de la Fée

Val-Jalbert is a deserted village standing in the centre of the provincial park of that name (established 1960; open: end of May–beginning of Sept. daily 9am–7pm) near the mouth of the Ouitchouane. Here, close to a spectacular 72m/236ft-high waterfall capable of providing almost unlimited water power, the industrialist Damas Jalbert built, in 1901, a sawmill and paper and cardboard factory, together with a village to accommodate the work-force which was 1000 strong. By 1927 the factory had closed down and the settlement became a ghost town. Part of the factory and the machinery survive and can be seen. A number of buildings including the school, butcher's shop and grocer's shop, have recently been restored and there is also an interesting little museum documenting the history of the project.

★ Val-Jalbert
Historic Village

In the island zoo north-west of St-Félicien (open: mid-May–end Sept. daily 9am–5pm, 7pm in July), caribou, black bear and many of Canada's other wild creatures can be seen at very close quarters. An Indian village and a lumberjack camp are also among its attractions.

St-Félicien

Writer Louis Hémon (1880–1913) lived for several months in Péribonca, and made it the setting for his novel "Maria Chapdelaine" (1916), a major work of Canadian literature, and a glorification of the settler ethos.

Péribonca

The Louis Hémon Museum, dedicated to the life of the author, is open June–Sept. daily 9am–6pm; Sept.–June Mon.–Fri. 9.30am–4pm.

Lake of the Woods (Lac des Bois)

Provinces: Ontario and Manitoba
Area: 4860sqkm/1876sq.miles

See Ontario, Manitoba

Information

TransCanada Highway 1; VIA-Rail

Access

On the borders of the Canadian provinces of Manitoba and Ontario, Lake of the Woods is half in Canada and half in the US State of Minnesota. In a very scenic setting, its waters, fed by the Rainy River and draining into Lake Winnipeg through the Winnipeg River, are between 25 and 27m/82 and 87ft

★Setting

deep, and full of fish. Islands and islets fringe the heavily indented Canadian north shore, while the south shore is flat, sandy and very marshy in places.

Lake of the Woods was discovered in 1688, providing trappers and "voyageurs" with a passage westwards. Nowadays it is a popular holiday hideaway.

Kenora   Kenora on the north-east shore of Lake of the Woods is in Ontario Province and the centre for the many hydroplanes and other light aircraft that ferry adventurous holidaymakers around on their fishing and hunting trips out of the many lodges.

Rushing River   Rushing River Provincial Park is a park of over 160ha/395 acres around a
Provincial Park   series of cascades in the Rushing River about 40km/25 miles below the lake.

Sioux Narrows   The village of Sioux Narrows is on the narrows between fingers of Lake of the Woods on Whitefish Bay, at one time the scene of skirmishes between the Sioux and the Ojibwa.

The Laurentians (Les Laurentides)   Q/P 8

Province: Québec

Information   See Québec (Province)

★★Topography   The Laurentian uplands extend from Ottawa in the west to the Saguenay River in the east, with the St Lawrence (see entry) as their southern boundary. They also form part of the southern Pre-Cambrian Canadian Shield. Throughout the year this rolling mountain range, with its maple woods, plentiful game – including the mighty moose – secret lakes, romantic waterfalls and lovely valleys, is a favourite playground not just for the city folk from Ottawa, Montréal and Québec, but for the whole of the densely populated St Lawrence seaboard (see entries).

Generally speaking the Laurentians are understood to mean the whole of the upland area of the Laurentine massif between the Ottawa and Saguenay rivers north of the St Lawrence, and more specifically the resort area north-west of Montréal. They were opened up between 1870 and 1891 through Antoine Labelle, a priest of St-Jérome, who founded twenty homesteads here since he feared many of his fellow countrymen would otherwise be tempted to emigrate to New England in search of better farming land.

However, it was not until the development of tourism after the Second World War that the Laurentians became less the kind of recreation area they are today, offering countless lakes and rivers, about 30 golf courses, over 20 winter sports resorts (including Mont-Tremblant, Morin Heights, Mont-Olympia), and facilities for riding, hunting and fishing. One of North America's most attractive and popular recreational areas, enjoying a reputation as Québec Province's "Switzerland", the Laurentians boast the greatest concentration of hotels, restaurants and holiday homes in North America.

★Montréal Laurentians

Access   By road
Laurentian Autoroute 15 (toll-road), then Highway 117; frequent buses from Montréal at peak holiday times, i.e. July/August, Christmas and February/March.

The Laurentians north of Montréal are the setting for some of Canada's most famous resorts, such as Ste-Adèle, Ste-Agathe, St-Donat, St-Sauveur, Estérel and Val Morin. On a par with the best in Europe, they attract visitors throughout the year, offering top hotels, plenty of entertainment, including Canadian folksong bars, a good network of walks and trails, water sports on the lakes, horseback riding, golf and tennis, and full winter sports facilities such as ski-lifts, cross-country routes, etc.

Built in 1975, Montréal's international airport at Mirabel is one of the largest in America.

Mirabel

The gateway to the Laurentians is the town of St-Jérome. A statue opposite the Cathedral commemorates its famous priest, Antoine Labelle.

St-Jérome

One of Québec's finest resorts, St-Sauveur-des-Monts is well-known for winter sports with its 30 ski-lifts.

St-Sauveur-des-Monts

The little township of Laurentides, with a population of 2000, just 30km/19 miles north of Montréal, is the birthplace of Sir Wilfred Laurier (see Famous People). Maison Laurier, the pretty house where Canada's first French-Canadian Prime Minister spent his childhood, is now a national monument, with guided tours daily between May and September.

Laurentides

Maison Laurier

Mont Gabriel, a summer and winter resort, boasts one of the biggest and highest priced hotels in the Laurentians.

Mont Gabriel

Founded in 1852, the little town of Ste-Adèle (pop. 5000) on the slopes of Mont Ste-Adèle, is picturesquely located by Lac Rond and has long been a favourite haunt of writers and artists.

Ste-Adèle

Ste-Adèle's Village de Séraphin, famous as the setting for a television series, recaptures the life and times of the Laurentians in the 19th c. (open: mid-May–mid-Oct.; admission fee). Séraphin Bastien, the inspiration of Claude-Henri Grignon's 1933 novel "Un homme et son péché", lived in the Jos Malterre inn from 1832.

Séraphin

Ste-Agathe-des-Monts (pop. 7000), the lively and scenic resort on Lac des Sables in the Laurentians near Montréal, is full of town dwellers holiday homes. There are boat cruises around the lake between May and October and a music and folk festival in July.

Ste-Agathe-des-Monts

Mont Tremblant, the highest peak in the Laurentians (960m/3151ft) and about 150km/93 miles north of Montréal, is at the heart of the Mont Tremblant Provincial Park, a particular favourite with visitors in the Indian Summer when the leaves change colour and for its skiing in winter.
   Established in 1894, the park and nature reserve covers about 3200 sq.km/1235 sq.miles. It has two well-signed trails, and camping and canoeing is allowed.
   The mountain owes its name to the roar of the rushing streams, sounding like the boom of an earthquake to the Indians. The park's wildlife includes deer, black bear, moose, lynx, otter, mink and beaver.

★Mont Tremblant

Close to Mont Trembland is St-Jovite and the Weir Satellite Reception Station which has public guided tours from mid-June to September.

St-Jovite, Weir Satellite Station

See entry

Joliette

★Laurentides near Québec (town)

Half an hour by car north-east of Québec City is the glorious scenery of the Mont Ste-Anne Park, a favourite recreation area summer and winter for the people of Québec, with its wildly romantic river valleys, Black Forest type mountains, and its uplands and mountain valleys with good grazing for dairy cattle and for raising livestock.
   Mont Ste-Anne is also good for winter sports, and has numbers of chalets and holiday homes, plus a reputation for gourmet eating.

★Parc du Mont Ste-Anne

Réserve faunique des Laurentides	The vast Laurentides wildlife conservation area lies about 60km/37 miles north of Québec City and takes in the Parc de Conservation Jacques-Cartier, the Parc de Conservation des Grands-Jardins, Lac Beauséjour and Lac Jacques-Cartier at the foot of Montagne Camille-Pouliot. The highway passing through this section of the Laurentians, drained by the Montmorency River, is Route 175, with plenty of roadside accommodation where the traveller can stay overnight or stop for a meal.

Extending over 10514sq.km/4058sq.miles of lakes and forests, with some peaks above 900m/3000ft, this park in the Canadian Shield was designated a protected area as early as 1895. It was originally intended as an enormous reserve for the conservation of the caribou, and after they became extinct here in 1930 some were reintroduced in the western half of the park in 1969.

The park is also home to black bear, lynx, deer, wolf and many other smaller creatures. Although hunting is forbidden fishing in its lakes and rivers is permitted. There is also kayaking on Lac Jacques-Cartier, and over 50km/31 miles of cross-country skiing trails around Mercier in winter. The reception centres at Jacques-Cartier, Mercier and Grands-Jardins can all provide plenty of information and literature.

Lac St-Jean	See entry

Lesser Slave Lake   F/G 6

Province: Alberta. Area: 1150sq.km/444sq.miles

Information	See Alberta
★Setting	About 90km/56 miles long and up to 20km/12 miles wide, Lesser Slave Lake covers an area of 1150sq.km/444sq.miles, its waters filling a great Pre-Ice Age valley that became the catchment area for the Ice-Age glacier. The dunes and broad sandy beaches around the lake – where stormy weather can bring 9ft high waves at times – are indicative of considerable fluctuations in the water level.
★Lesser Slave Lake Provincial Park	Lesser Slave Lake Provincial Park lies on the flat east shore of the lake, about 5km/3 miles north of the town of Slave Lake. It has a campsite, with swimming, fishing, surfing and canoeing in summer. Keen anglers can take part in the Golden Pike Fish Derby between May and September.

Birdwatchers can see over 170 species, while osprey and bald eagle breed on Dog Island.

Other park wildlife includes moose, black bear and beaver, together with grizzlies and wolves when the year is at its coldest.

Marten Mountain	Marten Mountain is the highest point (1030m/3380ft) of the Pelican Mountain Uplands adjoining the park, with a panoramic view over the surrounding countryside from the firetower on the top.
Grouard	The little village of Grouard (pop. 200) at the west end of the lake is named after an earlier Catholic Bishop of Athabasca. Its population was in thousands rather than hundreds at the start of this century until the decision was taken not to route the railroad to the north through the town.

It is possible to see round the Indian Museum and the mission that Bishop Grouard founded in 1884 and to visit his grave in the mission cemetery.

Hillard's Bay Provincial Park	Hillard's Bay Provincial Park on the lake shore about 13km/8 miles east of Grouard dates from 1978. A lovely recreation area, it has campsites and good sandy beaches, with a nature trail of just over a mile outlining the ecology of the northern pinewoods.
Shaw's Point	Shaw's Point, the ½-mile spit of land where the lake's old paddle-steamers used to come alongside, was once the start of the Grouard Trail, an alterna-

The Lesser Slave Lake

tive route from Edmonton to the goldfields of the Yukon. The old wagon trail, which early settlers also travelled to reach Peace River territory, can still be seen today.

For lovers of the great outdoors the forested uplands of the Swan Hills, south of Lesser Slave Lake and over 1200m/3928ft at their highest point, are something of a promised land, to which access can only be gained via the tracks laid down for hauling out the oil and timber.

Swan Hills

The expanding township of Swan Hills (pop. 2500) is capitalising on the five oil companies that operate nearby.

Fort Assiniboine (pop. 200), on the Athabasca River, dates from 1824 when the Hudson's Bay Company founded it as a trading post on the Beaver Route. It boasts a reconstruction of the old fort, which holds a small local history museum. Open: mid-May–Oct. daily 1–4pm; at other times Wed. and Sun. only.

From Lesser Slave Lake to Edmonton

Fort Assiniboine

Barrhead (pop. 4000) is a township serving an area of farming and forestry.

Barrhead

From here Highway 33 runs south for 72km/45 miles through undulating farmland to the Yellowhead Highway (see entry).

In the past Slave Lake (pop. 6000), at the south-east end of Lesser Slave Lake, lived primarily from the timber trade, but owes its rapid expansion since the 1960s to the petroleum and natural gas industry.

★Slave Lake

David Thompson, in 1799, was the first European to reach Lesser Slave Lake and realise the territory's potential for the fur trade. The North West Company's first trading post on Lesser Slave Lake went up that same year, followed by the Hudson's Bay Company in 1815. The trading posts developed into a general centre for servicing the north, known until 1923 as Sawridge, with landing stages for the paddle-steamers that plied the lake. Many prospectors passed through here during the Klondike Goldrush, and the paddle-steamers carried on until 1915, when the railroad first reached Slave Lake. The town is still the point of departure for trekking northwards today, as hunters take off from here after bear and moose in the hunting season. The lake gets its name from the Slave Indians who lived here when the first Europeans arrived. Like the Beaver Indians further north, they were among the Athabascan tribes, but subservient to the Cree Indians, part of the Algonquin nation. The 18th c. was a time of intertribal strife, particularly once the Cree became the first to obtain guns from the White Man, and a peace treaty only came when the Cree had been decimated by smallpox. Descendants of the original local peoples, along with the more recently arrived Métis, live on in Lesser Slave Lake territory today.

The Slave Lake Native Friendship Centre (408 5th Ave. NE, open: 8.30am to 4.30pm), with its own management structure and leisure facilities, helps with integration, and also has handmade moccasins, jewellery and Indian garments for sale.

Lethbridge   G 8

Province: Alberta. Population: 60,000

Information

See Alberta

The fast-growing city of Lethbridge on the Oldman River mainly owes its prosperity to the oil and gas industry. Other important local industries are tourism and farming (livestock, corn, sugarbeet and vegetables).

History

Lethbridge was founded in the 1870s when it was called Coalbank, a reference to the coal found nearby. It soon became a centre for farming and, at the turn of the century, was the site of Canada's first large-scale irrigation system.

Nearby townships like Coaldale and Coalhurst are reminders of the fact that up until 1965 coal was still being mined in the region's deep valleys where previously there had been only outposts set up in 1869 for the benefit of the unscrupulous liquor runners.

Sights

★Nikka Yuko Gardens

The Nikka Yuko Japanese Gardens (8th Ave.S/Mayor Magrath Drive, open: mid-May–mid-Oct. daily 9am–7pm) are the pride of Lethbridge. The beautiful, carefully tended gardens are a symbol of Canadian-Japanese friendship. The bridges and buildings were constructed in Japan in 1967 before being reassembled in Lethbridge.

★Indian Battle Park

Indian Battle Park on the Oldman River commemorates the great Indian battle in 1870 between the Blackfoot Confederation and the Cree Indians, when an attack by the Cree with their allies the Assiniboine on the camp of the Blackfoot, already weakened by an outbreak of smallpox, was repulsed but at the cost of almost 400 lives.

Surroundings

★Writing-on-Stone Provincial Park

Writing-on-Stone Provincial Park is reached by first going to Milk River (pop. 1000) 85km/53 miles south of Lethbridge, then travelling east on Highway 501 for 32km/20 miles and turning south down a tarmac road for another 10km/6 miles.

The park gets its name from the many Indian drawings on the sandstone rocks, eroded into bizarre shapes, that form the steep gulch of the Milk River.

These lands were of great spiritual significance for the Plains Indians who believed the spirits of the departed would "write" messages on the rock walls. Warrior braves came here to try and discover what might happen if they went on the warpath, but they never stayed long since it was too dangerous to linger near the spirits of the dead.

In 1908 the graves of five men, a woman and a child were found here, together with items from the US Cavalry. It is thought they could have been survivors of the Nez-Percé who were almost wiped out in 1877 by the US Cavalry near the Canadian border, or they could have been from the tribe of Sitting Bull who fled into southern Canada after their victory over General Custer in 1876 at the Battle of the Little Bighorn.

The bare rocks and hoodoos on the valley edge and the semi-arid prairie contrast starkly with the lush vegetation in the valley itself, where the Milk River lends itself well to canoeing. The Indian petroglyphs can only be seen on guided tours. These last about an hour.

Highway 4 runs south-east from Lethbridge to the only frontier crossing into the States from Alberta which is open 24 hours a day.   US border

Lloydminster   H 7

Province: Saskatchewan. Population: 15,000

See Saskatchewan   Information

Founded in 1903 by British colonists headed by the cleric Isaac Barr, Lloydminster is on the Yellowhead Highway close to the border with Alberta, and the centre of a thriving region that owes much of its prosperity to oil and farming.

The Barr Heritage Cultural Centre (open: end May–beginning Sept. daily 10am–8pm; in winter Mon.–Fri. 10am–8pm, Sat., Sun. 1–5pm) contains several kinds of cultural displays and function rooms.   **Sights**
Barr Heritage
Cultural Centre

The Barr Colony Antique Museum, has exhibits from the founding of the town, including a completely furnished schoolroom and a model oil refinery.   The Barr Colony
Antique Museum

In the Fuchs' Wildlife Display can be seen dioramas with about 1000 mounted birds and other animals.   The Fuchs'
Wildlife Display

The Imhoff Art Gallery shows the works of Berthold von Imhoff, an artist well-known for his religious pictures and his landscapes.   The Imhoff Art
Gallery

It is worth paying a visit to Weaver Park (Hwy. 16E, 44th & 45th St., open: mid-May–mid-Sept. 9am–9pm) where the restored buildings show the place as lived in by the first settlers.   ★ Weaver Park

The local Chamber of Commerce runs trips to some of the petroleum plants in and around Lloydminster, taking in a visit to the Char-Mil model drilling rig on 46th Street.   ★ Petroleum
industry
sightseeing tours

London   N 9

Province: Ontario. Population: 290,000

See Ontario   Information

London – on the Canadian River Thames – is the centre for Ontario's prosperous agricultural and industrial south-west, the seat of a Catholic and an Anglican Bishop, and the cultural focus, with its university, symphony orchestra, theatre and museums, for a large area.

The city was founded in 1792 by John Graves Simcoe who named it after London, England. This was because Niagara-on-the-Lake, the provincial capital at that time, was right on the American frontier and he wanted his   History

London

London – as in London, the capital of England, and also as a city deeper into Canada – to become the province's new capital.

Sights

★Art Gallery

London's main attraction is its art gallery, completed in 1980 and designed by Raymond Moriyama. Open: Tues.–Sun. afternoons. This unusual building on Ridout Street shows the work of 18th and 19th c. Canadian artists, together with temporary exhibitions covering the whole range of old and new North American art.

Eldon House

Also on Ridout Street, just north of the gallery, Eldon House was the elegant home of an English naval captain, who moved here in 1834. It is now a museum (open: Mar.–Nov. Tues.–Sun. afternoons).

Ridout Street

Close by Eldon House Ridout Street also has several beautifully restored Georgian buildings.

Labatt Pioneer Brewery

The Labatt Pioneer Brewery is a charming replica of the wooden brewery built here in 1828. Demonstrations inside the brewery, which is open on weekday afternoons from June to September, show how beer was brewed over 100 years ago, when they produced 300 barrels a year. Today's modern brewery next door, which can also be visited weekdays from June to September, between noon and 5pm by appointment (tel. 673–5211), turns out more than 1.2 million barrels of beer a year.

Springbank Park

Springbank Park, on the western edge of the city, has a small zoo, fairy tale garden and flower beds, also boat trips by little paddle-steamers on the Thames in summer.

Royal Canadian Regiment Museum

The museum holds Canada's oldest infantry regiment's notable collection of weapons. These can be viewed Tuesday to Saturday, but not on public holidays.

★Museum of Indian Archaeology

Located near a prehistoric Indian burial ground, the museum, at 1600 Attawarndaron Road, has 40,000 exhibits and tells the story of the 11,000 years of Indian settlement in Ontario. (Open: Apr.–Nov. Wed.–Sun. 10am–5pm; and from 1 to 4pm for the rest of the year.)

Surroundings

Fanshawe Pioneer Village

Fanshawe Pioneer Village, about 16km/10 miles north-east of London (open: May–Sept. daily 10am–4pm; by arrangement at other times) is the reconstruction of a settlement showing what life was like here before the coming of the railroad. It is on the shore of Fanshawe Lake, and its buildings include a Presbyterian church, grocery store, smithy, fire brigade storeroom and an assembly room recalling the influence in Ontario of the Orange Order founded in Ireland at the end of the 18th c. This is open between 10am and 4.30pm weekdays from October to December and daily from May to September.

★Ska Nah Doht Indian Village

Ska Nah Doht Indian Village (open: Mon.–Fri. 9am to 6pm), about 30km/19 miles south-west of London, is the palisaded replica of a 10th–12th c. Iroquois village, with three longhouses, a steam-room, areas for drying meat and fish, storage, etc., and patches of Indian crops such as squash, maize and beans.

St Thomas

St Thomas, a railroad junction and industrial town also some 30km/19 miles south-west of London, shows clear signs of the influence of Belgian and Hungarian immigrants. Elgin County Pioneer Museum of regional history and Pinafore Park, with its flowerbeds, miniature railway and children's zoo, are worth a visit.

★Stratford

Just 60km/39 miles north-east of London, Stratford (pop. 25,000) is internationally famous for its Festival. Named after the Bard's birthplace by 19th c. immigrants from Stratford, England, it sprang to fame in 1950 when a local newspaper editor organised the first festival. The 2250–seater Festival Theatre has been staging plays between May and October since 1953, with pride of place going to Shakespeare, but also, by public demand, putting on Molière, Brecht, and the like, not to mention the occasional Mozart opera.

Louisbourg (Forteresse de Louisbourg)　　　　　　　　　　　　R 8

Province: Nova Scotia. Population: 1500

Louisbourg, once an important French military base and now one of the most visited historical sites in Canada, lies on the eastern side of Cape Breton Island about 40km/25 miles south of the town of Sydney. | Situation

Visitor Reception Centre (about 1km/½ mile from the fortress, and where the bus leaves for the the park). The address for information on special events is: Forteresse de Louisbourg, National Historic Park, P.O. Box 160, Louisbourg. | Information

Louisbourg Fortress, which has been reconstructed, is open to visitors from the end of May until September daily 9am–6pm. | Visiting

Under the terms of the Treaty of Utrecht which ended the War of the Spanish Succession, France was forced to cede Newfoundland and large tracts of Acadia to Britain, retaining only the Îsle Royale (now Cape Breton Island) and the Îsle St-Jean (now Prince Edward Island). These two islands became the hub of the exceptionally lucrative French cod fishing industry centred on the waters of the Grand Banks off Newfoundland. The port of Louisbourg was established by the French on the east side of the Îsle | History

Fortress of Louisbourg

Royale in 1719, at which time the substantial fortifications were also built. All around Louisbourg long rows of wooden racks were constructed on which the cod were salted and dried before being exported as "klipfish". Trade with France, Québec, the islands of the Caribbean and parts of Newfoundland flourished. In 1745, the French having declared war on Britain, Louisbourg came under attack. Being difficult to defend on the landward side, it fell to the British after seven weeks. The 1748 Treaty of Aachen however returned Louisbourg to France. Ten years later the British again laid seige to the port, this time with a force of 16,000 men and 150 ships. On this occasion too Louisbourg held out for seven weeks. Afterwards the British razed the fortress walls to prevent the town from being fortified anew.

Reconstruction

In 1961 Canada's federal government undertook the reconstruction of part of the Forteresse de Louisbourg. The result is that fortifications, the harbour, buildings, courtyards and gardens can today be seen very much as they appeared in 1740. In the course of the rebuilding archaeologists excavated the old foundation walls.

★★Louisbourg Fortress

Louisbourg Fortress, or "la Forteresse de Louisbourg", is Canada's most famous historical reconstruction, the prototype of a "Living History Museum" offering visitors an opportunity to experience at first hand the rigours of mid 18th c. life on the far from hospitable, frequently mist-shrouded, east coast of Canada. Throughout the main tourist season appropriately costumed "townspeople" – servants, soldiers, merchants, maids and fishermen – re-enact the arduous daily round of those times. Two restaurants serve speciality dishes prepared from old recipes.

The Forteresse de Louisbourg, modelled on those built by Vauban, is surrounded by a wall with towers and bastions, and encompasses more than forty buildings. The town, of which seven blocks of houses were rebuilt, was right on the water, so that ships could moor there. The most luxurious buildings are in the "Bastion du Roi", and these were occupied by the French King's representative who was both Governor and Commandant. The ordinary soldiers' barracks, in which several had to share a room, were simply furnished. Among the numerous service facilities were a bakery, stores, a smithy, etc. The entrance to the fort is via the Porte Dauphine, close to the Armoury, and there is a museum by the Bastion du Roi.

Lunenburg   R 9

Province: Nova Scotia. Population: 3000

Information

See Nova Scotia

Access

From Halifax (see entry) south on Highway 3.

Lunenburg, is a little fishing port on a peninsula on the Nova Scotia coast between the town of Mahone Bay and the mouth of the La Have River. Because of its geographical position the town has two harbours, Back Harbour in the North and Lunenburg Harbour on the bay of the same name.

History

Lunenburg got its name from the many settlers from Lüneburg in northern Germany who came here when the British colonial government founded it in 1753 as a settlement for Protestants in Nova Scotia, and the social and cultural life of Lunenburg, as well as its traditions and townscape, still bear the imprint of those early northern European settlers.

Lunenburg's main claim to fame is its harbour and the shipyard that make it the home port of the famous "Bluenose" schooner, built here in 1921 when it was the world's best racing schooner, and the winner of many an in-

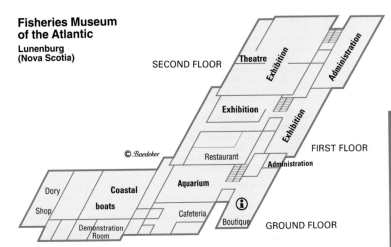

Fisheries Museum of the Atlantic
Lunenburg (Nova Scotia)

SECOND FLOOR — Theatre, Exhibition, Administration

Exhibition — FIRST FLOOR

© *Baedeker* — Restaurant, Administration

Dory Shop — Coastal boats — Aquarium

Demonstration Room — Cafeteria — Boutique — GROUND FLOOR

ternational race. It can still be seen today on one side of Canada's ten-cent coin. The sailing ship used in the "Mutiny on the Bounty" was also built in the Lunenburg shipyard.

The town's position as the centre of Canada's east coast fishing is reinforced every September when the Nova Scotia Fisheries Exhibition is held here. Besides the latest developments in shipping there is plenty of entertainment, on and off the water.

The Fisheries Museum of the Atlantic, in a former fish factory on the waterfront at Duke Street, is well worth a visit (open: mid-May–Oct., 9am–6pm, tel. 634–4794).

Sights
★★Fisheries Museum of the Atlantic

Spread over three floors, it also has an aquarium, souvenir shop and restaurant, and tells the history of sailing and fishing along eastern Canada's coasts, enlivened by old prints, photographs, illustrations of fishing methods and equipment old and new, audiovisuals, etc. to make a visit here a memorable experience.

The museum's star attractions, moored in the port, are the "Cape Sable" trawler, and the "Theresa E. Connor", a 1938 schooner, where the museum staff vividly demonstrate the traditional methods of cod fishing and what life was like on board.

Between mid-June and mid-September there are two-hourly harbour trips, starting at 10.30am, from Lunenburg Harbour on the historic schooner "Timberwind".

Trips on the "Timberwind"

Mackenzie District

B–J 4/5

Province: Northwest Territories

See Northwest Territories

Information

Mackenzie District forms the western section of Canada's Northwest Territories, a vast expanse covering 1.5 million sq.km/579,000sq.miles and bounded by Yukon Territory in the west, the continental coastline in the north, 120° longitude W in the east, and 60° latitude N in the south, with a population numbered only in several tens of thousands. Just on half of it is in the Arctic, and the forested sub-Arctic section of the district is home to a few thousand Indians.

The Mackenzie Mountains in the north-west of the district are a spur of the Cordilleras (see below), while the eastern section of this vast District is part of the Pre-Cambrian Canadian Shield. At its heart, however, is the alluvial valley of the Mackenzie River and the delta of this mighty north American river (see below).

Economy	In the 19th c. trade came from the few trappers and fishermen who lived here from time to time but in the first half of the 20th c. the forests in the Mackenzie Valley attracted the attention of the paper industry. This was followed by the discovery of oil at Norman Wells in the 1920s, pitchblende at Port Radium and gold at Yellowknife (see entry) in the 1930s, with mining becoming a thriving industry after the Second World War.
Mackenzie Mountains	The Mackenzie Mountains extend north-west into the Canadian Arctic as a spur of the North American Cordilleras, forming the frontier between Yukon Territory and the Mackenzie lowlands. Largely unexplored and relatively dry, with only sparse vegetation, the Mackenzies consist of two mountain chains, with the eastern one also known as Canyon Range. They cover about 800km/497 miles and have peaks as high as 2900m/9518ft in the west.
Mackenzie Highway	The Mackenzie Highway was built shortly after the Second World War and is an all-weather road covering the 600km/373 miles from Peace River in Alberta to Great Slave Lake and the territorial capital Yellowknife (see entry), serving to open up the mining district around Pine Point.

Mackenzie River   B–F 4/5

Administrative unit: Northwest Territories

Information	See Northwest Territories
Access	By air (Fort Simpson, Inuvik) or by road via the Mackenzie Highway

With a length of 4250km/2641 miles, the Mackenzie is the second largest river in North America, one of the longest in the world (from the mouth to the source of the Finlay River, its longest tributary) and has a catchment area of 1.8 million sq.km/69,480sq.miles. The main sources of the Mackenzie are the Peace River and the Athabasca which merge to form the Slave River. On leaving Great Slave Lake this becomes the river bearing the name of the Scottish explorer Sir Alexander Mackenzie (see Famous People).

The river was already an important artery for the canoes of the fur trade in the 18th c. and is navigable today in summer by steamers as far upriver as Fort Smith, about 2000km/1243 miles.

Big oil and natural gas reserves have been discovered in the Mackenzie Delta and the Beaufort Sea, which opens out into the Arctic Ocean.

Most of the towns along the Mackenzie River were North West or Hudson's Bay Company trading posts, used for storing and trans-shipping skins and furs.

★★Mackenzie Delta	The Mackenzie Delta can be reached by road along the Dempster Highway (see entry) or by air from Edmonton, Yellowknife and Whitehorse (see entries). Sightseeing charter flights can be booked in Inuvik.
Access	The Mackenzie River Delta extends over about 12,000sq.km/ 4632sq.miles between the Richardson Mountains in the west and the Caribou Hills in the east, and its origins are partly interglacial, possibly

In the Mackenzie Delta

pre-glacial. About 200km/124 miles before the river enters the Beaufort Sea its broad stream meanders and breaks up into countless smaller rivers and lakes.

The vegetation of this delta landscape is mostly low bushes and shrubs, junipers, lichens and mosses, with magnificent displays of colour from flowers and mosses during the brief but intensive summer (from June to late July this is the land of the midnight sun). To complete the picture, this very special environment also has a great variety of wildlife on water as well as on land (see Facts and Figures, Flora and Fauna).

Flora and Fauna

There are no more than about 7000 people in the delta. Their homes are in Aklavik, Tukoyaktuk, Inuvik (see entry), Fort McPherson and Arctic Red River, and they still live mostly from hunting and fishing.

The discovery of enormous gas and oilfields in the Mackenzie Delta and offshore in the Beaufort Sea is likely to alter the structure of the whole region and have a lasting impact on life in this remote landscape.

Population and economy

Fort Simpson is a community of about 1000 people where the Liard runs into the Mackenzie River west of Great Slave Lake about some 480km/298 miles from the Northwest Territories' southern boundary with Alberta.

It is the oldest settlement on the Mackenzie River and was founded by the North West Company in 1804 for the trans-shipment of skins and furs at this strategic junction.

The town got its name from the Governor of the Hudson's Bay Company, Sir George Simpson, after the two companies merged in 1821. In the decades that followed Fort Simpson was vital as a staging post for the vessels carrying furs, food and raw materials up the Mackenzie River.

Fort Simpson

The fur traders, gold and oil prospectors were followed here by Christian missionaries who began tilling the fertile soil which has since earned the

"Mackenzie Garden"

291

region the nickname of "Mackenzie Garden" on account of the vegetables and cereals grown in the area. Besides having a Roman Catholic mission, Fort Simpson has since 1858 also been a base for the Anglican Church.

Manitoba   J–L 6–8

Geographical situation: 88°–102° longitude W, 48°–60° latitude N
Area: 650,000sq.km/250,900sq.miles
Population: 1.1 million
Languages: English, French, many Indian and Inuit languages
Capital: Winnipeg

Information

Travel Manitoba, Dept. 2036, 7th Floor, 155 Carlton St, Winnipeg, Manitoba R3C 3H8; tel. (204) 945–3777.

Access

By air: Flights to Winnipeg from many places in Canada

By road: TransCanada Highway from Ontario in the east and Saskatchewan in the west

By rail: By VIA Rail

Manitoba gets it name from "manito waba", an Ojibwan phrase used for the narrows on Lake Manitoba where the sound from the pebbles being ground against the shore by the storm-tossed waves seemed to the early Indians to have come from Manitou, the great spirit.

Manitoba is bordered by the US State of North Dakota in the south, Saskatchewan in the west, Ontario in the east and the Northwest Territories in the north.

Lakes and rivers cover just on a sixth of its surface area. It is 1225km/761 miles from north to south and 793km/493 miles from east to west. Manitoba's coastline, on Hudson Bay, runs for 645km/401 miles, and its port there is Churchill.

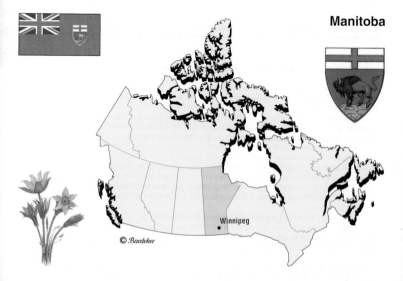

Manitoba

© Baedeker

Winnipeg

Manitoba's landscape bears the mark of the Ice Age, with its grassy prairie, uplands, dune wildernesses and craggy pine-covered hills, and criss-crossed by rivers flowing into Hudson's Bay.

The Hudson lowlands, with their layers of clayey topsoil, fringe the bay and stretch as far as 150km/93 miles inland, before gently rising to the uplands south and west, the highest point being Baldy Mountain, at 831m/2727ft, in the Duck Mountains.

The biggest lakes in this "land of many thousand lakes" are those left from Lake Agassiz, the vast post-glacial lake that covered most of the province.

In the east and, above all, the north the Canadian Shield, consisting mostly of Pre-Cambrian granite, gneiss, quarzite, etc., covers over half the province.

Eastern Manitoba's highlands and plateaux were covered by glaciers. These massive moving icesheets carved deep clefts and depressions that eventually filled with water, and laid bare quartz and granite strata that were smoothed down to gentle hills. The thin covering of soil that these acquired was sufficient to support shallow-rooted dense evergreen vegetation.

The summers are hot, with average temperatures of between 17° and 24°C/62 and 75°F, and as much as 30°C/86°F in high summer, although it can be quite cool at night, especially on the lakes.

Winters are long and very cold, getting as low as −40°C/−40°F.

In the intensively farmed south-west the frost-free period is about 100 days, but in the far north it is only 60 to 80 days.

Precipitation is comparatively low. Winnipeg, for example, only has about 120 days with significant precipitation a year.

Because of the differences in climate vegetation follows a particular sequence with the prairieland of the south bordered by a belt of parkland – open country dotted with trees, especially poplars – to the north. The dense forests begin around the southern lakes, starting with mixed woodland of poplar, birch, fir and pine, then becoming entirely coniferous before gradually giving way to tundra on Hudson Bay.

The ancestors of the native peoples of Manitoba got there from Asia over 12,000 years before the first Europeans. Around 1600 there were four Indian tribes in what is now Manitoba. The Chippewa lived in the bleak tundra around Hudson Bay, the Cree and Salteaux moved around the great forests of the Canadian Shield further south, while the Assiniboine, famous as buffalo-hunters, followed the herds on the prairies in the south-west along today's Canadian border with the USA.

The first European to explore the territory was Thomas Button, who sailed along the west coast of Hudson Bay in 1612 on a voyage of discovery, and spent the winter in Port Nelson, claiming the land for England. Like other later European explorers he was looking for the fabled Northwest Passage to India and instead of finding a sea route to the riches of the Orient had stumbled upon Hudson Bay and a land rich in game and wildfowl. The day of the lucrative fur trade had dawned.

A year earlier Henry Hudson and his son John, along with seven loyal seamen, had been cast adrift in an open boat in James Bay after a mutiny by the crew of his ship "Discovery". They were never seen again. Hudson had sailed along the east coast of Hudson Bay in 1610, also in search of the Northwest Passage. The harsh winter came on and along with it the mutiny, just as he had planned to head west again.

In 1631 and 1633 two English seafarers, Luke Fox and Thomas James – who gave his name to James Bay – explored the west coast of Hudson Bay and its southern inlet, James Bay, again in search of the Northwest Passage.

In 1670 King Charles II granted the Hudson's Bay Company the trading rights to all territories draining into Hudson Bay. They were named

Rupert's Land after the king's cousin, who was also titular head of the company which now had control of an area of about 8 million sq.km/3.08 million sq.miles, one-twelfth of the land on earth! Thus the foundations were laid for the world's oldest company still active today, and its most far-flung. The company established trading posts and forts along the coast, then penetrated to the south and inland. Henry Kelsey set out a few years later from York Factory, at the mouth of the Nelson River, in search of yet more fur animals and lived for two years with the Plains Indians, travelling as far as what is today the boundary between Saskatchewan and Alberta.

The British and French were constantly at loggerheads over the fur trade and in 1731 Sieur de la Vérendrye began building a line of forts between Lake Superior and the lower Saskatchewan River. These included Fort Rouge, now Winnipeg, in 1738, as he sought to extend France's North American sphere of influence.

The rivalry lapsed with the defeat of the French in 1763 until the founding of the North West Company in 1779 to compete with the Hudson's Bay Company. The two companies were eventually merged in 1821, and the Hudson's Bay Company that emerged is still one of Canada's leading store chains, although it abandoned the fur trade in 1991.

While the fur-trading companies were still competing with one another the first farming settlement was planned, and in 1811 Lord Selkirk received over 260,000sq.km/100,360sq.miles from the Hudson's Bay Company, taking in parts of what is now Manitoba, the States of North Dakota and Minnesota, and north-west Ontario. The company wanted to get down the cost of importing foodstuffs, and thus gain a competitive advantage over its North West rival. Scottish and Irish settlers arrived a year later, to be joined by colonists from French Canada and a great many Métis. The North West Company tried in vain to destroy the settlement, and in 1816 Commander Robert Semple and 20 other men were killed at the battle of Seven Oaks near Winnipeg. But the settlement carried on and farming began to prosper, attracting more and more people to come and settle to farming out on the prairie.

When the Dominion of Canada came into being in 1867 it wanted to buy Rupert's Land from the Hudson's Bay Company and in 1870, in the biggest land deal in history, it bought this enormous territory, which then had a population of 170,000, from the company for 1.5 million dollars.

However, the settlers, led by Louis Riel, were opposed to this union by acquisition, in which they had had no say. Métis descendants of Indians and French fur traders, they feared for their special lifestyle, their language and their culture, as well as for their land rights. The threat to these led to an armed struggle at the Red River before the land purchase was finalised. Louis Riel, their leader, set up a provisional government and tried through negotiation to dictate the conditions for the territory's entry into the Dominion. Although his government collapsed and Riel was executed, the Bill of Rights he had negotiated, guaranteeing equal French and English language rights in school and church, was upheld and incorporated in the Manitoba Act that established the territory as the fifth Province. Those rights were to be the source of further conflict later on.

When Manitoba entered the confederation on July 15th 1870 it was known as the "postage stamp province", since it only covered 215×170km/134×106 miles, with Winnipeg its centre. Large parts of the province were not settled until late in the 19th c. Manitoba was extended west to its present boundary with Saskatchewan in 1881 and north to Hudson Bay and its present boundary with the Northwest Territories in 1912.

The railroad from the east reached Winnipeg in 1881, making it possible to export its grain. The influx of settlers that followed included many Mennonites, Icelanders and Ukrainians. The population soared from 62,000 in 1881, to 153,000 in 1891, 255,000 in 1901 and 461,000 in 1911. Winnipeg became a melting pot as immigrants of many nationalities – German, Scandinavian, Polish, Hungarian, Ukrainian and Jewish – stopped off in the city on their way west.

The policies enacted between 1890 and 1900 were to have a negative impact that is still making itself felt today. In 1890 the government of Manitoba passed the Public Schools Act, discontinuing public funding of Catholic schools and teaching in the French language. Manitoba's Official Language Act of the same year forbad the use of French in the courts and Parliament. These laws were condemned as a denial of equal rights by the French-speaking minority, and Catholic parents feared they would have to send their children to church schools. Both groups campaigned for almost a hundred years to get these statutes reversed until Canada's Supreme Court repealed the Language Act on the grounds that the Provincial Act could not take precedence over the Federal Act which proclaimed Manitoba a French-English province in 1870.

The Provincial Parliament has 57 deputies. In Ottawa it is represented by 14 members in the House of Commons and 6 in the Senate.	Province and Administration

Manitoba's economy gradually recovered from the 1982 recession and has been experiencing above-average growth over the past few years. More than 300,000 of its 490,000 workforce are employed in the services sector, mostly in banking, insurance, retailing, hotels and restaurants, schools, universities and government.

Economy

Although not as rich in raw materials and renewable resources as its neighbours Alberta and Saskatchewan, Manitoba does have significant mineral deposits in the north. Its nickel, copper and zinc mines are working as normal again after closing down during the 1982/1983 recession, but the price fluctuations have caused limits to be set on how much can be mined. Mining companies have been moving into the Lynn Lake area in the north in recent years prospecting for gold.

Minerals

In 1987 mining earned around 400 million dollars, the major minerals being nickel and copper.

Manitoba does not have much oil. For thirty years Virden in the southwest had a small-scale oil industry but output fell sharply in the 1890s.

Manitoba's energy reserves are in hydro-electric power. A billion dollar hydro-electric project is under way on the Nelson River. Work was begun in 1985 on the fourth of seven power stations on this river which is the Province's last exploitable watercourse.

Manitoba's timber trade brings in over 35 million dollars a year.

Timber

The importance of agriculture to the province's economy is demonstrated by the fact that it employs 40,000 people and is responsible for 20% of the productive sector. Although the low grain prices of the 1980s have meant that many of the 20,000 farms have had a struggle to survive the 1987 harvest still brought in receipts of one billion Canadian dollars, while livestock only earned 724 million dollars in the same year.

Agriculture

Wheat is the main crop, followed by barley, oilseed rape, flax and rye. The short growing period in the north, where there are fewer than 90 days without frost, and the quality of the soil mean that further expansion of agricultural output is virtually impossible.

Manitoba's fisheries bring in about 15 million Canadian dollars. Two-thirds of the total catch comes from its three large lakes, and 90% is exported to America's northern cities.

Fisheries

There are many different sides to Manitoba's economy. Manufacturing is the biggest sector, followed by farming, mining and hydro-electric power. The primary sector accounts for 38% of producing industry, including energy generation. The remaining 62% is spread over the secondary sector, such as building and construction.

Industry

The range of products extends from foodstuffs and farm equipment through vehicles and aircraft to energy plant and fibre-optics.

295

Manitoba

Tourism
Tourism is growing in importance, with about 3 million visitors to the province every year.

Population
English-speaking settlers from eastern Canada and the USA formed the first great wave of newcomers. These were followed by the Mennonites in 1874, then a great many Icelanders and French-speaking families from France and Québec in 1875. There was another big wave of English immigrants in 1891 and the first of a large number of Ukrainians. The fast-growing population went up from 62,000 in 1881 to 1.1 million in 1991, with about half of them living in and around Winnipeg.

Manitoba is a multicultural society, composed of many different ethnic groups. Almost 400,000 Manitobans are of English descent. Other important ethnic groups include Germans, Ukrainians, French, Dene Indians, Inuit, Poles, Dutch, Scandinavians, Hungarians, Jews and Italians. In recent years they have been joined by many Asians, especially Philippinos and Vietnamese, as well as South Americans. They have all managed to retain their cultural identity, so that in Winnipeg's Folklorama, Canada's National Ukrainian Festival, etc. Manitoba now hosts several of North America's biggest folk festivals.

According to the 1986 census, 758,310 of the population were English-speaking, 45,600 spoke French and 259,105 other languages. In terms of religion, 57% of the population is Protestant, 31% Catholic and 12% of other faiths.

Suggested routes

★Whiteshell Route
(about 340km/211 miles)

From Winnipeg the Whiteshell Route passes through the Mennonite village of Steinbach, then on to Whiteshall Provincial Park, Falcon Lake, Winnipeg River and Pinawa.

Leaving Winnipeg on the TransCanada Highway the route enters the region of the Canadian Shield, its hills, lakes, valleys, forests and rivers abounding with opportunities for hunting and fishing or just relaxing. At Steinbach it is possible to visit an authentic Mennonite village. The resorts of Falcon Lake and West Hawk Lake further east offer fine beaches, sailing and waterskiing. Most of the route winds through the Whiteshell Provincial Park, along the Winnipeg River, criss-crossed by trails through forests that are home to moose, deer and black bear. Anglers can fish for pike and perch in the deep lakes but inside the park there are also shallow, marshy lakes, left by the Ice Age, and the haunt of wildfowl. Rocky crags to the north are covered with spruce and evergreens.

Cornbelt
(805km/500 miles)

The Cornbelt route runs west out of Winnipeg on the TransCanada Highway across Whitehorse Plain to Brandon and south through the Turtle Mountain Provincial Park to the International Peace Garden.

It passes through the heart of the cornbelt, thousands of acres of wheat, barley and oats, the "breadbasket of the world", but also important for its livestock farming.

Many farmers and ranchers take in visitors as guests who can help with such farm chores as haymaking or doing the milking, or sample the pleasures of the lakes, rivers and streams. Spring is the best time for a farm visit since summer temperatures can be as high as 38°C/100°F.

Interlake
(306km/190 miles)

The Interlake route follows the western shore of Lake Winnipeg north through Netley March and Gimli to the Hecla Provincial Park.

When in 1875 Iceland suffered intense and destruction volcanic eruptions many of its people chose to leave their beautiful but bleak homeland in search of a similar but more hospitable country where they could carry on with their farming and fishing. Liking what they saw of Manitoba, with its broad fertile prairie and many lakes they settled around Lake Winnipeg and Lake Manitoba.

The first stretch of the route along the western shore of Lake Winnipeg takes in what was once New Iceland, an independent territory where lived and ruled the descendants of those first Icelandic settlers, and where their Icelandic traditions still live on today.

It is worth making a stopover in one of the Icelandic-style vacation resorts that have sprung up amidst the forests of spruce, aspen and Scotch pine. The lakes provide excellent swimming and sailing, and there are small car-free islands where moose and bear can be encountered, while in spring the skeins of geese and duck fly in to breed. The landscape is at its most scenic in the autumn, when the woods become a riot of colour and the ripe corn stands high in the fields.

The North Route takes the TransCanada Highway west out of Winnipeg to Portage La Prairie then north-west to the old fur-trading post of Neepawa and further through the Minnedosa River Valley to the Riding Mountain National Park and The Pas and Flin Flon.

The North

It goes from the cornbelt towns deep in the interior to the lowlands around Hudson Bay, Riding Mountain National Park with its nature reserves and the timber and mining towns of Flin Flon and The Pas, where it is possible to get a flight to visit Churchill, Canada's only sub-Arctic seaport (see entry).

La Mauricie

P 8

Province: Québec

See Québec Province

Information

La Mauricie refers to the very scenic area along both sides of the Saint Maurice River, a mighty river used for carrying timber, with Route 156 following the twists and turns of the narrow valley. This is also a good way of getting to Lac Saint-Jean (see entry).

★Route (about 170km/106 miles)

See entry

Trois-Rivières

The Forges de St-Maurice, 13km/8 miles from Trois Rivières, leaving by the Blvd. des Forges, were Canada's first ironworks. They date back to 1730, and produced a whole range of items such as boilers and stoves until 1883 when the nearby stocks of iron ore and timber ran out and the works closed.

Forges de St-Maurice

A pretty road leads to the river and the Fontaine du Diable, where there is an escape of natural gas that can be set alight.

Shawinigan, 31km/19 miles further on, owes its rapid development since early this century to the hydro-electric potential of its 50m/164ft waterfalls. The two power plants are open to visitors from June to Dec. on weekdays; guided tours at 10am, 1.30 and 3pm (reservations tel. 372–3801).

Shawinigan

The Centre Culturel (2100 Rue Dessaules, open: 5–9pm) has a collection of contemporary art and sculpture, and puts on exhibitions of work by Québec artists.

An industrial town with a population of 16,000 41km/25 miles along the road, Grand-Mère is another place that owes its existence to the power generated by the Mauricie River. Its name came from a nearby black rock with the craggy profile of an old grandmother, subsequently removed to the town park to make way for the power plant.

Grand-Mère

A road leads from Grand-Mère via Saint-Jean-des-Piles to the south-east entrance to the Mauricie National Park.

★★Parc National de la Mauricie	The Parc de la Mauricie covers 544sq.km/210sq.miles and extends into the Laurentians that are part of the Canadian Shield. Its many kinds of tree range from maple, ash, cherry, lime and birch to a variety of conifers such as Scotch pine and cedar. It is a reserve rich in wildlife, with black bear, wolf, fox, beaver, otter, mink, lynx and musk rat, and such birds as bittern, geese, snipe, osprey, hazelhen, etc. For the wildfowl there are close on fifty lakes, the finest being Lac Wapizagonke, 8km/5 miles long, in the park's south-eastern section.
Saint-Tite	Saint-Tite (pop. 4000), reached after 44km/27 miles, and important for its leather industry, was founded in 1859 at the start of La Mauricie's timber trading, and in early September hosts a grand Western-style festival complete with rodeo, horse-races and processions.
Grand Piles	The Musée du Bûcheron in Grand Piles, on the steep bank overlooking the river, provides a glimpse of the life of Canada's first lumberjacks. Route 155, which runs from here along the Parc National de la Mauricie, is reached by a road which turns off about half a mile beyond Mattawin. Near Rivière-aux-Rats a roads leads off to the Saint-Mauricie Nature Reserve. Both roads are passable from mid-April to mid-November.
La Tuque	167km/104 miles further on, La Tuque (pop. 12,000), which was founded to exploit La Mauricie's timber, owes its industrial development to the building of a hydro-electric plant (216,000kW). When the French first arrived here it was a major trading post. The town owes its name to a rock by the river that looks like a "tuque", the knitted cap worn by the early Canadians.
Hydro-Québec paper factory	Hydro-Québec's hydro-electric complex about 30km/19 miles north of La Tuque is also associated with a big Compagnie International du Papier papermill which can be visited between 9 and 11am and 2 to 4pm. From La Tuque the railroad to Senneterre (449km/278 miles) passes through the indescribably lonely terrain of Haute-Mauricie.

Medicine Hat G 7

	Province: Alberta. Population: 43,000
Information	See Alberta
	Medicine Hat, on the South Saskatchewan River, is Alberta's fifth largest city. It gets its name from an Indian legend. During a battle between the Cree and the Blackfoot the Cree medicine man's headdress was blown off into the river. This was taken to be a bad omen by the Cree braves, who fled, and over time "the place where the medicine man lost his hat" became just plain "Medicine Hat". Rudyard Kipling described it as the place "with the whole of Hell as its cellar" when he visited the town in 1907, because enormous natural gas deposits had already been found when drilling for water in 1883.
Economy	This natural gas today forms the basis for Medicine Hat's thriving petro-chemical industry. Underground rivers also contribute to its intensive horticulture, the growing of flowers and vegetables in enormous greenhouses and highly irrigated fields. South-eastern Alberta's ranching tradition is reflected in July's annual Agricultural Show and especially its rodeo and stampede.

Sights in Medicine Hat

City centre	There is a downtown walking tour which takes in buildings still left in the city centre from the turn of the century.

The Medicine Hat Mall (Dunmore Rd. S.E.) includes over 60 different stores and boutiques. | Medicine Hat Mall

Medicine Hat's award-winning City Hall, supremely modern in its architecture and completed in 1986, is the pride of this mid-Western city. | ★City Hall

The Historical Museum, which tells the story of the Canadian West – the Plains Indians, pioneering days, etc. – also serves as the National Exhibition Centre (1302 Bomford Crescent S.W., Hwy. 1/Hwy. 3; open: Mon.–Fri. 10.30am–noon and 1–5pm, Sat., Sun. and public holidays 1–5pm). | Historical Museum

The Riverside Waterslide, with a variety of waterchutes, offers a chance to cool off in summer. | Riverside Waterslide

Medicine Hat's annual three-day Rodeo and Stampede takes place in July. | ★Rodeo and Stampede

Mission   E 8

Province: British Columbia. Population: 22,000

See British Columbia | Information

About 70km/43 miles west of Vancouver, the township of Mission in the Fraser Valley gets its name from the mission station founded here in 1861 which soon became a staging post for trappers and "voyageurs" on the Fraser River. The annual Mission Pow Wow in June still serves as a reminder of its Indian missionary past.

The intensively farmed land around it is famous as having the longest growing period in Canada, thanks to the protection afforded it in the lee of the mountains. The Dutch who settled around the lower reaches of the Fraser after 1848 built dykes to create a polder like their landscape back home, and black and white cows can still be seen grazing the meadows here.

From Mission Highway 11 proceeds to the southern bank of the Fraser River and the TransCanada Highway.

Westminster Abbey, a Benedictine abbey and seminary overlooking the town, is an impressive modern cathedral (reached via Dewdney Trunk Road; viewing Mon.–Sat. 1.30–4pm, Sun. 2–4pm). | ★Westminster Abbey

The region's first bank, built in 1907, now contains the local museum (33201 2nd Ave., open: Mon.–Fri. 10am–4pm, Sat., Sun. 2–4pm) with exhibits of life among the pioneers and the Indians. | Mission Museum & Archives

Moncton   R 8

Province: New Brunswick. Population: 56,000

Moncton Marketing & Promotions, 774 Main St, Moncton, New Brunswick E1C 1E8; tel. (506) 853–3590. | Information

An Acadian city in the south-east of the Province of New Brunswick, Moncton is at the end of the narrow estuary of the Petitcodiac, one of the tips of the Bay of Fundy, famed for having the world's highest tides.

Often hailed as the capital of Acadia, Moncton is an important east Canadian road and rail junction, as well as having a French-speaking university.

The French settled in the northern end of the Bay of Fundy in 1638, but the English destroyed their settlement a few years later and the inhabitants were abducted. | History

German settlers, previously from Pennsylvania, arrived here in the second half of the 18th c.

The east Canadian city owes its name to Robert Moncton, the British commander who took the nearby Fort Beauséjour in 1755.

Sights
Galerie d'Art
Musée de l'Acadie
(AcadianMuseum
& Art Gallery)

Moncton University has a very interesting collection of works of art by modern Acadians. It also maintains a small museum on Acadian history. Both are open from June to September Tuesday to Friday 10am to 5pm, Saturday and Sunday 1 to 5pm; the rest of the year they are open Tuesday to Friday noon to 4pm and 2 to 4pm at weekends.

Coliseum

Moncton Coliseum is one of the biggest venues of its kind in eastern Canada, staging big sporting events as well as gala balls, rock concerts and regional fairs.

★ Magnetic Hill

Magnetic Hill north-west of the city is one of Canada's most visited natural wonders. It owes its fascination to the fact that a driver can put a car in neutral, release the brake and feel that it is being drawn uphill as though by some ghostly hand!

Magic Mountain
Water Park

The giant waterchutes of Magic Mountain Water Park and its many other attractions make it very popular with visitors, especially in the summer.

★ Tidal flow

Twice a day the high tide of the Atlantic Ocean flows through Fundy Bay and sweeps into the Petitcodiac estuary, swelling its trickle into a broad lake and covering the mudflats and salt-marsh all around.

Hillsborough

Hillsborough, which is about 32km/20 miles south of Moncton on the east side of the Petitcodiac, has a historic steam train, of the Salem & Hillsborough Railroad (operating July, Aug. daily; mid-May–June and Sept.–mid-Oct. Sat and Sun.; tel. (506) 734–31 95 for information).

★★ Hopewell Cape

Hopewell Cape juts out into the Bay of Fundy's Shepody Bay and is just on 43km/27 miles south of Moncton on Highway 114. Here the world's highest tides have sculpted an incredible coastal landscape, carving away at the soft rock to form the "flowerpots", strange pillars of granite topped with fir and spruce, apparently standing offshore but, as can be seen at low tide, still connected to the mainland.

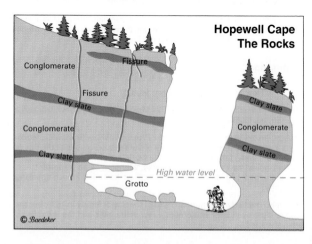

**Hopewell Cape
The Rocks**

Conglomerate

Fissure

Fissure

Clay slate

Clay slate

Conglomerate

Conglomerate

Clay slate

Clay slate

High water level

Grotto

© *Baedeker*

The Tidal Trail leads from Moncton south on Highway 114, along the Petitcodiac estuary to Hopewell Cape (see above), where it turns south-west along Shepody Bay and Chignecto Bay. At Riverside-Albert a slight detour along the 915, a very narrow and fairly basic little road, leads to Cape Enrage, with its lighthouse, jutting out into Chignecto Bay, part of the Bay of Fundy (see entry). Bathing from the steep, stony beach below the cape is highly dangerous. Next come Waterside, a little resort, and Alma, the delightful fishing port at the entrance to the Fundy National Park (see Bay of Fundy).

★Tidal Trail
★★Route
Moncton–
Hopewell Cape–
Fundy National
Park (Hwy. 114)

Fort Beauséjour is a national park about 60km/37 miles south-east of Moncton where Nova Scotia and New Brunswick meet (see entries). From the earthworks which are all that is left of the fort there is a fine view over the Cumberland Basin and Chignecto Bay. The fertile fen below the fort was farmed by French settlers as early as the 18th c.

★Fort Beauséjour

The French settled here in the second half of the 17th c., calling the land around "Beau Bassin", but it passed to the Scots and English under the Treaty of Utrecht in 1713. The frontier between British Novia Scotia (New Scotland) and French Acadia ran then, as it does today, along the narrow land-bridge between New Brunswick and Nova Scotia. The British built Fort Lawrence on their side and the French built Fort Beauséjour on theirs. Fort Beauséjour was captured in 1755 by the British who then proceeded to drive out or deport the French-speaking Acadians who lived there.
     Since 1926 Fort Beauséjour has been a protected national historic monument.

History

The information centre at Fort Beauséjour recounts this place's turbulent history using various exhibitions and other visual aids.

Information

New Brunswick's South-east Shore stretches north-east of Moncton along the Northumberland Strait, part of the Gulf of St Lawrence, and strung out along it are Canadian Atlantic seaside resorts where the bold actually venture into the water, mainly when summer is at its height.

New Brunswick's South-east Shore

Shediac, on the Acadian "Costa del Sol" about 18km/11 miles north-east of Moncton, is very popular with visitors in the summer months, priding itself on being the lobster capital of the world.
     St Martin in the Wood, Shediac's Anglican church, built of Canadian red fir in 1821, is worth seeing.

Shediac

Shediac's Parlee Beach Provincial Park is reckoned to have the finest sandy beach on Canada's Atlantic coast, and in summer the relatively shallow water here can get as warm as 20°C/68°F.

★Parlee Beach
Provincial Park

Cap-Pelé, 60km/37 miles north-east of Moncton, is a picturesque Acadian fishing village dating from 1780. It also has a lovely beach and the well-stocked fish market is particularly worth a visit.

Cap-Pelé

Bouctouche, about 50km/31 miles north of Moncton, is another traditional Acadian fishing place, and the birthplace of K. C. Irving, the industrialist reputed to be one of the richest men in the world.
     The Sacred Heart Chapel contains work by the Acadian artist Léon Léger (1848–1918).

Bouctouche

An international hydroplane regatta takes place off the mouth of the Cogagne River, south of Bouctouche, every year. This is also a place for deepsea fishing expeditions.

Cogagne

Kouchibouguac National Park is two hours' drive north of Moncton, along the Gulf of St Lawrence, where inland once lived the Micmac Indians.
     The National Park of 238sq.km/92sq.miles has a unique ecosystem, with all kinds of coastal vegetation, including around 25 species of orchid,

★★Kouchibouguac
National Park

saltmarsh, high dunes, long sandbars and tidal lagoons stretching for close on 30km/19 miles, its coastline different after every storm.

| Wildlife | The marshes and lagoons are breeding grounds for a whole world of waterloving creatures. It is a birdwatcher's paradise, with thousands of duck, geese, and other wildfowl, while seals love to bask on the sandbanks offshore.
Further inland the park supports black bear, beaver, moose, deer, fox and coyote. |

Recreational facilities

The park has its own campsites and trails, and can be explored by bike or canoe. There are obviously plenty of picnic sites, as well as a number of good beaches for bathing in summer, and skiing trails in winter.

Visitor centre

A visitor centre of generous proportions provides plenty of information about the plants and creatures of the National Park. There are also audiovisual shows and guided nature trails.

Information

Kouchibouguac National Park, Kent County, New Brunswick, E0A 2A0; tel. (506) 876–24 43.

Montréal   P 8

Province: Québec
Population: 1,015,420. Altitude: 233m/765ft

Situation

Montréal, in the south-west corner of Québec Province (see entry), is situated on the largest of the 234 islands that form the Hochelaga archipelago in the St Lawrence River. The heart of the city is the Île de Montréal (158sq.km/61sq.miles) at the confluence of the Ottawa River and the St Lawrence, which also takes in the slopes of the ancient volcano of Mont-Royal, or Mount Royal (238m/260ft), the mountain park in the city centre.
There are eight hills in and around Montréal, peaking as high as 527m/1730ft, the remnants of ice-age Devonian volcanoes.

Montréal in general

The city actually gets its name from one of the hills, the Mont-Royal already mentioned, and nowadays a very popular park with a view. Jacques Cartier (see Famous People) landed here in 1535 and took the territory for his King, François I of France. Officially founded in 1642, Montréal is one of North America's most important cities. Not only is it the second biggest city in Canada, it is also the second largest French-speaking city in the world.

Located as it is on the St Lawrence Seaway, the city has prospered since the 18th c. as a hub of communications and trade, a port of call for seagoing vessels from the Atlantic and the waterborne traffic along the St Lawrence and westward to the Great Lakes. It also has its share of administration and academic life, and is the seat of the bishopric.
Having also won itself a high international profile with the Expo in 1967 and the Olympic Games in 1976, in 1992 Montréal celebrated the 350th anniversary of its foundation.
An impressive view of the city is to be had from Mount Royal or one of the skyscraper viewing platforms. Another way of enjoying the city skyline is from a boat trip on the St Lawrence.

Climate

Montréal's climate swings between the extremes of high humid heat in summer and heavy snowfalls in winter. The average temperature in January is −10°C/14°F, and −20°C/−4°F is not unusual. In July the thermometer hovers around 22°C/72°F, occasionally reaching 30°C/86°F. Mean precipitation over the year is around 750mm/30in.

The City Hall in Montréal ▶

Montréal

Montréal's population growth has always tended to be dominated by immigration, whether from overseas or elsewhere in North America. This was at its highest between 1851 and 1861, and 1951 to 1961. The city's population in the 19th c. was 82% British and French in origin, but since the second half of the 19th c. it has been overwhelmingly French-Canadian. At the turn of the century there was an influx of Jews from Eastern Europe, followed by Southern Europeans. In 1971 the city had 64% French Canadians, 11% English Canadians, with 25% ethnic minorities including Jews and Italians as the largest groupings, followed by German, Poles, Ukrainians and Dutch, Greeks and Portuguese, as well as Asians and Afro-Caribbeans. The number of inner-city dwellers has fallen sharply in recent years as many have moved out into the suburbs, and this exodus from downtown Montréal, and from elsewhere in Québec Province to suburbia for that matter, is continuing. While many small ethnic minorities get along with one another in the everyday way of city life, this is not the case with the French and English Canadians, for whom the gulf between their cultures seems as wide as ever, and the demands for autonomy of Canada's French-speaking population have intensified considerably in the recent past.

When Jacques Cartier (see Famous People), on his 1535/1536 voyage of discovery, was the first European to set foot in what is now Montréal, he found an Indian village of some thousand souls, called "Hochelaga" by the Huron, just below a hill (where McGill University stands today), which he named "Mont Réal", the royal mount, in honour of his French king. It was almost three-quarters of a century before the territory was visited again, this time by Samuel de Champlain (see Famous People), the founder of Québec, who came here in 1603. He found no trace of the Indian village, and in 1611 established a short-lived trading post called "Place Royale".

Another 30 years later Paul de Chomeday the godfearing Sieur de Maisonneuve, founded a small mission station here in 1642. Called Ville Marie de Mont-Réal this was the original settlement that today is Montréal. He had accommodation built including a chapel and a hospital, run by Jeanne Mance, and built a palisade around it as protection against the Indians. Their conversion to Christianity was the object of the missionaries, foremost among them the Congrégation Notre-Dame and its Mother Superior Marguerite Bourgeoys, and the Compagnie de Saint-Sulpice, who had been given the Seigneurie of the Île Montréal in 1663 by the French king. By 1672 Montréal's population had grown to about 1500, the figure it remained at till the end of the 18th c.

In the comparatively calmer times following the peace treaty with the Iroquois in 1701 Montréal profited from its role as a centre of the fur trade, and farming began in the country round about. The burgeoning disputes between the British and the French finally erupted into war in the mid-18th c. when the British succeeded in taking the city without a fight in 1760. During the American War of Independence the American revolutionary troops besieged the city briefly in the winter of 1775/76, but withdrew when its people sided with the British, refusing to take part in the Americans' fight for freedom.

In the time that followed Montréal benefited from an influx of Loyalists, fleeing from an America no longer loyal to the king, and from growing numbers of British traders, mainly Scots and Irish, who together formed the North West Company, stepped up the fur trade, and set Montréal up as an important trading post and rival to the Hudson's Bay Company. By 1792 Montréal's population, at about 6000, was enough to give it township status.

A further boost came with the opening of the St Lawrence to steamer traffic in 1809 and completion of the Lachine Canal in 1825, allowing shipping to get from the Atlantic to the Great Lakes. Population numbers soared from 22,500 in 1825 to 44,000 in 1844 as immigrants flooded in from Great Britain. A dynamic business community invested heavily in timber and shipbuilding, then in import/export, and, after 1836, in railways and all the ancillary trades. Montréal became the most important centre of commerce, as well as an arena for social tensions, not only as between capitalism and the workers, but also between French-speaking and English-speaking factions as they struggled for political supremacy.

The Anglophile middleclass gained the upper hand with the defeat inflicted on the French patriots during the 1837 uprisings only to see their privileges swept away after 1867 as the French-speakers came to dominate the population. For a time, between 1844 and 1849 during the Canadian struggle for unification, Montréal became the capital, only to lose this status after the Parliament building fire during the unrest of 1849. Growing immigration from eastern and southern Europe meant that after 1900 the city became an even richer ethnic mix, its population soaring to close on 470,000 in 1922.

The boom for industry, trade, transport and financial institutions that followed the First World War gave way to the deep depression of the Thirties, when three-quarters of the million working population were forced on the dole, causing the collapse of the city budget.

The recovery, when it did come, was after the Second World War, when it was due to high demand from abroad and cheap immigrant labour, together with an army of refugees from rural life streaming into the cities. Montréal's economy received another boost from the joint venture with the USA to build the St Lawrence Seaway. The post-industrial era began in the Sixties with the demolition of much of the old centre of Montréal in order to construct the subway system, and massive expansion of the services sector. Giant multi-purpose building complexes sprang up while, below ground, a whole new town was built as a shopper's paradise, away from the harsh extremes of the Canadian winter. In fact there was virtually nothing that needed doing to improve on the already ideal business conditions. But all this actually had the opposite effect. The enormous infrastructure costs drove up prices, and this, together with political decisions to go for an independent French-speaking Québec, had industries and corporations in the 1970s moving away in droves to set up their headquarters in Toronto, where the business climate was better. Since then the two cities, Toronto and Montréal, have been vying for the position of Canada's business capital. Montréal's staging of high-profile international events – Expo in 1967, the Olympics in 1976, Floralies Internationales 1980 – have taken a heavy toll of the city's finances to an extent well beyond the power of any short-term world-wide publicity to offset. In 1989 Montréal also played host to a major international conference on the hole in the ozone layer. The 350th anniversary of the city's foundation was celebrated in 1992 with a wide-ranging programme of cultural and other events, as well as in more permanent fashion by the opening of several fine new museums.

After the city's fortunes had been founded for a century and a half on the fur trade, the mid-19th c. brought a great shift towards industrialisation, followed on in the 20th c. by an expanding services and high-tech sector. In 1971 only 16% of the active population worked in industry as compared with almost 26% in management and administration and 24% in services.

The availability of cheap electrical power has always been an important factor underpinning the city's industrial development. The major manufacturing industries are the construction of aircraft and rolling stock, electronics, textiles, petro-chemicals (oil refineries in east Montréal), food and drink (including breweries) and leather goods.

Montréal is the headquarters of a great many financial corporations, including Canada's oldest bank, the Bank of Montréal, founded in 1817, and other trading and money market concerns.

Economy

From its earliest days, Montréal's favourable location has made it a hub of communications. Its port caters for vessels engaged on both maritime and inland waterway trade, and is the second largest, after New York, on North

Transport

America's Atlantic coast, covering 24sq.km/9sq.miles and with berths for well over 120 ships. Thousands of freighters can be unloaded here during the ten ice-free months. There are enormous silos for handling the grain, and container terminals numbered amongst the most advanced of their kind in the world. All of Canada's main shipping lines are based in Montréal which has continued to gain in international importance for shipping since the opening of the St Lawrence Seaway.

The city is also traditionally the hub of Canadian rail traffic, astride all the transcontinental connections both east and west, and with the USA as well. It is the headquarters of Canadian National Railways, a conglomerate formed from a number of mergers, and of VIA Rail, Canada's rail passenger carrier. Canadian Pacific has also been duly represented since 1881.

Air traffic also figures prominently in Montréal, home to the national airline, Air Canada, and with two major international airports, Dorval for Canadian and US domestic flights, and Mirabel for all other international flights. Both IATA, the International Air Transport Association, and ICAO, the International Civil Aviation Organisation, with over 800 employees, have their headquarters here as well.

Road traffic is a big problem for the inner city, where it impinges on the quality of people's lives by wasting space or acting as a pollutant. There is an extensive network of urban motorways such as the six-lane Boulevard Metropolitain, crossing Montréal from east to west, and there are many bridges – 15 road and 5 rail – linking the suburbs with the Île de Montréal.

The city has a good public transport system, with a modern underground and plenty of local buses. The "Metro", a subway named after its Parisian counterpart, and opened in 1966, has 65 stations, each one different in its art and design, and about 60km/37 miles of line running between all the important points in "Underground Montréal".

The Olympia site in Montréal

Sights in Montréal

Said to be North America's most remarkable concentration of 17th, 18th and 19th c. buildings, "old Montréal" is the delightful Parisian-style quarter between the harbour and the banking district. Lovingly restored over the past thirty years, and very popular with visitors, it is best explored on foot, starting from the Metro for the Champ de Mars, just south of the station. A one-time drillground, then a promenade for the bourgeoisie, and now a square on the Rue Notre-Dame, this is overlooked by the two imposing 19th c. buildings of City Hall and the Palace of Justice.

Vieux-Montréal

The City Hall was designed by Perrault with an eye to the French Empire style of Napoleon III. Built between 1872 and 1878 it had to be restored following a fire in 1922.

★ Hôtel de Ville

Its hall of honour, which can be viewed daily between 9am and 4.30pm, is resplendent with marble and bronze, and has a bust of Jacques Viger, Montréal's first mayor in 1833.

It was from the balcony of City Hall that on July 24th, during his visit to Canada in 1967, the French President Charles de Gaulle uttered his clarion call "vive le Québec libre!" – long live free Québec – meeting with an enthusiastic response from the crowds on the Place Cartier below but considerably upsetting Canada's Federal Government.

"Vive le Québec libre" (see Baedeker Special p. 393)

The old palace of justice, opened in 1856, is modelled on classical Greek lines and was completed in 1891 with the construction of the dome and the top floor.

Vieux Palais de Justice

Place Vauquelin is a square between the two public buildings, with a fountain and a statue of Jean Vauquelin (by Eugène Bénet, 1930), the officer who tried in vain to defend New France against the British in 1759/60.

Place Vauquelin

Not far east along the Rue Notre-Dame, the Musée du Château Ramezay, which is open 10am to 4.30pm, Tuesday to Sunday, is an elegant mansion dating from 1705. It was the residence of Claude de Ramezay, Governor of Montréal from 1703 to 1724 and his successors, and provides a period setting for a collection of 18th and early 19th c. costume, furniture, and paintings.

Musée du Château Ramezay

The nearby Maison de George-Etienne Cartier is a Gothic revival building, originally two stone dwellings which were the home of the first Canadian Prime Minister from 1841 to 1871. It is open daily from 9am to 5pm, mid-May to September, and from 10am to 5pm Wednesday to Sunday for the rest of the year. Part of the building has an exhibition of the life and work of Jacques Cartier (see Famous People).

Maison de George-Etienne Cartier

The delightful Rue Bonsecours, off the Rue Notre-Dame, is one of Vieux-Montréal's oldest streets, with a whole range of the French architectural styles that went to make up the townscape of New France right through from the 17th to the 19th c.

Rue Bonsecours

By the Rue Saint Paul is the Maison Pierre du Calvet, dating from 1770, with a rustic façade, asymmetric windows and a pointed roof, and containing a little museum with exhibits from the pioneer days.

Maison Pierre du Calvet

Les Filles du Roi, now a restaurant, is where the young women lived who were brought to Montréal by the King of France to become wives for the settlers whom he had heard were taking up with Indian women because of a shortage of females.

Les Filles du Roi

The city's oldest church, the Chapel of Our Lady de Bonsecours, at the end of the street, was rebuilt in its present form in 1772 after a number of fires.

★ Notre-Dame-de-Bonsecours

Montréal

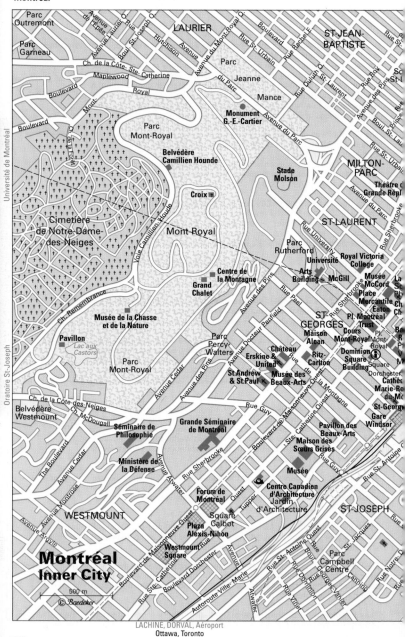

Montréal Inner City

500 m

© Baedeker

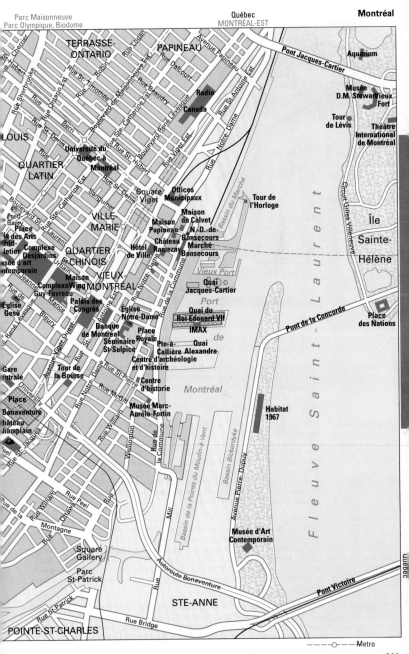

Parc Maisonneuve
Parc Olympique, Biodome

Québec
MONTRÉAL-EST

Montréal

TERRASSE-ONTARIO

PAPINEAU

Aquarium

Pont Jacques-Cartier

Musée
D.M. Stewart
Vieux Fort

Radio

Canada

Tour
de Lévis

Théâtre
International
de Montréal

LOUIS

QUARTIER
LATIN

Université du
Québec à
Montréal

Île

Sainte-

Hélène

Square
Viger

Offices
Municipaux

Tour de
l'Horloge

Circuit Gilles Villeneuve

VILLE-
MARIE

Maison
Papineau

Maison
du Calvet

N.-D.-de-
Bonsecours
Marché
Bonsecours

Place
des Arts

Fred-
letier

Complexe
Desjardins

usée d'art
ntemporain

QUARTIER
CHINOIS

Château
Ramezay

Hôtel
de Ville

Vieux Port

VIEUX-
MONTRÉAL

Maison
Wing

Complexe
Guy-Favreau

Quai
Jacques-Cartier

Port

Église
Gesù

Palais des
Congrès

Église
Notre-Dame

Quai du
Roi Edouard VII

IMAX

de

Banque
de Montréal

Place
Royale

Pont de la Concorde

Place
des Nations

Séminaire
St-Sulpice

Pte-à-
Callière

Quai
Alexandra

Gare
entrale

Tour de
la Bourse

Centre d'archéologie
et d'histoire

Centre
d'histoire

Montréal

Place
Bonaventure
hâteau
hamplain

Musée Marc-
Aurèle-Fortin

Habitat
1967

Fleuve Saint-Laurent

Bassin Bickerdyke

Rue de la Commune

Bassin de la Pointe du Moulin-à-Vent

Mill

Square
Gallery

Parc
St-Patrick

Musée d'Art
Contemporain

Autoroute Bonaventure

STE-ANNE

Pont Victoire

POINTE-ST-CHARLES

Rue Bridge

- - - ○ - - - Metro

Maison "Les Filles du Roi"

Notre-Dame-de-Bonsecours

It replaced the original wooden building put up by the founder of the Congrégation-de-Notre-Dame, Margeurite Bourgeoys, canonised in 1982.

★★Madonna

The church long contained a miraculous little madonna made of oak and given by the Baron de Fancamp in 1672. It was much venerated by the Congrégation de Notre Dame, and by seafarers, many of whom left offerings to the Virgin. Although today's madonna is a copy, the offerings, including some model ships, can still be seen.

Musée Margeurite Bourgeoys

The adjoining museum to Margeurite Bourgeoys tells of her Christian works.

★Marché Bonsecours

The Marché Bonsecours nearby was built between 1845 and 1853 as a multi-purpose building in the Neo-Renaissance style by William Fortner. The Parliament of the unified Canada met here for a time in 1849 then it served as the town hall before becoming Montréal's vegetable market from 1878 to 1963 when, following restoration work in 1964, it became the offices of the City Administration.

★Vieux-Port

Extending along the river close to the Marché is the site of the old port, restored at great cost in recent years and today enjoying a new role as an entertainment and leisure centre. Special attractions include an ultra-modern IMAX cinema, a large junk market, and the Quai Jacques Cartier where, every July, the Festival of Laughter is held ("Juste pour rire"; festival office in the Rue St-Denis). From the old port a magnificent view is obtained of the impressive Montréal skyline. Boat tours run from the Quai Victoria.

Festival of Laughter

★Place Jacques Cartier

Immediately to the north-west and stretching as far as the Rue Notre-Dame are the gardens of Place Jacques Cartier, where, under its Nelson's Column, there is a popular market of arts, crafts and souvenirs, surrounded by inviting street cafés and fine 19th c. townhouses and mansions.

The Place d'Armes is another square reached by taking the Rue Notre-Dame west out of the Place Jacques Cartier. The statue in the centre is by Philippe Hébert (1895) of Paul de Chomedey who in 1642 founded the mission Ville-Marie de Montréal from which the city is regarded as having developed.

★ Place d'Armes

The Palais des Congrès, the futuristic conference centre at 201, avenue Viger Ouest (main entrance opposite the Complexe Guy-Fatreau), was built in 1983 on the Place d'Armes, over the Ville-Marie expressway. It is linked underground with the Place d'Armes and Place des Arts Metro stations, and has a unique five levels of the very latest in convention facilities on the grand scale, where 10,000 people at once could all take part in conferences, exhibitions and other events. One hall can seat 6,000 delegates. This is where the world climate conference was held in 1990, using its state of the art technology (e.g. satellite communications).

Palais des Congrès

Also on the Place d'Armes, the Neo-Gothic façade of the Basilica of Our Lady, built in 1829, with its twin towers (69m/226ft) fronts Montréal's oldest Catholic parish church (founded 1656). The amazing interior is the work of Victor Bourgeau, resplendent with woodcarving and stained glass illustrating the history of the city.
  The Sacré Cœur altar (1982), in the chapel of the same name, consists of 32 bronze panels by Charles Daudelin.
    The great organ is a Casavant and the recitals held in the church throughout the year are very popular.

★★ Notre-Dame Basilica

The Old Seminary of Saint Sulpice adjoining the Basilica dates from 1685. The foundation still belongs to the order of Saint Sulpice, a non-ordained priestly order. It began in Paris in 1642 with Jean-Jacques Olier at its head, and much of the land of Montréal was gifted to it by the king in the 17th c. The seminary is the oldest stone dwelling in a city where originally most buildings were constructed more cheaply and simply in timber.
  The building, which is not open to the public, is of a refined simplicity, with some late-Renaissance style embellishment. Through the grille can be glimpsed the oldest clocktower in North America, dating from 1710.

Vieux Séminaire Saint-Sulpice

The Rue Saint Sulpice, as it runs down to the waterfront, is crossed by Montréal's oldest street, the Rue Saint-Paul, nowadays lined with all kinds of shops, but originally completed in March 1672 as the road between the fort and the Hôtel Dieu, the old hospital. It gets its name as much from Paul de Chomedey, the city's devout founder, as from St Paul the Apostle.

★ Rue Saint-Paul

The Place Royale, a short distance to the west of the Rue Saint-Paul, was the heart of French colonial life, its market and its parade ground until transformed in the 19th c. with various government buildings.
  The Neo-Classical customs house (1837) stands at the northern end.

Place Royale

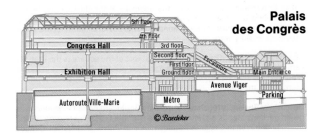

311

Montréal

Pointe-à-Callière
★Musée
d'archéologie et
d'histoire

To the south-east lies the Pointe-à-Callière, the "cradle of Montréal city". Two plaques and an obelisk, the work of Québécois artists, unveiled in 1894, commemorate the founding of the French settlement of Ville-Marie here in the late spring of 1642. The Musée d'archéologie et d'histoire (open: Tues.–Sun. 9am–5pm), in buildings which are themselves of architectural interest, documents the city's beginnings. Remains of 17th and 18th c. foundations can be seen in the basement.

Place Youville

Place Youville nearby was where in the 17th/18th c. canoes plied the waters of the Saint-Pierre River, now underground, as it flowed into the St Lawrence. Today the square is surrounded by 19th and 20th c. buildings. The courtyard of the Écuries d'Youville, close by, has some interesting old warehouses dating from about 1825.

Centre d'Histoire
de Montréal

The Centre d'Histoire de Montréal is in the old redbrick fire station (1903), and recounts Montréal's 350 year history (Open: mid-May–mid-Sept. daily except Mon. and public holidays 10am–6pm; mid-Sept.–mid-May 11am–4.30pm.)

Obelisk

East of the Place Youville stands the massive obelisk, the work of Québec artists, which was erected in 1894 to commemorate the 250th anniversary of the founding of the city.
The nearby Youville Stables, the Ecuries de Youville, were actually warehouses from around 1825 and are well worth seeing.

Hopital général
des Sœurs Grises

The Hopital général des Sœurs Grises is a short distance down the Rue Saint-Pierre. Montréal's second hospital dating from 1694, it was where Margeurite d'Youville founded the Congrégation des Sœurs Grises in 1753, the charitable order of the Grey Sisters. The wing of the building that the Mother Superior lived in was restored in 1980 and can be visited by prior appointment (tel. (514) 842–9411).

Musée Marc-
Aurèle-Fortin

Also in the Rue Saint-Pierre the Musée Marc-Aurèle-Fortin concentrates on works by this Canadian painter, but also shows pictures by artists from Québec Province. (Open: Tues.–Sun. 11am to 5pm.)

Downtown Montréal · Ville-Marie

★Place Ville-Marie

Ville-Marie Square is a good starting point for a look round the ultra-modern buildings of downtown Montréal, whose revitalisation began in 1962 with the cross-shaped towers of the Royal Bank of Canada building, 223m/732ft and 49 floors high, its shops and offices providing employment for 15,000 people. The sculpture in the square is "Female Landscape" by Gerald Gladstone, a profound statement on modern architecture. Although there are plenty of stores at groundfloor level, the real shopper's paradise is below ground in the vast "Ville Souterraine", Montréal's subterranean city.

★Place du Canada

Other downtown sights include the spacious Place du Canada, with a statue (1895) to Sir John Macdonald, the country's first Prime Minister (1867), in a group representing Canada and her seven children, or the seven provinces as they were then.

★Cathédrale
Marie-Reine-du-
Monde

The church of Mary, Queen of the World, east of the square is the Catholic cathedral which was built in 1894 as a smaller version of St Peter's in Rome. The massive statues represent the patron saints of the Archbishopric of Montréal in the 19th c.

★Dorchester
Square

Dorchester Square is reached by crossing Boulevard René-Lévesque. In its green gardens stands a statue by Emile Brunnet (1953) honouring Wilfrid Laurier, the French-Canadian statesman and Prime Minister of Canada from 1896 to 1911. Buildings around the square, which is also graced by Henry Moore's sculpture "Reclining Figure" (1962), include the Victorian bulk of the former Hotel Windsor (1878, renovated in 1985), the Neo-Classic Sun Life skyscraper, the city's oldest and put up between 1918 and 1933, and the towering Banque de Commerce Canadienne Impériale (1962), its 45 floors an example of a very fine architectural style that stands out from the often monotonous functionalism of many modern structures.

Rue Ste-Cathérine, which can be reached from Dorchester Square, is Montréal's main shopping thoroughfare, bustling with life and lined with department stores and shops of all kinds, as well as a host of eating places, ranging widely in the type of food on offer, as well as price.

★Rue Ste-Cathérine

It also leads to such other commercial centres as Cours Mont-Royal and the Promenade de la Cathédrale.

This futuristic marble-and-glass "megastructure", the creation of César Pelli and Mario Botta, has become one of the city's most popular meeting places. In addition to expensive shops the complex houses a number of service enterprises.

Place Montréal Trust

Christ Church Cathedral stands at the junction of Rue Ste-Cathérine and Rue University. The Gothic revival Anglican Cathedral dates from 1859. The statue in front of the cathedral (1870) is of Francis Fulford, the city's first Anglican Archbishop.

Cathédrale Christ Church

The Maison des Coopérants further along the Rue University is a massive glass and concrete tower, its own twin spires more or less a counterpoint to those on the façade of the cathedral.

Maison des Coopérants

Also further along the Rue University, heading towards McGill University, the McCord Museum of Canadian History houses an outstanding collection of exhibits on Canada's social history, featuring the country's native peoples such as the Inuit and Pacific Coast Indians, and colonial life in the 18th c. Re-opened in 1992 following major restoration the museum also possesses an extensive pictorial archive comprising both contemporary and historical material. Museum opening times: Tues.–Fri. 10am–6pm (Thur. until 9pm), Sat., Sun. 10am–5pm.

★Musée McCord d'histoire canadienne

Not far from the museum is the extensive campus of McGill University, its student body currently numbering about 30,000. This major university was founded in 1821 thanks to the generosity of one James McGill, politician and fur trader, whose statue (1875) stands on what was once the site of Hochelaga, the Indian village. Also on the campus is the Redpath Museum of Natural History. (Open: Oct.–May Mon.–Fri. 9am–5pm; June–Sept. Mon.–Thur. 9am–5pm.)

★McGill University

Musée Redpath

The Place-des-Arts metro station, on the northern edge of downtown Montréal, gives access to the city's modern centre for the performing arts, the Place des Arts, built in 1964. It contains four venues – the Salle Wilfried-Pelletier (capacity about 3,000), home to the Orchestre Symphonique de Montréal and where Canada's top ballet companies take the stage, the Théâtre Maisonneuve, seating about 1300, the Théâtre Port-Royal, seating 755, and the recital room, the Café de la Place, with seating for 138.

★Place des Arts

The Musée d'art contemporain (MAC; exhibitions of contemporary art; open: Tues.–Sun. 11am–6pm), on the south side of the square, is particularly worth a visit. Young French-Canadian artists are accorded special prominence.

Musée d'art contemporain

To the south-east, between Rue Sainte-Cathérine and Boulevard René-Lévesque, stands the huge imposing Complexe Desjardins, 1976, with numerous shops, cinemas, banks and a post office.

★Complexe Desjardins

Montréal

Complexe Guy-Fabreau	There are more shopping arcades in the nearby Complexe Guy-Fabreau.
★Chinatown	Montréal's Chinatown is centred around the Rue de la Gauchetière, with two Chinese arches marking the heart of the quarter. This dates from the late 1860s when many of the Chinese labourers who had come to work in the mines and on building the railroad moved into the cities in search of a better life. Today's Chinatown is no longer exclusively Chinese but a place where anyone can relax and enjoy a good meal.
★Musée des Beaux Arts	The Musée des Beaux Arts (open: Tues.–Sun. 11am–6pm, Sat. until 9pm), situated on the western edge of downtown Montréal, is the oldest museum in Canada, having been founded in 1860. Several dozen rooms house the city's public art collection comprising paintings, sculpture and items of applied art of all periods from Europe and Canada. For some years now the museum has also mounted major exhibitions of modern art. Equally noteworthy, this time from an architectural point of view, is the museum's annexe by Moshe Safdie (see Famous People).
★Centre Canadien d'Architecture	Further to the south-west, in the Rue Baile, is an attraction of a rather special kind – the Centre Canadien d'Architecture. This quite exceptional museum, housed in an elegant post-modern building by Phyllis Lambert and Peter Ross, boasts an unusually comprehensive collection of architectural drawings and photographs, together with a library and archive.
★Rue Sherbrooke	Named after Sir John Sherbrooke, Governor General of Canada from 1816 to 1818, Rue Sherbrooke is probably the city's most elegant main shopping thoroughfare, still retaining in the downtown section something of its 19th c. charm as it cuts across the Île de Montréal from east to west. At the turn of the century the few thousand people living in this quarter on the slopes of Mont-Royal owned about 70% of Canada's wealth, earning it the title of the "Golden Square Mile".
Île de Montréal	Around downtown Montréal, and easily reached by metro, there are several other places worth seeing between Mont-Royal in the west, Parc Maisonneuve and Parc Olympique in the north, Île Sainte-Hélène in the east and Parc Agrignon and the Jardin zoologique in the south.
★★Mont-Royal	Mont-Royal rises 233km/765ft above the city and is the green lung near the city centre. A stroll through this lovely park enables the visitor to see monuments from Jacques Cartier to King George VI, to spend some time by the Lac-aux-Castors and to have a look at the cemeteries on the western slope where the city's different ethnic groups have rested in peace together for centuries. From the summit, or rather from a platform below the cross, there unfolds a magnificent panorama of the whole of the 51km/32 miles length of the Île de Montréal and the St Lawrence. On clear days the view extends to the Adirondack Mountains in the USA.
★Oratoire Saint-Joseph	The Oratoire Saint-Joseph (metro: Côte-des-Neiges), near the western exit from the park, is dedicated to Canada's patron saint, and is a mecca for pilgrims. A huge Renaissance-style domed basilica was built in 1924, at the instigation of Brother André of the Congrégation de Sainte-Croix who had already built a small chapel here in 1904, where he performed miraculous acts of healing for which he was canonised in 1982. His tomb is in one part of the sanctuary in the original chapel. Votive gifts are displayed in a second chapel. A cloister behind the church leads up to Mont-Royal. Brother André's monument is by Emile Brunnet and that for St Joseph by Alfred Laliberté. A small museum exhibits religious art. There is a good view from the observatory over north-west Montréal and Lac Saint-Louis.
Université de Montréal	Close by is the campus of the Catholic, French-speaking University of Montréal, founded in 1876 and with 17 faculties, plus a polytechnic and a business school. The University buildings are chiefly by Ernest Cormier and date from between 1924 and 1943.

Oratoire St-Joseph

Cross on the Mont-Royal

Montréal's Anglo-Canadian Westmount district south-east of Mount Royal centres around the square of the same name (metro Atwater). Its steel and glass office buildings are by Mies van der Rohe and were completed in 1966, typifying the highrise international architecture of the mid-20th century.

It forms quite a contrast with the late 19th c. mansions and villas still very much a feature of the surrounding streets.

★Westmount Square

Across on the other side of the city is another oasis of greenery, the Parc Maisonneuve (metro Pie IX), incorporating North America's leading botanical garden, the lay-out of which is wonderfully imaginative. Visitors are drawn in particular to the Japanese Garden. The glasshouses too are exceptional, especially the displays of orchids and bonzai. The gardens contain in all some 26,000 species of plant. Open: mid May to mid Oct., gardens 8am–8pm, glasshouses 9am–6pm.

★★Jardin botanique

The Olympic Park, to the east, was the site of the 1976 Summer Olympics.

The Olympic Stadium, at its centre, takes between 60,000 and 80,000 spectators and is nowadays used for baseball, football, fairs and shows. Looking like a great seashell, the bowl can be covered over against the elements by a roof attached by cables to the mast looming above it. A platform at the top of the mast reached by a lift affords a magnificent view, in fine weather, over the city and its surroundings.

The Olympic Stadium, one of the most visited sports arenas in North America, is the home of Montréal's famous baseball team, the "Montréal Expos".

★★Parc Olympique (map page 316)

In 1992 the former Olympic Velodrome, another of the Parc's architecturally eye-catching structures, was officially renamed the "Biodome", marking its transformation from sports arena to covered botanic-zoological garden. Visitors to this absorbing exposition are taken on an ecological

★Biodome

Parc Olympique

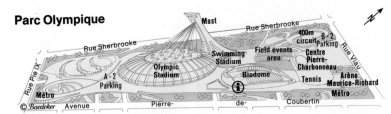

journey through four different habitats – tropical rain forest, the St Lawrence River, the northern coniferous forest, and the arctic – travelling in effect from the equator to the pole. Every attempt has been made to reconstruct as accurately as possible the conditions typical of each environment, so providing a natural setting for the characteristic flora and fauna.

★Chateau Dufresne, Musée des Arts décoratifs

To the west of the Parc Olympique, on the other side of the Rue Pie IX, stands the palatial villa built in 1918 for the shoe manufacturer Thomas Dufresne. Modelled on the Petit Trianon at Versailles it today houses the Musée des Arts décoratifs (open: Wed.–Sun. 11am–5pm), an exhibition of international design from 1940 onwards.

Le Village

It is worth paying a visit to the "Village" on the way back downtown. Between the Rues Saint-Denis and Papineau, it is a lively, colourful quarter comparable with New York's Greenwich Village. The restoration of the old houses has been going on for years, as its developing social and cultural life has unfolded around them.

★★Square Saint-Louis

Square Saint-Louis, reached by taking the metro to Sherbrooke Station, is one of Montréal's prettiest old squares, set in a turn-of-the-century French-Canadian residential quarter. In the little streets around the tree-shaded square there are still a few of the attractive Victorian houses, some of them now pleasant restaurants. Part of the Rue Saint-Denis and the pedestrian mall along the Rue Prince-Arthur at the western end of the square are given over in summer to outdoor cafés, etc., in fact all the lively streetlife of a modern bohemian quarter.

Boulevard Saint-Laurent

The Boulevard Saint-Laurent close by, one of Montréal's main shopping streets, marks the dividing line between the French-Canadians on one side and the Anglo-Canadians on the other, but in fact is highly cosmopolitan along its length, especially around the Rue Laurier where newcomers tended to first settle down in the 18th c. Between 1900 and 1930 the district was predominantly Jewish, then Greek, followed by Eastern Europeans and most recently Hispanics. As all the different cultures mix and mingle in a welter of languages, the many small stores selling specialities from all over the world give parts of the street quite a bazaar-like atmosphere.

Île Sainte-Hélène · Île Notre-Dame

There are two islands in the St Lawrence: Sainte-Hélène, which its named after the wife of Samuel Champlain (see Famous People), and Notre-Dame which is artificial. Both have several features worth seeing (metro: Île Sainte-Hélène).

Expo '67

The two islands were the site of Expo '67, the theme of which was "Terre des Hommes" (Man and his World). Many of the national pavilions, in varying states of repair, still remain to give a flavour of the 1967 world fair, its architecture and the progressive spirit that marked the Sixties.

Île Ste-Hélène · ★L'Homme

This monumental work by Alexander Calder, created for Expo, is 22m/72ft high and weighs 60 tonnes. It symbolises Man's vigour, strength and progress.

Every year at the end of May/beginning of June, La Ronde, Île Sainte-Hélène's big amusement park (open: mid May to Sept., daily 11am–midnight) is the venue for a firework spectacular known as the Benson & Hedges Fireworks Competition.

La Ronde
Amusement Park
★ Firework display
(May/June)

Of historical interest is a visit to the Vieux-Fort, the old fort built as an arsenal by the British in 1820 and restored to hold the D. M. Stewart Museum (open: May–Aug. Wed.–Mon. 10am–6pm, Sept–Apr. until 5pm), a collection of firearms, maps, navigational instruments, etc. In the summer uniformed soldiers recreate the military drill of the 18th c. (daily 10am–6pm).

Vieux-Fort, Musée
David M. Stewart

Being so close to the city this man-made island with its lake of the same name and Bassin Olympique (where the Olympic rowing events were held) is an immensely popular recreation area.

Île Notre-Dame

In 1980 Île Notre-Dame played host to "Les Floralies", the world-famous International Garden Festival. Flower lovers can still enjoy the splendour of the displays adorning the lovely gardens.

Les Floralies

At least once a year – in June – Île Notre-Dame again becomes the focus of world attention when the Molson Grand Prix du Canada, a Formula 1 World Championship event, is staged on the Circuit Gilles Villeneuve, named after Canada's best known racing driver. The lap record for the 4.43km/2¾ mile track, still one of the more challenging despite having been "made easier" in 1994, is at present held by Michael Schumacher with a time of 1min 21.5secs (195.68kmph/121.59mph).

Circuit Gilles
Villeneuve

Renamed the "Palais de la Civilisation", the French pavilion for Expo '67, an impressive ultra-modern building by Jean Faugeron, is today used for a wide range of cultural events.

Palais de la
Civilisation

The principal attraction of the Cité du Havre (across the Pont de la Concorde from Île Sainte-Hélène) is the housing project known as Habitat '67. It was designed by the Israeli-born architect Moshe Safdie as one of the grandiose schemes of Expo '67 to provide low-cost futuristic inner-city housing, but was never actually completed in its entirety. Now rather past their prime, these precast concrete uniform building blocks with their terraces and in their great variety of combinations do provide a far from standard alternative to municipal housing in boring tower blocks or monotonous estates.

Cité du Havre

★★ Habitat '67

The Maison Saint-Gabriel, a charming old stone farmhouse in the Saint-Gabriel district (metro Lasalle), dates from 1698. It was restored in 1960 and turned into a museum of colonial life, with exhibits from the 17th to 19th centuries (guided tours: mid Apr. to mid Dec. Tues.–Sat. 1.30 and 3pm, Sun. 1.30, 2.30 and 3.30pm).

Maison Saint-
Gabriel

Originally the farmhouse was where the "filles du Roy" lived, the unmarried young women sent over by the King of France to provide Nouvelle France with plenty of offspring to carry on the French line.

Surroundings of Montréal

Lachine, with a population of 45,000 on the south-east bank of Montréal Island (in Lac St-Louis), got its name from the first pioneers who in the 17th c. made their way up the St Lawrence looking for a route to China (in French "la Chine"). It became an important staging post for conveying goods round the famous Lachine Rapids. Today it is an important industrial base. It offers plenty of opportunities for charming trips along the banks of the St Lawrence. The Lachine Canal, which was first begun as a way of getting round the rapids in the 17th c., was eventually dug in 1825. It is twenty years, however, since it was last used for shipping and nowadays forms

Lachine

★ Rapides de
Lachine, Canal de
Lachine

part of a park which includes an Interpretation Centre, telling the story of the canal and providing guided tours. (Pavillion Monk, 7e Ave./Blvd. Saint-Joseph; open: mid May–mid Sept. Mon. 1–6pm, Tues.–Sun. 10am–noon and 1–6pm.) In summer it is possible to ride along the park's 11km/7 miles of cycletracks, while in winter there is cross-country skiing.

★Boat trips

Daily between the end of April and middle of October powerful motorboats specially designed for the purpose run exciting – and usually very wet – trips through the rapids from the Vieux Port (Quai Victoria), departing 10am, noon, 2pm, 4pm and 6pm.

Musée de Lachine

The Musée de Lachine (open: mid Mar.–Dec. Tues.–Sun. 11.30am–4.30pm) is in a restored building dating from 1669, and contains many of the items used in everyday life in the colonial days of la Nouvelle France.

Musée du Commerce de la Fourrure

The Musée du Commerce de la Fourrure in an old fur warehouse (1803) illustrates impressively, various aspects of the fur trade in the 17th/18th c., long the mainstay of Montréal's existence.

Sainte-Anne-de-Bellevue

On the south-west tip of Montréal Island, Sainte-Anne-de-Bellevue is the pleasant home to the Macdonald Agricultural College, founded in 1906. Much of its acreage is used for research, and there is an experimental farm that can be visited. The Morgan Arboretum, covering 24ha/59 acres, has woodland trails, walks and ski-runs that are popular with visitors from much further afield as well.

Buildings of historic interest in the early 18th c. Rue Sainte-Anne in the township centre include the house of Simon Fraser (1793), one of the heads of the North West Company of fur traders, the Victorian town hall and Saint Anne's Church (1853). A pleasant hour or so can also be whiled away in the cafés and restaurants along the waterfront promenade.
From Saint Anne's Sluice – l'Ecluse de Sainte-Anne – dating from 1840, below the old iron railway bridge that linked the Île Montréal with the Île Perrot, there are boat trips on Lac Saint-Louis or Lac des Deux-Montagnes.

Sault-au-Récollet

The Église de la Visitation in this part of town, on the Rivière des Prairies, is worth a visit. Built between 1749 and 1752, it is one of Montréal's oldest Catholic parish churches and has an interior covered with wood carvings by local artists. The monuments (1903) in front of the church are to Père Nicolas Vill and Ahnntsic, the Indian chief who lost his life during the Iroquois wars.
The riverside park is a lovely place for a walk or a picnic.

Moose Jaw   H 7

Province: Saskatchewan. Population: 36,000

Information

See Saskatchewan

Moose Jaw, the "friendly city", is in the heart of the grain country, at the confluence of the Moose Jaw River and Thunder Creek. It is an industrial town and has a turbulent history; there are at least three versions of how it got its name, the most popular being that it comes from "moosegaw", the Cree word for warm breezes, since it is warmer here in winter than elsewhere in the vicinity.

Airfield

Moose Jaw has Canada's busiest airfield (at the Canadian military base, south of the town) which is also home to the famous Snowbirds aerial acrobatic group.

History

In 1881 two land surveyors from Canadian Pacific decided that the point where the railroads met should be where the Moose Jaw River met Thunder Creek. The fertile soil soon meant that people settled here permanently once the railroad was finished and Moose Jaw became a town in 1903 after it had grown to be an major junction. It also became important for its grainstores and meat-processing.

In the Roaring Twenties Moose Jaw, at the end of a direct line from Chicago, was from where Al Capone and his fellow gangsters ran their liquor empires during Prohibition. A few of the old buildings are still to be seen on Main Street.

Sights of Moose Jaw

The Western Development Museum (open: Apr.–mid-June daily 10am–5pm; mid-June–beginning Sept. 9am–8pm) on Diefenbaker Drive, which was opened in 1976, is worth a visit since it is the only museum documenting the history of transport on the prairies. It gives an account of transport by road, rail, water and air, and includes automobiles, horse-drawn ambulance (1907), trucks, steamers and locomotives, even a ferry, as well as a railway station complete with telegraph office.

Western Development Museum

This museum and exhibition centre in Crescent Park puts on touring exhibitions of art, history and science. Among the 3000 items are clothing, Sioux and Cree beadwork, farming tools, etc. There is also a permanent exhibition of Canadian art. (Open: June–Sept. Tues.–Sun. noon–5pm and 7–9pm; Oct.–May Tues.–Sun. noon–5pm, Thur., Fri. also 7–9.30pm.)

Art Museum & National Exhibition Centre

The Wild Animal Park, established in 1929, covers about 203ha/502 acres in the river valley south of Moose Jaw (open: May–Oct. daily 10am till dusk); it has about 300 native and exotic creatures, as well as a children's zoo and amusement centre.

Wild Animal Park

Open all year round, Wakamow Valley is a scenic new park on the Moose Jaw River east of the town. Its name is Cree for loop and alludes to the spot where the Moose Jaw River loops abruptly from north to east.

Wakamow Valley

At Plaxton's Lake there are footpaths and cycletracks and opportunities for picnicking, canoeing and skating in winter.

Plaxton's Lake

Moosonee   N 7

Province: Ontario. Population: 1300

See Ontario

Information

Moosonee is the seat of administration for the north-east region of Ontario. It is at the mouth of the Moose River on James Bay (see Baie James) and there are no roads to it, so it can only be reached by rail (see Cochrane, Ontario, "Polar Bear Express") or plane.

In 1673 the Hudson's Bay Company built a fortified trading post on an island in the Moose River near where Moosonee is today. It was destroyed by French troops a few years later, but what remains can be seen in a little museum (open: mid-June–beginning of Sept. 9am–6pm). The smithy, about 200 years old, is the oldest wooden building in Ontario Province.

★Moose Factory

The Révillon Frères Museum sets out to throw some light on the rivalry between the English Hudson's Bay Company and their French competitor which dogged Moosonee's history as they each sought to win the upper hand, both militarily and economically, in the territory around the mouth of the Moose River.

Révillon Frères Museum

Muskoka   N 8

Province: Ontario
Area: over 650sq.km/250sq.miles

Nahanni National Park

Information	Georgian Lakelands Travel Association, P.O. Box 39, 66 Coldwater St E, Orillia, Ontario L3V 6H9; tel. (705) 325–7160
Access	Take Highway 400 north out of Toronto to Coldwater, then continue on Route 69; the roads around Muskoka are 118 (Glen Orchard–Port Carling–Muskoka Falls) and 169 (Foot's Bay – Gravenhurst).
Situation and ★★Landscape	Muskoka, about two or three hours' drive north of Toronto (see entry), is one of North America's prettiest lake districts, bounded by Georgian Bay (see entry) in the west and the Severn River in the south.

Geologically, Muskoka is part of the Pre-Cambrian Canadian Shield, its granite and gneiss shaped by the last Ice-Age, which left behind hundreds of lakes as the glaciers receded. This allowed a slight rise in ground levels as the weight of the ice was removed.

This lake district is very reminiscent of parts of central Sweden, with a landscape of lakes and islands, rocky outcrops and crags amidst pine forests with occasional groves of mixed woodland.

Recreational area — Thanks to its relative closeness to the cities on Lake Ontario and Toronto Muskoka has become a place for holidaymakers and weekenders, with many marinas and holiday homes to prove it. Its waters are full of fish and ideal for angling, canoeing and in many cases even sailing. There are some beautiful trails that can be followed on foot or mountain bike. It is a landscape that is particularly attractive in winter as well.

★Port Carling — For visitors the main centre is little Port Carling (pop. 700), on the site of an Indian settlement where sluices regulate the turbulent waters of the river running from the upper lakes (such as Lake Rousseau and Lake Joseph) into the much bigger Lake Muskoka. This is very busy especially in the summer. The town's Pioneer Museum is worth a visit. Open: daily from June–mid-Oct., it gives an account of the history of the area, including its long tradition of boat-building.

Huntsville — The township of Huntsville (pop. 12,000) in the north of the Muskoka district is also the western entrance to the Algonquin Provincial Park (see entry). Lion's Lookout Park has a fine view over the town and the district. For a good idea of the history of settlement locally visit the Muskoka Pioneer Village on the Brunel Road (open from June to mid-October).

Nearby Williams Port has a botanical garden around the Dyer Memorial, commemorating a lawyer from Detroit.

Nahanni National Park   D/E 5

Administrative unit: Northwest Territories
Area: about 4,700sq.km/1814sq.miles

Information — Nahanni National Park, P.O. Bag 300, Fort Simpson, Northwest Territories X0E 0N0; tel. (403) 695–3151

Access — By air: From Fort Simpson, Fort Liard, Fort Nelson or Watson Lake.

By road: By the Liard Highway to Blackstone Territorial Park (information centre) then from here by boat.

★★National Park — Nahanni National Park is in the Mackenzie Mountains and takes in much of the South Nahanni River. In 1978 it was put on UNESCO's World Heritage List.

The park's magnificent scenery is of a wild beauty that has deliberately been kept unspoilt. No building of roads or hotels is permitted, but it is precisely this tranquillity and lack of development that makes this landscape so inviting, with its breathtaking mountains, canyons and waterfalls.

The labyrinthine karst ridges of the South Mackenzie Mountains are full of caves and gorges, hollowed out by water as softer minerals were dissolved from the limestone. The region's complex landforms are the result of its having been free from ice cover for some 250,000 years.

Geology

Nahanni means "people from over there" and is supposed to refer to a vanished Indian tribe.

History

Stories about the region began with the gold prospectors who travelled up the Liard River on their way to the Klondike. They were also drawn to the valley early this century when the three McLeod brothers came here and word got around that gold nuggets the size of grapes had been found. Three years later the headless bodies of two McLeods were found in the valley where their cabins stood, henceforth to be known as Headless Valley. The vein of gold was sought long but in vain. Albert Faille spent a lifetime trying to find out about the brothers, but what exactly befell them remains a mystery. Other people also disappeared, by 1969 as many as 44 of them. Tall tales and legends grew up and South Nahanni became somewhere to be avoided.

There are unusual plants to be found there such as orchids, and the wildlife includes bear, moose and caribou.

Flora and Fauna

The Nahanni River flows through the Selwyn, Mackenzie and Franklin Mountains before running into the Liard River, a tributary of the Mackenzie, at Nahanni Butte. On its way it passes through awe inspiring gorges, over wonderful waterfalls and hot mineral springs, their heat producing vegetation unusual for these climes.

South Nahanni River

The South Nahanni's rapid changes in gradient and speed of current make canoeing suitable only for those with whitewater experience. A permit must be obtained from the park authorities. Anyone planning a trip

The Virginia Falls in the Nahanni National Park

	should for safety's sake inform the park authorities in Fort Simpson or the Nahanni Butte station at the entrance to the park.
White water trip	The 200km/124 mile trip up the Nahanni River from Nahanni Butte to the Virginia Falls is an unforgettable experience of the great outdoors, taking in a change in level of 200m/656ft.
	From Nahanni Butte the first stretch is to about 80km/50 miles upstream, where the river divides itself into a number of "splits" and there are sulphurous hot springs (about 37°C/99°F). Since the ground never freezes such exceptional plants grow there as ferns, roses, and wild cherries.
	Soon the river passes through the towering walls of the first canyon, some around 1200m/3950ft high, then after 27km/17 miles Deadmen Valley opens up before, after 34km/21 miles the second, dizzyingly high, canyon rears up, only to be followed by a third, where the river makes a turn of 90° through what is known as "the Gate", guarded by the mighty Pulpit Rock.
	Beyond the canyons come the foaming torrents of Hell's Gate then, finally, after the fourth canyon the river rounds a bend to give a sudden breathtaking confrontation with the famous Virginia Falls.
Virginia Falls	In a magnificent setting, and twice as high as Niagara, the Virginia Falls plunge 90m/295ft into a cauldron of foam encircled by rocks. From the Albert Faille Portage around the waterfall a road takes the canoeist to the rim of the cataract, where there is a beautiful view of this great natural spectacle.

New Brunswick/Nouveau Brunswick   Q/R 8

	Maritime Province in eastern Canada Area: 73,500sq.km/28,370sq.miles Population: 715,000. Capital: Fredericton (pop. about 45,000)
Information	Tourism New Brunswick, P.O. Box 12345, Fredericton, NB, E3B 5C3; tel. (506) 453–2377.
	The name New Brunswick comes from the German Duchy of Braunschweig ruled by George III of England in the late 18th c. Virtually rectangular in shape, it borders on the Province of Québec and the St Lawrence in the north, and the US State of Maine to the west, with the Bay of Fundy and Nova Scotia to the south, and the Gulf of St Lawrence and Prince Edward Island to the north-east.
Topography	The province has three kinds of landscape. In the south, along the Bay of Fundy, stretch the Southern Uplands, their highest point, Mount Pleasant, barely 400m/1,312ft. These are joined to the north by the Central Uplands, through which flows the Saint John River. The fertile lowlands in the south-east form the border with Nova Scotia. Like the eastern part of Québec Province, New Brunswick has the low relief of the paleolithic spur of the Appalachians – the undulating plateau rises from around 250m/820ft to 820m/2700ft at Mount Carleton in the north. A number of rivers – Saint John, Saint Croix, Petitcodiac, Miramichi, Nepisiguit and Restigouche – divide the province up into lots of shallow valleys that make good farmland, the most important being the valley of the Saint John River.
Climate	Along the coast New Brunswick has a relatively mild maritime climate. Inland, on the other hand, there are mostly continental extremes of temperature with hot dry summers and cold snowy winters, when the average temperature is around −10°C/14°F. In July the average is 19°C/66°F, although it has been known to soar to a record 38°C/100°F.
Vegetation	About four-fifths of the province is wooded, with only about 7% used for farming, mainly potatoes.
History	The Indians, who were here long before the arrival of the Europeans, were mainly Micmac, one of the Algonquin tribes. They lived mainly by hunting

New Brunswick

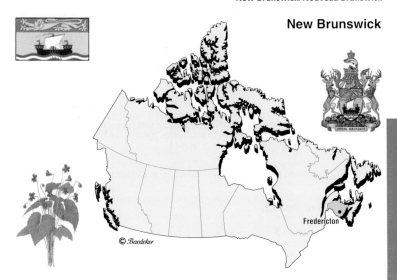

© Baedeker

Fredericton

and fishing, using the rivers to make their way far inland. Many of the place names still show their Indian origin. Miramichi Bay (Miramichi means "Micmac country") was also presumably where the first contact was made with Europeans when Jacques Cartier (see Famous People) landed here with his French expedition in 1534. Early in the 17th c. his fellow countryman, Samuel de Champlain (see Famous People), began the systematic colonisation of Canada, claiming the territory for France as part of "la Nouvelle France".

Few French settlers came here to begin with, preferring other parts of Canada such as the Saint Lawrence lowlands. However, the Treaty of Utrecht in 1713 gave "Acadia" – the pseudo-Classical name for original French lands on the Atlantic coast, now Maine, New Brunswick and Nova Scotia – to the British, and the following years saw the population growing, with the French contingent mostly in the north and east, many of them Acadians driven out of nearby parts of Nova Scotia.

The southern part of the province was settled by about 14,000 English Loyalists after the American War of Independence in 1776, mainly around the lower reaches of the Saint John River. This led to New Brunswick becoming a separate province from Nova Scotia in 1784. The colony became internally self-governing in 1847 and in 1867 it was one of the four provinces to found the Canadian Confederation.

New Brunswick can rightly claim to be Canada's only truly dual-language member of the Confederation. Its French-speaking minority of 35% lives in close contact with the English-speaking majority. The official languages are French and English. All the road signs, for example, are in both languages, while ability to speak and write in both is a precondition of employment in the civil service. The province is officially called New/Nouveau Brunswick. The rest of the population are mostly of German, Dutch and Scandinavian origin.

Population

Where people live depends on the lie of the land, so that while very few live in the forested interior, the river valleys, lowlands and coastal strip are relatively densely populated. The larger towns are Saint John, Moncton and the provincial capital, Fredericton (see entries).

323

Newfoundland

Economy	Traditionally the economic mainstay of New Brunswick is the felling and processing of timber, which still grows over 80% of the province, and about 30,000 people are employed in forestry and allied industries such as paper and pulp.
	Tourism is coming to play an increasingly important part in the economy, centred mainly on the Baie des Chaleurs and in Restigouche. New Brunswick's fisheries have long been another important part of the economy, albeit not to the extent of the other Maritime Provinces, providing over 15,000 jobs in various branches of the industry.
Agriculture	Intensive arable farming is mainly on the higher ground of the Saint John Valley, with potatoes the main crop, but some grain, fruit and vegetables as well. Between Saint John and Sussex agriculture predominantly takes the form of livestock and dairy farming.
Mining	Mining in New Brunswick did not get under way until after the Second World War. Besides coal there is zinc (at Bathurst), lead and copper.

Newfoundland (Province)   S 7/8

Situation: latitude 46°30′–60°30′N and longitude 52°30′–67°30′W
Population: 620,000
Area: 405,664sq.km/156,586sq.miles
Capital: St John's

Information

Department of Development and Tourism
P.O. Box 8730, St John's
Newfoundland A1B 4K2;
tel. (709) 729–2830 or (800) 563–6353

Transport and access

The main airports on the island of Newfoundland are St John's, Gander, Stephenville and Deer Lake, which also take flights from Europe. Those

Newfoundland

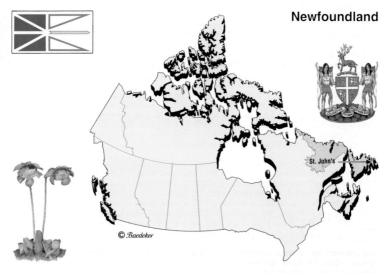

© Baedeker

St. John's

324

worth mentioning in Labrador are Goose Bay, Churchill Falls and Wabush, all of which, apart from Churchill Falls, can be reached from the larger Canadian airports.

There are ferry services to Newfoundland from North Sydney (Nova Scotia) to Port-aux-Basques (all year round) or Argentia (mid-June–mid-September), and to Labrador from St Barbe (Newfoundland) and Blanc Sablon (May–December) and Lewisporte and Goose Bay.

A partly tarmacked road runs between Baie Comeau (Québec) and Labrador City.

The old narrow-gauge railway on Newfoundland which linked Port-aux-Basques with St John's was closed in the 1960s. The line from Schefferville to Sept-Îles carries iron ore.

Newfoundland, Canada's youngest province, is actually a twin dominion consisting of the island of Newfoundland, with countless other small islands, and, on the mainland, 296,804sq.km/114,566sq.miles of Labrador. Newfoundland Island, the tenth largest island in the world at 108,860sq.km/42,020sq.miles, is in the Atlantic off Canada's north-east coast, separated from Nova Scotia by the Cabot Strait and from Labrador by the narrow Strait of Belle Isle, and measures 525km/326 miles from north to south and 515km/320 miles from east to west. Labrador, the peninsula called by Jacques Cartier "the land that God gave Cain", is bordered on the west and south by the Province of Québec and is 1046km/650 miles north to south and 724km/450 miles east to west.

Situation

Newfoundland Island is part of the Appalachian system and sits on the Continental Shelf. The famous "Grand Banks" offshore to the east and south of the island, which are only 200m/656ft deep, are the world's richest fishing grounds. Newfoundland's varied landscape was shaped by the ice ages, leaving big fiords, moorland, lakes and gentle valleys. The highest point is Lewis Hill (814m/2,672ft) in the Long Range Mountains on the west coast. These are wooded, as are the river valleys, with the rest a rocky wasteland.

Topography

From the Long Range Mountains the land falls away to the east and north-east. The Central Newfoundland plateau is one of North America's oldest geological formations, going back 400 million years to when it was part of the old Afro-European continent. The landscape in east Newfoundland, with the Bonavista, Burin and Avalon peninsulas, is pleasantly hilly.

Labrador is part of the east wing of the Canadian Shield surrounding the vastness of Hudson Bay. The undulating plateau of Pre-Cambrian granite and gneiss is 200–500m/656–1,641ft above sea level, rising up to 1800m/5908ft in the north-east. The coast is a typical fiord landscape.

Newfoundland's island climate is characterised by the fogs which occur all year round, caused in summer by the cold air from the Labrador current meeting the warmer air from the landmass, with the process reversed in winter. There are no great swings in temperature, the weather tends mainly to be rainy and cool. Average winter temperatures are between −2°C/28°F and −9°C/16°F, often accompanied by violent storms, and in the middle of the island the thermometer can fall to −20°C/4°F and below. Summer is fairly hot and wet on the coast and warmer further inland: the average July temperature is 15.3°C/59.5°F. The island has plenty of rain or snow all year round, especially in the east and on the coast (St John's 1346mm/53in. a year).

Climate

Labrador has a much more severe climate, with greater extremes of temperature, but less rain. Its northern climate is arctic, with winter temperatures of below −40°C/−40°F for six months of the year. In the three months of summer the average temperatures are around 10°C/50°F. The southern coastal areas are distinctly warmer. Goose Bay averages −14°C/7°F in January and 21°C/70°F in July, with an annual rainfall of 737mm/29in.

The northern part of Newfoundland Island is largely covered with fir and spruce, while the south is moor and marsh, with a few stunted trees growing on the barren podzol.

Vegetation

Newfoundland

Labrador's vegetation is predominantly conifers in the south giving way to sparser subarctic birch and small conifers and then the tundra of the far north.

History

Excavations at Port-au-Choix show that Indians were living in Newfoundland, the "cradle of the New World", at least 6,000 years ago. The Beothuk, the original North American Red Indians, were first known to Europeans as "redskins" because of the red ochre they used to decorate their bodies, and hence the name for them brought back to Europe by John Cabot.

The sensational diggings at L'Anse aux Meadows between 1961 and 1967 revealed traces of a Viking settlement from around 1000 A.D., possibly making the legendary Leif Erikson, one of their number, the first discoverer of Newfoundland and hence North America. The island was rediscovered in 1497 by John Cabot, an Italian whose real name was Giovanni Caboto, but who was in the service of England, although Basque fishermen were already fishing the rich waters of the Grand Banks as early as the 14th c., but keeping the existence of those waters to themselves. Soon the seas off the "new found land" were keeping the whole of Europe supplied with fish. This contact with Europe had fatal consequences for the native peoples, and the last Beothuk died in St John's in 1829. Labrador's Montaignais and Inuit only managed to avoid the same fate because their lands were of no interest to the colonialists.

Newfoundland effectively became Britain's first colony when Elizabeth I was declared its Queen in St John's in 1583. For a century the island was in practice ruled by the "Fishing Admirals", the British West Country merchants who made rules to prevent any permanent settlement that would provide them with competition. Some small English fishing communities managed to establish themselves nevertheless, although they never actually succeeded in getting colonial status. The French, however, did set up a colony, with a Governor, in Plaisance (Placentia) in 1662, and conflict between the French and the British over the island only ended in 1713 with

Newfoundland: Bay of Quidi Vidi

the Treaty of Utrecht when the British got Newfoundland and the French ended up with just St-Pierre and Miquelon.

In the years that followed Newfoundland was settled by the Irish, Basques and English West Countrymen. Newfoundland became a self-governing dominion within the British Commonwealth in 1855. During the Second World War an economic boom was created by the Allied military bases. Although Newfoundland took part in the Québec Conference in 1867 it did not become the tenth province of the Canadian Confederation until March 31st 1949, following a 52% vote in favour at a referendum.

Labrador has known human habitation for about 8,000 years (L'Anse Amour), and the Inuit in the north and the Naskapi Indians in the south long resisted French and English attempts to settle the coastline. John McLean began exploring the interior on behalf of the Hudson's Bay Company in 1839, and iron ore deposits were discovered in 1890. The military airbase at Goose Bay, used by the allies in the Second World War, subsequently became a civil airport, and the railway line between Sept-Îles (Québec) and Schefferville in Central Labrador, which made it possible to transport the iron ore was completed in 1954.

Newfoundland is unusual for Canada in having a very homogenous population: 99% of the "Newfies" are English-speaking and more than 95% were born on the island. About 2700 speak French, and they live mainly in the north-east and south-west of Newfoundland (St George's, Port-au-Port) and in Labrador. The only native peoples to have survived are the Micmac Indians.

Population

About 95% of the population of the province live on Newfoundland, although at 5.1 persons per sq.km/2 per sq.mile it is still very thinly populated. About a fifth of the population live in the St John's commuter area, while the rest are in the fishing villages along the coast, or the "outports" to give them their local name. Originally people lived along the whole length of the coast but in the 1970s they were grouped into small communities of one to two hundred as part of a resettlement campaign.

With a population of only 0.1 per sq.km/0.03 per sq.mile, Labrador is virtually uninhabited, apart from the coast and the iron ore workings. Two Indian tribes live in the north-east and south-west of Labrador, the Naskapi and Montagnais. The Inuit community numbers about 2600, and they get their living from the sea.

The Newfoundlander is an unusually large and heavy breed of dog, bear-like in appearance, with a flat coarse coat. The first settlers told of a breed of dog, around 1500, which lived on the island and was black, black and white, brown and grey in colour. These wild dogs had thick waterproof coats, and were used by the native Beothuk Indians to help haul in the fishing boats or pull sledges. Their appearance and their use in fishing caused speculation that they could be descendants of the Norwegian boarhound, since become extinct, and possibly brought to the island by the Vikings around the year one thousand. Another theory is that the Vikings first brought the Newfoundland to Europe and inter-bred their dogs with the North American races to make the boarhound.

Newfoundland dog

The Newfoundland was first brought to England and the North American mainland in the 17th c. where the massive, friendly dog was so popular it was much in demand, leading to such a drain on the native stock that systematic breeding of the strain was begun in Europe and North America towards the end of the 18th c. However to maintain the purity of the breed it was constantly necessary to import original native dogs from Newfoundland. By 1907 all the Newfoundlands living in the wild in Canada were extinct. Recently consideration has been given to creating a new race of dog in Newfoundland by re-importing from Europe and America. Nowadays Newfoundlands are used as guide dogs for the blind and for rescue at sea.

Molly Mill's Beppo, a typical Newfoundland thoroughbred

Economy

The fishing for which Newfoundland was famed in the 15th c. is still its main industry, providing about half the island's jobs. Most of Newfoundland's 32,000 fishermen are in co-operatives, fishing mainly for cod but also taking herring, halibut and salmon. Increasing demand, penetration by Japanese and Russians fleets, and the building of enormous factory ships had such a devastating impact on the seemingly inexhaustible fish stocks after the Second World War that strict quotas and a 200 mile limit had to be imposed. Despite considerable subsidy, the industry is still in recession, its difficulties compounded by distribution problems and high interest rates, with many fishermen having to work as lumberjacks at times in order to survive. Since Newfoundland's earliest history seals have also been hunted for their meat and their skins, and this still contributes to many families' livelihoods. The seal pups are particularly prized for their valuable furs. There have been protests about the hunting of seals since the mid-Fifties due not so much to the numbers that are taken as to the method of killing, when they are clubbed to death.

Farming is not important since very little land is suitable, and it employs only about 4,000 out of Newfoundland's workforce of 200,000. The farms on the Avalon Peninsula and in the Codroy Valley only supply the local markets.

In recent years mining and forestry have outstripped fishing in terms of production. Iron ore has been mined in the province since the turn of the century, principally in the Labrador Trough in western Labrador; Labrador City, where there is one of the biggest opencast iron mines in the world, and Wabush produce almost half of Canada's iron ore. Other minerals mined include lead, copper, gold, silver and gypsum. In the late 1970s large offshore oil and gas reserves were found off the coasts of Labrador and Newfoundland. There is estimated to be at least 1.85 billion barrels of oil in the Hibernia Field about 300km/186 miles east of St John's, and deposits of the same order are believed to lie under the Grand Banks, although icefloes and pack ice will make extracting it very difficult.

The completion of the TransCanada Highway in 1962 gave a substantial boost to Newfoundland's paper industry (Grand Falls, Corner Brook), kept supplied by the province's timber on a sustainable basis thanks to the reforestation programme. Labrador's hydro-electric reserves are put at 7500 to 10,500 MW, and the hydro-electric power station at Churchill Falls supplies Québec with an output of 5600 MW.

Unemployment in Newfoundland is a major problem, touching on almost every sector of the economy and reaching record levels for Canada in May 1988 at 17.2%.

Suggested routes

This short route round the Avalon peninsula can be covered in one or two days, starting at St John's and following the north coast, with its picturesque fishing villages.

North Avalon

Marine Drive, one of the oldest roads in Newfoundland, begins in St John's on Highway 30 and meets Highway 20 in Torbay. There are good views of the Atlantic from several points.

Logy, in North America, means slow or listless, and is also the name given to the big, slow fish caught in this bay.

Logy Bay

The Marine Sciences Laboratory located here carries out oceanic research, and has guided tours on Mondays and Fridays in summer at 3pm.

Flat Rock has a history going back at least to 1689. The village, where the sea has a very heavy swell, has indeed a huge flat rock forming a natural jetty and beach.

Flat Rock

A difficult landing in Pouch Cove, Newfoundland (see page 330)

Flat Rock is also known for its cave containing an altar to the Virgin which brings many pilgrims to the village every year.

Pouch Cove

There is proof of the existence of Pouch Cove, one of Newfoundland's oldest settlements, as far back as 1611. Its rather perilous harbour offered sanctuary to illegal immigrants in the 17th and 18th c. when permanent settlement was banned.

The Community Museum (open: 9am–5pm) recounts the history of this little place which, like Flat Rock, has a very impressive swell, so that boats have to be hauled out of the water on sledges since there is nowhere for them to anchor with safety.

Portugal Cove

Close on 30km/18½ miles south of Pouch Cove lies one of the very oldest villages in Newfoundland, Portugal Cove, where the inhabitants still mainly rely for a living on fishing (cod and salmon in particular).

Harbour Grace

Highways 72 and 70 lead onto the Port-de-Grace Peninsula, with its lovely coast and scenic fishing settlements, chief among them being Harbour Grace (population 3,100). This flourishing little town on Conception Bay gets its name from "Havre de Grace", as it was christened by the French in the early 16th c. At one time the second biggest town on Newfoundland, a series of massive fires between 1814 and 1944 slowed down development of this "harbour of grace".

It is probably the only place in Canada to have a monument to a pirate. Captain Peter Easton based himself here in 1610 and pressed hundreds of Newfoundlanders into his buccaneer fleet, beating a French squadron in 1611. Eventually, having amassed an immense fortune from plundering the ships of all nations, he retired to Savoie in France as a Marquis. His pirate fort was in the east part of town where the old Customs House (1790) stands today. Now an excellent local museum, open every day in summer and with a beautiful view of Conception Bay, it has a large local history collection, including model ships, 19th c. furniture, photographs, etc. Harbour Grace also has the oldest stone church in Newfoundland, St Paul's Anglican Church, which was built in 1835.

A number of transatlantic flights set out from here, such as the Wiley Post world trip of 1931.

Heart's Content

Heart's Content, in its lovely setting, was founded in 1650, making it one of the oldest places on the coast.

In 1866 the first transatlantic cable reached here, covering a distance of about 4440km/2760 miles from Ireland, and for a century it remained North America's most important relay station, taking 3000 messages a day, until automation led to its closure in 1965.

The cable station has been declared a provincial historical site and has been converted into an interesting museum which is open daily in July and August. It tells the story of communications from earliest times to the present, with a separate section dedicated to the transatlantic cable and the role that Heart's Content played in it, plus a replica of the cable station's first office.

The 81km/50 mile journey south back to St John's via Highway 80 passes through scenic fishing villages such as Heart's Delight, Cavendish, Whiteway (strange rock formations) and Green's Harbour, picking up the Trans-Canada Highway at the end of Trinity Bay.

South Avalon

This tour follows the eastern and southern coastline of the Avalon Peninsula from St John's to Argentina, taking in two of the world's most important reserves for seabirds at Bay Bulls and Cape St Mary's and starting out on Highway 10 south out of St John's.

Cape Spear
National Historic
Park

Open all year round, Cape Spear National Historic Park, on Highway 11 11km/7 miles south of St John's, is the most easterly point in North America, and has Newfoundland's oldest lighthouse. Dating from 1835 it was in operation until 1955 and is now an interesting museum. In addition there are massive half-ruined gun emplacements from the Second World War, including the barrels of two guns each weighing 30 tonnes and having a range of 13km/8 miles.

Castle Hill National Historic Park is between Placentia and Highway 100. Open: mid-June–beginning of Sept. Mon.–Fri. 9am–8pm, and until 5pm for the rest of the year. It is the site of English and French fortifications, whose history is told in the Interpretive Centre. Fort Royal was built by the French in 1693 then handed over 20 years later to the British, who renamed it Castle Hill. There is a magnificent view from here over Placentia Bay, and from Le Gaillardin, 10 minutes' walk away, a redoute built by the French in 1692.

★Castle Hill National Historic Park

Central Newfoundland is still largely untouched wilderness. Mostly marsh and moorland, it is covered with typical northern vegetation such as sheep laurel, caribou moss and Labrador tea, from which the Indians used to make a brew when they travelled.

Central Newfoundland

This route covers 676km/420 miles and traverses the island almost to the Avalon isthmus before turning south to the Burin Peninsula. The main stretch of the route is along the TransCanada Highway, Newfoundland's only east/west road, which at Springdale touches on Notre Dame Bay, where there are many picturesque little fishing villages.

From the Burin Peninsula it is possible to make a trip to enjoy the French atmosphere of St-Pierre and Miquelon.

Highway 1 runs along the north shore of Grand Lake and Sandy Lake between the two ranges of the Long Range Mountains. Lobster House and Mount Sheffield stand out on the other side of the lakes.

Western Newfoundland is a land of rugged grandeur, with fast-flowing rivers, pine forests and rich and unusual flora and fauna.

West Coast

The route down the west coast again mainly follows the TransCanada Highway, starting at Port aux Basques, where the ferry berths from North Sydney, Nova Scotia. Taking the highway northwards the Gulf of St Lawrence is on the left and the barren Long Range Mountains are on the right.

Halfway between Port aux Basques and Corner Brook is the Port au Port peninsula. Corner Brook is a popular starting point for trips into the centre of the island and for getting to Labrador. Gros Morne National Park, the next stop, is about 1000sq.km/386sq.miles and has the most spectacular fiords in North America.

From the park Highway 430 runs close to the west coast of the Great Northern peninsula.

Niagara

O 9

Province: Ontario

Niagara Tourist Board, Rainbow Bridge, Niagara Falls, Ontario; tel. (416) 356–6061
Niagara Park Commission, Niagara Falls, Ontario; tel. (416) 356–2241
Niagara National Historic Parks, Box 787, Niagara-on-the-Lake, Ontario

Information

The Niagara Falls are in the extreme south of the province of Ontario where the waters of Lake Erie plummet down almost 60m/197ft into Lake Ontario below.

★★ Niagara Falls

Niagara Falls are amongst the largest, most beautiful and certainly most famous waterfalls in the world. They were first chronicled in 1678 by Jesuit missionary Louis Hennepin, who followed the sound of the rushing waters upstream along Lake Ontario to discover this great body of falling water, nowadays seen by over 12 million visitors a year.

Niagara

"Lady of the Mist"

Spanish Aerocar

★★ Horseshoe
Falls
★ American Falls

The falls are in two parts, the concave Horseshoe Falls, 640m/2100ft across, which are Canadian, and in the Province of Ontario, and the American Falls, about 330m/1083ft across, in the State of New York, so the national boundary between Canada and the States runs through the middle.

Before the waters were used for hydro-electric power almost six million litres of water a second hurtled over the rocky rim. A Canadian/American agreement in 1951 for joint use guaranteed close on 3 million litres a second in summer and 1.4 million in winter. The spray rising from the foaming cauldron at the foot of the falls has beautiful rainbows when the sun shines.

★ Gorge

Below the falls the Niagara River flows through the deep walls of the gorge, between 80 and 300m/263 and 985ft across, forming the Whirlpool Rapids as the gorge narrows to the north-west.

★ Whirlpool

Just 6km/4 miles below the Horseshoe Falls the river changes course and turns north-east, and at that point swirls around in another seething cauldron, this time known as the Whirlpool, before plunging down through the Lower Rapids into Lake Ontario.

Erosion

The falls came into being during the last Ice Age, when the river ran over a chalk plateau, part of the Niagara Escarpment, before dropping to the level of Lake Ontario where the city of Lewiston stands today. As the water undercut and wore away its rim, the falls moved upstream relatively quickly, and in the last 3000 years have moved from the point of Rainbow Bridge to where they are today. The pace of erosion depends on the volume of water rushing over the crest. At present the cut-back in the area of the Horseshoe Falls is from 6–10cm/2–4in. a year. It can thus be estimated that in a few hundred thousand years they will be level with the American city of Buffalo.

The American and Canadian Falls

At present hydro-electric stations with a total capacity of 3 million KW are installed at the Niagara Falls. Plans for extension have been strongly opposed.

Energy potential

There are wonderful views of Niagara from the viewing platforms on the Canadian side. There are also a number of towers, open day and night, such as the Skylon and the Minolta Tower, which are amongst the best points for night viewing, since the falls are floodlit at night.

Views of the Falls

From the ground

Helicopters fly continuously from Niagara Falls station, taking passengers down to the Whirlpool, up the Gorge and then over the lip of the Falls.

Bird's eye view

A walk along the river front from Rainbow Bridge, through Queen Victoria Park, gives a good view of the American Falls, while it is even possible to take a trip under the falls, through the Table Rock Scenic Tunnels, starting beneath Table Rock House, near the lip of the Horseshoe Falls.

Frog's eye view

The "Maid of the Mist" sightseeing boats take visitors, duly provided with waterproofs, right to the foot of the Horseshoe Falls and past the American Falls, really the best way to get an idea of the amazing force of the waters.

"Maid of the Mist"

The Niagara Parkway from the falls to Niagara-on-the-Lake, where the river enters Lake Ontario, is administered by the Niagara Park Commission, who are responsible for the gardens and viewing points along the way. From the waterfalls the path leads under the Rainbow Bridge through an attractive residential area.

★★Niagara Parkway

A lift down to the bottom of the Niagara Gorge gives access to a breath-taking walk past the foaming rapids along the Gorge Trail.

★★Gorge Trail

The Spanish Aerocar is a cablecar that slowly makes its way over the face of the swirling waters of the Giant Whirlpool.

★★Whirlpool, Spanish Aerocar

Niagara

Niagara: the Canadian Horseshoe Falls, seen from a helicopter

Niagara Parks Commission School of Horticulture

Students of this technical school raise flowers, bushes and trees. In June the rose garden is particularly attractive. About 1.5km/1 mile further on the Canadian side of the river is the Robert Moses and Sir Adam Becket Generator Stations and nearby can be seen a large floral clock.

Queenston Heights

These heights are part of the Niagara escarpment where the falls once plunged into the river. Nowadays there is a park with a view over the river, with a statue in the middle to General Sir Isaac Brock, a hero of the 1812 war.

Queenston

This cluster of lovely homes and gardens at the foot of the escarpment contains the Laura Secord homesteads. Laura Secord was responsible for the British winning the Battle of Beaver Dam, since she warned them of the Americans' planned attack.

Niagara Falls, Canada
(Province of Ontario)

The Canadian Niagara Falls (pop. 73,000) is a clean and pleasant city on the more attractive west side of the Niagara Gorge. Its views of the falls make it a leading tourist centre, in fact there's no other place on earth quite like it. It has attractions to suit all tastes, honeymoon hotels to Monster Show.

Rainbow Bridge, Railroad Bridge, Whirlpool Rapids Bridge

There are three bridges linking the city of Niagara Falls with its American counterpart, all of them with fine views into the gorge that divides the two.

The view of the falls from Rainbow Bridge is particularly impressive.

Niagara Falls, USA
(New York State)

The American Niagara Falls (pop. 70,000) on the east side of the gorge also does well from the falls, and the accompanying tourism.

It is also an industrial area with unattractive factory sites.

★★Niagara-on-the-Lake

Niagara-on-the-Lake (pop.13,000) is a delightful small picture-book town at the northern end of the falls and on the shores of Lake Ontario. The first

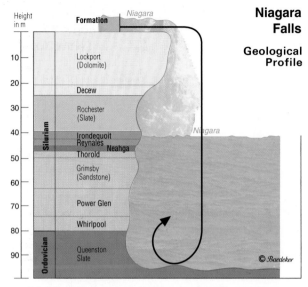

Niagara Falls

Geological Profile

Height in m — Formation

- 10 — Lockport (Dolomite)
- 20 — Decew
- 30 — Rochester (Slate)
- 40 — Irondequoit / Reynales — Neahga / Thorold
- 50 — Grimsby (Sandstone)
- 60
- 70 — Power Glen
- 80 — Whirlpool
- 90 — Queenston Slate

Siluriam — Ordovician

© Baedeker

capital of Upper Canada, it was razed to the ground by American troops during the War of 1812 against the British, but rebuilt with all due speed.

The town is full of pretty 19th c. houses set in their lovely gardens. Queen Street, its main street, has a clock tower in the middle and many little boutiques, eating places and hotels. The Niagara Apothecary, built in 1866, is especially quaint.

The little town has three theatres and is especially famous for its annual George Bernard Shaw Festival. — Theatregoing

The fertile hinterland of Niagara-on-the-Lake has a favourable climate for vine-growing and large vineyards have been established here. Some vintners and cellar-masters of German descent have settled here. — Viticulture

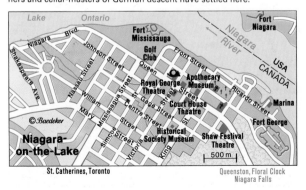

335

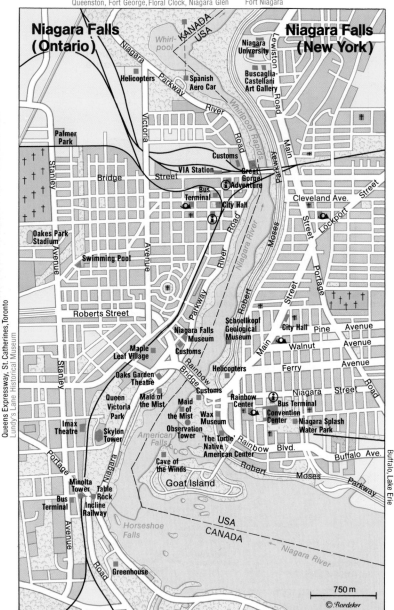

Lake Ontario
Queenston, Fort George, Floral Clock, Niagara Glen   Fort Niagara

Niagara Falls (Ontario)

Niagara Falls (New York)

KANADA
USA

Whirl-pool

Niagara

Parkway

Helicopters

Spanish Aero Car

Niagara University

Buscaglia-Castellani Art Gallery

River

Whirlpool Rapids

Victoria

Road

Lewiston Road

Main

Palmer Park

Customs

VIA Station

Great Gorge Adventure

Bridge   Street

Stanley

Bus Terminal

City Hall

Cleveland Ave.

Kennedy Street

Street

Lockport Street

Oakes Park Stadium

Swimming Pool

River

Avenue

Niagara River

Moses

Street

Robert

Portage

Street

Roberts Street

Parkway

Schoellkopf Geological Museum

City Hall   Pine   Avenue

Walnut   Avenue

Stanley

Niagara Falls Museum

Customs

Main

Ferry   Avenue

Maple Leaf Village

Helicopters

Niagara   Street   Road

Oaks Garden Theatre

Rainbow Bridge

Customs

Rainbow Center

Bus Terminal
Convention Center

Buffalo, Lake Erie

Queen Victoria Park

Maid of the Mist

Maid of the Mist

Wax Museum

Niagara Splash Water Park

Imax Theatre

Skylon Tower

Observation Tower

'The Turtle' Native American Center

Rainbow   Blvd.

American Falls

Cave of the Winds

Buffalo Ave.

Minolta Tower

Table Rock

Goat Island

Robert   Moses   Parkway

Bus Terminal

Incline Railway

Horseshoe Falls

USA
CANADA

Niagara River

Avenue

Road

Greenhouse

750 m

© Baedeker

Queens Expressway, St. Catherines, Toronto
Lundy's Lane Historical Museum

Chippawa, Fort Erie

336

The southern parkway leads to Dufferin Island which has a superb park where the Niagara becomes a broad gently flowing stream. There is a fine view here of the American shore and Grand Island. At Fort Erie the Peace Bridge crosses to the huge US city of Buffalo.

Dufferin Island

Fort Erie a reconstruction of the former fort which was completely destroyed. The officers' quarters, barracks, guardrooms and armouries can be visited.

Fort Erie

Fort George dates from the end of the 18th c. and was erected here to protect the area against attack by the Americans in their revolt against the British. The Commander at that time was Major General Isaac Brock. During the skirmishing of the War of 1812/1813 the fort fell into the hands of the Americans who took it under fire from the lake. Abandoned in 1820, the fort was declared a National Historic Park in 1969 and has since been lovingly restored, with visitors flocking here every year to learn more about the history of the area. At the height of the tourist season there are enactments of the military drills, firing practice and cookhouse activities of the early 19th c.

★Fort George

North Bay

O 8

Province: Ontario. Population: 52,000

Tourist Board; tel. (705) 472–8480

Information

North Bay, a lively little town on the north-east shore of Lake Nipissing, in a pleasant setting about 300km/186 miles from Toronto, is popular with visitors for its long sandy beach, good lake fishing, wide range of leisure facilities, and, not least, the riches and beauties of the hinterland in the north-east of the province.

The town was once on the fur traders' route from the Ottawa River to Georgian Bay, and still plays an important part in the trade today, staging public auctions five times a year – January, March, April, June and December – where the skins of beaver, marten and other valuable Canadian fur animals are offered for sale.

Fur trade

Ontario Marine Service operates a cruise that is particularly to be recommended. The "Chief Commander II" Cruise traces the route of the early "voyageurs" over Lake Nipissing along the French River to the Dokis Indian Reserve, making it possible to enjoy North Bay and the shoreland landscape from the lake.

★Lake cruise

From North Bay to Kirkland Lake

Highway 11 towards Kirkland Lake, after a drive of about 60km/37 miles, reaches the Marten River Provincial Park where there is the first opportunity to go for a good walk or enjoy some fishing.

Marten River

The Trapper Museum, which brings to life the times of the trappers and the fur trade, is open daily from mid-May to October.

Trapper Museum

One hundred kilometres/60 miles down the road, Timagami Lake is ideal for anyone who enjoys watery pursuits such as fishing and canoeing, with its 500km/310 mile shoreline, 1600 islands and ample stocks of fish. The town of Timagami Lake is on one of the long arms of the lake. A former trading post, it owed its subsequent wealth to timber and then mining. The largest mine in the district is the Sherman Mine, which offers a chance to see iron ore mining at first hand (sightseeing tours by arrangement May–Aug., Mon.–Fri. 9am–4pm).

Timagami, Timagami Lake

Provincial Forest   Provincial Forest, covering about 15,000sq.km/5790sq.miles, is impressive because of its great stands of conifers.

Cobalt   Cobalt (140km/87 miles) just off the highway, came into being in 1903 when a blacksmith, Fred LaRose, stumbled here on what turned out to be the richest silver vein in the world. Cobalt was found somewhat later, leading to a mining boom that lasted until the 1930s. The story of the town's rise to fame and its mining history are recounted in the Mining Museum.

Kirkland Lake   Kirkland Lake (240km/149 miles) is another old boom town, dating from 1912 when gold was first found here, and the supreme haunt of the prospector, achieving international fame for its legendary gold mile, a main road where gold was found at 12 spots. The Macassa Mine is the only mine still working Kirkland Lake's goldfields which are among the richest and largest in Canada.

Anyone wanting to be shown round should contact the Kirkland Chamber of Commerce, 20 Duncan Street N; tel. (705) 567–5444.

Northwest Passage   A–N 3–5

The Northwest Passage is the waterway on about 73° of latitude north along the north coast of the American continent, passing from the Atlantic through the Canadian Arctic archipelago and the Beaufort Sea and the Bering Straits to the Pacific Ocean.

History   The search for the Northwest Passage was begun in the 16th c. by Dutch and English navigators hoping to find a favourable sea route for trade with the Far East and thus circumvent the Portuguese monopoly on trade round the Horn of Africa. Martin Frobisher, in 1576, made the first attempt, assuming that this could not be the legendary sea of ice but just a frozen lake since saltwater never froze. In 1585–87 John Davis penetrated through the strait later to bear his name as far as Baffin Bay. Henry Hudson was looking for the Northwest Passage when he discovered Hudson Bay in 1609/1610. In 1616 William Baffin got as far as Lancaster Sound, but since he concluded that the Northwest Passage simply did not exist there was no more exploration for another 200 years.

It was 1818 before John Ross resumed the search at the head of an English expedition, although the motive this time was scientific rather than

A walrus in the Northwest Passage

Nanuvut – Land of the Inuit

On May 25th 1993, at a ceremomy in Iqaluit, "capital" of the Canadian Arctic, Prime Minister Brian Mulroney put his signature to the Nanuvut Agreement, a compromise hammered out following tough protracted negotiations, and endorsed by the indigenous inhabitants of the region, the Inuit, in a plebiscite held in late autumn 1992. As a result, before the century is out, the internal boundaries in north-east Canada will be redrawn, and what is today the eastern part of the Northwest Territories, an area extending from the north pole to Hudson's Bay, will become Nanuvut ("our land" in the language of the Inuit).

The newly created political entity comprises a region of some two million sq.km/772,000sq.miles, roughly a fifth of the total area of Canada. Of this vast new territory, ownership of about 350,000sq.km/135,000sq.miles passes directly to the 18,000 resident Inuit who, in addition, retain their traditional hunting and fishing rights throughout the whole of Nanuvut. The prospecting rights of the native inhabitants of the Arctic, on the other hand, are restricted to an area of barely 360,000sq.km/139,000sq.miles.

From its inception the new territory faces immense social and economic difficulties. The encroachment of the "western" way of life into the Arctic has proved deeply disruptive for the Inuit, a people whose lives hitherto have been closely attuned to nature and whose society remains archaic in structure. Many have now become addicted to alcohol and gambling, and there is a high rate of suicide. A large proportion of the Inuit population, whose traditional livelihood came from hunting and fishing, are now dependent on the state. More than a third of employable adults fail to find work. With the prospecting rights of these indigenous people of north-east Canada restricted to a relatively small area, the major share of the wealth generated by mining will continue to flow, as it always has done, into the coffers of Montréal, Toronto and big business elsewhere.

**Nanuvut
Territory**

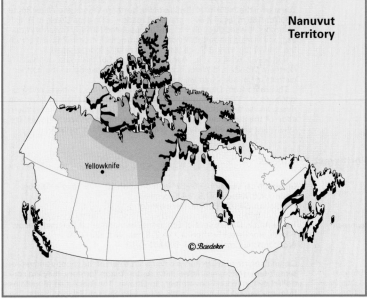

Yellowknife

© Baedeker

commercial. In 1829 he discovered the magnetic north pole on the Boothia-Felix Peninsula. The doomed expedition of John Franklin followed in 1845. After last being seen in July of that year in the Lancaster Sound, the members of the expedition were finally found dead, after numerous searches, on King Williams Island, having succeeded in exploring much of the Arctic coast of North America. McClure was the first, in 1850 to 1853, to be able to trace the passage on foot, coming over the iced up straits from the west, but the first person to manage finally to navigate the Northwest Passage from east to west was actually Roald Amundsen, the Norwegian polar explorer in 1900–03.

Present
importance

Since the way the ice forms in the Arctic Ocean can vary enormously from year to year and decade to decade its reconnaissance has always been of prime importance. This has improved over the years firstly with the use of planes and then, since 1960, of satellites. The first submarine, the US nuclear sub "Sea Dragon", went through the Barrow Strait in 1960, and in 1969 the special tanker "Manhattan", assisted by the Canadian icebreaker "St Laurent", succeeded in sailing through the Northwest Passage to Alaska, with the aid of satellite and aerial reconnaissance, and in the knowledge that the ice in the Arctic is at its thinnest between August and October and the Barrow Strait is largely ice-free.

The Northwest Passage has gained in importance of late with the discovery of oil in the Arctic off Alaska and Canada.

Northern Woods and Water Route   F–J 6/7

Provinces: British Columbia, Alberta, Saskatchewan

Information

Northern Woods and Water Route, The Secretary, Box 699, Nipawin, Saskatchewan S0E 1E0

The start of the 2400km/1419 miles of the Northern Woods and Water Route – 300km/186 miles of it over gravelled roads – is Dawson Creek, in British Columbia. It leads through virtually unpopulated territory towards Winnipeg, and there is the possibility of catching a quick fish or seeing game from the road on the way. Service stations are a day's journey apart.

Highway 2, west of Athabasca, becomes part of this route, dubbed the Northern Woods and Water Route in 1974, and opening up the northern districts of Canada's four western provinces.

This route from Dawson Creek through the north of Alberta and Saskatchewan to Winnipeg in Manitoba gives access to a chain of lakes and rivers, and to delightful, but little visited, provincial parks. At the northern edge of the settlement cornfields and grazing meadows, villages and lonely farmsteads alternate with great expanses of timberland.

Northwest Territories   B–R 1–5

Geographical situation: 60°–82° latitude north/60°–135° longitude west
Area: 3,400,000sq.km/1,312,400sq.miles
Population: 54,000. Capital: Yellowknife

Information

Travel Arctic, Department of Economic Development & Tourism, Yellowknife, Northwest Territories X1A 2L9; tel. (403) 873–7200
Arctic Hotline: freefone tel. 1–800 661–0788

Canada's Northwest Territories cover a large part of the country and represent its largest administrative unit. Like the Yukon Territory, they are controlled by the federal government in Ottawa. The Mackenzie Mountains form the natural boundary in the west, with Hudson Bay and Baffin Bay

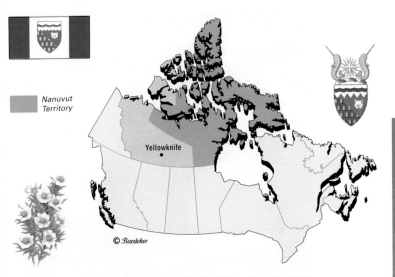

Nanuvut
Territory

Yellowknife

© Baedeker

defining the east. The southern boundary is the 60° line of latitude and in
the north the territories reach to within 800km/500 miles of the North Pole.
The lines of land communication are mostly north to south, such as the
Mackenzie Valley to Edmonton, or Baffin Island to Montréal.

In geographical terms there are two distinct regions, above and below
the timberline running more or less diagonally from around Inuvik in the
north-west corner to Churchill, Manitoba, on Hudson Bay in the south-east,
with Arctic above the line, and sub-Arctic, with trees, below. For administrative purposes there are three districts, Mackenzie in the west, Keewatin
in the east and Franklin in the north.

The District of Mackenzie is essentially the valley of Canada's longest river,
the Mackenzie, with a total length, counting Peace River (see entry), of
4240km/2635 miles, but also taking in Great Bear Lake and Great Slave Lake
(see entries) and the Mackenzie Mountains (2700m/8861ft), the eastern
section of the American mountain chain.

District of
Mackenzie

Keewatin, part of the Canadian Shield, was virtually levelled in the Cambrian period and nowhere rises above about 500m/1640ft. Known as the
Barren Lands because of its lack of trees, this area east of Hudson Bay is
dotted with thousands of lakes.

District of
Keewatin

Franklin District, all of it above the Arctic Circle and in the grip of the
permafrost, takes in the islands of the Canadian archipelago such as Baffin
and Ellesmere Island (see entries) with their countless fiords and glaciers,
and some highlands of the Canadian Shield that were not levelled by the
last Ice Age.

District of
Franklin

Since the Northwest Territories extend so far from north to south their
northern climate can vary in intensity so that Mackenzie and Keewatin
Districts have a largely sub-Arctic climate, while in Franklin it is the Arctic
climate that predominates. In all three districts, however, the average
minimum temperature is less than −30°C/−22°F, while in Yellowknife the
summer temperatures can reach 21°C/70°F but in Frobisher Bay the maximum reading will be only 12°C/53.6°F. Winter passes almost imperceptibly

Climate

Northwest Territories: Tuktoganiuk settlement

into brief summer, so that Great Slave Lake can still be covered in ice while the temperature is already over 20°C/68°F. North of the Arctic Circle is the land of the midnight sun in summer and of polar night in winter, while the bitter cold is the result of there being nothing to stop the Arctic winds sweeping down from the North Pole.

The mountains in the west hold back the softening effects of the Pacific, while the temperature is kept down in the east by the Labrador Current and the icy waters of Hudson Bay. There is little precipitation in the Northwest Territories – less than 250mm/10in. a year in parts.

Vegetation

Because of the brief growing period vegetation is very sparse. The timberline runs diagonally from the Mackenzie Delta to the southern tip of Hudson Bay (see entries), so that the south-west is thinly wooded with fir, spruce and birch, while the Barren Lands in the north and the Canadian archipelago are treeless tundra, with mosses, lichens, grasses and dwarf shrubs. Depending on drainage, the tundra can also be dry or wet, as in the swampland around Hudson Bay.

History

In the centuries following the Ice Age, these territories were inhabited solely by the Inuit (formerly known as Eskimoes) and Indians.

The first Europeans came with the founding of the Hudson's Bay Company in 1670 and its voyages of exploration to the north. Peter Pond, who actually preceded Alexander Mackenzie (see Famous People), was the best authority on this region as well as making discoveries such as Great Slave Lake.

Mackenzie joined the Western Fur Company in 1779. Ten years later he traced the course of the river that now bears his name from where it left Great Slave Lake and became the first European at its delta in the Arctic Ocean. Mackenzie District was declared an independent district within the Northwest Territories in 1895, the same year as Franklin District.

Sir John Franklin had led two expeditions into the Canadian Arctic, and the territory between Hudson Bay and the Coppermine River had been explored between 1819 and 1822. From 1825 to 1827 he followed the coastline to the Mackenzie, carrying out surveying work.

Keewatin, the smallest district, was founded in 1876. Its name comes from the Indian for "north wind". In 1869 Canada purchased all the land-rights from the Hudson's Bay Company and the Northwest Territories came under its administration. The present boundaries between the districts were drawn in 1918.

The Northwest Territories have a population of 54,000 – a density of only 0.02 per sq.km/0.007 inhabitants per sq.mile. 58.7% are Indians and Inuit, representing 4.3% of Canada's total original/native population, but also making the Northwest Territories the last of Canada's territories where the native peoples still form the majority. Europeans were very late arrivals, and it was 1931 before their numbers exceeds a thousand. Today there are still fewer than 25,000.

Population

Despite their small numbers the Europeans brought great problems for the Inuit. Although the situation is not quite as bad here as in other Canadian provinces the native people have undergone considerable changes in their lifestyle, bringing social problems in their wake. One marked feature of this is, for example, the four times as high suicide rate, while only about half the Inuit children attend school.

Social problems

Besides English and French there are an additional eight official languages in the Northwest Territories, although only about a third of the native population still speak their own language. The federal government has earmarked $580 million for the social integration of the Inuit, who also have 225,000sq.km/86,850sq.miles of their own land.

A division of the Northwest Territories into administrative units under the control of the native populations and the whites is under consideration. However, in this area there are still territorial problems, for the representatives of the natives claim areas with mineral deposits and touristic potential. The inhospitable conditions in the north and east are responsible for a concentration of population in the Mackenzie District where the capital Yellowknife (see entry) with 12,000 inhabitants is situated.

In recent years the Northwest Territories have increasingly gained in importance for Canada, as hunting and fur trading have come to be replaced in the economy by mineral extraction. Copper, zinc, silver, lead and uranium are all present, while gold has been mined around the Great Slave Lake (see entry) since 1896 and the time of the Gold-rush.

Fur trading, Mining

Growing importance has been attached to drilling for oil and gas in the Canadian archipelago from such fields as the Normann Wells, although the Arctic climate makes commercial exploitation of the north very difficult. The oilfields in the Beaufort Sea can only be worked in the brief summer, for example.

Oil

Other contributors to the economy include the fisheries on Great Slave Lake, timber in the south of Mackenzie District, and, continuing the tradition, breeding animals on special farms to cater for the fur trade.

Other industry

Although the climate and terrain mean that tourism here very much has its limitations, the conditions for anglers and some boat trips are ideal. Anyone wanting to cover a lot of ground can hire a hydroplane, and the Barren Lands and High Arctic provide the best territory for adventure holidays. The only road into these unspoilt landscapes is the Mackenzie Highway from Peace River (Alberta) to Yellowknife or Fort Simpson (see entries). The Mackenzie and Alaska Highways (Fort Nelson, B.C.) are linked by the Liard Highway, opened in 1983.

Adventure holidays

Tourists to the Far North who like their comfort as well can get Wilderness Tours in good wilderness lodges. The Northwest Territories have four wonderful National Parks, but these can be difficult to get to. The only one easy to reach by road is Wood Buffalo National Park (see entry), on the border with Alberta, while Auyuittuq (see Baffin Island) and Ellesmere Island National Park (see entry) are extremely remote. Nahanni National Park Reserve (see entry) is ideal for canoeists, as it can only be reached by air or water, and has been recognised by UNESCO as a World Heritage site.

Huskies

Huskies are Siberian in origin and found throughout Canada as pets, watchdogs and, of course, between the traces of dogsleds.

They are very similar to the wolf, reaching 50–60cm/19–24in. in height when fully grown, with thick coats in every shade between black and white. Brought here from their homes in northern Asia by the Inuit, in the settlements of the far north they haul sledges of mail and supplies, and also are used as police dogs.

Races between dog-teams were first started during the Gold Rush at the turn of the century, and this form of dog racing has since become very popular in Canada.

Nova Scotia

Q–S 8/9

Geographic situation: 43°–47° latitude north/58°–67° longitude west
Area: 55,000sq.km/21,230sq.miles
Population: 900,000. Capital: Halifax

Information

Nova Scotia Department of Tourism, P.O. Box 456, Halifax, Nova Scotia B3J 2R5; tel. (902) 424–5000.

The most important of Canada's Atlantic provinces, the Maritimes, is the only one to have a Latin name – Nova Scotia, or New Scotland.

Nova Scotia is a peninsula on the eastern edge of the Canadian mainland, to which it is joined by the Chignecto isthmus, only about 30km/19 miles wide. Between latitudes 43° and 47° north and stretching for 610km/380 miles from north-east to south-west, the peninsula varies between 80 and 160km/50 and 100 miles across. Canada's second smallest province, at around 55,000sq.km/21,230sq.miles, Nova Scotia also in-

Nova Scotia

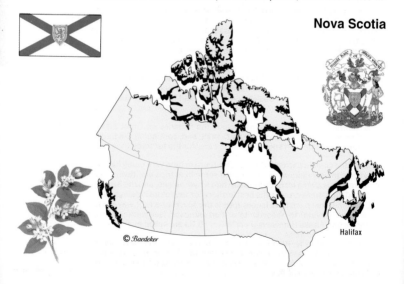

© Baedeker

Halifax

cludes Cape Breton Island to the north, from which it is separated by the narrow Canso Strait, although linked by the Canso Causeway over a dam built in the 1950s.

In broad morphological terms Nova Scotia is part of the Appalachian system, from which the peninsula is only separated by the Bay of Fundy, which itself splits into two narrow arms of the sea, Chignecto Bay and the Minas Basin. Its rocks are part palaeozoic granite and sediment, Pre-Cambrian slate and quartz, but also part magmatic.

The landscape of much of the peninsula is determined by the Atlantic uplands (150 to 300m/492 to 985ft) which gradually slope down to the coast, and the Cobequid Mountains, 350m/1149ft high in places, the Pictou-Antigonish Range and the North and South Mountains. Nova Scotia's highest point, at 532m/1746ft, is on Cape Breton Island.

The scenery often shows the telltale signs of the last Ice Age – glacially rounded outlines to the hills, drumlins showing the direction of the flow of the ice, and over 3000 lakes completing the picture of a morainal landscape. The biggest of these is Bras d'Or Lake on Cape Breton Island, linked to the Atlantic both in the north (Great Bras d'Or, Little Bras d'Or) and the south (channel to St Peter Inlet). Nova Scotia's coastlines are very different, with the Atlantic coast an indented mass of fiords and bays, while the Bay of Fundy has saltmarsh and mudflats. Here too is Nova Scotia's most amazing natural phenomenon, the greatest tidal fall in the world which can be as much as 15m/49ft in its uppermost reaches, and even 20m/65ft at spring tides. With this enormous difference between high tide and low tide the surging seawater rushes in at a speed that may be only 5kmph/3mph at the mouth of the bay, but can reach about 17kmph/10.5mph where the estuary narrows in the Minas Basin. Owing to the braking effect exercised by the floor of the bay, as the tidal surge spills into the river estuaries in Fundy's furthest reaches, such as the Petitcodiac out of Chignecto Bay, it pushes before it an advance wave, a tidal bore sometimes up to 1m/3ft high, travelling at a speed of up to 17kmph/10½mph, with a roar like a distant express train. For visitors, it is an unforgettable sight.

In these maritime latitudes Nova Scotia has a pleasantly breezy if rather damp climate. Average temperatures in July are around 17–18°C/62–64°F, and in January around −3°C/26°F. Total rain and snowfall is generally between 1200 and 1300mm/47 and 51in. Weather conditions can often cause fog in winter, and when the Arctic winds blow in from the north Nova Scotia can suffer from blizzards combined with a sharp drop in temperature.

A good 80% of Nova Scotia is still covered with woodland, mostly deciduous and predominantly ash, alder, maple and larch, but fir and pine can also feature prominently in places. Those worth mentioning include the Kejimkujik National Park in the west and the Cape Breton Highlands National Park.

Nova Scotia's culture has largely been shaped by almost 500 years of European colonisation. Before the advent of the Europeans all of what is now Nova Scotia (including Cape Breton Island), Prince Edward Island and the north and east of New Brunswick was the hunting grounds of the Micmac Indians who, unlike the Huron, a tribe of gatherers rather than hunters, roamed the land as nomads, hunting elk, bear, beaver, porcupine and caribou in winter, and camping on the coast under their skin wickiups in spring and summer, trapping sea otters and catching fish. They had no metal tools but fashioned implements from animal bones, stone or wood. Unfortunately Nova Scotia has not retained any Indian settlement as such.

European settlement, and the consequent inroads into Indian lands, began around 1500, although there is a theory that Leif Erikson may have also touched the coast of Nova Scotia around A.D. 1000, but there is still no historic confirmation of this.

Geology

Climate

Vegetation

Indians

History of European settlement, present population

Nova Scotia: the lighthouse on Cap d'Or

The actual history of the discovery by Europeans began with John Cabot, originally Venetian Giovanni Caboto, in 1497/1498, sent by the English king to look for a shorter way to the Far East, in higher latitudes. He reached either Labrador or the northern tip of Cape Breton, but failed to leave records on the subject.

The area was explored in 1528 by Verrazano, a Florentine merchant working for the King of France, and he christened the peninsula New France. In 1604 the French, including Samuel Champlain (see Famous People), settled the Annapolis Valley, founding Port-Royal, the first lasting European settlement north of Florida. They called it Acadia, a name that eventually came generally to refer to French settlement on Nova Scotia.

In 1621 the British succeeded in their attempt at settlement. King James I had granted landrights to Scottish noblemen led by Sir William Alexander, hoping for settlement by British colonists, on the grounds that the discovery by John Cabot duly entitled him to do so. Hence the peninsula came to be called "Nova Scotia".

Disputes between the two nations over the territory continued until finally Nova Scotia, if you were British, or Acadia, if you were French, was assigned to Great Britain in 1713 by the Treaty of Utrecht. The first large British settlement to be founded was Halifax, in 1749, as a garrison to counter the French's Vauban-type fortress of Louisbourg built on Cape Breton Island after 1719. Captured by the British in 1745, then returned to the French in 1748, Louisbourg was finally retaken by the British in 1758, and this time destroyed. Also in order to counter the French and their Catholicism the British encouraged Protestant settlers in the late 18th c., including the 2000 Germans who founded Lunenburg. Because about 10,000 French settlers refused to swear England unqualified allegiance, most of them were deported and their lands confiscated. With the ending of the American War of Independence about 7000 Loyalists came and settled here (around Shelburne, for example), and in time many of the Acadians eventually returned to their former territory.

In 1867 Nova Scotia joined Québec, Ontario and New Brunswick to form the Dominion of Canada, and became a Canadian Province.

The place names in Nova Scotia already indicated that the people living there came from England, Scotland, France, Germany and Holland. When Nova Scotia became Canadian about 350,000 people lived on the peninsula. The figures rose steadily to 883,000 in 1986, and by now they are over 900,000. At the last census 75% put themselves down as originally British, 11% French, 5% German and 3% Dutch. In terms of religion, 34% were Catholic, 22% United Reformed, 18% Anglican, 14% Baptists, and 7% Presbyterian.

Three-quarters of the people live in towns. The largest of these is Halifax, which, together with Dartmouth, has a population of around 300,000.

The fishing industry has long been traditionally Nova Scotia's chief source of employment, apart from a modest amount of farming, which tends to be confined to local needs. About 11,000 people, 3% of the workforce, earn their living from catching fish, which in the north-west Atlantic and the coastal waters of the continental shelf tend to be mainly cod and sole, but also lobster and shell-fish.

Fisheries

Falling catches due to overfishing forced the Canadian government to extend territorial waters to 200 sea miles in 1977. In terms of numbers of fishermen, Nova Scotia comes second in Canada after British Columbia. Much of Nova Scotia's fishing industry is centred around Yarmouth and Lunenburg, together with Halifax and its ice-free harbour. The old fishing villages on St Margaret's Bay also have a claim to fame.

Agriculture has been declining for decades both in terms of cultivated area (only about 4% of the province) and the number of farms. Dairy farming is the main form of agriculture but fruit and vegetables are also grown quite intensively in the Annapolis Valley.

Agriculture

Nova Scotia's timber industry is of supra-regional importance, but its vast woodland, covering about 80% of the province, only permits an annual felling of 300,000 cubic metres, most of which is processed for the construction industry, with the rest going for paper and cellulose (in Port Hawkesbury, for example).

Forestry

Mining, like agriculture, is also a declining industry. Coal was found in 1865 on Cape Breton Island at Inverness and, using iron ore imported from Newfoundland, Sydney's steel industry developed near the coalmines. Other coalfields exist at Pictou, on the coast at Northumberland Street and at Springhill. Also found are iron ore (Annapolis, west Westville, south New Glasgow, at Cape George and on Cape Breton Island), manganese (southwest of Windsor, together with tin, and north-west Halifax), copper (chiefly on Cape Breton Island), gypsum and antimony. Sherbrooke even experienced a brief gold rush in the 19th c. (Nova Scotia Gold District). Its decline is partly because these minerals are only found on a small scale, and partly because of anticipation of imminent closures. In value terms, Nova Scotia's mining only accounts for about 1% of the total for Canada.

Mining

The most important sector of the economy is manufacturing and processing (timber, engineering, etc.).

Manufacturing

The Okanagan

Province: British Columbia

Oakanagan-Similkameen Tourist Association, Dept. 5, 104–515 Highway 97 South, Kelowna V1Z 3J2; tel. (604) 769–5959

Information

See British Columbia

The Okanagan

Transport

By air:
Airports at Kelowna and Penticton. Scheduled flights to and from Vancouver/Calgary.

By bus:
Greyhound Bus Lines on Highway 97: Osoyoos, Oliver, Penticton, Summerland, Kelowna, Armstrong, Enderby.

★★Natural features

The Okanagan, the Ticino of Canada as it's often known, is a lush, sunny valley south of British Columbia's High Country, with sandy lakeside beaches, abundant orchards and excellent vineyards which make it a favourite destination for holidaymakers. Drained by the Okanagan River, a tributary of the Columbia River which rises in the US State of Montana, the valley, between 4 and 19km/2½ and 12 miles wide, nestles in the rolling uplands, as high in places as 2000m/1243ft, of the Southern Interior Plateau, and extends for about 160km/99 miles from Osoyoos, a village on the US border, to Armstrong in the north. From here it continues north of a barely perceptible watershed in valleys running more or less parallel to the main direction to Sicamous and Salmon Arm on Suswap Lake. The largest in its chain of lakes is Okanagan Lake, about 120km/75 miles long, east of which, in the northern part of the valley, lie Swan Lake, Kalamaka Lake and Wood Lake still in the broad valley floor, joined by Skaha Lake, Vaseux Lake and Osoyoos Lake to the south.

Climate

Thanks to its exceptionally mild climate, with dry, hot and sunny summers (often with temperatures topping 30°C/86°F) and relatively mild winters (average January temperature 0°C/32°F), giving about 150 frost-free days a year – Okanagan and Skaha Lakes very seldom freeze over – the Okanagan is Canada's orchard. In season the produce of the fruit trees planted all over the valley floor and its terraced slopes can be bought from roadside stands.

★Wine producers

Eleven of the fourteen wine producers of British Columbia are now located in the Okanagan area; their wines have gained international acclaim.

Vegetation

Unlike the Okanagan Valley with its lush greenery which is mostly artificially watered, the relatively bare semi-arid plateau uplands are in the rain-shadow of the steep Coastal and Cascade Mountains, with an annual rainfall usually well below 400mm/16in. Consequently the vegetation is sparser, mostly sagebrush or Ponderosa pine, cactus can often be found and, in Vaseux Lake Provincial Park Canada's only desert, stretching for about 40km/25 miles from Osoyoos Lake north to Skaha Lake. Here too, early in the morning, Californian Bighorn sheep can often be seen close to the road or on the rocky slopes.

History

Before the advent of Europeans the Okanagan was the preferred territory of the Salish peoples, and it was their Indian trails that the fur traders followed in the early 19th c. In 1811 men of the North West Company set up an outpost where the Okanagan flowed into the Columbia River, from which they explored the hitherto unknown south-east of British Columbia, competing all the time with their American rivals, the Pacific Fur Company, already established at the mouth of the Columbia River.

Until 1846, when it was agreed latitude 49 should be the frontier between the USA and Canada, a busy trail led through the Okanagan Valley to Kamloops. Fearing trade restrictions, this trail was abandoned and a new, more difficult route to the coast was sought through the canyons of the Fraser and Thompson Rivers. Hard on the heels of the fur trappers now came goldminers and prospectors, stock-farmers and settlers. As artificial irrigation increased the turn of the century brought fruit farming which is now the mainstay of the economy of the Okanagan Valley.

Highway 97

Highway 97 runs through the Okanagan linking Osoyoos on the Crowsnest Highway (see entry) in the south with Kamloops and the TransCanada Highway in the north.

Surrounded by orchards and vineyards. the little township of Oliver (pop. 2000, 304m/998ft) came into being after the First World War when the Canadian government gifted returning soldiers with 3000ha/7413 acres of irrigated land. The Oliver Heritage Society Museum (106 West 6th St). Open: June–Aug. 9.30am–8.30pm, and at other times Mon.–Thur. 9am–4pm. It has displays on the natural history of the Canadian desert, and on the pioneer days in and around Oliver and the old mining town of Fairview (1887 to 1906) and Camp McKinney.

Oliver

The 4km/2½ mile long shores of Vaseux Lake 17km/10½ miles to the north are a bird sanctuary where Canada Geese nest and it is possible to see the rare Trumpeter Swan.
  Bighorn sheep can be found among the rocks, but so can rattlesnakes, so care is necessary.

Vaseux Lake
Provincial Park

In a scenic setting between Lakes Skaha and Okanagan, Penticton (pop. 24,000, 351m/1151ft) has miles of sandy beaches and marinas. A popular pastime in summer is rafting from here 8km/5 miles down the Okaganan River Channel to Lake Skaha.

Penticton

The town gets its name from the Salish "Pen-Tak-Ton", or "place to stay", since the Indians found that the good climate and wealth of fish and game meant it was a place where they could stay all year round. Irishman Thomas Ellis was the first European to settle here when he started farming cattle on this land in 1866, then in the 1890s the ranch gradually turned into a settlement.
  Only 400 people lived here when plans were announced to build the Kettle Valley Railway in 1912, but irrigation projects, land speculation, steamboats chugging up and down the lake, and fruit farms, followed by packing and canning plants, not to mention sawmills, soon transformed the area. Today fruit and tourism are the town's two main industries.

Name and history

Waterslides, whirlpool and miniature golf are among the attractions offered by White Water Slide (3235 Skaha Lake Rd., open: May–Labour Day) and Wonderful Waterworld (225 Yorkton Ave., open: May–Labour Day). Other amenities available include golf, ranch horseback riding, and paddle steamer trips.

Leisure amenities

Okanagan Game Farm, 8km/5 miles south of the town on Highway 97 and open daily from 8am, has large paddocks holding about 130 species of animals from all over the world, most of them endangered, and including Bighorn Sheep, rhinos, bear, wolf, reptiles, etc.

Okanagan
Game Farm

Penticton Museum, at 785 Main Street, has a good collection drawing on local history and Indian cultures (open: June–Sept. 10am–5pm, at other times Mon.–Sat. 10am–5pm).

Penticton Museum

Apex Alpine, about 30km/18½ miles south-west, is a modern ski station with descents of 610m/2002ft, ski-lifts, etc., and a season from December to April.

Apex Alpine

A good excursion out is to Munson Mountain (1680m/5513ft), with a magnificent view, and along a winding road round the eastern lake shore to Naramata.

Munson Mountain

Most of the township of Summerland (pop. 8000, 411m/1349ft) is on terracing above the lake shore amid fruit trees and vineyards.

Summerland

There is a wonderful view of Okanagan Lake from Giant's Head Park (910m/2987ft), reached by about half a mile of narrow mountain road.

Giant's Head

Peachland (pop: 3000) lives from its thriving orchards and molybdenum mining in the Brenda Mine (29km/18 miles into the mountains above Highway 97).

Peachland

The Okanagan

Kelowna

On the eastern shore of the narrowing Okanagan Lake, Kelowna, a town of 65,000 people (344m/1129ft), is the centre of the Okanagan Valley, and has developed into a popular resort, thanks to its sandy beaches and more than 2000 hours of sunshine a year, it has over 2000 beds and an enormous camp site for visitors.

There is good fishing in the surrounding mountains in the many lakes, most of them used to irrigate the valley, and the town also serves as an important marketing and processing centre for the fruit and vegetables produced around the valley. Other major industries are timber (Crown Forest Industries) and manufacturing (Western Star Trucks).

The town is also popular with retired people on account of its mild climate and lovely setting, plus its good social facilities and a large number of golf courses.

History

Before the arrival of the first fur trappers in the early 19th c. this was the site of one of the ten main Salish villages of the interior. Around 1859/60 Father Charles Pandosy, a Catholic missionary, with two theological students, built a mission station here where Mission Creek runs into the lake. Persuaded by the Father's farming success the first European settlers soon began moving into the valley, and in the 1890s a town started to grow up on the lakeshore. A number of the larger farms were split up into fruit orchards. Around the turn of the century Kelowna became the landing for the sternwheel steamers of the Canadian Pacific Railway which operated on Okanagan Lake, steadily bringing in new settlers. By about 1909 the thrusting new town already had a population of 1800, and it received a further boost at the end of the Second World War with the opening of the Hope-Princeton Highway in 1949 and the building of the Okanagan Lake Bridge in 1958. This replaced the ferry that was the only link between Kelowna and Westbank, and is still, at a length of 650m/2133ft and carried on 60m/196ft high pontoons, Canada's longest floating bridge.

International Regatta

Kenowna is famous today for its annual international regatta, held every year since 1906 at the end of July, with sailing and waterskiing, plus tree-felling contests and the "Across-the-Lake Swim".

Big White Ski Village

The Big White Ski Village, a new ski resort with a fall of 658m/2160ft, has 45 ski runs, 5 chair-lifts and a ski tow. It lies about 60km/37 miles to the east at Big White Mountain (2317m/7604ft), which is part of the Monashee Mountains.

Father Pandosy Mission Historical Site (Oblate Mission of Immaculate Conception

The cabins built from tree-trunks by the missionaries at the Father Pandosy Mission (2685 Benvoulin Rd/Casorso Rd; access daily from 9am) show just how hard and full of deprivation their life was. Besides the plain little church, the school and simple homes of the mission, there are also two typical pioneer cabins that have been brought here.

Kelowna Centennial Museum

This local history museum vividly recreates scenes from the town's past, including a reconstructed kekuli, the winter home of the Salish, a typical street around 1910 and a trading post from 1861. The museum is at 470 Queensway and is open: July/Aug. Tues.–Sat. 10am–5pm, and Sun. 2–5pm.

Sun-Rype Tours

Sun-Rype Products, at 1165 Ethel Street, produces juice from about 65,000 tonnes of fruit every year in one of Canada's biggest plants, have guided tours from June–Sept. 9am–2.30pm.

Hiram Walker & Sons

In Winfield, a few miles to the north, it is possible to visit the Hiram Walker distillery, makers of the famous Canadian Club whisky (Jim Bailey Rd, June–Aug. 9.30, 10,30am, 1 and 2pm, otherwise 9.30am and 1pm only).

By the Okanagan Lake ▶

The Okanagan

Flintstones Bedrock City

Flintstones Bedrock City at 990 McCurdy Road, 7km/4 miles north-east on Highway 97, is a pleasure park and an imitation Stone Age village in the style of the television series, complete with Fred and Wilma and their Stone Age friends (open: Apr.–Oct. 10.30am–4pm).

Wild Waters Waterslide Park

Wild Waters Waterslide Park nearby, also on McCurdy Road, has, of course, lots of waterslides, as well as miniature golf (open: May–Sept. 11am–6pm, and till 7pm in peak season).

Old MacDonald's Farm

Old MacDonald's Farm (13km/8miles south on Highway 97) is a children's theme park with baby animals which can be stroked.

M.V. "Fintry Queen"

The "Fintry Queen", the ferry that ran between Kelowna and Westbank from 1948–58, now takes people on pleasure trips round the lake from the town marina (refreshments on board).

The "Okanagan Princess" also leaves on excursions from Kelowna Marina at the end of Queensway.

Vernon

A little town between three lakes, Vernon (pop. 22,000, 381m/1250ft) is the point where all roads meet in the northern Okanagan Valley. Its history goes back to 1864 when the Vernon brothers, after failing to strike it rich as prospectors in the Monashee Mountains, were encouraged by the valley's fine weather to turn their hand to farming, and started a cattle ranch on the site of what is now the Coldstream Ranch today. The B.X. Ranch also came into being at the same time nearby, providing horses for the Cariboo mail coaches and Barnard's Express.

This sleepy little hamlet began to thrive with the advent of the Shuswap & Okanagan Railway in the early 1890s, and irrigation projects brought fruit and vegetable farming.

Nowadays tourism is Vernon's main industry, together with the fruit processing, and visitors come for the watersports, diving, fishing, hang-gliding, golf, riding and hiking.

Vernon Museum

Vernon Museum and archives in the Civic Centre, at 3009 32nd Avenue, tells of the Canadian Pacific sternwheel steamers which used to ply the lake, and the pioneers and Indians who used to live here (open: Mon.–Sat. 10am–5pm).

Atlantis World of Water, Okanagan Bob Slide

Atlantis World of Water, with waterslides, etc., is about 7km/4 miles north on Highway 97A (open: June–Sept. 10am–8pm). Just over a mile further north there is the Okanagan Bob Slide, about 580m/1903ft long (open: Easter–mid-Oct. 10am–8pm).

★Silver Star Recreation Area

Silver Star Mountain Resort, 87sq.km/34sq.miles of recreation area, lies about 22km/14 miles north-east along Silver Star Road – unsurfaced for the last 10km/6 miles. It has 35 ski runs, descents of 485m/1591ft, several chair-lifts and ski-tows, and at summer weekends a chair-lift takes visitors up Silver Star Mountain (1885m/6187ft) where there are attractive walks and fabulous views.

O'Keefe Historic Ranch

One of the biggest ranches in the Okanagan Valley, the O'Keefe Ranch, 12km/7 miles north on Highway 97, goes back to 1867, and the O'Keefe family actually lived there until 1977. Nowadays an open-air museum (open: May–mid-Oct. 9am–5pm, and July/Aug. until 7pm) it has a dozen historic buildings, furnished according to the period, from the first block-house up to the pretty 1890s Victorian O'Keefe Mansion and St Ann's Church.

Armstrong

The township of Armstrong (pop. 3000, 362m/1188ft) lies in the Spallum-cheen Valley, the northern continuation of the Okanagan, where the fruit trees gradually give way to fields of vegetables and dairy farms.

Armstrong's first settlers arrived around 1866, and the many wooden buildings have retained something of a Western atmosphere. Main Street is still shared by automobiles, pedestrians and Canadian Pacific's freightcars.

The little place is particularly known for its "Cheddar" cheese, which visitors can watch being made at the Armstrong Cheddar Cheese Plant on Pleasant Valley Road.

Ontario   L–P 6–9

Geographic situation: Canada's central province
Area: 1,070,000sq.km/413,020sq.miles
Population: 9.3 million. Capital: Toronto

Ontario Travel, Queen's Park, Toronto M7A 2E5; tel. (416) 965–4008/ (800) 668–2746.

Information

Ontario Province is the political, industrial and cultural heart of Canada and its second largest province, situated between Québec and Manitoba. An inland province, it nevertheless has 7600km/4723 miles of freshwater shoreline along the Great Lakes in the south and 1200km/746 miles of saltwater coast on James and Hudson Bay in the north.

A fifth (200,000sq.km/77,200sq.miles) of Ontario's surface area is not land but water, and its highest point is Mt Ogidaki, at 665m/2183ft. The province extends for 1730km/1075 miles from north to south, and 1690km/1050 miles from east to west.

Apart from a few exceptions in its extreme north and the south, Ontario belongs to the world's earliest geological era, its bedrock being the Pre-Cambrian Canadian Shield, mostly slate, granite and gneiss.

Geology and morphology

Geographically the province can be divided into two parts. The northern, larger part, with some of the Hudson Bay coastal lowlands, the Patricia and Kesagami Plains and the Central Highlands and the Cochrane Plain are

Ontario

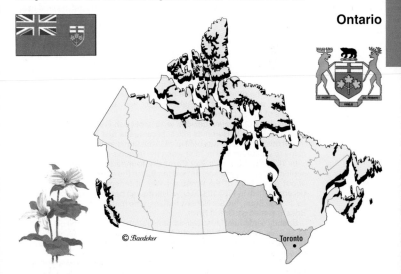

© Baedeker

Toronto

Ontario

geologically part of the Canadian Shield, but the southern part, with only 12% of the total area, is formed by the Niagara Escarpment. South of Hudson Bay is a district area, of 50,000sq.km/19,300sq.miles which belonged to a much larger lake after the Ice Age, where the sediment deposited makes the land good enough for farming. The variation in sea-level is due to the land being raised several hundred feet after the melting of layers of ice that were miles thick.

Ice-ages

All life in the province was frozen out by the massive ice-sheets of the Laurentide Glacier at most 18,000 years ago. The glacier's retreat, begun in the south about 12,000 years ago, and lasting until about 7000 years past in northern Ontario, left its enduring mark on the landscape as it scooped out lakes and briefly blocked the St Lawrence, the whole of the meltwater flowing south along the Mississippi. The morainal scenery shows the direction taken by the long-gone glacial flows – particularly evident from the air – leaving a hilly landscape with many lakes and swamps.

Climate

Ontario has a distinctly continental climate, although marked differences exist between north and south. Its southern part, especially the Ontario "peninsula", has milder winters, thanks to the Great Lakes, but wetter summers than the north of the province, where the winters are long, bright and very cold and the summers are short but sunny and hot. In Toronto the average July temperature is 22°C/71.6°F and the frost-free period lasts from early May to mid-October. In Thunder Bay the average July temperature is 17.6°C/63.7°F and in January a frosty −13.7°C/9°F, while it is without frost only from early June to mid-September. Annual rainfall varies in the province from 650 to 1020mm/25½ to 40in., and is thus evenly distributed throughout the year. Three to six feet of snow is normal in winter, and from autumn until well into spring blizzards can bring heavy snowfalls and abrupt drops in temperature. In spring and early summer the weather can be very capricious.

Vegetation

Most Europeans will feel very much at home in the deciduous woodlands of the south. The transition to boreal conifers begins north of the River Severn as spruce, fir and pine come increasingly to dominate the landscape. The wildlife and vegetation of the fen and marshland is particularly interesting.

History

Before the Europeans came, the land was the home of the Eastern Woodland Indians, among them the Iroquois and Algonquin, particularly in the south. They lived mostly from cultivating maize, beans and squash; they knew nothing of rotation of crops or of fertilising the land, and after ten years, when the soil was exhausted, simply moved on, taking the whole village, where large families lived in longhouses, to another place. The Huron, on the other hand, were nomadic traders in fur and other goods, and they were the first to make contact with the French on the lower reaches of the St Lawrence.

Samuel de Champlain decided in 1610 to push French influence further west and, with the Huron as allies, became the first missionary. The first Jesuit mission station was built in 1639 but Christian attempts at expansion came to an abrupt end in 1650 when the Iroquois destroyed it.

In 1673 the Hudson's Bay Company founded Moosonee, the oldest settlement in the province, on Hudson Bay in the north. Ontario itself came about as a result of the American War of Independence. After Canada became British in 1763 10,000 Loyalists moved here from America, and, led by Joseph Brant, the Six Nations Indians, who had fought on the side of the British, settled on Grand River.

Speedy settlement led to self-administration and in 1791 the old province of Québec became divided into Upper and Lower Canada, with Upper Canada becoming Ontario after 1867, at first with Niagara-on-the-Lake as its capital, and then Toronto.

In 1812 the Americans attempted to capture Canada and declared war. Since England was busy fighting Napoleon at the time the Americans

Ontario: an old fire-station   *Trillium, the flower of the province*

thought it would be an easy conquest, but they met bitter resistance on the Niagara Peninsula. Success in this struggle sharpened local self-awareness and gave Upper Canada a sense of its own identity.

After the Anglo-American war the policy of encouraging immigration with land-grants and other inducements led to a quadrupling of the population. Between 1820 and 1840 1.5 million people emigrated to Upper Canada from Europe alone, in search of a better life and bringing with them new strengths and political ideas. The successful struggle for democracy and parliamentary government in Europe made Canada appear backward, with power residing in the hands of the British Governor and a few influential groups. The armed uprising led by William Lyon Mackenzie in 1837 was soon put down but it set the struggle for independence on the move again and in 1867 Ontario and Québec headed the Confederation of provinces, set free from England.

There are 125 seats in the provincial parliament and thanks to the British first-past-the-post voting system the Conservatives have held power since 1943. Ontario, on the basis of its population, is entitled to 95 members in the Federal Parliament and 24 senators in the Senate.

Province and Administration

Together with Québec, Ontario is one of the two Canadian provinces to have two-tier local government, with counties as well as parishes and towns. Planning committees, especially in the Toronto conurbation, have recently been set up in an attempt to control urbanisation.

Since the first census in 1871 Ontario has demonstrably been the Canadian province with the largest population. From 1.6 million it reached 3.7 million in 1941. There was a new influx of immigrants after the Second World War, particularly from Europe. In recent years emigration from Asia has increased, and with the Crown Colony due to be handed over to China in 1997 a great many of the newcomers are Chinese from Hong Kong.

Population

Since the Second World War Ontario's population has risen up by about 1 million every decade. The most densely populated area is greater

Ontario

Toronto, with over 3 million people, tending to be concentrated in the urban areas, with over 65% in townships of more than 10,000 people.

Geographically speaking, 85% of the population live in the south on only 15% of the surface area. The north is virtually unsettled apart from mining, timber and fishing settlements.

The largest ethnic group is the 65% or so of originally British Canadians, followed by the French, Germans and Italians.

Farming and forestry

The southern part of the province has good fertile soil, and the growing period is one of the longest in the whole of Canada, yielding tobacco as well as maize, soya beans and sugarbeet. Fruit and wine can only be produced in very sheltered locations.

Furs, whether farmed or trapped, make a very important contribution to the economy in the north, and although timber does not play as great a part as in some other provinces its economic potential should not be underestimated.

Mining and Energy

Sudbury Basin was discovered in 1883 when the railroad was being built. It conceals the largest nickel deposits in the world, much of the output going to the USA. The primary deposits of plutonium also contain extractable amounts of platinum, gold, silver, cobalt, copper and tellurium.

In 1903, not long after Sudbury Basin, large silver deposits were found at Cobalt, again as a result of the railroad.

During the Second World War there was an economic boom in Atikokan as its iron ore was mined, then in the 1950s and 1960s the first uranium began to be brought out.

The Canadian Shield still has many mineral resources that can be tapped in the future, and outside the Shield, in the extreme south, salt and gypsum are also to be found in abundance. The absence of fossil fuels has inevitably led to the development and generation of waterpower.

Industry

About 50% of the goods that Canada produces come from Ontario. In value terms supply and vehicle manufacture are the main industrial sectors, but heavy engineering, iron and steel, rubber, paper and food and drink all make important contributions to the economy. Industry tends to be centred on Toronto, Hamilton (iron and steel), Windsor (vehicles) and Sarnia (petro-chemicals).

USA/Canada

Thanks to its common boundary with the States Ontario has closer links with the USA, and therefore greater economic interdependency, than any other Canadian Province.

Leisure, sport, tourism

Its many lakes, National and Provincial Parks, resort areas and magnificent scenery make Ontario an unforgettable holiday destination, with canoeing, camping, hiking and fishing in such lovely places as the Haliburton Highlands, Georgian Bay, Karwatha Lakes and Thousand Islands on the St Lawrence.

Canoeing

For Ontario canoeing is the national sport, whether it be on the clear waters of a quiet lake or shooting the rapids. Probably the best known mecca for canoeists is Algonquin Park, with 1600km/994 miles of water trails. Quenitico Provincial Park is on a similar scale, with 525km/326 miles of fur trapper canoe route and 43 cross-country routes. Details of routes and maps can be obtained from Ontario Travel (see Information section in Practical Information).

Another exciting experience is whitewater rafting on the Ottawa River.

Walking

There are good wilderness walks along the shores of Lake Superior in Pukaskwa National Park, a chance to observe nature in all its beauty. In fact all the other parks also have walks of various lengths and degree of difficulty.

Winter sports

Like everywhere in Canada, Ontario is good for winter sports, with cross-country trails and snowmobile tracks always accessible. There is also some downhill skiing at, for example, Thunder Bay and the Blue Mountains, which have fine, challenging pistes.

The fishing will gladden any angler's heart, particularly in the rugged north. All non-residents need a licence which can be obtained at specialist stores or from the Ministry of Natural Resources (see Practical Information, Fishing).

Fishing

Orillia   O 9

Province: Ontario
Population: 25,000

Georgian Lakelands Travel Association, P.O. Box 39, 66 Coldwater St. E, Orillia, Ontario L3V 6H9; tel. (705) 325–7160

Information

From Toronto on Highway 400 north to Barrie, then on Route 11 to Orillia.
    Orillia is a little town about 120km/75 miles north of Toronto (see entry) on the northern end of Lake Simcoe. It is also the gateway to the Muskoka Lakes region (see entry).

Access

For centuries Orillia was at the heart of lands that were home to many Indians. Samuel de Champlain passed through here in 1615.

History

Sights of Orillia

Couchiching Beach Park, with its statue of Champlain, is part of Orillia's bustling and attractive lakeshore area.

Couchiching Beach Park

The town's opera house is famous for its good acoustics.

Opera House

The town's great son was Stephen Leacock (1869–1944), Canada's famous author and humourist. A professor of political science at Montréal's McGill University, Leacock spent his summer holidays here, from where there are fine views over Brewer Bay, and he drew on the town for his book "Mariposa".

Stephen Leacock

His pretty holiday home, built in 1908, is off Highway 128 on Old Brewery Bay, and is now a museum (open: mid-June–end August daily 9am–5pm, mid-Apr.–mid-June and Sept.–mid-Dec. Mon.–Fri. 9am–noon).

Museum

Surroundings of Orillia

The Mara, who have their reserve outside Orillia, belong to the Ojibwa Indians. They make and sell fine examples of their native crafts and also act as guides on hunting, fishing and canoeing trips around Orillia's scenic lakeland.

Mara Reserve

There are boat cruises from Orillia in July and August on Lake Simcoe and Lake Couchiching.

Boat cruises

Lindsay is a resort about 80km/50 miles from Orillia via Highway 7, set in farmland with two big mills. It is a good place for fishing in the well-stocked local waters.

Lindsay

Lindsay is also a good base for trips to Kawartha Lakes, in their lovely setting, and the Haliburton Hills.

Kawartha Lakes

The Trent & Severn Canal is a whole system of waterways linking Lake Ontario with Georgian Bay on Lake Huron, wending its way through various river and lake systems, such as the Trent River and Lake Simcoe, in the east of Ontario Province.

★**Trent & Severn Canal**

The changing levels mean that it needs over 40 locks, including the world's highest hoist, built in 1905 at Peterborough (see entry), to operate a travelator covering a height of 20m/66ft.

In the past the Canal was mainly used for carrying grain and timber, and there were lots of mills along its banks, but these have nowadays been replaced by power stations. Visitors enjoy cruising the waterways too, and Orillia is a good place to start.

Muskoka   See entry

Oshawa   O 9

Province: Ontario
Population: 120,000

Information   Tourist Office, 13 John Quest Street; tel. (416) 728–1683

South-western Ontario is the commercial centre of Canada, and this is particularly true of the "golden horseshoe" which starts at Oshawa, on the northern shore of Lake Ontario, about 50km/31 miles from Toronto, and is the area between Lakes Michigan and Ontario where almost a third of Canadian industry is based and which is highly populated. The mainstay of Oshawa's business is the car industry, founded by the efforts of Robert McLaughlin, who began building automobiles here, starting with the McLaughlin Buick, in 1907 with his son, Robert Samuel McLaughlin (1871–1972). His plant eventually merged with the USA's General Motors in 1918, thus taking Oshawa from a lake port to being one of the main centres of the automobile industry in Canada.

Sights

★Parkwood   At 270 Simcoe Street in the north of the city, in a beautiful park stands the mansion of the industrialist, art collector and patron Robert Samuel McLaughlin. After the death of the owner the luxurious mansion was given to Oshawa in order that it might be opened to the public.

Robert McLaughlin Gallery   The Robert McLaughlin Gallery, downtown near the Civic Centre, built in 1969 and designed by Arthur Erickson, houses works of the "Painters' Eleven", a group of abstract artists founded in 1953. Open daily except Mondays the gallery has temporary exhibitions by contemporary Canadian artists as well as the permanent collection.

★Canadian Automotive Museum   This extremely interesting museum, charts the history of the automobile in Canada, using models, design drawings, photographs and other documents, best of all, its collection of over 80 vintage cars from between 1898 and 1930, including the 1912 McLaughlin Buick. Open: daily; tel. (416) 576–1222.

Surroundings

Cullen Garden   Whitby, on the way from Oshawa to Toronto (see entry), is definitely worth a visit to see Cullen Garden, a park of over 20ha/49 acres which, in addition to its masses of flowerbeds and other park features, also has painstakingly accurate miniature versions of Ontario's historic buildings, monuments, farms, etc. (open: daily; tel. (416) 668–6606).

Othello-Quintette Tunnels Historic Park   E 8

Province: British Columbia

Information   See British Columbia

★Old railroad   To get to the Othello-Quintette Tunnels Historic Park, in Coquihalla Canyon Recreational Area, take the Kawkawa Lake road and the Othello road. The tunnel in the Coquihalla Canyon for the Kettle Valley Railway (closed in 1959) will give the visitor the feeling of being back in the good old days of steam, when the Canadian Pacific line was laid between 1911 and 1918 linking the Kootenays with the Pacific.

The old railway bridges between the tunnels were replaced with hair-raising foot bridges in the 1960s. Anyone wanting to follow the tunnel trail should definitely take a good torch!

See Fraser Valley

Yale
Fraser Canyon

Ottawa   O 9

Province: Ontario
Population: 305,000 (Greater Ottawa 820,000)

Ottawa Tourist Office, Metcalfe St (on Parliament Hill); tel. (613) 239–5000   Information

Canada's capital is more strictly bilingual than any other place in the country.   Languages

By air: Access
Ottawa International Airport has commuter airlines from most large Canadian cities, especially Toronto and Montréal, plus direct flights, particularly in summer, to the major European cities.

By rail:
VIA Rail – Ottawa's station was relocated a few years ago from the centre to the south-east of the city. Trains run several times daily to Toronto and Montréal.

By bus:
The city is well served by the Canadian intercity bus lines.

Ottawa Transit's city buses run at short intervals on an extensive and closely integrated system of routes.   City buses

Ottawa stands at the confluence of the Ottawa and Rideau rivers, and is also the starting point of the Rideau Canal linking it to Lake Ontario. The city grew up between 1820 and 1840 from the construction base which had been set up where the Rideau Canal diverged from the Ottawa River. In charge of the project was the British Colonel John By (1779–1836) and consequently the town was known until 1853 as "Bytown". In 1854 the town changed its name to Ottawa.   History

From 1864 Ottawa was developed as the Canadian capital. The Parliament buildings were built in 1865, high above the Ottawa River, and this is where, in 1867, the first Canadian Parliament met following the founding of the Dominion of Canada.

In the course of time Ottawa has become a busy government seat, with all the marks of the federal city, but it has some industry too, especially timber, paper and printing.

Although the city may have been considered rather provincial in the past, it now has a very real feeling of the international metropolis, due in no small measure to the cosmopolitan nature of the many people who have come to live here.   Capital city

As Canada's capital Ottawa not only houses the national parliament but also the Supreme Court, as well as the many government departments and cultural institutions such as major museums and two universities, plus a Catholic and an Anglican bishop.

As the seat of government of a nation that is an economic force to be reckoned with, Ottawa has also been able to develop into a top-ranking venue for conferences, many of them of worldwide significance.

Conferences

Together with Hull (see entry) in Québec Province on the other side of the Ottawa River, Ottawa has succeeded more than any other Canadian city in developing a life of lively intellect and culture. The Royal Society of Canada, University of Ottawa, Carleton University and several research institutes have all contributed to this, as have such internationally famous venues as the National Arts Centre (since 1969; opera, concerts), the National Library and Archives, the National Gallery (since 1988 in a fine new building by Moshe Safdie) and the Canadian Museum of Civilization (since 1989 in an imposing new building by Douglas Cardinal, see Hull).

Science and culture

Although Ottawa cannot be said to have the commercial importance of Montréal or Toronto (see entries), in recent years a great many major companies have made it their headquarters, particularly in the high-tech sector, and its status as a capital city and centre for the arts have also attracted bankers, stockbrokers, and insurers, together with publishers.

Business interests

Parliament Hill · Rideau Canal

The Parliament Buildings, in all their splendour of Victorian Gothic sandstone, are quite an imposing sight on their 50m/165ft high hill looking out over the Ottawa River, and, with the highrise towers that have grown up around them of late, seem to frame the city skyline.

The building of the Houses of Parliament was begun in 1860. In their Neo-Gothic style, they look as though they have been transplanted straight from Westminster. The part that was destroyed by fire in 1916 has been completely restored.

★★ **Houses of Parliament**

The Peace Tower (glockenspiel with 53 bells), in the centre, was built in 1927 to commemorate the Canadian dead of the First World War.

Peace Tower

The two houses of Parliament, the House of Commons and the Senate, are in the buildings on either side of the Peace Tower, and can be visited, as part of a guided tour, along with Confederation Hall and the Hall of Honour (tickets can be obtained from the Information Service in the grounds, but apply in good time).

Legislative Building

The Parliamentary Library, at the back of the building opposite the entrance, is a wonderfully furnished octagon that was untouched in the 1916 fire. Its beautifully panelled interior is very reminiscent of the Reading Room of the British Museum in London.

★★ Library

The east wing houses the Government offices, some of them restored to look as they did in the 1870s in the time of Lord Dufferin and Premier John Macdonald.

East Wing

The MPs and Senators have their offices in the west wing, which also used to contain support services such as the printroom and the employees' quarters.

West Wing

In front of the Parliament buildings extends an attractive grassed area which is patrolled in summer by members of the Canadian Mounted Police, looking very dashing in their Mountie uniform of scarlet jackets, stetson, riding breeches, and kneeboots.

★ Grounds

◄ *Ottawa: Parliament*

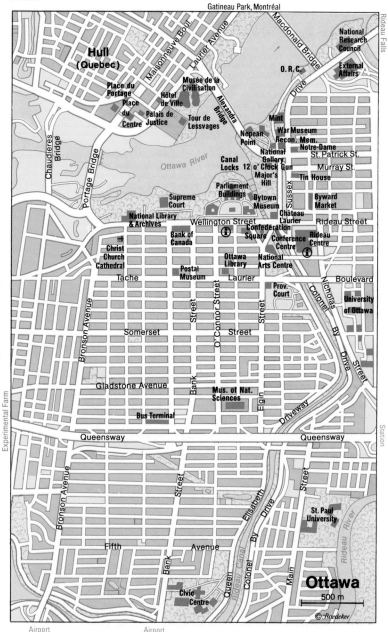

Gatineau Park, Montréal

Hull (Quebec)

National Research Council

O.R.C.

External Affairs

Rideau Falls

Macdonald Bridge

Laurier Avenue

Maisonneuve Boul.

Place du Portage

Place du Centre

Hôtel de Ville

Palais de Justice

Tour de Lessvages

Alexandra Bridge

Musée de la Civilisation

Mint

War Museum

Recon. Mem.

Notre-Dame

St. Patrick St.

Murray St.

Tin House

Nepean Point

National Gallery

Ottawa River

Canal Locks

12 o' Clock Gun

Major's Hill

Chaudières Bridge

Portage Bridge

Supreme Court

Parliament Buildings

Bytown Museum

Byward Market

National Library & Archives

Wellington Street

Confederation Square

Château Laurier

Rideau Street

Christ Church Cathedral

Bank of Canada

Conference Centre

Rideau Centre

Tache

Postal Museum

Ottawa Library

National Arts Centre

Boulevard

Bronson Avenue

Street

O'Connor Street

Laurier

Street

Prov. Court

University of Ottawa

Nicholas

Colonel

By

Drive

Street

Somerset

Street

Street

Gladstone Avenue

Bank

Mus. of Nat. Sciences

Elgin

Driveway

Bus Terminal

Queensway

Queensway

Station

Experimental Farm

Bronson Avenue

Street

Elisabeth

Drive

Street

St. Paul University

Rideau River

Fifth

Avenue

Bank

Queen Canal

Rideau

Colonel

By

Main

Ottawa

500 m

© Baedeker

Civic Centre

Airport

Airport
Kingston, Toronto

Houses of Parliament

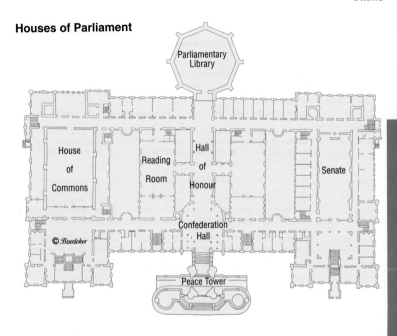

The Changing of the Guard takes place on the front lawn every morning at 10am in July and August, weather permitting.

Changing of the Guard

The Centennial Flame in front of the main building was lit in 1966 to commemorate the centenary of the Canadian Confederation.

★Centennial Flame

The sculpture in the grounds behind the Parliament building, from which there is a fine view across the Ottawa River, includes statues of Queen Victoria and several famous Canadian prime ministers. Many of them are by Philippe Hébert, a notable sculptor from Québec Province.

Sculpture Garden

Below Parliament Hill there is a really lovely walk that runs alongside the Ottawa River.

★River walk

Canada's Supreme Court is to the south-east of the Parliament and has a glistening green roof. Built in 1875, it also has a good view of the Ottawa River.

Supreme Court

Colonel By's Rideau Canal starts east of the Houses of Parliament, in a gully taking it up from the Ottawa River to the Rideau valley through a system of 9 locks that bridge the difference in height between the two rivers. The War of 1812 with the young United States had shown how easily the US could threaten the St Lawrence. After the war the Duke of Wellington despatched scouts to upper Canada to see if a solution could be found to the difficult situation. Colonel John By was sent to Canada in 1826 to oversee the building of a canal that would circumvent the dangerous waters of the St Lawrence and provide an alternative route for navigation as far as Lake Ontario 200km/124 miles to the south-west. The canal was finished in 1832 but never achieved its anticipated strategic or economic importance.

★★Rideau Canal

Ottawa

★★Locks	The locks were completely overhauled some years ago, and an interpretive trail runs alongside the canal.
Old Commissariat	Ottawa's oldest surviving stone building, the Commissariat, built in 1827 as a depot for military supplies, is now the Bytown Museum (open: mid-May–mid-Oct. daily, mid-Oct.–Nov. and Apr.–mid-May weekends only), and tells of the early days of Ottawa, or Bytown as it was called at the time.
Canal, Colonel By Drive	By climbing up alongside the staircase of locks the level stretch of the canal is reached. Here in summer there are boat trips and in winter, when the canal is frozen over, hundreds of skaters enjoy themselves on the ice.
Events by the canal	The canal banks provide space for all kinds of activities. Winterlude/snow-balling: in February the winter festival takes place. Then the canal becomes a gigantic fair on ice. At many places professional and amateur artists try their hand at ice-sculpture.
Festival of Printemps	Festival of Spring: in mid-May this spring festival marks the ending of winter as the tulips – given by Queen Juliana of the Netherlands in grati-tude for the city's hospitality during the Second World War – come into bloom all over the city. The canal banks are the scene of general festivities, full of festival-goers, including those from the nearby Arts Centre.
Fête du Canada	Ottawa Festival: this lively event takes place in July, complete with flower parade and waterborne procession and entertainment to suit every taste.
★Château Laurier	An ornate building, with the air of a medieval castle but actually built in 1912, the Château Laurier, at the upper end of the canal locks, is a prime example of the grand hotels built by the big Canadian railroad companies, which is what it still is today.
Conference Centre (former rail station)	The splendid conference centre in front of the Château Laurier was actually Ottawa's central station until that was transferred to the south eastern edge of the town in the 1980s.
Rideau Centre	Ottawa's latest grand mall, the Rideau Centre, is an ultra-modern complex of shopping arcades, cinemas, restaurants and conference rooms, on what was railway land behind the former station.
★National Arts Centre	Set amidst lawns, in themselves a kind of sculpture park, the National Arts Centre, the cultural "pulsating heart" of Ottawa, has three auditoria famous for their acoustics. Leading national and international orchestras, appear here, as do opera, theatre and dance companies.

Upper Town

	The fashionable Upper Town extends below Parliament Hill and south-west of the Rideau Canal. The streets are laid out in a checkboard pattern. The busy thoroughfares are Wellington Street, Kent Street, O'Connor Street, Metlalfe Street and Sparks Street pedestrian precinct.
Confederation Square	The principal square of the city is Confederation Square at the upper end of the Rideau Locks staircase, below the Parliament Buildings. It is also the eastern gateway to the Upper Town. The main post office is situated here.
★Sparks Street	Canada's first pedestrian mall, Sparks Street can be said to be the Upper Town's shop window, a string of top department stores and smart bou-tiques, together with banks and business houses, interspersed with gour-met eating places.
★Bank of Canada	Probably the most striking architecture of the Upper Town is the Bank of Canada building, by the famous architect Arthur Erickson. The atrium

behind the twelve-storey tinted glass façade has the feeling not so much of a bank as of a great greenhouse, with works of art, plants the height of trees, and the splashing of fountains.

The Currency Museum is inside the original Bank of Canada building, and has a cross-section of coinage ranging from ancient China, Greece, Rome and Byzantium, through medieval Europe and the Renaissance, to the detailed evolution of currency in North America as it is today. This includes playing cards from "Nouvelle France" and the tokens used for payment by the Hudson's Bay Company.

★Currency Museum

Place de Ville is at the south-west end of Sparks Street.

Place de Ville

Not far from Sparks Street several ultra-modern highrise buildings, such as Minto Place, the Metropolitan Centre and the Four Seasons Hotel, thrust their way into the Ottawa skyline.

Highrise buildings

Lower Town · Major's Hill

Ottawa's busy Lower Town, the city's market place, full of food stores and market stalls, lies to the north of the Rideau Canal, with Rideau Street its main thoroughfare.

Byward Market has enjoyed a colourful existence since 1846. In summer the food stores in the main market hall are supplemented by stalls in the streets between the market buildings where fruit, flowers and vegetables are on sale. In fact around the whole market area, lovingly restored a few years ago, with lots of restaurants, smart boutiques, etc., there are delicacies on sale from all over the world, further proof of just how cosmopolitan a city this is.

★Byward Market

Just north-west of the market hall, Tin House Court with a pretty fountain is a delightful little courtyard with some of the city's oldest buildings, including the façade of a house owned by a former tinsmith, and decorated by him with examples of his work.

Tin House Court

On Sussex Drive, at St Patrick Street opposite the new national gallery, Notre Dame is the church of the Catholic bishopric. Consecrated in 1846 it contains beautiful mahogany carving by Ph. Parizeau, figures of the four evangelists, prophets and apostles by Louis-Philippe Hébert, and some particularly fine stained glass.

★Basilica of Notre Dame

Major's Hill Park, south-west of the basilica, aflame with thousands of tulips in May and June, is where the noonday gun stands, an old ship's cannon which since 1869 has been fired at noon on weekdays and 10am on Sundays and public holidays.

Major's Hill
12 o'clock gun

Protruding into the river at the southern end of Alexandra Bridge, Nepean Point has a fine view over the river, and on clear days it is sometimes possible to see as far as the Gatineau hills to the north.

On the point stands an idealised version of a statue to Samuel de Champlain (see Famous People), who passed this way in 1613 to 1615.

Nepean Point

Also on Sussex Drive, the Canadian War Museum (open: daily 10am–5pm) concerns wars fought on Canadian soil and others that Canadian forces took part in, including the fighting between the French and the Iroquois in the 16th c. and the Canadian contribution to the First and Second World Wars (e.g. diorama on the Normandy landings).

Canadian War Museum

Erected in 1994 the bronze Reconciliation Memorial near by provides a fitting monument to the dedication of Canadian Blue Caps in fulfilling a

Reconciliation Memorial

Basilique Notre-Dame

Tin House Court

12 o'clock gun

peace-keeping role – in Korea (1947), Palestine (1948) and more recently the Golan Heights, the former Yugoslavia and Somalia.

The National Gallery of Canada, designed by Moshe Safdie, is an architectural masterpiece, a highly successful, ultra-modern building that, with its prism-like glass towers, echoes the lines of the nearby Parliament Buildings, and while strongly contrasting with their Neo-Gothicism and the mock medieval Château Laurier nevertheless fits very well into Ottawa's cityscape.

★★ National Gallery

Location
Sussex Drive, near Nepean Point

Open:
May–Sept.
Tues.–Sun.
10am–6pm;
Oct.–Apr.
10am–5pm

Ground Floor:
The gallery shop, auditorium, lecture rooms and cafeteria are on the ground floor, with a colonnade leading to the prism-shaped great hall.

First Floor:
The first floor traces the development of Canadian art, including early religious art from Québec and Nova Scotia (much of it 19th c.), the reconstructed late 19th c. convent chapel, works by Tom Thomson and the Group of Seven, by Paul Kane, Emily Carr and Cornelius Krieghoff, and by Jean-Paul Lemieux, the Canadian Group of Painters, and L. L. Fitzgerald, as well as such contemporary artists as Ian Carr-Harris, Yves Gaucher and Guido Molinari.

Second Floor:
The second floor covers a wider spectrum, ranging from European art of the 17th and 18th c., through Impressionism, and up to American art after 1945, in addition to 20th c. British artists, international Modernism, and art from Asia and the Far East.
    The rooms of Inuit art between the library and the great hall are particularly worth looking at.
    Print, graphics and photography are shown in temporary exhibitions.

Among the gallery's major works, those by Canadian artists include "Joseph Brant" (1805) by William Berczy, "North Shore, Lake Superior" (1926) by Lawren S. Harris, "Blunden Harbour" (1930) by Emily Carr, "Journey on Foot" (undated) by Pitseolak, and "Reason over Passion" (1968) by Joyce Wieland.

Major works
(selection)

From Europe come Hans Memling's "Virgin and Child with St Antony", Lucas Cranach the Elder's "Venus", and El Greco's "St Francis of Assissi", together with "The Mechanic" (1920) by Fernand Léger; also works by Gustav Klimt, Pablo Picasso, Claes Oldenbourg, George Segal and Andy Warhol.

Other sights around Ottawa

Laurier House, halfway between the Rideau Canal and the Rideau River, stands on Avenue Laurier. It was the residence of a number of Canadian Prime Ministers including Sir Wilfrid Laurier, Prime Minister from 1896 to 1911, and William Mackenzie-King, Premier from 1921 to 1930 and 1935 to 1948, and also contains reminders of Nobel Peace Prizewinner Lester Pearson, Prime Minister from 1963 to 1968.

Maison Laurier
Laurier House

Since 1989 the National Museum of Natural Sciences has occupied the beautiful building that was the National Museum of Man (see Hull, Canadian Museum of Civilization), on the southern rim of downtown Ottawa. The museum traces the earth's geology and the making of seas and continents, focusing particularly on North American aspects such as meteor strikes, mineral deposits, etc. Highlights include the dinosaurs found in the Alberta Badlands, and there are wildlife dioramas showing North American and mammals such as Arctic musk oxen, moose from eastern Canada and grizzly bears from British Columbia, as well as birds of Canada and the distribution of the country's flora and fauna.

★National Museum
of Natural Sciences

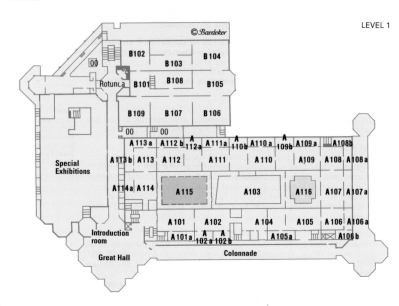

National Gallery of Canada · Ottawa

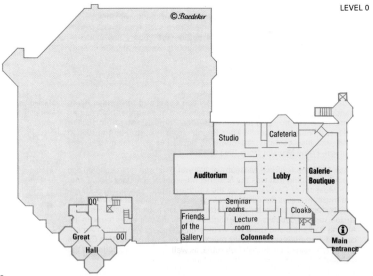

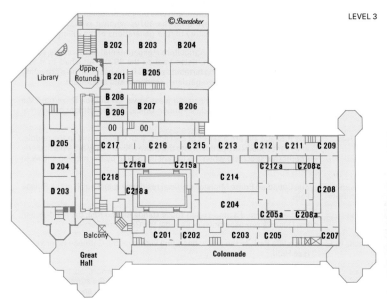

L'Outaouais

Billings Estate	Billings Estate, in the south of the city near the Rideau River, is one of the oldest estates still left in Ottawa, and was built by Braddish Billings in 1828. His descendants lived here until the 1970s when it was made into a museum tracing the life history of four generations of the Billings family.
★Experimental Farm	The Canadian Ministry of Agriculture's experimental farm, on the south-western edge of the town, dates back to the 1920s. Attached to it is a farming museum, showing farming as it was in the past, and also providing guided tours of the kitchen-gardens, seedbeds and arboretum.
Pearson Building	The Pearson Building, a gleaming glass tower on Sussex Drive near the Rideau Falls, houses Canada's Foreign Office, the Department of External Affairs.
★Rideau Falls	The Rideau Falls are a series of cascades, with Green Island in the middle, where the Rideau drops down into the Ottawa River. They are a particularly impressive spectacle when the torrent is swollen by the melting snows in spring.
Prime Minister's official residence	The Canadian Prime Minister's official residence is just north of the Rideau Falls.
Rideau Hall	Further east amid a green open space stands Rideau Hall, the residence of the Queen's representative in Canada, the Governor General.
★Rockcliffe Park	Rockcliffe Park, to the north, has a fine view over the Gatineau River valley (see Hull).
★National Aviation Museum	The National Aviation Museum is at Rockcliffe Airport, on the northern edge of town, and dates from 1988. Telling in detail the story of Canadian civil and military aviation, among the aircraft on display are a replica of the Silver Dart, which in 1909 made the first flight in Canada, fighter planes from the First and Second World Wars, and some of the seaplanes and other aircraft that helped open up Canada's uncharted northern wilderness. The Royal Canadian Airforce Hall of Tribute commemorates the exploits of the service.
★National Museum of Science & Technology	On the eastern edge of the town, this is another museum worth visiting. Exhibits include a Nova Scotia lighthouse, old boats and farming equipment, a whole series of vintage cars and an Atlas rocket, vintage steam engines and steam locomotives. There are also special exhibitions about communications and modern physics, and an interesting collection of timepieces. Astronomy and space exploration are also covered and the museum has an excellent observatory for stargazing on clear nights.
Portage	At the south-western end of Wellington Street lies the southern end of Portage Bridge. Here there is a little park by the rapids of the Ottawa River containing a number of panels showing the development of industry in the Ottawa area, alongside an ageing hydro-electric plant, and some unsightly industrial buildings and old mills.

L'Outaouais

	Provinces: Québec, Ontario
Information	See Québec and Ontario
	The area known as "l'Outaouais" stretches along both sides of the Ottawa River between the cities of Ottawa and Montréal (see entries). North of this 300km/186 mile-wide stretch of land there are the low hills where the tumbling tributaries of the Ottawa River such as the Rouge, Lièvre and Gatineau have their source.

The Ottawa River always has been of major importance. Samuel de Champlain (see Famous People) had already realised on his first expedition in 1603 that the Huron and Algonquin used it to get from the Great Lakes to the St Lawrence to barter their furs. From then on it was the crucial transport link in the Canadian fur trade. Its history is one of strife, punitive expeditions and bloody massacres, as well as treaties.

In the 18th c. Canadian "voyageurs", such as the fur company men, took over from the Indians, travelling in fleets of canoes, hundreds of men at a time every year, to the Great Lakes in spring, even getting as far as James Bay (see entry), and returning laden with furs in the autumn.

As the fur trade began to decline in importance in the early 19th c. the American Philemon Wright started up a new industry by commercially exploiting the forest timber, an industry that is still of considerable importance in the Québec economy today, albeit beset with problems. Wright set himself up near what is now Hull (see entry) in a beautiful country estate. He had no income to start with that would cover the vast expense that his plans involved, but finally he saw his chance. Deprived of its timber sources in Scandinavia by the Napoleonic Wars, England was desperately looking to its American colonies to meet its demand for wood. The densely forested Outaouais had plenty, and it could easily be floated down in rafts to the next port, Québec, so in the winter of 1805/1806 Wright had his men felling the pines and the other trees.

The first consignment of timber was finally despatched on June 11th 1806 down the Ottawa River from Gatineau to the St Lawrence (see entry). After this success the lumberjacks of Québec in their thousands fell upon the timber on the banks of the Ottawa River and its tributaries. In 1860 the Bishop of Ottawa estimated that there were more than 20,000 "Hommes des Bois" in his diocese alone.

In Gatineau Park, just outside Hull and Ottawa (see entries), the Outaouais has one of the province's most beautiful parks, as well as the Papineau – Labelle nature reserve.

The Papineau – Labelle nature reserve, named after the Canadian politician who had his home there, has rivers, lakes, waterfalls, dams and his "Petite-Nation" estate.

There is plenty going on in the constantly expanding towns of the Outaouais. Hull, its capital (see entry), has changed a lot since the 1970s, and is now home to over 20,000 Federal government employees.

★ Tour of the Outaouais (from Montréal, about 430km/267 miles)

This route is mostly along Highway 148 to Hull, and then Highway 17. Ferries can provide shortcuts – it is possible to cut 260km/162 miles off the journey just by taking the ferry from Fasset to Lefaivre. From Montréal, take Autoroute 40 towards Ottawa, then after 13km/8 miles Autoroute 13 towards St-Eustache.

St-Eustache (pop. 34,000), after 33km/21 miles, is on the eastern part of Lac des Deux-Montagnes. Its church still shows signs of the fighting in 1837 when about 250 of the "patriot" rebels, only half of them armed, made a stand in the church, the presbytery and the adjoining buildings, but were unable to withstand the English soldiers and their cannon.

From St-Eustache continue on Route 344, passing Park Paul-Sauvé. This is an estate leased by Louis XV to the Siegneur of St-Sulpice, and acquired by the province in 1962. Walnut trees, oak and elm grow right down to the lakeshore. Fishing is allowed, but not hunting.

The resort of Oka (pop. 1500), almost 60km/37 miles further on, is famous for its "Oka" cheese, at one time made by the Trappist monks of Notre-Dame-des-Lacs, a foundation dating from 1831. Of the pilgrimage chapels

(1740–42) that used to stand on the hill near the lake, only three remain (date of pilgrimage September 14th).

Como ferry Como can be reached by a ferry that operates from 6.30am to 5pm or 11pm, depending on the season (tel. (514) 458–4732 for information).

Sainte-Placide The village of Sainte-Placide, on Lac des Deux-Montagnes, is the birthplace of Sir Adolphe Routhier (1839–1920), who wrote the French words to the Canadian national anthem.

Carillon Carillon, a former trading post, was a popular base for travellers en route to the high country. A monument commemorates Adam Dollar des Ormeaux and his companions who, together with a number of Huron and Algonquin, held out behind a palisade for days against several hundred Iroquois at the Long Sault rapids.

Ferry to Pointe-Fortune There is a ferry to Pointe-Fortune that operates from April to December between 7am and 9pm.

Grenville Grenville, after 103km/64 miles, is an industrial town that grew up out of a trading post, founded by English settlers in 1809, where a canal was built between 1819 and 1823 to bypass the Long Sault rapids. This was replaced by a new one in 1963, leading to Carillon. A bridge over the Ottawa River makes it possible to get to Hawkesbury.

Calumet Calumet is a timber town beyond Grenville.

Fasset Between April and December, from 6am to 10pm, Fasset has a ferry service over to Lefaivre (Ontario).

Montebello Montebello (pop. 1500) is a pleasant village in what were the hunting grounds of the Algonquin.

Château Montebello's Château, near the Château de Montebello Hotel, was built in 1850 by Louis Joseph Papineau. A liberal deputy to Lower Canada's legislative assembly, and subsequently leader of the rebel "Patriots" in 1837, he returned to Canada in 1845 from exile in the USA and Paris, where he had become friends with the Count of Montebello. The château was also the childhood home of Henri Bourassa (1868–1952), the liberal politician and founder of the newspaper "Le Devoir", and it was his father Napoléon Bourassa (1827–1916), an architect, artist, sculptor and writer, who was responsible for building Montebello church.

Plaisance Plaisance is a village built on part of the Petite Nation estate, which was leased by the East India Company to the Sieur de Laval in 1674, when the company held the monopoly for the fur trade.

Thurso The industrialised village Thurso (pop. 3000) was founded in 1886 to take out the timber from this part of the Ottawa valley. There is a ferry to Rockland from April to December between 7am and midnight (tel. (819) 423–5025 for information).

Masson Masson is mainly concerned with producing pulp for the paper industry. It has a ferry to Cumberland between April and December (on request).

From Masson Route 309 proceeds towards Mont-Laurier and the mining town of Buckingham, and to Val-des-Bois, near an entrance to the Papineau–Labelle nature reserve.

Hull
Gatineau (Park) See Hull

Peace River

Province: Alberta

Information See Alberta

The Peace River, which gets its name from "Peace Point" on its lower reaches, rises in the Rocky Mountains of British Columbia. Its two main tributaries are the Smoky River and the Heart River. On leaving the Rockies, it flows east through the Peace River Valley, and then turns northwards. After 1920km/1193 miles, just north of Lake Athabasca, it joins the Athabasca River (see entry) to form the Slave River, the largest of the rivers flowing into Great Slave Lake.

The middle section of the Peace River Valley, in the eastern Rockies, with places such as Grand Prairie, Peace River and High Prairie – an area of 65,000sq.km/25,090sq.miles – is famous as fertile farmland with higher-than-average yields of grain and vegetables (potatoes, wheat, rye, etc.). Its good climate and topography meant that the valley was settled very early on, developing into an important farming region and centre for the fur trade, particularly with the coming of the railroad in 1915.

Farming

Peace River (town)

Province: Alberta. Population: 6000

Land of the Mighty Peace Tourist Association, P.O. Box 3210, Peace River T0X 2X0

Information

The little town of Peace River, on the banks of the river of the same name, lies in the heart of the Peace River Region. Its history goes back to the early 18th c., when it was already a meeting place for traders and fur trappers. The explorer Sir Alexander Mackenzie (see Famous People) set out from here in 1742 on his expedition to the north.

The town has a larger-than-life wooden statue of its most famous son, the legendary Henry Fuller Davis. A spectacular gold discovery made the "little" man – his nickname was "Twelve-Foot Davis" – into a local celebrity overnight, and the town still likes to remember the kindness and generosity of its esteemed citizen.

Henry Fuller Davis

See John Hart Highway

Peterborough

O 9

Province: Ontario. Population: 62,000

See Ontario

Information

Peterborough is the gateway to the Kawarthas, part of the Trent–Severn Waterway lake district and the centre of a recreational area extending from Rice Lake in the east to Lake Suncoe in the west.

Peterborough was founded in 1818 when a sawmill was built on the river here. The area around it has many traces of Indian settlements.

History

The area just north of the town on Lake Story, now protected as a Provincial Park, has more Indian rock drawings than anywhere else in Canada, with about 900 which are between 500 and 1000 years old. The park is open from mid-May to mid-October between 9am and 6pm.

Sights

★ Petroglyph National Park

Peterborough's locks are one of its special attractions. Uptown it has three locks regulating the waterlevel for shipping, among them the famous hydraulic lock built in 1904. One of only eight of its kind in the world, it enables vessels to overcome a difference in waterlevel of 20m/66ft.

★ Locks

The Interpretive Centre has exhibitions and audio visuals showing how the locks were built and how they work (open: mid-May–mid-Oct. 9am–5pm). The centre also covers the Trent–Severn Waterway, popular for boating holidays, which has another hydraulic lock and more than 36 ordinary locks.

★★Waterway cruises

In summer and autumn cruises on the waterways depart from the landing in the town centre. The various trips are particularly enjoyable when the leaves are changing colour in the autumn.

Surroundings

Lang Century Village Museum

It is worth taking a trip just 20km/12½ miles along the TransCanada Highway to Lang Century Village Museum which is a reconstruction of a 19th c. pioneer village. The old mill, dating from 1845 and in full working order, is particularly interesting. There are displays of the old craftsmen's tools in, for example, the mill, smithy, and sawmill, etc. The museum is open 1 to 5pm from mid-May to mid-October.

Point Pelee National Park N 9

Province: Ontario

Information

See Ontario

Point Pelee National Park is at the southernmost point on the Canadian mainland, an almost triangular peninsula which juts out into Lake Erie. It has long been famous as a resting place on the path of many migratory birds, and for its now very rare Monarch butterflies.

Morphology

The sandy peninsula of Point Pelee came into existence about 10,000 years ago, when wind and water deposited great quantities of sand here from the slowly retreating glaciers of the last Ice Age. In places this sand is still as much as 60m/200ft deep.

★Plantlife

Its favourable climate has given the peninsula lush mixed woodland, mostly deciduous, but also some evergreens. Its trees include mountain maple, walnut, mulberry, hickory (pecan), and red cedar, along with various kinds of hops, climbers and creepers. There are also plenty of prickly pears, with their lovely yellow flowers.

★★Bird reserve

Point Pelee is where two major bird migration routes meet so that in spring and autumn often over a hundred different bird species can be seen in a day, and there are more than 300 species recorded in the course of the year.

★Monarch butterfly

In September the trees of this national park are full of beautiful Monarch butterflies resting, like some of the birds, on their migration to the south.

Boardwalk

From the boardwalk with two tower hides on the edge of the marsh it is possible to see fish, turtles and musk rats as well as birds.

Lighthouse

A lighthouse off the southern tip of Point Pelee warns passing ships of the shallows around the peninsula.

Visitor Centre

The Visitor Centre, open daily, has films and slideshows about various aspects of the National Park, plus very interesting leaflets, etc. (canoe and bike rental, picnic sites, refreshments; tel. (519) 326–3204 for information).

Park railway

A little train takes visitors round the park, starting from the Visitor Centre.

Portage la Prairie H 7

Province: Manitoba. Population: 13,000

Information

See Manitoba

A rare visitor to the most southerly point of Canada

Many early French explorers passed through here on their way to Lake Manitoba, in their vain search for the Northwest Passage to the Far East, and this is where, in 1738, Sieur de la Vérendrye built Fort La Reine as his base for exploring the prairies. The town's name dates from that time, when it was on the portage between the Assiniboine River and Lake Manitoba. John Sutherland Sanderson made it the first settlement in western Canada.

Manitoba's history is vividly illustrated by the displays in Fort La Reine Museum and the Pioneer Village on the outskirts of the town at the intersection of Highways 1A and 26 (open: May–mid-Sept. Mon.–Fri. 8am–6pm, Sat. and Sun. 10am–6pm).

Sights

★ Fort La Reine Museum, Pioneer Village

The museum complex includes a trading post, a smithy and stables, and the Pioneer Village has an early wooden house, a trapper's cabin, the "Farm of the Century", a country church and an 1880s schoolhouse. Other exhibits include a reconstructed York boat and a Red River wagon, brought here from Joliette, Québec, for Manitoba's centenary. These carts drawn by oxen were the principal means of transport of the early settlers. Built entirely of wood they were very noisy because their wheels were not greased against the dust. A railway service wagon can also be seen.

Island Park and Crescent Lake Nature Reserve, with its horseshoe-shaped lake, are also worth a visit to see the deer and wildfowl, including the large colony of captive Canada geese.

Surroundings

★ Island Park, Crescent Lake

The park also has a little zoo, a golf course, tennis courts and picnic sites, as well as canoeing and swimming facilities. The monument to Arthur Meighen commemorates this son of Portage La Prairie who was elected Canada's Prime Minister in 1920.

Prescott   O 9

Province: Ontario. Population: 5000

Information

See Ontario

Founded by Loyalists in 1784, Prescott was for a long time an important port on the St Lawrence because of the rapids downstream. These held up the grain shipments so they had to be loaded onto barges here to continue the journey, or to be ground into flour in the town.

★ Fort Wellington

The main building of Fort Wellington is the restored blockhouse, but the officers' quarters and fortifications can also be seen. The fort was the scene of heavy fighting when William Lyon Mackenzie led his supporters and American allies in rebellion.

Museum

Nowadays the fort is a military museum, and stages re-enactments of the old military drill parades in the British and American uniforms of the time.

Lighthouse

East of Fort Wellington is a former windmill that was converted into a lighthouse in 1838. Mackenzie's supporters took refuge here during the uprising (open: mid-May–Sept. daily 10am–8pm; and Mon.–Fri. 9am–4pm at other times).

Prince Albert   H 7

Province: Saskatchewan. Population: 34,000

Prince Albert, a lively town on the North Saskatchewan River, is an important centre for the timber and farming areas of northern Saskatchewan. It is also the gateway to the Prince Albert National Park (see entry) north of the town.

Historical Museum

The Historical Museum (open: May–Aug. daily 10am–6pm, and by arrangement in winter) is housed in the Old Fire Hall (view over the river) and provides an interesting account of the history of the locality and the town (North West Rebellion, pioneers, Indians, mineral resources), with interesting photographs, documents and objects as well as staging annual photographic exhibitions.

Diefenbaker House

Diefenbaker House (open: mid May–beginning of Sept. daily 10am–8pm) commemorates the close links between Canadian Premier John Diefenbaker and the town, which was his constituency, telling his life story through photographs and other memorabilia.

Grace Campbell Gallery, The Little Gallery

Art lovers will be interested in the Grace Campbell Gallery (open: Sept.–June, Mon.–Fri. 9am–9pm, Sat. 9am–5.30pm, Sun. 1–5pm; and on Fri. and Sun. until 6pm in summer), the John Cuelenaere Library and the Little Gallery (open all year) in the Prince Albert Art Centre. These galleries show works by local, provincial and national artists (painting, photography, etc.).

Lund Wildlife Exhibit

The Lund Wildlife Exhibit on River Street, west of the river (open: June–Aug. daily 10am–10pm, Sept. and Oct. daily noon–9pm), has an outstanding collection of North American wildlife.

Prince Albert National Park   H 7

Province: Saskatchewan
Area: 3875sq.km/1496sq.miles

Prince Albert National Park, P.O. Box 100, Waskesiu Lake, Saskatchewan
SOJ 2YO; tel. (306) 663–5322

Probably Saskatchewan's most attractive park, Prince Albert National Park
is on the edge of the Canadian Shield as it stretches away to the north. The
gently undulating landscape is a mixture of spruce swamp, large lakes and
aspen-dotted uplands, the legacy of the ice that retreated from here about
10,000 years ago, but has continued to leave its mark on the park's flora and
fauna. The park is in an area of transition from aspen parkland to boreal
northern forest, and this is reflected not only in the park wildlife, but also in
the course of this area's history.

★★**National Park**

Native Americans have lived here for thousands of years, and there is
archaeological evidence that in severe winters tribes from the prairies
moved north up here to its sheltered woodlands, intermingling with the
people who lived here.

History

The park's creatures vary according to the habitat, with moose, wolf, black
bear, fox, lynx, caribou and eagles in the northern forests, and elk, deer,
badger, coyote and squirrel in the parkland in the south. The park has some
species that are unique in their national significance. There are also unique
resources of natural importance.

Wildlife

Lavallée Lake holds Canada's second largest colony of white pelican, and a
limited area in the north-west of the park is given over to one-third of
Canada's fescue grassland, once a widespread habitat, where one of the
park's two herds of buffalo still roam.

★★Lavallée Lake

Grey Owl, the best-known, colourful and at the same time controversial
naturalist of the 1930s, lived in this park for seven years in a small log cabin
called "Beaver Lodge" on Ajawaan Lake. A trapper turned conservationist
and author, his popular books, inspired by the woodland and wildlife of the
park, tell of his love for the wilderness and the people and creatures who
live there, threatened by the advance of civilisation. He returned to the lake
after his triumphant lecture tour of England and the States, and died in
1938, but his message – "remember you belong to nature, not it to you" –
lives on, and has even greater significance today. His cabin can be reached
by boat or canoe across Kingsmere Lake, or by a 20km/12½ mile trail from
the south end of the lake, where there is a campsite.

Grey Owl
★Beaver Lodge

The busy little resort of Waskesiu Lake which serves the park, at the edge of
its wilderness, gets its name from the Cree word for "red deer".

Waskesiu Lake

The Prince Albert National Nature Centre (open: end June–beginning Sept.
daily 10am–5pm) and has exhibitions on the themes of Grey Owl, the

★Nature Centre

M.S. "Neo Watkin" in the Prince Albert National Park

377

boreal wilderness, and the transition from the prairies grasslands, through parkland, to the northern boreal woodlands.

Recreation   Several hundred miles of trails and canoe routes allow the visitor the chance to see moose, wolf, fox and black bear in their natural surroundings, and well over 200 species of bird have been recorded. With one-third of the park area taken up by water, it is also possible to observe beaver, musk rat and otter. There is canoeing and boating on the many lakes, and Kingsmere, Crean and Waskesiu Lakes are all very popular with anglers. The park also boasts picnic areas, riding stables, beaches, tennis courts, good golf courses and fully serviced campsites, not to mention 150km/93 miles of cross-country skiing trails.

Prince Edward Island/Île Prince Edouard   R 8

Indian name: Abegweit ("cradled on the waves")
Situation: in the Gulf of St Lawrence
Area: 5657sq.km/2184sq.miles
Population: 123,000
Capital: Charlottetown
Language: English

Information   Department of Tourism, P.O. Box 940, Charlottetown C1A 7M5, Prince Edward Island; tel. (902) 368–4444.

Access   By plane:
Direct daily flights to Charlottetown from Toronto, Montréal, and Halifax.

By ship:
Car ferries from Cape Tormentine/New Brunswick to Borden and from Caribou/Nova Scotia to Wood Islands; also a ferry from Souris to the Magdalen Islands.

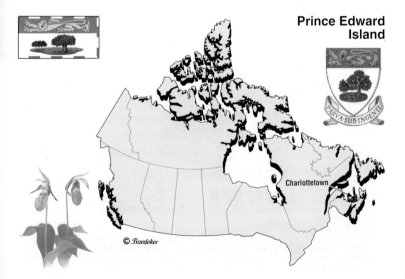

Prince Edward Island

Charlottetown

© Baedeker

By train/bus:
By train to Moncton/New Brunswick, then by bus to Cape Tormentine, and on the ferry to Borden and then to Charlottetown.

The Micmac Indian legend tells how the god Glooscap painted all of the world's beautiful places then dipped his brush in every colour and created Abegweit, his favourite island. Canada's smallest province, but one of its loveliest, Prince Edward Island's natural beauty lies in its gently rolling hills and scenic beaches of powdery white sand in the north, and edged with red sandstone cliffs in the south. Its pleasant climate, good beaches and rural charm make it a favourite with holidaymakers who swell its population every year to well over half a million. Unlike its neighbours, most of the island's countryside is farmland, thanks to its exceptionally fertile, brick-red soil.

Situation

The island nestles in the Gulf of St Lawrence, separated from the mainland by the Northumberland Strait, only 14km/8½ miles across at its narrowest point. It extends between longitude 61° and 64° and between latitude 45° and 47°.
It stretches 224km/139 miles and is from 6km/4 miles to 64km/40 miles across. The coastline is broken up by a mass of bays and inlets, and its highest point, at 150m/492ft, is in Queens County.

Geology

Prince Edward Island is very young in geological terms. Its sandstone was formed by sediment deposited about 250–300 million years ago. The oldest sediments were found in the Miminegash region and the striking redness of the soil is due to the high iron oxide content. The whole island bears the imprint of the Ice Age. As the ice retreated about 15,000 years ago the sea level rose, and the three small islands that appeared in the Gulf of St Lawrence gradually grew together to form the present landmass.

Present morphology

The most spectacular morphological change is currently along the coast-line, where the erosive forces of wind and rain, waves and frost have created long beaches and sandbanks, and vulnerable sandstone can be worn away at the rate of several inches a year.

Climate

Thanks to its position in the Gulf of St Lawrence, Prince Edward Island has pleasantly moderate temperatures, although it can become very cold in winter. In high summer the thermometer can climb up to 30°C/86°F. The precipitation of 1090mm/43in. falls on only 160 days of the year. July and August are the driest and warmest months, when the water around the island can be as warm as 21°C/70°F.

Vegetation

About 90% of the land on the island is farmed. Potatoes are the main crop, but some cereals and other vegetables are grown as well. There are size-able orchards, but no real woodland.

Wildlife

Over 300 bird species have been recorded on Prince Edward Island. These include albatross, petrels, cormorant, gannet, heron, osprey, etc.

History

The mainland Micmac Indians, who came here about 2000 years ago and named the island "Abegweit". As nomadic people they lived in small groups, fishing in summer and hunting on the mainland in winter.
France laid claim to the island as early as 1523, even before Jacques Cartier sailed here in 1534. He was fascinated by the glorious beauty of the island. The French named it Île St Jean, and the first of them arrived in 1663. In 1719 the first influx of immigrants of any size settled in Port de la Joie, now Fort Amherst. Jean-Pierre de Roma founded a settlement at Three Rivers, Brudenell Point, in 1732, and French Acadians came here in 1755, driven out of Nova Scotia by the British. Apparently the Micmac and the early French settlers managed to live in relative harmony with one another.
After the French fortress of Louisbourg on Cape Breton Island fell into British hands in 1758 many of the local French settlers fled to Prince Edward

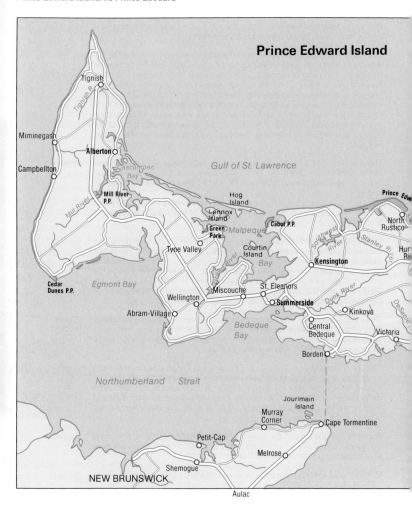

Prince Edward Island

Tignish
Tignish R.
Miminegash
Alberton
Campbellton
Cascompec Bay
Mill River P.P.
Mill River
Gulf of St. Lawrence
Hog Island
Lennox Island
Green Park
Malpeque
Cabot P.P.
Prince Edw
North Rustico
Tyne Valley
Courtin Island
Bay
Southwest River
Stanley River
Hur R.
Kensington
Cedar Dunes P.P.
Egmont Bay
Wellington
Miscouche
St. Eleanors
Dunk River
Kinkova
DeSable
Abram-Village
Summerside
Central Bedeque
Victoria
Bedeque Bay
Borden
Northumberland Strait
Jourimain Island
Murray Corner
Cape Tormentine
Petit-Cap
Melrose
Shemogue
NEW BRUNSWICK
Aulac

Island, prompting the British to occupy the island and deport the Acadians because of their questionable loyalty to the British crown. They were sent either to British North America, or to England to be returned to France after the war. The few who remained on the island escaped deportation by fleeing into the woods.

Under British rule, St John's Island (as the British called it) was annexed to the colony of Nova Scotia in 1763. In 1764/65, General Samuel Holland divided the island into three administrative districts and 67 lots, each of 20,000 acres, and these were drawn for in London by wealthy Englishmen at a grand lottery for the distant colony. This led to a century of struggle against absentee landlords and harsh rent collectors until finally, in 1853,

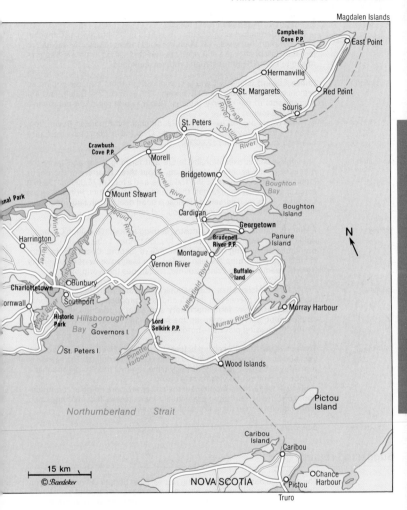

the Land Purchase Act enabled the island government to buy back most of the land. When Prince Edward Island joined the confederation in 1873, the rest of the land was acquired and sold. In 1769 the island won independence from Nova Scotia and became a British colony in its own right.

Many British settlers, mostly Scots, came here during the 18th and 19th c. The Montgomerys arrived around 1770, and early Scottish immigrants settled in Scotchfort and Tracadie. After 1803 the Selkirks from the Scottish Highlands settled around Eldon, to be joined on the island by many loyalists who moved north following the American War of Independence.

The legislative assembly named the island Prince Edward in 1798 after the Duke of Kent who was later to become the father of Queen Victoria, and who was commander of the English troops in Halifax at that time, and the island got its own government in 1851.

The Conference of Charlottetown was held in 1864 to discuss Canadian Confederation, but it was 1873 before the islanders reluctantly decided to join the Union, after the still relatively new federal government had promised to set up communications with the mainland.

Population	Prince Edward Island is Canada's smallest but most densely populated province. Its population is 80% British, 17% French, 2% Dutch, and 4% descendants of the original Indians. About two-thirds of its people live outside the towns. There was a big increase in population after the American Revolution, when the British loyalists fled to Canada. Over the last ten years the figure has held steady at about 123,000.
Agriculture	The island soil is exceptionally fertile and farming is far and away the mainstay of the economy, employing about three quarters of the population. Each farm is around 63ha/156 acres, and a total of 70,000ha/172,970 acres is given over to potatoes, the island's main product. Prince Edward produces all its own cereals, as well as a good deal of fruit and vegetables such as apples, strawberries, broccoli and tomatoes.
Fishing	Fishing is another important industry, earning almost 180 million Canadian dollars a year, with catches totalling 100,000 tonnes. Lobsters are the most profitable, accounting for half this source of income. Cod, sole, herring, salmon, trout and tuna are also landed, and Malpeque oysters, originally from Malpeque Bay in Prince County, are famous the world over.
Industry	Prince Edward Island has little manufacturing, and what there is is mostly associated with processing its fish and farm products, but there is some printing, glass fibre, farm machinery and paint production. In terms of employment, services make up the largest and fastest growing sector. Timber processing plays a subordinate role.
Tourism	Tourism is the island's second biggest earner, with over 700,000 visitors a year and bringing in more than 110 million Canadian dollars. The season is from May to October, but is at its peak in the summer months, although the number of year-round visitors is growing. Many of the farmers supplement their income by providing accommodation for tourists, and there are actually more tourist flats, cottages and rooms in farms than there are hotel and motel rooms.
Charlottetown	See entry

Suggested routes

The province has three sightseeing routes, Lady Slipper Drive, Blue Heron Drive and Kings Byway Drive, all of them scenic routes around the island's beautiful coast which also take in other major attractions. They are clearly marked and can be followed by car or bicycle.

Although varying in length from 190km/118 miles to 375km/233 miles, each of them can be done in a day by car. There are other attractions not actually on the route, but because distances on the island are surprisingly short none of them are much of a detour.

Although these routes are signposted clockwise along the highways they are, for convenience described here in an anti-clockwise direction.

★**Lady Slipper Drive (about 300km/186 miles)**   Named after the Lady Slipper orchid, Prince Edward Island's floral emblem which grows in its shady woodland, the drive is signed by a red orchid in a red frame on a square white background. The drive follows the coastline in the western part of the island, with its red sandstone cliffs, silvery sands and lush green meadows, passing through peaceful farmland growing mostly potatoes.

This part of Prince County has lots of little villages, many of them quite old and still following a traditional way of life. Here live the descendants of the French-speaking Acadians who since 1884 have had their own flag as a symbol of their cultural unity.

The Acadian Pioneer Village (open: in summer daily 10am–7pm) at Cape Egmont, 5km/3 miles west of Mont Carmel on the Acadian Shore, is a recreation of an authentic early 19th c. village, with a church, village hall, store, school, a well and smithy. The houses have objets d'art and restored furniture of the period.

★Acadian Pioneer Village

Further north along the coast, at the island's westernmost point, the 2km/ 1 mile white-sand beach of Cedar Dunes Provincial Park is overlooked by the West Point Lighthouse, an old wooden lighthouse from 1874 that had its own keeper until thirty years ago. It was restored a few years ago and now contains a little museum a shop for craftwork and rooms for visitors.

★West Point

Early this century Alberton was a centre for silver fox farming for the fur trade, which had started up here in 1894 and flourished for four decades until it was badly hit by the depression of the 1930s. The tree-lined streets and fine big houses are a reminder of these prosperous times.

Nowadays Alberton is one of the home ports for Canada's deep-sea fisheries, and it is possible to make long-shore fishing trips from here.

Alberton

Alberton Museum is in the town's first courthouse, built in 1878 on the corner of Church Street and Howlan Street. It is a local history museum, with special emphasis on the silver-fox farming, as well as displays of Indian items, farm tools, books and photographs as well as other memorabilia (including furniture) of the early European settlers (open: July/Aug. Mon.–Sat., 10am–5pm).

★Alberton Museum

Lennox Island is the biggest Indian reserve in the province, and home to many descendants of the Micmac, whose history is recounted in its little museum.

Lennox Island

Malpeque Bay is where Prince Edward Island's world-famous oysters have their main beds. It is the centre of Canada's oyster-farming, yielding about 5 million oysters a year. In the west of Malpeque Bay numerous branches of the fishing industry have their bases.

★Malpeque Bay

The road to Green Provincial Park winds its way through woodland groves and open fields. At the centre of the park is the elegant villa of shipbuilding magnate James Yeo Jr. Built in 1865, the villa has been restored and filled with period furniture. The history of shipbuilding on Prince Edward Island is told in a modern exhibition building and a 19th c. shipyard at the water's edge shows how a wooden ship was built.

The park has what are probably the finest campsites on the island.

★Green Provincial Park

Blue Heron Drive, in the central part of the island, has as its main attraction the long silvery beaches of the North Shore – the best are in Prince Edward Island National Park (entrance fee only if by car). The drive passes through many little holiday resorts and many of the island's tourist attractions and leisure parks, the most interesting being places connected with that famous book "Anne of Green Gables".

From Charlottetown Blue Heron Drive follows the North Shore, with its fine beaches and red sandstone cliffs, then at New London Bay, further west, it comes to the home of the blue heron after which it is named (the sign is a blue heron on a blue-framed square white background). From here it turns south to the South Shore, with several Provincial Parks and their beaches, campsites and picnic areas, ending up back at Charlottetown.

★**Blue Heron Drive (about 200km/124 miles)**

Prince Edward Island/Île Prince Edouard

York

From Charlottetown take Highway 2 to Marshfield then Highway 25 to York. Jewells Gardens & Pioneer Village is a restored early 19th c. village surrounded by gardens, with a shop, smithy, school and chapel. There is also a glass museum.

★Prince Edward Island National Park

Take Highway 25 out of York, then turn right onto Highway 220 to Grand Tracadie, then left to Prince Edward Island National Park. This extends from Tracadie Bay in the east to Cavendish Bay in the west, a long line of lovely white-sand beaches. Over 200 species of birds can be seen here, including the superb blue heron. Despite the enormous influx of tourists in summer, the park has surprisingly managed to maintain its ecological balance.

★Cavendish

Cavendish has one of Canada's most popular beaches. Its Rainbow Valley amusement park of about 9ha/22 acres has pleasant gardens, a boating lake and a barn (open: June–Sept. Mon.–Sat. from 9am and Sun. from 11.30am until dusk; admission fee).

★Green Gables Farmhouse

The countryside around Cavendish was the setting for Avonlea, Lucy Maud Montgomery's fictional farming community of her famous novel "Anne of Green Gables". The Green Gables Farmhouse, about 2km/1 mile west of the town on Highway 6 near the Cavendish entrance to the national park, is an enduring reminder of this popular children's classic (open: mid-June–mid-Aug. 9am–8pm, otherwise 9am–5pm).

★Anne of Green Gables Museum

The "Anne of Green Gables Museum" is in the house built in 1872 where Lucy Maud Montgomery lived from time to time, and is packed with Montgomery memorabilia including signed copies of the first edition of the famous novel (open: daily, 9am–9pm).

★Malpeque

Malpeque is one of Prince Edward Island's historic sites. A home to the Micmac, it was settled by the French in the early 18th c. Captain Samuel Holland, sent here by the British in 1765, named the place "Princeton", but it later reverted to its old Indian name. Much of the later immigration was from Scotland, and many of their descendants still live here today.

★★Malpeque Gardens

One of the finest gardens in eastern Canada, Malpeque has several hundreds of different kinds of flowers, including dahlias and roses, and contains such interesting features as an old windmill and a showcase beehive.

Port de la Joie ★Fort Amherst National Historic Park

Port de la Joie, was the first place on the island to be settled by the French in 1720. The British built Fort Amherst here in 1758 after they captured the settlement, but today only the earthworks remain. The whole site has been declared a National Historic Park. The museum is open daily.

★Micmac Indian Village

Micmac Indian Village, near Rocky Point, is the reconstruction of a 16th c. village showing how the Micmac lived before the Europeans came; contains wigwams and canoes, hand-made hunting and fishing implements, and life-sized sculpture. The museum showing how the island's first inhabitants used their weapons and tools is particularly interesting.

Kings Byway Drive (about 380km/ 236 miles)

Kings Byway Drive, signed by a purple crown on a square white background with a purple border, is mostly in Kings County, hence its name, and takes the visitor through the most interesting parts of the island. The people who live here are predominantly the descendants of early Scottish settlers. Its special attractions include red and white sandbanks, photogenic lighthouses, and North Lake Harbour, which prides itself on being "the tuna fishing capital of the world". Anyone wanting to cover the whole drive should plan for two overnight stops on the way.

The drive starts from Charlottetown in the strawberry fields above the Hillsborough River, then runs south to Elden, and cuts across the hilly tobacco-growing district to the east coast. The provincial parks along the route provide plenty of opportunities for swimming and camping. The drive then follows the east coast up to North Lake Harbour then turns along the rugged north coast, passing through several little fishing villages before coming full circle in Charlottetown.

Prince George   E 7

Province: British Columbia
Population: 70,000. Height: 570m/1871ft

See British Columbia   Information

Prince George, on the upper Fraser River at its confluence with the Nechako, is the busy hub of northern British Columbia, with about 165,000 people living in its commuting area. It is an important junction, at the crossroads of the Yellowhead Highway (Hwy 16), Northern Canada's main east–west link, with Highway 97, which as the John Hart Highway runs north to Dawson Creek at the southern end of the Alaska Highway, and as the historic Cariboo Highway (see entry) runs south to Highway 1, the TransCanada Highway. Prince George is also a rail junction on the C.N. Railway route from Prince Rupert to Edmonton and the B.C. Railway route from Prince Rupert to Vancouver.

During his first expedition Alexander Mackenzie (see Famous People)   History
camped briefly at the confluence of the two rivers in 1793, and thought it a suitable place for later settlement. He was followed in 1806 by Simon Fraser of the North West Company, who founded Fort George here a year later as an outpost of Fort St James.
   Despite its strategic position the fur trade and the 1858 Cariboo gold-rush largely passed Fort George by, and it only began to boom with the building of the Grand Trunk Pacific Railway, which brought with it a flood of settlers and trades people.

In 1915 the two rival townships of Fort George and South Fort George (south of the Fraser) joined forces to become the new town of Prince George. By 1951 this had a population of 5000, mostly making their living from timber.

When three big paper and cellulose factories were built here in the 1960s, the population shot up to over 60,000. The advent of more industry resulted in Prince George becoming one of Canada's highest per capita income areas in the 1970s.

This pretty park on the bank of the Fraser River holds a replica of the old Fort   **Sights**
George, complete with palisades. The Fort George Regional Museum (20th   ★Fort George Park
Avenue; open: May–Sept. 10am–5pm) outlines the history and the background of the region (timber, ethnography, temporary exhibitions). There is also an Indian burial ground that can be visited.

There are several other older buildings worth seeing, including the school-   Other buildings
house and the station, with a steam train that runs at weekends in summer.

The Prince George Railway Museum in Cottonwood Island Park was   Prince George
opened in 1986 (River Road; open: May–Sept. Thur.–Mon. 10am–5pm).   Railway Museum

Prince Rupert   C 7

Province: British Columbia. Population: 17,000

See British Columbia   Information

The port of Prince Rupert is scenically located on Kaien Island among the fiords of Canada's often rain-shrouded Pacific coast just 60km/37 miles from the southern tip of Alaska. Its large ice-free natural harbour near the mouth of the Skeena soon made Prince Rupert one of Canada's prime fishing ports, but it is also important as the terminus of the Grand Trunk Pacific Railway, now Canada National Railway. Grain, coal and timber are shipped out through the port, which is also the main destination of B.C. ferries, sailing between here and Vancouver Island (see Inside Passage) and the Queen Charlotte Islands (see entry), and along the Alaska Marine Highway. The town and its fisheries expanded considerably after the Second World War, adding paper and cellulose to its other industries, and more recently tourism as well.

History

The town was founded in 1906 by Charles Hays, the ambitious General Manager of the Grand Trunk Pacific Railway, as a northern rival to Vancouver, and the railway line was completed in 1914. During the Second World War it served as a base for the Canadian and American forces.

Sights of Prince Rupert

Downtown walking tour

Downtown Prince Rupert still retains many of the buildings from its earliest years.

★Totem poles

Haida and Tsimshian beautifully carved totem poles can be found throughout the town as a reminder of the peoples who originally lived here. There are some particularly fine examples at Harbour Viewpoint, at Summit Avenue on the edge of Roosevelt Park, from where there is also a good view over the bay and the harbour, especially at sunset.

★Museum of Northern British Columbia

The Museum of Northern British Columbia (1st Ave./McBride St; open: mid-May–Labour Day, Mon.–Sat. 9am–9pm, Sun. 9am–5pm; at other times Mon.–Sat. 10am–5pm) is devoted primarily to the Indian culture of the Pacific coast. Outside the building is a brakeman's cabin of 1917, a former Skeena fishing boat; native carvers can be watched at work in the adjoining carving shed.

Court House

Near the museum stands the B.C. Court House, a building of 1921 in Neo-Classic style.

Sunken Gardens

Behind the museum lie the so-called "Sunken Gardens" which attract many visitors. They were laid out after the Second World War on the site of a munitions dump.

Kwinitsa Railway Museum

Next to the modern VIA rail station stands the former Kwinitsa Station. Built originally in 1915 and moved here in 1985, it contains a little museum on the subject of the building of the Grand Trunk Pacific Railway.

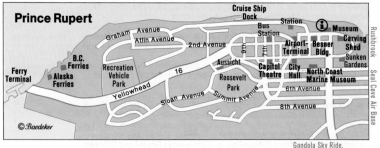

Gondola Sky Ride,
Terrace, Yellowhead

The Indian Cultural Days are in June every year and feature traditional Indian dances and crafts.

Indian Cultural Days

Surroundings of Prince Rupert

From the summit of Mount Hays (732m/2402ft) there is a magnificent panoramic view of the Pacific coast. On a clear day it is possible to see as far as the Queen Charlotte Islands (see entry) and the Alaska Panhandle. The cable railway from Prince Rupert (Wantage Road) takes four hours to reach the summit and operates in July and August (timetable available from the Tourist Information Centre, good skiing in winter).

Mount Hays

Hovercraft trips lasting several hours operate from Prince Rupert to Port Simpson, a remote Indian village about 30km/19 miles to the north. Set up as an outpost of the Hudson's Bay Company in 1834, Port Simpson is also served by a twice-weekly ferry or by hydroplanes from of the Seal Cove hydroplane terminal.

Port Simpson

Pukaskwa National Park

M 8

Province: Ontario

Pukaskwa National Park, Bag Service No. 5, Marathon, Ontario P0T 2E0; tel. (807) 229–0801

Information

Pukwaskwa National Park is 24km/15 miles south-east of Marathon on Highway 627.
    A vast park of 1900sq.km/733sq.miles on the shores of Lake Superior on the south-west edge of the Canadian Shield, with typical boreal pine forest.

The park centre is Hattie Cove, where the visitor centre has various displays and can provide information on the park's campsites, canoe routes and wilderness trails. The scenery is particularly pleasant along the shores of Lake Superior on the 64km/40 mile Coastal Trail where there are walks lasting one or several days.

Recreational facilities

Qu'Appelle Valley

J 74

Province: Saskatchewan

The Qu'Appelle Valley gets its name from the Indian legend about a young brave who is going on a journey in his canoe, but soon after setting out the beautiful young maiden he loves falls ill, and calls his name. Although some miles away, he hears her voice and turns around with the cry "qu'appelle?" – who's calling? When he gets back home the maiden is dead, and it is said that ever since his cry can be heard echoing through the valley.
    Pauline Johnson, the well-known Indian writer at the turn of the century, enshrined the valley in several of her poems.

Legend

The beautiful Qu'Appelle Valley, north of Regina between the TransCanada and Yellowhead Highways, extends along the Qu'Appelle River which rises in Lake Diefenbaker to the west of the province. In the floor of this steep-sided valley, carved out of the gently undulating prairie by the glacial waters following the Ice Age, there is a rich garden-style landscape.
    With good timber for both fuel and building it became a staging post for the fur traders before later attracting the pioneers. Eight lakes are strung out along the valley, from Buffalo Pound in the west to Round and Crooked Lake in the east, as well as several scenic parks and little townships.

Situation

387

| Katepwa Provincial Park | Katepwa – which is Cree for "calling river" – is a pretty little provincial park (8ha/20 acres) on the shores of Katepwa Lake, and has a lovely beach, particularly suitable for families with children. |

Lebret

In 1865 Lebret's Sacred Heart Church, also known as Fieldstone Cathedral, was the first church to be built in this district. The present building dates from 1925.

Fort Qu'Appelle

Fort Qu'Appelle museum (open: mid-May–Labour Day 10am–noon and 1–5pm, at other times by arrangement) is worth seeing. It is linked to an original Hudson's Bay Company trading post, and has displays covering the Indians, the pioneers and the North West Mounted Police.

★Echo Valley Provincial Park

Echo Valley Provincial Park, west of Fort Qu'Appelle, is in the heart of the Qu'Appelle Valley, and extends over 650ha/1606 acres between Lakes Pasque and Echo. It has scenic trails and good swimming in the lakes, as well as particularly fine fishing.

The Saskatchewan Fish Culture Station in the eastern part of the park, on Highway 210, is the only fish farm in North America that breeds fish for both cold and warm waters, raising about half a million trout and 20 million walleye and whitefish every year. The information centre is open to visitors May–Aug. 9am–noon and 1–4pm. There are guided tours throughout the year, by arrangement, and the best time for a visit is between January and July.

Buffalo Pound Provincial Park

The 1900ha/4695-acre Buffalo Pound Provincial Park (open all year), west of Regina in Qu'Appelle Valley, is where the Indians used to round up the wild buffalo herds, and there are still buffalo herds in the park today.

Buffalo Pound Lake within the park is ideal for all kinds of watersports, and the park has a big swimming pool, tennis courts, riding stables, campsites, a beach and trails, as well as downhill and cross-country skiing and ice-fishing in winter.

Québec (Province)   O–S 5–8

Area: 1.65 million sq.km/636,900sq.miles
Population: 6.6 million
Capital: Québec. Language: French

Information

Tourisme Québec, C.P. 20000 (Ville) G1K 7X2; tel. (418) 873–2015.

Québec reaches almost to the Arctic Circle in the north, and borders on Labrador, Newfoundland and New Brunswick in the east, the American States of Vermont and New York in the south and south-east, and Ontario Province and Hudson Bay in the west. It encompasses the east Canadian land mass north of the Ottawa and St Lawrence Rivers, while south of the St Lawrence it takes in the lowlands as far as the US border, as well as the Gaspé Peninsula projecting out into the Gulf of St Lawrence. In the west an artificial line divides Québec from Ontario, and in the east the border with Labrador is still a matter of dispute.

A vast province about one-sixth of the whole of Canada, Québec could accommodate the United Kingdom five times over, but has a population of only 6.6 million people representing a population density of just 4 per sq.km/10.4 per sq.mile. Most Québécois live in the two large conurbations of Montréal (about 3 million) and the provincial capital Québec (about 600,000). The province's lifeline is the St Lawrence, almost 1200km/750 miles long, which, with the St Lawrence Seaway, has since 1959 been the direct link between the Atlantic and the Great Lakes.

Natural features

Québec Province can be divided into three major physical regions. Firstly, the north belongs to the primeval Laurentian mountains, and is part of the

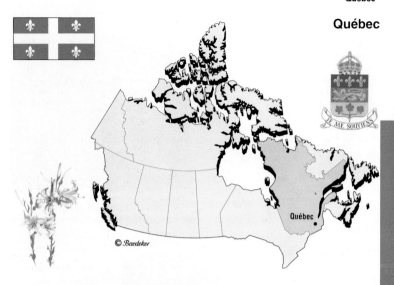

Canadian Shield. These rounded uplands, dotted with lakes, rise up to about 1000m/3,300ft, then slope gently down towards Hudson Bay and James Bay in the north. The Torngat Mountains in the north-east are the highest part of the Canadian Shield, reaching over 1500m/4900ft, while the densely wooded Laurentians form the southern edge of the Shield. The extreme south of the province and the Gaspé Peninsula, are considered part of the Appalachians, which extend as far as Newfoundland, and rise to between 970m/3184ft and 1270m/4168ft. The third region, the St Lawrence Lowlands between the Laurentians and the foothills of the Appalachians, was the first part of the province to be settled, and is today where 90% of the population live, on the rich land along both banks of the great river.

Québec's climate is influenced by its northerly position (45°–74°N) and the cold Labrador current. The north, and particularly the north-west, is sub-Arctic with bitterly cold, dry winters and cool summers, while the south of the province is subject to strong seasonal variation. With no high mountains to contend with, the air masses can circulate freely. Spring begins in April/May, and often lasts for only two weeks before the onset of the often humid heat of summer. Average temperatures are around 20°C/68°F, but records of 35°C/95°F are not unusual. Although it may have started abruptly, summer is slow to fade and there can still be a few warm, autumn days in late October, and sometimes even early November, those days of Indian summer when the bright autumn colours permeate the leaves of the mighty forests. Winters are cold, with a great deal of snow. The average January temperature in Montréal is −8.9°C/16°F, and further north up the St Lawrence River is even colder, with more and more snow. The average January temperature in Québec City is −11.6°C/11.1°F, and while Montréal gets 2.5m/8ft of snow, Québec gets over 3m/10ft, and Sept-Îles, still farther east, has more than 4m/13ft. It is thanks to this cold winter that the Canadians can rely on getting ideal conditions for their national game of ice-hockey.

Climate

As the climate varies from one zone to another, so does the vegetation, with fruit and vegetables being intensively farmed around the St Lawrence

Vegetation

The Gaspésie

and then, on the poor soil stretching far to the north, come the vast tracts of mixed timber (maple, birch and pine) which cover two-thirds of the province. Then as these woods peter out in the far north, the mosses and lichens take over.

History

In 1534 the Breton Jacques Cartier reached the mouth of the St Lawrence on his quest for a Northwest Passage, and on the shore of the Gaspé Peninsula he claimed the land on behalf of the King of France. The Algonquin and the Iroquois Indians lived at that time in large villages along the St Lawrence. On his second journey a year later Cartier got as far as the Indian settlements of Stadacona (now Québec) and Hochelaga (Montréal). However, when he returned to Paris from his third voyage in 1542 bringing only "worthless" minerals, interest in this far land waned for a while. This was to change in 1600 when Canada's wealth of furs, especially beaver, prompted Pierre Chauvin to set up a first trading post at Tadoussac. Samuel de Champlain set out to explore the St Lawrence, founding the settlement of Québec in 1608. He immediately began establishing links with the local Indians, and bartering for furs. Conflict with the Iroquois, who were allied with the British, began soon after, inhibiting further settlement, and the few colonists that there were lived in daily fear of attack.

It was Louis XIV who made the region the crown colony of "Nouvelle (New) France". Wanting to increase France's fame and prestige, he sent over troops and settlers, appointing the Comte de Frontenac, Louis de Buade, its governor. The province owed its stability to three factors: the absolutist government, the strong Catholic Church, and the seigneurial system, based on the French feudal system, whereby the landed gentry (seigneurs) rented out land to settlers (habitants) who paid their rents in kind.

Between 1641 and 1760 the French-speaking population grew from 500 to over 80,000. In the 18th c., however, the conflicts between the British and the French intensified, but the Seven Years' War (1756–63) put an end to

France's colonial aspirations and "New France" was ceded to Britain by the Peace of Paris in 1763.

In the Québec Act of 1774 the British Parliament guaranteed the French Canadians a say in their government and the right to their own language, religion and culture. When many English Loyalists moved up here after the American War of Independence, and the two differently structured national groupings fell out, it was decided, by the Constitutional Act of 1791, to divide the territory into Upper Canada (more or less present-day Ontario) and Lower Canada (Québec). The limitations on the rights of the elected parliament, which had no authority over the British Governor, led to unrest in both colonies. This was put down and well over half a million Québécois subsequently emigrated to the USA.

In 1840 Upper and Lower Canada joined together to become the "Province of Canada", and in 1867 the British North America Act made Québec a province in its own right in the Dominion of Canada, together with the other three provinces of Ontario, New Brunswick and Nova Scotia.

Little changed in the decades that followed in this province of farmers and lumberjacks, where the exploitation of its raw material resources was mainly in the hands of Anglo-Canadian and US business.

The end of the 1940s saw Québec's French-speaking majority starting to take up the cudgels against the overbearing role of the Anglo Canadians. The movement gathered strength in the 1960s and the "Parti Québécois" went as far as to demand full independence from the state of Canada. In 1974 French was declared the sole official language, and two years later the "Parti Québécois" won the provincial elections. A provinical referendum held in 1980 produced a majority against secession but following the separatists' spectacular election victory of 1994 the question once again has been re-opened.

Iroquois

In the 17th c. the powerful Iroquois Nations represented a great threat to the settlers of New France. In 1657 they even besieged Québec. Armed with muskets and tomahawks by the Dutch and the British, the war-like Iroquois were greatly feared, often luring soldiers and traders into ambushes or falling unexpectedly on homesteads. Their great rivals were the Huron, but they managed to eliminate them in the mid-17th c. This was despite the arrival of the Carignan-Salières Regiment and the bounties offered by the French – 20 crowns for every Iroquois captured, and 10 crowns for every Iroquois scalp.

The Iroquois settled around Lake Erie and Lake Ontario, living in large families in the longhouses of their little villages. They grew some crops but lived mainly from hunting, fishing, and fur trading, and usually wore garments of deer-skin. They also held great religious festivals every winter, and celebrated harvest with ritual dances by masked men swinging axes and spears.

Population

Québec is the French province of Canada – 82% of its 6.6 million people are of French origin. The 11% who have British ancestors live mostly in and around Montréal. The rest are mainly descendants of Italian, Jewish, Greek and German settlers, and in recent years there has been an influx of Vietnamese and Hispanics. The Indians and Inuit, who live in small settlements in the north of the province, are becoming an ever smaller group.

Québec's present-day French-speaking population can actually be traced back to a very small group of immigrants. These were the 10,000 or so French people who came here between 1608 and 1759. It was their birthrate of 10–15 children per family that led to the present population figure. In the recent past, however, as in other industrialised countries, the birthrate has declined sharply and, according to the statistics, there is now only an average of 1.5 children per family.

Economy

The three mainstays of the Québec economy can be summed up as wood, minerals and water.

Over half the province's vast forests are used commercially for timber, of which about three-quarters is softwood which is turned into cellulose and

Tapping maple syrup

paper. Québec supplies one-fifth of the world's newsprint, and has no fewer than 60 paper mills producing over 7 million tonnes of paper a year.

Mining

The province's mineral resources are concentrated in the rocks of the Canadian Shield, which abound in various ores. The large deposits in the Abitibi and Témiscamingue region in the west account for one-fifth of Canada's copper and gold; silver, zinc, lead and nickel are also there in smaller amounts. Iron ore has begun to be mined on the Ungava Peninsula in Labrador (see entry) relatively recently. Québec is also the world's largest producer of asbestos, with what is reckoned to be over one-third of all the asbestos in the world in the south-east of the province, in the foothills of the Appalachians at Estrie (see entry).

Farming

In the late 19th c. 70% of the people of Québec were still engaged in farming but today that proportion is down to less than 30%, and agriculture's contribution to total production has dropped to about 4%. Very little of the land actually lends itself to farming, yet the regions around Montréal, the St Lawrence lowlands, parts of southern Québec and the Lac St Jean district (see entry) produce fruit and vegetables, meat and dairy products in sufficient quantities to feed the people of the province.

Energy

Richly endowed with waterpower, the province has enormous hydro-electric power stations on the Rivers St Lawrence, St Maurice and Manicouagan, but the largest and most modern is on the Grande Rivière (see Baie James) and produces over 10 million kW. Much of Québec's energy is exported to the USA. Its power sources have also led to Québec becoming one of the world's top aluminium producers. The services sector makes another considerable contribution to the prosperity of the province.

New technology

In recent years a number of high-tec companies based in Québec province have made names for themselves, in electronics and telecommunications in particular.

Vive le Québec – libre . . .

Charles de Gaulle's rallying call during a visit to Montréal in the summer of 1967 was deeply ambiguous: was he simply applauding the achievements of the largest francophone community in the western hemisphere; or was he expressing his support for the separatist vision of a free (i.e. independent) Québec? Certainly his remarks caused deep offence to some members of the federal government of the day.

The seed sown by the French president quickly took root. A great many French Canadians, especially Québécois, considered themselves, as still today, imposed upon in numerous aspects of their lives by the English-speaking majority. In the 1960s and 1970s the Québécois independence movement grew significantly, eventually forcing a referendum on the issue in Québec Province in 1980 and 1995; more than 40% voted in favour of secession from federal Canada.

Although a majority of the electorate in Québec Province, in which approximately a quarter of all Canadians reside, have long demanded greater, more far-reaching powers of self-government, a nationwide referendum in 1992 voted against granting special status to the province with its distinctive language and culture.

That the dissatisfaction of French Canadians had diminished not a whit in the intervening year was made abundantly clear by the parliamentary election of autumn 1993 from which the francophone separatist Bloc Québécois emerged the second most powerful political force in Canada. French-speaking members of parliament from Québec Province, whose declared aim is secession from the Canadian federation, now form the strongest opposition group in the Lower House in Ottawa.

Québec Province itself was led until recently by a committed federalist and Liberal, Robert Bourassa. In elections which took place in 1994 the Québécois Separatist Party emerged the victors. This gave fresh impetus to the movement fuelled by the deep economic recession.

Québec

St Lawrence River   As far as transport is concerned, the St Lawrence River is the backbone of the province; Québec City, Montréal, Trois Rivières and Rimouski all have important freight and container ports.

Tourism   Tourism also plays a large part in Québec's economy, with many of Canada's visitors arriving at Montréal's two international airports, Dorval and Mirabel, probably the most important airports in the east of the country for both domestic and international air traffic.

Québec (City)   P 8

Province: Québec. Population: 170,000 (Greater Québec: 605,000)

Information   Office de Tourisme et des Congrès de la Région de Québec, Rue d'Auteuil 60, Québec, G1R 4C4; tel. (418) 692–2471.

Access   By plane: Québec has an international airport which foreign airlines and charter companies make use of mainly in the summer months. There are good connections with Canadian domestic flights, particularly to Montréal and Toronto (the hub of Canada's air network) as well as to New York (USA).

By rail: Several trains a day run between Montréal and Québec.

By coach: Being one of the most popular tourist destinations in North America Québec enjoys the benefit of excellent long-distance coach services. These include services to the big east coast cities of the USA.

★★Location and general   Québec City (the name derives from the Indian word "kebek" meaning "at the meeting of the waters") is situated at the mouth of the Rivière

The idyllic situation of the City of Quebec

394

St-Charles which flows into the St Lawrence River at the head of the St Lawrence Estuary. The city, built on a rocky spur reaching a height of 100m/330ft, considers itself the "cradle of North America" and still retains something of a European air. Ever since its foundation in 1608 by Samuel de Champlain (see Famous People) Québec has been the political, spiritual and intellectual heart of "la Nouvelle France" (New France). As well as being the capital of Québec Province it is a university city and the seat of both Roman Catholic and Anglican archbishoprics.

Québec is also an important commercial and industrial centre (e.g. for the food and brewing industries, leather goods, textiles, wood and metal processing, engineering, shipbuilding and the printing trade). Its port handles more than seven million tonnes/tons of merchandise a year.

95% of Québécois are French speaking. Wherever the visitor goes – be it to a shop, a restaurant or the theatre – the French way of life is always in evidence. Québec Old City has been designated a historical monument and is listed by UNESCO as a World Heritage Site.

Tourist centre

There are four reasonably large ski resorts and 20 golf courses all within a radius of 40km/25 miles of the city. Hunting, fishing, tennis and watersports (including white-water rafting on the Rivière St-Charles and sailing on the St Lawrence) are among other leisure activities also well catered for.

In 1608, having penetrated as far as this stretch of the St Lawrence River, Samuel de Champlain (see Famous People) established a small settlement on the northern bank close to the confluence with the Rivière St-Charles. Initially a centre for the trade in furs, within a few years the arrival from Paris of Louis Hébert, an apothecary, saw the infant colony developing a thriving agriculture. The soils of the nearby Île d'Orléans were found to be extremely fertile, as were those of the north bank of the St Lawrence below the Montmorency Falls where climatic conditions also proved especially favourable. The colony grew rapidly to become the administrative centre of French America. From Québec expeditions pushed upstream into what is now the province of Ontario, as well as southwards to the foothills of the north-east Appalachians and beyond to where the city of New York would later be founded.

History

Despite its defensively strategic position on a rocky spur protected on two sides by rivers, Québec fell to the British in 1629, only to be returned to France in the Treaty of St-Germain. In the autumn of 1690 a British fleet of some three dozen ships commanded by Admiral Sir William Phipps appeared off the town, carrying more than 2000 troops. Bad weather intervened however to thwart their assault.

The British under General Wolfe again laid siege to Québec in the summer of 1759. This time the fleet of more than 40 ships carried 2000 cannon and an army 10,000 strong. Wolfe stationed his troops on the Île d'Orléans – abreast of Lévis on the southern bank of the St Lawrence – and also near the Montmorency Falls. Québec was subjected to heavy bombardment. In September 1759 a force of 5000 led by Wolfe made a landing on the north bank of the St Lawrence and a bloody battle ensued on the Plains of Abraham between the British and the French under Montcalm. Both Wolfe and Montcalm lost their lives in the carnage. A few days later the British entered Québec. The French, having retreated to their winter quarters near Montréal, returned the following April to defeat the British at the Battle of Ste-Foy. Little was gained by the victory however, New France being finally ceded to Britain in the Treaty of Paris of 1763.

In 1774 the "Québec Act" was passed by the British Parliament guaranteeing religious freedom for the French population and ensuring the survival of the French Civil Code.

In the winter of 1775/76 troops from Britain's rebellious American colonies tried to enlist the aid of their northern neighbours in the struggle for independence, laying siege unsuccessfully to Québec. When in the following spring the British frigate "Surprise" appeared in the river the Americans withdrew.

Chûtes Montmorency, Ste-Anne-de-Beaupré, Île d'Orléans

Nouvel Palais de Justice

Gare du Palais

CHARLESBOURG, BEAUPORT

Parc de la Jeunesse

Rue Prince Edouard

Rue Mgr-Gauvreau

Rue de la Reine

Rue du Pont

St-François

Rue St-Paul

Rue des Prairies

Barra

Rue Côte Samson

Centre d'Achat

Rue Ste-Marguerite

Rue de l'Église

Fleurie

Rue de la Couronne

Rue Dorchester

Rue

Artille
Sœurs
Grise

Sœurs
de la Charité

Patronage
St-Vincent de Paul

Olo
Foun

Rue Côte d'Abraham

Avenue Dufferin-Montmorency

Pa
Montc

Richelieu

Rue St-Jean

Rue St-Joachim

Rue St-Olivier

Rue Ste-Geneviève

St-Mathieu

Centre
Municipal
des Congrès

Rue Ste-Claire

Rue Sutherland

Rue

St-Jean
Baptiste

Rue St-Gabriel

Hôtel
Parlem

Rue St-Jean

Rue Lockwell

Rue Claire Fontaine

Boulevard St-Cyrille Ouest

Rue Lachevrotiere

Parc de
l'Amérique-
Française

Marie-Guyart

St-Amable

Manège
Militaire

Bon-Pasteur

Rue

Grande Ouest Allée

Avenue Laurier

Grand
Théâtre

Synagogue

Boulevard St-Cyrille Ouest

Rue Turnbull

St-Cœur-
de-Marie

Grande Ouest Allée

La Laurentienne

Grande Ouest Allée

Avenue Laurier

Avenue Georges VI

Parc des

Champs de Bataille

Avenue Cartier

Aquarium, Airport

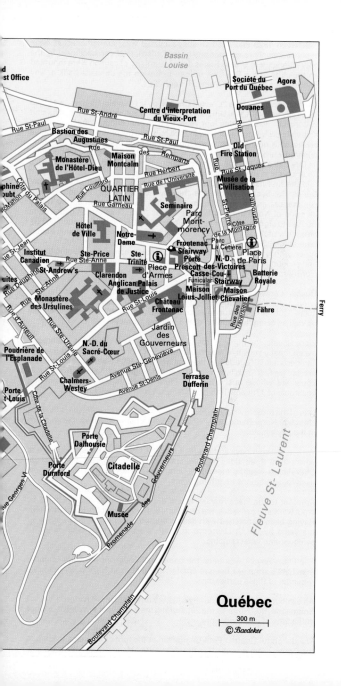

Québec

300 m

© Baedeker

Between 1820 and 1850 Québec's citadel was strengthened at huge expense, mainly to counter any further attempts at encroachment by the now independent United States. Large numbers of cannon were mounted on the cliffs of the Old City, trained to fire on the opposite bank or any hostile ships in the St Lawrence River.

The first meeting of the "Conseil Général de la Nouvelle Québec" was held in the city in 1648. Laval University – now the foremost institution of its kind in Canada – was founded four years later. Within another fifteen years the erstwhile proud capital of New France had also become the administrative centre of a new French speaking province of Québec. Over the next hundred years or so the city acquired its very Parisian parliament building, its City Hall and, in 1892, its most famous landmark, Château Frontenac, a luxury hotel in the style of a medieval château.

In the first half of the 20th c. Québec endured a period of stagnation. During the Second World War the city was the venue for some major conferences and it was here in 1943 that the Allies planned the D-Day invasion of Normandy. In 1945 delegates from 31 countries gathered in Québec to sign the charter setting up the World Food Organisation (WFO), an agency of the United Nations which had itself been founded only a short time before. Since the 1960s the city, one of the most beautiful in North America, has enjoyed something of a renaissance as the administrative and economic capital of its region and the focal point of French culture in North America.

Lower Town

Québec's Lower Town, site of the original settlement, is built on the low-lying ground bordering the St Lawrence. The Upper Town, atop the 100m/330ft cliffs, grew up to accommodate the government of New France as well as being the location of the military barracks.

★★ Place Royale

Place Royale, the nucleus from which the city developed, has undergone exceptionally sensitive restoration in recent years. It stands on the site of Québec's actual foundation, the spot where, in 1608, Samuel de Champlain erected his first "habitation", a farm and storage shed. Named in honour of Louis XIV whose bust adorns it, Place Royale is the largest surviving ensemble of 17th and 18th c. buildings in North America.

★ Notre-Dame des Victoires

One of the most lovingly restored buildings on the Place Royale is the little church of Notre-Dame des Victoires (1688), a name which evokes so much in the city's history.

★ Maison Chevalier

With its tall chimneys and red tiled roof this fine stone house the wings of which form three sides of a square was built in 1752 for Jean-Baptiste Chevalier, a wealthy merchant. Completely renovated in 1959 it is now used for exhibitions on ethnography.

★ Batterie Royale

Adjacent to the Place Royale, facing out over the river and encircled by stout walls and palisades, the little Batterie Royale was constructed in 1691. Having been threatened with destruction on a number of occasions over the years by the St Lawrence in spate, a way has now been found of safeguarding what remains.

Maison Nicolas Jérémie

The Place Royale was once the commercial heart of old Québec and a merchant's shop has been re-created in the Maison Nicolas Jérémie as a reminder of those earlier days.

Maison Soumande

An exhibition devoted to the city's history is housed in the restored Maison Soumande (Rue Notre-Dame 29). Among the displays is a model of Québec at the time of its foundation.

Quartier Petit-Champlain

The delightful Quartier Petit-Champlain at the foot of the steps leading to the Upper Town is nowadays much favoured by artists and crafts people,

The Batterie Royale   *In the Upper Town*

many of whom have set up business there. Indian leather goods and furs in particular, also examples of Inuit art, are among the many items offered for sale.

Built to designs by the well-known architect Moshe Safdie the new Musée de la Civilisation (Rue Dalhousie 85; open: Tues.–Sun. 10am–5pm, Wed. 10am–9pm) is of great architectural interest in its own right. In addition to its permanent collection the museum mounts a variety of temporary exhibitions on different aspects of human civilisation. Among its prize exhibits are what is thought to be the earliest barque built in America (in Québec soon after 1608), vaulting from the Maison Pagé-Quercy, remains of the old town wharf and items of modern sculpture. Old furniture and various articles of everyday life contribute to a thoroughly fascinating re-creation of the early days of Québec.

★ Musée de la Civilisation

Every bit as interesting are the special exhibitions, many sponsored by business and industry, on the theme of technical innovation and its effect on people's lives.

In the last few years the area around the 19th c. Old Port has been turned into a National Monument. What was once a hive of commercial activity centred on the Bassin Louise now has more the air of a leisure park. But the 19th c. is brought vividly to life again in the new Centre d'Interprétation (open: May–Aug. Tues.–Sun. 11am–6pm) where visitors are treated to an excellent audio-visual presentation on the shipbuilding industry, the lumber trade, and Québec's commerce. Fine views of the picturesque Old City, the St Lawrence River, and the Laurentian Mountains can be enjoyed from the special observation platform in the Centre.

★ Vieux Port (The Old Port)

Built in 1894 for the Canadian Pacific Railway the majestic Château Frontenac, visible for miles around, is Québec's most famous landmark. The palatial hotel, standing on the site once occupied by Fort St-Louis, the governor's residence in colonial times, is named after the Comte de

Upper Town

★★ Château Frontenac

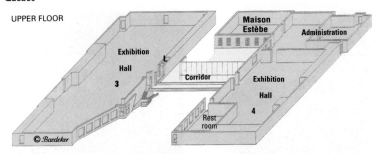

UPPER FLOOR

Maison Estèbe

Administration

Exhibition Hall 3

L

Corridor

Exhibition Hall 4

Rest room

© Baedeker

Musée de la Civilisation — Québec

GROUND FLOOR

Entrance

Maison Estèbe

Vault of the Maison Pagé-Quercy

Boutique

Administration

Exhibition Hall 1

Internal Courtyard

L

ℹ️

Old Quay

L

Exhibition Hall 2

Auditorium 1

Sculptures

Entrance

Café du Musée

Cloakroom

L

Auditorium 2

Studios

L = Lift

BASEMENT

© Baedeker

Frontenac, a French nobleman who was a leading figure in "la Nouvelle France".

From the moment the huge building was completed it became adopted as a fitting emblem for Québec City. Still the provincial capital's foremost hotel, it was here at the Québec Conference in August 1943 that the Allied Powers in the persons of Winston Churchill, Franklin D. Roosevelt, William L. M. King, Vice-Admiral Lord Mountbatten and the US Chief of Staff, General George C. Marshall, and others, laid preparations for the D-Day landings in Normandy (June 6th 1944).

Jardins du Gouverneur

Adjoining the Château on its southern side are the pretty Jardins du Gouverneur. Here Generals Montcalm and Wolfe, adversaries in life but united in death, are honoured by a single monument (see History).

★Terrasse Dufferin

The Terrasse Dufferin with its oriental-style baldachins (also the entire length of the Promenade des Gouverneurs) affords stunning views northwards to the Laurentians (see entry) and south-eastwards where, in good visibility, it is possible to make out the foothills of the Appalachian Mountains in the north-east USA.

★★Promenade des Gouverneurs

From Dufferin Terrace the Promenade des Gouverneurs – a footway high (about 90m/300ft) above the St Lawrence in places – leads southwards from the Château Frontenac, past the Citadel and then along the cliffs of Cap Diamant to the Plains of Abraham.

The world-famous Château Frontenac

The Place d'Armes (Arms Square) in the Upper Town is Old Québec's busy main square.

Place d'Armes

The little Musée du Fort in the Place d'Armes is well worth a visit by anyone with an interest in history. The story of the city and the various battles for Québec are vividly recounted with the aid of a son et lumière show.

Musée du Fort

The Catholic cathedral with its lovely façade was designed by the architect Baillairgé and completed in 1844.

Cathédrale Notre-Dame

In the basement of Québec's venerable old city hall (directly opposite the cathedral) there is an interesting exhibition on urban life and history. A statue of Cardinal Taschereau (1820–98) stands in the hotel forecourt, which once served as a marketplace. Taschereau, a former rector of Laval University, was the first Canadian to be made a cardinal.

Hôtel de Ville

Established by Bishop Laval in 1663 to provide training for the priesthood Québec's Jesuit Seminary quickly became, under the guidance of its founder, the leading institution of learning in New France and the nucleus from which the Université Laval was formed. With upwards of 22,000 students the university now has its own campus in the south-western suburb of Ste-Foy.
    A number of university faculties (e.g. architecture) still occupy some of the Seminary's historic old buildings.
    The Seminary's Briand Chapel was built in 1785 and its 18th c. interior remains unchanged. Many of the wood carvings are masterpieces of their kind.

★Séminaire

In addition to notable works by local artists the Seminary museum has a collection of European religious and secular art, including a portrait by Joshua Reynolds of the British General Wolfe, killed in battle on the Plains

Musée du Séminaire

of Abraham. The skill and artistry of Québec's goldsmiths are specially featured in the museum, which also has an interesting collection of scientific instruments.

★Rue du Trésor

The Place d'Armes leads into the colourful Rue du Trésor, Québec's equivalent of Montmartre. Like its Parisian counterpart the street is usually crowded with artists exhibiting their work. Paintings and prints in particular are among the many items offered for sale.

Musée du Cire

The Musée du Cire, its waxwork scenes illustrating the history of Québec City, is housed in a 17th c. building at the southern end of the Rue de Trésor facing the Cathédrale Notre-Dame.

★Cathédrale
Anglicane

The exterior of Québec's Anglican cathedral is very similar to London's St Martin's in the Fields. It was the first Anglican cathedral to be consecrated outside the United Kingdom (in 1804). The interior has a very fine choir installed in honour of the British monarch, with beautiful choir stalls.

Rue St-Louis

The Rue St-Louis, main thoroughfare of the Upper Town, extends southwestward as far as the old Porte St-Louis. Along it are found some of the city's oldest stone buildings including the Maison Kent, Maison Maillou and Maison Jacquet.

★★Vieux
Monastère des
Ursulines

Just off the Rue St-Louis stands the old Ursuline convent. Founded in 1639 by Madame de la Peltrie it provided an education for young girls, Indian as well as French.

The convent's first Mother Superior was Marie de l'Incarnation who came from Tours in France. She made great efforts to get to know the Algonquin and Iroquois Indians, compiling the first ever dictionaries in their two languages. Surrounded by an aura of mystery during her lifetime and already revered as a saint in the 17th c. she was beatified in 1980.

The convent church is exceptional, being adorned with beautiful early 18th c. altars and statues by Levasseur, an artist very well known in his day. A small chapel next to the church contains the tomb of Marie de l'Incarnation. This has become an occasional place of pilgrimage.

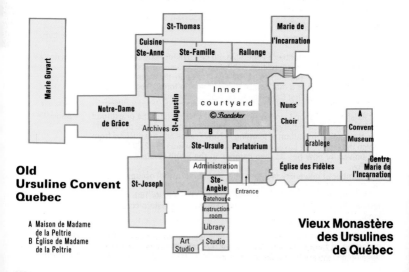

Old Ursuline Convent Quebec

A Maison de Madame de la Peltrie
B Église de Madame de la Peltrie

Vieux Monastère des Ursulines de Québec

Also full of interest is the convent museum, vividly conveying to 20th c. visitors the realities of convent life in earlier days. The lives of the convent's foundress and its first Mother Superior are thoroughly documented too. Among items of interest preserved in the museum is the skull of the French Général Montcalm who died in battle on the Plains of Abraham.

Visitors to the old powder magazine near the Porte St-Louis can see a film tracing the various stages in the development of the city's defences.

La Poudrière

Proceeding northwards from La Poudrière leads in the first instance to the partly restored Porte St-Jean. Beyond the old gate lies the Parc de l'Artillerie (open: May to Oct. Mon. 1–5pm, Tues.–Sat. 10am–5pm) into which a number of ancient buildings have been incorporated (part of a military complex including barracks which was constructed here in the 17th and 18th c.). The Logis d'Officiers (officers' quarters) and the neighbouring Redoute Dauphine with its mighty walls have been excellently restored. In 1879 an arsenal was established on the site, and afterwards a factory making munitions and other military equipment. The latter closed in 1964. The factory building now houses an information centre devoted to the city's history (with an enthralling model of 19th c. Québec).

★ Parc Historique de l'Artillerie

In the more than 300 years of its history Québec has come to possess a variety of fortifications, all of which can be explored on a (fairly long) circular walk. The bastions, walls, towers, gates and countless old cannon leave no doubt as to the thoroughness with which the former French colony was protected.

★ City fortifications

Completed in 1832 the 4.5km/2¾ miles of defensive ramparts on the west flank of the Old City were constructed of granite and sand, the only fortifications of this kind in North America.

The numerous pieces of weaponry positioned along the ancient parapets and terraces encircling the Upper Town are a constant reminder of Québec's troubled past.

A short distance north-east of the Parc de l'Artillerie stands the Hôtel Dieu, an Augustinian hospital built in the 1640s. The small museum contains some handsome pieces of old furniture and a variety of domestic items from days gone by. There are also displays of old surgical instruments and a collection of religious art.

Hôtel Dieu

The hospital's well preserved vaults were used as workshops and stores and also as places of refuge.

The Voûtes du Palais, to the north-west and a little way down from the Hôtel Dieu, were once the cellars of the Intendant's Palace. They now house exhibitions on the city's history.

Voûtes du Palais

Thrusting upwards from the west towards the St Lawrence, Cap Diamant reaches a height of 100m/330ft and commands an extensive and varied panorama. On it stands Québec's Citadel, completed in 1832, a massive fortress with hardly an equal anywhere in the world. Within the protection of its thick walls, ramparts and ditches (laid out roughly in the shape of a star) are military quarters for generals, officers and men. One of the excellently restored buildings is now the summer residence of the Governor General of Canada while the mid-18th c. powder magazine in the southern corner of the Citadel has been converted into a military museum.

Citadel and Battlefield

Cap Diamant, ★★ La Citadelle

Today the Citadel is the headquarters of the 22nd Canadian Regiment which, formed at the beginning of the First World War, boasts a distinguished record including action at the Battle of the Somme and – much later – in the Korean War.

Guided Tours: mid-May to mid-Oct. daily (tickets need to be obtained in plenty of time). Colourful "Changing of the Guard" ceremony: daily 10am.

To the west of the Citadel stretches the green expanse known as the Plains of Abraham (Champs de Bataille) where in 1759 the British led by General Wolfe fought the French under Montcalm.

★ Plains of Abraham (Champs de Bataille)

"Living history" on the Plains of Abraham

Information boards are provided, making it possible to trace the course of events. Also to be seen are the remains of two Martello towers, later additions to Québec's fortifications.

Musée de Québec There is an excellent collection of work by Canadian artists in the Musée de Québec (in the Parc des Champs Bataille on the former battlefield).

Monument de Wolfe In front of the museum stands an imposing monument to General Wolfe.

Terrasse Grey South-west of the museum Terrasse Grey provides a lovely view of the wide St Lawrence River valley.

Parliament Hill

★Hôtel du Parlement The spaciously laid out district immediately south-west of the old Upper Town is the seat of Québec's provincial government. The Parliament, completed in 1877 but later extended, could have been modelled on any number of Parisian public buildings. The Salle de l'Assemblée Nationale (National Assembly) and Salle du Conseil Législatif (Legislative Council) are open to the public (tickets should again be obtained in plenty of time). Both are fine old chambers, sumptuously furnished.

Palais des Congrès Still on Parliament Hill but a little further down, the Palais des Congrès is a large hotel/shopping/entertainment complex. It includes a 3800sq.m/41,000sq.ft congress centre capable of accommodating up to 5000 people.

Grand Théâtre As well as plays the Grand Théâtre de Québec (along the Boulevard St-Cyrille Est) also stages concerts by the Conservatoire and the Québec Symphony Orchestra, the latter being the oldest orchestra of its kind in Canada.

The northern part of the Lower Town

Centre Commercial The vast Centre Commercial on the northern side of Parliament Hill is Québec's answer to the Underground City in Montréal (see entry). The

The Provincial Parliament of Québec

completely roofed over and centrally heated complex with its many arcades is an ideal place for shopping or just walking around, even in the harshest winter weather.

Further north again, on the lower ground bordering the Rivière St-Charles, is the eye-catching, shimmering green outline of the ultra-modern Palais de Justice.

Palais de Justice

Québec's main railway station near the Palais de Justice was rebuilt a few years ago. The former station building next to it has been converted into an old people's home.

Gare du Palais

South-west of the Plains of Abraham lies Sillery, a suburb with attractive villas. Pleasant views can be had from a number of vantage points on the elevated ground sloping down to the St Lawrence.

Sillery

Québec's well-stocked aquarium is situated overlooking the Boulevard Champlain at the northern end of the Pont de Québec, the older of the two bridges over the St Lawrence.

Aquarium

Spanning the St Lawrence River at a slight narrows the massive iron frame of the Pont de Québec, built between 1899 and 1917, became familiar to the world even before its completion. During construction two serious accidents occurred in which more than 80 workmen lost their lives.

★Pont de Québec

The Pierre-Laporte Bridge was opened just a few years ago. Its span of 1040m/3400ft and the height at which it crossed the river (40m/130ft) made it one of the most ambitious bridge-building projects ever undertaken in North America.

Pont Pierre-Laporte

Not far from the southern end of the two bridges a pleasant picnic area has been created at the Chûtes de la Chaudière where the Rivière Chaudière plunges over an escarpment into the St Lawrence.

Chûtes de la Chaudière

Québec

Sainte-Foy

West of Sillery is the modern residential and commercial suburb of Sainte-Foy.

Université Laval

Having outgrown Québec's Old City the tradition-rich Université Laval now occupies a large modern campus in Ste-Foy. About 25,000 students attend what is the oldest French speaking university in America.

Charlesbourg

Situated on Québec's northern side, across the Rivière St-Charles, Charlesbourg is an industrial suburb and the site of a large timber processing factory.

★ Parc Historique Cartier-Brébeuf

The open-air Cartier-Brébeuf Museum (open: May–Sept. Mon. 1–5pm, Tues.–Sun. 9am–5pm) stands on the banks of the St-Charles River in the city's Limoilou district, an evocative monument to events in the very early history of colonial New France. It was here, on his second voyage to Canada, that Jacques Cartier and his men passed the winter of 1535/36 aboard their ship "La Grande Hermine". There is a reconstruction of the vessel which can be visited. Another pioneer to spend a winter here was the missionary Jean de Brébeuf, later destined to enter ecclesiastical history as Canada's first martyr (he was killed by the Iroquois at Ste Marie among the Hurons). A palisaded long-house provides some insight into the life of the indigenous peoples at that time. The influential role of the Jesuits during the early days of French colonisation is one of the themes explored in the museum's information centre.

Parc de l'Exposition

Not far from one another in the suburb of Vannier are a sizeable Centre Commercial and the Parc de l'Exposition, an exhibition site which is also the location of the city's racecourse (known as the Hippodrome).

Jardin Zoologique

Québec's very fine zoo is situated to the north-west of the city, on the outskirts of Charlesbourg.

Village Huron

Also on Québec's north-western periphery is an Indian settlement called Village Huron where traditional art and craftwork is found on sale.

★ Île d'Orléans

A few kilometres downstream from Québec the Île d'Orléans splits the St Lawrence waterway into two. 35km/22 miles long and 9km/6 miles wide the island has kept its rural character almost intact. Despite a recent influx of prosperous Québécois in search of their own small haven of peace, life on the island still evokes something of the pioneering spirit of the earliest colonists of New France.

Jacques Cartier originally christened the island the "Isle of Bacchus" (having found wild grapes there, so the story goes). Later it was renamed in honour of the Duke of Orléans. The Marquis de Roberval visited the island in 1542, and Samuel de Champlain in 1608, but the first settlement by Europeans only began after 1648. Colonisation was completed under Bishop Laval.

In 1759 the British General Wolfe attempted to mount his assault on Québec from the island but was repulsed by Montcalm's French.

A steel suspension bridge linking the island to the mainland was built in 1935.

There are six delightful villages on the Île d'Orléans well worth visiting.

Ste-Pétronille

In the early days of French colonisation Huron Indians, converted to Christianity by Jesuit missionaries, established a retreat on the island, building a chapel at the south-western end in 1651. It was from here that the island was settled by French colonists.

St-Laurent

St-Laurent, on the east side, was founded in 1675, though the present church dates only from 1862. This is where General Wolfe came ashore in 1759 to set up his headquarters.

St-Jean

Further to the north-east stands the village of St-Jean, its church dating from 1732. The village's major attraction however is the Manoir Mauvide-Genest, a 1735 manor house complete with valuable period furniture.

The parish of St-François occupies the north-east tip of the island, from where the much smaller Île Madame and Île-aux-Réaux are plainly visible lying a little way offshore. In 1759 the village church, built in 1734, was used as a hospital for the wounded. The church was damaged by fire in 1988. There are fine carvings to admire in the interior.

St-François

Ste-Famille, on the north-west side, is almost certainly the oldest European settlement on the island.

Ste-Famille

On the way back to the mainland the road passes through the village of St-Pierre. The church was built in 1717. Wood carvings by the artist Vézina on the altar and pulpit also date from the 18th c.

St-Pierre

From Québec to Ste-Anne de Beaupré–Avenue Royale

Heading north-east from Québec towards Ste-Anne de Beaupré both the newer (and faster) Highway 138 and the older more leisurely Highway 360 follow the direction of North America's first paved road, the Avenue Royale, constructed in the early 18th c.

N.B.

A bare 10km/6 miles north of Québec the Montmorency River plunges over an 84m/275ft high escarpment. Despite being 30m/98ft higher than the Niagara Falls (see entry) the Chûtes Montmorency are not nearly so spectacular.
   Trails with many fine views and attractive picnic places have been marked out in the vicinity of the Falls.
   In the 1790s Maison Montmorency (also known as "Kent House") to the left of the Falls was a great favourite of the Duke of Kent (father of the Victoria who later became Queen). From the house there are particularly fine views.

★★Chûtes Montmorency

Québec City: A cellar in the Avenue Royale

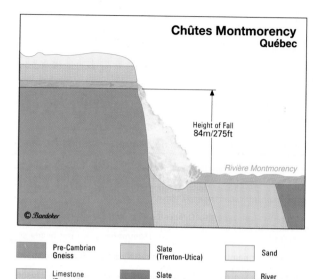

Chûtes Montmorency
Québec

Height of Fall
84m/275ft

Rivière Montmorency

© *Baedeker*

Pre-Cambrian Gneiss	Slate (Trenton-Utica)
Limestone (Trenton)	Slate (Lorraine)
Sand	River Montmorency

★ Côte de Beaupré

Beyond Montmorency the road passes through the agricultural "garden" of Québec Province, an area of countryside blessed with a particularly favourable local climate and dotted with old mills, farmsteads and unusual cellars half-buried in the valley sides. At some of the attractive old farmhouses and country inns travellers stopping for a welcome rest can savour the local produce (especially the bread, butter and maple syrup). This is a part of Québec also popular with artists; their work, religious and non-religious, is to be seen displayed in a number of places.

Petit-Pré

Where the little Petit-Pré flows into the St Lawrence there is an old mill open to visitors during the tourist season.

Château-Richer

A small exhibition in the village of Château-Richer (population 4000) is devoted to local agriculture and the local economy.

★ Ste-Anne de Beaupré

Location

The little monastery town of Ste-Anne de Beaupré (pop. 3000) is situated on the banks of the St Lawrence only 40km/25 miles north-east of Québec.

★ Church

The first chapel dedicated to St Anne was built here in the 17th c., quickly becoming a place of pilgrimage following reports of miraculous events. The original wooden building fell victim to a flood however, and in 1661 a new stone-built chapel was erected on the valley side. Fifteen years later it too was replaced.

In 1872 a basilica was constructed at St-Anne, only to be destroyed soon afterwards in a fire. The present massive neo-Romanesque church, designed by the Parisian architect Maxime Roisin and completed in 1923, was the work of Louis Audet, a master-builder from Sherbrooke. Among the most pleasing features of the spaciously proportioned interior are the mosaics and colourful stained glass windows. However there are also fine sculptures and paintings by European and Canadian artists. Some services are held in the basement of the church.

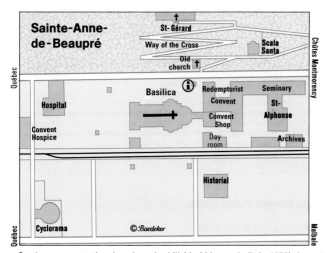

On the way up to the chapel on the hillside (this one built in 1878) the Stations of the Cross are marked by beautifully executed life-size metal figures. The altar dates from the 18th c. while the clock tower, designed by Claude Baillif, was already there in 1678.

Stations of the Cross

The nearby Scala Santa Chapel (Chapel of the Holy Steps) was built in 1871. The steps are a replica of those which Christ mounted to be taken before Pontius Pilate.

Scala Santa

Located on the large car park in front of the basilica the waxworks museum known as the Historial is dedicated to the cult of St Anne in North America and the history of the shrine at Beaupré.

Historial

Painted in the 1880s this intriguing oddity consists of a huge 360° panorama of Jerusalem on the day of the Crucifixion. It shows the places where Christ paused on the way to Golgotha.

Cyclorama

Around Ste-Anne de Beaupré

About 10km/6 miles east of Ste-Anne, at Cap Tourmente, a wildlife reserve has been established on the northern shore of the St Lawrence Estuary. Here each spring and autumn thousands upon thousands of migrating snow geese break their long northward or southward journey.

Cap Tourmente

Some 7km/4 miles north of Ste-Anne de Beaupré the Ste-Anne River has carved a romantically wild gorge through the foothills of the Laurentians (see entry) on its way down to the St Lawrence Estuary. Although certainly impressive the Ste-Anne's Falls scarcely deserve the accolade of "Grand Canyon of Québec".

★ Chûtes Ste-Anne

A few kilometres/miles beyond the Chûtes Ste-Anne on Highway 360 are the equally impressive Sept-Chûtes (access from mid-June to mid-Sept). There are a number of fine viewpoints and an ecology trail. A large hydro-electric station has been built to harness the energy of the falls.

★ Sept-Chûtes

Also to the north of Ste-Anne de Beaupré lies Mont-Ste-Anne, the slopes and surrounding areas of which have been turned into a provincial park

★ Parc du Mont-Ste-Anne

(one of many popular leisure areas in the Laurentians close to Québec). There is good walking and in winter excellent skiing. There are a number of establishments offering accommodation and also restaurants. Facilities include ski-lifts on the slopes of Mont-Ste-Anne where snow is guaranteed and several restaurants. An emergency rescue service operates in the Park.

Lévis

Lévis, situated on the east side of the St Lawrence opposite Québec, is today a heavily industrialised suburb of the city. In earlier times its fortifications stood guard over the waterway.

Fort No. 1

Foremost among the sights around Lévis is Fort No. 1 (open: mid-May to Aug. daily 10am–5pm), constructed by British troops between 1865 and 1872. Built on Pointe-Lévis (115m/375ft) just across the river from Québec's Citadel, the fort was one of three defence works erected on the south shore of the St Lawrence for the protection of Québec City.

Lauzon

Also situated on the east side of the river, a little lower down abreast the southern tip of the Île d'Orléans, Lauzon has a number of dry-docks.

Queen Charlotte Islands–Haida Gwaii   C 7

Province: British Columbia
Location: Between 52° and 54°N
Population: 6000

Information

Queen Charlotte Islands Chamber of Commerce, P.O. Box 357, Queen Charlotte City, B.C. V0T 1S0, tel. (604) 559–4661.

Access

By plane:
Daily flights operate between Vancouver International Airport and Sandspit (Moresby Island), also between Prince Rupert and Sandspit and between Prince Rupert and Masset (seaplane).

By ferry:
Three to five sailings a week from Prince Rupert to Skidegate Landing. Several sailings a day between Graham Island and Moresby Island.

By bus:
Buses run between Masset, Port Clemens, Tiell and Sandspit Airport; also between Queen Charlotte City and Sandspit Airport.

The Queen Charlotte Islands are an isolated group of more than 150 islands lying out in the Pacific at the western edge of the continental shelf. The two main islands, Graham and Moresby, are about 50km/30 miles and 150km/90 miles respectively off the coast of British Columbia. The Queen Charlottes are often called "the Misty Islands", partly because the sky is usually overcast and the deeply indented cliffs on their western sides frequently enveloped in mist, partly on account of the enigma of their native inhabitants, the Haida Indians. The Haida, thought to have lived on these islands for at least 8000 years, were known and feared as proud warriors and daring navigators. With their awesome 20m/65ft long warcanoes they traversed the length of the Inside Passage as far south as Puget Sound. Nowadays they are rather more famous for the skill and artistry of their carving. Their totem poles and wonderfully elaborate argillite carvings (argillite is a black slate-like but soft stone found only at Slatechuck Mountain in south Graham Island, which only the Indians are allowed to work) occupy pride of place in every ethnographic museum on the Canadian Pacific coast. The Haida were also notorious for their lavish potlatches – ceremonial feasts at which the distribution of gifts served not only to display the wealth and status of the tribe but also to consolidate the often extremely complex systems of kinship and allegiance.

Canada's western isles were discovered in 1774 by the Spaniard Juan Pérez. In the 19th c. skilled Haida hunters kept white traders supplied with sea-otter pelts, which at that time fetched particularly high prices in China. But the white man also brought European diseases and epidemics soon decimated the native population. Several Haida coastal settlements were abandoned and numbers fell from an estimated 8000 or more to just 588 in 1915. Today most of the 1300 surviving Haida Indians live on reservations at Skidegate Mission and Haida on Graham Island, the largest island in the group. A permit issued by the Indians themselves is required for visiting the reservations or abandoned Haida villages (for south Graham Island apply to the Skidegate Band office in Skidegate Mission, tel. 559–4496; for north Graham Island and Langara Island apply to the Masset Band office in Haida, tel. 626–3337).

White settlement of the isolated Queen Charlotte Islands began relatively late at the beginning of the 20th c. A number of homesteads and small self-sufficient rural communities were set up, mainly on the flatter eastern side of Graham Island. Most however soon failed. Today four fifths of the islands' population live in twelve villages and logging camps on Graham Island, generally close to the Yellowhead Highway (Hwy. 16). Since 1980 when the new, non-tidal ferry terminal was completed near Skidegate, there have been several sailings a week to and from Prince Rupert (6–8 hours, depending on the weather).

History

Owing to the influence of the warm Japanese current the climate stays relatively mild throughout the year. Precipitation though is high, averaging 1260mm/50in. per annum. May and April – the driest months – are best for travelling. Mean daily temperatures in August are around 17°C/63°F and in January 4°C/39°F. Cool, wet and windy or misty weather must be expected at any time of year.

Climate

What to see in the Queen Charlotte Islands

This fishing port and Canadian army base in sheltered Masset Inlet is the Queen Charlotte Islands' largest settlement (population about 2000).

Masset

An Indian reserve of some 600 inhabitants situated 3km/2 miles north of Masset near the abandoned Haida village of Ka-Yung. Numerous fairly recent totem poles celebrating important events and people. Ed Jones Haida Museum in the old school house. Sale of typical Indian handwork. Beaches strewn with agate, cornelian, large shells and "sand dollars" (a type of sea urchin).

★Haida (Old Masset)

This stunningly beautiful 726sq.km/280sq.mile Provincial Park on the north-eastern tip of Graham Island is accessible either from Masset or from Tiell on the island's east coast. From Masset a spit of sand 26km/16 miles long runs along the northern coast as far as the basalt Tow Hill (109m/360ft; splendid views). Old planking, still visible in places, is all that remains of the original road which once served a remote settlement. The present vehicle track ends at Agate Beach (campground). Some of the beaches around McIntyre Bay are more than 300m/330yd wide, superb for walking on in fine weather. Metres-high piles of driftwood thrown up by the sea fringe the sand dunes behind the beach. A very pleasant 10km/6 mile walk (the Cape Fife Trail) crosses "Argonaut Plain" – which Ice Age glaciers have left dotted with small lakes, bogs and meandering streams – to Fife Point on the east coast.

The 5km/3 mile Rose Spit after which the park is named ("naikoon" means "long nose") can only be reached on foot. This ecologically fragile area of dunes is now a reserve and an ideal place to watch waterfowl.

The Park Headquarters (brochures, cards, etc.) are at the southern entrance near Tiell, set amongst massive sand dunes. From the entrance a 10km/6 mile circular trail winds through typical lichen-rich rainforest to the

Naikoon Provincial Park

Tiell River estuary, then north for a short distance to the wooden wreck of the "Pesuta" which ran aground here in 1928. This marks the start of the 64km/40 mile trail along East Beach to Tow Hill (for the experienced only; 4–6 days; good equipment, up-to-date guide and tide tables essential).

★ Queen Charlotte Islands Museum

The Queen Charlotte Islands regional museum, a modern glass and native cedarwood building located right by the sea at the western end of the Skidegate Mission reserve (Second Beach; open: May–Sept. 9am–5pm, at other times from 1–5pm) is devoted chiefly to the history and culture of the Haida Indians (totem poles, carvings, wickerwork). It also has a fine collection of old photographs from pioneering days as well as displays on natural history. The old photos show numerous totem poles standing in front of traditional long-houses. Today though only one pole survives. About 350 Haida Indians live on the Skidegate Mission reserve. The most striking building houses the new tribal administration offices. Built in the style of a long-house it has a totem pole by the celebrated carver Bill Reid towering in front of it.

Indian dancing

Every year on the first Saturday in June a festival is held to mark the building of the long-house (traditional Indian dancing).

Moresby Island

South Moresby Island

The large south island is for the most part accessible only to people with their own boats or travelling on foot. The only public roads (32km/20 miles in all) run between the ferry landing and Sandspit – though at weekends it is also possible to drive on the privately-owned forestry roads (guides and cards from the Crown Forest Industries office in Sandspit).

Tours

Boat trips and bus tours are a good way of getting to know the islands, even some of the remoter parts (details from the information centres in Queen Charlotte City, Masset and Sandspit).

South Moresby

412

Plant and animal species now scarcely found anywhere else in the world survive on South Moresby, which was made a National Park in 1989 to protect the remaining rainforest and the alpine-like mountain meadows. Some of the best preserved remains of the extraordinarily rich Haida Indian culture are also to be seen on the island.

★★South Moresby National Park

The ruins of the long abandoned Haida village of Ninstints are included on UNESCO's list of the world's most important cultural heritage sites.

Ninstints

Regina   J 7

Province: Saskatchewan. Population: 180,000

Tourism Saskatchewan, 1919 Saskatchewan Drive, Regina S4P 3V7; tel. (306) 787–9685.

Information

Regina is a cosmopolitan commercial, cultural, industrial and tourist centre which, in addition to being the agrarian capital of Canada, boasts a major oil refinery, the country's biggest steelworks, numerous other factories and a number of research establishments. As the seat of the Saskatchewan provincial government and also of several federal government departments, a high percentage of Regina's citizens are employed in the public sector. This economic diversity has enabled the city to prosper, making it a desirable place to live.
  A rich programme of drama, music and dance (including performances by ethnic groups) and the presence of the Saskatchewan Centre of Arts, one of the best concert halls in North America, testify to the city's long-established cultural tradition. The Regina Symphony Hall prides itself on being the home of Canada's oldest permanent symphony orchestra founded in 1908.

General

Regina's history can be traced back to a time when the locality was known as "Pile o'Bones" on account of the huge quantities of buffalo bones to be found here. It would seem that, in yet earlier days, native hunters drove these animals down to Wascana Creek for slaughter.
  A settlement first grew up on the site with the building of the railway. When in 1882 the little township became capital of the Northwest Territories it was rechristened Regina in honour of Queen Victoria. Having been granted city status in 1903 just two years later it was pronounced capital of the newly created province of Saskatchewan.
  Towards the end of the 19th c. Regina was the headquarters of the North West Mounted Police – later to become the Royal Canadian Mounted Police (RCMP). In 1920 RCMP headquarters were moved to Ottawa but the RCMP Academy, the sole training centre for the "Mounties", remains located in Regina.
  In the early 20th c. immigrants from all over the world flocked to Regina helping to transform the region into a highly productive wheat growing area.

History

The Royal Canadian Mounted Police Museum (open: June–mid-Sept. daily 8am–8.45pm; mid-Sept–May daily 8am–4.45pm) is located in the west of the city at the RCMP Academy in Dewdney Ave. W. Both the Sergeant Major's Parade (Mon.–Fri. 12.45pm; venue: Parade Square or, in winter or bad weather, the Drill Hall) and the Sunset Retreat (July–mid-Aug. Tues. 7pm) attract large crowds. The latter, a colourful lowering the flag ceremony involving a parade of recruits and a marching band, was re-introduced to mark the centenary of the force. It harks back to the tattoos of the 18th c. and to 19th c. British military tradition.
  The museum, which attracts over 250,000 visitors a year, is Canada's largest devoted to the Mounties and includes items of equipment, weaponry, uniforms, photographs, archive material, personal effects and

Sights

★★Royal Canadian Mounted Police (RCMP) Centennial Museum

413

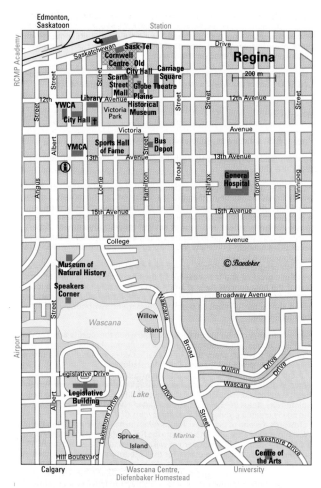

memorabilia. One theme of the museum is the history of the force from its foundation to the present day, setting it in the context of Canada's development as a nation. Another theme is the celluloid image of the RCMP as portrayed in innumerable Hollywood films about the Mounties. Famous personalities and historic events are also featured in the museum, among them Chief Sitting Bull who took refuge in Saskatchewan after the massacre of Custer and his men at the Little Big Horn. A substantial part of the museum is given over to the North West Rebellion of 1885 and its leader Louis Riel.

Other items on display include Red Indian artefacts and clothing. The large, painted buffalo skin on which an entire history is recorded in pictographs is one of the most valuable of its kind in Canada.

The historic RCMP chapel, one of the oldest buildings in Regina, is also well worth a visit. It began life in 1883 as a casino before being partly destroyed by fire in 1895. Following restoration it was turned into a chapel, made particularly attractive by the contrast between the richness and variety of its splendid stained glass windows and the simplicity of the basic structure and original pews. Finest of all are the two superbly coloured windows behind the altar depicting red-uniformed Mounties. One is dedicated to the many police wives who played such an important role in their husbands' absence on duty, manning telephones and taking care of prisoners.

Laid out on the shores of an artificial lake in the middle of Regina the 930ha/2300 acres of the Wascana Centre form one of the largest city parks anywhere in the world. The park is the setting for Saskatchewan's Legislative Building, the Museum of Natural History, the Saskatchewan Science Centre, the Diefenbaker Homestead, the Saskatchewan Centre of Arts and the University of Regina.

★Wascana Centre

Wascana Lake is also a bird sanctuary, its islands and reedbeds providing refuge for ducks, geese, swans, pelicans and a variety of other birds. Picturesque Willow Island at the northern end of the lake makes an ideal spot for picnicking (open: Mon.–Fri. noon–4pm; reached by ferry).

Located just to the west of Broad St. the Diefenbaker Homestead (open: daily 10am–5pm) was the childhood home of J. G. Diefenbaker, Prime Minister of Canada from 1957 to 1963 and Saskatchewan's most famous son. It was brought to Regina in 1967 from Borden and contains some personal possessions and memorabilia of the Diefenbaker family.

Diefenbaker Homestead

The Legislative Building (open: end of May–beginning of Sept daily 8am–5pm) was built between 1908 and 1912. Shaped like a cross it shows the influence of both the English Renaissance and the Age of Louis XVI. In addition to the local Tyndall limestone 34 kinds of rare marble were used in its construction. The building has a total area of about 19,000sq.m/205,000sq.ft.

★Legislative Building

Regina: the Legislative Building

Included among the 265 rooms are the Prime Minister's Office and Cabinet Chamber. The Legislative Building also houses various items of historical interest and a number of works of art.

One wing is occupied by the Canadian Native Gallery. It has displays of native Indian art and a photographic collection.

★Mackenzie
Art Gallerie

The Mackenzie Art Gallery in the south-west corner of the Wascana Centre (open: Tues.–Sun. noon–6pm, Wed. noon–10pm) possesses an excellent collection with exhibits ranging from the art of ancient Mesopotamia to contemporary Canadian works. The Gallery also puts on important temporary exhibitions.

★Saskatchewan
Science Centre

Regina's newest tourist attraction, the 464sq.m/5000sq.ft Saskatchewan Science Centre, opened in 1989. Occupying a converted former power station on the north bank of Wascana Lake the Centre is rather special in encouraging "hands on" involvement with the sciences (e.g. geology and astronomy). Visitors are able to handle the exhibits, perform experiments and ask questions as well as experiencing simulated space travel and "seeing" their voices reproduced on a computer screen.

Museum of
Natural History

Visitors to the Museum of Natural History on the corner of College Ave and Albert St. (open: May 1st–Labour Day daily 9am–8.30pm; Sept.–Apr. daily 9am–4.30pm) find themselves taken back 2 billion years in time. There are over 100 glass display cabinets devoted to geology, palaeontology, archaeology and anthropology. The new Earth Sciences Gallery is quite exceptional with its fascinating series of extremely lifelike dioramas showing mastodons, dinosaurs, etc. (also contemporary wildlife) in their natural environment.

★Plains Museum

The Regina Plains Museum (open: Mon.–Fri. 11.30am–5pm, Sat., Sun. 1–5pm, winter Wed.–Fri. 11.30am–5pm, Sat., Sun. 1–5pm) occupies the former Post Office in Scarth St. It recalls the lives of the plainsfolk, Indians, Metis and early pioneers and there are reconstructions of a typical turf hut, schoolroom, church, saloon and Red River cart as well as displays of old photographs and artefacts.

Library

The Dunlop Art Gallery (open: Mon.–Fri. 9.30am–9pm, Sat. 9.30am–6pm, Sun. 1.30–5pm) in the Central Library on 12th Ave. is used for exhibitions of one sort or another – art, crafts or theme-related.

Also in the Library the Prairie History Room (open: Mon.–Wed. 9.30am–9pm, Thur., Fri. 9.30am–5pm., Sat. noon–5pm, Sun. 1.30–5pm) contains a large collection of items relating to the history of the prairies and the prairie provinces (including photographs and newspaper cuttings).

Goverment
House

Goverment House in Dewdney Ave. (open: Sept.–June Tues.–Sat. 1–4pm, Sun. 1–5pm, July, Aug. Tues.–Sun. 1–5pm) was built in 1891 and until 1945 was the official residence of the Lieutenant Governor. Now all the elegance of the turn of the century is again reflected in its restored rooms.

Every summer Government House is the setting for "The Trial of Louis Riel", a dramatic reconstruction based on documents from the original trial.

Saskatchewan
Sports Hall of
Fame

The Sports Hall of Fame (open: Mon.–Fri. 9am–5pm, Sat., Sun. noon–4pm) in Victoria Ave celebrates the province's sporting achievements. Exhibits include portraits and a variety of memorabilia.

IPSCO Wildlife
Park

The IPSCO Wildlife Park (open: mid-May–Sept. 1–6pm, June, Aug. 11am–8pm) about 4km/2½ miles north of Regina is home to a variety of animals including buffalo, elk, deer and pheasant.

Repulse Bay

Administrative unit: Northwest Territories, District of Keewatin

Travel Keewatin, Department EG, Box 328, Rankin Inlet, NWT, X0C 0G0, tel. (819) 645–2618

Information

By plane: Via Winnipeg–Churchill (Manitoba)–Rankin Inlet to Repulse Bay (Canadian Airways Partner Companies).

Access

The most north-easterly point of mainland Northwest Territories, Melville Peninsula (part of the Franklin District), is joined to the remainder by an isthmus, 70km/43 miles wide, between Hudson Bay and the Gulf of Boothia. Repulse Bay sits on its southern shore, exactly on the Arctic Circle (marked by an arc of stones at the airfield). It is served by scheduled flights from Churchill, Eskimo Point and Rankin Inlet.

The "European" chapter of this part of Canada's history opened in 1741 when Captain Middleton sailed into the deep bay – known to the Inuit as "Naujaat" (= gulls' nesting place) – in search of the Northwest Passage. In his disappointment Middleton christened the bay Repulse. In the mid-19th c., Roses Welcome Sound, with Repulse Bay at its northern end, was a much frequented British and American whaling ground, many Inuit (called "Avilingmiut") being employed as "scouts" on the whale boats. Their local knowledge proved to be of inestimable value. When the American explorer Hall arrived here around 1864 an Inuit from Repulse Bay was able to draw him an astonishingly accurate map of Foxe Basin (between the Melville Peninsula and Baffin Island). The same traditional experience, handed down from generation to generation, is still made use of today by Inuit tourist guides. Until 1954 Repulse Bay was simply a Hudson's Bay Company (H.B.C.) settlement (H.B.C. standing, so it is said, for "Here before Christ"!) and a Catholic mission. Now there are about 420 inhabitants, virtually all of them Inuit. While a subsistence economy based on hunting still survives, Arctic tourism has also brought new opportunities for employment. Thus the wealth of flora and fauna on land and sea continues to support the Inuit way of life, albeit in a rather novel manner.

History and the present

Réservoir Manicouagan

Province: Québec

Highway 389 from Baie-Comeau (on the north shore of the St Lawrence Estuary). Distance: 430km/270 miles.

Access

Association touristique régionale de Manicouagan, Rue de Puyjalon 871, Baie-Comeau, Québec, tel. (418) 589–5319.

Information

About 210 million years ago a meteorite struck the Canadian Shield north of the St Lawrence Estuary to the north-east of the Laurentians (see entry). Its highly destructive impact resulted in the formation of a crater some 100km/62 miles across. So much energy was released that part of the meteorite itself and some of the surface rock evaporated, the tremendous pressure causing an explosion in which vast quantities of rock were hurled into the air and scattered over the surrounding countryside. At the same time metamorphosis of the rock produced mineral concentrations which today form important raw material deposits (including iron ore).

General situation

Taking advantage of the valleys and depressions produced in the vicinity of the meteorite crater by erosion and glaciation, a huge reservoir was constructed to exploit the electricity generating potential of the area. The

★★ Barrage
Daniel-
Johnson

Manicouagan: the huge Daniel Johnson Dam

214m/700ft high Daniel Johnson Dam, built in the 1960s by the Hydro-Québec Company, resulted in an artificial lake covering some 2000sq.km/770sq.miles.

The gigantic barrage was inaugurated in 1968 by Canada's then Prime Minister Daniel Johnson.

Complexe Manic-Outardes

Ever since 1958 work has also been in progress to harness the hydro-electric potential of the Manicouagan and Outardes rivers, which flow parallel to one another from the north-east Laurentians.

Over this period two Hydro-Québec Co. generating plants known as Manic 5 and Manic 2 have come into operation.

★ Manic 5

This ultra modern power generating plant started producing electricity in 1990. With a capacity of 1064 megawatts it is one of the biggest of its kind anywhere in the world.

Centre d'Interprétation

Visitors to Hydro-Québec's Centre d'Interprétation can learn anything and everything about power generation. Bus tours are arranged from mid-June to the beginning of Sept.
   Departure: daily 9 and 11am, 1.30 and 3.30pm.
   Information: tel. (418) 294–3923.

Manic 2

The 70m/230ft dam powering Hydro-Québec's Manic 2 generating station is situated on the lower reaches of the Rivière Manicouagan about 20km/12 miles north of Baie-Comeau. Tours: mid-June to beginning of Sept. daily 9 and 11am, 1 and 3pm.
   Information: tel. (419) 294–3923.

Revelstoke

Province: British Columbia
Population: 9000

The town of Revelstoke lies between the snow-clad ranges of the Selkirk and Monashee Mountains, where the Illecillewaet flows into the Columbia River (see entry). It marks the western end of Rogers Pass through the Glacier National Park (see entry), which posed so many problems to the road builders and railway engineers. Both upstream and downstream of Revelstoke the once raging waters of the Columbia River have been tamed to form a string of sizeable lakes extending for more than 300km/186 miles. Lakes Revelstoke and Kinbasket (north) and Arrow (south) offer good facilities for watersports.

First settled in 1883, Second Crossing/Farwell (as it was originally called) was renamed in honour of Lord Revelstoke whose bank contributed substantially to the financing and completion of the Canadian Pacific Railway. As early as the beginning of the 19th c. however, fur trappers had already penetrated this far up the Columbia River – the great 2000km/1250 mile waterway of the Canadian West – followed soon afterwards by traders, missionaries, gold prospectors and the earliest settlers. | History

Revelstoke is a popular summer and winter holiday resort for hill walking, heli-skiing, white-water rafting, fishing, etc. (see also Mount Revelstoke and Glacier National Park). | Revelstoke today

A redevelopment project in the early 1980s saw a number of the town's early 20th c. buildings restored, including the Court-House (1912), the King Edward Hotel, the McKinnon Building and the Roxy Theatre. At the same time parts of the town centre were pedestrianised and greened. | Architecture

The former Post Office at 315 West 1st St, built in 1926, now houses the Revelstoke Museum (open: June to Sept. Mon.–Sat. 2–9pm). Old photographs, etc. are used to document local history, mainly the building of the railway and the era of river navigation. | Revelstoke Museum

The Mount Mackenzie Ski Area (610m/2000ft vertical drop, 20 ski runs, 2 chair lifts, T-bar), 6km/4 miles from the town centre, is well known for its abundant snow (3–5m/10–16ft a year). Heli-skiing; cross-country skiing and ski touring (mainly in the Mount Revelstoke National Park); snowmobile trails. | ★Mount Mackenzie

About 5km/3 miles north of the town on Highway 23 the Revelstoke Canyon Dam, a 175m/570ft high concrete barrier completed in the early 1980s, controls a stretch of the Columbia River extending as far as the Mica Dam 144km/90 miles to the north. B.C. Hydro's new hydro-electric station will eventually produce 2.7 million kilowatt hours of electricity a year making it one of the biggest in the province. | ★Revelstoke Canyon Dam

Even today scars inflicted on the Mount Revelstoke landscape during the building of the dam are clearly visible. A modern Visitors Centre opened in 1985 (open: June–Aug. 8am–8pm, at other times 10am–6pm) explains technical aspects of the barrage and generating plant and the operation of the Columbia River system. An elevator takes visitors up to a view point on top of the dam.

Highway 23 North continues along the east side of the reservoir to Mica Dam

Heading in the other direction from Revelstoke towards Nakusp (altitude: 415m/1360ft; population: 1000) Highway 23 South skirts Upper Arrow Lake through a densely forested, sparsely inhabited area. | Nakusp

At Nakusp Hot Springs, about 100km/62 miles south of Revelstoke, there are two thermal swimming pools with water temperatures in the region of 40°C/104°F (open: daily 10.30am–9pm). | Nakusp Hot Springs

Highway 23 South links up with Highway 6 at Nakusp, leading in one direction to Okanagan (see entry) and in the other to Kootenay Lake and then on to Crowsnest Highway 3, the main east–west route in the south.

Shelter Bay, Galena Bay

Ferries run across Arrow Lake between Shelter Bay and Galena Bay and between Fauquier and Needles. At Halcyon and St Leon there are more hot springs. Being as yet undeveloped however, they are accessibly only via poorly signposted minor roads.

Albert Canyon Hot Springs

Tourist facilities at Albert Canyon Hot Springs (35km/22 miles east of Revelstoke on the TransCanada Highway) include a thermal pool, camping ground, cafeteria and souvenir shop.

★ Rogers Pass

Rogers Pass (1327m/4350ft) cuts through the high mountains and breathtaking, glacial scenery of the Glacier National Park (see entry).

Rideau Canal O 8/9

Province: Ontario

History and function

The 200km/124 mile long Rideau Canal, only 1.6m/5¼ft deep, connects Ottawa with Kingston on Lake Ontario. It was originally intended as a second strategic route between Montréal and Lake Ontario, the military need for which was demonstrated during the war with the United States in 1812.

At the time of building (1826–32) the canal was a triumph of constructional engineering. More than four dozen dams were required to control the water levels, and the 83m/272ft ascent to the summit between Ottawa and Lake Ontario meant that boats had to pass through numerous locks.

Although steamers plied the canal for over a hundred years it never came to have any major economic significance. Today the waterway with its 24 operational locks is used mainly by pleasure boats and for tourism.

Ottawa

It is one of history's curiosities that a camp for 2000 construction workers employed on building a branch of the canal from the Ottawa River should eventually become the capital of Canada.

The staircase of eight locks on Parliament Hill is highly photogenic. Ottawa's first stone building was on a site next to the canal.

Jones Falls

Among the many interesting features on the canal is Stone Arch Dam at Jones Falls.

Kingston Mills

As well as the Visitors Centre the Block House (museum) at Kingston Mills is also worth visiting.

Boating season, Information

Mid-May to mid-October. Information: 12 Maple Ave N., Smiths Falls, Ontario, K7A 1Z5; tel. (613) 283–5170.

Riding Mountain National Park J/K 7

Province: Manitoba
Area: about 3000sq.km/1158sq.miles

Information

Superintendent, Riding Mountain National Park, Wasagaming, Manitoba, R0J 2H0; tel. (204) 848–2811

★★ Nature park

Riding Mountain National Park is located 310km/190 miles north-west of Winnipeg (see entry) on Highway 10. Accessible throughout the year this scenic park is a combination of recreation area and nature reserve, a varied landscape of prairie, aspen parkland, fir and deciduous forest and wonderfully clear lakes and streams. The park extends over part of the glacially formed Manitoba Escarpment where a series of plateaux rising to heights of about 340m/1100ft overlook the surrounding prairie with its gentle hills, meadows, lakes and watercourses.

The cold deep lakes such as Clear Lake, Lake Katherine and Deep Lake are rich in pike, whitefish, walleye and trout (good angling). Beavers live in the shallow, marshy bays.

Near Lake Audy a herd of buffalo roam freely about a 552ha/1360 acre enclosure. There is a special look-out from which the animals can be observed in their natural environment, and an informative display about bison – now virtually extinct except for this one remaining species. Bears, wolves, elk and deer also inhabit the park ("The Duke", the largest brown bear ever reported in Canada, was killed by poachers here in the autumn of 1991).

Yellow potentilla and violet gaillardia are among the flowering plants which grow on the prairies of the Canadian West.

Fauna and Flora

The park has innumerable trails for use by walkers, cyclists and riders. One trail leads to the log cabin formerly belonging to the English naturalist Grey Owl who, in the early 1920s, wrote books about the wildlife of the area.

There are winter sports facilities for downhill and cross-country skiing (Mt Agassiz).

Leisure activities

Wasagaming (Indian for "clear water") at the southern entrance to the park is a leisure resort on the shores of Clear Lake (18–hole golf course, tennis, badminton, roller-skating rink and camping).

Wasagaming

Housed in a fine 1930s wooden building at Wasagaming the Interpretive Centre focuses on Riding Mountain's rich natural history.

Interpretive Centre

Clear Lake, 33m/108ft deep and largest in the park, has facilities for swimming, angling (pike, walleye, trout, whitefish), boating, wind surfing and sailing.

Clear Lake

Saguenay (Fiord)   P/Q 8

Province: Québec

The Saguenay is the major tributary of the St Lawrence River. Tremendously deep in places (up to 275m/900ft), all sorts of marine life including whales and salmon are found in its tidal, salt water reaches.

The countryside through which the Saguenay Fiord twists and turns (sometimes between cliffs 180–300m/590–980ft high) presents three quite different faces, dense forest giving way in turn to agricultural land and industrial development.

By far the best – and in some parts the only – way to see the Saguenay is by water. There are cruises daily from Chicoutimi between June and September.

The Saguenay Fiord was discovered by Jacques Cartier on his second expedition up the St Lawrence in 1535/36. Having largely escaped colonisation by Europeans until the mid-19th c. the sunken valley underwent its most dramatic transformation following the Second World War. Exploitation of the Saguenay for hydro-electric power led to the construction of one of the world's largest aluminium plants at Jonquière. Meat processing and paper are other industries which now play an important role in the local economy.

History and economy

Saguenay

Whale-watching

Every year between the end of July and October hundreds of whales congregate where the Saguenay flows into the St Lawrence. The result is a unique spectacle – and an unmatched opportunity to observe these magnificent creatures at close quarters from aboard one of "whale-watching" boats from Baie Ste-Catherine, Tadoussac or Rivière-du-Loup. As many as ten different species of whale have been identified among those which gather here, including the huge fin whales and white whales. Plans are afoot to create a special reserve to protect these splendid mammals, now threatened with extinction.

Sights along the Saguenay

Rivière-Eternité

From Rivière-Eternité a 9km/5½ mile footpath leads to the 457m/1560ft high Cap-Trinité with its statue of the Virgin Mary erected in 1881. Of interest in Rivière-Eternité itself is the Parc national du Saguenay Interpretation Centre (open: mid-May–mid-Oct. daily 9am–5pm).

La Baie

Primarily an industrial town, La Baie nevertheless boasts the Musée du Fiord (3346, bd. de la Grande-Baie S.) with worthwhile collections of ethnography and regional art treasures (open: end of July–beginning of Sept. Mon.–Fri. 8.30am–5pm, Sat. and Sun. 1–5pm. Tues.–Sat. also 7.30–9pm; Sept.–June Mon.–Fri. 8.30am–noon and 1.30–5pm, Sat. and Sun. 1–5pm).

Chicoutimi

Attractively situated on a hill in heavily wooded country on the south bank of the Saguenay, the town of Chicoutimi more than lives up to its sobriquet of "Queen of the North".

Musée
du Saguenay,
Centre Culturel

Among Chicoutimi's attractions is the Musée du Saguenay-Lac St-Jean in the Cultural Centre (534 rue Jacques-Cartier). There are comprehensive ethnological and archaeological displays of Indian artefacts, etc. as well as

Saguenay Fiord

Chicoutimi

a collection of early 20th c. furniture (open: end of June–beginning of Sept. Mon.–Fri. 8.30am–5pm, Tues. and Thur. also 7–9pm, Sat. and Sun. 1–5pm; Sept.–June Mon.–Fri. 8.30am–noon and 1–5pm, Sat. and Sun. 1–5pm).

Built in 1921 and dedicated to St-François-Xavier the cathedral has a lovely painting in the transept vaulting.   Cathedral
   A magnificent view along the southern shore of the sunken valley is obtained from the Pont Dubuc which crosses the Saguenay.

Jonquière, another industrial town, has a most unusual church, Notre-Dame-de-Fatima, shaped like a wigwam.   Jonquière

Also worth seeing is the Musée de la Nature (open: daily 8.30am–9pm) in picturesque little Ste-Rose-du-Nord. It has extensive collections of stuffed animals and wooden artefacts (magnifying glasses, witches broomsticks).   Ste-Rose-du-Nord

See entry   Tadoussac

Saint John   Q 8

Province: New Brunswick. Population: 90,000

See New Brunswick   Information

Saint John (the name is always written in full and without an apostrophe "s" to distinguish it from St John's which, as the locals are quick to point out, is in Newfoundland), New Brunswick's largest town, is also the province's major industrial centre and a thriving port. It stands on a rocky estuarine spur at the point where the Saint John River disgorges into the

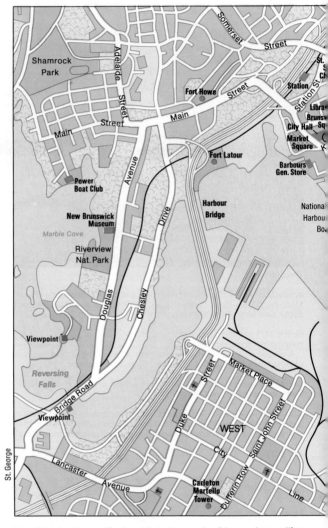

Bay of Fundy. Known affectionately to the people of the province as "fog city" (on account of the sea fogs which from time to time roll in off the Bay), the peculiarities of its site mean that Saint John has few straight roads, and a great many cul-de-sacs instead.

On a clear summer's day, with a wind to blow the smell of wood pulp (emanating from the big, riverside paper mills) away from the town, there are few more attractive and interesting places than Saint John.

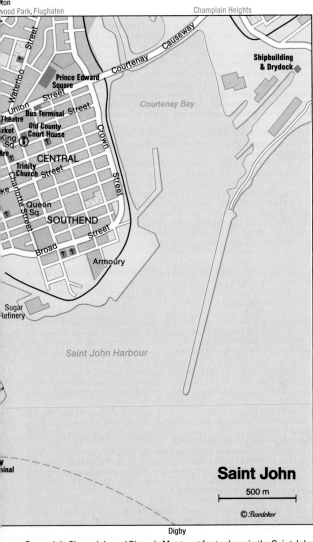

Saint John

500 m

© Baedeker

Digby

Samuel de Champlain and Sieur de Monts set foot ashore in the Saint John   History
Estuary in 1604. They were followed a few years later by their compatriot,
Charles de la Tour, who established a trading post. In 1645 Sieur de
Menou d'Aulney, a fellow Frenchman from Port Royal, destroyed the
post, initiating a period of intense internecine rivalry among the French in
Acadia (see entry) – at a time also of almost continuous Anglo-French
hostilities.

Eventually the area was ceded to Britain at the Treaty of Paris in 1763 and a new trading post was set up.

The town of Saint John is regarded as having itself been founded in 1783. On May 18th of that year the sails of a huge fleet were sighted in the mouth of the river. Aboard the ships were 3000 Loyalists fleeing the American War of Independence and with their arrival the little settlement was transformed almost overnight into a boom town. By the end of the year the number of newcomers had risen to 4200, many of whom made their way north along the river to settle at Fredericton. Most of the new arrivals were well-to-do people who had lost nearly everything during the revolution. Few came equipped with the necessary pioneering skills for wresting a home from the wilderness. But somehow they survived and in due course built up a prosperous maritime city known in addition for its lively social life.

In the 19th c. the city's flourishing shipbuilding industry and many trading links earned Saint John the reputation of being North America's Liverpool.

In 1877 more than half the town was burned down in a catastrophic fire. When some years later the era of wooden ships came to an end, Saint John fell into decline, a fate shared with other communities on the Atlantic seaboard. Although the port continued in operation it was only in the 1960s that prosperity returned, with vast sums of money being invested in the paper industry and sugar and oil refineries. Harbour facilities were improved by the construction of a container terminal and deep water berths (for supertankers) and Saint John experienced both a resurgence of its shipyards and the growth of a number of newly diversified industries responsive to the needs of its port.

Events

In July each year the founding of the city is celebrated in style with a re-enactment of the Loyalist landing. Everyone dresses up in 18th c. costume and there is a big parade. Wining, dining and dancing in the street complete the festivities.

Sights

★★Reversing Falls Rapids

The Saint John River flows south-east through New Brunswick from its source in the US state of Maine, spilling out into the Bay of Fundy (see Fundy Bay) at Saint John where the tidal range is 8.5m/29ft. At low tide the sea level is more than 4m/13ft below that of the river, and a torrent of water pours into the Bay. As the tide rises the flow of the river slackens, then becomes still as a mill pond before eventually being reversed. At high water the level in the Bay rises more than 4m/13ft above the river and the sea forces its way powerfully inland, the effects of the incoming tide being felt as much as 130km/80 miles upstream at Fredericton.

The most spectacular reversal of flow occurs at Reversing Falls Rapids where, prior to reaching the Bay of Fundy, the river narrows, plunging through a deep gorge. With a strong current flowing (in either direction) impressive rapids and eddies form.

The Reversing Falls can best be appreciated in all their variety by making a number of visits at different states of the tide (e.g. at low water when the river pours towards the Bay, at slack water to observe the flow reverse, and on the full flood as the water surges upstream). The exact times of the tides can be obtained from the Tourist Office.

Reversing Falls Bridge

From the bridge craft can be seen making their way up and down river at slack water, movement being impossible at other times because of the strong currents.

Falls View Park

Good views of the rapids (though not nearly as dramatic as the views from Reversing Falls Bridge) can also be obtained from the park at the end of Falls View Ave.

Fort Howe Lookout

There are two places from which, on a fine clear day, attractive views can be had over the attractively situated town. One is Fort Howe Lookout (reached

Reversing Falls Rapid

from Main St. via Metcalfe St. and Magazine St.). From the site of this wooden blockhouse perched high on its rocky cliff a magnificent panorama unfolds of the shipyards, harbour, river and town.

The Carleton Martello Tower (open: mid-May–mid-Oct. daily 10am–7pm) stands in what is now a National Historic Park. The tower was built in 1813 to protect the port against possible attack by the United States. It had various uses from time to time in the 19th c. and again during the two World Wars. In the Second World War it served as area headquarters for the anti-aircraft defence and fire fighting services, a two-storey steel and concrete structure being added for the purpose.

Carleton Martello Tower

Today the tower houses an exhibition of military life in the 18th c. with guides in historical costume. The general history of the region is also the subject of several displays.

Rising high above its surroundings the tower is the second vantage point from which fine views can be enjoyed over the town, the harbour and far out to sea across the Bay of Fundy.

Founded more than a century ago the museum is devoted to the natural history, life and art of the province. The "golden age" of New Brunswick's shipbuilding industry in the 19th c. is especially well represented, with collections of model ships, paintings and other items of interest. Various exhibits pay tribute to the city's role as a major trading centre during that period, quite apart from its shipbuilding. A vivid picture emerges of the huge quantity of goods of all kinds which passed through the port.

★New Brunswick Museum

There is an interesting section on the indigenous Indian culture of New Brunswick including artefacts made from birchbark, quill and bead work, traditional furnishings and clothes, etc.

In addition the museum possesses an outstanding collection of watercolours, drawings and photographs of Saint John, New Brunswick and other parts of Canada. The collection is used to mount a series of temporary exhibitions based on different themes.

The natural history section concentrates on flora and fauna native to New Brunswick (especially birds, insects, fish and mammals) as well as the geology of the province.

Open: May–Sept. daily 10am–5pm, Oct.–Apr. 2–5pm.

Town centre

Downtown

In recent years new life has been breathed into the city centre making it a particularly pleasant place to explore on foot. Various tourist "trails" have been marked out (information from the Tourist Office).

Market Place

Opened in 1983 the Market Place is actually an attractive multi-level shopping centre with atrium-like inner courtyard, part of a complex which also includes a hotel, conference centre, a number of flats. A street of 19th c. warehouses incorporated into the complex now faces a pretty "plaza" around Market Slip (where in 1783 the Loyalists came ashore from their ships).

"Ocean Hawk II"

Today Market Slip provides a berth for an elderly deep sea tug "Ocean Hawk II". In summer the plaza is a lively place, with street cafés and musical entertainment.

Barbour's General Store

On the south side of the plaza Barbour's General Store (open: daily except mid-Apr.–mid-May) occupies a red and cream coloured building erected in 1867. On display is a wide range of merchandise typical of the times.

Dock Street, City Hall, Brunswick Square

An elevated walkway crossing over Dock St. links Market Square with the Saint John City Hall and Brunswick Square (a complex of shops, offices and hotels). There is an observation gallery in the City Hall (open on weekdays).

Loyalist House

Built in 1817 by David Merrit, a Loyalist who fled New York in 1783, the house was among the few to survive the great fire of 1877 and is thus one of the oldest buildings in Saint John. The plain, partly shingle-clad façade conceals a spacious and elegant Georgian interior. Notice especially the arches between the rooms, and the curved staircase. The solid rock foundations on which the house is built, visible on the Germain St. side, are typical of houses in Saint John. (Guided tours daily June and Sept. at half hourly intervals.)

★King Square

Generally regarded as the centre of Saint John, King Square with its two-storey bandstand is planted with trees and flowerbeds in the form of a Union flag. Almost any product of New Brunswick – including the edible seaweed known as dulse – can be found at the old City Market off one corner of the square.

Burial Ground

Situated off the side of the square opposite the market is the old Loyalist Burial Ground.

Saint John River Valley   Q 8

Province: New Brunswick

Information

See New Brunswick

The Saint John River, 660km/410 miles long with a catchment area of more than 67,000sq.km/25,800sq.miles, rises in the US state of Maine before flowing south-eastwards through the Canadian province of New Brunswick. For some 100km/62 miles of its length it forms the frontier between the two countries. It enters the sea at Saint John on the Bay of Fundy (see entries).

★Geography

After emerging from the northern-most foothills of the Appalachians the river traverses New Brunswick's agriculturally rich "potato belt", reaching the relatively flat coastal region near Fredericton.

Throughout its history the valley of the Saint John River has served as an important highway. European immigrants, arriving in numbers from the 17th c. onwards, settled in the valley, at the heart of the region which came to be known as Acadia (see entry). The river itself was christened by Samuel de Champlain, who landed in the estuary on St John's Day (June 24th) 1604.

History of settlement

The natural route represented by the valley is still followed today by two major links in Canada's modern transport system, the TransCanada Highway and the railway.

Several big dams have been constructed on the Saint John River, producing between them enough hydro-electric power to meet a large part of New Brunswick's needs.

Hydro-electric power

A drive down the valley of the Saint John River

The route described follows the Saint John River downstream from the provincial boundary between New Brunswick and Québec.

N.B.

Set in an otherwise largely rural area the small industrial town of Edmundston (population 12,000) lies at the centre of the mainly French-speaking and Catholic "République de Madawaska", a relic of the old Acadia dating back to the end of the 18th c.

Edmundston

The twin spires of Edmundston's Catholic cathedral are a striking landmark, visible for miles around. Also worth seeing is the Musée Madawaska (Bd. Hébert; open: mid-May–mid-Sept. Tues.–Sun.) which traces the history of the area.

An hour's drive beyond Edmundston, at the little town of Grand Falls, the Saint John River is transformed into a thundering cascade as it squeezes through a picturesquely wild gorge. A large hydro-electric power station harnesses the water's energy.

★ Grand Falls (Grand Sault)

The most interesting section of the gorge is now a Provincial Park and a Visitors Centre (open: mid-May–mid-Sept.) has been built beside the falls.

South of Grand Falls Highway 105 offers a pleasant alternative to the TransCanada Highway, passing through an attractive agricultural landscape with many lovely views down into the valley.

Florenceville

Potato fields dominate the scenery around the village of Hartland (population 1000). McCain's is one of the potato processing companies to have a factory here, products such as frozen potatoes being exported all over the world.

Hartland

Hartland used to be better known for its covered bridge, built over the Saint John River in 1897. At 391m/1280ft it is the longest of its kind in the world. The bridge has suffered serious damage on a number of occasions in its lifetime and requires almost continual repair.

Covered Bridge

Next stop downstream is the attractive township of Woodstock, not far from the Canada-US frontier.

Woodstock

The King's Landing outdoor museum south of Woodstock (open: daily, end of May to mid-Oct.) vividly re-creates village life in 19th c. New Brunswick. The houses of the restored village, in an attractive setting at the mouth of a little creek, were originally built by King's American Dragoons who settled along the river after the American War of Independence. When the river was dammed some years ago all the buildings had to be moved to a more elevated site.

★ King's Landing

The working sawmill and King's Head Inn (restaurant, refreshments) are particularly enthralling, the latter the epitome of a 19th c. country coaching inn. Various scenes of "Living History" are enacted during the main tourist season.

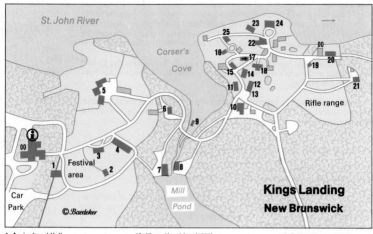

1 Agricultural Hall
2 Print Shop (1890)
3 Hagerman House (1850)
4 Carriage Shop
5 Joslin House (1860)
6 Jones House (1830)
7 Gristmill (1880)
8 Sawmill (1830)
9 Brunswick Lion

10 Kings Head Inn (1855)
11 Lint House (1830)
12 Horsepower & Dragsaw (1890)
13 Lint Barn
14 Blacksmith Shop (1870)
15 Long House (1845)
16 Heustis House (1850)
17 St. Mark's Church (1890)

18 Perley House (1870)
19 Parish School (1840)
20 Snack Bar
21 Killeen Cabin (1830)
22 Morehouse House (1820)
23 Kings Theatre
24 Ingraham House (1840)
25 Fisher House (1820)

Mactaquac
Provincial Park

About half an hour's drive from the New Brunswick capital of Fredericton (see entry), Mactaquac Provincial Park (boating, walking and a variety of other leisure facilities) provides opportunities for relaxation in delightful surroundings.

Saint John's   T 8

Province: Newfoundland. Population: 160,000

Information

Tourism Newfoundland, P.O. Box 2016, St John's, A1C 5R8; tel. (709) 576–2830.

General

The capital of Newfoundland, undisputedly the oldest "European" town in North America, occupies a spectacular site on one of the finest natural harbours in the world. Entered through "the Narrows", a 207m/226yd wide passage flanked by cliffs 150m/490ft high, the harbour widens out into a basin some 800m/875yds across, surrounded by steep rocky slopes on which St John's is built.

Typical of St John's are the traditional square, flat-roofed, wooden houses painted in different colours. Because of the many fires to engulf the town, these now date back only to Victorian times.

Name

The city was named after St John the Baptist, John Cabot having reputedly discovered Newfoundland on June 24th (sic!) 1497.

History

Whatever uncertainty surrounds the exact date of its discovery, there is no doubt that, from about 1500, the harbour was used as a base by fishing vessels from various European countries, leading to Britain's claiming official possession in 1583 in the reign of Elizabeth I.

The centre of St John's, capital of Newfoundland

There followed a long period during which, having developed into a thriving fishery and trading post, St John's "governed" by a succession of ruthless "Fishing Admirals".

In subsequent centuries British possession was disputed with the Dutch, Portuguese, Spaniards and particularly the French. In addition St John's was attacked on a number of occasions by pirates. British sovereignty was finally confirmed in 1762 following a short period of French occupation.

In the 19th c. under British rule the city developed rapidly as a centre of commerce, despite being devastated several times by fire – in 1892 it was almost completely rebuilt. Its prosperity continued into the early 20th c. and was revived during the Second World War when St John's became the departure point for North Atlantic convoys. In 1949 Newfoundland joined the Canadian Confederation, a development which resulted in the city's decline. But recent years have seen the capital revitalised, especially following the discovery of oil reserves offshore.

The city played an historic part in the development of transport and communications. It was in St John's that the first transatlantic wireless signal was received in 1901 and it was also from St John's that John Alcock and Arthur Brown took off on the first successful non-stop flight across the Atlantic.

Transatlantic communication

Signal Hill, the steep cliffs of which make up the north side of the harbour entrance, was the scene of the final engagement of the Seven Years' War between Britain and France. During the annual Military Tattoo, held here mid-July–end of Aug. (Tues., Thur., Sat. and Sun. 3 and 7pm), the battle is commemorated by the sounding of the last post.

Despite its strategic position Signal Hill remained unfortified following the Seven Years' War until the present defences were built during the hostilities of 1812. The hill traditionally served as a marine look-out however, which is how it acquired its name.

Sights

★★Signal Hill National Historic Park

431

Saint John's

The thump of cannon can still be heard each midday, echoing round the Signal Hill National Historic Park (open: mid-June–beginning Sept. daily 9am–8pm, at other times daily 8.30am–4.30pm). The Park is one of the largest of its kind in Canada and, being situated 152m/500ft above the sea, affords superb views day and night over the city, the harbour and the adjacent coast.

Visitor Centre

The Visitor Centre has several interesting displays illustrating the history of Newfoundland, especially the development of St John's.

Cabot Tower

Cabot Tower (open daily) was built in 1897 to mark the four hundredth anniversary of the discovery of Newfoundland. It also now commemorates Guglielmo Marconi's reception here in 1901 of the first transatlantic radio telegraphy signal, transmitted over a distance of 2700km/1700 miles from Poldhu in England. In the tower are exhibitions on the history of Signal Hill and the history of communications (with a special section on Marconi). From the top there is a panoramic view of the city and the coast as far as Cape Spear – the most easterly point of North America.

Queen's Battery

An excellent view of the harbour can be had from the 18th c. Queen's Battery overlooking the Narrows.
The lighthouse on the other side of the Narrows stands among the remains of an old fort – Fort Amherst.

★Quidi Vidi

Quidi Vidi, a delightful little fishing community which forms part of St John's, is situated on a small cliff-enclosed inlet on the north side of Signal Hill. A narrow channel links the inlet with Quidi Vidi Lake, where the oldest sporting event in North America, the annual St John's Regatta, is held.
The now restored Quidi Vidi Battery (open daily in summer) overlooking the inlet was built during the French occupation of St John's. In 1780, after the British regained control, the battery was strengthened and used as a garrison by British troops until their withdrawal from Newfoundland in 1870. What is possibly the oldest house in British Canada, built in 1740, survives within the fort (it was used by the British as a dressing post during the Battle of Signal Hill). In 1967 the Battery was restored for the centenary celebrations.

Commissariat House

Standing next to one another in King's Bridge Road Commissariat House and the little Anglican Church of St Thomas make an attractive ensemble. The house (built between 1819 and 1821) and the church (1836) are among the few buildings to have escaped the devastating fires in the 19th c. The restored Georgian-style house (open: daily in summer; in winter by appointment only) was the headquarters of a Commissariat responsible for keeping the St John's military post supplied. An Interpretive Centre in the adjoining reconstructed coach house illustrates how the house was restored.

Colonial Building

Built in 1850 of white Irish limestone and embellished with a Classical portico, the Colonial Building in Military Road was until 1960 the seat of the Newfoundland government (afterwards the provincial parliament moved into the newly erected Confederation Building). The old building now houses the provincial archives (open: in summer Mon.–Fri. 9am–4.15pm, in winter Mon.–Fri. 9am–5pm).

★★Basilica of St John the Baptist

Also in Military Road, on the highest point of the ridge above the city (fine view over the Narrows), stands Newfoundland's architecturally most important building, the Basilica of St John the Baptist (1842–92). Built in the form of a Latin cross and graced by slender twin towers 42m/138ft high, the Basilica is noted for some fine statues and its beautiful ornate gold leaf ceiling. The statue of Our Lady of Fatima in one of the transepts was a gift from Portuguese sailors who were fortunate enough to survive being shipwrecked on the Banks. The basilica is now a National Historic Site.

Also dedicated to St John the Baptist, the Anglican cathedral on Church Hill (a short distance south of the basilica) is likewise a National Historic Site. The cathedral, the foundation stone of which was laid in 1849, was designed by Gilbert Scott and ranks among the finest examples of pure neo-Gothic architecture in North America. It also has fine interior furnishings.

★ Anglican Cathedral of St John the Baptist

After suffering serious damage in two major 19th c. fires the cathedral was not restored until 1905. Among other valuable treasures kept in the chapter-house is a gold communion vessel presented by William IV.

The Newfoundland Museum, just across the road from the Anglican cathedral, traces the history of Newfoundland and Labrador back 9000 years, with exhibits dating from prehistoric as well as colonial times (open: Mon.–Wed., Fri. 9am–5pm, Thur. 9am–9pm, Sun. and holidays 10am–5pm). One section includes an excellent collection of Indian art while another is devoted to the lives of the European pioneers who settled the province – from the hardships of the fisherfolk to the elegant drawing rooms of the prosperous city dwellers.

★ Newfoundland Museum

The War Memorial (1924) in Water Street E. stands on the spot where in 1583 Sir Humphrey Gilbert claimed possession of the colony in the name of Queen Elizabeth I.

War Memorial

The harbourside Murray Premises are restored mercantile buildings dating from 1847, now converted into shops, restaurants and offices and containing a branch of the Newfoundland Museum. Opened in 1983 the branch is devoted to the natural, military and maritime history of the province, including the development of maritime trade, underwater archaeology, navigation, cartography and shipwrecks (open: Mon.–Fri. 9am–5pm, Sat. and Sun. 10am–6pm).

★ Murray Premises

With its many bars and restaurants George Street is a popular city centre rendezvous.

George Street

For more than 400 years Water Street, one of the oldest streets in North America, was the commercial centre of St John's. It is still the meeting place for sailors from all over the world, with a host of inviting shops, restaurants and bars.

Water Street

Occupying a site high above the rest of the city the Confederation Building (guided tours Mon.–Fri.) is the seat of Newfoundland's provincial govenment. It is also the location of a permanent exhibition which includes some of the best of the province's art both traditional and experimental.

Confederation Building

Strikingly modern in its architecture the Arts and Culture Centre in Prince Philip Drive was built in 1967 for the centenary celebrations. It plays a leading part in the province's cultural life and incorporates a quite exceptional theatre, two art galleries, a museum of the sea, three libraries and a commercial art school.

★ Arts and Culture Centre

The Centre is the venue for the Summer Festival of the Arts (theatre, concerts, etc., including some open air performances).

The Longshoremen's Protective Union Hall at the bottom of Victoria St. (referred to simply as the LSPU) is home to the highly successful Newfoundland Theatre. The company stages a wide variety of modern and classical plays, including works by Newfoundland authors. Interesting art exhibitions are mounted in the gallery of this lively cultural and social centre. It is also a centre for municipal activities.

Longshoremen's Protective Union (LSPU) Hall

Situated on the northern perimeter of St John's, C. A. Pippy Park (opened in 1968) extends over nearly 1400ha/3460 acres. There are walkers' trails, picnic places, a golf course and a children's animal farm.

C. A. Pippy Park

Botanical Gardens C. A. Pippy Park is also the location of a botanical garden belonging to St John's Memorial University. The garden (open: May to Nov. Wed.–Sat. 1.30–5.30pm, Sun. 10am–5.30pm) occupies some 42ha/100 acres of undulating ground and incorporates the about 6ha/15 acre Ox Pond. Spruce and fir, bog, heath and alder intersperse with rocky outcrops and natural landscape.

St Lawrence Waterway

Major axis of development The St Lawrence River is Canada's main transport corridor, along which lies the country's major axis of development. The river is a highway serving all the regions most favoured in terms of climate, soil and raw materials, areas incalculably rich in timber, mineral resources and agricultural potential. No wonder then that Canada's oldest and most densely populated areas of settlement lie in a ribbon along its banks. Aptly referred to as the "Main Street" of this vast country, 60% of all Canadians live within this belt. Just as importantly the St Lawrence is the gateway to Canada, and running east–west links several of the country's differing geographical regions. In this it contrasts strikingly with what also purports to be a "natural" route to the heart of North America, Hudson Bay, which in fact leads only into a cul-de-sac of inhospitable and largely unexploitable wastes. The importance of the St Lawrence even extends beyond the frontiers of Canada. On the one hand it forms a continuation of major transatlantic routes and thus a direct link with Europe; on the other it opens the way to the Mississippi river system, completing a line of communication used by the French as early as the 17th c. to maintain their colonial empire.

This draws attention to another factor – the significance of the St Lawrence to the neighbouring USA. Around the Great Lakes is concentrated one of the largest agglomerations of population and industry in the whole North American continent. As well as Chicago and Detroit with their millions of inhabitants and cities such as Milwaukee, Cleveland and Buffalo with populations of around half a million each, the industrial centres of the Prairies and the Mississippi basin all lie within the river's reach.

Even this is not yet the whole story. The great US east coast megalopolis with its more than 40 million inhabitants, seemingly cut off from the lowlands of the St Lawrence by the barrier of the Appalachians, is in practice easily accessible thanks to the Hudson–Champlain and Hudson–Mohawk depressions. The important New York–Montréal–Toronto transport triangle created by these natural routeways brings together the two largest concentrations of population and economic activity in the USA and Canada (Boston–New York–Philadelphia–Baltimore–Washington and the Québec–Windsor corridor i.e. "Main Street"). This same valley system also provides traffic on the St Lawrence with access to ice-free Atlantic ports (as does the St John River Valley in New Brunswick). Last but not least, not only does the St Lawrence form with Lake Superior by far the most important waterway in North America, the course of the river is also followed by Canadian Pacific (CP) and Canadian National (CN) Railways' busiest lines, by most VIA Rail routes, by the major highways (including the Trans-Canada Highway) and the busiest air corridors.

Traffic travelling up and down the St Lawrence Seaway maintains an almost perfect balance. Shipped east from the ports on Lake Superior (Duluth and Thunder Bay) are bulk cargoes of iron ore and grain, the latter carried the length of the St Lawrence on its way to ports abroad, the former, from the Mesabi Range, bound for the centres of US heavy industry (Sault Ste-Marie, Chicago–Gary and Detroit–Toledo).

In the opposite direction comes Pennsylvanian coal, heading west from ports on Lake Erie towards those self-same blast-furnaces or destined for the industrial cities on Lakes Erie (Cleveland, Ashtabula, Buffalo) and Ontario (Hamilton). These latter are in turn supplied, not with American iron ore from Lake Superior (Duluth) but with Canadian ore from further east (from

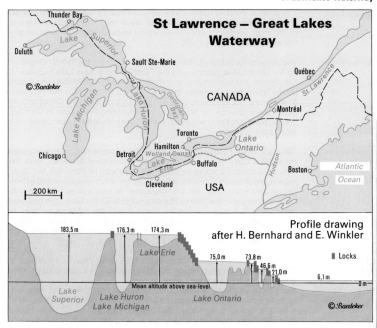

St Lawrence – Great Lakes Waterway

Profile drawing after H. Bernhard and E. Winkler

© Baedeker

the deposits in Labrador, opened up after the Second World War). This pattern of shipment means that upstream of the Niagara Falls (bypassed by the Welland Canal) most of the tonnage carried is of lowland origin whereas on the St Lawrence itself about half the tonnage comes from mountain areas.

The winter freeze-up poses a great problem for shipping – in the Toronto area for instance it lasts for 90 days.

Winter freeze-up

Topography throws down other sorts of challenges to navigation, the first being met with as the St Lawrence crosses the foothills of the Canadian Shield – a landscape of rocks worn smooth by glaciers – in the vicinity of the Thousand Islands. The second is faced on the middle section of the waterway where, at Niagara Falls and the adjacent Niagara Gorge, a difference in height of 100m/330ft between Lakes Ontario and Erie has to be overcome. Without the removal of these two barriers – not to mention the 7m/23ft height difference at the Sault Ste Marie Rapids between Lakes Superior and Huron – no truly efficient through route would be possible.

Topography

The existence of these three natural obstacles determined the character of the eventual waterway, involving the bypassing of Niagara Falls and construction of lock staircases at Sault Ste Marie and below Kingston.

Although the Niagara escarpment with its massive Falls represented a seemingly insurmountable obstacle, it was precisely at this point (between Lakes Erie and Ontario) that the need for an efficient transport link was most acute. As a result no less than four successive canal and lock systems were constructed, not all being on the same route.

Niagara escarpment

St Lawrence Waterway

Welland Canal

The present Welland Canal (see entry) overcomes the 100m/330ft difference in level by means of a staircase of seven huge locks. The result is one of the most prodigious feats of structural engineering to be seen on any transport system in the world.

St Mary's River

The locks on the St Mary's River at Sault Ste Marie are the hub of navigation on the Great Lakes, neutralising the 7.2m/23ft drop from Lake Superior to Lake Huron. The first canal to be built at this strategic point was constructed by the North West Company in 1798, but was destroyed in the 1812 war. Next came a lock in 1855, followed in 1895 by a canal on the Canadian side and lock staircase on the American, circumventing the rapids. Today there are five parallel locks of which the 9m/29ft deep McArthur Lock (on the USA side) is the largest.

Lake Ontario–Montreal section

The most difficult problem on the whole St Lawrence Waterway was posed by a 300m/328yd section between Lake Ontario and Montréal. Here the river crosses the Canadian Shield, dropping a total of 75m/246ft and forming a series of rapids. The idea of building a canal to circumvent the Lachine Rapids above Montréal was first canvassed as long ago as 1680, but only came to fruition in the 19th c. The original 5km/3 mile long Lachine Canal was 1.50m/5ft deep and ascended 13m/43ft with the aid of seven locks. In subsequent years more canals and locks were built until, by about 1900, a system of shallow water canals was in operation all the way from Lake Superior to Montréal.

Creation of the Seaway

In 1954, after initial resistance from the USA (which feared the effects of competition on other American shipping routes), the long awaited construction of the St Lawrence Seaway began. The Seaway was completed and officially opened in 1959. The installations on this major waterway comprise efficient technologically advanced canals navigable by vessels of 8.2m/26ft draught, with locks 233.5m/766ft long, 24.4m/80ft wide and 9.1m/30ft deep, together with several large hydro-electric stations (some new, some enlarged).

The 22 old locks formerly needed to surmount the 75m/246ft rise on this section of the river are today replaced by just seven large ones, with lifts of between 1.8 and 15.2m/6 and 50ft. But the massive engineering project inevitably had a profound effect on the local environment; traffic routes had to be relocated, bridges built, and industrial plant and harbour installations constructed or enlarged. In many places what had previously been cultivated land was flooded, and a total of 500 buildings and 6500 people were moved to new sites on higher ground.

The benefits which this has brought in terms of improved transport efficiency have been felt over a wide geographical area. Before the Seaway opened, ocean-going vessels would off load their cargoes at Montréal onto small "canallères" with a capacity of 2000–3000 tonnes. At Lake Ontario the freight would be transferred for a second time, aboard the big "lakers". Today this three-stage operation is no longer necessary and ocean-going ships and "lakers" of more than 25,000 tonnes ply the whole length of the St Lawrence. As a result many ports and industrial areas have seen their economies expand. Total shipments increased from 12.5 million tonnes in 1956 to 20 million tonnes by 1959; by 1984 they had more than doubled again to some 48 million tonnes. In that same year, on the Montréal–Lake Ontario section of the Seaway, wheat accounted for 15.9 million tonnes (33.5%), iron ore 11.4 million tonnes (24%) and iron and steel 4.5 million tonnes (9.5%).

Of all the freight carried on the Seaway, 42.2% was transported within Canada, 15.6% went from Canada to the USA, and 7.7% from the USA to Canada. Exports from Canada to countries other than the USA accounted for 4.6%, imports for 3.2%. Non-Canadian imports to the USA amounted to 13.7%, exports from the USA 10.0%. These figures are eloquent testimony to the huge national and international importance of the St Lawrence Seaway.

Saskatchewan (Province)

Geographical location: 49° to 60°N 102° to 110°W.
Area: 651,900sq.km/251,633sq.miles
Population: 1,046,862. Capital: Regina

Tourism Saskatchewan   Information
1919 Saskatchewan Drive, Regina S4P 3V7; tel. (0306) 787 9685.

Saskatchewan, which extends some 1125km/700 miles from north to
south, has shared borders with Manitoba in the east, Alberta in the west
and the two US states of Montana and North Dakota in the south.

Two-thirds of the province belong to the Interior Plains of Canada, the
remaining (northern) third being part of the Canadian Shield. As a result
Saskatchewan reveals two very different topographical faces. The north,
shaped long ago by glaciation, is a landscape of extensive bogs with
literally thousands of lakes. In the south gently rising prairies of fertile
brown and black earth merge into the hill country further west. The province's highest point (1392m/4570ft) is found in the Cypress Hills, the lowest
at Lake Athabasca (65m/213ft). Half the province is wooded, a third is arable
land, and one eighth (totalling 80,000sq.km/30,880sq.miles) is covered
with freshwater. The vast majority of the almost 100,000 lakes, relics of Ice
Age glaciation, are found in north Saskatchewan.
  Of the major river systems three, the Assiniboine, the North and South
Saskatchewan and the Churchill, all flow into Hudson Bay; the Frenchman
River (in the far south-west) flows into the Mississippi.
  To the Cree Indians living on the Great Plains centuries ago the biggest of
these waterways was "the river that flows swiftly" or "Saskatchewan". It
was from this that the province later took its name.

Saskatchewan has a distinctly dry continental climate with temperatures   Climate
that increase progressively from north to south. The long cold winter

Saskatchewan

begins in October, average temperatures being below freezing point (January temperatures in the north range from about −20° to −25°C/−4° to −13°F). But the sun alleviates the cold even when the thermometer falls to −30°C/−22°F, and the warm chinook wind can lift the temperature within hours by up to 25°C/77°F. The north averages 130cm/51in. of snow, the south 76cm/30in.

Spring generally arrives in April. In the very short but extremely hot summer temperatures of up to 38°C/100°F can be reached, though from May through to August they most often hover between 20°C/68°F and 35°C/95°F. Saskatchewan is Canada's sunniest province and Estevan the country's "Sunshine Capital" (averaging 2540 hours of sunshine a year). Nights are usually quite cool. Rain accompanied by violent thunderstorms is a quite frequent feature of the late afternoon or evening. Annual rainfall ranges between 250 and 600mm/10 and 24in.

Vegetation

Influenced by the climate the vegetation also varies progressively from north to south. The sub-Arctic coniferous forests of north Saskatchewan give way to mixed coniferous forests (spruce, aspen, poplar and birch), these latter yielding in turn to the prairie grasslands of the south.

History

The history of the area now comprising Saskatchewan can be traced back at least 30,000 years, to the time when nomadic hunting tribes crossed from Asia into North America over the land bridge which then connected the two. These first inhabitants of North America migrated with the seasons, moving between the prairies and the forests and river valleys. They lived primarily by hunting buffalo. Few vestiges of their presence now remain though archaeological excavations near Saskatoon have revealed some evidence of Indian tribal culture from 8000 years ago.

Saskatchewan's more recent history reflects the complex interplay of differing ethnic groups. Its opening chapters were written centuries ago when the native Assiniboine, Blackfoot, Chipewyan and Cree Indians, living on the Great Plains, came into contact with the first European adventurers pushing west into the interior from the shores of Hudson Bay.

The earliest recorded arrival (1690) was that of Henry Kelsey, commissioned to reconnoitre the area on behalf of the British Hudson's Bay fur trading company. Soon other explorers followed, also making their way inland from Hudson Bay or from the Great Lakes, men such as La Vérendrye, Hearne and Pond, who helped map out Canada and in doing so opened the hinterland to the growing trade in furs. Rupert's Land, as it was then called, remained in the possession of the Hudson's Bay Company for 200 years, before recognition of the vast mineral wealth led to its purchase by the Canadian government in 1870. This was followed by large-scale settlement of the prairies where plots of arable land were sold to pioneer farmers for just a registration fee.

In 1873 the Canadian government appointed a provisional administration for the region (renamed the Northwest Territories and incorporating the bulk of western Canada). Battleford became the territorial capital in 1876.

It was also at this time that the police force known today as the Royal Canadian Mounted Police came into existence. It was formed in 1874 when 300 police recruits, charged with establishing the rule of law in the North-West, set out on an incredible 1300km/800 mile trek from Fort Dufferin in Manitoba,.

In 1885 simmering unrest in the new frontier region boiled over into armed conflict between the Metis and the Canadian government. The root cause of the North West Rebellion (as the conflict became known) was the failure of the federal authorities to concern themselves with the problems of the frontier folk. Several clashes took place between government troops and the insurgents led by Louis Riel before the rebellion was finally quashed. Riel was found guilty of treason and hanged the same year.

The population of Saskatchewan and Alberta increased rapidly in the first decades of the 20th c. with the arrival, in wave after wave, of 700,000 new settlers. Attracted to the prairies by cheap land they quickly established agriculture as a major sector of the country's economy.

Saskatchewan only became a province in 1905 and has the reputation of being the most politically radical in the Canadian federation.

The 1930s were a turning-point for the economy. First came the stock market crash of 1929 and the worldwide Great Depression which followed. Then drought and failed harvests brought the country to the edge of ruin. Within a short time, however, Saskatchewan had recovered and today enjoys the benefits of a stable economy based on a wealth of natural resources.

In 1944 the people of the province elected the first socialist government in North America, keeping it in power until 1967. A series of measures were introduced to improve living conditions. These included the creation of state enterprises, modernisation of schools and expansion of electricity supplies throughout the region.

Many of the more than one million Saskatchewans trace their roots back to Europe, to Russia, Scandinavia and the British Isles.

About 55% of the population are urban dwellers, of whom a third live in Regina and Saskatoon. Most people are concentrated in the south of the province, 40% of them in farming communities.

Saskatchewans have the highest life expectancy in Canada – 78.6 years for women, 71.1 years for men.

Population

The Saskatchewan economy reflects the richness of its natural resources, particularly the mineral deposits, energy reserves (mineral oil, natural gas) and huge supplies of timber.

Economy

Between 1982 and 1987 skilful management of the economy saw Saskatchewan's GNP rise from $14.7 billion to $18.4 billion. 40% of goods produced in the province are exported, three quarters of them beyond Canada. Almost half (45.2%, mainly oil, potash and uranium) go to the USA. The second most importance market (24.7%) is in Asia and the countries of the Pacific basin, which between them import $1.4 billion worth of produce, primarily cereals, potash and uranium. Exports to western Europe account for 8.8%.

Saskatchewan is a major source of potash, oil, gold and uranium. It is the world's leading supplier of potash possessing almost two-thirds of the planet's known reserves. 25% of world demand is met by ten mines.

The richest deposits of heavy oil in Canada are also found in the province, a total of 662.7 million barrels (1988). Production in 1987 was 76.2 million barrels.

Saskatchewan is the world's largest exporter of uranium, more than 300 million kg/661 million lb of uranium bearing ore (about 80% of the earth's total) having been discovered in the Athabasca basin. Annual production is presently running at 8.2 million kg/18 million lb.

In its first year the Star Lake mine, one of a number of gold mines opened in 1987, produced 1056kg/2328lb of gold valued at $20 million.

Saskatchewan also exports increasingly large quantities of natural gas. Reserves are estimated at more than 69 billion cu.m.

Lignite deposits totalling 7.6 billion tonnes/tons supply almost 75% of the province's electricity requirements.

Mining of all kinds contributes 9% of the province's GNP.

Saskatchewan's largest renewable resource is its forests, barely half of which are exploited commercially. The most important woods are spruce, aspen, poplar and birch. In 1987/88 timber production was worth $258 million.

As a result of deliberate economic diversificiation into new technologies the province is today a world leader in the fields of bio-technology, fibre optics and satellite communications. SaskTel developed and installed the world's first commercial fibre optics telephone, television and data communications system (still one of the largest) and, with telecommunications

"Echo Valley Farm" in Saskatchewan

playing an increasingly important role, runs a worldwide service network (video conferences, data and teleprinter communications, etc.)

Agriculture, cereal production in particular, continues to be a major source of income for Saskatchewan, possessing as it does 44% (20 million hectares) of the federation's agricultural land. Canada's "bread basket" produces 60% of the country's wheat and meets 12% of total world demand.

Livestock represent another important branch of agriculture, with more than 25% of the country's cattle and 20% of its sheep, pigs and poultry being reared in the province.

The food processing industry also contributes substantially to the economy (meat and potato products, pasta, etc.)

Leisure, sport, tourism

In its still largely unspoilt landscape Saskatchewan has a further resource, particularly attractive to anyone with a love of the great outdoors and the untouched, tranquil beauty of the land. While canoeing, angling and swimming can all be enjoyed on the numerous lakes, many visitors want nothing more than the opportunity to observe wild creatures in their natural environment. But for those keen to participate in any of the various sports and leisure activities excellent facilities are provided by the National and Provincial Parks (walkers' trails, swimming and a wide range of other pursuits).

Suggested route

TransCanada Highway (about 600km/370 miles)

A substantial part of the province can be seen by following the Trans-Canada Highway as it runs across the prairies and wheatfields of southern

Saskatchewan. It is best to start from the province's south-east border with Manitoba (see entry) and drive east–west along the Highway (which passes through the capital Regina and the town of Swift Current). Detours can then be made either north or south to visit the many places of interest (Moose Mountain Provincial Park, Qu'Appelle Valley (see entry), Cypress Hills Provincial Park (see entry), etc.). Plenty of opportunities for swimming, fishing and hunting will be found along the way.

Saskatoon   H 7

Province: Saskatchewan. Population: 185,000

Tourism Bureau, 345 3rd Ave., Saskatoon; tel. (306) 242–1206   Information

Saskatoon, the province's biggest city and a melting pot of different cultures, lies on the banks of the South Saskatchewan River. Known as "the city of bridges" it has wide tree-lined streets and 1620ha/4000 acres of parks and green spaces. It is the acknowledged "mining capital" of Canada and is often referred to as a mini Silicon Valley because of its leading role in Canada's high-tec and mining industries. It is the home of the highly respected University of Saskatchewan with some 17,000 students.   General

Before the arrival of Europeans this area was inhabited by Cree Indians, the dominant prairie tribe. Each spring and summer they hunted buffalo on the Great Plains, setting up camp in the vicinity of Saskatoon.   History

The town itself was founded in 1882 by Methodists from Ontario who, led by John Lake, intended to establish a temperance colony. In due course the settlement was named Saskatoon (from "misakwatomin", the Indian word for the red berries which grew locally). Already by this time the great buffalo herds had disappeared and the days of the Indians' nomadic existence were numbered. For the new arrivals life was far from easy. Floods, blizzards, prairie fires and mosquitoes exacerbated the normal hardships of the daily round, instilling into the early pioneers a stubborn determination to overcome adversity.

The temperance ideal attracted few settlers however, and 20 years on the township could still only claim 113 inhabitants. This soon changed, partly because by 1901 agricultural production was on the increase, and partly because, with the opening of the railway in 1908, the entire region saw an influx of new immigrants. The result was that people of many different nationalities – Germans, Scandinavians, Ukrainians and Britons – have all contributed to the development of the town. By 1911 Saskatoon had a population of more than 11,000. In the years that followed both population and economy continued to grow, slowly but steadily.

Highly recommended is a visit to this, the largest of Saskatchewan's four Western Development Museums (open: in summer daily 9am–9pm, reduced opening in winter) which authentically recreates and documents the history of the Canadian west. "Boomtown 1910", the reconstructed main street of a typical prairie town (the longest such street anywhere in North America), is lined with old-style shops – including a Chinese laundry and a barber's shop – as well as a church, fire-station, railway station, and other period buildings. There is also a collection of vintage cars (priceless today) and ancient tractors.   **Sights**

★Western Development Museum

The John Diefenbaker Centre (open: Mon.–Fri. 9.30am–4.30pm, Sat., Sun. and holidays 12.30–5pm) on the University campus is a combined archive and museum devoted to the life and times of Canada's 13th Prime Minister. In addition to its permanent displays, among which are replicas of the Cabinet Chamber and Prime Minister's office in Ottawa, the Centre is used for temporary exhibitions on history, politics, science and art. Diefenbaker and his wife are buried nearby.   John Diefenbaker Centre

Saskatoon

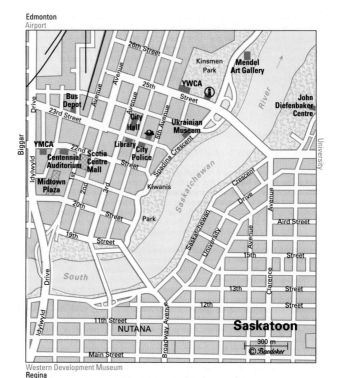

Western Development Museum
Regina

Little Stone School House	Also located on the University campus is a restored school dating from 1905 (open: May–Sept. Mon.–Fri. 9.30am–noon and 12.30–4.30pm, Sat., Sun. and holidays 12.30–5pm). Victoria School was Saskatoon's very first school and is its oldest surviving public building.
★Ukrainian Museum of Canada	The Ukrainian Museum of Canada (open: mid-Sept.–mid-June Tues.–Fri., Sun. 1–4.30pm, mid-June–Labour Day Mon.–Fri. 10am–4.30pm, Sat., Sun. 1–8pm) is dedicated to the many settlers who came here from the Ukraine and who contributed in such large measure to the country's development. Craftwork on display includes embroidered fabrics, wood carvings, traditional items of a religious kind (such as decorated Easter eggs) and ceramics.
★Museum of Ukrainian Culture	Other Ukrainian memorabilia, some dating from the 18th and 19th c., are collected together in the Museum of Ukrainian Culture (open: June, July, Aug. Mon.–Sat. 11am–5pm, Sun 1–8pm, winter Sat., Sun. 2–5pm) in Ave. "M" S. This ethnographic museum, founded by the Ukrainian Catholic Church, has various collections devoted to the religious, secular and folk heritage of Ukrainian immigrants.
Memorial Art Gallery	The Memorial Art Gallery in 11th St. (open: Mon.–Fri. 8am–noon and 1–4pm) commemorates students who lost their lives in the First World War. On display are paintings and wood cuts by 20th c. Canadian artists.

The Mendel Art Gallery (open: daily 10am–10pm) in Spadina Cres. East has temporary as well as permanent exhibitions of international, national and regional art.

Adjoining the gallery is a conservatory filled with colourful tropical plants.

Located about 3km/2 miles north of Saskatoon the Wanuskewin Heritage Park – from the Cree word "Wanuskewin" meaning "living together in harmony" – aims to encourage a better understanding of the indigenous peoples who inhabited the region in earlier times.

The park, spread over land purchased in 1983 from the Meewasin Valley Authority (the body responsible for the river valleys around Saskatoon) is the site of some exciting archaeological discoveries, research into which has established that Plains Indians lived in the area at least 6000 to 7000 years ago.

Among the major archaeological finds is a "medicine wheel", estimated to be about 1500 years old, consisting of a central cairn enclosed in a ring marked by three smaller cairns. Other cairns have been found marking the trail along which buffalo were herded before being driven over a precipice to their deaths. The animals were butchered in the valley below, the meat being preserved and the hides, bones, etc. processed for making into clothing, tools and tepees.

Sault Ste Marie

N 8

Province: Ontario
Population: 82,000

Algoma Kinniwabi Travel Association, 616 Queen St. E., Suite 203 M, Sault Ste Marie, Ontario, P6A 2A4; tel. (705) 254–4293.

Information

The Canadian border city of Sault Ste Marie, principal town of Algoma County, is situated on the delightful St Mary's River which joins Lake Superior to Lake Huron.

Long before the arrival of Europeans the significance of this particular location was appreciated by the native Indians for whom it was a place to meet and trade. As early as the first half of the 17th c. French "voyageurs", fur traders and timber raftsmen had already formed close links with local tribes. In 1667 the Ste Marie Mission was founded by French Jesuit missionaries and in 1671 possession was taken of the land in the name of the French king, Louis XIV.

Increasing numbers of settlers, the majority British but also some French, came to Sault Ste Marie after 1797/98 when a canal was dug to by-pass the rapids. In 1861 the town became a free port, and 26 years later was granted civic status. A second canal built on the Canadian side in 1895 and a rail-link to the Canadian Pacific Railway further quickened the pace of settlement. In 1899 the (iron and steel producing) Algoma Steel Company was established, to be followed in later years by numerous other industries (including timber processing, paper and chemicals). The city is also well known for its long established and highly regarded forestry and land research institute.

The waterway connecting Lakes Superior and Huron forms the frontier between the USA and Canada. Like Sault St Marie, Ontario, to which it is joined by a bridge, Sault Ste Marie, Michigan, has a number of major industries (timber, leather and food processing, ship building, rail repair shop, etc.).

Sault Ste Marie (USA) ("The Soo")

Navigable only from mid-April to mid-December the 2km/1¼ mile long canals on the US and Canadian sides of the frontier at Sault Ste Marie

Sault Ste Marie canals, ★locks

443

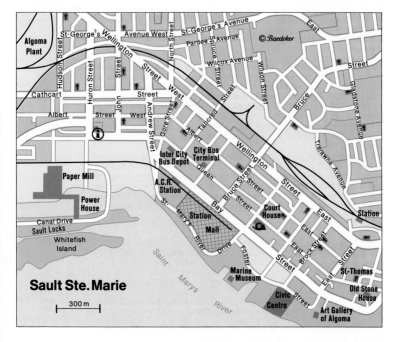

together make up the world's busiest waterway. Well over 100 million tonnes/tons of freight (mainly mineral ore and grain) pass through the locks en route from the industrial centres, mining and wheat growing areas around Lake Superior. A boat trip through the "Soo Locks" – those on the Canadian side of the St Mary's Rapids were completed in 1895 – is an experience not to be missed. Boats leave from Norgoma Dock (near Foster Drive) daily between the end of May and mid-October.

Sights in Sault Ste Marie

Art Gallery of Algoma	An eye-catching modern building on the St Mary's embankment houses the Art Gallery of Algoma (10 East St.; open: Mon.–Sat. 9am–5pm, Sun. 1–5pm) where the County's extensive art collection is on display. Temporary exhibitions.
★Ermatinger House	This attractive solid 1814 stone-built house (831 Queen St. E.; open: Apr.–Nov. every afternoon) originally belonged to a fur trader whose wife came from the local Ojibwa tribe. Now restored it provides a graphic insight into what life was like here almost 200 years ago.
Bellevue Park	Queen Street East is the location of the lovely Bellevue Park with its conservatories, small zoo, lighthouse and marina.
Sault Ste Marie Museum	The Sault Ste Marie Museum occupies a listed building in East Street (no. 107). Use is made of temporary exhibitions to illustrate 10,000 years of the area's history. Open daily.
M.S. "Norgoma"	The M.S. "Norgoma" was the last passenger ship built for service on the Great Lakes. Now on permanent moorings and converted into a museum the 24m/79ft vessel can be visited daily from June to mid-October.

Around Sault Ste Marie

Reached via Highway 565 the Forest Ecology Trail ("Deer Run" and "Wind-fall" trails) is open to walkers from the end of June until August. Guided walks.

Forest Ecology Trail

The Great Lakes Forestry Centre (1219 Queen St. E.; guided tours: mid-June–Aug. Mon.–Fri. 10am–2pm) provides a feast of interesting informa-tion about forestry in the Great Lakes region.

Great Lakes Forestry Centre

Searchmont, a winter sports resort, is situated about 50km/31 miles north of Sault Ste Marie on Highway 556. It is open from mid-December to well into April.

Searchmont winter sports resort

★ Algoma hill-country

Between June and mid-October the Algoma Central Railway (ACR) runs a particularly delightful excursion from Sault Ste Marie to the Agawa Canyon (dep. 9am daily). The train winds its way along the 183km/114 miles of track amidst the mountainous Algoma scenery, taking about 2½ hours to reach the impressive gorge through which wild, amber-coloured water rages and roars (the most striking views are obtained by walking up to the Bridal Veil and the Black Beaver Falls). The journey is at its loveliest in autumn when the leaves are on the turn.

★★ Agawa Canyon

The ACR also runs excursions to the Agawa Canyon in winter (Jan.–Mar., Sat., Sun.; 8 hour round trip), continuing beyond Agawa as far as Eton. This is an opportunity for nature-lovers and photographers alike to revel in the entrancing winter landscape – the trees with their thick caps of snow, the streams and lakes covered with ice, the waterfalls frozen into the strangest shapes. Information: Algoma Central Railway, Sault Ste Marie, Ontario; tel. (705) 254–433.

★ St Joseph Island

St Joseph Island lies in the channel leading from Lake Huron to Lake Superior, at the western end of the Manitoulin chain of islands in Lake Huron. It is of some geological interest on account of its jasper con-glomerate or "pudding stone".

Location and geography

Still very rural in character the island is becoming increasingly popular as a leisure area, with good angling and swimming.

On the south-west side of the island stands the ruined Fort St Joseph (1796–1812), now designated a historical monument. The Visitors Centre (open: May–Oct. daily) explains the one time military and economic signi-ficance of the fort (the fur trade, European–Indian relations, etc.). Nearby is an extensive animal reserve and bird sanctuary.

★ Fort St Joseph

About 6km/4 miles south of the bridge linking the island to the mainland there is a museum of local history (open: daily July–beginning Sept.) with an interesting collection of memorabilia from pioneer days.

St Joseph Island Museum

Thessalon

The old lumber town of Thessalon (population 1500), north of Sault Ste Marie, occupies a pleasant river-mouth site at the head of Lake Huron. During the warmer months it is busy with holidaymakers, one of the attractions being its marina.

These falls are situated just off Highway 129 between Thessalon and Chapleau. The now dammed Mississagi River plummets over a distinctive 39m/128ft escarpment, carving a path for itself through a gorge.

★ Aubrey Falls

Province: Manitoba
Population: 10,000

Information   See Manitoba

General situation A 9m/30ft high sculpture on Selkirk's Main Street underlines this agreeable
                   east Manitoban town's claim to be North America's Mecca for anglers in
                   pursuit of catfish. Indeed, so many catfish have been caught between
                   Selkirk and Lockport that restrictions on fishing have had to be introduced.
                   There is a well appointed yacht marina on Lake Winnipeg.

Sights   Several historic ships have been brought together in a park to form this
                   interesting Marine Museum (Eveline/Queen St.; open: mid-May–June
Marine Museum   Mon.–Sat. 9am–6pm, Sun. 10am–7pm, July, Aug. daily 9am–8pm). The
                   main attraction is an old steamship, the S.S. "Keenora", which operated
                   cruises on Lake Winnipeg from 1923 to 1965. Other vessels on show are the
                   icebreaker "C. G. S. Bradbury", the passenger and cargo carrying "Chick-
                   ama", and an elderly fishing cutter, the "Lady Canadian".

City Park   A reproduction Red River cart has been placed in the City Park to com-
                   memorate the early pioneers. Carts such as this were the sole means of
                   transport in those days for goods of every kind.

Around Selkirk The Fort Gary National Historic Park outside Selkirk has as its centre-piece
                   the only stone fort from the fur trading era to survive intact anywhere in
★Fort Gary   North America (the park itself is open throughout the year; the buildings
National Historic mid-May to beginning of Sept. daily 9.30am–6pm, Sept. Sat., Sun.
Park   9.30am–6pm.). Lower Fort Gary was erected by the Hudson's Bay Com-
                   pany in the 1830s, becoming an important centre for the fur trade and
                   serving as a base for the exploration of the Northwest Territories. It was
                   built to replace an earlier fort which originally stood at the confluence of the
                   Red and Assiniboine Rivers in what is now the centre of Winnipeg. This old
                   fort was destroyed by floods in 1826, after which George Simpson, Gover-
                   nor of Rupert's Land, ordered the construction of the Lower Fort on a more
                   elevated (but more isolated) site at some distance from the existing busy
                   settlement.
                     In later years the fort was used successively as a training camp for the
                   Royal Canadian Mounted Police, a prison, a mental institution, and a
                   company headquarters, before eventually being leased to the Manitoba
                   Motor & Country Club in 1911. It was handed over to the Crown by the
                   Hudson's Bay Company in 1951. In 1964 Parks Canada began a programme
                   of restoration.
                     The fort has been equipped with period furniture, crockery, pictures, etc.
                   painstakingly gathered together over a period of years not only from within
                   Canada but also from Britain and the USA.
                     Costumed Parks Canada employees act out the roles of the fort's earlier
                   inhabitants, e.g. smiths, labourers, servants and "voyageurs" (i.e. traders
                   who travelled by canoe bringing back pelts from the territories further
                   north). Visitors are able to talk to the "Governor" and his wife and to
                   various employees and domestic staff, as well as enjoying oatmeal biscuits
                   in the basement kitchen. The result is a vivid impression of the complexities
                   of life in a fur trading community.
                     Displayed in the building where the furs were stored are samples of pelts
                   of every kind – lynx, fox, beaver, racoon, mink and wolf. On the ground
                   floor, a Hudson's Bay Company shop has been re-created, stocked with
                   everything from clothing and household goods to beads, horse bells, traps,
                   brooms, boots and blankets. The settlers were entirely dependent upon
                   such shops to keep their needs supplied.
                     Standing beside the storehouse is an example of a "York Boat". Hun-
                   dreds of these solidly built craft (capable of carrying up to 2 tonnes/tons)

plied the lakes and rivers all the way from Hudson Bay to the Rocky Mountains and from Red River to the Arctic.

An audio-visual presentation on the history of the fort greets visitors arriving at the Reception Centre (opened in 1980) which also has excellent displays on the fur trade and the lives of the early settlers, illustrated with the aid of a variety of artefacts, pictures and models.

After visiting the Fort continue on Highway 9 via Petersfield to Netley Marsh.

The 36,000ha/89,000 acre Netley Marsh is one of the largest waterfowl breeding grounds in North America, the permanent home of 18 varieties of duck as well as of geese, herons, pelicans, terns and various kinds of diver. In spring the population is swollen by thousands of migratory birds.

★Netley Marsh

The best way to see the marsh is by canoeing along its narrow waterways, the alternative being to follow the footpath which runs through the wetland reserve. Between 4am and 6am in the morning there is a good chance of spotting more than a hundred different species of bird.

Sudbury

N 8

Province: Ontario
Population: 97,000 (160,000 if the environs are included)

Sudbury Welcome Centre, Highway 69 S., Whippoorwill, Box 29 M, Sudbury, Ontario, P3E 4N1; tel. (705) 522–0104.

Information

Sudbury, often referred to as the mining capital of the world, is situated beside Ramsey Lake in northern Ontario, about five hours' drive north of Toronto (see entry).

Location and general

Iron bearing lodes of mineral ore were first noticed here in 1883 during construction of the Canadian Pacific Railway. Before long other minerals were discovered, massive deposits of sulphurous nickel in particular. The latter have been mined on a large scale ever since and today more than three quarters of the world's output of nickel comes from the Sudbury Basin. Platinum, gold, silver, copper, cobalt, lead, zinc and iron are among the other metals found in the area.

The huge smokestacks towering above the copper and nickel processing plants are among the town's many landmarks. Sudbury also possesses a first-class technical university. As for the surrounding landscape, it is reminiscent of the surface of the moon.

Up-to-date research into the geology of the region suggests that the depression or "basin" in which Sudbury lies is a massive crater formed by a meteorite striking this south-western part of the Canadian Shield with enormous velocity many millions of years ago. Particles of material from the impact were condensed into the existing rock or transformed by metamorphosis into new rocks, minerals and ores. The shock waves of the collision scattered debris over a wide area. This cataclysmic event is believed to have been responsible for the formation of the sulphurous nickel deposits which lie in extensive fields about 60km/37 miles long, and of other ores.

Geology

The latest theory has superceded an earlier one which sought to explain the origin of the crater together with the presence of large quantities of minerals as the product of a violent volcanic eruption in Palaeozoic times.

Until just a few years ago toxic gas emissions were allowed into the atmosphere at a rate of 3600 tonnes per day, resulting in acid rain which attacked and destroyed vast tracts of vegetation over a wide area. Damage was even caused to forests as far afield as the Labrador Peninsula, 1200 to

Environmental problems

447

1500km/750 to 930 miles to the east. Nowadays, thanks to the installation of efficient desulphurising systems, the gas plumes issuing from the tall chimneys (up to 350m/1150ft high) are much less toxic and dangerous to the environment. Both local industry and the government (provincial as well as federal) are committed to further reductions in pollution levels.

Sights in Sudbury

★Copper Cliff Museum

Copper Cliff Museum (open: June–beginning Sept. Mon.–Fri. 10am–4.30pm) is a rich source of interesting information about copper mining in and around Sudbury.

★Big Nickel Mine

The Big Nickel Mine (open: mid-May–mid-Oct.; tel. (705) 522–3701) is operated by Science North. Visitors are able to descend more than 300m/985ft to the workface.

The Big Nickel itself is a massive (about 10m/33ft high) replica of the Canadian commemorative coin minted in 1951.

Giant Stacks

The mining and industrial area around Sudbury boasts the highest smoke-stacks in the world (350m/1150ft), built in the hope of preventing toxic gases emitted by local industries from laying waste the entire surrounding countryside. It soon became clear however that the poisonous fumes from the new chimneys were simply being carried further afield (as far as Labrador for example) before wreaking similar havoc there. Now waste-gas purification plants have been installed to reduce the damaging effects of the emissions.

The celebrated "Gold Coin" of Sudbury

The Flour Mill Heritage Museum (a former mill; St Charles St.; open: mid-June–beginning Sept. Mon.–Fri. and Sun. afternoons) contains old furniture, domestic equipment, tools and weaponry.

Flour Mill Heritage Museum

The Galerie du Nouvel Ontario (No. 20, Rue St Anne) provides an opportunity to see works by French Canadian painters, sculptors and potters and is well worth the visit.

Galerie du Nouvel Ontario

The bilingual Laurentian University specialises in science and technology. There are guided tours of the super-modern campus beside Ramsey Lake and of the Doran Planetarium adjoining it.

Laurentian University

The University Museum in the W. J. Bell House (built 1906; corner of John St. and Nelson St.; open: Tues.–Sun. afternoons) is also full of interest.

Accommodated in a striking modern building designed to resemble a snowflake this extraordinary Science Centre (Ramsey Lake Rd./Paris St.; open daily) vividly conveys a wealth of information about the geology and landscape of North Ontario and the Canadian Arctic. There are also various fascinating presentations (e.g. films and demonstrations) on the history of the universe and the development of communications. Visitors are invited to conduct scientific experiments for themselves, with the assistance of the staff.

★★Science North

Everything from classical drama to the most recent plays is performed in the very modern Sudbury Theatre (near City Hall).

Sudbury Theatre

Attractively laid out on the shores of Ramsey Lake, Bell Park is Sudbury's most popular recreation area. It has an outdoor theatre where various festivals and open-air concerts are held.

Bell Park

Around Sudbury

Lake Ramsey

Some very pleasant boat trips can be enjoyed on Lake Ramsey (mid-May to Sept. daily from the Science North pier).

★★Path of Discovery

The "Path of Discovery" bus tour (taking several hours) is highly recommended for anyone visiting Sudbury in the summer months. Starting at the Big Nickel Mine this mini geological field-trip makes a circuit of the Sudbury meteorite crater. There are various stops en route for guides to point out traces of the meteorite's impact on the earth's surface and to explain its consequences in terms of the geological composition and present day topography of the area and the formation of the mineral fields.

★French River

French River, the 112km/70 mile long waterway between Lake Nipissing and Georgian Bay (see entry), is about an hour's drive south of Sudbury. A group of French "voyageurs" and missionaries, Samuel de Champlain among them (see Famous People), set off into the interior from here in 1620. Nowadays the river is very popular with canoeists, anglers, and outdoor enthusiasts generally.

★Killarney Provincial Park

Also about an hour's drive from Sudbury, but to the south-west, lies the 363sq.km/140sq.mile Killarney Provincial Park. This area bordering on Georgian Bay (see entry) is still a part of the Canadian Shield, and includes the La Cloche mountains – sometimes snow capped even in early autumn. The Park is another much favoured haunt of canoeists.

Tadoussac

Q 8

Province: Québec. Population: 1000

Access

Highway 138

General situation

Tadoussac lies surrounded by the most delightful scenery north of the junction of the Saguenay Fiord and St Lawrence River. Jacques Cartier made a stop here in 1535 and before long the burgeoning trade in furs saw it develop into something of a centre. It was the site of the first trading post established in New France (built by Pierre Chauvin in about 1600) and fifteen years later of the first mission station. Tadoussac's importance diminished following colonisation of the upper Saguenay.

Sights in Tadoussac

★Riverside walk, Comptoir de Pierre Chauvin

A very pretty walk runs along the banks of the St Lawrence, from where in summer boat trips depart for the Saguenay Fiord (for whale-spotting in particular). There is an interesting reconstruction of Pierre Chauvin's trading post from 1600 (open during the summer tourist season only). Also worth seeing is the mid-18th c. wooden fisherman's chapel nearby.

Around Tadoussac

Le Désert

About 3km/2 miles outside Tadoussac sand has been blown by the wind into great dunes over 100m/330ft high. Known locally as "Le Désert", sand ski races are held here in summer.

Les Escoumines

The harbour at Les Escoumines, just 35km/22 miles north of Tadoussac on the St Lawrence River, has been a port of call for Basque fishermen since the 17th c. From the middle of the last century it has also been an increasingly important outlet for the timber trade.

Les Escoumines is one of Canada's most popular centres for underwater sports.

Terra Nova National Park

Province: Newfoundland
Area: about 400sq.km/154sq.miles

Terra Nova National Park, Glovertown, Newfoundland A0G 2L0;
tel. (709) 533–2801

Information

The Terra Nova National Park on the shores of Bonavista Bay south-east of
Gander is a heavily glaciated region of wooded hills and indented coastline, with deep, narrow fiords extending far inland. In spring the coastal
waters are dotted with icebergs carried down by the Labrador current. The
beaches in the Park are extremely beautiful but the coldness of the water
makes them unsuitable for bathing.

★Topography

The Park supports a rich and varied wildlife. While animals such as black
bear and moose can often be seen from the road others including beaver,
red fox, lynx and Canada geese are best observed by taking to the 80km/
50 miles of hiking trails.

Fauna

Bluehill Pond Lookout is situated some 9km/5½ miles from the northern
entrance of the Park (turn off for the fire tower after about 7km/4 miles,
continuing for a further 2km/1¼ miles). There are superb panoramic views
over the whole Park, with Newman Sound, the Southwest Arm and Alexander Bay all clearly visible.

Bluehill Pond
Lookout

To reach Newman Sound head for the Information Office which is about
12km/7½ miles from the Park's northern entrance. The Sound is a deep inlet
with low cliffs rising directly from the water. A short walking trail leads
along the shore.

Newman Sound

About 23km/14 miles from the north entrance a road branches off to the
Ochre Lookout Tower (3km/2 miles). From here there are more panoramic
views to be enjoyed over Clode and Newman Sounds. A display at the
tower explains how Newfoundland was shaped by Ice Age glaciation.

Ochre Lookout
Tower

The Park offers a host of leisure facilities including canoeing, cycling,
angling, cross-country skiing, and a 9-hole golf course by the sea. It also
boasts some very attractive camp sites.

Leisure facilities

Thunder Bay

Province: Ontario
Population: 115,000

North of Superior Tourism, 79 North Court St., Thunder Bay, Ontario,
P7A 4T7; tel. (807) 345–3322

Information

Thunder Bay, on the north-east shore near the head of Lake Superior, is the
furthermost port on the St Lawrence Seaway/Lake Superior accessible to
sea-going vessels. It is the primary outlet for grain exported from the
Canadian Prairies. Grouped around the docks are a whole series of gigantic
grain elevators and storage silos with a total capacity of about 4 million
cu.m./141 million cu.ft.

Location and
general

The city came into being in 1970 with the amalgamation of two existing
communities, Port Arthur and Fort William. The latter began life as a
trading post in the second half of the 17th c., the former being founded
some 200 years later.

History

Sights

Fort William (open: mid-May–Sept. daily 10am–4pm) is the reconstruction
of an old British fort originally erected in 1816. Situated on the banks of the

★Fort William

Kaminiskwia River in south Thunder Bay it comprises some 40 buildings enclosed within exceedingly substantial palisades. Long before the fort was built the site was occupied by a French trading post, and it was from here that Pierre de Varennes set off in 1731 to explore the American West. When possession of Canada passed to the British the post was handed over to the North West Company, serving as the company's headquarters from 1803. Throughout the summer months European and Indian trappers would converge on Fort William to trade their pelts and furs with the "voyageurs" from Montréal (who brought with them all sorts of goods to barter in return).

★ Centennial Park

Among the attractions of the spacious Centennial Park in north Thunder Bay (open: end of May–beginning Sept. daily 10am–7pm) is the re-creation of a logging camp, complete with log huts, smithy and a canteen serving "loggers' steaks" and other equally "hearty" meals. There is plenty in the park to keep children amused.

Centennial Conservatory

The Centennial Conservatory (Balmoral St./Dease St.; open: every afternoon) boasts an incredible variety of plants.

Hillcrest Park

From Hillcrest Park excellent views are obtained over Thunder Bay, the port, and across to the Sleeping Giant (see below).

International Friendship Gardens

The different ethnic groups who have made a new home for themselves in Thunder Bay each find recognition among the flowerbeds of the International Friendship Gardens (Victoria Avenue).

★ Art Gallery

Thunder Bay Art Gallery (Confederation College Campus; open: Tues.–Sun. afternoons) is mainly devoted to Red Indian art. The impressive collection of pictures, weaving, sculptures and pottery by Indian artists is the equal of any in the country.

Auditorium

Opened in 1985 and acknowledged as one of the best equipped theatres in Canada, the Auditorium (Beverly St./Winnipeg Ave.) stands as a tribute to the city's prosperity.

Canada Games Complex

Thunder Bay's "state of the art" sports complex on Winnipeg Ave. (open: every day) includes an Olympic swimming pool and huge water slide.

Historical Museum

Among items of interest in the town's Historical Museum (219 S. May St.; open: Tues.–Sun. daily) are examples of Indian art pre-dating the arrival of Europeans. The museum also focuses on the history of navigation and the military history of this central part of Canada.

★★ Harbour tour

The opportunity to see at close quarters the impressive installations of the largest grain-handling port in the world (enormous silos, grain elevators, loading bridges, 30,000 grt grain ships, etc.) turns this tour of the harbour into a thoroughly fascinating experience.

Chippewa Park

Chippewa Park on the shores of Lake Superior south of the town (Highway 61B; open: end June–beginning Sept.) has a sandy beach as well as a whole range of recreational and pleasure facilities.

Mount McKay

From 183m/600ft up the slopes of Mount Mckay (part of an Ojibwa Indian reservation on the south side of Thunder Bay) more fine views are gained over the town.

Paipoonge Museum

The Paipoonge Museum (on the Rosslyn road on the western edge of the town; open: mid-Apr.–beginning Sept. daily) has memorabilia from the pioneering days and interesting material relating to the growth of industry in and around Thunder Bay.

Ski resorts

There are four excellent ski areas close to Thunder Bay (also two large ski jumps).

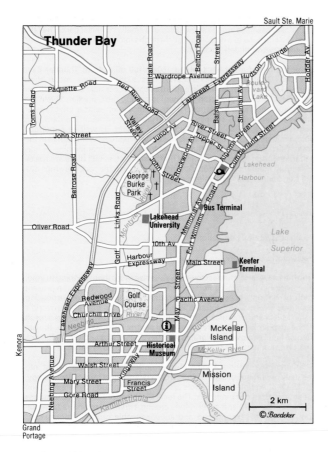

Thunder Bay

Sault Ste. Marie

Wardrope Avenue
Paquette Road
Red River Road
Hittdale Road
Belton Road
Street
Lakehead Expressway
Hudson
Arundel
Shuniah Av
Boulevard
Lake
Hodder Av
Toms Road
John Street
Valley Street
Junot Av
River Street
Tupper St.
Balsam
Algoma Street
Cumberland Street
Betrose Road
Rockwood
John Street
George Burke Park
Lakehead Harbour
Links Road
McIntyre River
Memorial Av
Fort William Road
Bus Terminal
Oliver Road
Lakehead University
Lake Superior
10th Av
Harbour Expressway
Main Street
Keefer Terminal
Golf Course
May Street
Pacific Avenue
Redwood Avenue
Lakehead Expressway
Churchill Drive
Neebing River
McKellar Island
Kenora
Arthur Street
Historical Museum
McKellar River
Neebing Avenue
Kaministiquia
Walsh Street
Kingsway
Mary Street
Francis Street
Mission Island
Gore Road
Missouri River

2 km

© *Baedeker*

Grand Portage

The about 250sq.km/96sq.mile Sibley Provincial Park occupies most of the Sibley Peninsula, which juts out into Lake Superior on the east side of Thunder Bay. Large numbers of black bear, deer, lynx, fox and beaver still inhabit the heavily ravined and scenically delightful outliers of the Canadian Shield, the extremities of which lie hidden beneath the waters of the Lake. The Park is also home to more than 200 species of bird.

At the tip of the peninsula the land rises to form the 304m/1000ft hill known as the Sleeping Giant.

A number of open-cast amethyst mines are found in the area between 55 and 75km/34 and 47 miles north-east of Thunder Bay. Local dealers usually have some fine quality stones for sale.

About 80km/50 miles north-east of Thunder Bay the Ouimet River has carved a canyon 5km/3 mile long and up to 150m/490ft deep through solid rock. Even in the height of summer snow and ice lingers on in nooks and crannies where sunlight scarcely penetrates, despite which the canyon still manages to support an interesting plantlife.

Around Thunder Bay

★Sibley Provincial Park

Sleeping Giant

★Amethyst Mines

★Ouimet Canyon

Timmins

★ Kakabeka Falls

Barely 30km/19 miles west of Thunder Bay the wildly beautiful 33m/108ft high Kakabeka Falls are the show-piece of a small provincial park. The falls form the entrance to a narrow gorge through which the Kaminiskwia River thunders between dark rock walls.

★ Quetico
Provincial Park

Some distance further west (about 160km/100 miles from Thunder Bay) lies the Quetico Provincial Park. This extends over more than 4500sq.km/1740sq.miles and is for the most part accessible only on foot, on horseback or by canoe. Belonging geologically to the Canadian Shield the landscape shows all the familiar signs of glaciation with a multitude of lakes and hummocks sculpted by ice from the crystalline Pre-Cambrian bedrock. There are still some black bears around, as well as numerous animals such as otters and beavers (also some ospreys) which thrive in the water-filled environment. Although a stranger might imagine him- or herself transported to a truly primeval northern forest, in fact there are traces of lengthy human occupation. Among them are simple rock drawings of a hunting people and their animal quarry.

Timmins

Province: Ontario. Population: 47,000

Information

See Ontario

North-east Ontario's largest town owes its rise more than anything to gold, discovered in the nearby Porcupine field at the beginning of the present century. Not only does output exceed that of all but a few gold producing countries in the world, in addition Timmins boasts one of the world's richest silver and zinc mines. The population, which grew rapidly as a result of the gold strikes, is largely made up of central European, Italian, British, Finnish and Ukrainian immigrants who have helped foster other industries apart from mining, the timber and brewing industries in particular.

Porcupine
Outdoor Mining
Museum

The Porcupine Outdoor Mining Museum offers an intriguing insight into the daily operations of a mine, and an understanding of mining technology. All kinds of equipment and tools are on display including mine cars and steam-powered track vehicles. The local Chamber of Commerce arranges visits to other gold and silver mines around Timmins, the tours being on foot and led by experienced and knowledgeable guides. (Information: Timmins-Porcupine Chamber of Commerce, P.O. Box 985, Route 101, Timmins, Ontario, P4N 7H6, tel. (705) 264–4321.)

Kettle Lakes
Provincial Park

This nature reserve with its many little lakes just 32km/20 miles from Timmins on Highway 101 is an open invitation to anyone keen on canoeing, fishing or swimming.

Toronto

Province: Ontario
Population: 650,000 (city), 3.5 million (metropolitan area)

Information

Metropolitan Toronto Travel Association, 207 Queen's Quay W., Suite 509, P.O. Box 126, Toronto, Ontario, M5J 1A7; tel. (416) 368–9821.
Free telephone information: tel. 1–800–363–1990.
Information kiosks at the Queen's Quay Terminal and the corner of Yonge St. and Dundas St.

Toronto: Central Business District ▶

Toronto

Toronto (Indian for "meeting place"), capital of the Canadian province of Ontario (see entry) and the country's leading industrial metropolis, stands on the north-west shore of Lake Ontario (see entry) bordering Toronto Bay. For quite some time now the city has found itself being swept along by a tidal wave of dynamic development, evidenced by the construction of not only numerous hyper-modern skyscrapers but also the highest television tower in the world and the huge sports arena known as the Skydome. In the last two decades the already highly industrialised conurbation has expanded deeper and deeper into what was once its hinterland. The original relatively small city centre is today ringed by a succession of interconnecting fast roads and highways, and one after another new communities spring up along the big main roads leading from the town.

History

In 1793 the then Governor of Ontario John Graves Simcoe selected the north side of Toronto Bay for the site of a new settlement, to be laid out on the model of a European city. Christened York and made the capital of Upper Canada, the town was subjected to military attack on a number of occasions in the decades which followed.

One such occasion was in the spring of 1813 when a fleet belonging to the now independent United States of America bombarded the town. A number of important buildings were destroyed by fire. In retaliation the British burned down part of the US federal capital Washington.

By 1834 the population had risen to almost 10,000 and the burgeoning community on the shores of Lake Ontario was granted civic status. At the same time its name was changed from the English "York" to the Indian "Toronto".

The combination of a good road system and its status as provincial capital soon led to a further rapid increase in the city's population and, in particular, economic growth. The harbour was enlarged and numerous industries established. A second wave of industrialisation starting at the end of the 19th c. gave a particularly strong boost to the economy. By the turn of the century the population had passed the 200,000 mark.

The two World Wars were a further stimulus to Toronto's prosperity. Statistics from the end of the 1950s show as many as 3000 companies with in excess of 120,000 employees. By then the port was handling more than 3500 ships annually, with freight totalling 4 million tonnes/tons.

This present century has also seen Toronto develop into a major cultural centre. The city has two universities, some excellent colleges and a number of leading theatre companies and orchestras. It is justifiably proud of its fine museums and galleries. Its cultural standing is further reflected in its religious life, Toronto being a Catholic archbishopric and seat of the United Ruthenian Church's apostolic exarch for eastern Canada.

Economy

Toronto's continuing development has already transformed it economically speaking into by far the most important city in Canada, wielding immense financial influence through its concentration of banks and insurance companies and its stock exchange (the fourth largest in North America). Modern industrial plants and factory units representing a wide range of industries (construction, machine and vehicle manufacture, electronics, chemicals, food processing, brewing, textiles, paper manufacture and printing) can be seen all over the city, but especially around the harbour and the airport. The Toronto trade fairs attracts several million visitors every year.

Both Toronto's airport and its seaport are of major economic significance, the latter benefiting from its position on the St Lawrence Seaway, the former from being located at an important junction of routes.

★★Skyline

Few cities have a skyline to rival Toronto's – particularly impressive given a bird's eye view and even more striking when seen from the offshore islands which encircle the harbour. The tallest skyscrapers, mostly financed through investment by banks and insurance companies, cluster together in the old city centre, constantly augmented by new ultra-modern structures

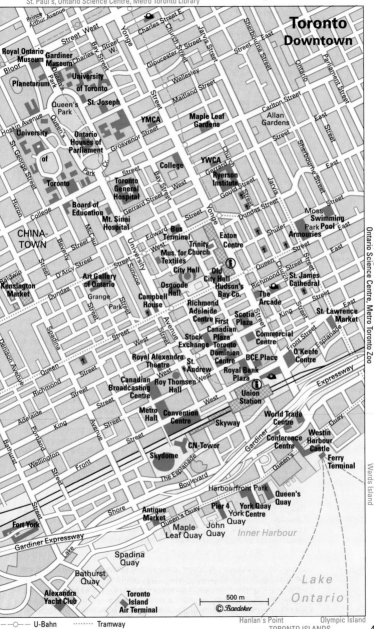

sheathed in aluminium, eloxal and glass. The 553m/1815ft high CN Tower completed in 1976 points skywards like a gigantic antenna, with at its foot the huge arched canopy of the 1989 Skydome (the roof of which can be opened in fine weather).

City lay-out

The old city centre, relatively small and rectangular in shape, is laid out on a "grid-iron" pattern. Now known as the "Central Business District" it is bounded by Yonge St. or Church St. (east), Spadina St. (west), Front St. (south) and Bloor St. (north). Two large thoroughfares – Yonge St. and University Ave. (beneath which the city's subway runs) – bisect the CBD from north to south. These are crossed at right angles by several streets and lead to Toronto's main railway station and the harbour. With street by street redevelopment being carried out apace, very few old buildings now remain. The original two-storey stone and timber houses, dating from the settlement's earliest days, have almost entirely disappeared. Even the first generation of skyscrapers are today being replaced by taller, more up-to-date blocks. The only old buildings to have survived this apparently insatiable urge for modernisation are some of the larger, more splendid and historic edifices such as the railway station, the old City Hall, parts of the old University, one or two venerable buildings housing the provincial government, and a few palatial dynastic family mansions. Many of these lovely old buildings are of course almost submerged in the sea of glass and reinforced concrete, as are numerous ageing churches the survival of which is becoming a major cause for concern.

Mount Pleasant
(Richmond Hill)

The residential area of Mount Pleasant (pop. 20,000), about 20km/12 miles north of the city centre, is the site of the University of Toronto's David Dunlab Observatory (interesting and worth a visit). The district is also known as Richmond Hill, having been named after the Duke of Richmond in 1819.

Harbourfront Park

Location

Toronto's old waterfront, which until a few years ago was dominated by storage sheds and wholesale warehouses, is now transformed into the 38ha/94 acre multipurpose Harbourfront Park. This incorporates everything from hotels, to luxury flats, the offices of various utilities, art galleries, a range of boutiques, shops, restaurants and cafés, theatres, a French cultural centre, a yacht marina (with a sailing school) and the railway museum.

**Railway
redevelopment–CN
Tower–Skydome**

Union Station

Toronto's huge main railway station belonging to the Canadian National Railway Company was opened in 1927 by the Prince of Wales (later King Edward VIII). Today it stands as a reminder of the vigour of the Canadian economy in the 1920s when vast quantities of rail freight in the form of wheat, timber, cellulose and non-ferrous metals passed through Toronto. Passenger traffic, especially holidaymakers travelling by rail, also provided important business until well into the 1950s. Nowadays the station is the terminus for fast inter-city trains from Montréal, Ottawa and New York (via Niagara Falls), as well as express services to the Canadian West and northern Ontario. Recently Union Station became the hub of a local fast transport system serving Toronto and its suburbs.

Railway
redevelopment

The declining importance of rail transport in the Toronto area forced the Canadian National Railway Company to find new uses for its growing stock of surplus property. Today the tallest television tower in the world is just one of the buildings which have been erected on what was formerly railway land.

★★CN Tower

The 553m/1815ft high CN Tower, constructed between 1972 and 1976, can claim to be the tallest building ever. This modern landmark beside Lake Ontario is more than two and half times the height of Stuttgart's television tower (which, built just 20 years earlier, was the prototype of all such towers). About two-thirds of the way up the Tower (335m/1100ft) the seven-story "Skypod" houses the biggest revolving restaurant in the world, and observation platforms from which, in clear weather, views extend for 120km/75 miles. On occasions it is even possible to make out the cloud of mist and spray which hangs above the Niagara Falls. Anyone so inclined can take the lift even further up, to the 447m/1470ft high Space Deck, above which rises the Tower's enormous aerial.

Being in the Tower during a thunderstorm is particularly dramatic. The view from above as lightning flashes and wind and driving rain rage below, is quite simply awe-inspiring.

Strobe lighting has been installed on the Tower to warn not only approaching aircraft but also birds, especially the many which fly past on migration in spring and autumn.

The Tower also carries a rich assortment of aerials belonging to a host of television, radio and telephone companies.

The Tour of the Universe at the foot of the Tower is very popular with visitors. It simulates a journey into space aboard a replica of the Hermes Space Shuttle.

Tour of the Universe

Immediately adjacent to the CN Tower is Skydome, a massive domed sports arena the roof of which slides back allowing it to be opened in favourable weather. This mega-structure, completed in 1989, is Toronto's answer to the ambitious Olympic Stadium built by its arch rival, Montréal. Skydome can accommodate many thousands of spectators and is a venue for every kind of sport – baseball and football in particular – as well as for rock and pop concerts.

★Skydome

The ultra modern Convention Centre immediately north of the CN Tower was completed within the last three years. This, too, is built on former railway land.

Convention Centre

North again is the new and equally modern Toronto Opera House.

Opera House

Beyond the Opera House the circular Roy Thomson Hall was designed by the famous architect Arthur Erickson. The concert hall is known throughout Canada for the excellence of its acoustics.

Roy Thomson Hall

A vast number of commercial, financial and professional institutions and services together with several government agencies are concentrated in the Central Business District, easily recognised by its towering skyscrapers. Every weekday a multitude of bankers, stockbrokers, insurance and property agents, lawyers and business people join with an army of civil servants to squeeze themselves into this relatively small downtown area. Their reinforced concrete office blocks, encased – some attractively, some rather less so – in glass and eloxal, bear fine sounding names such as the Sun Life Centre (28 storeys), Commerce Court (57 storeys), the Toronto Dominion Centre (designed by Mies van der Rohe and others) and First Canadian Plaza (consisting of the 72-storey Bank of Montréal, the 36-storey Stock Exchange and the massive Sheraton Hotel). Also prominent is the 70-storey Nova Scotia Bank. The majority of these modern high-rise developments have shopping levels with supermarkets selling food and household goods, fashion boutiques, banks, medical practitioners, hairdressers, hi-fi and camera shops and a variety of similar facilities including, of course, cafés, bistros and restaurants.

★**Central Business District (CBD)**

Central Area

The high-rise office blocks in the CBD are virtually all connected to one another by underground walkways and shopping concourses. Whatever the weather – rain or snow, strong winds or bitter cold – shoppers can make their way dry shod along the 1½km/1 mile from Union St. to Dundas St. (north). Outlets selling all the daily necessities stay open till well into the evening. The large Toronto department stores are also linked into this system of subterranean precincts, and at various points there is access to the big city centre car parks and the subway.

★Underground Toronto

CN Tower

TECHNICAL DATA

Building begun
1972

Inauguration
1976

Height
553.35m/1816ft
(tallest building in the world)

Weight
143,299 tonnes

Volume of mast
48463 cu.m/1,711,713 cu.ft

Lifting capacity
68,343 tonnes

Viewing platforms
Space Deck (446.5m/
1465ft)
Sky Pad (335.3m/1100ft)

**Range of View (in good
weather)**
south to the Niagara Falls in
the area of Rochester and
New York (USA), north to
Lake Simcoe

Transmitters
6 TV and 8 radio

Stairs
1760 steps

Revolving restaurant
Diameter: 45.75m/150ft
Radius: 137.15m/444ft
Rotation cycle: 90 minutes

Speed of lift
365.75m/1200ft per minute

Frequency of storms
60–80 per annum

Movement in strong winds
Top of tower: 2.5m/8ft
Shaft of tower: 0.25m/
9 inches

© Baedeker

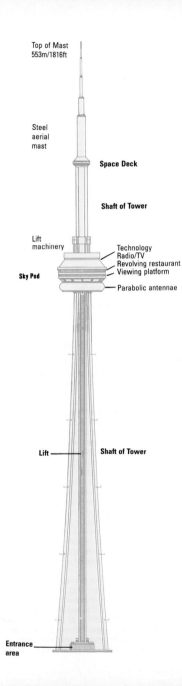

Top of Mast
553m/1816ft

Steel
aerial
mast

Space Deck

Shaft of Tower

Lift
machinery

Technology
Radio/TV
Revolving restaurant
Viewing platform

Sky Pod

Parabolic antennae

Lift

Shaft of Tower

Entrance
area

Skydome

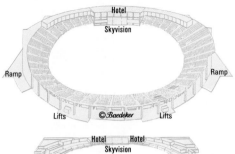

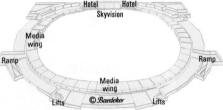

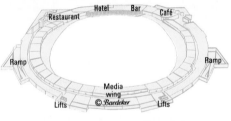

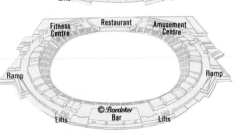

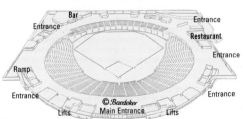

SKYDECK
Level 500
17,506 seats

UPPER SKYBOXES
Level 400
100 suites (2238 seats)

LOWER SKYBOXES
Level 300
61 suites (1180 seats)

SKYCLUB
Level 200
5800 seats

ESPLANADE
Level 100
21,295 seats

Toronto

Toronto: Old City Hall . . .   *. . . and New City Hall*

Old City Hall	The Old City Hall (as it is called) stands on the corner of Bay St. and Queen St., a magnificent stone building dating from the end of the 19th c. Following the completion of the new City Hall near by, various branches of the Justice Department (including the Law-Courts) were transferred to the old building.
★New City Hall	Dominating the spacious Nathan Philips Square with its bronze sculpture "The Archer" by Henry Moore is the still highly acclaimed new City Hall, designed by the gifted Finnish architect Viljo Revell and built in 1965. It consists of two arc-shaped high-rise blocks (20 and 27 storeys high respectively), wrapped around a lower central building topped by a flattened cupola (housing the chamber in which meetings of the Toronto and Greater Toronto councils are held).
★Eaton Centre	Anyone taking a car into the city centre for some shopping should make for the huge Eaton Centre at the north end of the CBD. With its own subway station and indoor parking for several hundred cars this ultra-modern shopping complex extends over several blocks and is continually being renovated and enlarged. Strangers can quite easily lose their way in the bewildering maze of department stores, specialist shops, boutiques, restaurants, caféterias and snack bars which crowd the different levels above and below ground. There is hardly a speciality from anywhere in the world which cannot be found for sale here. The original Eaton department store opened in Toronto in 1869. Since then it has grown into an enormous retail business, with branches in all the larger Canadian towns and cities and as well as abroad.
Yonge Street General	Yonge Street was one of the original streets built by Toronto's founder Governor John Simcoe at the end of the 18th c. Running north to south it is now the city's primary thoroughfare and stays busy day and night. The 2½km/1½ mile section between Bloor St. (north) and the main railway

station (south) is a sort of microcosm of the city as a whole, epitomising its dynamism and the unceasing cycle of renewal. Yesterday's "small town" shops and businesses housed in modest old-fashioned premises have today given way to the glitzy shop fronts of the latest in fashionable boutiques, each intent on seducing eager shoppers with plenty of money to spend. By tomorrow these too will probably have been swept away to make room for the next generation of ultra-modern skyscrapers. A huge and immensely varied selection of food and entertainment is available along Yonge St., ranging from the most luxurious of restaurants to the seediest of dives.

The five-storey red brick and glass encased Metro Toronto Library was completed in 1979, one of architect Raymond Moriyama's acknowledged masterpieces. Mounting a wide-ranging programme of cultural events the library has become a popular focus for the activities of Toronto's middle class intelligentsia.

★ Metro Toronto Library

Osgoode Hall (1835–55), a former law-courts situated immediately west of the new City Hall, was named after Upper Canada's first High Court Judge. Its gardens, bounded by heavy iron railings, have a special charm, especially in the spring.

Osgoode Hall

Campbell House (guided tours: Mon.–Fri.) once belonged to Sir William Campbell, chief justice of Upper Canada from 1825 to 1829. It was moved to its present site on the west side of University Ave. in 1972. The house is well worth a visit for its 19th c. furnishings and displays on local history.

Campbell House

The renowned Art Gallery of Ontario occupies a pleasing modern building on the west side of the city centre.

The handsome old building in the garden (known as "The Grange", and in which the Art Gallery was formerly housed) was built in 1816/17 by a prosperous New England family. For a time it was a meeting place for the political opponents of William Lyon Mackenzie. The house was restored to its 1830s elegance some years ago.

★ **Art Gallery of Ontario (AGO)**

Location:
Dundas St. W.

Open:
Tues.–Sun.
11am–5.30pm

A whole series of temporary exhibitions are mounted throughout the year by this exceptionally well endowed gallery. There are three main collections – Canadian art, European art and sculptures by Henry Moore.

The collection of Canadian paintings is particularly impressive. The work of the early Québécois painters is well represented, as is that of Cornelius Krieghoff, Tom Thomson and the Group of Seven, Emily Carr, David Milne and Paul Peele. Contemporary Canadian artists are accorded special attention.

Collections

Paintings by old and modern masters alike feature in the European collection. Included are works by Pieter Brueghel the Younger, Tintoretto, Rembrandt, Frans Hals, Gainsborough, Van Gogh, Monet, Gauguin, Dégas, Renoir and Picasso.

The Gallery has a complete wing devoted to the English sculptor Henry Moore, more than a dozen of whose large bronzes are on display. Sketches, lithographs and miniatures offer illuminating insight into the creative genesis of his work.

Toronto's Chinatown occupies the district immediately north and west of the Art Gallery of Ontario, extending along Dundas St. and into some of the adjacent side streets. Crowding together into this small area are people from every part of East and South-east Asia, some of whom are the descendents of Chinese contract workers but many others being more recent arrivals from Hongkong and Vietnam. At all hours the place buzzes with commercial activity, the selection of goods in the innumerable shops being correspondingly wide. All the delicious aromas of the orient waft from the restaurants and snack bars.

Chinatown– Kensington Market

Chinatown

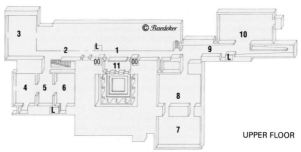

1 Exhibition Gallery
(modern art)
2 Walter Trier Gallery
(temporary exhibitions)
3 Signy Eaton Gallery
(contemporary collection)

4 J. S. McLean Gallery
(historical collection)
5 John Ridley Gallery
(historical collection)
6 Georgia Ridley Gallery
(historical collection)

7 Zacks Gallery South
8 Zacks Gallery North
9 Irina Moore Gallery
10 Moore Sculpture Centre
11 Members' Lounge
L Lift   00 Toilets

UPPER FLOOR

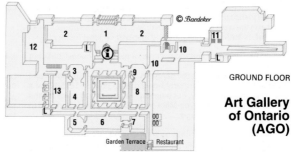

GROUND FLOOR

Art Gallery
of Ontario
(AGO)

1 Main Lobby
2 Gallerie-Boutique
3 Fudger Rotunda
4 Fudger Gallery
(old masters)
5 F. P. Wood Gallery
6 E. R. Wood Gallery
(old masters)

7 Laidlaw Gallery
8 Leonard Gallery
(19th and 20th c.
modern art)
9 Leonard
Rotunda
10 Gallery of
Contemporary Art

11 Moore Atrium
12 Edward P. Taylor
Audio-Visual Centre
13 Margaret Eaton Gallery
(prints and drawings)

L Lift
00 Toilets

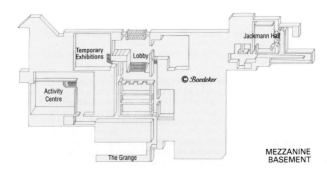

MEZZANINE
BASEMENT

Kensington Market is situated on the far side of the Dundas St./Spadina Ave. intersection in a district peopled at one time by newly arrived Jewish and other European immigrants, the latter mainly from southern Europe and the Balkans. Later they were joined by members of Toronto's Portuguese community and today the area between Spadina Ave. and Augusta St. is home to immigrants and "tourists" from every corner of the globe. From the very beginning this formerly residential suburb seems to have evolved a lifestyle of its own, with a motley selection of colourful little shops, flower stands, pleasant bars, cafés and snack bars. During the year the Asian community holds a number of lively celebrations.

The market itself, some of whose traders seem to deal in a highly exotic assortment of wares, is open: Mon.–Sat. 7am–7pm.

★ Kensington Market

Running north–south along the west side of the CBD parallel to Yonge St., University Ave. passes through Toronto's university quarter and the district which houses Ontario's provincial parliament.

In addition to a great many government buildings the Avenue is also the site of several scientific institutions and clinics. North of Queen's Park are a number of important museums.

University Avenue– Queen's Park

The Royal Ontario Museum (open: daily 10am–6pm) on the corner of University Ave. and Bloor St. W. ranks high on the list of places of interest in Toronto. Unusually for such a museum it brings together a series of outstanding collections in the fields of both science and the arts.

★★ Royal Ontario Museum

The opening section "Mankind Discovering" is an imaginatively presented introduction to the work of a museum. It traces in a clear and informative way all the stages from the moment a "find" is uncovered to the time it is labelled and then eventually goes on display.

The natural history section concentrates primarily on the evolution of life on earth. Among its highlights are a superb display of dinosaur skeletons and a series of fascinating wildlife dioramas (including some featuring mammals native to Ontario).

Also of great interest are the museum's gem collection and the sections devoted to the pre- and early history of Ontario (with e.g. Indian rock drawings) and the period since the arrival of the first Europeans. Then there are the exhibitions on the Mediterranean World (including the civilisations of ancient Egypt, Greece and Rome) and European decorative crafts since the 17th c., each occupying several rooms. Many rewarding hours could be spent just looking round the wonderfully comprehensive textiles section and the small collection of musical instruments!

Collections

The Royal Ontario Museum is known throughout the world for its magnificent Far East collection of Chinese art covering four millennia – from the Shang Dynasty (c. 1500 B.C.), through the Tang Dynasty (7th to 10th c. A.D.) and Ming Dynasty (14th to 17th c.) right up to the period of the Manchu Emperors (early 20th c.). Wonderful examples of religious (temple) art are displayed alongside exquisite ceramic figures and superb vases. Normally the centre of attention in this section of the museum is the arresting ceramic figure of "Yen Lo Wang", King of the Underworld. Also quite exceptional however is the Ming tomb (17th c.).

The special exhibition on Imperial China since the 10th c. succeeds brilliantly in bringing its subject to life.

★★ Far Eastern Collection

On display in the Bishop White Gallery are some huge Chinese temple paintings. The largest, a Buddhist work, dates from about 1320.

★ Bishop White Gallery

Adjoining the main museum on its south side is the McLaughlin Planetarium and Astrocentre.

McLaughlin Planetarium

Situated opposite the Royal Ontario Museum and definitely worth a visit, the Museum of Ceramic Art (open: Tues.–Sun. 10am–6pm) owes its existence to a pair of private collectors, Mr and Mrs George Gardiner. On

★ Gardiner Museum of Ceraamic Art

Royal Ontario Museum (ROM)

GROUND FLOOR

G Cloakroom
R Escalator
W Temporary exhibitions
00 Toilets

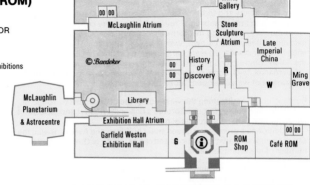

FIRST BELOW

1 ROM Theatre
2 Creative Arts Studio
3 European musical instruments
4 Portraits
5 Canadiana
6 Pre-history of Ontario
7 Toy Boutique

G Cloakroom
R Escalator
00 Toilets

SECOND BELOW

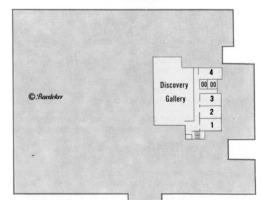

1, 2, 3, 4 Instruction rooms

Discovery Gallery
Here items from the museumn
can be examined. Minimum
age for visitors 7 years

00 Toilets

Royal Ontario Museum (ROM)

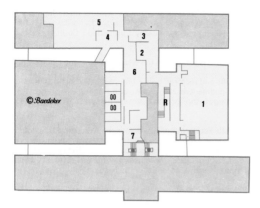

THIRD FLOOR

1 Caravans and Clipper Ships
  (History of East–West trade)
2 Egypt and Mesopotamia
3 Near East
4 Etruscans
5 Greeks
6 Romans
7 Islamic civilisation

R Escalator
00 Toilets

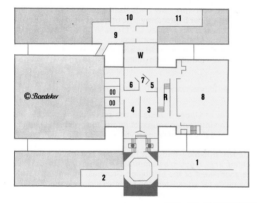

SECOND FLOOR

1 Dinosaurs
2 Fossils
3 Evolution
4 Reptiles
5 Botany
6 Arthropods
7 Living invertebrates
8 Interdisciplinary Gallery
9 Forest
10 Bat cave
11 Mammals

R Escalator
W Temporary exhibitions
00 Toilets

exhibition are objets d'art representing over four thousand years of mankind's creativity, including American pottery from the Pre-Columbian period (e.g Nazca, Peru and Mexico), European porcelain (e.g. Delft, Meissen, Vienna, Sèvres and various British manufacturers) and Italian Majolica. Also rather special is a delightful series of "Commedia dell'arte" figurines.

A short distance south of the Royal Ontario Museum lies the spacious and beautifully maintained Queen's Park, dominated by the Neo-Gothic outline of the Ontario Parliament buildings (1885–92). Guided tours are organised during the summer recess and at other times by arrangement.

Queen's Park

Houses of
Parliament

East of the Parliament are more provincial government buildings.

Government
buildings

Housed in a building just to the west of the Ontario Parliament this quite exceptional collection of "Canadiana" (open: daily 10am–5pm) includes splendid items of Colonial period furnishings and furniture brought together from all over eastern Canada. There are also some very fine works by Canadian artists (e.g. portraits of Generals Montcalm and Wolfe, adversaries in that famous battle fought on Québec's Plains of Abraham in 1759).

Canadian
Decorative Arts
Collection

Toronto

Yorkville
The tastefully redeveloped district of Yorkville with its many high-class boutiques, galleries and elegant restaurants extends northwards from Bloor St. Hazelton Lanes and the nearby Cumberland Court represent luxury shopping at its most stylish.

Spadina Avenue
Spadina Ave. runs north–south along the western side of the city centre.

★Spadina
Mansion
Dating from the 1880s and restored only a few years ago the splendid old Spadina Mansion (Spadina Ave. 285; at the north-western extremity of the city centre) now belongs to the Toronto Historical Society. There are guided tours daily.

★Casa Loma
Standing in beautifully kept grounds just across the Avenue from Spadina Mansion, Casa Loma is an extraordinary building somewhat reminiscent of a medieval castle. It was originally constructed for Sir Henry Pellatt, an eccentric Canadian multi-millionaire who was among the first to recognise and exploit the money-making potential of the Niagara Falls.

With close to 100 rooms (including three dozen bathrooms) the house is now a museum (open: daily).

City centre south-west

★Old Fort York
Located at the south-western end of what used to be a huge block of CNR-owned land, Old Fort York now finds itself penned in between the railway line and the Gardiner Expressway. The original fort, built by Governor Simcoe in 1793, was destroyed by US forces in 1813. It was quickly rebuilt but soon lost any strategic importance.
Inside the fort (open: end May–Sept.) is a small museum devoted to its history. During the main tourist season military parades are held in period uniform.

Exhibition Grounds
Beyond the Gardiner Expressway lies Toronto's exhibition site.

Marine Museum of Upper Canada
The Marine Museum of Upper Canada in the surviving part of the old Stanley Barracks is an interesting source of information about navigation on the Great Lakes and the St Lawrence River.

★Ontario Place
Ontario Place (open: mid-May–mid-Sept.) is a large and inviting pleasure park and recreation area. It occupies a number of man-made islands close offshore to the south-west of the Exhibition Grounds. As well as a wide range of amusements for youngsters the facilities include a marina, various restaurants and shops, neat gardens, a large open-air theatre (where e.g. pop concerts are held in summer), a six-storey Cinesphere and a captivating Children's Village.

HMCS "Haida"
Now permanently berthed at Ontario Place and always a popular attraction with visitors is the destroyer HMCS "Haida" which saw service in the Second World War and Korean War.

Old Town
What few traces remain of Toronto's predecessor York are largely to be found in the area just to the east of the Central Business District. In addition to one or two elderly churches, and the St Lawrence covered market, the "Old Town" has some rather pleasant places at which to eat.

O'Keefe Centre
The O'Keefe Centre (close to Union Station) is a theatre with a long established reputation for the performing arts.

Mackenzie House
Also worth visiting in the Old Town is the modest Bond Street home of William Lyon Mackenzie, Toronto's first mayor and leader of the "Upper Canada Rebellion". Open daily.

★Toronto Islands
The ferry trip from Queen's Quay Terminal to the Toronto Islands (about a kilometre offshore) is the prelude to a thoroughly enjoyable outing. There

are lovely walks on the islands, and the opportunity for rowing, sailing, swimming, etc. or simply to relax. One or two marinas and the odd cluster of weekend homes bring a touch of variety to the scene. In summer the islands are the venue for numerous open-air events, including the occasional Indian pow-wow.

In favourable visibility there is a stunning view of the Toronto skyline.

The Ontario Science Centre (open: daily) occupies a site overlooking the Don Valley, about 10km/6 miles north-east of the city centre. Designed by the virtuoso architect Raymond Moriyama this extremely modern building was completed in 1969. Visitors to the Centre are brought face to face with the latest developments in e.g. laser technology, telecommunications, optics, biology, atomic physics, space travel and meteorology, all presented in an absorbing and imaginative way. The emphasis is very much on visitor participation, with many inter-active displays and widespread use of suitably installed computing and other equipment.

Around Toronto

★★Ontario Science Cetre

Toronto's huge zoo with its collection of several thousand animals is situated on the Red River some 40km/25 miles north-east of the city centre. In concept the zoo is similar to Munich Zoo (though on a very much larger scale) and is divided into four sections, each representing a major region of the globe. The North American section is unique, enthralling the visitor with its spacious grizzly bear enclosure, vast bison park and impressive polarium, etc.

★★Toronto Zoo

The farm making up the nucleus of Black Creek Pioneer Village (about 30km/19 miles north-west of the city centre and well worth a visit) originally belonged to a Dutch Pennsylvanian of German extraction who settled here in the early 19th c. The village consists of more than two dozen homesteads and other buildings (including a mill, cartwrights shop and smithy). Some are original, some rebuilt and some are replicas. Together they provide a

★Black Creek Pioneer Village

Skyline of Toronto

469

fascinating glimpse of pioneer life during the last century, with costumed museum staff demonstrating the old crafts and re-enacting everyday scenes from those far-off times. Visitors can even sample some of the exceptionally tasty food enjoyed by the early pioneers.

Canada's Wonderland

Also about 30km/19 miles north-west of the city centre is Canada's Wonderland. The theme park's many attractions make for an enjoyable family day out.

Kleinburg

Kleinburg is a small town situated about 40km/25 miles north-west of the city centre in the wooded Humber Valley.

★★McMichael Collection

Anyone with an interest in art will certainly wish to see the McMichael Collection which is located here. Although started only a few decades ago, the collection encompasses a wide range of works by Canadian artists, including Tom Thomson and the Group of Seven, Emily Carr, David Milne, Lawren Harris and Clarence Gagnon. Also noteworthy are sculptures by North-west Coast Indians, and Inuit carvings and lithographs.

★Ontario Agricultural Museum

Ontario's Agricultural Museum (open: mid-May–Sept.) is to be found a few kilometres/miles south of the international airport.

Mississauga

★City Hall

Devotees of contemporary architecture make pilgrimages to Mississauga (15km/9 miles south-west of the city centre) from all over the world, drawn by its striking post-modernist City Hall. Constructed a few years ago, the distinctive complex with its clock tower, rotunda, large hall and office wing was designed by architects Jones & Kirkland and is now considered the finest expression of modern Canadian architecture.

Trois-Rivières   P 8

Province: Québec. Population: 115,000

Information

See Québec (Province)

General

Trois-Rivières was founded in 1634 when Sieur de Laviolette built a fort to regulate the fur trade in the Saint-Maurice Valley and protect the local Indians from raids by the Iroquois. The settlement flourished and was the home of some famous pioneer explorers, including, for example, La Vérendrye. When first established the iron smelting works here (see below) was the only industry in the whole colony. Exploitation of the great forests to the north of town began this century, transforming the economic outlook of the area.

Trois-Rivières takes its name from the once wild Saint-Maurice River, which divides into three island-separated channels before flowing into the St Lawrence. The delta still survives today, but hydro-electric schemes have tamed the river's rapids and falls. With water and timber both in plentiful supply, paper manufacturing has prospered on a vast scale and the town is often referred to as the "newsprint capital of the world".

Quite apart from its thriving modern industries Trois-Rivières has also managed to preserve something of its past, particularly in the "old" quarter near the river. The beautifully restored Manoir Boucher de Niverville, built in 1729, was originally the residence of the town's first seigneur. Now, in addition to a couple of rooms of old French-Canadian spruce furniture and works of art, it houses the local tourist office (168 rue Bonaventure, tel. (819) 375–9628).

Standing next to the Manoir is a statue of the town's most illustrious citizen, Maurice Duplessis, Prime Minister of Québec from 1936 to 1939 and again from 1944 to 1959.

The archaeological museum belonging to the University of Québec is also worth visiting (3351 Blvd. des Forges).

Truro

Province: Nova Scotia. Population: 13,000

Truro Tourist Office; tel. (902) 893–2922 (open: only in summer)

Information

Situated near the mouth of the Salmon River at the extreme head of the funnel-shaped Bay of Fundy, the small town of Truro experiences the highest tides in the world (normally around 15m/49ft but reaching heights of up to 21m/69ft at spring tides!).

Today Truro is a highly industrialised town with agricultural and teacher training colleges.

Truro, or "Cobéquid" as its Acadian inhabitants called it, was first settled in the 17th c. When the Acadians were deported in the mid-18th c. they were replaced by incoming settlers from Northern Ireland. These were later joined by Loyalists from New Hampshire (in the US) and new immigrants from Scotland.

History

The several hundred hectares/acres of Victoria Park make for excellent walking (with some longer trails as well as short ones). But this scenic park is also a pleasant place in which simply to relax, retaining something of the wild with its delightful little streams and romantic ravines. People come to swim and jog and there are some beautiful picnic spots.

Sights

★Victoria Park

The twice daily tidal bore on the River Salmon makes a marvellous natural spectacle. The river level can rise a metre in just five minutes and reaches high water mark (15m/49ft) within an hour. The phenomenon is particularly dramatic at spring tides when the water can rise as high as 21m/69ft!

These huge tides are responsible for some very striking coastal scenery in the Truro area.

★★Tidal bore (ebb and flood)

Minas Basin–Northumberland Strait

From Truro it is possible to combine drives by car to the Northumberland Strait and the Minas Basin (coal mining district) in a very pleasant circular tour.

Note

From Truro follow Highway 2 westwards for about 100km/60 miles. The road runs along the north side of the Minas Basin, crossing the slopes of the Cobequid Mountains to Parrsboro (population 2000). Here, in addition to the impressive tides which characterise this arm of the Bay of Fundy (see entry), agates and amethysts can also be found.

Parrsboro

From Parrsboro the route heads north for 35km/22 miles to the former mining town of Springhill (population 5000). Set in the midst of delightful scenery the town is nevertheless the centre of what was once a coal mining district, the history of which is recorded in Springhill's mining museum (open: May–Oct. 10am–6pm).

Springhill

30km/19 miles or so beyond Springhill the pleasantly green city of Amherst (pop. 10,000) stands at the "gateway" to Nova Scotia. Amherst evolved from a former Acadian settlement founded in the 17th c. beside a Micmac Indian village. When English-speaking colonists took over in 1760 it was renamed after Baron Amherst, the British general who captured Montréal in that year and later became Governor of the US state of Virginia.

Today Amherst is a lively industrial town (e.g agricultural machinery, railway).

Amherst

Province: Ontario

Hwy. 2 (eastbound) from Morrisburg, exit to Hwy. 401 at Upper Canada Road for Cryslers Farm Battlefield Park.

"Living history" is a speciality of the Canadian museum service and Upper Canada Village near Morrisburg is one of the most outstanding and fascinating examples of the technique which involves faithfully reproducing a period from the past in every living detail. Many of the buildings in the village came from sites in the old St Lawrence Valley condemned to extinction by the great new inland waterway. Now re-erected here they convey all the appearance and atmosphere of a real 19th c. community, a community which has progressed over the years between 1780 and 1867 through the efforts of its white settler inhabitants.

Upper Canada Village vividly re-creates the everyday lives of people in the St Lawrence Valley from the beginnings of settlement and the initial cultivation of the land to the first phase of industrialisation.

★★A walk around Upper Canada Village

Entrance	A bridge and a gate lead into the museum village.
Houses	The village has 35 houses in all. These range from simple timber shacks built by fur trappers and pioneer settlers to homely farmsteads, brick-built houses exuding solid middle-class comfort, and the refined elegance of a Greek Revival villa.
Public buildings	Everything a 19th c. community would have possessed in the way of public buildings is reproduced here – schools, an Anglican church, shops, bar and even a doctor's surgery; likewise tradesmen's premises – bakery, smithy and sawmill.
	A great bustle of activity prevails in the streets and houses of Upper Canada Village. Dressed of course in the costumes of the day, the "villagers" go about their routine daily business (visitors are welcome to join in if they feel so inclined).
Asselstine Factory	The Asselstine Factory is a reconstruction of a textile mill. Regular demonstrations are given showing how cloth was manufactured in the early days of industrialisation.
Farm life	Life on a 19th c. North American farm is portrayed in detail, all kinds of authentic farmyard activities being carried out for real.
Willard's Hotel	In Willard's Hotel the meals as well as the architecture are in the style of the 1850s.
Boats and horse-drawn carriages	Anyone wanting to try out the transport of the time can venture on a boat trip or take a drive in a horse-drawn carriage.
Opening times	Daily from mid-May to mid-Oct. 9.30am to 5pm. Admission fee.

Vallée Richelieu   P 8

Province: Québec

Information	See Québec (Province)

The Richelieu is an important tributary of the St Lawrence, having its source in Lake Champlain and entering the St Lawrence at Sorel. The 130km/80 mile long river played a significant role in the history of both New France and New England, but even before the arrival of Europeans it was a busy trade route and communications corridor for the Indians. During the period of Anglo-French conflict, especially the years between 1754 and 1763, the Richelieu gave the warring nations and their Indian allies two-way access to the area east of Montréal.

General

Nowadays the Richelieu Valley is best known for its delightful scenery.

Boucherville still has a large number of 18th c. houses, among which are La Chaumière (416 rue Ste-Famille; built 1741), the Manoir Pierre-Boucher (468–470 Bd. Marie-Victorin) and the Maison Lafontaine (1780). In addition the church of St-Famille possesses some of the finest wood carvings in the whole of Canada, including side altars (dated 1808) by Louis Amable Quévillon and a 1745 tabernacle by Gilles Bolvin.

Boucherville

The small industrial town of Sorel is situated at the confluence of the Richelieu and the St Lawrence. It owes its name to an officer of the Carignan-Salières Regiment engaged in the 1665–66 campaign against the Iroquois. At that time Sorel was an important forward post for the French. Between 1781 and 1830 the Manoir des Gouverneurs (rue du Roi) served as a summer residence for a succession of governors of Canada. Today the country house is a conference and exhibition centre.

Sorel

St-Ours, founded in 1672, is the region's oldest parish after Sorel.

St-Ours

Mont-St-Hilaire nestles at the foot of a hill bearing the same name. The town is best known for its orchards while the hill, 411m/1350ft high and volcanic in origin, offers splendid views across to Lake Champlain and the US states of New York and Vermont.

Mont-St-Hilaire

Chambly, another industrial town, lies on the edge of the Montréal plain. Its principal tourist attraction is the well-preserved Fort St-Louis, steeped in 18th c. French colonial history. The stone fort was built in 1709, replacing the wooden fortifications constructed earlier by Jacques de Chambly in 1655. In 1760 the fort fell to the British, and in 1775 to the Americans. It was used to hold American prisoners of war during the 1812–14 conflict and in 1837–38 Québécois "Patriotes" were also interned here (open: May–beginning Sept. daily except Mon.).

Chambly

Vancouver

E 8

Province: British Columbia
Altitude: 0–12m/40ft
Population: 430,000 (Vancouver City), 1.4 million (Vancouver Metropolitan Area).

Vancouver Travel Information Centre, Suite Pavilion, Four Bentall Centre, 1055 Dunsmuir St., P.O. Box 49296, Vancouver B.C. V7X 1L3; tel. (604) 683–2000.

Information

By plane:
Most of the major airlines fly to Vancouver. The International Airport is on Sea Island (Richmond), about 11km/7 miles south of the city centre.
Airport buses depart for the city centre from Level 2.
There are regular flights by seaplane between Vancouver (city centre: Seaplane Terminal in Coal Harbour) and Victoria (Inner Harbour).

Access

By rail:
VIA Rail: Vancouver–Banff–Calgary–Winnipeg or Vancouver–Jasper–

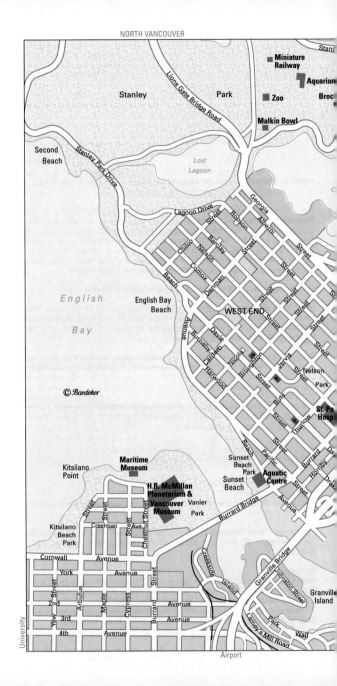

NORTH VANCOUVER

Stanl

Miniature Railway

Aquariu

Stanley   Park

Zoo   Broc

Lions Gate Bridge Road

Malkin Bowl

Second Beach

Stanley Park Drive

Lost Lagoon

Lagoon Drive

Georgia   Street

Robson   Street

Alberni   Street

Barclay   Street

Chilco   Street

Nelson   Street

Comox   Street

Beach   Avenue

Denman   Street

English

Bay

English Bay Beach

WEST END

Davie   Street

Burnaby   Street

Cardero   Street   Nicola   Street

Jervis   St

Nelson Park

Harwood   Street   Broughton   Street

© *Baedeker*

Birte   Street

St. Pa Hosp

Thurlow   Street

Kitsilano Point

Maritime Museum

Sunset Beach Park

Beach   Avenue

Pacific   Street

Burrard   Street

Da

Hornby

Dre

H.R. McMillan Planetarium & Vancouver Museum

Sunset Beach

Aquatic Centre

Street

Street

Ave.

Creelman

Chestnut Street

Vanier Park

Avenue

Kitsilano Beach Park

Cornwall   Avenue

York   Avenue

Avenue

Street

Burrard Bridge

Creekside   Island

Granville Bridge

Johnston Street

Granville Island

University

Yew   Street

2nd

3rd

4th

Arbutus   Street

Maple   Street

Cypress   Street

Burrard   Street

Avenue

Avenue

Avenue

Park

Lamey's Mill Road

Wall

Airport

474

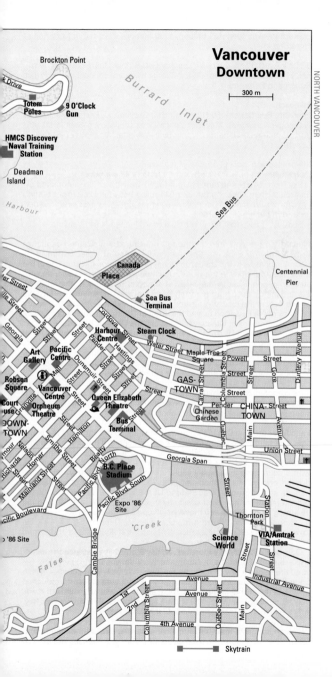

Vancouver
Downtown

300 m

Brockton Point

Burrard Inlet

NORTH VANCOUVER

k Drive

Totem
Poles

9 O'Clock
Gun

HMCS Discovery
Naval Training
Station

Deadman
Island

Harbour

Sea Bus

Canada
Place

Centennial
Pier

er Street

ille Street

Georgia

Street

Street

Street

Street

Cordova Street

Sea Bus
Terminal

Steam Clock

Water Street

Maple Tree
Square

Powell

Street

Street

Gore

Dunlevy Avenue

Harbour
Centre

Art
Gallery

Pacific
Centre

Dunsmuir Street

Hastings

Cambie Street

Carral Street

Columbia Street

Street

GAS-
TOWN

Street

Robson
Square

Vancouver
Centre

Main Street

Street

Street

Queen Elizabeth
Theatre

Pender

Street

Abbott Street

CHINA-
TOWN

Street

Court
use G

Orpheum
Theatre

Granville Street

Chinese
Garden

Main

Avenue

DOWN-
TOWN

Hamilton

Street

Bus
Terminal

Union Street

eymour

Nelson

Homer

Smithe Street

Beatty Street

Georgia Span

Richards
Street

Mainland Street

North

Pacific Blvd.

B.C. Place
Stadium

Station

cific Boulevard

Pacific Blvd. South

Expo '86
Site

Street

o '86 Site

Cambie Bridge

'Creek

Thornton
Park

VIA/Amtrak
Station

False

Science
World

Street

Industrial Avenue

Avenue

1st

2nd

Columbia Street

Avenue

Quebec Street

Main

4th Avenue

Skytrain

475

Edmonton–Winnipeg (CN Station, 1150 Station St., at the eastern end of False Creek).

BC Rail: North Vancouver–Whistler–Lillooet–Prince George (BC Rail Terminal, 1131 W. 1st St.). From Prince George there are connections to Prince Rupert and Edmonton.

By coach:
Inter-City Bus Depot (150 Dunsmuir St.), Greyhound, Pacific Coach Lines (Vancouver–Victoria), Maverick Coach Lines (Vancouver–Seattle Int. Airport; Vancouver–Nanaimo; Vancouver–Whistler; Vancouver–Sunshine Coast).

City transport:
Vancouver Regional Transit System: buses to all suburbs.
SkyTrain: (ALRT=Advanced Light Rapid Transit), a fully automated urban rail system covering the 22km/14 miles between Waterfront Station (downtown Vancouver) and New Westminster. (The track runs underground in the inner city area.)
SeaBus: (passenger ferry) across Burrard Inlet to North Vancouver.

General

Vancouver, the commercial (though not the administrative) capital of British Columbia, lies in Canada's extreme south-west corner, only 40km/25 miles from the US border. It has the reputation of being one of the most beautiful cities in the world. Downtown Vancouver is superbly situated on a peninsula in the Strait of Georgia, bounded to the north by Burrard Inlet, a deep fiord reaching far inland, and to the south by the delta of the Fraser River. Curbing any westward expansion are the sandy beaches of the Pacific coast and the Strait of Georgia, to the west of which rise the mountains of Vancouver Island and the Olympic Peninsula. Further to the north, beyond Burrard Inlet, gleam the often snow-covered ranges of the Coast Mountains.

With its relatively equable climate keeping temperatures mild throughout the year and its delightful surroundings, extensive parks, green spaces and busy cultural life, Vancouver is a paradise for leisure activities.

In the last 20 years increasing numbers of skyscrapers, bank and insurance company offices, apartment blocks and hotels have sprung up in the city centre, many of them incorporating modern shopping precincts – the clearest possible sign of the city's economic vitality.

Vancouver today is Canada's gateway west (i.e. to the Far East), the country's access route to the markets of Asia. As such it is the premier port on Canada's Pacific coast, in addition to being a financial, industrial and cultural centre. Even so Vancouver remains a thoroughly attractive city, with a downtown area easily explored on foot. The city also reflects the diverse origins of its inhabitants with many an echo of other parts of Canada and of Europe, Asia and the USA (Vancouver's Chinatown is the second largest of any west coast city in America). Concealed among the gleaming tower blocks and modern building complexes are some delightful shopping streets (Robson St., Granville St., Denman St.), while Gastown, the oldest district, has recently been carefully restored and turned into a major tourist attraction.

Opposite downtown Vancouver, across Burrard Inlet, stretch the extensive residential suburbs of North and West Vancouver. Immediately beyond them, just a few minutes by car from the bustling city centre, British Columbia's untamed wilderness begins – a vast area of forest untouched by all but the timber companies. There are good, properly surfaced roads only along the coast (Hwy. 101) and along the shores of Howe Sound (Hwy. 99) to Whistler, an increasingly popular holiday resort.

History

Research suggests that the Vancouver area was already inhabited thousands of years before the start of the Christian era. Archaeologists now believe that the Fraser Estuary was a centre of the Pacific Coast Indian fishing culture.

Prior to the coming of Europeans the land on the southern shores of the Strait of Georgia was occupied by the Salish tribe of Coast Indians. The first recorded arrival of a white man was in 1791 when the Spaniard José Navéz sailed into and explored English Bay. A year later he was followed by an Englishman, Captain George Vancouver, seeking the elusive Northwest Passage. For a time after that only fur hunters and trappers penetrated to these western shores, but in 1808 Simon Fraser, travelling overland, reached the Fraser Estuary, having followed the river all the way from the Rocky Mountains. Even then, when gold diggers passed through on their way to the Cariboo Mountains in 1858, there was still no permanent settlement in the area. It was only later in the 1860s that, first lumberjacks and other frontiersmen, and then settlers, finally established themselves on the peninsula. In 1886, by which time the population was still barely 2000, Vancouver was officially declared a town – only to be destroyed by fire the same year.

Boom time came when the Canadian Pacific railway reached Burrard Inlet, eventually transforming Vancouver into North America's principal Pacific coast port (today handling 50 million tonnes/tons a year). The major exports are mineral ore, cellulose, and timber, mainly bound for Asia. Long freight trains also bring wheat from Canada's prairie provinces to Vancouver for onward shipment.

In just 100 years Vancouver has grown to become the third largest metropolitan area in Canada, a conurbation whose inhabitants number 1.4 million. Almost half the population of British Columbia now live here at the mouth of the Fraser River. In addition to overseas trade and the service industries, wood processing and fishing are also economically important.

Situated on a small peninsula immediately west of the city centre Stanley Park is a 405ha/1000 acre park-cum-nature reserve with a host of sights and leisure facilities including a zoo and an aquarium. Particularly on the western side of the peninsula there are numerous huge, centuries-old, red cedar and Douglas fir trees. Being earmarked for use if repairs were needed to sailing ships of the British navy, they escaped the woodcutter's axe and saw. The park, now criss-crossed by more than 80km/50 miles of trails and roads, was handed over to the then new town of Vancouver in 1888 by the Governor General of Canada, Lord Stanley.

★★**Stanley Park**

Coal Harbour (where a small coal seam was discovered in the 19th c.) is the start of an 11km/7 mile walk/cycle ride along the top of the low sea wall encircling the peninsula. One splendid view follows another – of Vancouver's towering skyline, of Burrard Inlet with shipping inward and outward bound, and across First Narrows to North Vancouver and the mountains beyond.

Seawall Promenade

The one-way, about 10km/6 mile Scenic Drive round the park begins from Georgia St., branching off past Coal Harbour with its view of the Vancouver Rowing and Yacht Club.

Scenic Drive

"Discovery", the ship in which Captain George Vancouver surveyed the waters around Vancouver Island in 1792, is now permanently berthed at Deadman's Island (naval base).

From Halleluja Point there is a very fine view of downtown Vancouver.

Deadman's Island

Standing almost opposite are the famous Stanley Park totem poles, the work of various North-west Coast Indian tribes. The oldest erected here were acquired by the city in 1912. Also worth seeing is the more than 100 year-old Nootka canoe.

Totem poles

Every day without fail an old cannon known as the 9 O'Clock Gun is fired from its position near the tip of Brockton Point. Manufactured in England in

Brockton Point, 9 O'Clock Gun

View from Stanley Park of the skyline of Vancouver

1815 it was brought to Vancouver in the late 19th c. and used to be fired at 6pm to signal the end of the fishing day.

From Brockton Point (lighthouse) there are fine views of the Lions Gate Bridge and the port of Vancouver. The cross commemorates the victims of a 1906 shipwreck.

"Empress of Japan"

Adding a touch of history at another viewpoint is a replica of a figurehead from the Canadian Pacific Line's "Empress of Japan". The ship plied the Pacific Ocean between Vancouver and east Asian ports from 1891 to 1922. A rock at the water's edge in front of the figurehead provides the setting for Vancouver's equivalent of the Copenhagen Mermaid, although Elek Imredy's Canadian girl, sports a wet suit.

Beaver Lake

The walk to attractive Beaver Lake (so-called because it was once home to a beaver colony) is well worth the effort. In summer the lake, the only natural freshwater lake in the park and haunt of herons and trumpeter swans, is a mass of variously coloured waterlilies.

Prospect Point

Only a few metres from Prospect Point (at the north-western tip of the peninsula) the Lions Gate Bridge spans First Narrows, linking North Vancouver to the city centre. Both the bridge and the nearby totem pole date from 1939. The pole was carved by Chief Joe Capilano and commemorates George Vancouver's original meeting with the Salish Indians in 1792.

Hollow Tree

From the "Hollow Tree", a partly hollow red cedar estimated to be between 800 and 1000 years old (about 1km/½ mile beyond Prospect Point) walking trails lead to Third Beach (very popular in summer) and Shiwash Rock lying close offshore.

Ferguson Point Teahouse

As recently as 1945 Ferguson Point, another "look-out", was the site of some important military installations. The Teahouse restaurant, formerly the CO's quarters, is a great favourite on account of its views.

Second Beach is a much frequented part of Vancouver. In 1912 sand dredged from False Creek was used to build up the beach and bathing huts were erected. Today the large swimming pool and wide range of leisure facilities draw crowds of visitors.

Second Beach

Prior to construction of the road and causeway the marshy Lost Lagoon was part of Coal Harbour and virtually dried out at low water. In 1936 an electrically lit fountain was installed. Despite so much human intervention large numbers of waterfowl continue to gather here; the Canada geese, swans and ducks clearly enjoy being fed.

Lost Lagoon

This small zoo with its unusually interesting bear enclosure is located off one of the side roads in Stanley Park.

Stanley Park Zoo

There is a children's zoo in the north-west corner where youngsters can hold and feed the animals and have pony rides, etc.

Children's Zoo

The Miniature Railway (open: daily 11am–5pm) is just one more of Stanley Park's many attractions.

Miniature Railway

When it was built in 1911 the wooden Dining Pavilion housed the park administration. Today it is used as a restaurant.

Dining Pavilion

Next to the Pavilion there is a pretty rose garden, first laid out in the 1920s.

Rose Garden

Also situated in Stanley Park is the internationally renowned Vancouver Aquarium (open: May–Aug. 9.30am–9pm, at other times daily 10am–5pm). In the Max Bell Marine Mammal Centre performing dolphins, white and killer whales, captivating otters and powerful sea-lions attract large audiences. In addition however the aquarium provides a fascinating introduction to the marine life of the North Pacific (Sandwell North Pacific Gallery) while salmon and other freshwater fish can be seen in the nearby R. Gibbs Hall.

★Vancouver Aquarium

Right in the centre of Vancouver the Robson Square complex extends across three blocks between the old court-house (now the Vancouver Art Gallery) and the seven-storeyed glass pyramid housing the new court-house (designed by the Vancouver-born architect Arthur Erickson and built in 1979). Various government departments occupy the different levels in the complex. With roof garden terraces, small waterfall, pond and well-designed foyer the Square lends itself to open-air events in summer.
Off Robson St. there is a wide shopping concourse with restaurants, outdoor cafés and roller skating rink (ice skating in winter).

Downtown Vancouver (old city centre)

Robson Square

The excellent collection of paintings by Emily Carr (1871–1945) ranks high among the attractions of the Vancouver Art Gallery at the northern end of Robson Square (750 Hornby St.; open: Tues.–Sun. and holidays 10am–6pm). One of the best-known of all Canadian artists, much of her work depicts scenes of British Columbia and reflects her fascination with the art and culture of Canada's North-west Coast Indians. The Gallery also mounts temporary exhibitions.

Vancouver Art Gallery

Robson St. always seems to be busy, attracting the crowds with its high-class boutiques and galleries (Indian arts and crafts) and huge range of restaurants and shops selling goods from all over the world. The two blocks between Burrard St. and Bute St. are known locally as "Robson-strasse" because many of the shops were at one time German-owned.

Robson Street

This covered market on the corner of Robson St. and Cardero St. was obviously influenced by London's Crystal Palace. A variety of nationalities are represented among the several small restaurants serving fast food on the first floor.

Robson Public Market

There are more little shops and restaurants in Denman St. (city centre west). At its northern end is the wharf used by the harbour ferries.

Denman Street

Vancouver

On the "Britannia" and the "Royal Hudson"

In summer the excursion to Squamish (Wed.–Sun.) aboard the MV "Britannia" or the "Royal Hudson" (an old steam train) is immensely popular. It takes the same time (7½ hours) by ship or train and passengers can sample both forms of transport by switching for the return journey.

Harbour tour

Harbour tours on the paddle steamer "Constitution" are a delight. (Wed.–Sun. 1½ hours)

Granville Mall

Since 1976 Granville Mall between Nelson St. and Hastings St. has been Vancouver's main shopping street (closed to all private traffic). The Pacific Centre and the Vancouver Centre (at the Georgia St./Granville St. intersection) are two big shopping complexes with numerous shops and cinemas above and below ground. The Orpheum Theatre (865 Seymour St., off the Mall) used to be the Variété Théatre of Vancouver. Today the lovingly restored building is the concert hall home of the famous Vancouver Symphony Orchestra.

Further along the Mall a number of large Canadian department stores have branches.

Arts, Science and Technology Centre

Granville Mall is also the location of Vancouver's museum of technology (600 Granville St.; open: Mon.–Sat. 10am–5pm, Sun. 1–5pm or later in summer). Visitors are able to handle or operate most of the exhibits on the museum's three floors and are encouraged to try out some experiments for themselves. In addition the museum has a programme of science lectures and films.

CP Waterfront Station

At the north end of Granville St. the CP Waterfront Station (the old Canadian Pacific Railway terminal) is now the point of departure for the city's "SkyTrain" and "SeaBus" services.

The 15 minute passenger ferry crossing to North Vancouver gives superb views of the city skyline.

★ Canada Place, convention centre

British Columbia pier just to the west of Waterfront Station is the site of one of Vancouver's newest landmarks, "Canada Place". The unusual roof of this architecturally remarkable structure creates the impression of a huge sailing vessel. Built for Expo '86 the complex houses a convention centre with a hotel, restaurants, a number of exclusive shops and an ultra-modern IMAX film theatre. Cruise liners can berth at the pier alongside the centre, which itself has a series of "promenade decks" on different levels like those of a ship. These make excellent vantage points for viewing the activities in the harbour, including the Air B.C. seaplanes as they take off and land.

Harbour Centre

A few steps in the opposite direction from the north end of Granville Mall are all that is needed to reach the Harbour Centre (555 W. Hastings St.), a modern highrise development incorporating a large shopping precinct. The topmost storey (167m/550ft up) has a revolving restaurant and viewing platform, both of which are served by "Skylift" – a pair of glass enclosed external lifts operating daily 10am–10pm (Fri. and Sat. 10am–midnight). On clear days the view extends to Vancouver Island and Victoria (in the south-west) and south-east as far as the snow-covered peak of Mt Baker.

Vancouver Discovery Show

The "Vancouver Discovery Show", a rousing, 25 minute, multi-media presentation, tells the story of Vancouver throughout its 100–year history.

★ Gastown

The old part of Vancouver known as "Gastown" begins just beyond the Harbour Centre, at the eastern end of the city's main shopping and banking quarter. It occupies the area bounded by Richard St., Columbia St., Hastings St. and Water St. Carefully restored Victorian buildings and old warehouses put to new uses (full of restaurants, bars, boutiques, art galleries and souvenir shops) give the district its distinctive atmosphere.

History

Gastown came into existence in 1867 when a man called John Deighton (1830–75) arrived on the scene with a barrel of whisky and set up a saloon

Vancouver: Canada Place

for the benefit of the thirsty employees of a nearby sawmill (the nearest bar at the time was some 20km/12 miles away in New Westminster). Deighton had a habit of launching into lengthy, bragging monologues and soon acquired the nickname "Gassy Jack". As a result the vicinity of the saloon (on the corner of Water St. and Carrall St.) became known as "Gassy's Town" or "Gastown".

As Vancouver grew the city centre gradually expanded in the direction of Gastown, as well as further to the west.

In the 1960s the charm of this old district came to be appreciated anew and renovation of the run-down buildings began. In 1972 Gastown was declared a historical monument.

With its cobblestones and gaslights Water St. is particularly attractive.

Standing on the corner of Cambie St. and Water St. is a steam operated clock which toots every quarter hour. Made in the 1870s it is today linked to the district heating system. ★Steam Clock

Gassy Jack and his whisky barrel are commemorated by a statue in Maple Tree Square at the end of Water St.

Vancouver's exotic and interesting Chinatown, the largest in North America apart from San Francisco's, extends east of Carrall St. as far as Gore Ave. Set among the modern functional buildings are many older ones dating from Victorian times, some with typically Chinese features. E. Pender St. and Keefer St. (the main shopping streets) are crowded with restaurants. At lunchtime these serve "dim sum", a sort of Chinese brunch which can sometimes include less familiar Chinese dishes. Many of the shops describe their wares only in Chinese and some of the foodstuffs on display are to say the least unusual to European eyes. Vegetables and fruit are sold on the streets. Even the telephone kiosks are shaped like pagodas. Running between the streets proper are narrow alleyways such as the Truance or "Blood" Alley. These are used for deliveries to the shops and also give **Chinatown** access to the flats and habitations. Every year the Chinese New Year festival is celebrated with a procession and fireworks.

History

The first Chinese came to western Canada in the 19th c. during the gold-rush and most of the labourers hired in the 1880s to build the railway were also Chinese coolies. Those who survived the rigours of such a hard life settled mainly in the Vancouver area. With their alien ways the Chinese were generally looked down upon and their preparedness to work for low rates of pay led to friction with white workers. As a result they suffered numerous attacks. With its opium cellars and secret societies the Chinese quarter used to be regarded with the utmost suspicion and was long considered a place to be avoided. Not only were the Chinese population denied Canadian citizenship, they were also made to pay additional taxes and had special conditions of employment imposed. They were only granted the right to vote in 1949.

Today there are about 100,000 inhabitants of Vancouver who are of Chinese origin, only a few of whom live in Chinatown.

Sam Kee Building

Look out for the newly renovated Sam Kee Building (8 W. Pender St.) which being barely 2m/6½ft wide claims to be the narrowest office building in the world.

Dr Sun Yat Sen Garden

Artisans and landscape gardeners from the city of Suzhou (China) laid out this classical Chinese garden (in Carrall St. on the edge of Chinatown) for Expo '86.

Chinese Cultural Centre

The Chinese Cultural Centre (housed in a modern building at 50 E. Pender St.) provides visitors with an opportunity to learn about the history and cultural life of Vancouver's Chinatown. Temporary art exhibitions.

Tymac

A harbour tour (1hr) aboard the little "Tymac" leaves from the wharf at the northern end of Main St.

Queen Elizabeth Theatre & Playhouse

The Queen Elizabeth Theatre & Playhouse (Cambie St./Dunsmuir St.) is Vancouver's largest theatre. It stages opera, ballet and musicals as well as drama.

B.C. Place Stadium

The B.C. Stadium on the north side of False Creek is a huge multipurpose amphitheatre capable of accommodating up to 60,000 spectators for large sporting and other cultural events.

Additional sights in Vancouver

Granville Island

The once mainly industrial Granville Island (beneath Granville Street Bridge, Hwy. 99) has recently undergone transformation – part of a major redevelopment scheme encompassing the entire False Creek basin. The result is a thriving new centre of activity with a relaxed and distinctive atmosphere. Artists and art students have moved into the converted warehouses beside the houseboats and theatres, shops, galleries and restaurants have all been opened (together with a marina and a number of greened areas). Granville Island Public Market is one of the most popular attractions, selling fruit and vegetables, seafood and a great variety of other specialities. The island is linked to the residential suburbs on the south bank of False Creek by road and foot bridges. Ferry from Burrard Bridge.

Vanier Park, ★ Vancouver Museum

Located in Vanier Park on the south side of False Creek (cross via Burrard Bridge) the Vancouver Museum (1100 Chestnut St.; open: Tues.–Sun. and holidays 10am–5pm) is the biggest municipal museum in Canada and definitely worth visiting. It has sections devoted to the history of the city and the Pacific coast as well as collections on natural history and ethnography (the culture of the North-west Coast Indians in particular). Also housed in the modern domed building, completed in 1968, is the H. R. MacMillan Planetarium (several programmes, laser show) while adjacent to it stands the Gordon Southam Observatory (with a 15cm/6in. Zeiss telescope). Instructive audio-visual presentations accompany the displays. From the museum splendid views can be enjoyed over English Bay and Sunset Beach to the city and the North Shore mountains beyond.

H. R. MacMillan Planetarium, Gordon Southam Observatory

The nearby Maritime Museum (1905 Ogden St.; open: daily 10am–5pm) covers various aspects of the maritime history of the area (from the exploration of British Columbian waters to the development of navigation, the fishing industry and the port of Vancouver).

A number of old vessels are moored in the Heritage Harbour. Most interesting of all however is the "St Roch", lying in the dry dock. Built in 1928 for use by the Royal Canadian Mounted Police (RCMP) as an Arctic patrol and supply ship, this wooden two-master successfully negotiated the Northwest Passage to Halifax and back in a single year (1944). She was taken out of service in 1954.

Vancouver Maritime Museum, "St Roch" National Historic Site

The main attraction at the Kitsilano Beach Park is a heated seawater swimming pool.

Kitsilano Beach Park

Of Vancouver's first sawmill only the store and post office survived the 1886 fire and the later rapid development of the city. Built in 1865 the Old Hastings Mill Store is today a museum (1575 Alma Rd.; open: June–Sept. daily 10am–4pm, at other times Sat. and Sun. 1–4pm) housing items from pioneering days and the period of Indian settlement.

Old Hastings Mill Store Museum

From the end of 4th Ave. North West Marine Drive continues past delightful stretches of beach along the south side of English Bay to the University of British Columbia at Point Grey. The extensive 2470ha/6100 acre campus is also the site of the university's renowned anthropological museum, housed in a quite exceptional building designed by Arthur Erickson (6393 North West Marine Drive; open: Tues. noon–9pm, Wed.–Sun. 11am–5pm).

The many items of Indian culture on display include totem poles, carved wooden posts from long-houses, and sculptures by the Haida woodcarver Bill Reid. These are augmented by glass cabinets filled with eye-catching masks, textiles, jewellery and smaller objects of wood, bone, horn, ivory and argillite – eloquent testimony to the highly developed skills and artistry of Indian craftsmen. Completing the collection are anthropological exhibits from all over the world. Visitors are recommended to join one of the theme-related guided tours.

North West Marine Drive, University of British Columbia, ★ UBC Museum of Anthropology

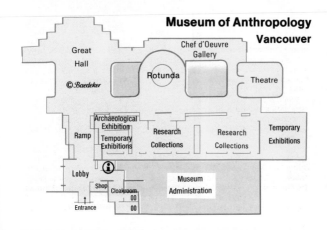

Museum of Anthropology
Vancouver

Great Hall

Chef d'Oeuvre Gallery

© *Baedeker*

Rotunda

Theatre

Archaeological Exhibition

Ramp

Temporary Exhibitions

Research Collections

Research Collections

Temporary Exhibitions

Lobby

ⓘ

Shop

Cloakroom

Museum Administration

Entrance

More Indian totem poles and long-houses, etc. can be seen in the museum grounds.

UBC Botanical Garden, Nitobe Memorial Garden	Also on North West Marine Drive is the University of British Columbia's botanical garden, divided into sections to facilitate teaching and research. Among the highlights are the austere, contemplative Nitobe Japanese Garden (with pretty tea-house) and a gem of a herb garden established more than a century ago.

Van Dusen Botanical Gardens

Of considerable interest too are the Van Dusen Botanical Gardens (5251 Oak St., east of Granville St. between 34th St. and 37th St.). Each of the 40 or so plots is given over to a different geographical region or botanical species and the collection includes a number of exotic plants from around the world.

MacMillan Bloedel Place

Canada's biggest timber company has an information centre in MacMillan Bloedel Place (Oak St./37th St.) where it is possible to learn all about the forests of British Columbia and their economic significance.

Queen Elizabeth Park, Bloedel Conservatory

Just to the east the 53ha/130 acre Queen Elizabeth Park (W. 33rd and Cambie Sts.) extends up the slopes of Little Mountain – at 150m/500ft the highest point in the Vancouver municipal area. There are excellent views of the city centre and the mountains to the north. The park's major attraction however is the Bloedel Conservatory, a 15m/49ft high dome made up of 1490 triangular plexiglas panels.

Vanterm

At the northern end of Clark Drive, east of the city centre, there is public access to part of Vancouver's port (Vanterm) where container ships can be watched loading and unloading. (Guided tours: Sun.–Thur. 9am–noon and 1–3pm; reservations tel. 666–6129; diashow and information on port.)

B.C. Sugar Terminal

One block further east the B.C. Sugar Company museum at the end of Rogers St. (open: Mon.–Fri. 9am–3.30pm) is full of interesting information

Totem pole . . .   *. . . in the Anthropological Museum*

on beet and cane sugar production. Old equipment and machinery can be seen displayed next to it.

Around Vancouver

Port Moody (population 17,000), now a suburb of Vancouver, lies at the head of Burrard Inlet some 20km/12 miles east of the city centre. For just one year it was the terminus of the Trans-Canadian Railroad – hence the Golden Spike Festival held annually at the end of July/beginning of August. Built in 1907 the restored CPR station has now been converted into the Station Museum (2734 Murray St.; open: July/Aug. daily 1–8pm, at other times Sat. and Sun. 1–4pm) recalling the early days of the railway era on Canada's west coast.

Port Moody, Port Moody Station Museum

Now just a continuation of Vancouver Burnaby (population 145,000) is the home of Simon Fraser University. The university campus, another of Vancouver architect Arthur Erickson's striking designs, occupies a beautiful site in Burnaby Mountain Park – atop Burnaby Mountain from which magnificent panoramic views unfold over the south-west mainland of British Columbia. The Museum of Archaeology & Ethnology displays the results of research into the about 10,000 years of Indian settlement in the province. There are also a number of totem poles and everyday items of contemporary North-west Coast Indian culture, together with a small ethnographic collection (open: Mon.–Fri. 10am–4.30pm, Sat. and Sun. noon–3pm). In addition to mounting special exhibitions of contemporary art the Simon Fraser Gallery owns some 900 works by Inuit artists.

Burnaby, Simon Fraser University

Museum of Archaeology & Ethnology, Simon Fraser Gallery

With its 30 or so replica buildings the open-air Burnaby Village Museum on the north side of Deer Lake (4900 Deer Lake Ave.; open: Mar.–Oct. daily 11am–4.30pm, at other times limited opening hours) offers an insight into British Columbian life in the years between 1890 and 1925.

Burnaby Village Museum

Situated on the Fraser River about 25km/15 miles south-east of Vancouver, adjoining Burnaby to the south-east, New Westminster (present population about 40,000) is the oldest town on mainland British Columbia. Founded in the 1850s it was a boom town during the gold-rushes and by 1868 had been elevated to provincial capital. In the town centre are many Victorian buildings which, having survived a major fire in 1898, have now been carefully preserved. Particularly worth seeing are Irving House (302 Royal Ave. open: May–Sept. 11am–5pm, at other times Sat. and Sun. 1–5pm), the impressive home of a riverboat captain, and (beyond it) New Westminster's Museum.

New Westminster, New Westminster Museum, Irving House Historic Centre

New Westminster Waterfront, a recent development on the banks of the Fraser River, features a small promenade and modern shopping centre. Westminster Quay Public Market aims to create all the colour and atmosphere of a weekly market.

New Westminster Waterfront, Westminster Quay

Richmond (23km/14 miles south of Vancouver; population 96,000) was founded in 1879 on a large island in the Fraser River delta. On its south-west side (and now incorporated into the town) is the picturesque former fishing village of Steveston with delightfully restored old timber houses, boatsheds and landing stages. Scores of fishing craft still bring their catch ashore here. Located in Moncton Street is the Steveston Museum.

Richmond, Steveston Heritage Fishing Village

Built in traditional Chinese style the Buddhist temple at 9160 Steveston Hwy. (open: 10am–5pm) has some valuable interior furnishings. As well as religious ceremonies, lectures and tea ceremonies are also held. Attached to the temple are a small museum and library.

Buddhist Temple

From downtown Vancouver North Vancouver is just a few minutes drive on Highway 99, crossing First Narrows by the Lions Gate Bridge. The latter was constructed in 1939 to give the Guinness brewery convenient access to

West Vancouver, North Vancouver, Lions Gate Bridge

company property on the north side of the inlet. Adorned with twin lions the bridge is named after "The Lions" (two peaks a little way up the coast which from a distance resemble a pair of lions).

For an outing with numerous superb views follow Marine Drive through West Vancouver (a prosperous satellite of Vancouver with 40,000 inhabitants), past Lighthouse Park (excellent for walking), to the very attractive Horseshoe Bay (and Whytecliff Park). From the north side of the Bay ferries depart for Nanaimo (Vancouver Island), Bowen Island and Langdale.

Marine Drive
Horseshoe Bay

About 12km/7 miles from downtown Vancouver a winding 8km/5 mile long access road branches off TransCanada Highway 1 in West Vancouver to the Cypress Provincial Park. At the heart of the park Hollyburn Ridge (Mt Hollyburn 1325m/4350ft, Mt Strachan 1454m/4772ft) offers more magnificent views and splendid walking.

Cypress Provincial
Park

North Vancouver's Lonsdale Quay can be reached in 15 minutes by Sea-Bus. In the course of redevelopment over the last ten years it too has acquired a public market – also a small shopping centre (boutiques), street musicians, open-air waterside cafés and weekly market atmosphere. From the Observation Tower there is a fine view of Vancouver city centre opposite.

Lonsdale Quay

North Shore Museum (209 W. 4th St.; open: Wed.–Sun. 1–4pm) is mainly devoted to the history of the area since the arrival of Europeans though some Salish Indian artefacts are to be seen as well. Changing exhibitions.

North Shore
Museum and
Archives

Since 1899 people with a good head for heights have been able to cross the 70m/230ft deep Capilano Canyon on foot by suspension bridge (3735 Capilano Rd.; access daily from 8am). The 140m/460ft long bridge is now something of a tourist attraction in its own right. On the far side are a number of massive old red cedar and Douglas fir trees.

Capilano
Suspension Bridge

Just beyond the suspension bridge Capilano Park Rd. branches off left and descends to the Capilano Salmon Hatchery (4500 Capilano Park Rd.) in the Capilano River Regional Park. When the impressive Cleveland Dam was constructed to secure Vancouver's water supply, salmon returning from the Pacific to spawn found themselves cut off from their traditional breeding grounds. The hatchery was created in an effort to maintain stocks. The spawning cycle of the salmon is explained in informative detail and from July to October fish can be observed ascending the salmon-ladder.

Capilano Salmon
Hatchery

From the 1250m/4100ft high Grouse Mountain – Vancouver's "private" peak – an unmatched panorama can be enjoyed in clear weather, especially in the evenings when the city lights are on. A cable car (Skyride; operating daily 10am–10pm) runs from the end of Nancy Greene Way to the summit restaurant (at 1128m/3700ft) from where a chair-lift continues to the summit itself. In winter Grouse Mountain is a popular skiing area. (Hang-gliding and helicopter tours.)

★Grouse
Mountain

The Royal Hudson Steam Train leaves from the foot of Pemberton St. on a 60km/37 mile excursion to the small town of Squamish. Hauling the train on its approximately two hour journey through the delightful scenery beside Howe Sound is CP Rail's legendary steam locomotive No. 2860, the engine which in 1939 hauled a train carrying King George VI from Québec to Vancouver (hence the title "Royal Hudson").
  Departure times: May, June, Sept. Wed. and Sun., July, Aug. Wed.–Sun. 10.30am.
  Information: tel. 687–9558.
  The return journey can if desired be made by boat (M.V. "Britannia").

★Royal Hudson
Steam Train

◀ *Log transportation in the Burrard Inlet, Vancouver*

Vancouver

Lynn Canyon Park   Lynn Canyon Park on the east side of North Vancouver is a good place for short hikes and walks. Here too a suspension bridge spans the 83m/270ft deep gorge (waterfalls). The Lynn Canyon Ecology Centre (3663 Park Rd.; open: Mar.–Nov. daily 10am–5pm, at other times weekends only) has all sorts of interesting displays on the ecology of the area.

★Mount Seymour
Provincial Park   Extending around the 1453m/4768ft Mount Seymour and almost on Vancouver's doorstep (8km/5 miles north-east of North Vancouver; 15km/9 miles north-east of the city centre by Second Narrows Bridge), the 35sq.km/13sq.mile Mount Seymour Provincial Park is a popular skiing and recreation area criss-crossed by several trails. A winding but good road with frequent impressive views climbs to about 1000m/3282ft, from which point hiking trails continue to the summit and to some small karst lakes (more views). While racoons, eagles and other birds of prey are relatively common the park's black bears are generally only encountered in remoter areas. The 42km/26 mile "Baden Powell Centennial Trail", starting at Deep Cove on Indian Arm and continuing west through the Cypress Provincial Park to Horseshoe Bay on Howe Sound, is much favoured. In summer the Mystery Peak chair-lift takes visitors up to an altitude of 1200m/3938ft.

This particular provincial park was established in 1936. Although the first recorded ascent of Mount Seymour was in 1908, it, like other peaks in the Coast Mountains, was largely neglected until the end of the 1920s. In 1929/30 however the Alpine Club of Canada began to take an interest and the first skiing facilities were installed shortly afterwards.

Deep Cove   Tucked away on the west shore of Indian Arm at the foot of Mount Seymour lies the picturesque little village of Deep Cove, a good place for boat trips and also for diving.

Nugget Route (Circular drive)

The route
Vancouver–
Squamish–Lytton–
Hope–Vancouver   Leave Vancouver via Georgia St. (Hwy. 99) and the Lions Gate Bridge heading for Horseshoe Bay (21km/13 miles) where the B.C. Ferries terminal is situated.

★Howe Sound   From Horseshoe Bay Hwy. 99 runs along the east side of Howe Sound, its route blasted directly out of the rock in places. The scenery here is exceptional.

Britannia Beach
B.C. Museum
of Mining   56km/35 miles: When in production between 1930 and 1935 the Britannia Beach copper mine was the largest in the British Empire. Today there is an interesting mining museum (open: May–Labour Day daily 10am–5pm) with collections of old photographs, equipment, machinery and minerals. Visitors are taken by mine railway to a specially laid out gallery underground.

Squamish   66km/41 miles: In its spectacular setting at the head of Howe Sound the old logging town of Squamish (population 10,000) is the destination for excursions aboard the Royal Hudson Steam Train and the M.V. "Britannia". The trunks of trees felled in the Squamish Valley are rafted together here before being towed down to Vancouver.

The first Europeans to arrive (in 1888) were quick to appreciate the value of the sheltered harbour, and consequently founded a settlement around it. Until 1956 when the line was extended as far as Vancouver, Squamish was at the southern end of the Pacific Great Eastern Railway from Prince George (operated today by B.C. Rail). There is a small museum devoted to the Squamish Valley in old Brightbill House (2nd Ave.; open: Wed.–Sun. 10am–4pm).

Shannon Falls   The Shannon Falls are located about 3km/2 miles south of Squamish.

Stawanus Chief   A popular challenge for rock climbers, the "Stawanus Chief" is a 510m/1673ft high granite monolith.

Guided treks on horseback into the still largely undeveloped interior are another much indulged form of recreation.

Flights over the ice-fields and glaciers of the Coast Mountains can be arranged from Squamish Airport (with a landing on the remote glaciers one of the highlights).

The town's annual Squamish Days (at the end of July/beginning of August) are to all intents and purposes a full-scale international lumberjacks' championship. Teams come from all over the world to compete in the traditional logging contests.

Squamish is also a starting point for visits to the southern part of the 1950sq.km/750sq.mile Garibaldi Provincial Park, including a trip to one of the most popular areas – Diamond Head. One or two alpine refuges and a few basic campsites are provided in this magnificent and still largely untouched mountain wilderness centred on the majestic, glacier-clad Mt Garibaldi (2678m/8790ft).

Signs of relatively recent volcanic activity abound in the park, many of the peaks, especially in the vicinity of Garibaldi Lake, being volcanic in origin. The waters of the lake itself are contained by a about 300m/985ft high lava wall known as "The Barrier". This is believed to have been formed about 12,000 years ago when lava flowing from Mt Price cooled rapidly on contact with a glacier. The present physiognomy of the mountains is also partly the result of a landslip, probably caused by an earthquake in 1855.

About 4km/2½ miles north of Squamish a 16km/10 mile long access road (mainly unsurfaced) branches off Hwy. 99 to Diamond Head from where there are marvellous views over the Squamish Valley and Howe Sound. The Elfin Lakes refuge (trails to Mamquam Lake and Little Diamond Head) can be reached in about four hours from the car park.

Garibaldi Provincial Park

Access to the Black Tusk area (at the heart of Garibaldi Park; highest summit 2316m/7600ft) and also to the delightful Garibaldi Lake is from the car park at Rubble Creek (37km/23 miles north of Squamish).

Rubble Creek

123km/76 miles: Whistler (see entry).

Whistler

157km/97 miles: Leaving the asphalted Hwy. 99 at the scattered settlement of Pemberton (90m/295ft above sea level; population 350) follow instead the gravelled Duffy Lake Road. In summer this is usually problem-free as far as driving is concerned and crosses the about 100km/62 miles of virtually uninhabited country to Lillooet on the Fraser River. (Continuing on Hwy. 99 beyond Pemberton leads first to Birken – 33km/20 miles – and then to D'Arcy on Anderson Lake – a further 16km/10 miles.)

Pemberton

260km/161 miles: Lillooet (population 2000) owes its existence to the so-called "Cariboo Gold-Rush" of 1858. It stood at the end of the Harrison trail, a canoe route up the Fraser River bypassing the Fraser Canyon.

It was here that the gold hunters exchanged their canoes for ox-carts before setting off up the "Cariboo Road", and to cater for them a settlement quickly became established on the Cayoosh Flats. By 1860 the shanty town of log huts and tents was at times filled to overflowing with as many as 16,000 inhabitants. The Pacific Great Eastern Railway line reached Lillooet in 1912.

Be sure to visit the Lillooet Museum in the former Anglican Church (Main St.; open: July/Aug. 9.30am–5.30pm, May/June and Sept./Oct. 1–4pm). It is full of memorabilia from the gold-rush days. Also interesting are the "0" milestone on the old Cariboo Road and the "Hanging Tree" where rough frontier justice was meted out to law-breakers. In 1980 the name of the old Fraser Bridge was changed to the "Bridge of the 23 Camels", commemorating the animals imported from Asia in 1862 by an enterprising entrepreneur who intended to introduce them into the mines as beasts of burden. Having frightened the life out of the local people and their horses the

Lillooet

camels were eventually set free. Mineral collectors will enjoy sifting through the gravel for jade and semi-precious stones.

Lytton

330km/205 miles: From Lillooet take Hwy. 12 to Lytton (population 400) at the confluence of the Fraser and Thompson rivers. From here TransCanada Highway 1 offers a quick route back to the Vancouver area.
670km/416 miles: Vancouver

Tour of the Fraser River Valley

The route
TransCanada
Highway 1
Port Coquitlam

37km/23 miles east: From Port Coquitlam (population 30,000) the 30km/19 mile Poco Trail provides splendid walking upstream along the Pitt River to Widgeon Creek Lodge and the large Pitt Lake (where the effect of the tides is still felt). Canoes can be hired at the Pitt River Bridge.

Maple Ridge

42km/26 miles east: Maple Ridge (15m/49ft above sea level; population 38,000) has an interesting local museum (22535 River Rd.; open: May–Aug. Tues.–Sat. 9am–5pm, Sun. 1–4pm, at other times Wed. and Sun. 1–4pm) in a former private house dating from 1907. There are also fine views of the Fraser River and the historic part of Port Haney.

Golden Ears
Provincial Park

Trips are run from Maple Ridge to the Golden Ears Provincial Park in the Coast Mountains (close to the southern extension of the Garibaldi Provincial Park (see Vancouver, Nugget Route) which is only about 10km/6 miles to the north). Most of the park's leisure activities are centred on Alouette Lake (dam); these include watersports, horse riding, hiking and nature trails. The approximately ten hour hike to Alouette Mountain (1371m/4500ft) where the views are quite outstanding, and the one hour walk to the Lower Falls can both be thoroughly recommended.

Fort Langley
Ferry

5km/3 miles further east at Albion the Fort Langley ferry crosses the Fraser River.

Fraser River
Heritage Park

The recently established Fraser River Heritage Park in East Mission (5th Ave.; see entry) occupies the site of the original St Mary's Mission. The park contains a museum and a small arts centre and there are delightful views of the river.

Kilby Provincial
Historic Park

100km/62 miles east: The highlight of Kilby Provincial Historic Park, on the Harrison River 1km/⅔ of a mile south of TransCanada Highway 1, is a General Store from the 1920s. The accommodation at the rear and the "hotel" rooms on the first floor say much about living conditions in the first half of this century. Settlement of the area took place as early as 1870, by which time the first sawmills had also been built. In the latter part of the 19th c. many pioneers and gold diggers took the Harrison River route north in order to avoid the treacherous Fraser Canyon.

Harrison Mills

From the 1880s freight brought by rail was loaded onto sternwheel paddle-steamers at Harrison Mills (on the opposite bank) for onward shipment by river. It was in 1904 that Thomas Kilby opened the "Th. Kilby Hotel & General Store", a two-storey building supported on piles. His son was still running the business in 1976.

Agassiz

120km/75 miles east: Standing in the grounds of the agricultural research station at Agassiz (18m/59ft above sea level; population 4000), the old CPR building (1893; renovated) now houses the Agassiz-Harrison Historical Museum (6947 Hyw. 7; open: May–Labour Day daily 10am–3pm). The telegraph office and waiting room have been restored to their original state.

Harrison Hot
Springs

Situated on the exceptionally attractive Harrison Lake some 6km/4 miles north of Agassiz, Harrison Hot Springs (13m/43ft above sea level;

population 700) has a public thermal pool and a 3km/2 mile long sandy beach (excellent for sunbathing in summer).

Boats run trips to Port Douglas at the northern end of the 70km/43 mile lake.

The Sasquatch Provincial Park, 10km/6 miles further north, is a favourite leisure area for local people (sailing, windsurfing, waterskiing, canoeing, etc.). Canoes and pedalos can be hired.

From Harrison Hot Springs follow the Fraser River eastwards for another 33km/20 miles, rejoining TransCanada Highway 1 about 3km/2 miles north of Hope.

145km/90 miles: Deer Park exit, Burnaby Village Museum: see Vancouver

152km/94 miles: New Westminster: see Vancouver

170km/105 miles: see Fort Langley

185km/115 miles: The roomy enclosures of the Vancouver Game Farm (open: daily from 8am) are home to more than 100 species of large animal from all over the world. Access to the farm, located 1km/⅔ of a mile south of TransCanada Highway 1 near Aldergrove (pop. 10,000), is via Hwy. 13. | Vancouver Game Farm

220km/137 miles: see entry | Clearbrook Abbotsford

Vancouver Island   D/E 7/8

Province: British Columbia
Population: 400,000

Tourist Association of Vancouver Island, 302–45 Bastion Square, Victoria, B.C. V8W 1J1; tel. (604) 382–3551 | Information

By plane: | Access
Victoria International Airport (Saanich Peninsula). Scheduled flights from Vancouver and Seattle/Wash. Regional airports at Campbell River, Comox, Nanaimo, Port Hardy. Numerous connections by seaplane to out-of-the-way places or camps.

By rail:
VIA Rail: Victoria–Duncan–Ladysmith–Nanaimo–Qualicum Beach–Courtenay (225km/140 miles)

By bus:
Pacific Coach Lines: Victoria–Vancouver
Maverick Coach Lines: Nanaimo–Vancouver
Island Coach Lines: Victoria–Nanaimo–Campbell River–Port Hardy; Nanaimo–Port Alberni

Ferries:
Swartz Bay–Tsawwassen (–Vancouver); Swartz Bay–Gulf Islands; Victoria–Port Angeles/Wash.; Victoria–Seattle (passengers only); Sidney–Anacortez/Wash.; Departure Bay–Horseshoe Bay (–Vancouver); Courtenay/Comox–Powell River; Port Hardy–Prince Rupert; numerous local ferry and boat services.

450km/280 miles long, 100km/62 miles across at its widest, and with an area of more than 32,000sq.km/12,000sq.miles, Vancouver Island is the largest island on the Pacific coast of North America. Lying close to the west of the Canadian mainland it is rich in contrasts. The extremely rugged and still largely virgin western coast is deeply indented, with numerous inlets and bays extending far inland. The majority of its small Indian communities can only be reached by boat or seaplane and because of the remoteness many of the Nootka traditions have survived.

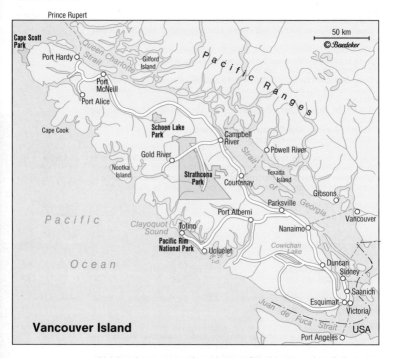

Prince Rupert

Cape Scott Park

Port Hardy

Port McNeill

Port Alice

Queen Charlotte Strait

Gilford Island

Pacific Ranges

50 km

© Baedeker

Cape Cook

Schoen Lake Park

Campbell River

Powell River

Gold River

Nootka Island

Strathcona Park

Courtenay

Strait

Texada Island

Gibsons

Pacific

Clayoquot Sound

Tofino

Pacific Rim National Park

Ucluelet

Parksville

Port Alberni

Nanaimo

Cowichan Lake

of Georgia

Vancouver

Ocean

Duncan

Sidney

Saanich

Esquimalt

Victoria

Juan de Fuca Strait

USA

Port Angeles

Vancouver Island

Dividing the west coast from the rest of the island are virtually impassable mountain ranges – in particular the central Vancouver Island Mountains, a permanently snow-covered chain. The dense forests which here envelop the valleys and hillsides are the mainstay of the island's thriving economy. In contrast to the west coast, where the high rainfall produces a thick covering of rain forest overgrown with mosses and ferns, the landscape of the gently rolling and relatively sunny hill country in the south and east is mainly agricultural. Although likewise relatively flat, the northern tip of the island beyond Port Hardy is again predominantly wooded and scarcely touched. Being separated from the mainland by the Johnstone and Georgia Straits, Vancouver Island lacks many of the mammals found in other parts of Canada. Racoons, wapiti, blacktail deer and marmots are plentiful, particulary in the Provincial Parks and the remoter areas, but black bear, wolf and cougar are seldom seen.

The island is customarily divided into three regions: Southern Vancouver Island from Victoria to Nanaimo, Central Island from Nanaimo to Campbell River, and Northern Vancouver Island from Campbell River to Port Hardy.

History

At the time of the first contacts with Europeans three different West Coast Indian language groups were represented among the tribes of Vancouver Island. The Nootka hunted and fished from settlements on the island's west coast while the north was inhabited by bands of Kwakiutl and the southeast by the coast Salish.

The first European to reach the area was probably Sir Francis Drake. Voyaging along the Pacific coast of America at the end of the 16th c. Drake reached as far as present day Vancouver. It was not however until the end

Pacific Coast, Vancouver Island

of the 18th c. that Spanish, Russian, British and American seafarers explored the west coast of Canada more extensively. In 1778 Captain James Cook, sailing up the west coast of Vancouver Island, landed at a small Indian settlement on Nootka Sound, presumably the first white person to do so. Cook recognised the possibilities for the fur trade and the potential for trade with China and soon British and American ships were making regular visits to the west coast Indians to exchange pelts. This growing British and American presence in territory to which Spain had formal claim quickly led to disputes, and in 1790 the Spaniards built a modest fort on Nootka Island, at Friendly Cove. Subsequently four British ships were seized. In 1795 however a new agreement was reached by the two sides which resulted in the Spanish relinquishing their remote outpost.

It was during the 1790s also that Captain George Vancouver, successfully negotiating the Johnstone Strait, established that the territory he took possession of for Britain and to which he gave his name was indeed an island. Later Vancouver Island came under the control of the Hudson's Bay Company which dominated the fur trade and in 1843 the company founded the first European settlement – at Fort Victoria – to which, in 1846, its western headquarters were transferred. The island would probably have long remained the exclusive domain of fur traders had not the discovery of gold in the Cariboo Mountains brought thousands of gold prospectors and settlers to Victoria.

Today as many as 400,000 people live on the island, over 80% of them at its southern end between Victoria and Nanaimo. Here the climate is drier and milder and the conditions generally more favourable to agriculture. Most of the island's settlements are on the east coast, spaced out along the TransCanada Highway (Hwy. 1) and its northern continuation (Hwy. 19) which runs from Nanaimo to Port Hardy. Branching off this main north–south artery (properly surfaced in 1980) are a small number of roads into

Population

493

The Interior . . .   *. . . Vancouver Island*

the interior and across to the west coast. The northern part of the island is very sparsely populated.

Economy

Timber is still the island's primary industry. In consequence large tracts of ancient forest, much of it many hundreds of years old, have already been destroyed. The larger tree trunks are shipped away elsewhere while the smaller ones end up at the cellulose factories and paper mills of Duncan, Nanaimo, Campbell River, Port Alberni and Port Alice. The rest of the tree is burned. The timber companies are nowadays required to replant de-forested areas, which they do mainly with fast-growing Douglas firs to yield another "harvest" in 50 to 70 years time. Estimates suggest that with the exception of protected areas Vancouver Island will have lost all its ancient forests within half a century. But it would be difficult to over-estimate the importance of the timber trade to the economy, particularly the contribution made by the logging companies and related industries to the island's infrastructure. Outside working hours private cars are able to use most of the unsurfaced forestry roads. Fishing and tourism are Vancouver Island's other major activities.

Victoria

See entry

Saanich Peninsula

See Victoria

Duncan

The little town of Duncan (population 4100) lies 60km/37 miles north of Victoria on Hwy. 1. It now depends for its livelihood primarily on the timber trade and a modest degree of agriculture. The first settlement of the Cowichan Valley took place in 1887 and in its early days Duncan was little more than a railway halt known as "Duncan's Farm". The town itself came into existence in 1912 when greater numbers of settlers were attracted to the area by the discovery of what turned out to be limited copper and coal deposits at nearby Mt Sicker. Today only abandoned mines and the

On the trail of Canadian timber?

In 1993 the Canadian economy earned in excess of 21 billion Can.$ from the export of timber and derivative products. In the same year more than 166 million cu.m/217 million cu.yds of forest was cut down. Forestry has always been one of the pillars of the Canadian economy and about a million people are estimated to be employed in timber-related industries.

Today about half of Canada's "timber harvest" comes from British Columbia. Every year in this "Brazil of the North", one percent of the currently 6.5 million ha/ 16 million acres of virgin forest disappears. On the abundantly wet Pacific coast of Vancouver Island grow the largest, oldest and most valuable trees in the world; giant moss- and lichen-covered arbores vitae, Sitka spruces and hemlock firs several hundred years old, and red cedars not far short of a thousand years old. The coastal areas of British Columbia with their year-round comparatively mild and very wet climate, are one of the few regions on earth where temperate coastal rain forest still flourishes. This unique eco-system, not unlike tropical rain forest in its organic richness and diversity, has in the course of time evolved more than 120 different species of tree and no less than 48,000 species of animal. Now it is endangered. The provincial government proposes to open up to forestry Canada's largest remaining continuous and as yet virtually untouched area of virgin rain forest, around Clayoquot Sound. Only a third of the existing forest would be protected, the rest being available for exploitation, for which reason, in the summer of 1993, a massive campaign was mounted against the plan by environmental groups and conservationists. The fear is that even greater damage will result here than is already evident elsewhere on Vancouver Island, where forest clearance has caused irreparable harm, leaving mountain tops denuded of trees, soil erosion and nutrient loss on a large scale, and natural freshwater fish stocks under threat.

The temperate coastal rain forest is capable of absorbing seven times the quantity of carbon-dioxide as the same area of tropical rain forest and is therefore of inestimable importance from the point of view of the dynamics of global climatic change. Yet as long as, for example, a tenth of all the paper used by the German printing industry is manufactured from Canadian cellulose and annual per capita paper and cardboard consumption in German-speaking countries remains at 200kg/440lb, what hope is there for the "Brazil of the North"?

Rain forest around Clayoquot Sound

remains of buildings and camps bear witness to the short lived "boom". From Mt Prevost there are splendid views.

Ghost towns

Information about the "ghost towns" around Duncan can be obtained from the Duncan–Cowichan Travel Infocentre (381 TransCanada Highway 1; tel. 746–4421).

Cowichan Indian Sweaters

Duncan and its environs are rightly known for the grey and white sweaters which the Cowichan Indians, a coast Salish tribe, handknit from coarse homespun wool. In recent years also several totem poles, many carved by craftsmen from the local Cowichan band, have been erected in the town.

British Columbia Forest Museum

The open-air, 40ha/99 acre, British Columbia Forest Museum (about 2km/1¼ miles north of Duncan; open: May–Sept. daily 10am–5.30pm) provides a vivid introduction to the history and development of the timber industry – from the first primitive logging camps, 100 year old sawmills and old steam engines of yesteryear to the cellulose factories and paper mills of today. There is even an old narrow-gauge railway.

Whippletree Junction

Whippletree Junction on Hwy. 1 about 5km/3 miles south of Duncan comprises a group of fourteen simple buildings, now restored, which were once part of the local Chinatown. On sale in this re-created village atmosphere are a variety of souvenirs, handicrafts, Christmas decorations and refreshments. The "Glass Castle" near by is a real curiosity – a house constructed from more than 180,000 glass bottles.

From Duncan to Parksville (Hwy. 19)

Cowichan Valley Demonstration Forest
Cowichan Lake

From near Duncan, Hwy. 18 heads westwards to Lake Cowichan (31km/ 19 miles), the largest freshwater lake on the island. Posted at various viewpoints along the way are boards with information about the local forestry. Cowichan Lake Village is a good place from which to set out on the 75km/47 mile drive round the lake (only the western section of the road is asphalted).

Satellite station

4km/2½ miles west of Cowichan Lake on the Youbou road is the Teleglobe Canada Satellite Earth Station which links western Canada with the rest of the world (open to the public: June–Sept., Tues.–Sun. 10am–5pm).

Chemainus

Chemainus (population 2000), 16km/10 miles north of Duncan on Hwy. 1, used to be a quiet little spot entirely dependent on its sawmill. Spurred by the closure of the mill it has since acquired fame and fortune from larger-than-life-size murals illustrating the history of the town painted by well-known artists on the walls of many of its houses. A "Festival of Murals" is held every year in July. Restored Victorian buildings have been turned into restaurants and shops and street musicians and puppeteers entertain visitors. The big waterwheel in the town centre is a relic of the first sawmill, constructed here in 1862. From Chemainus a ferry runs to Thetis Island (boat trips).

Ladysmith

9km/6 miles north-west of Chemainus at Ladysmith (population 4500) the TransCanada Highway crosses the 49th Parallel. In addition to its various species of tree Ladysmith's Canada Crown Zellerbach Forest Arboretum also has a collection of vintage locomotives and steam engines.

Nanaimo

The Vancouver Island section of the TransCanada Highway terminates at Nanaimo (population 51,000; the island's second largest town) where ferries leave Departure Bay on the 67km/42 mile crossing to Horseshoe Bay (Vancouver). Nanaimo evolved from a Hudson's Bay Company settlement called Colville Town, which owed its existence to the alertness of Company agents who saw the potential in the coal deposits they were shown by local Indians. The first settlers, mainly English and Scottish miners, arrived in

1851 and for the next 75 years coal dominated Nanaimo's economy. Demand fell sharply after the Second World War however and in 1953 production ceased at the town's last remaining mine. Today Nanaimo makes its living from the timber and fishing industries, from its harbour, and to an ever increasing extent from tourism. The offshore islands in the Strait of Georgia, and the surrounding mountains and lakes, all offer good opportunities for recreation. Indisputably the highpoint of Nanaimo's year is the "Great International Bathtub Race" in mid-July. Nothing daunted the participants in this now classic event set out to cross the 55km/34 mile Georgia Strait to Vancouver in a flotilla of variously modified, outboard-engined bathtubs.

Nanaimo Centennial Museum (100 Cameron St.; open: May–Sept. Mon.–Sat. 10am–6pm, at other times Mon.–Fri. 10am–4pm) concentrates on the area's local history. Among the well-presented displays are a re-created coal mine, an old miners' hut and a diorama on the coastal Salish. The museum also has an interesting collection of coast Salish masks, basketwork and carvings. Tourist information available.

Nanaimo Centennial Museum

Standing on Front St. is a small wooden tower known as the Bastion. The only remaining one of its kind it was built by the Hudson's Bay Company in 1853 as protection for the settlement's pioneer miners in the event of Indian attack. Inside today is a little museum. Every noon throughout July and August soldiers in period uniform fire one of the two cannon with appropriate ceremony. The old town centre overlooking the picturesque little smallcraft harbour (also the seaplane terminal) has been rejuvenated with many restored old buildings, re-cobbled streets and sidewalks, and open-air cafés in which to sit and relax. The walk along Waterfront Promenade, past Georgia Park with its display of authentic Indian canoes and totem poles, to Swy-A-Lana Lagoon is really delightful.

Bastion

Popular with trippers (passenger ferry in summer) the 300ha/740 acre Newcastle Island which directly faces the harbour provides fine views of the coast and the mountains (Nares Point). The Pavilion, built in 1931, contains a Visitors Centre (information about walks, coastal flora and fauna, and the island's interesting history). Boat hire and beach.

Newcastle Island Park

Definitely to be recommended is the tour of MacMillan Bloedel Ltd.'s fascinating Harmac Pulp & Lumber Mill (a sawmill and cellulose factory open to visitors: Mon., Wed. and Fri. 1pm).

Harmac Pulp & Lumber Mill

20 minutes away by ferry Gabriola (population about 3000), the northernmost of the Gulf Islands, is a quiet holiday retreat with little chalets and holiday homes, enchanting bays and eye-catching viewpoints. Scuba diving.

Gabriola

Rather than the work of the coast Salish living in the area at the time of their discovery, the Indian rock drawings preserved in Petroglyph Park (3km/2 miles south of Nanaimo) are believed to be more than 1000 years old.

Petroglyph Park

26km/16 miles north-west of Nanaimo, Nanoose Bay has some well-frequented bathing beaches and a large, sheltered yacht harbour (sailing school, boat hire, Naval submarine training establishment).

Nanoose Bay

With its long sandy beaches on tranquil Georgia Strait, Parksville (population 6000) is a favourite summer holiday resort. Be sure to visit the Craig Heritage Park, a small local museum with a number of historic buildings (open: Sun. noon–4pm).

Parksville

Among its many attractions this much-visited Provincial Park, about 3km/2 miles south of Parksville, has a level sandy beach over 2km/1¼ miles long. At the Park office information can be obtained about guided tours of the

Rathtrevor Beach Provincial Park

"Horne Lake Caves" situated some 20km/12 miles to the north (there are many more caves than those so far open to the public).

West coast detour to the Pacific Rim National Park

About 4km/2½ miles south of Parksville, Hwy. 4 branches off at the start of a thoroughly rewarding 185km/115 mile detour to Tofino on the west coast.

Little Qualicum Falls Provincial Park	Just 20km/12 miles west of Parksville Little Qualicum Falls is one of Vancouver Island's loveliest Provincial Parks, a forested upland area with numerous little ravines and waterfalls and glorious sparkling blue-green pools irresistably inviting for a swim.

Cathedral Grove
In the MacMillan Provincial Park some 15km/9 miles further on, a stand of towering Douglas firs known as "Cathedral Grove" (which somehow managed to escape a ferocious forest fire about 300 years ago) includes several specimens between 600 and 800 years old. A forest walk winds through the grove past trees up to 75m/245ft tall with trunks as much as an impressive 3m/10ft across. Beyond the Park the road continues westwards across the Beaufort Range, where Mount Arrowsmith (1806m/5930ft) is a popular ski area (Dec.–Apr.).

Port Alberni
With a population of 20,000 Port Alberni (16km/10 miles) is the largest town on the west coast of Vancouver Island as well as a major port; despite its length Alberni Inlet, which penetrates 50km/31 miles inland, is deep enough for ocean-going ships. Fishing vessels operating out of Port Alberni account for about 20% of all the salmon caught in British Columbian waters. Huge cellulose factories, paper mills and sawmills (the earliest of which was built in 1864), process the region's wealth of timber. From Port Alberni a 69km/43 mile unsurfaced road goes to Bamfield at the northern end of the West Coast Trail (a six to eight day hike).

"Lady Rose"
In summer the little M.V. "Lady Rose", built in Scotland in 1937, makes her way along the Barkley Sound to Bamfield or (on alternate days) north through Broken Group Islands (part of the Pacific Rim National Park) to Ucluelet, delivering passengers, post and freight to outlying communities en route.

Alberni Valley Museum
The Alberni Valley Museum in the Echo Recreation Centre (4255 Wallace St., open: daily 10am–5pm, Thur. till 9pm) has among other things displays of pioneer artefacts and baskets and tools made by west coast Indians. It is also a mine of information about fishing.

Bamfield
Seaplane, boat or 100km/62 miles of gravel road from Port Alberni (thrice-weekly bus service) are the only ways of reaching the picturesque little fishing community of Bamfield (population 240), snugly situated in the shelter of Bamfield Inlet on the eastern side of Barkley Sound. Here instead of a village street there is just open water and a boardwalk over a kilometre long. Bamfield is also the start of the 72km/45 mile West Coast Trail to Port Renfrew (see Pacific Rim National Park). There are a couple of reasonably short and entirely delightful walks, one to Keeha Bay on the Pacific, the other to the lighthouse at Cape Beale. Boat hire; scuba diving on sunken wrecks off the deeply indented coastline; excursions by boat to the Broken Group Islands, part of the National Park.
See Pacific Rim National Park (91km/56 miles from Port Alberni).

Ucluelet
Situated on a promontory right on the Pacific coast, the small fishing village of Ucluelet (Indian="safe harbour"; population 1600) is a convenient gateway to the northern section of the Pacific Rim National Park (see entry). Near Ucluelet itself Amphitrite Point with its lighthouse and Marine Tracking Station is exceptionally scenic. In years past the tortuous,

Vancouver Island: In Tofino

often storm-battered and mist-shrouded coastline brought disaster to many ships.

Trips to the Broken Group Islands, big game fishing, scuba diving and whale-watching are also possible from Ucluelet. In April and again in late autumn Pacific grey whales pass by on their long migration.

Also at the end of a promontory, some 42km/26 miles north of Ucluelet, Tofino (population 1000) is another very attractive little fishing village and one of the oldest settlements on the west coast, a trading post supplying local settlers having first been established on Stubbs Island in 1875. There are boat trips to Hot Springs Cove (Maquinna Marine Park, 30km/19 miles north) where the water temperature reaches almost 50°C/122°F, and to Meares Island. Whale-watching trips and scuba diving can also be arranged. West Coast Maritime Museum (open: June–Aug., Mon.–Sat. 10am–5pm). Scenic flights by seaplane.

Tofino

Around Tofino there are magnificent beaches of fine sand, Long Beach included, where in summer it is possible to bathe.

Long Beach

Clayoquot Sound, which with its deep fiords and countless little islands opens out north-west of Tofino, is one of the last surviving areas of temperate rain forest. A recent decision by the provincial government to allow clearance of half the remaining 3500sq.km/1350sq.miles of virgin wilderness has met with increasingly fierce opposition (see Baedeker Special, page 495).

Clayoquot Sound

Detour to Strathcona Provincial Park, Gold River (Hwy. 28)

About 10km/6 miles north-west of Campbell River there are more gigantic Douglas firs to be marvelled at in the Elk Falls Provincial Park, as well as several waterfalls plummeting as much as 25m/80ft. Nowadays these latter

Elk Falls Provincial Park

can only really be appreciated in the Spring, when the flow of water from the nearby dam is increased following the melting of the snow.

Quinsam River Salmon hatchery

When the Quinsam River was dammed in 1974 a hatchery was established in an attempt to counteract the effect of the dam on salmon stocks. Although in 1976 only 2000 fish returned to spawn, by 1986 the numbers had recovered to several hundreds of thousands. The Visitors Centre at the hatchery (variable opening hours) provides imaginatively presented and comprehensive information on the life cycle of the Canadian salmon.

Strathcona Provincial Park

Created in 1911 in a mountainous area of exceptional scenic beauty to the west of the Campbell River, the Strathcona Provincial Park can claim to be the oldest in British Columbia. Included in its more than 2300sq.km/ 900sq.miles are over 100km/62 miles of hiking and nature trails, good watersports facilities on Upper Campbell and Buttle Lakes (accommodation, campsites) and three Nature Conservancy Areas, virgin wilderness accessible only on longer hiking tours. Strathcona is a magnificent landscape of clear mountain lakes, waterfalls, exceptionally rugged peaks snow-covered throughout the year, small glaciers and karst country (caves). The "Canadian Outdoor Leadership Training School" (Strathcona Lodge) organises various courses (mountaineering, canoeing and kayaking, survival in the wild, etc.). Information about the Park can be obtained from the Park headquarters at Buttle Lake. A good 40km/25 mile road runs alongside the lake to the Westmin Resources Mines (mining and logging co-exist in the Park together with nature conservancy). In summer there are free guided tours of the mine (zinc, copper, lead).

Northern Vancouver Island

Alert Bay

Alert Bay, on the small, crescent-shaped Cormorant Island (45 minutes by ferry from Port McNeill via Sointula), is the site of one of the earliest Nimpkish Indian (Kwakiutl) coastal settlements. At the end of the 18th c. Indians were encouraged to move to the island to make up a workforce for salmon curing during the fishing season. This in turn led to the establishment of a mission station (Church Mission). Today the inhabitants of the delightful little fishing village and the Nimpkish Indian Reserve total about 1100. Twelve elaborately carved totem poles adorn the Indian cemetery while in nearby Fir St. a small local museum has been set up. A short distance along is the Village Office (information). Sunday services at the charming Anglican church (on the waterfront; built in 1879) are in Kwakiutl.

U'Mista Cultural Centre

As well as displays of the typical Indian masks and everyday artefacts the U'Mista Cultural Centre (open: May–Sept. Mon.–Fri. 9am–5pm, Sat. 1–5pm), about 2km/1¼ miles west of the ferry terminal, houses a collection of potlatch gifts confiscated in 1921 when potlatch ceremonies were banned. Guided tours of the centre (Mon., Tues., Sat.) sometimes also feature dancing, films, or demonstrations of traditional food preparation (reservations required, P.O. Box 253, Alert Bay, B.C. V0N 1A0; tel. (604) 974–5403).

Totem pole

Not far from the Centre stand a traditional long-house (used as a community centre) and the "world's tallest totem pole" 73m/240ft high. Made by Indian craftsmen in 1971 it is carved from top to bottom.

Port Hardy

500km/310 miles after leaving Victoria the Island Highway terminates at Port Hardy (population 5300) on Vancouver Island's northern end. From here ferries make the trip through the Inside Passage (see entry) to Prince Rupert, departing from the new Bear Cove ferry terminal on the east side of Hardy Bay. In addition to the income generated by tourism and the ferry services, the economy of this increasingly prosperous, sprawling little town is dominated by the fishing and timber industries and more especially

Totem poles in Alert Bay

Tallest totem pole in the world

by the big copper mine at nearby Rupert Inlet. Utah Mines Ltd. is the largest employer in the area and responsible for 10% of Canada's entire copper production. The original settlement at Port Hardy, founded in 1904, was on the east side of the bay. When the government decided to locate the new harbour installations on the west side, the inhabitants had either to cross the bay or drive round. Beyond Port Hardy the extreme north of Vancouver Island remains virtually untouched, just as it was when the earliest settlers first saw it.

Not far from the airport a chimney stack is now all that remains of the Hudson's Bay Company's old fort, erected in 1849 to serve as an Indian trading post as well as a base for workers at the Beaver Harbour colliery. It was destroyed by fire in 1890. In 1912 the Indians of the Kwakiutl village at Beaver Harbour were the subject of an early documentary film "In the Land of the Canoes" (of which there are showings at the Provincial Museum in Victoria). The Port Hardy Museum (Market/Shipley St.; open: in summer daily 10am–4pm, in winter Tues.–Sat. noon–4pm) has exhibitions devoted to the history of the region as well as an excellent collection of Kwakiutl artefacts. Nature trails.

Fort Rupert

Created in 1973 the 151sq.km/58sq.mile Cape Scott Provincial Park on the north-west tip of the island is virgin countryside, accessible only on foot and completely unexploited even from a tourist point of view. Almost permanently drenched in rain throughout the year this inhospitable coast is pounded by mighty Pacific rollers which surge in over vast tracts of sand. The Park is about 60km/37 miles from Port Hardy. After 37km/23 miles the more than adequate gravel surface gives way to a good forestry road, which continues as far as Holberg (since the Second World War a Canadian military base/radar station; small motel, pub, small shop and filling station). Anyone intending to make the trip on a working day is advised to call in at the Western Forest Products (WFP) Ltd. office first, to enquire about

**Cape Scott
Provincial Park**

road conditions. This is also where the drivers of the huge timber transporters operating in the area get their information from.

★★Pacific Rim National Park

Location
Central west coast of Vancouver Island
Area: 5110sq.km/2000sq.miles
Established: 1970

Information
The Superintendent, Pacific Rim National Park, P.O. Box 280, Ucluelet, B.C. V0R 3A0; tel. (604) 762–7721.

Access
From Victoria: Hwys. 1 and 19 to Parksville, then Hwy. 4 westwards via Port Alberni to Tofino or Ucluelet. (Beyond Port Alberni the road deteriorates.)

Long Beach
The best known part of the Park is the Long Beach section which begins a few kilometres/miles south-east of Tofino. Here on the superb long sandy beaches massive piles of driftwood testify to the violence of the ocean waves. Away from the beach are areas of moss- and fern-covered rain forest typical of the Pacific north-west, and also stretches of swamp and bog. Various hiking and nature trails cross the Park. Beach combing is a more popular pastime than bathing on the magnificent beaches – even in high summer the water is cold (6 to 15°C/43 to 59°F) and the currents strong. All kinds of flotsam comes ashore (the glass floats from Japanese fishing nets being much sought after) and sea creatures and flora abound. Whales can often be spotted, especially in spring and autumn.

Although the maritime climate is relatively mild it tends to be very changeable and damp. Blanketing mist and lengthy rain showers can be expected at any time even in summer.

Tree trunks washed ashore on the coast of the Pacific Rim National Park

The Wickaninnish Centre is worth visiting (information, natural history displays, films, Park Ranger programmes, restaurant, terrace with telescope for sea-lion and whale-watching). North-west of the Centre the beach extends for 16km/10 miles.

Wickaninnish Centre

The Broken Group Islands lie a short distance south-east of Ucluelet in the Barkley Sound, a multitude of characteristically densely wooded small islands and islets separated by a labyrinth of narrow channels. For the most part completely undeveloped they can be reached only by boat. There are eight campsites, all without facilities of any kind, and a Park Ranger on Nettle Island. This section of the Park is popular mainly with canoeists and the more adventurous outdoor enthusiasts who enjoy camping in the wildest of the wilds. Ospreys are a common sight. Access from Port Alberni, Bamfield and Ucluelet.

Broken Group Islands

Until the beginning of this century Canada's stormy Pacific coast with its treacherous shallows and rocky headlands was known to sailors as the "graveyard of the Pacific"; a great many ships were lost in storms and fog. To give survivors a means of escape from this otherwise impassably rocky coastline backed by impenetrable rain forest, a primitive trail was opened in 1906, following the route of the telegraph lines laid in 1890 between the various lighthouses. About 40 years ago, having lost its raison d'être with the advent of modern navigational aids, communications and aircraft, the trail was allowed to lapse. In the 1960s however, the 6 to 10 day hike along the West Coast Trail was discovered by backpackers, and when the National Park was created the authorities set about restoring and extending the route. Throughout the summer Park Rangers now regularly patrol the 72km/45 mile trail, a richly rewarding but extremely arduous hike across challenging terrain. The trail is still only roughly marked out and the very basic campsites along the way have no sanitary facilities. Nor can any supplies be obtained. In the season Indians will ferry hikers across the Nitinat Narrows for a small fee; other rivers have to be waded or crossed by simple bridge or (in some cases) primitive cable-car. Good equipment and waterproof clothing are essential – it can be soaking wet or foggy and cool even in July and August. At Pachena Bay, 5km/3 miles south of Bamfield at the northern end of trail, there is an Information Centre where maps are available. Most people begin the hike from there.

West Coast Trail

Victoria

E 8

Province: British Columbia. Altitude: 17m/56ft
Population: 70,000 (Greater Victoria 263,000)

Tourism Victoria, 812 Wharf St., Victoria, B.C. V8W 1T3; tel. (604) 382–2127.

Information

By plane:
Victoria International Airport near Sidney, 20km/12 miles to the north on Hwy. 17; regular scheduled flights from Vancouver and Seattle (USA), regional Vancouver Island services.
Airport bus to/from the Empress Hotel.

Access

By rail:
VIA Rail station, 450 Pandora St.: daily service between Victoria and Courtenay (Vancouver Island).

By bus:
Pacific Coach Lines: Victoria–Vancouver, as well as regional Vancouver Island services.
Island Coachline: Victoria–Port Hardy.

City transport:
Vancouver Island Transit System: buses from downtown Victoria to Sooke and Sidney.

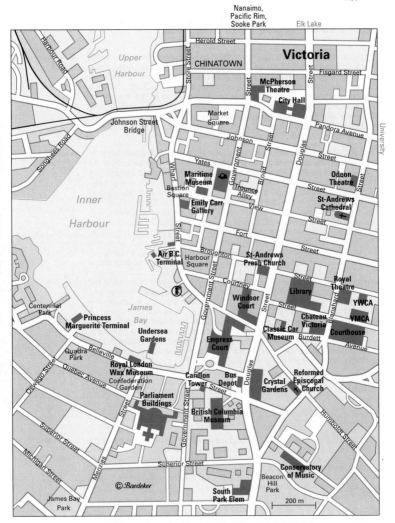

Nanaimo,
Pacific Rim,
Sooke Park

Elk Lake

Herold Street

CHINATOWN

Victoria

Fisgard Street

Upper
Harbour

Store Street

McPherson
Theatre

City Hall

Market
Square

Pandora Avenue

Johnson Street
Bridge

Johnson

Street

Douglas

Johnson

Street

Yates

Wharf

Government

Maritime
Museum

Trounce
Alley

Broad

Street

Odeon
Theatre

St-Andrews
Cathedral

Street

Bastion
Square

Emily Carr
Gallery

View

Street

Street

Inner

Fort

Street

Street

Harbour

Street

Air B.C.
Terminal

Harbour
Square

Broughton

St-Andrews
Presb Church

Street

Royal
Theatre

Blanshard

Courtney

Library

Centennial
Park

James

Windsor
Court

Street

Street

YWCA

Bay

Chateau
Victoria

YMCA

Princess
Marguerite Terminal

Undersea
Gardens

Classic Car
Museum

Burdett

Courthouse

Avenue

Belleville

Quadra
Park

Quebec Avenue

Royal London
Wax Museum

Confederation
Garden

Empress
Court

Carillon
Tower

Bus
Depot

Douglas

Crystal
Gardens

Reformed
Episcopal
Church

Oswego Street

Parliament
Buildings

Street

British Columbia
Museum

Humboldt Street

Superior Street

Michigan Street

Menzies

© Baedeker

Superior Street

Beacon
Hill
Park

Conservatory
of Music

James Bay
Park

South
Park Elem

200 m

Ferries:
Victoria–Port Angeles/Wash. (Olympic Peninsula).
Sidney–Anacortez/Wash.
Swartz Bay (29km/18 miles north)–Tsawwassen (Vancouver).
Victoria – Seattle/Wash. (only in summer).
Nanaimo (111km/69 miles north-west)–Horseshoe Bay (West Vancouver).
Victoria Clipper (passengers only) Victoria–Seattle.

Victoria, provincial capital of British Columbia since 1871, lies at the
southern tip of Vancouver Island (see entry), the largest island on the

Empress Hotel and Harbour

Pacific coast of North America. Only the narrow Juan de Fuca Strait separates it from the USA's Olympic Peninsula with its often snow-covered peaks. Sheltered in the lee of mountains and influenced by the warm North Pacific current the city enjoys the mildest climate in the whole of Canada. Even in January the temperature averages 5°C/41°F (August 17°C/63°F) as a result of which Victoria's parks and gardens are festooned with foliage and flowers throughout the year. In comparison with Vancouver (the province's commercial capital on the nearby mainland) Victoria is quiet, skyscraper-free and largely administrative and residential. To these charms is added a downtown area around the snug Inner Harbour which retains its Victorian buildings and atmosphere. Well-tended parks, flower baskets hanging from bright blue lamp standards, red double-decker buses and a leisurely rhythm to life, all help to foster the impression of a typically English colonial town. In the Empress Hotel people still gather for afternoon tea at five. Victoria today is more British than the UK and has been a favourite destination for American tourists since the early part of this century.

Victoria was founded in 1843 as a Hudson's Bay Company fort. Faced by the impending loss of its Oregon territories to the USA, the Company abandoned its western headquarters at the mouth of the Columbia River and moved to Vancouver Island, christening the new trading post Victoria in honour of the British Queen. Six years later the island became a British Crown Colony. When in 1858 there was a gold strike in the Cariboo Mountains, being the southernmost harbour on the west coast of Canada Victoria and its 800 inhabitants experienced turbulent times. More than 20,000 gold hunters and adventurers flocked to the province from California (among them a great many Chinese, and for a time Victoria had the largest China-town north of San Francisco). Overnight the little port became the base and supply depot for the prospectors. A town of tents sprang up around the harbour, the surrounding forest was cleared and a frantic building boom got under way. In next to no time new arrivals from America made up the

History

505

vast majority of its residents and the sleepy pioneer settlement had become a typical gold-rush town with all the trappings of saloons, bars and dives. Even so Victoria's founding Governor James Douglas managed to maintain some semblance of law and order and in less than ten years the gold fever had subsided. In 1866 Vancouver Island and mainland British Columbia were united into a single Crown Colony with Victoria as its capital, joining the Canadian Confederation five years later in 1871. With the arrival in Vancouver of the trans-continental railroad Victoria gradually yielded economic supremacy to its mainland rival while itself remaining the seat of provincial government. Even as long ago as the turn of the century Victoria's peaceful ambience and mild maritime climate attracted more and more visitors, and the south-east coast of Vancouver Island quickly found favour among wealthy Canadians for holiday, second or retirement homes. Together with the provincial government and the tourist industry the Canadian armed services are today among the area's major employers, in particular the naval base at Esquimalt. Fishing, timber and horticulture play a subsidiary role.

Sights

Inner Harbour

Despite its Pacific coast location Victoria has a unique "Merry England" atmosphere. The city's attractions are easily explored without transport. Maps and leaflets detailing circular walks (e.g. "Victoria on Foot") are available from Tourism Victoria's information centre at the north-east end of the Inner Harbour (Government/Wharf Sts.). Daily guided tours are arranged in summer.

Government Street

The city's main shopping thoroughfare is Government St. (lots of small shops and historic buildings – among them old-fashioned shops such as Roger's Chocolate at No. 913 and E. A. Morris's tobacconists at No. 1116) adjoining which to the west lies the Wharf Street Old Town area. Renovated houses on Bastion Square, site of the original fort erected in 1843, now accommodate boutiques, art galleries, restaurants and the Maritime Museum.

**Trounce Alley
Market Square
Johnson Street
Bridge**

Fishermen's Wharf

Tucked away in Market Square the attractive Trounce Alley shopping centre, a redevelopment of some old warehouses, makes another pleasant place to stroll, as does the Harbour Walkway, a waterfront promenade. Start at the light blue painted Johnson Street suspension bridge, recently restored, and walk round the sheltered Inner Harbour with its moored yachts, excursion boats, Air B.C. seaplane terminal and ferry terminal, as far as Laurel Point and Fishermen's Wharf, Victoria's busy fish dock.

James Bay

The James Bay district, until not so long ago a run-down area of slums, has lately blossomed and become the "in" place to live as far as Victoria's "yuppies" are concerned.

Lower Causeway

The flower-decked Lower Causeway beside the delightful Inner Harbour provides a convenient starting point for a round walk exploring some of Victoria's chief sights.

★ Empress Hotel

Built in 1905 for Canadian Pacific the ivy-covered Empress Hotel is one of the town's best-loved landmarks. Afternoon tea at the Empress, elegantly served, certainly counts as one of the highlights. The building on the northern side of the hotel (entrance: 649 Humboldt St.) houses the Miniature World (8.30am–10pm in summer, 10am–5pm in winter), a collection of over 40 different miniaturised scenarios. Among them are a model railway journeying through a variety of typical Canadian settings, 19th c. London, a circus and various battle scenes.

Red double-decker buses leave on sightseeing tours of the town and harbour (about 1 hour) from in front of the stately hotel.

Parliament Buildings

The Parliament buildings, silhouetted in lights at night, are set in spacious gardens on a slightly elevated site at the southern end of the harbour. A

Victoria: Parliament Buildings

statue of Queen Victoria surveys the port from in front of the palatial complex, designed by the Yorkshire architect Francis M. Rattenbury and completed in 1897. Perched high above the massive dome is a gilded statue of Captain George Vancouver who achieved the first circumnavigation of Vancouver Island.

Figures of famous personalities from the province embellish the façade. (Guided tours of the magnificently furnished building daily throughout the summer season, at other times Mon.–Fri. only. Visitors can also attend parliamentary sittings.) Tours of the town centre by horse-drawn carriage (one is called "The Tallyho") depart from in front of the building.

The Royal London Wax Museum (470 Belleville St.; open: May–Oct. 9am–9pm, at other times 9.30am–5pm) occupies the former Canadian Pacific steamship terminal (built by Rattenbury in 1924) at the harbourside west of the Parliament. Its groups of wax figures reflect more than 50 different themes. Just north of it a modern building houses the Pacific Undersea Gardens (490 Belleville St.; open: in summer 9am–9pm, winter 10am–5pm) where there is a large underwater viewing window for observing marine life.

Royal London Wax Museum

Pacific Undersea Gardens

In Heritage Court (adjacent to the Parliament building) the three-storeyed British Columbia Provincial Museum (675 Belleville St.; open: beginning May–beginning Sept. 9.30am–7pm, at other times 10am–5.30pm) has quite outstanding collections on the natural and human history of British Columbia, presented with the aid of all the latest museum techniques. On the first floor a spectacular still-to-be-completed series of dioramas re-creates the landscape and wildlife of the province – including life-size mammoth which is featured to particular effect. On the second floor visitors are taken on a journey through time, the most fascinating stage of which is the pioneering age (with reconstructed turn-of-the-century street, sawmill, farm, fish processing factory, gold mine, etc.). The museum's

★★British Columbia Provincial Musuem

British Columbia Provincial Museum

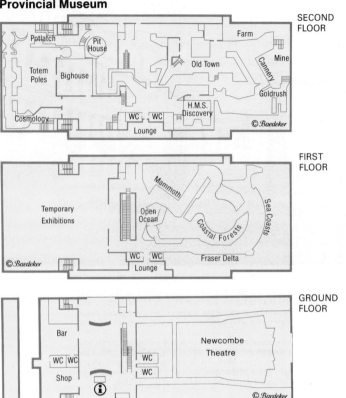

SECOND FLOOR

Potlatch — Pit House — Farm — Mine — Totem Poles — Bighouse — Old Town — Cannery — Goldrush — Cosmology — H.M.S. Discovery — WC — WC — Lounge — © Baedeker

FIRST FLOOR

Temporary Exhibitions — Mammoth — Open Ocean — Coastal Forests — Sea Coasts — WC — WC — Fraser Delta — Lounge — © Baedeker

GROUND FLOOR

Bar — Newcombe Theatre — WC WC — WC — WC — Shop — ⓘ — © Baedeker

Indian History Gallery contains what is almost certainly the finest and most comprehensive exhibition of any on the history, culture and art of the Canadian Pacific Coast Indians (including totem poles, canoes, textiles, masks, a Salish earth house and a traditional Kwakiutl Big House). Haunting Indian songs are played through loudspeakers.

The Glass House at the northern end of the museum contains a large collection of North-west Coast Indian totem poles.

Thunderbird Park

There are many more totem poles (mainly copies) in Thunderbird Park (Douglas/Belleville Sts.), adjoining the museum. On working days in summer Indian craftsmen can be seen carving new poles in the studio (a reproduction Haida Big House).

Helmcken House

At the southern end of the park stands one of Victoria's oldest buildings Helmcken House (1852; open: daily 10am–5pm), furnished and decorated in period style. J. S. Helmcken, a practising doctor as well as a politician, played a decisive role in negotiating British Columbia's entry to the Canadian Confederation.

Situated diagonally opposite Helmcken House the Crystal Garden is a large glass building constructed in 1925 (again to plans by Rattenbury) and modelled on London's Crystal Palace. When first completed it housed what claimed to be the biggest salt water swimming pool in the British Empire. At the time of its renovation (at great expense) in 1977, the pool was converted into a delightful tropical conservatory with exotic plants, parrots, flamingoes and monkeys. Also in the building are a restaurant, tea room and shops.

Crystal Garden

Reproductions of the British Crown Jewels can be seen at the Classic Car Museum (813 Douglas St.; open: May–Oct. 8.30am–9pm, at other times 9am–5pm), in addition to its superlative collection of 40 vintage cars.

Classic Car Museum

The Emily Carr Gallery (1107 Wharf St.; Old Town Area; open: May–Sept. Mon.–Sat. 10am–5pm, at other times Tues.–Sat. 10am–4.30pm) features the work of the well-known Victoria painter (1871–1945; predominantly western Canadian landscapes, Indian villages and Indian art). The gallery also shows films about her life and achievement.

Emily Carr Gallery

The Maritime Museum of British Columbia (28 Bastion Square; open: July–Sept. daily 10am–6pm, at other times Mon.–Sat. 10am–4pm, Sun. noon–4pm) took over the old 1889 law-courts in 1926. Among the exhibits is the "Tillikum", a 11.5m/38ft long wooden canoe which Captain Voss sailed from Victoria to England in 1901–04.

Maritime Museum of British Columbia

Victoria's small Chinese quarter occupies just two blocks on Fisgard St. (beyond the red Gate of Harmonious Interest west of the Government St. intersection). Despite its popular restaurants and one or two exotic shops the district today hardly bears comparison with a hundred years ago when Victoria Chinatown had over 8000 inhabitants and was notorious for its gambling and opium dens (not to mention its brothels). In those days Fan Tan Alley, one of the narrowest streets in Canada, was best avoided by white folk; nowadays it is just another tourist attraction.

Chinatown

The Scenic Marine Drive runs for about 13km/8 miles along Victoria's southern and south-eastern shores, as far as Cattle Point on Oak Bay (Dallas Rd., Hollywood Cres., Crescent Rd., Beach Dr.). One superb view follows another of delightful bays and the Juan de Fuca Strait. Where the route skirts Beacon Hill Park a post at the end of Douglas St. marks mile "0" on the TransCanada Highway. From here the 8000km/5000 mile Highway 1 crosses the entire breadth of Canada to St John's Newfoundland.

Scenic Marine Drive

The 74ha/183 acre Beacon Hill Park, one of the favourite recreation areas within easy reach of the town, affords beautiful views of the Juan de Fuca Strait and the Olympic Peninsula. No prizes for spotting one of the tallest totem poles on Vancouver Island, carved by Chief Mungo Martin.

Beacon Hill Park

Sealand of the Pacific (1327 Beach Dr.) at the Oak Bay Marina is Canada's largest marine aquarium. Californian sea-lions and three killer whales keep visitors entertained (open: in summer daily, at other times Wed.–Sun. 10am–5pm).

Sealand of the Pacific

Craigdarroch Castle (1050 Joan Crescent; open: in summer daily 9am–9pm, at other times 10am–5pm), a small gem of Victorian architecture, was built in 1885 by the wife of Robert Dunsmuir, a Scottish immigrant who made his fortune from Vancouver Island coal. The view from the top of the tower takes in the greater part of Victoria.

Craigdarroch Castle

Her Majesty's representative in the province (the Lieutenant Governor) has his official residence at No. 1401 Rockland Ave. The extensive beautifully kept gardens are open to the public during the day.

Government House

509

Victoria Island

Around Victoria

Hill National
Historic Park, Fort
Rodd

The gun batteries at Fort Rodd in the Hill National Historic Park about 13km/8 miles west of Victoria (open: daily 8am–8pm), used to guard the sheltered waters of Esquimalt Harbour, a British naval base at one time. They were kept in service until 1956. Today the well preserved fortifications can be visited and in summer Park Rangers explain the layout of the fort and details of the weaponry. Fishguard Lighthouse, the oldest on the Canadian west coast, built in 1860 and still in use, makes an attractive picture on its rocky islet linked to the mainland only by a causeway. The light-keeper's brick-built house contains a small museum.

★ Butchart
Gardens

Deservedly considered one of the area's premier attractions Butchart Gardens at Brentwood Bay (some 22km/14 miles north of Victoria on the Saanich Peninsula; Hwy. 17A) were begun in 1904 in abandoned limestone workings by Jennie Butchart, wife of a wealthy quarry owner. They flourished in the mild climate and have been developed into a 20ha/50 acre horticultural tour de force without rival in Canada. Among the various formal and other specialist gardens are a sunken garden, a rose garden, a Japanese garden and an Italian garden. Open: Jul./Aug. 9am–11pm; May/Jun., Sept. 9am–9pm; Mar./Apr., Oct 9am–5pm; at other times 9am–4pm. Firework displays: Jul./Aug. Sat. evenings.

Victoria Island   F–J 3/4

Province: Northwest Territories. District: Franklin

Information

Arctic Coast Tourist Association
Box 91, Cambridge Bay, NWT, X0E, 0C0
Tel. (403) 983–2224 or Arctic Hotline 1–800–661–0788

Location and
terrain

Situated directly off the northern coast of mainland Canada the 211,000sq.km/81,500sq.mile Victoria Island is the third largest in the Canadian Archipelago being only marginally smaller than Ellesmere Island. Over 550km/340 miles from north to south and 650km/400 miles from east to west it lies well north of the Arctic Circle (the latitude of its southernmost point being 68°30'N). Ice-Age glaciers were responsible for the monotonous, mainly flat terrain (never more than 600m/2000ft above sea level) and moraines, drumlins and glacial lakes dominate the scene. The island was discovered in 1826 by Franklin but was not properly mapped until quite recently.

Cambridge Bay

Canada's central Arctic region is administered and supplied from Cambridge Bay on the island's south-east coast. European seafarers searching for the Northwest Passage, missionaries and fur traders were among the earliest to call in at this remote spot which, in 1839, was named after the Duke of Cambridge by a pair of English traders. Until the 1950s the area was used chiefly by the Copper Inuit as a summer camp; "Ikaluktutiak" it was called in Inuktitut, meaning "good place to fish". Then a LORAN radio beacon and a link in the Distant Early Warning chain were established, since when the population has risen to 1000. The little settlement has a stone-built Catholic church and a new wind-powered generating plant, also a fish canning factory processing mostly arctic char, a relative of the salmon with exceptionally good red meat. Other sources of income are handicrafts and servicing expeditions (fishing, trekking and birdwatching). The remains of Roald Amundsen's ship "Maud" add interest to the harbour. Cambridge Bay can be reached on scheduled flights from Edmonton, Yellowknife, Inuvik and Iqaluit.

Holman

The second place of any significance on Victoria Island is Holman on the west coast. Located at the tip of the Diamond Jenness Peninsula this small community of 300 offers visitors the kinds of tourist facilities generally found in the Arctic (though the 9-hole golf course can hardly be counted one of them). Holman is served by regular flights from Yellowknife, Coppermine and Inuvik.

This is an appropriate point at which to mention one of the area's more unusual tourist enterprises – courses on the preparation and use of "qiviut" i.e. musk ox hair (softer than camelhair, though not quite as soft as genuine cashmere). Those taking part learn to make dyes from lichen and to spin, weave, or knit the yarn (information from Wendy Chambers, 21 Boxwood, Whitehorse, Yukon Y1A 4X8).

"qiviut"

Waterton–Glacier International Peace Park

F/G 8

Province: Alberta. US State: Montana
Location: Rocky Mountains in the Canadian–American frontier zone, about 260km/160 miles south of Calgary.
Area: 4630sq.km/1787sq.miles
Established: Waterton Lakes National Park 1895; Glacier National Park 1910.

The Superintendent, Waterton Lakes National Park, Alberta T0K 2M0; tel. (404) 859–2262.

Information

The Superintendent, Glacier National Park, West Glacier, Montana, 59936; tel. (406) 888–5441.

Waterton Lakes Information Center in Waterton Townsite.
Entrance Rd./Prince of Wales Rd. (open: mid-May–mid-Sept. 8am–6pm, in the summer months until 10pm).
Glacier National Park: St Mary Visitor Center (open: mid-May–mid-Oct.)
Logan Pass Visitor Center (open: mid-June–beginning Sept.).
Apgar Visitor Center (open: mid-May–mid-Dec.).

Visitors Centers

The Canadian Waterton Lakes National Park and the American Glacier National Park were amalgamated in 1932 to create the Waterton–Glacier International Peace Park. Though bisected by the international frontier the two form a single unit, and as a UNESCO Biosphere Reserve (since 1979) they together protect a relatively unspoilt part of the Rocky Mountains close to the Continental Divide (watershed).
To the Indians the Waterton–Glacier area was "the land of the shining mountains"; to the American journalist and naturalist George Bird Grinnell it was "the crown of the continent".
The magnificent high mountain scenery with precipitous rock faces, more than 50 glaciers and over 200 lakes is to a large extent untapped wilderness traversed by a network of just under 1500km/930 miles of hiking trails and mountain tracks.
A number of strikingly scenic roads, generally closed in winter, make this mountain fastness accessible to anyone touring by car, rewarding them with superb views. There are excursions by boat on the larger lakes such as Waterton Lake and McDonald Lake.

★★ Mountain fastness

In the shape of their central mountain chain consisting of the Lewis and Livingston Ranges the two National Parks comprise a distinctly alpine section of the Rockies. The north-west/south-east orientated continental watershed forms the western border of the Waterton Lakes National Park and splits the Glacier National Park in two. Created by the Lewis overthrust which occurred over a period 200 to 40 million years ago, the mountains appear from the east like a huge wall rising abruptly out of the Great Plains. On the western side on the other hand they slope up more gradually.
During the formation of this segment of the Rocky Mountains, hard Pre-Cambrian sedimentaries were displaced eastwards some 70km/

Geology, geomorphology

43 miles and upward at an inclination of some 10°, coming in the process to overlie more recent chalk strata. Geologists believe that the resulting mountains originally reached heights of about 5000m/16,400ft.

Since then Ice-Age glaciation, at its most severe during the Wisconsin icing about 12,000 years ago (when only the highest peaks protruded), has eroded and re-shaped the range. Mt Cleveland (3190m/10,469ft) is the highest mountain in the Park today.

The principal features of the landscape are U-shaped valleys with high vertical rock faces, lateral hanging valleys from which countless waterfalls cascade into the main valley below, narrow sharp-edged ridges and crests, and more than 200 smallish karst lakes in addition to larger lakes in the terminal basins. All are testimony to the heavy glaciation occurring during the Pleistocene period. The 50 or so glaciers in the Park at the present time are not however relics of the great continental ice sheets, having formed more recently and after the intervening warm period. In contrast to the usual type of valley glacier they are mostly wide and relatively short. They are found on slopes exposed to the north-east wind, which piles the snow up in great accumulations below the normal snow-line

Climate, vegetation, wildlife

The prevailing winds are southerlies and south-westerlies, bringing with them moist air from the Pacific. The resulting precipitation mainly affects the western parts of the Park; on the eastern side the winds are felt as a "chinook" (a warm, dry wind occurring in the lee of mountains). Thanks to the chinook, winter in Waterton is normally milder than elsewhere in Alberta. Not only do these warm winds speedily melt any snow lying in the valleys, they also swiftly dispel the incursions of cold air from the Arctic which hold the rest of the province in their wintry grip. The onset of a strong chinook in January 1966 saw the temperature near Pincher Creek rise by 21°C/70°F in only four minutes, and though the average winter minimum temperature at Waterton Lake is −32°C/−26°F, the average maximum temperature is as high as 10°C/50°F. While in mild winters the lake only freezes for a few days, in severe ones it can be covered by a thick sheet of ice from January to April, making it possible to skate the 6½km/4 miles to the lake-end in Montana.

Summers are generally pleasantly warm and dry but unfortunately also short (mid-June to the end of August). In the relatively windless months of July and August maximum daily temperatures range between 23°C/73°F and 35°C/95°F.

Precipitation varies considerably within the Park. The prairie section near the eastern entrance averages only 760mm/30in.; below the ridge of mountains at Cameron Lake on the other hand, twice that amount is recorded (1520mm/60in.). As a result, while hemlock spruce, fir and red cedar forests (Lake McDonald Valley) clothe the valleys and slopes to the west of the watershed and thrive in the wetter, warmer Pacific air, on the drier eastern side the tree-line is considerably lower and the sub-alpine fir cover much less dense. Where to the east the mountains give way to prairie there are some open stands of aspen.

In the short snowfree summer months the mountain meadows of the Arctic sub-alpine vegetation zone are transformed into a gloriously colourful sea of wild flowers, vast in number and some being rare. Bear-grass (*Xerophyllum tenax*) is typical of the species found on the mountain slopes, a cyclical flowering plant which in many years carpets great tracts with its creamy-white petals on tall stalks and in other years is nowhere to be seen.

Botanists divide the Park into six bio-climatic zones. First comes a wet zone of many lakes and areas of swamp, populated by sedges, birch and willow (e.g. Maskinonge Lake and the beaver ponds at Blakiston Creek) and offering food and shelter to beaver, musk rat, mink, duck, geese and also moose. Second is a narrow prairie zone – the furthest western extremity of the Canadian Great Plains – intruding into the Park from the east and providing a habitat for coyote and bison (since 1952 the Park has once again come to support a small herd of bison in the special Bison Paddock near the entrance on Hwy. 5).

Next there is a parkland zone bordering the prairie, with open aspen stands and groves (e.g. Belly River, Vimy Peak Trail), followed by the "montane zone" of mountain valleys and lower slopes, where the pine and Douglas fir forests are the haunt of red deer, cougar and black bear. The fifth, sub-alpine, zone extends to the tree-line (Cameron Lake, Summit Lake Trail); here spruce, Englemann fir, larch and silver pine flourish along with bear-grass, gentian and – among other fauna – grizzly bears. Finally comes the alpine zone (above the tree-line; dwarf-pine) merging into alpine meadows, the home of marmot, Rocky Mountain goats and bighorn sheep (which make their way down to the valleys in the autumn).

234 different species of bird, 57 species of mammal and 17 species of fish have been recorded in the Park, emphasising its importance as a refuge for increasingly threatened wildlife. In autumn the lakes are a stopping place for countless migratory birds. None of the three types of snake found in the Park is poisonous. Since the 1980s there has again been a pack of grey wolves roaming the Park. These keep mainly to the more remote valleys of the North Fork Flathead River in the north-west together with the adjacent parts of British Columbia. Unlike bears, wolves pose no danger to visitors hiking in the Park.

Far more likely to be seen are bighorn sheep, white Rocky Mountain goats, wapiti, moose, whitetail and mule deer, beaver and marmot. One of the largest attractions though is the little herd of bison grazing its prairie pasture. With luck it is also possible to catch a glimpse of the white-headed osprey, sadly now facing extinction. In autumn kokanee salmon congregate to spawn in lower McDonald Creek.

Sights in the Waterton–Glacier International Peace Park

A road circuits the large buffalo enclosure situated north of the Park entrance (Hwy. 5). The little herd is kept as a reminder of the vast numbers of bison which once roamed the Prairies.

★ Bison Paddock

About 5km/3 miles beyond the Park entrance a narrow road branches off Hwy. 5 towards Red Rock Canyon, following Blakiston Creek which has here created a massive alluvial fan between Lower and Middle Waterton Lake. The road passes through successive bio-climatic zones between the prairie and Mt Blakiston (2940m/9650ft), highest peak in the Waterton Lakes National Park. The very attractive Red Rock Canyon, reached after 15km/9 miles, was formed by a small tributary cutting deep into the red sedimentary rocks (from the Pre-Cambrian Grinell Formation). The canyon's distinctive colouring is due to the high iron content of the rock, set off by patches of bluish green algae.

★ Red Rock Canyon Parkway

From its superb site above the narrow "Bosporus" which flows between Upper and Middle Waterton Lakes, the majestic Prince of Wales Hotel, designed by a Swiss architect and completed in 1927, enjoys magnificent views of the two lakes and the surrounding mountains. In the 1920s the President of the American Great Northern Railway hit upon the idea of offering coach tours from Glacier National Park to Jasper and Waterton Lakes was judged the ideal stop-over. With a depth of 152m/498ft Upper Waterton Lake (1279m/4197ft above sea level) is the deepest in the Canadian Rockies. Walkers can take advantage here of the water-taxi to Crypt Lake. All year round in Emerald Bay sub-aqua enthusiasts are to be seen diving to the wreck of a steamer that sank there in 1918. The vessel, built in 1907, was used to ship logs to a sawmill on the Waterton River.

Waterton Lakes, Waterton Townsite

The twin Canadian and US National Parks are linked by the Chief Mountain International Highway (Hwy. 6/SR 17), passable from mid-May to mid-September. Built in 1935 and running partly through the Park and partly through the Blackfoot Indian Reserve, the road initially provides exceptionally fine views of the Waterton Valley. Then follows a long stretch when

★ Chief Mountain International Highway

Chief Mountain (2763m/9068ft) is plainly visible, an isolated limestone relic of the Pre-Cambrian period which erosion has separated from the main mountain range. This furthermost manifestation of the Lewis overthrust towers above the rolling hills of the prairie, a sacred mountain to the Indians and a once important point of orientation. Crossing the US frontier after a drive of 22km/14 miles (the highest peak in the Glacier National Park, the 3190m/10,469ft Mt Cleveland, can be seen to the south-west), the road continues for a further 24km/15 miles before meeting US 89. Following this south for another 21km/13 miles leads to St Mary and the eastern entrance to the Glacier National Park. Outside the summer months access to the two National Parks is via US 89 and Hwys. 2 and 5 via Cardston (Alberta). This route also provides superlative views.

★ Many Glacier

At Babb, about 14km/8½ miles from St Mary, a 20km/12 mile side road (closed in winter) branches off to Many Glacier, an area of exceptional scenic beauty. Rocky Mountain goats and black bears can often be spotted from the road. Built in 1914 the Many Glacier Hotel on the shores of Swiftcurrent Lake is the Park's principal resort, conjuring up an image of Switzerland with staff dressed in lederhosen and dirndls. From here there are various walks and mountain hikes to e.g. the Grinnell Glacier, the Granite Park area, Iceberg Lake (where even in high summer ice-floes dot the sparkling emerald water) and Red Rock Falls. By following the 4km/2½ mile Swiftcurrent Lake Nature Trail starting from the hotel much of interest can be learned about beavers, geology and the forested mountain sides. Boat excursions are also run from the hotel on Swiftcurrent and Josephine Lakes. Boat rental, trail riding.

★ Going-to-the-Sun Road

Opened in 1932 the 80km/50 mile road from St Mary over the Logan Pass (2026m/6650ft) to West Glacier is considered one the loveliest mountain roads in North America, offering some of the very finest views. The narrow winding route is generally only passable from the second week in June to mid-September and is closed to vehicles over 2.5m/8ft wide or 9m/29ft in length. From St Mary it first skirts the northern shore of St Mary Lake (look out for the information board after about 6km/3½ miles giving details of the "Triple Divide" just to the south – the watershed of three drainage systems flowing into the Pacific, North Atlantic and Gulf of Mexico respectively). The view of St Mary Lake and the encircling peaks from the big bend beyond Rising Sun must be one of the most photographed in the entire Park. From the lake the road climbs steeply up to Logan Pass and Logan Pass Visitor Center, above which tower the imposing Reynolds (2782m/9130ft) and Clements Mountain (2674m/8776ft). From the Visitor Center a 2km/1¼ mile Nature Trail leads through the Hanging Gardens. The brilliant display of colour from the wild flowers blooming in the short summer season is a never-to-be-forgotten sight. There is also a good chance of seeing some of the inhabitants of this alpine ecosystem, the marmots and Rocky Mountain goats. Two of the mountain walks here deserve particular mention, one to the crescent shaped Hidden Lake and the other to the Granite Park Chalet (along the steep sided Garden Wall with its sharp ridge). Beyond Logan Pass the road down into the McDonald Valley is a marvel of highway engineering, snaking daringly through various curves and a big, sharp bend to the valley below.

From Avalanche Creek campsite in the McDonald Valley a popular walk along the "Cedar Trail" goes to Avalanche Lake, fed by five waterfalls. Built as a private house in 1913 the historic Lake McDonald Lodge, right on the lakeside, retains much of the atmosphere of the old West and acts a base for mountain hikes to Sperry Chalet and the Sperry Glacier (backpackers can carry on over Gunsight Pass to St Mary Lake). Boat trips on the lake are run from the Lodge. Boat rental, trail riding. From July to the beginning of September hikers can use the cabins at Sperry Chalet and Granite Park Chalet for overnight stops provided they book in advance (Belton Chalets, P.O. Box 188, West Glacier, MT 59936).

Welland Canal

Welland Canal Society, St Catharines, Ontario; tel. (416) 684–1135.   Information

The 42km/26 mile Welland Canal joins Lake Ontario (75m/246ft above sea level) and Lake Erie (at 174m/571ft above sea level almost 100m/330ft higher). The canal is situated not far from the world famous Niagara Falls and close to the Canadian–US frontier. It takes eight massive locks to surmount the so-called "Niagara Escarpment" separating the two large lakes.

Every year more than 1000 ocean-going ships and about 3000 other sea-going vessels pass through the locks, as well as "lakers" and other inland craft mostly sailing under the Canadian flag. Passage through the canal takes 12 hours on average. In 1990 freight carried totalled about 48 million tonnes, wheat, iron ore and coal being the principal commodities.

The first Welland Canal was opened in 1829. A second was built between   History
1845 and 1915, and a third between 1887 and 1930. Even this was unable to meet the demands of ever increasing traffic and larger ships however, and on August 6th 1932 the Governor General of Canada inaugurated a route designed for modern needs. Between 1967 and 1973 a 13km/8 mile stretch near the little town of Welland was re-aligned and straightened and the opportunity simultaneously taken to rebuild an important road and rail underpass. The old canal which leads directly through Welland is now used by pleasure craft and water-skiers.

The eight locks are each 261.8m/860ft long, 24.4m/80ft wide and 9.1m/30ft   **Welland route,**
deep. Ships using the seven lifting locks and the single containing lock   **locks**
which make up the canal staircase are restricted to a maximum length of 222.5m/730ft and 23m/75ft beam. The maximum permitted draught is 7.9m/26ft and the maximum air draught 35.5m/116ft. To raise or lower a ship 14.2m/46ft in one of the seven chamber locks involves sluicing 94.5 million litres/20 million gallons of water into or out of the lock, a procedure which normally takes about ten minutes.

Lock 1 is located right at the Lake Ontario entrance to the canal. Close by are   Lock 1
the Port Weller dry-docks.

The second lifting lock is at St Catharines a short distance inland. Picnic   Lock 2
place nearby.

An observation platform at Lock 3 (south of St Catharines) gives an excel-   Lock 3
lent view of the lock in operation. Information centre.

The three twin-flight locks (4, 5 and 6) are the most interesting part of the   Locks 4, 5, 6
canal. They can handle two ships simultaneously, one going up and the other in a parallel lock going down.

Situated at the small town of Thorold Lock 7 is the final lifting lock on the   Lock 7
Niagara Escarpment section of the canal.

The Thorold Tunnel (Hwy. 58), the first to pass under the canal, was opened   Thorold Tunnel
in 1968.

In August 1974 the M.V. "Steelton" rammed Bridge No. 12 at Port   Port Robinson
Robinson, destroying it.

The length of old canal made redundant by the new stretch completed in   Welland
1974 is now used for watersports and by pleasure craft. Leisure and sports   Recreational
facilities are provided on Merritt Island, which lies cut off between the two   Waterway, Merritt
canals. Information board (history of the canal).   Island

An ocean-going freighter in the flight of locks on the Welland Canal

Main Street Tunnel	Main Street Tunnel (road) under the canal at Welland was opened in 1972.
Townline Tunnel	The Townline Tunnel (road and rail) was built under the canal in 1973.
Lock 8	The regulating system at Lock 8 (at the Lake Erie end of the canal at Port Colborne) is one the largest in the world. Interested spectators can watch from the viewing tower in the adjacent park.
Merritt Trail	The interesting Merritt Trail takes in various old and modern sections illustrating different phases in the enlargement of the canal.

Whistler   E 7

Province: British Columbia. Population: 3000

Location and general

The famous ski resort of Whistler at the foot of the Whistler and Black Comb massifs is the centre of the biggest winter sports area in North America.

Two cable cars, 20 chair and four T-bar lifts give access to the two massifs. Downhill skiers can choose between about 200 pistes (the longest having a drop of 1600m/5250ft). Snowmobile trips, heli-skiing and ski marathons are all popular with visitors. The newest attraction is "7th Heaven", a summer ski area on the Horstman and Black Comb Glaciers.

Whistler has more than 1300 units of tourist accommodation ranging from apartment blocks to hotels. Activities such as tennis, golf and riding, as well as white-water rafting and kayaking on the area's untamed rivers, attract growing summer tourism, as do canoeing, rambling and backpacking in the peaceful isolation of the magnificent highland wildernesses (including the Garibaldi Provincial Park, Cheakamus Lake, Singing Pass Region).

Whitehorse

See Yukon Territory
Population: 19,000

Visitor Reception Centre, T. C. Richards Building
302 Steele St., Y1A 2C5; tel (403) 667–2915

Information

Whitehorse, capital of the Yukon Territory (see entry) since 1953, stands on the left bank of the Yukon River at the intersection of the Alaska and Klondike Highways (see Klondike), about 80km/50 miles north of the provincial border with British Columbia (see entry). As the administrative centre for the region and the home of half the territory's population the town is not short of modern facilities, old wooden cabins mingling with comfortable hotels, supermarkets and a shopping street. Included among the items in the shops are some especially typical of the area – gold nuggets, woodcarvings, Eskimo drawings, mukluks (Eskimo boots) and Indian handwork.

General

Whitehorse, like Dawson, owes its existence to the Klondike gold-rush which began in 1897. Having survived the arduous journey from Skagway over White Pass (in the course of which many lost their lives) the gold prospectors then had to negotiate the Miles Canyon and Whitehorse rapids before descending the Yukon River to Dawson (see entry). Almost from the first a small settlement grew up on the river's right bank opposite the present town. The seething, foaming waters of the rapids, rearing like white steeds, gave the settlement its name – White Horse. Although nothing remains to be seen of the rapids (the Sunwapta Lakes having since been dammed), driving through the canyon today still conveys a vivid impression of the hardship which this stretch of the river must have represented in those early days.

History

When in 1898–1900 the White Pass/Yukon Railway from Skagway was constructed, its northern terminus was on the western bank and so the present town was born. From Whitehorse the legendary Yukon River sternwheelers pounded their way downstream to Dawson (see entry). One of the largest, the S.S. "Klondike", is now permanently berthed in Whitehorse and forms one of the town's major landmarks. When the gold-rush subsided the population of Whitehorse fell dramatically. For a time copper mining kept the town alive but when this too halted in the 1920s numbers sank to fewer than 400 inhabitants. In 1942 however the building of the Alaska Highway (see entry) and with it an influx of more than 20,000 newcomers, provided a fresh impetus comparable to the first arrival of the railway. At the same time Dawson (see entry) was experiencing an ever deepening crisis which led eventually to its relinquishing its role as capital of the Territory to Whitehorse in 1953.

Sights in Whitehorse

The sternwheelers on the Yukon River remained the region's most important mode of transport for decades after the gold-rush. It was not until 1955 that the S.S "Klondike", built in 1937, gave up carrying ore from the silver mines in Mayo (see Klondike, Klondike Highway, Silver Trail) to Whitehorse for onward shipment by road. Today the restored and refitted paddle steamer welcomes visitors on the Yukon embankment in the town centre.

★ S.S "Klondike"

The McBride Museum in First Ave. has a large collection of relics and photographs from the gold-rush days. These include the log cabin belonging to Sam McGee about whom Robert Service, "Bard of the Yukon", wrote a famous ballad. There are also numerous bits of old machinery and implements and an interesting display on the wildlife of the Yukon (open: mid-May–Sept.).

McBride Museum

On the way from Skagway to Whitehorse

★Frantic Follies

The "Frantic Follies", a nightly revue (June–Sept.) in the Sheffield Hotel is hugely popular. Can-can girls and honky-tonk piano naturally feature in this 1890s-style vaudeville show. Book in advance: tel. (403) 668–7377.

Government Building

On weekdays there are guided tours of the Territorial Government Building in 2nd Ave.
  It is decorated with tapestries and paintings produced in the Yukon (particularly worth seeing).

Art Gallery

Works by local (as well as other Canadian) artists can also be seen in the Art Gallery, housed in the building next to the city library.

Old Log Church Museum

Standing on the corner of 3rd Ave. and Elliot St. the old wooden Anglican cathedral, built for the Rev. R. J. Bowen and completed in October 1900, has a collection of documents and photographs recording early missionary work in the Yukon Territory (see entry).

Yukon Gardens

A visit to Whitehorse's 9ha/22 acre botanical garden is the best possible introduction to the region's trees and other flora.

Town tour

Free history tours of Whitehorse are arranged by the Yukon Historical & Museums Association (tel. (403) 667–4704).

★Ascent of the king salmon

Once the ice has begun to break up in the spring, king salmon hurry upstream from the Pacific to their Yukon River spawning grounds. Some even journey as far as Whitehorse, taking about 60 days over the about 3000km/1860 mile trek. To watch as these magnificent fish climb the fish ladder provided for them is a unique and very moving experience.

S.S. "Klondike", Yukon sternwheeler ▶

Around Whitehorse

Tours	Members of the Conservation Society lead nature walks through the pleasant environs of the town (tel. (403) 668–5678). Local travel agents also lay on a variety of tours e.g. by bus, horse-drawn carriage or aboard the M.V. "Schwatka" to Miles Canyon and Schwatka Lake.
Yukon River trip	The twin-decked M.V. "Anna Maria" makes the traditional trip down the Yukon River to Dawson (see entry). Highly recommended: tel. (403) 667–4155.
Takhini Hotsprings	See Klondike, Klondike Highway.
Reindeer farm	Visitors are made welcome at the Yukon's solitary reindeer farm near Lake Laberge (Shallow Bay Road, about 30 minutes drive from Whitehorse).
Black Mike's Gold Mine	The museum at Black Mike's Gold Mine, 37km/23 miles south of Whitehorse, brings to life gold mining in the old Klondike days.

Windsor · N 9

Province: Ontario. Population: 250,000

General situation	The industrial city of Windsor is situated on the south (Canadian) side of the Detroit River, linked to the US city of Detroit by bridge and tunnel. Strategically positioned on the Great Lakes waterway Windsor's port comes second only to its car industry which, like Detroit's, is the main pillar of the local economy. The good neighbourly relations between the two cities are clear for all to see when they annually join forces to celebrate Canada's National Day (July 1st) and America's Fourth of July.
History	Windsor (founded in the 1830s) and Detroit lie in an area first settled by the French at the turn of the 18th c. A trading post established by Antoine de Lamothe de Cadillac in 1701 on the north side of the Detroit River quickly became the regional centre for the French fur trade before being captured by the British in 1760 and later handed over to the Americans after the War of Independence. Except for a short interval during the 1812 Canadian-American War the river has formed the frontier between the two countries ever since

Sights in Windsor

Hiram Walker Museum	This historical and ethnological museum which traces Windsor's development since the earliest days of colonisation, occupies the oldest house in the city, overlooking the river. The section on North American Indian culture is especially interesting. Open: Tues.–Sat. 9am–5pm, Sun. 2–5pm.
Jackson Park Sunken Gardens, Dieppe Gardens	The Jackson Park Sunken Gardens (Tecumseh Rd.) and the Dieppe Gardens (Ouellette St.) are particularly worth seeing for their roses (500 varieties in all totalling some 11,000 bushes).

Around Windsor

Fort Malden	Fort Malden (30km/19 miles from Windsor) was built between 1797 and 1799 by the British, after they were forced to abandon Detroit to the Americans. Only the base of some ramparts remain and a barracks restored to its 1840 state. The site commands a magnificent view of the Seaway. It was here that the Shawnee Chief Tecumseh met General Brock to negotiate peace. In the small museum in the grounds a slide show

illustrates the fort's history and its role during the 1812 war and the Mackenzie Rebellion of 1837 to 1838.

The Jack Minor Bird Sanctuary, 47km/29 miles away in Kingsville, was established in 1904 by the naturalist Jack Minor. It is at its best during the spring and autumn migrations (Mar./Apr. and Oct./Nov.) when huge flocks of Canada geese and wild duck call in on their flight north or south. Open: Mon.–Sat. 9am–6pm.

Jack Minor Sanctuary

Winnipeg

K 8

Province: Manitoba. Population: 690,000

Travel Manitoba, 155 Carlton St., Winnipeg, R3C 3H8; tel. (204) 945–3777.

Information

Winnipeg, capital of Manitoba, occupies a position equidistant from the Atlantic and Pacific coasts and 100km/62 miles north of the border with Minnesota (USA). It is located at the confluence of the Assiniboine and Red Rivers which together formed the main routes of communication for the early fur traders.

General

Winnipeg is now the fourth largest city in Canada, having evolved within a period of 117 years from a tiny outpost of the fur trade to one of Canada's foremost cultural centres and the hub of a stable provincial economy. It has six professional performing arts companies offering everything from drama and ballet to concert and opera, some of which e.g. the Royal Winnipeg Ballet and the Manitoba Theatre Centre, have won international acclaim.

Ethnic diversity is one of the hallmarks of the city, Britons, Germans and Ukrainians heading the list of more than 40 ethnic groups. St Boniface, the French quarter, has the largest Franophone community west of Québec.

Winnipeg is also a city of trees, an estimated 2 million in fact. Mostly planted before 1920 various species are represented including some 250,000 elms alone.

In 1738 Sieur de La Vérendrye chose the site for his Fort Rouge which later became the nerve centre of a flourishing fur trade marked by increasingly bitter rivalry between the North West and Hudson's Bay Companies. In 1821–22 the Hudson's Bay Company established its own Red River trading post, christened Upper Fort Garry. The settlement which grew up outside the fort took its name from the Cree word "win-nipi" meaning "murky water".

History

It was still a small community of only 215 inhabitants when the province of Manitoba was created in 1870. But by the time of its incorporation in 1874 the figure had grown to 1,879, and ever since then Winnipeg has been the premier manufacturing and marketing centre in western Canada. In 1882 it became an important stop on the first Canadian east–west railroad, soon developing into the financial, industrial and retailing capital for the entire West. At the same time, agriculture became a major factor in the province's economy. Following the first shipment of wheat from Manitoba in 1876 a multitude of grain trading businesses sprang up in the city and the Winnipeg Grain Exchange, now the Winnipeg Commodity Exchange, was founded.

The greatest period of expansion however occurred between 1901 and 1914. The population increased to 100,000 as immigrants from Europe and America poured into the prairies, among them large numbers of Ukrainians, French-Canadians, Germans, Poles and Scandinavians, producing the city's characteristic mix of ethnic groups each of which preserves its language and traditions.

This was the time also when the city centre began to take shape, the insatiable demand for housing, offices and business premises brought about by the influx of immigrants giving rise to a building boom.

Winnipeg

Logan

Avenue

Higgins

Henderson

Highway

Nairn. Ave.

CHINATOWN

Ukrainian
Cultural Centre

Manitoba Museum
of Man and Nature
Planetarium

Civic Centre

Centennial
Centre

Oak Point

Notre Dame Ave.

Whitler Park

Blue

Archibald

Thunder Bay

Winnipeg
Square

Portage
Place

Portage

Ave.

Smith

Main

Provencher

Boulevard

Airport
Winnipeg Gallery University
Western Canada Aviation Museum

Cathédrale
St. Mary's

Convention
Centre

Civic
Auditorium

Street

Union
Station

The Forks

Upper Fort
Garry Gate

College
St-Boniface

St. Boniface
Cathedral

St. Boniface
Museum

Government
House

Legislative
Buildings

Street

River

Assiniboine

Fort
Rouge
Park

Red River

Tache Avenue

Marion

Street

OSBORNE
VILLAGE

Osborne

Donald

Street

Eugenie Street

Dubuc Street

Assiniboine Park

Street

Street

Lyndale Drive

Highfield Street

St. Mary's

Road

Thunder Bay

Churchill Drive

Pembina

Bartlett Avenue

Winnipeg

500 m

© *Baedeker*

Winnipeg was hard hit financially in 1914 by the opening of the Panama Canal which proved to offer a cheaper route for freight to British Columbia and Alberta. The set-back proved temporary, being overcome in time by the city's transformation into the major manufacturing centre in the prairies with, amongst others, extensive clothing, food processing, furniture, farm machinery, machine tool and electronic components industries. It is this diversification which largely accounts for the city's enviable economic stability.

In the 1920s Winnipeg began to present a more outward-looking and cosmopolitan face, as well as acquiring a symphony orchestra, ballet company and professional theatre (it already had a university, the University of Manitoba founded in 1877). In the early 1970s the city enjoyed another building boom. Old and dilapidated downtown buildings were replaced and the centre was revitalised with numerous high-rise blocks. Following a period of recession at the start of the 1980s the pace of new building quickened again in 1983.

Sights in Winnipeg

Main Street is the heart of Winnipeg, a principal thoroughfare giving access to all parts of the city, and for over a century the throbbing artery of its business and commerce. At one time the houses were concentrated together and everything could be bought here. Today the street is a kaleidoscope of Winnipeg's past, present and future.

Main Street

Turn-of-the-century Victorian and Edwardian commercial architecture is most in evidence in the vicinity of the old market place neighbouring the present Civic Centre. This area is known as the Exchange District, its name a reflection of the many financial and commodity dealing houses which sprang up in Winnipeg between the 1880s and 1920s when the city was the undisputed centre of expansion in western Canada. Thanks to the Hudson's Bay Company's fur trade, the Stock Exchange, and the Winnipeg Grain and Produce Exchange, vast quantities of goods and money changed hands in the town.

★Exchange District

More recently the Exchange District has seen a revival of its earlier role as the hub of local commerce, with old warehouses, bank and business premises being converted into fashion boutiques, up-market shops, art galleries, bureaux and restaurants.

The area is also a focus for the city's cultural life with an impressive selection of venues including the Pantages Playhouse Theatre, the Manitoba Theatre Centre, the Prairie Theatre Exchange, the Manitoba Centennial Centre, the MTC Warehouse Theatre and the Artspace. Shoppers too will find plenty to interest them (fashions, art and furniture).

A weekend market is held in summer in the Exchange District's Market Square, a showplace for the city's wide range of ethnic products. On sale is a vast variety of traditional home cooking as well as work by local artists and craftsmen. Street musicians add their own distinctive flavour to the market atmosphere.

Old Market Square

The Manitoba Centennial Centre with its lovely terraced gardens embellished with attractive fountains and appealing sculptures, was built for the Canadian centennial celebrations in 1967. other features to date include a concert hall and planetarium. The province's own centenary was celebrated in 1970 when the Manitoba Museum of Man and Nature and the Manitoba Theatre Centre were opened.

★Manitoba Centennial Centre

While the outstanding and highly informative Museum of Man and Nature (Rupert Ave.; open: Mon.–Sat. 10am–5pm, Sun. and holidays noon–6pm) is primarily devoted to the human and natural history of Manitoba province, it also has sections covering the formation of the earth and universe,

★★Manitoba Museum of Man and Nature

early human history, and the regional environment, past, present and future. All are entertainingly and instructively presented with the aid of dioramas, reconstructions, original exhibits, graphics and audio-visual material. Among other things visitors can see the first sailing craft to cross the Hudson Bay in 1668, "journey" from the Arctic to the Prairies, and enjoy the experience of 1920s vaudeville theatre. They can also examine pieces of the most ancient rock on earth from the Canadian Shield, formed some 3.75 million years ago during the Pre-Cambrian era.

Planetarium

The excellent Planetarium has programmes illustrating the wonders of the universe as well as shows and films on topics such as the exploration of space. The superb "Touch the Universe" science gallery with more than 60 multi-dimensional exhibits and hands-on activities for all ages engenders a unique appreciation of the universe as we know it today.

★ **Ukrainian Cultural & Educational Centre**

The important Ukrainian Centre (Alexander Ave.; open: Tues.–Sat. 10am–4pm, Sun. 2–5pm (not the library); closed holidays, including Ukrainian ones) comprises a historical and ethnographic museum, art gallery (temporary exhibitions) and library. The folk art collection includes embroideries, weaving, pysanky (Ukrainian Easter eggs), wood carvings, ceramics and traditional costume.

The Centre also possesses stamp, coin and map collections.

City Hall

Standing on a site occupied by two generations of its predecessors, City Hall was completed in 1974. It consists of two buildings joined by an underground link. (Guided tours arranged by the Mayor's office.)

Winnipeg Square

Situated at the Main Street/Portage Avenue intersection, Winnipeg Square is an attractive modern shopping precinct.

★ **Portage Place**

A few blocks further west on Portage Avenue stands the complex of ultra-modern buildings known as Portage Place. Located in this architecturally

View of Winnipeg

striking development are numerous shops and offices, several restaurants, three cinemas and an IMAX theatre with a vast screen on which action movies in particular show to spectacular effect.

Founded in 1867 the University of Winnipeg (guided tours) enjoys something of a liberal reputation. The oldest building on campus dates from 1894. Also noteworthy are the Western Canada Pictorial Index, an archive of some 45,000 old photographs, and the splendid new Athletics Centre, a facility used by top athletes.

University of Winnipeg

This site on south Main Street near Union Station was where Upper Fort Garry formerly stood, close to the confluence of the Assiniboine and Red Rivers. Only the north gate survives from what was one of the Hudson's Bay Company's foremost trading posts in the Canadian West. Opposite, on the south-east side, stands the modern headquarters of the now almost completely restructured fur trading company.

Fort Garry Place

A few years ago the large open space adjoining to the east was successfully developed as "The Forks", a popular entertainment and shopping centre – a kind of vast multi-purpose indoor market.

The Forks

The Winnipeg Commodity Exchange (Main St.; open: Mon.–Fri. 9.30am–1.15pm) is the most important institution of its kind in Canada. There is a gallery from which visitors can watch trading.

Winnipeg Commodity Exchange

For all its modern appearance Knox United Church in Qu'Appelle Street (city centre) is one of Winnipeg's oldest places of worship. It was built during the First World War.

Knox United Church

Seven Oaks House (Rupertsland Ave., not far from Main St.; open: mid-May–mid-June Sat., Sun. 10am–5pm, July–Labour Day daily 10am–5pm) has the distinction of being the oldest habitable house in Manitoba. Built in 1851 the large two-storey dwelling was constructed entirely of wood without using a single nail. It is decorated and furnished in period style.

Seven Oaks House

Winnipeg has had a Chinese population for about 100 years, the earliest arrivals having migrated to Canada to work on the trans-continental railroad. The at first small and rather isolated Chinese community only really started to expand in the 1920s. From then on more and more businesses of every conceivable sort started to appear, ranging from exotic spice shops and porcelain and silk emporia to laundries and restaurants (some of which count among the city's best).

★Chinatown

History

Although a big tourist attraction Winnipeg's Chinatown still manages to preserve its distinctive oriental atmosphere.

Dedicated to the preservation and promotion of Chinese culture the Dynasty Building was part of a programme of redevelopment undertaken in the Chinese quarter. The Chinese gate between Logan Ave. and James Ave. was also erected as part of the same programme.

Dynasty Building

The St Boniface Museum (Tache Ave.; open: Mon.–Fri. 9am–5pm, Sat., Sun. and holidays noon–5pm), the oldest building in Winnipeg, was constructed in 1846 for the Grey Nuns and was the first convent, hospital, girls' school and orphanage in the Canadian West. After restoration in 1967 it became a museum. On display are 2300 items, pictures, photographs, etc. documenting the history of Manitoba's French minority; also an extensive collection of Canadian and Metis artefacts. There are reconstructions of a workshop, Metis hunting camp, spinning room, shop, dining, working and sleeping quarters and a kitchen. The display of religious objects and vestments in the chapel off the foyer includes a small bell, the first in western Canada, originally presented to the convent by Lord Selkirk.

St Boniface

★St Boniface Museum

St. Boniface Cathedral   **Winnipeg**

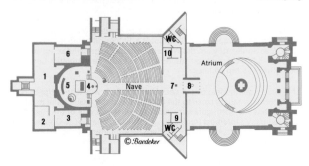

1 Catechism Room	4 Altar	7 Narthex
2 Workshop	5 Organ	8 Vestibule
3 Sacristy	6 Discussion Room	9 Cloakroom
		10 Vestry

★ St Boniface Cathedral

St Boniface Cathedral (Ave. de la Cathédrale) is the oldest cathedral in western Canada. Founded in 1818 fire caused it to be rebuilt on several occasions since. The façade and parts of the walls survived however and are incorporated in the latest (1970) building. The interior has modern furnishings. The grave of Louis Riel, born in St Boniface, can be seen in the churchyard.

More sights in the Winnipeg area

La Vérendrye Monument

On Tache Ave., facing St Boniface Hospital, a monument salutes Pierre Gautier de La Vérendrye, the first white man to sail west on the lakes and reach the confluence of the Red and Assiniboine Rivers.

Dalnavert-MacDonald House

No expense or modern comfort was spared when the now beautifully restored Victorian home of Hugh John MacDonald, former Prime Minister of Manitoba, was first built and furnished in 1895. Staff dressed in period costume escort visitors through the rooms (Carlton St.; open: June–Aug. daily 10am–6pm, Sept.–Dec., Mar.–May daily noon–5pm, Jan., Feb. Sat., Sun. noon–5pm; closed Mon., Fri. and holidays).

★ Riel House

Riel House (National Historic Park in River Rd.) belonged to Louis Riel's family. It has been restored to reflect the social, economic and cultural realities of life for the Lagimodière and Riel families in the 1890s.

★ Legislative Building

Built of local Tyndall stone and Italian marble the magnificent Neo-Classical Legislative Building (Broadway/Osborne St.; open: daily 9am–8pm, guided tours mid-May–beginning Sept.) was completed in 1919. It contains the provincial legislative chambers, Prime Minister's and other ministerial offices and some government departments.

Surmounting the 72m/236ft dome is a statue known as the Golden Boy, a 4m/13ft high bronze weighing 5 tonnes and plated with 23.5 carat gold. A torch in his right hand and sheaf of wheat on his left arm symbolise Manitoba's enduring agriculturally based prosperity.

The building is set in 12ha/30 acre grounds adorned with statues of Queen Victoria and various influential statesmen. A monument to Louis Riel stands by the riverside.

Orthodox Church, Winnipeg

St Boniface

Winnipeg

★ Art Gallery — Housed in its very modern building shaped like the bow of a ship, the Art Gallery (Memorial Blvd.; open: Tues., Fri., Sat. 11am–5pm, Wed., Thur. 11am–9pm, Sun. noon–5pm) not only possesses a fine collection of old and contemporary art by Canadian, American and European artists but also one of the world's best collections of Inuit art.

Living Prairie Museum — The Living Prairie Museum (Ness Ave.; open: July, Aug. 10am–6pm, at other times Mon.–Fri. 9am–1pm, Sat., Sun. noon–5pm) is an opportunity to visit one of the few remaining vestiges of natural prairieland. The 16ha/ 40 acre former conservation area harbours 200 species of native plants, including some now rare. Audio-visual and other explanatory material is provided in the reception area.

University of Manitoba — The University of Manitoba founded in 1877 is the oldest university in western Canada. It has its own art gallery, zoological museum, geological mineral collection, planetarium, greenhouses and many different displays.

The Historical Museum of St James Assiniboia — Regional history and the pioneering days are the subject of this small historical museum (Portage Ave.; open: daily mid-May–Labour Day, at other times workdays only).

Naval Museum, H.M.C.S. "Chippawa" — The Naval Museum in Smith St. (open: by appointment only) has an assortment of items of interest relating to the British and Canadian Navies from the First World War to the present day. Naval personnel from the prairies and naval vessels named after prairie towns are two of the principal themes.

Grant's Old Mill — The watermill known as Grant's Old Mill (in Portage Ave., near Grace Hospital; open: June–Aug. daily; May, Sept., Oct. weekends only) occupies the site of the Red River Settlement's first mill built in 1829.

St James Church — Dating from 1853 St James Church (Portage Ave., by Tylehurst St.) is western Canada's oldest timber church.

Royal Canadian Mint — The Royal Canadian Mint (Lagimodière Blvd.; open: Mon.–Fri. 9am–3pm) produces coins not just for Canada but for a number of other countries as well. Anyone interested can follow the whole minting process.
    The ultra-modern building also contains a tropical garden, fountain and museum.

Manitoba Children's Museum — The Children's Museum (Pacific Ave.; open: Tues.–Sat. 10am–5pm, Sun., and holidays 1–5pm) is a sort of activity centre for the young. In The Big Top, for example, they are able to re-create the world of the circus for themselves by dressing up, etc.

Winnipeg Police Museum — The museum at the Winnipeg Police Training Division in Vermilion Rd. brings together pictures, items of equipment and other memorabilia of the Winnipeg Police Department from its foundation to the present day.

Kildonan Presbyterian Church — Completed in 1854 Kildonan Presbyterian Church in John Black Ave. was the first of this particular denomination in western Canada.

Ross House — Ross House (in the Joe Zuken Heritage Park in Meade St.) was the Red River Settlement's first post office and is one of the area's earliest examples of a half-timbered building.

★ Western Canada Aviation Museum — The Aviation Museum at the airport (open: Mon.–Sat. 10am–4pm, Sun. and holidays 1–4pm) is the second largest of its kind in Canada. As well as several vintage aircraft (including a Tiger Moth, a Junkers JU 52, and a Bristol Freighter) the museum traces the significance of aviation in Canada's history. One section is dedicated to Canadian Women in Aviation.

★ Assiniboine Park — Assiniboine, Winnipeg's oldest park (Corydon Ave.; open: daily 10am till dusk) encompasses 150ha/370 acres of grass together with superb trees and an English garden.

The zoo is one of Canada's best, a collection of 1250 animals belonging to 300 species, many now threatened with extinction. Special emphasis is given to creatures of the northern latitudes (many of which are indigenous to Canada though there are also some rare exotic species such as the European bison, Siberian tiger and North Chinese leopard).

The zoo's internationally renowned tropical house is home to hundreds of free-flying birds, monkeys and reptiles. Also of interest are the Monkey House and the Native Bird Building. For children there are young animals at Aunt Sally's Farm.

The Winter Garden contains tropical plants and flower displays. Shows are held every month.

Adjoining Assiniboine Park on its southern side Assiniboine Forest (open: 8am–10pm) is a large, 280ha/692 acre nature reserve. Various wild creatures and plants can be seen and there is an observation area beside the pond for birdwatching.	Assiniboine Forest
Some of the province's most ancient trees are to be found in the delightful Kildonan Park (open: daily). There are also splendid flower gardens, a Hänsel and Gretel Witch's Hut, and an open-air theatre – the Rainbow Stage – where plays are performed in summer. Other attractions include a swimming pool and boat trips on the Red River.	Kildonan Park
The Fort Whyte Centre (McCreary Rd.; open: Mon.–Fri. 9am–5pm, Sat. and Sun. 11am till sundown) is known for its four lakes, grass and aspen parkland and areas of bog (accessible via boardwalks) where waterfowl and other wildlife can be observed. Walking trail. Information from the Interpretive Building.	Fort Whyte Centre
Uniforms, weaponry and a variety of other items illustrating the history of western Canada's oldest military unit are displayed in the Royal Winnipeg Rifles Museum in St Matthews Ave.	Royal Winnipeg Rifles Museum
The Pan Am Pool (Poseidon Bay) was built for the Pan American Games held in Winnipeg in 1967. The 65m/213ft by 25m/82ft pool is one of the largest in Canada. The Hall of Fame houses a collection of watersports memorabilia including a large array of stamps with designs reflecting sporting themes.	Pan Am Pool/ Aquatic Hall of Fame
Exhibited in the Red River House Museum are items belonging to a former Hudson's Bay Company fur trader and explorer.	Red River House Museum

Wood Buffalo National Park   F/G 5/6

See Northwest Territories/Alberta

Park Office, McDougal Rd. and Portage Ave, Fort Smith; open: Mon.–Fri. 9am–5pm; tel. (403) 872-2237.	Information
Hwy. 5 from Hay River (see entry) in the direction of Fort Smith. A few kilometres south of Fort Smith a road branches off at the start of a 300km/186 mile circuit of the south-eastern section of the Park.	Getting there
With a total area of about 45,000sq.km/17,370sq.miles Wood Buffalo National Park to the south of Great Slave Lake is one of the biggest national parks in Canada. Two-thirds of the Park lie in the province of Alberta, one-third in the Northwest Territories. The Slave River marks the eastern boundary of the Park.	General situation
Now listed as a World Heritage Site this huge conservation area extends across one of the world's largest inland deltas (the Athabasca-Peace River	★**National Park** Flora and fauna

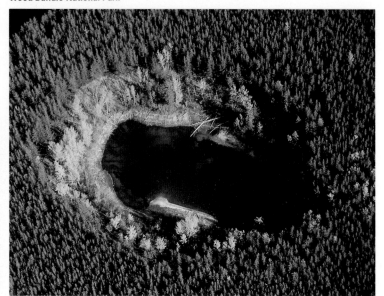

Sink hole

Salt plains in Wood Buffalo National Park

Delta), an immense wilderness of dried-out salt plains and wild landscape, dotted with lakes and swamps and traversed by rivers, the habitat of numerous now rare species of wildlife.

The Park was established in 1922 with the purpose of saving from extinction the last free-roaming herds of wood buffalo. Today more than 6000 of these animals graze the Park, together with moose, bear and cariboo.

Wood Buffalo
National Park

Every year whooping cranes arrive from Texas to breed and rear their young. Wood Buffalo National Park is one of the last, if not the very last, refuge for this extremely rare species of crane, now in desperate need of protection.

Whooping cranes

White pelicans breed beside the Slave River rapids, feeding from the Park's many lakes. The steep river banks afford good views of the nesting grounds.

Pelicans

Huge flocks of migratory birds visit the Athabasca-Peace River Delta on their annual pilgrimmage south.

Migratory birds

Fort Smith evolved from a one-time fur trading post on the Mackenzie River route to the far north of Canada. From 1911 to 1967 it was the administrative capital of the Northwest Territories, a role which was then assumed by Yellowknife (see entry). A number of NWT government departments are still located in Fort Smith and the town's schools and training colleges have a national reputation.

Fort Smith

Apart from various prehistoric finds such as mammoth remains, etc. the Northern Life Museum (110 King St.) concentrates on the human history of the region. Exhibits include everyday Inuit artefacts and handwork, photographs and other documents relating to the pioneering days and early settlers, and Indian craftwork.
    Open: May–Labour Day, Tues.–Sun. (excl. Sat.), Tues. and Thur. 7–9pm.

Northern Life
Museum

Yellowhead Highway (Highway 16)   D–H 7

Route:
Prince Rupert–Prince George–Jasper National Park–Edmonton

Completed only about 20 years ago the modern Yellowhead Highway, the most northerly road link to Canada's Pacific coast, extends for almost 3000km/1864 miles from Prince Rupert (see entry) on the west coast of British Columbia (or from Masset in the Queen Charlotte Islands – see entry – which lie off the coast) to Portage la Prairie in Manitoba. For the most part the well-surfaced road follows the traditional routes taken by fur trappers, prospectors and the early settlers. Roadside information boards (mileposts) detail important chapters in the opening up of western Canada.

General

The highway takes its name from Pierre Hatsination, a fair-haired Iroquois trapper who worked for the Hudson's Bay Company and was nicknamed "Tête Jaune" i.e "Yellowhead".

Name

Several roads branch off the Yellowhead Highway penetrating sparsely populated areas still very much in their wild state. Anyone embarking on one of the longer detours should recognise the element of risk involved and go properly equipped with adequate supplies of fuel, food, maps, etc.

Detours off
the Highway

See entry

Prince Rupert

Called "kaien" (meaning "frothing water") by local Indians, the Butze Rapids are an interesting tidal phenomenon produced by the strong currents at the edge of the Morse Basin. Viewpoint on Hwy. 16 (5km/3 miles east of Prince Rupert).

Butze Rapids

Yellowhead Highway

Port Edward

Another short detour leads to Port Edward (about 10km/6 miles south of Hwy. 16) where in 1987 a museum (open: summer daily 10am–5pm) was created in the remnants of the old North Pacific Cannery, shut down in 1981. The cannery, established in 1889, was one of nineteen which used to operate on the Skeena River. It employed as many as 400 people in its heyday and a small, still very picturesque settlement grew up around the isolated factory with its warehouses and wharves. Like the factory itself a number of the simple log cabins are supported on stilts and linked by boardwalks. Some are now used for selling souvenirs and refreshments.

Inverness Cannery

A few kilometres further on are the remains of the Inverness Cannery, burned down in 1973.

★Skeena River

The mighty, about 500km/310 mile long, fast flowing Skeena River (called "K-shian" or "water from the clouds" by the Indians) played an important role in opening up the Canadian north-west. In the second half of the 19th c. this ancient Indian trade route became much used by European settlers as well, and from 1889 onwards sternwheelers plied its waters until the coming of the railway. Huge quantities of wood were needed to fuel the steamers on their way upriver, leading to a string of little settlements with jetties where stockpiles were kept. Most of these were gradually abandoned after the railway was built.

The stretch of railroad across the Coast Mountains posed serious problems for the engineers, vast amounts of explosives being used to blast a route through the granite of the Skeena valley. The 150km/93 miles from Prince Rupert to Terrace cost $100,000 per mile, an enormous sum in 1910.

The Skeena River and its tributaries teemed with salmon, as a result of which canneries sprang up along its lower course. Fleets of fishing boats, generally two-man cutters, followed the shoals upstream. In the first half of the 20th c. depletion of salmon stocks caused by overfishing forced many plants to close.

Port Essington

40km/25 miles: An information board, some foundations, and a number of decayed wharves are a sad reminder of Port Essington, for 50 years the most important harbour on the Skeena River. It first came into existence in the 1870s during the Omineca gold-rush, quickly developing into a centre of river navigation and fishing. The arrival of the railway and the disappearance of the salmon led to its decline. By the 1950s only a few Indians and one or two fishermen remained. The bulk of the town was destroyed by a big fire in 1961.

Terrace

149km/92 miles: The small town of Terrace (67m/220ft above sea level; population 11,000) lies on the eastern edge of the Coast Mountains which rise here to more than 2000m/6500ft. Until the 1960s life in Terrace was shaped entirely by the timber trade, but gradually the town has developed into a commercial and cultural centre serving the some 40,000 inhabitants of the lower Skeena River. Being fairly low down and in the lee of mountains it enjoys a relatively mild climate for its northerly latitude.

For a number of years now Terrace has been a popular base from which to venture into the surrounding wilderness on hunting, fishing, white-water rafting or "survival" expeditions. Other possibilities include float-plane and helicopter flights over the snow and ice covered Coast Mountains, "flightseeing" tours (taking several hours) to Ketchikan in Alaska, and holidays at a very remote but exceptionally well-equipped lodge complete with its own lake and hunting-grounds. For those in search of even more excitement there is hiking in the mountains and exploring the river in an inflatable boat.

Climbing Thornhill Mountain (1500m/4923ft) brings rewards in the shape of marvellous views of the Skeena, Kalum and Kitimat valleys. The trip to the Sleeping Beauty Ridge area (Nass River) is equally full of delights.

Heritage Park

The fascinating Heritage Park outdoor museum (Kalum St./Kerby St.: open: mid-May–end Aug. daily 10am–6pm) features a number of log cabins and other interesting timber buildings dating from between 1910 and 1935. Some, furnished in the style of the period, evoke life in the pioneering days; others house various displays illustrating the region's history.

Across the new Skeena River bridge (completed in 1976) Hwy. 37 South branches off Hwy. 16 to Kitimat, a small town 60km/37 miles distant, at the head of a fiord penetrating deep inland. Some 26km/16 miles along the road lies Lakelse Lake (pronounced "La-kelse", Tsimshian for "freshwater mussel") where large quantities of mussels can be found even today.

Kitimat Road (Highway 37 South) Lakelse Lake

From an ecological point of view the Lakelse Provincial Park (campground, etc.) remains largely intact – hemlock fir, gigantic Sitka spruce and, not least, red cedar all being found in the area. There is good swimming and excellent walking.

In August thousands of sockeye and blueback salmon arrive to spawn in Williams Creek. Black bears are common in the Park and trumpeter swans, otherwise threatened with extinction, winter on the lake.

At the Lakelse Hot Springs, 6km/4 miles to the south, mineral water without taste or smell gushes out at a temperature of 42–72°C/108–162°F. The first albeit modest hotel was built here as long ago as 1910, but with Prince Rupert rather than Kitimat being chosen for the terminus of the transcontinental railway the spa was never fully developed.

Lakelse Hot Springs

The small town of Kitimat (altitude 35m/115ft; population 13,000) has been in existence only since the 1950s. In 1951 Alcan (the Aluminium Company of Canada) began constructing a huge aluminium smelter, now the second largest in the western world. The project came just at the right moment to exploit the area's enormous hydro-electric potential. Today the foundry employs more than 2000 workers and produces about 300,000 tonnes/tons of aluminium a year, 90% of which is exported.

Kitimat

Extending 100km/62 miles inland the deep Douglas Channel gives giant ocean-going freighters access to Kitimat's ice-free harbour.

Other companies besides Alcan have located here to take advantage of the cheap energy.

It is possible to see round the Alcan plant by joining one of the company's 90 minute "Alcan Smelter Tours" (June–Aug. Mon.–Fri. 12.45 and 1.30pm, Sept.–May Tues. and Thur. by appointment only, tel. (604) 639–8259).

Works tours

The Eurocan Pulp and Paper Complex, which came into operation in 1967, and the chemical firm Ocelot (1981; petro-chemicals, natural gas conversion to methanol and ammonia) provide interesting guided tours as well.

Also worth seeing in and around Kitimat are the Moore Creek Falls, the massive 500 year old Sitka spruce (diameter of trunk: 3.5m/11½ft) in Radley Park, the Kitimat Centennial Museum (town history, pioneer period, Haisla Indian culture), the Moore Creek Falls, and Kitimat Village (on the east bank of the Douglas, 13km/8 miles south of Kitimat; traditional Haisla community, Indian crafts).

More sights

From Terrace the exceptionally scenic Kitsumkalum (Kalum) Lake Rd. heads north into a largely undeveloped hinterland. Viewpoint after viewpoint reveals extensive views over the valley and west to the glacial peaks. The road is surfaced only as far as Rosswood (51km/32 miles), a small settlement at the northern end of Kitsumkalum Lake.

Kitsumkalum Lake Road

At Rosswood the Kalum Lake Rd. meets the Nass Rd., a gravelled logging road belonging to the Skeena Cellulose Company. The road is open to private vehicles but the big timber trucks, usually travelling at speed, always have right of way (keep headlights on and take avoiding action!). Black bear, moose, deer, Rocky Mountain goats and beaver are a common sight in this area. Look out also for the rare and seldom seen kermodei bear.

Nass Road

By the Skeena River

Lava on the Nass Road

64km/40 miles along the road Lava Lake lies contained by the Tseax lava stream. When the volcano (8km/5 miles further east) erupted sometime in the 18th c., lava poured into the Nass River Valley, diverting the river northwards. Since then there have been no more eruptions.

Lava Lake

The actual lava stream is another 14km/8½ miles beyond the lake itself. This area, known as the Tseax Lava Beds, remains largely denuded of vegetation, colonised only by lichens. As the lava cooled innumerable fissures, hollows and little lakes appeared. The expert eye can identify various different kinds of lava formation.

Tseax Lava Beds

After 94km/58 miles Greenville Rd. branches off left to Canyon City (8km/ 5 miles). Here the Nass River has cut deeply into the lava and the settlement can only be entered on foot across a swaying suspension bridge.

Greenville Road, Canyon City

The side road ends at the remote Nishga Indian village of Greenville (population 1000).

Greenville

98km/61 miles: New Aiyansh is now the main Nishga settlement, dating back only to 1958 when the road was laid. Note the richly decorated Tribal Council Hall and ornate totem poles. Permission can be obtained from the Band office to wander down to the river bank for a glimpse of the abandoned village of Old Aiyansh on the further side. It was founded by an Anglican missionary in 1885.

New Aiyansh

Continuing past the Nass Camp logging station the road eventually meets (after 138km/86 miles) the now tarmacked Stewart Cassiar Highway (Hwy. 37), principal route from British Columbia to Alaska. – A map of the Nass River region is available from the Terrace Chamber of Commerce (Terrace, 4511 Keith Ave.).

Stewart Cassiar Highway

From the road-end the detour can be extended by taking the Stewart Cassiar Hwy. north over Bear Pass to Stewart (147km/91 miles). Alternatively follow Hwy. 37 south again for 86km/53 miles, passing the Indian villages of Kitwancool and Kitwanga, to rejoin the Yellowhead Highway (Hwy. 16) north-east of Terrace.

168km/104 miles: North-east of Terrace the Skeena River divides into three narrow rock-girt channels, only two of which were navigable by sternwheelers. Even then the boats lacked the power to fight their way upriver under their own steam and had to be hauled through the Kitselas Canyon using strong hawsers. These were secured to massive iron rings cemented into the rock walls. A number of steamers came to grief and sank, including the "Mount Royal" in 1907. She reputedly carried a large shipment of gold which was never recovered.

Kitselas Canyon

A trail runs down to the river and along to Ringbolt Island (1hr) where some of the old iron rings can still be seen.

243km/151 miles: From a junction here on the Yellowhead Highway the Stewart Cassiar Highway runs north to Stewart (231km/143 miles), eventually (after 735km/457 miles) joining the Alaska Highway about 25km/15 miles west of Watson Lake. This route offers anyone making for the Yukon and Alaska a rewarding alternative to the Alaska Highway itself. The Stewart Cassiar Highway is also popular with tourists heading west from Prince George to explore northern British Columbia.

★**Stewart Cassiar Highway (Hwy. 37/37A)**

Formerly made up of private roads owned by logging companies, the highway evolved in stages from about 1926 onwards, being passable throughout its entire length only since 1976 (the surface is still mainly gravel, so it is essential to drive slowly). It traverses an extremely sparsely populated region in the north-west of British Columbia, with very few tourist facilities, shops or filling stations along the way. What there is however is a magnificent, largely undisturbed landscape of mountain ranges, glaciers, volcanoes (e.g. in the Mt Edziza Provincial Park), untamed rivers, lovely lakes and – perhaps the greatest attraction of all – an exceptionally varied plant and wildlife.

Kitwanga, Gitwangak	4km/2½ miles: Just north of the mouth of the Kitwanga River lie the settlement of Kitwanga and the neighbouring Gitwangak ('Ksan) Indian reserve. Gitwangak – which acts as a centre for the about 1500 inhabitants of the Kitwanga Valley (timber and modest farming), encircled by high, mostly snow-capped mountain peaks – boasts a number of very fine, typical 'Ksan totem poles some of which are more than 100 years old (look particularly for those in School Rd.). Also interesting is the Anglican church, built in 1893 and one of the oldest surviving wooden churches in British Columbia.
Kitwanga Fort	A short footpath leads up from Kitwanga Valley Rd. to Battle Hill, once the site of a palisaded Gitksan stronghold known as Kitwanga Fort where early in the 19th c. a battle took place between rival Indian tribes. – Kitwanga Fort is the first purely Indian "National Historic Site" in western Canada.
Kitwancool	19km/12 miles: Also famous for its totem poles is another Indian village in the Kitwanga Valley – Kitwancool. Many of the twenty poles date back to the 19th c. and are still in their original positions. One of the oldest is the "Hole in the Ice" totem, erected in about 1850. It symbolises the resourcefulness of a man who saved the people of his village from starvation one winter by catching fish through a hole hacked in the ice. A small local history museum (open: daily 10.30am–4.30pm but closed Tues. and Wed. in winter) is currently being expanded.
Cranberry Junction	86km/53 miles: Known as Cranberry Junction this is where the still largely unsurfaced Nass Rd. (see above) branches off south-west to Terrace (138km/86 miles; see entry).
Meziadin Jct. Hwy. 37A	172km/107 miles: At Meziadin Junction Hwy. 37A forks off to the left for Stewart (60km/37 miles). Meziadin Lake has a superb setting and, being popular with anglers, some modest tourist facilities as well. The road to Stewart is not only good but exceptionally attractive from a scenic point of view, passing a number of wild, roaring waterfalls and as many as ten magnificent glaciers cascading down from the peaks of the Cambria Range (up to 2700m/8860ft high).
Bear Pass, Bear Glacier	The scenery around Bear Pass and the Bear Glacier is incomparable. Keep a look-out for Rocky Mountain goats scaling the steep rock-faces – quite a common sight here.
Stewart	From Bear Pass the road follows the narrow, deeply incised valley of the Bear River to Stewart (population 1300), situated at the head of a 145km/90 mile long fiord known as the Portland Canal down the centre of which runs the Canadian-Alaskan (US) frontier. The harbour here, the most northerly on the Pacific coast of Canada, remains ice-free throughout the year and is a ferry stop for the "Alaska Marine Highway".
	With worthwhile deposits of gold, silver and copper in the surrounding, over 2000m/6550ft high mountains, Stewart started life at the beginning of the century as a mining town, its fortunes being closely linked to raw materials prices. In its short heyday around 1910 the population grew to over 10,000, but after the Second World War fell to below 20.
	The town's chequered history is recorded in the old Fire Station. Quite a number of films have been made on location in Stewart, and in the exceptionally attractive country around it.
Hyder	Hyder, only 3km/2 miles west of Stewart (Canada) but already in Alaska (USA), can be reached from Stewart either by road or across the Portland Canal. This must be one of the few places where the US frontier can be crossed without strict controls (the border post is nailed up!) Once a prosperous mining town like its neighbour but now with a population of barely 80, Hyder is to all intents and purposes a ghost town. There are three bars (which stay open virtually 24 hours a day), a souvenir shop and a post office.

Yellowhead Highway: the Bear Glacier

Grizzly Bear Lodge is full of atmosphere. Gigantic moose heads bedeck the restaurant walls and there is also a fully-grown grizzly (an awesome sight even when stuffed). The saloon walls are covered with dollar bills – in the old days prospectors and miners would leave a signed dollar bill nailed to the wall as insurance against being broke when they next returned!

Grizzly Bear Lodge

The one or two remaining wharves are a reminder that the town was once a busy little port shipping out ore.

Wharves

Be sure to make the 8km/5 mile drive to Fish Creek. This is a favourite spot with anglers and wildlife enthusiasts, where from August to October thousands of rare chum (or dog) salmon arrive to spawn. Since the 1960s the spawning grounds have been increasingly threatened by floods – from a glacial lake which periodically bursts its banks – so special channels have been built to protect the fish. Whiteheaded eagles and a relatively large number of bears also inhabit the area.

Fish Creek

The unsurfaced mountain road which continues over the 960m/3150ft high "Summit" to the Tide Lake Flats and the abandoned Granduc Copper Mine (58km/36 miles; back into British Columbian territory) is not recommended for private motorists. In summer however Seaport Limousine (tel. 636–2622) run trips there. Lasting several hours they provide some majestic views – on Salmon Glacier for example.

Yellowhead Highway (continued)

287km/178 miles: see 'Ksan

The Hazeltons

Gitanmaks was an Indian village where in 1866 a Hudson's Bay Company outpost was established, only for it to be abandoned shortly afterwards. White settlers arriving in the 1870s christened the place "Hazelton" on

Gitanmaks

account of its numerous hazelnut bushes, and from 1898 the settlement was the start of the so-called "poor folk's route" along the Telegraph Trail to the Yukon goldfields. With its many pioneer-age buildings and its location on the edge of the untapped wilderness, Hazelton still has very much the feel of a frontier town.

Kispiox Village

From Hazelton a road follows the valley of the Kispiox River for 14km/8½ miles to the small Indian village of Kispiox. Here permission should be sought from the Band office to visit the splendid group of carved red cedar totem poles standing at the junction of the Skeena and Kispiox Rivers. Originally these poles stood in front of the long-houses belonging to the individual clans whose status and family history they depict. The very popular Kispiox Rodeo is held here every year in June.

Moricetown Canyon

323km/200 miles: At Moricetown Canyon the Bulkley River suddenly narrows from almost 500m/550yd to a mere 15m/16yd, becoming a seething rapids in the process. During the salmon season Carrier Indians can be seen fishing its waters in their traditional way.

Smithers

355km/220 miles: The little town of Smithers (altitude 496m/1639ft; population 5000) started life in 1913 as a rail depot. Surrounded by fertile farmland and meadows it lies in the shadow of Hudson Bay Mountain (2576m/8454ft; a favourite winter ski resort) with its Kathlyn Glacier and Twin Falls.

The best vantage point from which to view the glacier and falls is on Kathlyn Lake Rd. which branches off about 10km/6 miles north-west of the town.

Much effort has gone into giving the town a Bavarian atmosphere with Bavarian-style architecture.

The Bulkley Valley Museum (Central Park Building on Hwy. 16/Main St.; open: in summer daily 10am–5pm at other times Tues.–Sat. 1–5pm) is devoted mainly to the history of settlement in the Bulkley Valley and to local Indian culture.

★Tweedsmuir Provincial Park

The 9810sq.km/3786sq.mile Tweedsmuir Provincial Park is the biggest in British Columbia, the northern part in particular being still largely undisturbed wilderness. Ootsa, Whitesail and Tetachuck Lakes have however been dammed and a pipeline runs through the Hazelton Mountains to Kemano (generating electricity for the huge aluminium smelter at Kitimat). Moose, deer, bear and also beaver are a relatively common sight along roads in the vicinity of the Park. A number of resorts catering for anglers offer accommodation (rustic cottages, little log cabins) and there are also boats for rental on the lakes.

Fraser Lake

570km/354 miles: For many years Fraser Lake (altitude 786m/2580ft; population 1500) consisted of just a railway halt and sawmill. Today most of the inhabitants are employed at the Endako Mine, 22km/13½ miles to the south-west (the biggest molybdenum mine in Canada; viewing by appointment only).

Highway 5 Wells Gray National Park

782km/486 miles: At Tête Jaune Cache Hwy. 5 – also known (confusingly) as the Yellowhead Highway – branches south off Hwy. 16 and makes a good route through to Kamloops and the TransCanada Highway (338km/210 miles; see entry).

Clearwater, Spahats Creek Prov. Park, ★ Wells Gray Provincial Park

On Hwy. 5, about 250km/155 miles south of Tête Jaune Cache, the little town of Clearwater (altitude 406m/1332ft; population 6000) on the North Thompson River is the gateway to Wells Gray Provincial Park, established in 1939. The northern section of this 5,200sq.km/2000sq.mile conservation area ranges over part of the heavily glaciated Cariboo Mountains and Wells Gray is renowned for its breathtaking waterfalls and picturesque lakes. Few tourist facilities exist in the Park.

From Clearwater a 40km/25 mile long minor road with many spectacular views follows the Clearwater Valley past Spahats Creek Provincial Park (15km/9 miles; Spahats Creek Canyon, 122m/400ft deep with a 61m/200ft waterfall – at its most attractive against a background of autumn foliage) to the main entrance at Hemp Creek (Park office, information; recreation area at Helmcken Falls Lodge with boat and canoe hire). From here a gravel road continues north to Clearwater Lake providing access to several superb hiking trails (e.g. Placid Lake Trail, Whitehorse escarpment) and some awe-inspiring waterfalls.

At Dawson Falls, 5km/3 miles beyond Hemp Creek, the waters of the 91m/300ft wide Murtle River plunge 18m/60ft into the depths. A small side road leads to a rugged gorge on the Murtle known as the Mush Bowls (Devil's Punchbowl).

From the end of the Mush Bowls road a path leads to the marvellously spectacular Helmcken Falls.

★★Helmcken Falls

The many volcanic features found in Wells Gray Park (e.g. cooled lava beds, volcanic cones and craters – the youngest between 4000 and 400 years old) point to almost continuous volcanic activity during the last 500,000 years. About 7000 to 8000 years ago, a 15km/9 mile long lava flow issuing from the now inactive volcanic cone east of Ray Lake blocked the valley of the Clearwater River and led to the creation of the present Clearwater Lake.

Wells Gray Park can also be entered by a road branching off Hwy. 5 just north of Blue River (altitude 680m/2231ft; population 1000), about 100km/62 miles north of Clearwater.

This south-eastern section of the Park, which includes the Murtle Lake, is a Nature Conservancy Area enjoying total protection. Vehicles must be left at the entrance (24km/15 miles down the gravel access road) from where a 2½km/1½ mile footpath leads to a bay on the lake – considered one of the loveliest in the whole of Canada. For the experienced canoeist this is the start of some superb canoe routes.

786km/488 miles: Rejoining the main Yellowhead Highway we come to Tête Jaune Cache, a short distance beyond which the Rearguard Falls can be seen from a vantage point barely fifteen minutes walk from the Highway. Although some 1200km/745 miles from the river mouth near Vancouver, these upper reaches of the Fraser nevertheless carry a considerable volume of water which here cascades down a low escarpment. In August leaping salmon can be seen tackling this final obstacle on the long journey to their spawning grounds.

Rearguard Falls

The Yellowhead Highway now makes its way along the upper course of the Fraser River and deep into the Rocky Mountains, crossing as it does so the Mt Robson Provincial Park (2200sq.km/850sq.miles; west entrance, information centre and campground 10km/6 miles east of Tête Jaune Cache), another area of breathtaking scenery close to the border with Alberta and a favourite with hikers, climbers and outdoor enthusiasts generally.

★Mount Robson Provincial Park

Adjoined by the Jasper National Park (see entry) to the east of Yellowhead Pass (77km/48 miles), the Park takes its name from the highest peak in the Canadian Rockies, Mt Robson (3954m/12977ft). This magnificent mountain landscape with its waterfalls, lonely tarns and glacier-capped peaks (including one of the few still advancing glaciers in the Canadian Rockies) was designated a provincial park as long ago as 1913. Even in those days mountaineers and tourists were drawn to the area undeterred by the distances involved.

One of the most popular hikes here is the 25km/15½ mile trail through the "Valley of the Thousand Falls" (Robson River Valley) to the lovely turquoise lake which nestles at the foot of the glacier-clad Mt Robson.

Other beauty spots along the Highway before it begins its climb to Yellowhead Pass are the Overlander Falls, Moose Lake (moose can often be seen on the swampy east shore) and Yellowhead Lake.

Mount Robson, the highest mountain in the Canadian Rockies

Yellowhead Pass

859km/534 miles: The 1131m/3712ft Yellowhead Pass is one of the lowest to cross the Rocky Mountains. It forms the divide between British Columbia and Alberta and also between two time zones (Pacific Time/Mountain Time). A centuries old Indian trade route went over this easily traversed pass; sometime around 1810 the first white North West Company trappers probably found their way over it too.

A group of Hudson's Bay Company trappers certainly used the pass to cross the Rockies in 1820, making their way down the Fraser River to what is now the little town of Prince George. Among them was a fair-haired Iroquois nicknamed "Tête Jaune" i.e. "Yellowhead", who in the 1820s set up a cache near the Fraser River (though not at the site of the present settlement known as Tête Jaune Cache). Subsequently employed by the Company as a guide, he and his family were killed by Beaver Indians in 1827.

For a time the pass was used by fur traders supplying much needed leather to the forts in New Caledonia, which led to its being called "Leather Pass". From the 1830s onwards however they favoured the alternative route along the Peace River, and until the building of the two railways (the Canadian Northern (1905) to Vancouver and the Grand Trunk Pacific (1910) to Prince George) the Yellowhead Pass was rarely used.

Then, having started out as rivals, the two railway companies merged. The abandoned track came to serve as a primitive road. After upgrading it became the Yellowhead Highway, officially opened in 1970. Particularly in winter the Yellowhead has considerable advantages over the shorter (by 177km/110 miles) TransCanada Highway further south, on which latter the Rogers Pass is frequently closed by heavy snowfalls and the risk of avalanches. East of Yellowhead Pass the Highway follows the narrow, thickly forested valley of the Miette River down to Jasper on its 74km/46 mile journey through the Jasper National Park (see entry).

Yellowhead Highway in Saskachewan (about 700km)

This section of the Yellowhead Highway is described from east to west; it begins near Langenburg and at Churchbridge there is a detour to Duck Mountain Park.

The Park caters for a wide range of leisure activities, particularly in the area around the lake. Near the Ministik Beaches, in addition to an 18-hole golf course, there are facilities for riding, tennis, cycling, boating and mini-golf, also angling on both Madge and Batka Lakes. In winter the possibilities include cross-country skiing and snowmobile trekking.

    As the route heads west again along Hwy. 5, the Ukrainian origins of many of the inhabitants of this part of Saskatchewan are everywhere evident, most noticeably the Ukrainian Orthodox churches with their silver domes.

Duck Mountain Provincial Park

21km/13 miles along the road in Veregin (population 128) an interesting stop can be made at the Doukhobour Heritage Village (open: mid-May–mid-Sept. daily 10am–6pm, mid-Sept–mid-May Mon.–Fri. 9am–5pm, Sat. and Sun. by appointment only). Among the nine buildings are a completely original turn-of-the-century gentleman's residence and older houses reflecting the lifestyle and customs of the Doukhobour pioneers. The career of their leader Peter Veregin is also charted in considerable detail. Other things to see include a brick oven, bath house, prayer house, museum, administration buildings, barns, a blacksmith's forge and farming implements.

Veregin

Canora (population 2569; 25km/15½ miles further on) has a Ukrainian Orthodox Church which is well worth visiting (Main St.; open by appointment only summer Mon.–Fri. during the day). Built in 1928 and later restored the church with its paintings and coloured glass might almost have been brought here straight from Kiev.

    On the south side of Canora stands the Ukrainian Welcome Statue, designed by the inhabitants themselves. The 7.6m/25ft high "Lesia", decked out in traditional Slav costume, is intended to symbolise the Ukrainian heritage.

    The route now follows Hwy. 9 southwards allowing an additional worthwhile detour via Hwy. 229 to Good Spirit Lake Park.

Canora

"Good Spirit Lake" is a translation of the Indian word "Kitchimanitou", a Hudson's Bay Company trading post of that name (established in 1880) being incorporated into the Provincial Park when it was created in 1931. The 1900ha/4695 acre Park extends along the shores of Good Spirit Lake with its inviting sandy beaches and warm, shallow water. Planted with poplars the Park is also well known for its fine dunes of beautifully clean sand up to 5m/16ft high which surround the lake. Being ecologically very sensitive these are out of bounds for walking.

Good Spirit Lake Provincial Park

    Continue south on Hwys. 229 and 9 to rejoin the main route (Hwy. 16) at Yorkton.

An important east Saskatchewan centre for local commerce Yorkton (population 16,000) is also characterised by ethnic diversity. In particular the Ukrainian heritage of many of the inhabitants of the area is manifest in its architecture, exhibitions, craftwork and fine European cooking.

    The town is also known for its internationally acclaimed Short Film and Video Festival.

    Yorkton's Western Development Museum – Story of the People (open: Apr.–Oct.) is full of interest, vividly illustrating the history and traditions of Canada's immigrant population.

    Also rewarding is a visit to the remarkable St Mary's Ukrainian Catholic Church (Catherine St.; open: in summer daily, at other times only by appointment), the first brick-built Ukrainian church in Canada. The

Yorkton

21m/69ft high dome is decorated with outstanding paintings (1939 and 1941) by Steven Meush.

The Yorkton Arts Council (in the Godfrey Dean Cultural Centre, Smith St.; open: daily 2–5pm) exhibits work by local artists.

Parkland Village (open: mid-May–mid-Oct. daily 1–8pm), about 10km/6 miles south-east of Yorkton on Hwy. 16 near Rokeby, has buildings and other exhibits dating from the early days of settlement in Saskatchewan.

From here the Yellowhead Highway makes its way westwards to Foam Lake across vast wheat-covered plains.

Foam Lake

Visits to the interesting Foam Lake Museum Association in Foam Lake (population 1443) are by arrangement only.

Foam Lake Heritage Marsh, a 1620ha/4000 acre area of wetland surrounded by hills about 7km/4½ miles to the north-west, is an excellent place for observing waterbirds.

Wynyard

Wynyard (population 2187) is another small place with something to see – in this case the Frank Cameron Museum (open: May, June daily 9am–5pm, July, Aug. 8am–8pm).

Only a short drive away to the north are the Quill Lakes.

Quill Lakes

Lying on a major bird migration route Quill Lakes are a resting place and breeding ground for many waterbirds.

At Plunkett a detour via Hwy. 365 leads to Little Manitou Lake.

Little Manitou Lake

The medicinal properties of the mineral rich, 19km/12 mile long Little Manitou Lake were well known to the early Indians, to whom it was the "Place of the Healing Waters". In its heyday the lake was called the "Karlsbad of Canada", the mineral content of the water being similar to that of the famous German spa. A new attraction has recently been added in the shape of the Manitou Springs Mineral Spa at Manitou Beach. Opened in 1988 this is now the largest indoor mineral bath in Canada.

Saskatoon

Return on Hwy. 365 to the Yellowhead Highway, continuing to Saskatoon (see entry) from where a day trip can be made to Pike Lake Park situated 30km/18 miles south-west (Hwys. 7 and 60).

Pike Lake Provincial Park

A long sandy beach and lush expanses of grass with aspen, ash and birch make Pike Lake Park (open all year) a pleasant place to relax. For the more energetic there are tennis courts and a new swimming-pool.

West of Saskatoon Hwy. 16 threads its way across farming country for 138km/86 miles to North Battleford.

North Battleford

See Battleford

By taking Hwy. 4 northwards from North Battleford, then branching off on Hwy. 26, a detour can be made to the lake district in north-west Saskatchewan.

Edam

The Washbrook Museum (open: May–Sept. Mon.–Fri. 10am–6pm, evenings by appointment) in Edam (population 463) provides an insight into Sakatchewan rural life.

St Walburg

St Walburg (population 731) also has an interesting museum, the St Walburg & District Museum (open: July–Aug. Mon.–Sat. 10am–noon and 2–5pm, Sun. noon–5pm) housed in the Old Church of the Assumption in Main St. Exhibits come from the village and its surroundings pre-1945 and include paintings by Imhoff. The church organ, made in 1885, still plays.

Loon Lake

Loon Lake's Big Bear's Trail Museum (open: July, Aug. Mon.–Fri. 10am–8pm, otherwise by appointment only) stands on the highway in this small community (population 401).

Yellowknife   G 5

Administrative unit: Northwest Territories
Population: 10,000

TravelArctic, Yellowknife, Northwest Territories, X1A 2L9; tel. (403)   Information
873–7200; Arctic Hot Line (freephone), tel. 800–661–0788.

By plane: Daily flights from Edmonton.   Access
Road: Mackenzie Highway No. 35.

The modern town of Yellowknife, the largest community in the Mackenzie   General
district and since 1967 capital of the Northwest Territories, lies south of the
tree limit on the shores of the Great Slave Lake. It was founded only in 1935
after gold was discovered there, the first such strike in the cold north
(average temperature: −6°C/21°F!). A second gold-rush occurred in 1944
since when the community, set in a landscape of dwarf firs, birch and
poplar, has developed steadily into the nerve centre of northern Canada.

The gold mines at Yellowknife are among the biggest in Canada and gold
has unquestionably been the spur to the town's growth. The population
figures tell the story: in 1961 Yellowknife had 3250 inhabitants, today that
total has trebled.

Indians have hunted in the Yellowknife area for thousands of years.
Europeans on the other hand made their first appearance in the third to last
decade of the 18th c., and settled permanently only after the gold-rush of
1934.

The name "Yellowknife" derives from the copper knives long used by the   Name
local Indians.

Yellowknife, the chief town in the Northwest Territories

Sights in Yellowknife

★ The Prince of
Wales Northern
Heritage Centre

The Prince of Wales Northern Heritage Centre (open: Tues.–Sun. 10.30am–5pm) is exceptionally interesting.

As well as displaying its large mineral collection and finds from the Centre's archaeological research, the museum explores in depth the culture of the Dene Indians and traces the pervasive influence of the fur trade, in operation here since at least the 18th c.

Well-known local artists and craftsmen also exhibit their work in the Centre and visitors can view the extensive collection of photographs and old documents in the Northwest Territories' State Archive.

★★ Giant
Yellowknife Mines

The gold mines are situated in an area about 4km/2½ miles north of the town. Tours of the Giant Yellowknife Mine can be arranged (summer only), and only by appointment, tel. 873–6301.

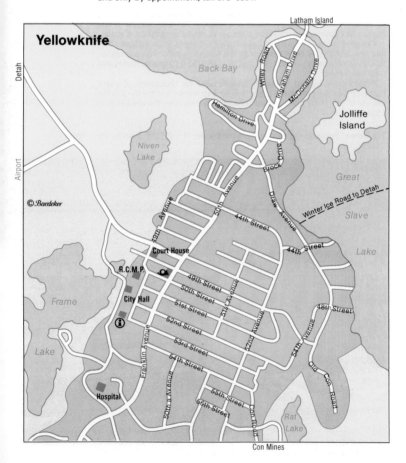

544

In the peak holiday season excursions are run on Great Slave Lake (from the Yellowknife Trading Post dock). These usually include a visit to the Indian village at Detah.

There are interesting drives around Yellowknife, one being eastwards along the Ingraham Trail (Hwy. 4) to Tibbet Lake, continuing to the Yellow-knife Preserve (conservation area). Another follows Hwy. 3 north-west through the unspoiled country beside Great Slave Lake to Edzo. The same road goes to the Mackenzie bison reserve.

The major event in Yellowknife's calendar is the annual Caribou Carnival in March, which includes a big dogsled race. The Canadian Flying Clubs' "Midnight Sun Golf Tournament" also takes place here every year on June 21st.

Yoho National Park   F 7

Province: British Columbia. Area: 1313sq.km/507sq.miles

The Superintendent, Yoho National Park, P.O. Box 99, Field, B.C. V0A 1G6; tel. (604) 343–6324.

Road:
TransCanada Highway 1 (Lake Louise–Kicking Horse Pass–Golden).

Rail: (Canadian Pacific Railway; VIA Rail):
Stations at Lake Louise, Field and Golden.

The Yoho National Park extends over part of the western flank of the Rocky Mountains, adjoining both the Banff and Kootenay National Parks. As the fourth largest nature reserve in the Canadian Rockies it encompasses some magnificent and extremely varied mountain scenery, with snow-covered peaks, thundering rivers, majestic waterfalls and delightful mountain lakes (especially in the eastern section of the Park in the vicinity of the main range). The Park's two chief areas of interest are the valley of the Kicking Horse River and the over 20km/12½ mile Yoho Valley ("yoho" is Cree for "awe").
    In 1985 all four National Parks in the Rocky Mountains were adopted by UNESCO's World Heritage Programme on account of their great scenic beauty and the extent to which they have preserved their natural environments.
    The TransCanada Highway passes through the Park making access very easy. There are viewpoints at three particularly scenic spots. Side roads branch off the Highway to major places of interest.

The history of the Yoho National Park is closely linked to the building of the trans-continental railway. The first white man to reach the area was almost certainly the geologist Sir James Hector, a member of the Palliser Expedition charged with reconnoitring road and rail routes through the Rocky Mountains. Hector made his way over the Vermilion Pass and into the Kootenay Valley which he followed northwards. Crossing another little pass he arrived at Beaverfoot Creek, a tributary of the Kicking Horse River. Near the Wapta Falls he was kicked so badly by his horse that his companions at first took him for dead. With great difficulty the little expedition struggled back to the valley of the Bow River by way of a pass they christened "Kicking Horse" on account of the incident.
    1884 saw the construction of the Kicking Horse Pass section of the Canadian Pacific Railway. Initially the gradient at some places on the descent to Field was as great as 4.5% (1 in 3½) and several serious accidents occurred when brakes failed on the downward run. In 1909 two spiral tunnels were built, reducing the gradient to 2.2%.
    Following completion of the railway, Canadian Pacific also built the first tourist accommodation in the area. A stretch of road laid along the disused

Mount Hungabee

section of the original track in 1927 eventually became part of the Trans-Canada Highway. In 1886 some 26sq.km/10sq.miles in the vicinity of Mt Stephen (3199m/ 10,500ft; near Field) were declared a protected area and named Dominion Park. This modest beginning was eventually to lead to the creation of the Yoho National Park in 1930.

Ascent to Kicking Horse Pass	The climb up to Kicking Horse Pass from the east (see above: "History", for the origin of the name) begins at the border between the two provinces of Alberta and British Columbia.
Avalanche Path	A broad scar down the nearby mountainside marks the track of an avalanche which some years ago thundered down the slope sweeping away an entire forest in its path.
Great Divide	A sign about 3km/2 miles east of the TransCanada Highway marks the continental watershed (Hudson Bay/Pacific Ocean).
Wapta Lake	Wapta Lake (1586m/5205ft), a pretty little mountain lake, is the haunt of some rare species of waterbird as well as being the source of the Kicking Horse River which flows west alongside the TransCanada Highway.
★★ Lake O'Hara	From Wapta Lake a road follows Cataract Creek southwards to Lake O'Hara (camp site), set against an impressive backdrop of high mountains – to the east Mt Huber (3368m/11,053ft), Mt Victoria (3364m/11,040ft; glacier) and Yukness Mountain (2847m/9343ft), to the south Mt Schaffer (2693m/8838ft, on the south side of Lake McArthur), and to the north-west Catherine Mountain (3189m/10,466ft; mountain trail) and Mt Vanguard (2469m/ 8103ft).
Old Bridge, Big Hill	The old bridge on the "Big Hill" (the notorious steep section where the height difference is 400m/1300ft) was once part of the original CPR track over Kicking Horse Pass.

An observation tower about 9km/5½ miles west of the 1625m/5333ft summit of Kicking Horse Pass provides a good view of the daringly engineered later section of track with its two spiral tunnels (modelled on the St Gotthard rail tunnels in Switzerland).

Lower Spiral
Tunnel Viewpoint

This is a fine vantage point from which to admire the hanging glacier on Mt Stephen (3199m/10,500ft). Below and to the right of the glacier the entrance to the now abandoned Monarch Mine is clearly visible. Lead, zinc and small amounts of silver were extracted until the mine was closed in 1952.

Mount Stephen
Viewpoint,
Monarch Mine

The best place from which to admire the upper of the two railway tunnels.

Upper Spiral
Tunnel Viewpoint

The supremely attractive, ice-field framed Yoho Valley has a 360km/224 mile network of hiking trails which make for some outstanding walking (details from the information centre at the Park office). A memorial near the information centre honours Edouard Gaston DeVille, Canada's Surveyor-General in 1885. A narrow 13km/8 mile long road (dead-end; closed to campervans) winds its way tortuously up the valley.

★★Yoho Valley

The Yoho Valley Rd. ends at the stupendous Takakkaw Falls (camp site), among the highest in North America. The main fall, where melt-water from the Daly Glacier (tip of the Waputik Ice-field) plunges 384m/1260ft over a rock-face, is a magnificent spectacle.
The ice-fields of Mts Yoho (2760m/9058ft), Gordon (3153m/10,348ft; Wapta Ice-field), Daly (3152m/10,345ft; Waputik Ice-field) and Niles (2972m/9754ft) ring the valley. West of the falls rises the glacier-covered Vice-President Massiv (3066m/10,062ft).

★★Takakkaw
Falls

During the age of steam when extra locomotives were needed to push or pull trains up or down Big Hill, Field (altitude 1224m/4017ft; population

Field

A natural bridge on the Emerald Lake   *Takakkaw Falls*

547

400) was a busy railway town. Nowadays it is the peaceful home of the Parks Administration (round-the-year information available at the side of the Highway). Fossil-rich Palaeozoic shales and sedimentaries are found on the slopes of Mts Field and Stephen nearby.

★★Burgess Shale Fossil Beds

The Burgess Shale fossil beds to the east of Field have proved of supreme importance to palaeontology. Fossils more than 530 million years old (Cambrian; esp. trilobites) recovered from these unique, undisturbed beds, have yielded major insights into the development of life on earth.

★Emerald Lake

About 2km/1¼ miles south of Field an 8km/5 mile long road (dead-end) branches off to Emerald Lake. This lovely, turquoise-blue lake, nestling at the foot of the over 3000m/9800ft glacier-capped President Range, is a popular tourist resort.

Natural Bridge

A little under 2km/1¼ miles along the Emerald Lake road, the Kicking Horse River is spanned by a natural bridge. An information board explains how this geological curiosity was formed.

Hamilton Lake

Several splendid hikes begin at Emerald Lake, among the most attractive being the Lake Circuit, the climbs to Yoho and Burgess passes, and the Hamilton Lake trail (to a small lake hidden in a typical hanging valley).
The view from Emerald Lake is dominated by Michael Peak (2696m/8848ft) to the north and Mt Burgess (2583m/8477ft) to the south.

Ottertail Viewpoint

An information board at Ottertail Viewpoint gives details of the rock formations exposed by the Ottertail and Kicking Horse rivers. In the valley below there used to be a sawmill owned by the Canadian Pacific Railway.

Misko Viewpoint

From this vantage point good views are obtained of Mts Hunter and King. The information board explains the effects of glaciation in high mountains.

Avalanche Nature Trail

This mountain trail leads to a huge avalanche slide on the 3320m/10,896ft Mt Vaux.

Deerlodge Trail ★★Hoodoo Creek

A well marked and scenically very attractive trail follows Hoodoo Creek to the Park's first wardens' cabin, built in 1904.
The pyramid-shaped "hoodoos" of hardened sand and clay with a capping of relatively hard rock are real oddities of nature.

Leanchoil Marsh

Given a little luck a visit to Leanchoil Marsh will be rewarded with sightings of some of Canada's high mountain fauna (including beaver).

Chancellor Peak Campground

On the way to the Chancellor Peak camp site (just off the TransCanada Highway, a short distance further on), a beautiful view unfolds across the valley of the Kicking Horse River to Mt Vaux (3320m/10,896ft), Chancellor Peak (3280m/10,765ft) and Mt Ennis (3132m/10,279ft; large glacier).

Wapta Falls

Before the western entrance to the Park is reached a side road branches off, terminating after 5km/3 miles in a dead-end. A trail then leads to the Wapta Falls where Sir James Hector suffered his near fatal accident (see above) and where, at a bend in its course, the Kicking Horse River cascades down over a wide rock-step.

Yukon Circle Route   A/B 5

See Yukon Territory

Route

The approximately 1500km/930 mile long Yukon Circle Route makes use of three highways through the south-west corner of the Territory, the Klondike Highway (see Klondike), the Top of the World Highway (see Dawson, Surroundings) and the Alaska Highway (see entry), each a heady mixture of exciting scenery and historical fascination.

The circuit is best begun at the Yukon capital, Whitehorse (see entry), following the Klondike Highway (see Klondike) to the famous gold-rush town of Dawson (see entry), situated where the Klondike joins the Yukon River. Those who prefer to retrace the actual route taken by prospectors at the turn of the century can book a river passage from Whitehorse to Dawson instead.

★Klondike Highway, Whitehorse, Dawson

From Dawson, having been sure to visit the legendary Klondike gold-fields, head west through the majestic scenery of the Top of the World Highway (see Dawson, Surroundings) across the US/Canadian frontier to Tetlin Junction in Alaska.

★Top of the World Highway

Joining up with the Alaska Highway in Tetlin Junction, drive south-eastwards into Canada again, continuing through Beaver Creek to the snow-covered peaks of the St Elias Mountains in the Kluane National Park (see entry). From there return via Haines Junction to Whitehorse (see entry).

★★Alaska Highway, ★★Kluane National Park

Yukon Territory

A–D 4/5

Location: 60°–69°N 124°–141°W
Area: 536,000sq.km/206,896sq.miles
Population: 30,000. Capital: Whitehorse

Tourism Yukon, P.O. Box 2703
Whitehorse, Yukon, 1A2C6. Tel. (403) 667–5340

Information

In contrast to the Canadian provinces which are largely self-governing within the federal structure, the "Territories" such as the Yukon (the name comes from the Indian "you-kon" meaning "big water") are administered directly by the Federal Government in Ottawa. To the Yukon's east the Mackenzie Mountains form the border with the Northwest Territories (see entry), to the west lie the Coast Range Mountains where the 6050m/19,856ft Mt Logan in the Kluane National Park (see entry) is the highest in Canada.

Location and geography

Yukon

© Baedeker

Whitehorse

Yukon Territory: expanses of unspoiled landscapes

The 60th Parallel divides the Yukon from British Columbia (see entry) to the south, while to the north the Territory has a short stretch of coastline on the Beaufort Sea. Encircled by high mountain ranges the Yukon Plateau forms a middle- to high-altitude upland region (mean altitude: 1000m/3282ft), mainly composed of lava-covered, mineral-rich, crystalline rock. Dominating influence over the entire Territory is the Yukon River, 3185km/1979 miles from source to mouth and disgorging into the Bering Sea via an immense 30,000sq.km/11,580sq.mile delta in Alaska. Having its headwaters in the southern Yukon (Pelly River, Lewes River) the great waterway has a total catchment area of 855,000sq.km/330,000sq.miles. It begins by flowing north through Whitehorse (see entry) and Dawson (see entry), then along the American Cordillera until, having reached the Arctic Circle, it makes its "big bend" to the west.

The Yukon is a gently flowing river, ice-covered from October to May. In summer melting snow causes it to flood. Made famous by the gold-rush at the end of the last century its best-known tributary the Klondike (see entry) joins the Yukon River at Dawson (see entry).

Climate

The climate of the Yukon is principally determined by the north–south alignment of its mountain ranges, as a consequence of which polar air is able to flow unhindered from the north in winter. This results in bitter winter cold and the lowest recorded temperatures on the North American continent (about −60°C/−76°F).

Owing however to the continental-type climate, summers (June to mid-September) tend to be dry and relatively warm, and 20 hours of sunshine a day are not uncommon in these high northern latitudes. The frost period extends from October to April, the transition to summer being comparatively short. In Whitehorse (see entry) the average minimum temperature in January is −25°C/−13°F, the maximum only −16°C/3°F; in summer the corresponding values are 8°C/46°F and 21°C/70°F respectively.

The Territory is divided into two regions as far as vegetation is concerned, boreal coniferous forest predominating in the south and coniferous tundra in the north. Altitude likewise produces distinct vegetation zones, coniferous and birch forests in the valleys, tundra on the heights. Owing to the permafrost numbers of plant species are relatvely low. The few which are adapted to the conditions have also had to battle hard to re-establish themselves following the retreat of the last (Wisconsin) Ice Age about 13,000 years ago.

Vegetation

Prior to the 17th c. any settlement of the Yukon was by the indigenous peoples only. Initial European exploration of the region – later part of the Northwest Territories (see entry) – was mainly by the Hudson's Bay Company following its foundation in 1670. Around 1850 the demand for furs increased, and not long afterwards, in 1880, the first gold prospectors

History

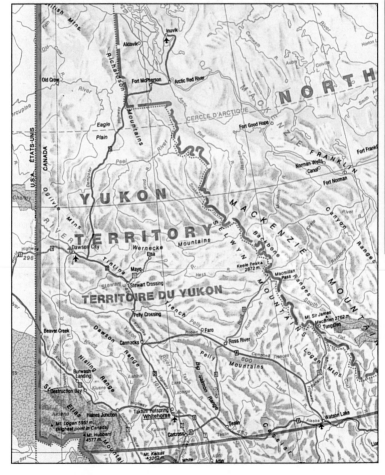

551

Canoeing on Yukon River

arrived in the Yukon as yields from the claims in British Columbia (see entry) began to fall. In 1887 Dawson reconnoitred for the first time the area around the town which now bears his name. These developments led to the Yukon being made a separate district of the Northwest Territories in 1895. When on August 17th 1896 George Carmack discovered fist-sized nuggets of gold in a tributary of the Klondike (Bonanza Creek) the find triggered a gold-rush of unbelievable proportions. Within a few months the population of Dawson City soared to 25,000 (some sources even suggest more than 50,000), and in the boom year of 1898 the Yukon proclaimed itself a Territory in its own right on the strength of its gold finds. Between 1897 and 1904 gold valued at almost 100 million dollars was extracted. From 1905 onwards a decline set in until the building of the Alaska Highway (see entry) in 1942 gave a fresh impetus to development. In 1952 White-horse (see entry) became the Yukon's administrative centre, replacing Dawson as Territorial capital. 1978 saw the opening of North America's only public road north of the Arctic Circle, Dempster Highway (see entry), named after Corporal Dempster who led an expedition there in 1911.

Population

With scarcely 30,000 inhabitants the population density in the Territory is a mere 0.05 per sq.km/0.02 per sq.mile. Before the influx of white settlers lured by the discovery of gold in the latter part of 1880, those living in the Yukon were mainly Athapaskan Indians who supported themselves by hunting and fishing (the Athapaskans are members of the large Na-Dené language family to which the Navajos and Apaches in the south also belong). Otherwise the only inhabitants were a very small number of Inuit settled on the coast. Although today about 21.4% of the people living in the Yukon are Indians, they constitute just 0.7% of Canada's indigenous population as a whole. Among the Yukon's white population 48% are of British extraction. Today the biggest towns in the Yukon Territory are Whitehorse (see entry) with about 19.000 inhabitants and Dawson (see entry) with fewer than 2000.

Cross Country skiing in Yukon Territory

Transport in the Territory relies on four major highways: the Alaska Highway (see entry) through Whitehorse, the Campbell Highway, the Klondike Highway (Whitehorse–Dawson; see Klondike) and the Dempster Highway (Dawson–Inuvik, NWT).

Transport

The bitterly cold climate and consequent permafrost mean that agriculture, normally the prime requirement for permanent settlement, is possible only to a very limited degree. Instead mining heads the list of economic activities. Of the ten minerals extracted, silver, lead, wolfram and antimony deserve special mention (the wolfram deposits, worked since 1961, are thought to be the biggest in America). Tourism has now overtaken forestry in second place.

Economy

The endless expanses of unspoilt wilderness are a paradise for the more adventure-minded. Canoeists in particular find conditions in the Territory ideal.

Leisure, sport, tourism

Of the Yukon's two national parks, the Kluane National Park (see entry) enjoys comparatively easy access via the Alaska Highway (see entry). As well as boasting Canada's highest mountains it is an area of huge ice-fields and calf glaciers – challenging country for experienced mountaineers. The Northern Yukon National Park on the other hand lies off the beaten track on the shores of the Beaufort Sea.

Dawson (see entry), reached via the Klondike Highway (see Klondike) or the Top of the World Highway from Alaska (see Dawson, Surroundings), has developed into quite a tourist centre. Something of the atmosphere of the old gold digging days can still be recaptured in the saloons, dance halls and houses of the now restored town. "Discovery Day" (August 17th) is celebrated annually with colourful cavalcades and a legion of other events. Anyone wanting to try their hand at gold panning will find plenty of opportunity on the special gold field tours.

Practical Information

For Canada the standards to apply beforehand to such matters as distance, travelling time, comfort, etc., are quite different in many respects from those for Europe. There is no problem so far as the relatively densely populated south of the country is concerned, but anyone planning to journey to the north or far from human habitation in the timberland would be well advised to take the proper precautions both in terms of equipment and personal fitness. Canadians are always willing to lend a hand in an emergency, but there can be times when travellers are thrown back entirely on their own resources, making it vital to acquire some knowledge of survival techniques before setting out – such as how to get through a blizzard or a tornado, or what to do when faced with a bear!

A certain degree of caution is also called for in urban Canada, especially at night. Although social strife here has not reached the extremes of New York or Los Angeles in neighbouring America, visitors should be on their guard against street crime, since attacks on the person do happen. And the same applies, albeit to a lesser degree, to places further off the beaten track.

Care and consideration should also be the watchword in dealings with Canada's native peoples, the Indians and the Inuit, as they increasingly assert their own identity. They are a dignified people who should be treated with respect, and the word "eskimo" should be avoided at all costs, since it is an insult.

Accommodation

See Bed and Breakfast, Camping, Hotels and Motels, Lodges, Ranch and Farm Holidays, Young People's Accommodation

Air Travel

In Canada travel by air is obviously the first choice for anyone whose time is limited and who has to cover long distances. Canada's air network is surprisingly closeknit for a country of its size, and it is possible to penetrate to the remotest corner through the gateways of the main cities.

Airports

The major airports which provide international services in Canada are Calgary, Edmonton, Halifax, Montréal (Dorval and Mirabel), Ottawa, Toronto, Vancouver and Winnipeg. Gander in Newfoundland, Goose Bay in Labrador, and Québec City airports are in a rather special position serving as transatlantic staging posts, military bases and tourist destinations respectively. Saskatoon and Regina, both in Saskatchewan, and Victoria, on Vancouver Island, are also international destinations but not by direct flights.

International airports

Most of Canada's international airports also connect with America's main cities, including New York and Chicago.

The services provided by Canada's larger airports are well up to international standards.

◀ *Toronto: Eaton Shopping Mall*

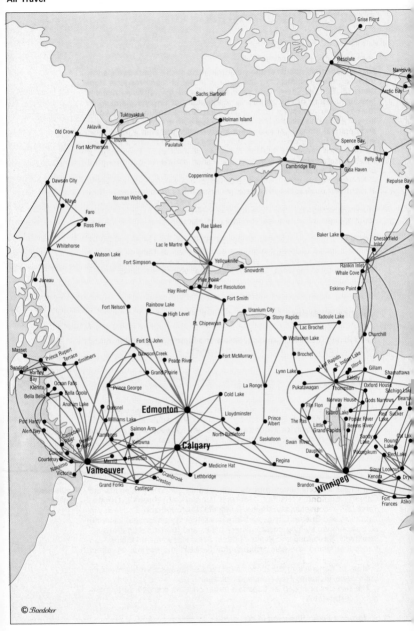

Air Services

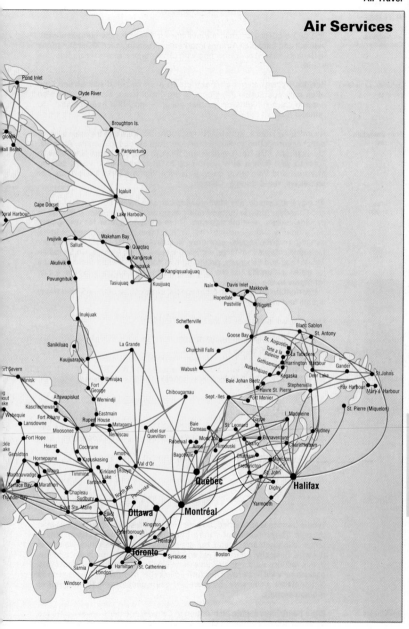

Airlines

Air Canada, Canadian Airlines
The two biggest Canadian airlines are Air Canada (now completely privatised) and Canadian Airlines International, serving over 100 destinations in Canada, as well as connecting with other major airports throughout the world.

Smaller Canadian airlines
Besides the two national airlines there are a number of smaller carriers who often only operate on a regional or provincial basis. Many of them also provide charter flights on smaller planes – including hydroplanes – to remoter places.

Non-Canadian airlines
Air India, Air France, British Airways, Lufthansa, KLM and Swissair all have direct or connecting scheduled services from Europe to Canada. Air India, for example, flies on Tuesdays and Fridays non-stop from Heathrow to Toronto, and British Airways has up to 23 services each week, serving Montréal and Vancouver daily, plus nine flights a week to Toronto. For addresses, see Getting to Canada.

Air fares in Canada
Air travel in Canada is relatively cheap compared with Europe. Air Canada and Canadian Airlines International link up with smaller internal airlines to provide cut-rate multiple ticketing. There are special rates for young people, students and senior citizens. In fact, there is a wide range of fares, varying from the regular economy, business and first-class, to the value-for-money Maple Leaf fares, the Pond-Hopper fares, Airpass, Go Canadian Travel Pass and Flexipass, providing two, four, six or eight flight coupons for travel in Canada and the USA (supplementary coupons available also for flights to the Caribbean).

Information on these and other special deals can be obtained from travel agents and airline offices.

Canadian airline offices in the United Kingdom:

Air Canada
7–8 Conduit Street, London W1R 9TG;
tel. (0181) 759 2636, fax (0181) 572 8727

Canadian Airlines International
23–59 Staines Road, Hounslow, Greater London TW3 3HE;
tel. (0181) 577 7722 (London Area), (0345) 616 767 (other areas)

Private pilots

Pilot's licence
Holders of a pilot's licence and an English radio-operator certificate can rent planes in Canada after taking a test. Further information from:

Aeronautical Information Service, Department of Transport,
Place de Ville, 7th Floor, Ottawa, Ont., Canada K1A 0N8

Bears

Where Canada is concerned, no animal is more fascinating to humans than the bear. The embodiment of the primeval wilderness, bears play an important role in myth and legend, but are also seen as a threatening danger in the wild. Basically, bears will eat anything, and are very much like humans in this respect. Although they live mainly on fruits and various plants they occasionally kill live prey. They turn up in larger numbers in places such as National Park picnic sites, for example, where people leave food, scraps or rubbish around.

Black bears
Black bears have a wide distribution in Canada, and there are estimated to be about 300,000 of them between the Atlantic, Pacific and Arctic Oceans.

Their preferred habitat should be more or less primeval forest, but they also enjoy tracking down the haunts of campers, tourists, etc.

Grizzlies are bigger, stronger and more determined, tending to occur in the Rockies and the Yukon. If attacked by a grizzly, get into a tree – they are poor climbers! | Grizzly bears

The few polar bears still roaming free can be found in the cold and remote fastnesses of Canada's uninhabited North. They can be very aggressive, and at certain times of year they gather in a few places in great numbers. One of these is Churchill, in Manitoba, where they congregate in autumn, making life quite difficult for the locals. | Polar bears

Although most visitors to Canada will never come face to face with a bear, polar, black, brown, or grizzly, there is still the question of what to do if and when . . . | In bear country
Bears can be kept at bay when backpacking or having to carry canoes for stretches overland by the occasional loud call, clapping or whistle (it is a good idea to take a whistle with you). Anyone travelling in bear country should take particular care, and know something about how to read tracks. Female bears with cubs should be treated with special respect. With warning grunts they will send their cub to safety and then take on the intruder.

No looking them straight in the eye. Speak softly, soothingly, drop to the ground on your stomach, protecting your head and shoulders with crossed arms. Don't scream or yell, just play dead. A rucksack can act as additional protection. However, if there is a chance to climb a tree, a dropped rucksack can serve as a distraction. | If a bear attacks

Whether out in the wilderness or stopping in civilisation at a campsite, never keep food in a canoe or tent, but do as the Canadians do and keep it in airtight drums or watertight containers and hang it from a branch which is at least six feet off the ground, placed so that it is no less than three foot from the trunk and hangs 18 inches below the branch. Leftovers should be buried deep in the ground as far away from sleeping places as possible. | Keeping foodstuffs

Bed and Breakfast (B & B)

Bed and Breakfast accommodation is widely available in Canada, and can be a real bargain. Local tourist offices keep lists of B & B providers, while some regions and provinces handle reservations and sell directories of homes taking part in bed and breakfast schemes.

Bed & Breakfast Homes of Toronto, P.O. Box 46093, College Park Post Office, 444 Yonge Street, Toronto, Ontario M5B 2L8; tel. (416) 363–6362 | Toronto

Bed & Breakfast à Montréal, P.O. Box 575, Snowdon Station, Montréal, Québec H3X 3T8; tel. (514) 738–9410 | Montréal

Bus Travel

There are bus services linking almost every town and city not on the national rail network. Buses are very comfortable, with air conditioning and on-board toilet, and the leg and head room are comparable to airlines or trains.

Reasonably-priced Canada Travel Passes are available from Greyhound Buslines of Canada. Valid for periods of 7, 15, 30 or 60 days, they must be purchased prior to arrival in Canada. | Canada Travel Pass

The Tourpasses issued by Voyager Bus, a provincial operator (Ontario and Québec provinces), represent excellent value for money. Available | Voyager Tourpass throughout the period May–Oct. they can be purchased in Canada as well as abroad.

Some bus companies

Canada
Acadian Lines, 6040 Almon Street, Halifax, Nova Scotia B3K 5M1

Brewster Transport Co. Ltd./Royal Glacier Tours, 100 Gopher Street, P.O. Box 1140, Banff, Alberta T0L 0C0 (scheduled bus service only Banff–Jasper)

Frame & Perkins Ltd., Box 400, Yellowknife, Northwest Territories X1A 2N3

Gray Coach Lines Ltd., 580 Commissioners Street, Toronto, Ontario M4M 1A7

Greyhound Lines of Canada Ltd., 877 Greyhound Way SW, Calgary, Alberta T3C 3V8

Ontario Northland Transportation Commission (Ont.), 555 Oak Street East, North Bay, Ontario H3C 3N3

Pacific Coach Lines Ltd., 710 Douglas Street, Victoria, British Columbia V8W 2B3

Pacific Western Transportation Ltd., 419 34th Avenue SE, Calgary, Alberta T2G 1V1

S.M.T.(Eastern) Ltd., 100 Midland Drive, Dieppe, New Brunswick E1A 6X4

Saskatchewan Transportation Co., 2041 Hamilton Street, Regina, Saskatchewan S4P 2E2

VIA Rail Canada Inc. (Motor Coach Service), C.P.8116, 2, place Ville-Marie, Montréal, Québec H3C 3N3

Voyageur Colonial Ltd., 505 Boulevard de Maisonneuve Est., Montréal, Québec H2L 1YA

Voyageur Colonial Ltd., 265 Catherine Street, Ottawa, Ontario K1R 7S5

United Kingdom
Greyhound World Travel Ltd., Sussex House, London Road, East Grinstead, West Sussex RH19 1LD; tel. (0342) 317317

Camping

Campsites
Canada has over 2000 campsites, some private, some official, located along the main highways – about every 160km/100 miles on the Trans-Canada Highway – and in almost all the national and provincial parks. They are very well equipped, usually with a table, benches and fireplace for every camper. The facilities provided vary according to the price, which ranges between 10 and 15 dollars a night.

Private campsites are more expensive and less spacious.

Many sites have places for buying camping equipment.

The Canadian Automobile Association (2525 Carling Avenue, Ottawa, Ontario, Canada K2B 7Z2; tel. (613) 820 1890, fax (613) 820 4646. The Canadian Automobile Association, Toronto, 60 Commerce Valley Drive Est., Markham, Ontario, Canada L3T 7P9; tel. (905) 771 3000, fax (905) 771 3101) and the provincial tourist offices have information on the most appropriate campsites.

Directories
Some provinces publish annually updated campsite directories, which can be obtained from the relevant tourism office (see Information).

Reservations
Advance reservation is not possible for many campsites, and this can cause considerable problems, especially at peak holiday times in the summer. It is advisable therefore to arrive at a campsite as early as possible.

Unauthorised camping
Camping outside an official site close to towns is not encouraged, and camping in parks in forbidden.

Campers and Motorhomes

Many holidaymakers explore Canada in motorhomes and campers. They can be rented in all the big cities and at all international airports. They differ considerably from their European counterparts, so it pays to familiarise yourself with how they handle. It also pays to book campers and motorhomes before departure with a reputable hire firm or a specialist travel agency, since this can be much cheaper than renting them on the spot.

Caravan Abroad Ltd., 56 Middle Street., Brockham, Surrey RH3 7HW; tel. (01737) 842735
Cruise Canada, The Old House, High Street, Balcombe Forest, West Sussex; tel. (01444) 811991

Motorhome rental in the United Kingdom

Be sure to read the small print of the contract. Find out what the procedure is in the event of an accident (repair costs, towing fees, extra hotel charges, etc.), and precisely what the insurance covers.

When taking over, record the state of the vehicle and put down any recognisable defects and damage. Check whether everything on the inventory is there, and that you also have the operating instructions and the address and telephone number of the rental company.

For most rented vehicles it is necessary to use a credit card as security.

Take care when loading a mobilehome or camper to store heavy items as low down as possible in front of the back axle. Fuel consumption is likely to rise by 1 to 2% per additional 100kg/220lbs. Empty the watertank before starting out then fill up with fresh water on arrival. Mobilehomes hold between 25 and 40 litres/5½ and 9 gallons of fuel, depending on the make. The most economic driving speed is between 70 and 80kph/43 and 50mph.

When renting a camper, besides Sales Tax – the equivalent of Europe's value added tax – the hirer also has to pay Goods and Services Tax, and additional insurance in the form of collision damage waiver (CDW) and vacation interruption protection (VIP).

Canoeing and Rafting

Canoeing in Canada in summer is as much a way of life as skiing in the Alps is in winter. Over thousands of years the Canadian canoe has been shaped and refined to suit the geography and materials found in North America to such good purpose that it has become the ideal craft, as regards weight, seaworthiness, carrying capacity, etc., for the job it has to do.

Canoeing

Canada was opened up by the canoe and the *voyageurs* and *coureurs de bois* who paddled it up and down the country's three million or so lakes, and countless other waterways. Nowadays, even though no longer of birchbark, but more likely polyester or aluminium, the canoe is still "the" way to explore the country. No one who has "discovered" Canada by canoe can say they have simply "been there".

The method of propulsion is simple enough – the paddlepower generated by a person's own biceps which, apart from the sheer exhilaration of the experience, gives the canoeist the kind of freedom and independence that enables him or her, preferably a crew of two anyway, to get to places quite different from the camper in his mobilehome. To where cruisers and sailing boats simply cannot pass, and where it is too rocky or shallow for small motorboats, or where the ground cannot take a heavy vehicle. With a canoe, one person picks up the canoe, the other the baggage, and in next to no time there's a whole different environment opening up – with no engine fumes, no traffic sounds, no mechanical breakdowns, but a world without noise, something quite new to many Europeans.

This freedom need not only be exercised on the rushing waters of a mighty river. It could be on a little chain of lakes, of which Canada has many thousands, or even just exploring one lone stretch of water in splendid isolation.

Rafting on the Ottawa River

Equipment

Canoes and equipment can be rented from "outfitters" in Canada, or experienced canoeists from abroad will probably bring with them their own lifejackets, watertight bags for food and clothing, even, possibly, their own inflatable canoe. Besides light footwear, a tent, good maps and insect repellent, another essential requirement is sturdy rubber shoes with soles that have a good grip, since in the event of capsizing keeping a firm footing can be a matter of life or death.

Various watertight bags will protect foodstuff against an involuntary ducking. Main stocks of sugar, flour, pasta, etc. are best kept in sealed muslin or linen bags packed in sturdy watertight plastic. Pepper, salt, jam, etc. can be kept in wide-necked plastic containers obtainable in Europe from camping shops and chemists. In Canada they are only available at specialist shops in big cities, and finding them can be time consuming and costly.

For emergency rations take good European chocolate (rather than American candy bars) and dried egg, plus dried fruit mixtures. Do not take bacon and salami since they will immediately be confiscated by Canadian customs.

Rafting

Rafting, which has become increasingly popular over the past twenty years, is more of a group activity, an organised thrill, and consequently a safer if no less exciting way of riding the white water of the bigger rivers. These are not as spectacular as the Colorado in America's Grand Canyon, but the Thompson, Fraser and Chilcotin Rivers in British Columbia have plenty of rock walls and rapids, while in the Northwest Territories there are tours on the Slave River, and even from the skyscrapers of Ottawa it is a relatively short step to the calmer waters of the Ottawa River at Beachburg, Ontario. Here the crew of eight or ten have to paddle themselves, whereas over in the West the heavyweight pontoons are propelled from behind by outboard motors. Early reservation is necessary in high summer. The equipment, i.e. wetsuits, life jackets, etc., comes as part of the package.

Guides to the rivers in particular provinces can be had from the local provincial offices, while newspaper kiosks, general stores, etc. also sell guides to the smaller rivers for certain areas.

Car Rental

Cars can be rented in most towns and airports. Rental rates are from about £115 a week, depending on the size of the car and whether or not there is unlimited mileage. A credit card or a cash deposit is usually required. If a car is rented in one city and returned in another, sometimes a quite substantial charge is made, depending on the final location. Most car rental companies do not rent vehicles to persons under 21 years of age. A full British driving licence is valid for driving in Canada for up to 3 months in most provinces. For longer an international driving licence is required.

The following are some of the UK offices/representatives that handle reservations for Canadian car rental:

Canadian car rental reservations in the UK

Avis Rent-a-Car Systems Inc., Avis House, Park Road, Bracknell, Berks. RG12 2DS; tel. (01344) 426 644.

Bricar International Car Rental Ltd., 28/30 Woodcote Road, Wallington, Surrey SM6 0NN; tel. 0181–773 2312.

Budget Rent A Car Ltd., 41 Marlowes, Hemel Hempstead, Herts. HP1 1LD; tel. (01442) 23 2555.

Hertz Europe Ltd., Hertz House, Bath Road, Cranford, Middlesex TW5 9SW; tel. 0181–759 2499.

Thrifty Car Rental, The Old Court House, Hughenden Road, High Wycombe, Bucks. HP13 5DT; tel. (01494) 44 2110.

Tilden Rent a Car (Europecar), Bushey House, High Street, Bushey, Herts. WD2 1RE; tel. 0181–950 5050

The following are some of the best-known car rental firms in Canada:

Car rental reservations in Canada

Aviscar Inc., 2 Eva Road, Etobicoke, Ontario M9C 2A8

Budget Rent A Car of Canada Ltd., 20 Eglinton Avenue West, Suite 1900, Toronto, Ontario M4R 1K8

Hertz Canada Ltd., 5403 Eglinton Ave. West, Suite 100, Etobicoke, Ontario M9C 5K6

Thrifty Car Rental, 6711 Mississuaga Road North, Mississuaga, Ontario L5N 2W3

Tilden Rent a Car System, 1485 rue Stanley, Bureau 905, Montréal, Québec, H3A 1P6

Currency

The Canadian dollar (1 Can.\$ = 100 cents) has notes in denominations of 1, 2, 5, 10, 20, 50, 100, 500 and 1,000 dollars, printed in English and French. The coins have a value of 1 cent (penny, sou), 5 cents (nickel, cinq sous), 10 cents (dime, dix sous) and 25 cents (quarter, vingt-cinq sous), plus the half-dollar (50 cents, cinquante sous) and one dollar. The rate of exchange for the Canadian dollar can fluctuate considerably, and it is possible to make quite a loss when changing notes upon returning home.

Canadian dollar

European visitors to Canada should take traveller's cheques in Canadian dollars, since these can be used like cash and there are very few places for cashing cheques in European currencies. Banks can often prove difficult, too, and will charge a fee. Always carry a driver's licence or passport for purposes of identification.

Traveller's cheques

Eurocheques, although popular in Europe, are virtually unknown in Canada and will not generally be accepted.

Eurocheques

Customs Regulations

Credit cards	The major international credit cards, especially American Express, Mastercard/Eurocard, Visa and Diner's Card, are accepted almost everywhere in Canada. Many top car-rental companies and hotel chains will only deal with credit card holders. The relevant company should be informed immediately a credit card is lost.
Banks	Canadian banks are usually open Monday to Friday between 10am and 3pm, although opening times can vary. For business transactions a letter of credit should be obtained from the visitor's own bank before leaving home.
Currency exchange	Foreign banknotes, traveller's cheques, etc., can be converted into Can. $ at many banks and special bureaux de change.
Currency import/ export	There is no limit on the amount of Canadian dollars or foreign currency that can be taken in or out of the country.

Customs Regulations

N.B.	Customs regulations on both sides of the Atlantic are currently under review. Up-to-date information should be sought from Customs & Excise or the nearest Canadian Embassy or Consulate prior to setting out. Visitors can take in personal items – including sporting equipment, cycles, cameras, portable radios and TVs – free of duty, but must be at least 18 or 19, depending on the province, to be able to do so in their own right. The duty-free allowances for import and export to and from Canada are 200 cigarettes or 50 cigars or 0.9kg (2lb) tobacco (persons aged 16 or over), 1.1 litre of spirits or wine (persons over 18 years of age entering Alberta, Manitoba or Quebec; 19 years other states), and gifts up to a value of Can.\$40. Absolutely no food, plants, drugs or narcotics may be brought in. Cars and motorcycles licensed abroad can be imported into Canada for periods of up to a year on issue of a Temporary Permit.

Cycling

	Cycling has become very popular in Canada, as it has in Europe. The big cities in particular, but many of the provincial and national parks as well, have also recognised the signs of the times, and established some fine trails for use as cycletracks. Mountain bikes are also popular, but their use in Canada's great outdoors is very much subject to restrictions.
"Green Corridor"	The network of cyclists' routes in the "Green Corridor" between the New England states of the north-east USA and Canada's Québec Province is currently being improved. Already there is a well-signposted cycleway traversing the 800km/500 miles from Connecticut, USA to Montréal, Canada.

Diplomatic Representation

United Kingdom	British High Commission, 80 Elgin Street Ottawa, Ontario K1P 5K7. Tel. (613) 237 1530
United States	US Embassy, 100 Wellington Street, P.O. Box 866, Station B, Ottawa, Ontario K1P 5T1. Tel. (613) 238 5335
	There are British and American consulates in the principal cities of Canada.

Electricity

In Canada the electricity supply is 110 volts (60Hz) AC, as in the United States. Europeans should get a plug adaptor in advance if they want to use their own electrical appliances, since plugs in Canada are the standard two-flat-prong American type.

110 volts AC

Emergencies

Dial 0 and ask to be put through to the police (or "sûreté").

Police

Dial 0 and ask for medical assistance.

Medical emergency

Dial 0 and ask for the fire brigade.

Fire

Inform the nearest police station immediately by dialling 0. In heavily populated areas emergency telephones are provided along the motorway-like "Highways".

Accident

Members of European automobile clubs can call out the Canadian Automobile Association, but must produce their membership card.

Breakdown

Events and Festivals (selection)

La Pérade (Québec): ice fishing

Winter

Québec (Québec): International Curling Tournament

January

Carleton (Québec): Grand Prix Baie-des-Chaleurs (snowcat racing)
Chetwynd (B.C.): Chinook Daze (winter carnival)
Chibougamau (Québec): Festival des Folifrets (ice and snow chase)
Chicoutimi (Québec): carnival
Courtenay (B.C.): winter carnival
Dawson Creek (B.C.): winter carnival
Golden (B.C.): snow festival
Hazelton (B.C.): ice carnival
Hull (Québec): marathon de ski de fond (ski marathon)
Jonquière (Québec): Jonquière en neige
Lac-la-Hache (B.C.): winter carnival
Prince Albert (Saska.): winter festival
Québec (Québec): ★Carnaval d'Hiver (winter carnival), world's biggest ice-sculpture competition
St Boniface (Man.): Festival du Voyageur
The Pas (Man.): Trappers' festival
Whitehorse (N.W.T.): Sourdorough Rendezvous

February

Baddeck (N.S.): S.A.N.S. tour
Elmira (Ont.): maple syrup festival
Hull (Québec): Salon du Livre (book fair)
Yellowknife (Yukon): Caribou Carnival

March

Inuvik (N.W.T.): top of the world ski meeting

Easter

Eastern Canada: maple sugar season, "sugaring off" parties
Snow geese northern migration, throughout Canada

March/April

Guelph (Ont.): Spring arts festival

April/May

Stratford (Ont.): Shakespeare festival
Niagara-on-the-Lake, Shaw festival

May to October

Events and Festivals

May	Campbell River (B.C.): Ishikari festival
	Chilliwack (B.C.): festival (including races)
	Creston (B.C.): flower festival
	Fort St John (B.C.): stampede
	Golden (B.C.): Columbia rafting
	Ladysmith (B.C.): festival
	Niagara Falls (Ont.): blossom festival
	New Hamburg (Ont.): Mennonite auction
	New Westminster (B.C.): Hyack festival, Fraser River canoe marathon
	Ottawa (Ont.): ★Canadian Tullip Festival
	Trois-Rivières (Québec): Classique de canot de la Mauricie (canoe classic)
	Victoria (B.C.): Victorian Days
Late May/early June	Digby (N.S.): Annapolis Valley apple blossom festival
Early June to mid-August	Banff (Alta.): arts festival
	Williams Lake (B.C.): stampede
Mid-June to mid-September	Charlottetown (P.E.I.): "Anne of Green Gables" summer festival (theatre)
June	Chetwynd (B.C.): rodeo
	Chilliwack (B.C.): Indian festival
	Cranbrook (B.C.): Sam Steele Day
	Forestville (Québec): Festival de la Pêche (fishing festival)
	Gaspé (Québec): international regatta
	Grande Prairie (Alta.): stampede
	Hazelton (B.C.): Kispiox rodeo
	Hope (B.C.): bluegrass festival
	Regina (Saska.): Western Canada Farm Progress Show
	Shelburne County (N.S.): Lobster Festival (regatta)
	Toronto (Ont.): international caravan show
	Yellowknife (Yukon): midnight golf tournament, Folk on the Rocks
Late June	Bridgewater (N.S.): bluegrass maritime festival
	Montréal (Québec): international jazz festival
	Cabano (Québec): Festival de Touladi (including angling contests)
	Chicoutimi (Québec): Jours de la Culture; regatta
	Québec (Québec): fête nationale (Québec Province national day festival)
	Cabot celebrations – 1997 marks the 500th anniversary of the historic journey of John Cabot, from Bristol to Newfoundland. Celebrations are due to be held throughout 1997, ending with the arrival of Cabot's ship "Matthew", for June and July.
June/July	Campbellton (N.B.): salmon festival
	Duncan (B.C.): Duncan-Cowichan summer festival
	Grand Falls (N.B.): potato festival
	Windsor (Ont.): freedom festival
	Winnipeg (Man.): Red River exhibition and fair
July	July 1st, National Day celebrations throughout Canada
	Antigonish (N.S.): Highland Games
	Austin (Man.): Manitoba Threshermen's Reunion
	Bella Coola (B.C.): rodeo
	Belleville (Ont.): agricultural exhibition
	Bridgetown (N.S.): American visitors' party
	Calgary (Alta.): ★stampede and exhibition
	Campbell River (B.C.): salmon festival
	Campbellton (N.B.): Festival du Saumon
	Drummondville (Québec): Festival de Folklore
	Edmonton (Alta.): international jazz festival; Klondike Gold Rush Commemoration
	Flin Flon (Man.): Flin Flon Trout Festival

Fort St. John (B.C.): stampede
Gaspé (Québec): Festival Jacques Cartier
Grand-Pré (N.S.): Acadian Days
Halifax (N.S.): Natal Day (24th); Scottish games
Howe Sound (B.C.): Salmon Derby
Îles de la Madeleine (Québec): Festival du Homard (lobster festival);
    Festival du Pêcheur
Jonquière (Québec): Jonquière en fête
Kamloops (B.C.): rodeo
Kelowna (B.C.): international regatta
Montréal (Québec): Festival International du Jazz; Bell just for laughs
    festival
Ottawa (Ont.): Ottawa Festival
Pugwash (N.S.): Gathering of the Clans
Québec (Québec): ★ Festival d'Été (summer festival with music, dance,
    folklore)
Saskatoon (Saska.): Pioneer Days
Selkirk (Man.): Manitoba Highland Gathering
Shediac (N.B.): lobster festival
Shippagan (N.B.): fisheries festival
St John (N.B.): Loyalist Day
Ste-Anne-de-Beaupré: international pilgrimage to Ste-Anne-de-Beaupré
Thunderbay (Ont.): Rendezvous Pageant
Valleyfield (Québec): international regatta
Vancouver (B.C.): sea festival, Nnaimo-Vancouver bathtub race
Windsor (Newfoundland): Exploits Valley Salmon Festival
Winnipeg (Man.): folk festival
Yorkton (Saska.): Saskatchewan stampede and exhibition

Alma (Québec): Festirama	Late July
Carleton (Québec): Festivoile	
Granby (Québec): Granby National (including classic car show)	
Mahone Bay (N.S.): Mahone Bay Wooden Boat Festival, street parties	
Robertval-Péribonka (Québec): Traverse du Lac St-Jean (trans-lake swim)	

Whalewatching on east and west coasts	July/August
Annapolis Royal (N.S.): King's Festival	
Baddeck (N.S.): Festival of the Arts	
Cheticamp (N.S.): Festival de l'Escauette (Acadian festival)	
Dauphin (Man.): National Ukrainian Festival	
Edmundston (N.B.): Foire Brayonne	
Lennoxville (Québec): Festival de Théâtre	
Magog (Québec): Orford Festival	
Penticton (B.C.): peach festival	
Regina (Saska.): Buffalo Days	
Steinbach (Man.): Pioneer Days	
Toronto (Ont.): Caribana (Caribbean festival)	

Abbotsford (B.C.): air show	August
Brandon (Man.): Manitoba Exhibition	
Brantford (Ont.): Six Nations Indian Pageant	
Bromont (Québec): Festival de la Musique Classique	
Campbell River (B.C.): arts festival	
Coaticook (Québec): Festival du Lait	
Courtenay (B.C.): Elks Rodeo	
Dawson (Yukon): Discovery Day	
Dawson Creek (B.C.): rodeo	
Fernie (B.C.): Rangler Valley rodeo	
Gimli (Man.): Icelandic Festival	
Grande-Prairie (Alta.): Muskoseepi Sunday	
Halifax (N.S.): arts festival	
Havre-St-Pierre (Québec): Festival de la Minganie	
Hazelton (B.C.): Pioneer Days	

Events and Festivals

Hull (Québec): Festival de la Chanson, Musique de l'Outaouais
Kamloops (B.C.): international aerial meeting
Lake Cowichan (B.C.): Youbou Regatta
La Malbaie (Québec): les 95km de Charlevoix (cycle race)
Liverpool (N.S.): Musique Royale
Lethbridge (Alta.): Whoop Up and rodeo
Manitoulin Island (Ont.): Wikwemikong Pow-Wow
Maxville (Ont.): Glengarry Highland Games
Ottawa (Ont.): Canada Exhibition
Québec (Québec): air show, craft fair, Québec province fair
Saskatoon (Saska.): folk festival
Squamish (B.C.): loggers' sports day
St Ann's (N.S.): Gaelic Mod
St Catherines (Ont.): Royal Canadian Henley Regatta
St John's (Newfoundland): Royal St John's Regatta
Sudbury (Ont.): Rockhound Festival
Winnipeg (Man.): Folklorama

| August 15th | Campbellton and Caraquet (N.B.): ★Fête Nationale des Acadiens |

Mid-August

Halifax (N.S.): ★Festival of Forts (commemoration of the Scots landing in 1629)
Bridgetown (N.S.): Black Powder Rendezvous
Les Becquets (Québec): Festival de la Tomate
Lunenburg (N.S.): Folk Harbour (festival)

August/September

Chester (N.S.): Nova Scotia crafts market
Louisberg (N.S.): Louisberg Crab Festival
Toronto (Ont.): Canadian national exhibition
Vancouver (B.C.): Pacific national exhibition

September

Blanc Sablon (Québec): Festival de la Morue (cod festival)
Courtenay (B.C.): Comox Valley exhibition
Golden (B.C.): rodeo
Granby (Québec): Festival de la Chanson
Grand Forks (B.C.): Western Week, rodeo
Halifax (N.S.): Joseph Howe Festival
La Malbaie (Québec): Charlevoix open golf tournament
Lunenburg (N.S.): Nova Scotia fisheries exhibition and fishermen's reunion
Montréal (Québec): Montréal Marathon
St Catherines (Ont.): Niagara grape and wine festival
Trois-Rivières (Québec): Molson Grand Prix
Victoria (B.C.): Fall flower show

September/October

Throughout Canada: spectacular Fall colours; snow geese fly south
Muskoka Lakes (Ont.): Cavalcade of Colour
Penticton (B.C.): harvest and grape fiesta

October

Granby (Québec): Festival Gastronomique
Kitchener-Waterloo (Ont.): October festival
Rimouski (Québec): Festival d'Automne

November

Québec (Québec): Beaujolais nouveau festival
Regina (Saska.): Canadian Western Agribition
Toronto (Ont.): Agricultural Winter Fair

December

Chilliwack (B.C.): Santa Claus Parade
Duncan (B.C.): Santa Claus Parade

Ferry Services

Along the Atlantic seaboard, the St Lawrence River and the Pacific Coast of British Columbia there are numerous medium- and short-distance ferry services, use of which can often avoid a much longer journey by road, particularly in the peak summer season. Detailed information and time-tables are available from regional and provincial tourist offices.

Note

Principal ferry routes

Saint John (New Brunswick) – Digby (Nova Scotia)

Bay of Fundy

Cape Tormentine (New Brunswick) – Borden (Prince Edward Island)
Caribou (Nova Scotia) – Wood Islands (Prince Edward Island)

Northumberland
Strait

Souris (Prince Edward Island) – Havre-Aubert & Grande-Entrée (Îles de la Madeleine, Québec)

Îles de la
Madeleine

North Sydney (Nova Scotia) – Argentia (Newfoundland)
North Sydney (Nova Scotia) – Channel – Port-aux-Basques (Newfoundland)
Lewisporte – Goose Bay (Labrador)

Newfoundland

Portland or Bar Harbour (Maine) – Yarmouth (Nova Scotia). Early booking essential!

USA/Nova Scotia

Several ferry services on the St Lawrence River

Québec

B.C. Ferries run services to no less than 25 ports on the Pacific coast and Vancouver Island, including the exceptionally busy Port Hardy – Prince Rupert route (early booking essential). Further information from:

British Columbia

B.C. Ferries, 1112 Fort Street, Victoria, B.C. V8V 4V2, tel. (604) 386–3431, fax (604) 381–5452; alternatively 1045 Howe Street, Vancouver, B.C. V6Z 2A9, tel. (604) 669–1211
Main UK agent; tel. (0181) 393–0127
The MV "Queen of the North" runs regular passenger and vehicular services (cars, campers and motorhomes) from Port Hardy on Vancouver Island to Prince Rupert, connecting with the Alaska Marine Highway ferry service.

B.C. Ferries

Alaska Marine Highway System, P.O. Box R, Juneau, Alaska 99811; tel. (907) 465–3941 Juneau
Regular passenger and vehicular services (cars, campers and motor-homes) from Seattle (restrictions apply) and Prince Rupert to Ketchikan, Wrangell, Juneau, Petersburg, Sitka, Haines and Skagway.

Alaska

Filming and Photography

Filming and photography in Canada pose no problems whatsoever. Processing is up to European standards and film, with DIN or ASA values, is easily available just about everywhere. The largest towns and cities have rapid processing labs, where colour prints can be ready in a few hours.

Filling Stations

In the more densely populated areas and along the main highways Canada has plenty of filling stations (gas stations), but away from the main roads they are few and far between. Anyone travelling in the far North should take spare petrol supplies. In British Columbia, Yukon and the Northwest Territories it is possible to drive for hundreds if not thousands of miles without finding a single filling station.

Fishing

With three oceans – the Atlantic, Arctic and Pacific – and countless lakes, streams and rivers, in fact half the world's stock of freshwater, Canada has everything to make the keen angler's heart rejoice.

Canada's inland waters hold fish to suit every angling taste, from superb salmon, fighting their way upriver every year, to perch, pike, all kinds of trout, bass, and the like, distributed virtually throughout the country's lakes and waterways, where, compared with Europe, they grow to a most impressive size. Among the many other species commonly caught are Dolly Varden, whitefish, barbel and eel. There is good deep sea angling off Canada's Atlantic seaboard and in the Pacific off the coast of British Columbia.

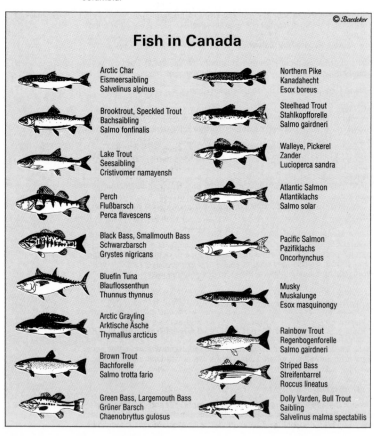

© Baedeker

Fish in Canada

Arctic Char
Eismeersaibling
Salvelinus alpinus

Brooktrout, Speckled Trout
Bachsaibling
Salmo fonfinalis

Lake Trout
Seesaibling
Cristivomer namayensh

Perch
Flußbarsch
Perca flavescens

Black Bass, Smallmouth Bass
Schwarzbarsch
Grystes nigricans

Bluefin Tuna
Blauflossenthun
Thunnus thynnus

Arctic Grayling
Arktische Äsche
Thymallus arcticus

Brown Trout
Bachforelle
Salmo trotta fario

Green Bass, Largemouth Bass
Grüner Barsch
Chaenobryttus gulosus

Northern Pike
Kanadahecht
Esox boreus

Steelhead Trout
Stahlkopfforelle
Salmo gairdneri

Walleye, Pickerel
Zander
Lucioperca sandra

Atlantic Salmon
Atlantiklachs
Salmo solar

Pacific Salmon
Pazifiklachs
Oncorhynchus

Musky
Muskalunge
Esox masquinongy

Rainbow Trout
Regenbogenforelle
Salmo gairdneri

Striped Bass
Streifenbarrel
Roccus lineatus

Dolly Varden, Bull Trout
Saibling
Salvelinus malma spectabilis

Many of Canada's best places for the sport can easily be reached by rail, road or plane, and are often close to campsites, hotels, lodges and other accommodation.

No special permit is needed to take in fishing tackle for personal use.

Import of fishing tackle

Fishing is governed by federal, provincial and territorial laws, and anglers must have non-resident licences for the provinces or territories where they plan to fish. Fishing permits can be bought at stores and lodges and cost between 10 and 30 dollars.

Fishing licences

A special permit is required to fish in all national parks. These can be obtained at any national park site for a nominal fee and are valid in all the national parks across Canada. In addition, tidal-waters sports fishing licences are required in some areas.

Dept. of Fisheries and Oceans, Communications Branch, 1090 West Pender Street, Vancouver, British Columbia V6E 2P1; tel. (604) 666–03 84

Information

Food and Drink

Shopping for food in Canada is very much like its European counterpart. So far as supermarkets are concerned, there is little to choose between them, and it is possible to eat well for about $30 a day.

Canadian cooking has won itself an international reputation in recent years, thanks to the richness of the country's ethnic backgrounds. There is actually no national dish as such, but there are several Canadian specialities such as steak, salmon and lobster.

Canadian cooking

Canada's culinary highpoint is the French-Canadian cuisine of Québec, where the sturdy old French traditions is augmented by the use of specific local ingredients such as maple syrup and Canadian cheese. The Atlantic provinces are famous mostly for their lobster suppers, while Nova Scotia is also known for its solomon gundy, a marinaded herring recipe brought from their homeland by immigrant Scots. Ontario's lake pike and trout are deliciously complemented by the wine, fresh vegetables and fruit from the Niagara Peninsula. The prairies mostly serve up fare that is simple but well cooked, while Alberta is known for its peerless steaks.

Regional specialities

The West Coast menu again features top quality shrimp and crab, as well as halibut and salmon – a poached salmon steak with vegetables from the Fraser Valley is a very special Canadian delicacy.

Although Canada is so rich in game it seldom appears on the menu, since officially it is not for sale and few restaurants have special permits. Canadians hunt exclusively for their own consumption, so that an invitation home to dinner is needed to sample the best of Canada's wild game.

Game

Canadian whisky, 40% proof, is usually drunk with ice and/or water, or with mixers. Canadian rye, a spirit made by distilling fermented cereals, matured and often blended, is reckoned to be one of the best of the Canadian whiskies. The popular brands are Seagram's and Canadian Club. Yukon Jack is a northern speciality, a very strong malt whisky.

Drink

Whisky

Canadian wine can be surprisingly good. The main wineries are around Niagara-on-the-Lake, south of Ontario, and the Okanagan valley in southern British Columbia. The grapes are chiefly Chardonnay, Riesling, Sylvaner and Gewürztraminer.

Wine

Wine is often only served in the better restaurants.

Beer is Canada's favourite drink, usually as lager, pils and ale, as well as the stronger porter and stout, with Carling Black Label leading the field. Canada's top brewers are Molson, Labatt's, Carling-O'Keefe and Moosehead.

Beer

Getting to Canada

Direct flights from Europe

Air Canada   From London, Heathrow, to Calgary, Charlottetown, Deer Lake/Corner
Brook, Edmonton, Fredericton, Gander, Halifax/Dartmouth, Moncton,
Montréal, Ottawa, Regina/Moose Jaw, Saint John, Saskatoon, St John's,
Sydney/Glace Bay, Thunder Bay, Toronto, Vancouver, Victoria, Windsor,
Winnipeg (for UK address, see Air Travel).
From Manchester to Toronto.
From Glasgow to Halifax, Toronto, Calgary and Vancouver.

Air India   From Heathrow to Toronto.
Air India Building, Mathison Way Colnbrook, Slough, Buckinghamshire
SL3 0HF; tel. (01753) 684828

British Airways   From London to Montréal, Toronto and Vancouver.
156 Regent St., London W1R 5TA; tel. (0181) 897 4000 (London Area), (0345)
222111 (other areas).

Canadian Airlines   From London and Manchester to Calgary, Edmonton, Ottawa, Toronto and
International   Vancouver (for UK address see Air Travel).

By road from the USA

The main road routes into Canada are, in the east, US Highways 87, 89 or 91
for Montréal, and Queen Elizabeth Way or Highway 401 for Toronto, and, in
the west, Interstate 5 and then Canadian Highway 99 to Vancouver.

Golf

Golfers will be in their element in Canada. There are more than 400 golf
courses in the Province of Ontario alone. Clearly the list that follows is only
a selection and for more detailed information write to the individual golf
associations.

Alberta   Banff Springs Golf Course
Banff, Alberta; tel. (403) 762–2211
18-hole, open April–October

Kananaskis Country Golf Club
Lake Kananaskis, Alberta
18-hole, open April–October

Mayfair Golf & Country Club
Edmonton, Alberta; tel. (403) 739–7544
18-hole

Jasper Golf Course
18-hole

British Columbia   Royal Colwood Golf & Country Club
Victoria, B.C.; tel. (604) 478–8331
18-hole, open all year

Capilano Golf & Country Club
West Vancouver; tel. (604) 922–9331
18-hole, open all year

Cordowa Bay Golf Course
18-hole

Olympic View Golf Course
Victoria, B.C.
18-hole

Uplands Golf Course (Oak Bay)
Victoria; tel. (604) 592–7313
18-hole, open all year

Whistler Golf Club
Whistler; tel. (604) 932–4544
18-hole, open May–October

Chateau Whistler Golf Club
Whistler, B.C.
18-hole

Hecla Island Golf Course (Gull Harbour)   Manitoba
Riverton; tel. 1–800–267 6700
18-hole

Falcon Beach Golf Course
Falcon Lake; tel. (204) 349–2554
18-hole

Wasagaming Golf Course (Clear Lake)
Wasagaming; tel. (204) 848–7445
18-hole

Mactaquac Provincial Park Golf Course   New Brunswick
Fredericton; tel. (506) 263–3011
18-hole, open March–October

Algonquin Golf Course
St Andrews; tel. (506) 529–3062
18 and 9 hole, open April–October

Ashburn Golf Course   Nova Scotia
Halifax; 2×18-hole, open May–October

Glen Abbey Golf Course   Ontario
Oakville; tel. (416) 644–1800
18-hole, open April–October

Niagara Parks Whirlpool Golf Course
Niagara Falls; tel. (416) 356–1140
18-hole, open April–October

The National Golf Club
Woodbridge; tel. (519) 426–0683
18-hole, open March–December

Windermere Golf & Country Club
Windermere; tel. (705) 769–3611, 18-hole

Knollwood Golf Club
Ancaster; tel. (416) 648–6687
18-hole, open April–November

Mill River Provincial Park Golf Course   Prince Edward
Woodstock; tel. (902) 859–2238   Island
6, 12 and 18-hole, open May–October

Hotels and Motels

Québec	The Royal Montreal Golf Club Montréal; tel. (514) 626–3977 18, 18 and 9-hole, open March–November
	Chateau Montebello Golf Course Montebello; tel. (819) 423–6341 18-hole
	Grey Rocks Golf Course St Jovite; tel. (819) 425–2771 18-hole
	Mont Ste-Marie Golf Course Lac Ste-Marie; tel. (819) 467–5200 18-hole
Saskatchewan	Waskesiu Golf Course Waskesiu Lake; tel. (306) 663–5488 18-hole, open June–October
Golf associations in Canada	Royal Canadian Golf Association c/o Glen Abbey Golf Club RR2, Oakville, Ontario L6J 4Z3; tel. (416) 844–1800
	Alberta Golf Association 200A Haddon Rd. SW, Calgary, Alberta T2V 2Y6; tel. (403) 259–6261
	B.C. Golf Association 322 1675 W. 8th Ave., Vancouver, B.C. V6J 1V2; tel. (604) 736–0488
	Ontario Golf Association 400 Esna Park Drive, Unit 11, Markham, Ontario L3R 1H5; tel. (416) 475–5238
	Quebec Golf Association 3300 Cavendish Blvd. Room 250, Montréal, Québec H4B 2M8; tel. (514) 481–0471

Hotels and Motels

Throughout Canada, countless hotels and motels of all categories offer accommodation of a generally high standard. Although many of these are in private ownership, including fine old establishments and delightful country guest houses, most hotels belong to large chains (such as Canadian Pacific, Best Western, Hilton, Holiday Inn, Hyatt, Meridien, Novotel, Westin, York Hanover, TraveLodge, Trust House Forte, Ramada and Sheraton) for which reservations can be made from Europe in advance.

Categories   Some chains, e.g. Canadian Pacific, Four Seasons, Hilton International or Westin Hotels, have very luxuriously appointed rooms, and all the larger establishments have bars, restaurants and coffee shops. In some cases the services offered include laundry, hairdressing and newspaper kiosks. Resort hotels with spacious buildings, first-class sports facilities and a high degree of comfort are quite expensive, but Canada has two inexpensive hotel chains, Journey's End and Relax Inn, and other attractive, clean and inexpensive accommodation can be found throughout the country. Carborne tourists are best accommodated in the better-class motels, usually found along the main highways. During the summer the large universities and colleges provide overnight accommodation for visitors at reasonable prices, and farms and ranches offer inexpensive bed and breakfast accommodation in informal surroundings.

The following list, intended only as a guide, refers to the cost per night of a double room (Autumn 1994):
Luxury hotel: minimum of 250 Can.$
High amenity hotel: 200–400 Can.$
Good quality hotel: 100–200 Can.$
Reasonably priced hotel: 80–180 Can.$
Very reasonably priced accommodation (principally motels and guest houses): from 30 Can.$

Prices

In the big cities it is best to make a hotel reservation even out of season, since some cities have convention centres, and when a big convention is taking place the hotels are usually full. Accommodation in farms and hotels near popular holidays areas should be booked as early as possible, as less overnight accommodation is available here than in the cities, although a last-minute cancellation can mean a room becoming available at short notice.

Reservations

Almost all provinces levy sales taxes on hotels, motels and restaurants. In Alberta the hotel "room tax" is currently 5%.

Taxes

B = beach; CC = convention centre; Disco. = discothèque; F = fishing; G = golf; H = hunting; r. = rooms; R = riding; Rest. = restaurant; S = sailing; Sh. = shop; Sk. = skiing; SP = swimming pool; T = tennis; u. = units; WS = watersports

Abbreviations

Alberta

Athabasca Inn, 5211 42nd Ave, 65 r., Rest.; tel. (403) 675–2294
Athabasca Lodge Motel, Hwy. 2, 22 r., SP; tel. (403) 675–2967

Athabasca

Banff Park Lodge, 222 Lynx St., 210 r., Rest., SP; tel. (403) 762–4433
★ Banff Springs Hotel, 850 r., 68 suites, G, R, Rest., Sk., SP, T; tel. (403) 762–2211
Cascade Inn; tel. (403) 762–3311
Homestead Inn, 217 Lynx St., 27 r.; tel. (403) 762–4471
Mount Royal, 138 Banff Ave., 97 r., Rest.; tel. (403) 762–3331
Rundle Ridge Chalets, 1km/½ mile east of Banff Park entrances, 37 chalets; tel. (403) 678–5387
Swiss Village, 600 Banff Ave., 47 r.; tel. (403) 762–4581

Banff

Lakelander Motor Hotel, Rest.; tel. (403) 826–3309

Bonnyville

Heritage Inn, 2nd St., 64 r., Rest.; tel. (403) 362–6666

Brooks

Bow Ridge, 8220 Bow Ridge Crescent NW, SP; tel (403) 288–4441
Calgary Centre Inn, 202 4th Ave.SW, Rest., SP; tel (403) 262–7091
Crossroads Motor Hotel, 2120 16th Ave. NE, 242 r.; tel. (403) 291–4666
Highlander Motor Hotel, 1818 16th Ave. NW, Rest.; tel. (403) 289–1961
★ The Palliser, 133 9th Ave. SW, 406 r., 20 suites, Rest.; tel. (403) 262–1234
Relax Inn-South, 9206 Macleod Tr. S, 270 r.; tel. (403) 253–7070
Skyline, 9th Ave./Centre St. SE, 387 r., Rest., SP; tel. (403) 266–7331
Stampeder Inn, 3828 Macleod Tr., 150 r., Rest.; tel. (403) 243–5531
Sun Bow Inn, 2359 Banff Trail NW, Rest., SP; tel (403) 289–1973
Westin Hotel Calgary, 4th Ave./Third St. SW, 525 r., Rest., Sh., SP; tel. (403) 266–1611

Calgary

Crystal Springs Motor Hotel, 3911 48th Ave., 68 u.; tel. (403) 672–7741

Camrose

Cee-Der Chalets, Harvie Heights, 1.5km/1 mile east of the Banff Park entrances; tel. (403) 678–5251
Rocky Mountain Chalets, Hyw. 1 A, 37 u.; tel. (403) 678–5564

Canmore

Hotels and Motels

Cardston	Flamingo Motel, 848 Main St. S, 20 u.; tel. (403) 653–3952
Claresholm	Sportsman, 42 r.; tel. (403) 625–3347
Drumheller	Drumheller Inn, 100 Railway Ave. SE, 100 r., Rest., SP; tel. (403) 823–8400
Edmonton	Agryll Plaza Hotel, 9933 63rd Ave., 48 r.; tel. (403) 438–5856 Chateau Lacombe, 101st St.; tel. (403) 428–6611 Coast Terrace Inn, 4440 Calgary Tr., 228 r., Rest., SP; tel. (403) 437–6010 Fantasyland, 87th Ave./170th St., 360 r., Rest.; tel. (403) 444–3000 Four Seasons, 10235 101st St., 314 r., Rest., SP; tel. (403) 428–7111 Kingsway Inn, 10812 Kingsway Ave., 70 r., Sh., Rest.; tel. (403) 479–4266 Relax Inn, 10320 45th Ave., 227 r., SP.; tel. (403) 436–9770 Relax Inn, 18320 Stony Plain Rd., 227 r., SP, tel (403) 483–6031 Rennford Inn at Fifth, 104th St./100th Ave., 107 r., Rest., SP; tel (403) 423–5611 Westin-Hotel, 10135 100th St., 416 r., Rest., SP; tel. (403) 426–3636
Fort Macleod	Sunset Motel, Hwy. 3, on the western approach to the town, 30 r.; tel. (403) 553–4448
Grande Prairie	Alpine, 10901 100th Ave., 62 r., SP; tel. (403) 532–1680 Grande Prairie Inn, 11633 100th St., 212 r., Rest., SP; tel. (403) 532–5221
Hinton	Greentree Motor Lodge, 100 u., SP.; tel. (403) 865–3321
Jasper	Jasper Park Lodge, Jasper, 436 r., 59 suites, F, G, Rest., Sk., SP, T, WS; tel. (403) 852–3301 Lobstick Lodge, Geikie St., 138 r.; tel. (403) 852–4431 Pyramid Lake Bungalows, about 6km/4 miles north-west of Jasper, 10 bungalows, SP, WS.; tel. (403) 852–3536 Whistler's, opposite the station, 40 r., Rest.; tel. (403) 852–3361
Kananaskis Country	★The Lodge and Hotel at Kananaskis, Kananaskis Village, 324 r., 80 suites, G, R, Rest., Sk., SP, T; tel. (403) 591–7711 Mount Engadine Lodge, Smith-Dorrien Road, south of Canmore at Mount Shark junction; tel. (403) 678–4080
Lake Louise	★Château Lake Louise, Lake Louise, 515 r., 66 suites, G, R., Rest., Sk., SP, WS; tel. (403) 522–3511 Deer Lodge, 74 r., Rest.; tel. (403) 522–3747 Lake Louise Inn, 186 u., Rest., SP, T; tel. (403) 522–3791 Paradise Lodge and Bungalows, about 1km/½ mile from Lake Louise, 21 cabins; tel. (403) 522–3595
Lethbridge	Lethbridge Lodge Hotel, 320 Scenic Dr., 190 r., Rest., SP; tel. (403) 328–1123 Lodge Motel, Mayor Magrath Dr./7th Ave., 94 r., Rest., SP; tel. (403) 329–0100 Park Plaza Hotel, 1009 Mayor Magrath Dr., 68 r., Rest.; tel. (403) 328–2366 Sandman Inn, 421 Mayor Magrath Dr., 138 r., Rest., SP; tel. (403) 328–1111 Sundance Inn, 1030 Mayor Magrath Dr., 54 r., SP; tel. (403) 328–6636
Medicine Hat	Imperial, 3282 13th Ave. S E, 103 r., SP; tel (403) 527–8811 TraveLodge, 1100 Redcliff Dr. S W, 92 r., Rest., SP; tel. (403) 527–2275
Peace River	Crescent Motel, 9810 98th St., 95 r.; tel. (403) 624–2584 Traveller's, 9510 100th St., 100 r., Rest.; tel. (403) 624–3621
Pincher Creek	Foothills Motel, 1049 Waterton Ave., 30 r., Rest.; tel. (403) 627–3341

Ponoka Stampeder Inn, 58 u.; tel. (403) 783–3804 — Ponoka

Black Knight Inn, 2929 Gaetz Ave., 100 r., Rest., SP; tel. (403) 343–6666 — Red Deer
Red Deer Lodge, 4311 49th Ave., 240 r., Rest., SP; tel. (403) 346–8841

Nash's Cabins, about 5km/3 miles north of Slave Lake, 3 cabins, B; tel. (403) 849–3977 — Slave Lake
Sawridge Motor Hotel, 183 r., Sh., Rest.; tel. (403) 849–4101

Bayshore Inn, 111 Waterton Ave., 70 r., Rest.; tel. (403) 859–2211 — Waterton
Kilmorey, 117 Evergreen Ave., 26 r., Rest.; tel. (403) 859–2334
Prince of Wales Hotel, 82 r., Rest.; tel. (403) 859–2231

British Columbia

Sundance Guest Ranch, 8km/5 miles south of the TransCanada Hwy., R, SP, T; tel. (604) 453–2554 — Ashcroft

Austrian Chalet Village, 462 South Island Hwy, SP; tel. (604) 923–4231 — Campbell River
Painter's Lodge, Rest., SP; tel. (604) 286–1104

Peace Villa Motel, Mile Point Zero, 1641 Alaska Ave.; tel. (604) 782–8175 — Dawson Creek

Fort Nelson, Rest., Sh.; tel. (604) 774–6971 — Fort Nelson

Alexander MacKenzie Inn, 9223 100th St.; tel. (604) 785–8364 — Fort St John

Coast Canadian Inn, 339 St Paul St., Rest., SP; tel. (604) 372–5201 — Kamloops
David Thompson Motor Inn, 650 Victoria St., SP; tel. (604) 372–5282
Four Seasons Motel, 1767 Hwy. 1, SP; tel. (604) 372–2313

Kelowna TraveLodge, 1780 Gordon Dr., SP; tel. (604) 762–3221 — Kelowna
Lake Okanagan Resort, 2751 Westside Rd., G, R, S, SP, T, WS; tel. (604) 769–3511

Radium Hot Springs Lodge, G., Rest.; tel. (604) 347–9622 — Kootenay National Park
Blakley's Bungalows; tel. (604) 347–9918

Yellowpoint Lodge, Rest., SP; tel. (604) 245–7422 — Ladysmith

Alexander MacKenzie, Rest., Sh.; tel. (604) 997–3266 — Mackenzie
Powder King Ski Village, 55 r., Rest.; tel. (604) 561–1776

Flying U Guest Ranch, R.; tel. (604) 456–7717 — 70 Mile House

108 Golf and Tennis Resort, 61 r., G, R, T; tel. (604) 791–5211 — 100 Mile House

Coast Bastion Inn, 11 Bastion St., Rest.; tel (604) 753–6601 — Nanaimo

Sandy Beach Lodge, on Okanagan Lake, SP, T; tel. (604) 496–5765 — Naramata

Bayside Inn, Rest., SP, T; tel. (604) 248–8333 — Parksville
Vancouver Island Parksville Motel, 414 W Island Hwy.; tel. (604) 248–2072

Delta Lakeside, 21 Lakeshore Dr., 200 r., Rest., SP, T, WS; tel. (604) 493–8221 — Penticton

Hospitality Motor Inn, 3835 Redford St., F; tel. (604) 723–8111 — Port Alberni

Coast Inn of the North, 770 Brunswick St., Rest., SP; tel. (604) 563–0121 — Prince George

Hotels and Motels

	Sandman Inn, 1650 Central St., Rest., SP; tel. (604) 563–8131
	Yellowhead Inn, 1445 W Central St.; tel. (604) 562–3171
Prince Rupert	Drifter, 1080 W Third Ave., Rest.; tel. (604) 624–9161
	Prince Rupert, 2nd Ave./6th St., Rest.; tel. (604) 624–6711
Princeton	Riverside, on the Tulameen River; tel. (604) 295–6232
Quadra Island	Petersons April Point Lodge, S, Sh., WS; tel. (604) 285–2222
Qualicum Beach	Best Western College Inn, Rest., SP; tel. (604) 752–9262
Quilchena	Quilchena, G, R, Rest.; tel. (604) 378–2611
Revelstoke	Three Valley Gap Motor Inn; tel. (604) 837–2109
Smithers	Hudson Bay Lodge, 3521 Hwy. 16 E; tel. (604) 847–4581
Terrace	Inn of the West, 4620 Lakelse Ave.; tel. (604) 635–9151
	Sandman Inn, 4828 Hwy. 16 W, Rest., SP; tel. (604) 635–9151
Vernon	Vernon Lodge, 3914 32nd St., Disco., SP; tel. (604) 545–3385

Vancouver
Blue Boy Motor Hotel, 725 S E Marine; tel. (604) 321–6611
Coast Georgian Court, 773 Beatty St., 180 r., Rest.; tel. (604) 682–5555
Delta's Airport Inn Resort, 10254 St. Edward's Dr., Richmond, SP, T; tel. (604) 278–9611
Delta Place, 645 Howe St., Rest.; tel. (604) 687–1122
Four Seasons, 791 W Georgia St., 430 r., Rest.; tel. (604) 689–9333
Georgia, 801 W George St., Rest.; tel. (604) 682–5566
Granville Island, 1253 Johnston St., 54 r., Rest.; tel. (604) 683–7373
Hyatt Regency, 655 Burrard St., CC, Rest.; tel. (604) 687–6543
Lloyd, 1348 Robson St., 80 r., Rest.; tel. (604) 588–8850
Méridien, 845 Burrard St., 408 r., SP; tel (604) 682–5511
New World-Harbourside, 1133 W Hastings St., Rest.; tel. (604) 689–9211
Pagebrook, 1234 Hornby St., 202 r.; tel. (604) 688–1234
Ramada Renaissance, 1733 Comox St., Sh., Rest.; tel. (604) 688–7711
Royal Garden, 1110 Howe St., 210 r., Rest., SP; tel. (604) 684–2151
Sylvia, 1154 Gilford St., Rest.; tel. (604) 681–9321
★Vancouver, 900 W Georgia St., 508 r., 42 suites, Rest. SP; tel. (604) 684–3131
★Waterfront Centre, 900 Canada Place Way, 489 r., 29 suites, CC, Rest., SP; tel. (604) 691–1991
Wedgewood, 845 Hornby St., 93 r.; tel. (604) 689–7777
Westin Bayshore Inn, 1601 W Georgia St., Sh., Rest., SP; tel. (604) 682–3377

Victoria
Château Victoria, 740 Burdett Ave., 181 r., SP; tel. (403) 382–4221
★The Empress, 721 Government St., 481 r., 41 suites, CC, Rest., SP; tel. (604) 384 8111
Laurel Point Inn, 680 Montréal St., Rest., SP, T; tel. (604) 386–8721
Oak Bay Beach, 1175 Beach Dr.; tel. (604) 598–4556
Olde England Inn, 429 Lampson St.; tel. (604) 388–4353

Whistler
★Chateau Whistler Resort, 4599 Chateau Blvd., 343 r., 24 suites, G, Rest., Sk., SP; tel. (604) 938–8000

Yoho National Park
Emerald Lake Lodge, 8km/5 miles north of Hwy. 1, Rest.; tel. (604) 343–6231

Manitoba

Brandon
Redwood TraveLodge, 345 18th St., 60 r.; tel. (204) 728–2200
Royal Oak Inn, 3130 Victoria Ave., 100 r., Rest., SP; tel. (204) 728–2200
Victoria Inn, 3550 Victoria Ave., Rest., Sh., SP; tel. (204) 725–1532

Seaport, Munck St./Kelsey Blvd., 21 r., Rest.; tel. (204) 675–8807	Churchill
Carpenter's Clearwater Lodge; tel. (204) 624–5467 New Vickery Lodge, WS; tel. (204) 624–5429	Clearwater Lake Provincial Park
Kelsey Trail Motor Inn, 76 u., Rest., SP.; tel. (204) 687–7555	Flin Flon
Shoreliner, 39 First Ave., 18 u.; tel. (204) 642–5992	Gimli
Hiwin Glen Farm, on Hwy 2, 4km/2½ miles west of the Hwy 5 intersection, SP; tel. (204) 827–2891	Glenboro
Gull Harbour Resort Hotel, 93 r., G, Sk, SP; tel. (0800) 442–0497	Hecla Provincial Park
Lundar, Route 6, 23 r.; tel. (204) 762–5855	Lundar
Valley View Farm, R.; tel. (204) 822–3731	Morden
Wescana Inn, 459 Fischer Ave., 80 u., Rest.; tel (204) 623–5446	The Pas
Chesley's, 7 u.; tel (204) 738–2250	Petersfield
Best Western Manitoba Inn, Hwy. 1/Yellowquill Tr., SP; tel (204) 857–9791 Westgate Inn Motel, 1010 Saskatchewan Ave.; tel. (204) 239–5200	Portage La Prairie
Inverness Fall Resort, Bereron Lake, 10 cabins, Sh., WS; tel. (204) 369–5336	Rennie
Elkhorn Ranch Resort, Mooswa Dr., Wasagaming, 52 u., R, Rest., SP; tel. (204) 848–2802 Frelo Farm, Angusville, about 1km/½mile from the park; tel. (204) 773–2956 Thunderbird Bungalows, near Clear Lake, 22 cabins, SP	Riding Mountain National Park
Frantz Motor Inn, Hwy. 52 E, 20 r., Rest.; tel. (204) 326–9831	Steinbach
Falcon Lake, Falcon Lake, 35 u.; tel. (204) 349–8400 Tallpine Lodge, 15 u., Rest., SP; tel. (204) 349–2209	Whiteshell Provincial Park
Birchwood Inn, 2520 Portage Ave., 200 r., Rest., SP; tel. (204) 885–4478 Delta Winnipeg, 288 Portage Ave., 272 r., Rest., SP; tel. (204) 956–0410 Grant Motor Inn, 635 Pembina Hwy., 65 r., Rest.; tel (204) 453–8247 Holiday Inn, Downtown, St Mary's Ave., CC, Rest., SP; tel. (204) 942–0551 Journey's End, Pembina Hwy., on Perimeter Hwy.; tel. (800) 268–0405 Marlborough Inn, 331 Smith St., CC, Rest.; tel. (204) 942–6411 Relax Plaza, 360 Colony St., 160 r., SP; tel. (204) 786–7011 Sheraton Winnipeg, 161 Donald St., 286 r., Rest., SP; tel. (204) 325–3535 TraveLodge, 20 Alpine, St. Vital; tel. (204) 255–6000 Viscount Gort Flag Inn, 1670 Portage Ave., Rest; tel. (204) 775–0451 Westin, 2 Lombard Pl., Rest., SP; tel. (204) 957–1350	Winnipeg

New Brunswick

Atlantic Host, Route 11, 106 u., Sh., Rest., SP; tel. (506) 548–3335 Fundy Line, 855 St. Anne St., 52 u., Rest.; tel. (506) 548–8805 Kent, 150 Main St., 5km/3 miles north of the city on Route 134, Rest.; tel. (506) 546–3345	Bathurst
Bouctouche Bay Inn, Route 11, 18 r., Rest.; tel. (506) 743–2726	Bouctouche
Motel du Village, Rte. 11, near the Acadian Village, 20 u., Rest.; tel. (506) 727–4447 Paulin, 143 St. Pierre Blvd., 12 r., Rest.; tel. (506) 727–9981	Caraquet

Hotels and Motels

Chatham	Morada, 64 King St., 28 r.; tel. (506) 773–4491
Doaktown	Inn by the Pond, 5 r.; tel. (506) 365–7942
Edmundston	Le Brayon, Ste. Basile, Rue de Rocher, 25 u.; tel. (506) 263–5514 Lynn, 30 Church St., 49 r.; tel. (506) 735–8851
Fredericton	City, 1216 Regent St., 56 r., Rest., SP; tel. (506) 455–9900 Condor Motel, Woodstock Rd. W, Rest., SP; tel. (506) 455–5537 Happy Apple Acres Bed and Breakfast, R.R. 4, 5 r.; tel. (506) 472–1819 Lord Beaverbrook, 659 Queen St., Rest., SP; tel. (506) 455–3371
Fundy National Park	Caledonia Highlands Inn and Chalets, 44 u.; tel. (506) 887–2930 Fundy Park Chalets, 29 u., Rest., SP; tel. (506) 887–2808
Grand Falls	Près du Lac, TransCanada Hwy., 96 u., Rest., SP; tel. (506) 473–1300
Grand Manan	Compass Rose, North Head, 9 r.; tel. (506) 662–8570 Marathon Inn, North Head, 55 r., SP, T; tel. (506) 662–8144
Moncton	Auberge Wandlyn Motor Inn, Magnetic Hill R.R. 8, Rest., SP; tel. (506) 384–3554 Beausejour, 750 Main St., 314 r., 15 suites, Rest., SP; tel. (506) 854–4344 Canadiana, 46 Archibald St., 73 r.; tel. (506) 382–1054
Newcastle	Governor's Mansion, Nelson-Miramichi, 21 u.; tel. (506) 622–3036 Wharf Inn, Jane St., 53 u., SP; tel. (506) 622–0302
Rothesay	Shadow Lawn Inn, Rte. 100, Rest.; tel. (506) 847–7539
Sackville	Different Drummer, 146 Main St., 6 r.; tel. (506) 536–1291 Marshlands Inn, 73 Bridge St., 20 r., Rest.; tel. (506) 536–0170
St Andrews by-the-sea	★Algonquin, on Passamaquoddy Bay, 250 r., 18 suites, F, G, Rest., SP, T, WS; tel. (506) 529–4194 Pansy Patch, 56 Carleton St., tel. (506) 529–3834 Rossmount Inn, R.R.2, Rest., SP; tel. (506) 529–3351
Saint John	Delta Brunswick, 39 King St., CC, Rest., SP; tel. (506) 648–1981 Hilton International, Market Sq., CC, Rest.; tel. (506) 693–8484 Park Plaza, 607 Rothesay Ave., Rest.; tel. (506) 633–4100 The Trellis Bed and Breakfast, 4247 Manawagonish Rd., 2 r.; tel. (506) 696–5397
St Martins	Quaco Inn, Rest.; tel. (506) 833–4772
St Stephen	Haun's Holiday Farm, Route 740; tel. (506) 466–4938 Wandlyn, 90 King St., 59 r., Rest.; tel. (506) 466–1814
Sussex	Maples, 1019 Main St., 22 r.; tel. (506) 433–1558
Woodstock	Wandlyn, on Route 95, Rest.; tel. (506) 328–8876 Atlantic Inns Ltd., R.R.6, 27 u., Rest.; tel. (506) 328–6688

Newfoundland

Calvert	Sullivan's, near Ferryland, 2km/1 mile from Route 10; tel. (709) 432–2474
Churchill Falls (Labrador)	Lobstick Lodge and Motel, F., Rest.; tel. (709) 925–3235
Corner Brook	Bridge Way Motel, Riverside Dr., SP; tel. (709) 634–4378 Glynmill Inn, 1 Cobb La., 92 r., Rest.; tel. (709) 634–5181 Jones Hospitality Home, 11 Noseworthy Rd., 2 r.; tel. (709) 785–7461

Deer Lake Motel, Rest.; tel. (709) 635–2108	Deer Lake
Airport Inn, 74 u.; tel. (709) 256–3235 Albatross Motel, Rte.1, 111 r., Rest.; tel. (709) 256–3956	Gander
Labrador Inn, 74 u., Rest.; tel. (709) 896–3351	Goose Bay (Labrador)
Granny's Motor Inn, 10 r., Rest.; tel. (709) 832–2180	Grand Bank
Mount Peyton Hotel/Motel, Rte.1, 214 Lincoln Rd., 150 r., Rest.; tel. (709) 489–2251 Town and Country Inn, 6 Church Rd., 9 r.; tel. (709) 489–9602	Grand Falls
Parsons Hospitality Home and Harbour View Cabins, Rocky Harbour, 8 u.; tel. (709) 458–2544	Gros Morne National Park
Carol Lodge, 214 Drake Ave., 24 u.; tel. (709) 944–3661	Labrador City
Golden Sands, near Rte. 222, 18 u. and 86 caravan spaces; tel. (709) 891–2400	Lewin's Cove
Atsanik Lodge, Rest., F; tel. (709) 922–2910	Nain (Labrador)
Harold, Rte.91, 23 r.; tel. (709) 227–2107	Placentia
Port aux Basques, Grand Bay Rd./TransCanada Hwy., 50 r., Rest; tel. (709) 695–2171	Port aux Basques
St Anthony Motel, Rest; tel. (709) 454–3200 Viking, Rtes. 430/437, 22km/13½ miles from the town, 11 r., Rest.; tel. (709) 454–3541	St Anthony
Battery, 100 Signal Hill, 155 r., Rest., SP.; tel. (709) 726–9143 ★ Newfoundland, Cavendish Sq., 302 r., 19 suites, Rest., SP.; tel. (709) 726–4980 Parkview, 118 Military Rd., 18 r., Rest.; tel. (709) 753–2671 Radisson Plaza, 120 New Gower St., 276 r., Rest., SP; tel. (709) 739–6404	St John's
Robert, 54 r.	St Pierre
Pelley Inn, Little Bay Rd., 23 r.; tel. (709) 673–3931	Springdale
Hotel Stephenville, 213 Oregon Dr., 50 u., Rest.; tel. (709) 643–5176	Stephenville
Weston's Terra Nova National Park Chalets, Rte. 1, 24 u., G, Rest.; tel. (709) 533–2296	Terra Nova National Park
Governor's Park, about 1km/½mile from Salmonier Nature Park, Rte. 10, T, SP; tel. (709) 438–2934	Trepassey
Village Inn, Rte. 339, 8 r., Rest.; tel. (709) 464–3269	Trinity
Anchor Inn, Rte. 340, 18 u., Rest.; tel. (709) 884–2776	Twillingate

Northwest Territories

Great Bear Lake, on Great Bear Lake, 4 r., Rest., WS; tel. (403) 589–3705	Fort Franklin
Fort Simpson, Rest.; tel. (403) 695–2201 Maroda, 8 r., Sh.; tel. (403) 695–2602 Nahanni National Park, in Nahanni National Park; tel. (403) 695–3151	Fort Simpson

Hotels and Motels

Fort Smith	Pelican Rapids Inn, in the centre, 50 r.; tel. (403) 872–2789 Pinecrest, near Wood Buffalo National Park, 28 r., Rest.; tel. (403) 872–2104
Hay River	Back Eddy; tel. (403) 874–6680 Caribou Motor Inn, 29 r., Rest.; tel. (403) 874–3732 Cedar Rest, 31 r.; tel. (403) 874–3732 Harbour House, 6 r.; tel. (403) 874–2233 Hay River, in the old town, 22/38 r., Rest.; tel. (403) 874–6792 Migrator Motel, on the highway between the old and new towns, 24 r.; tel. (403) 874–6792 Ptarmigan Inn, in the centre, 41 r., Rest.; tel. (403) 874–6781
Inuvik	Eskimo Inn, 78 r. Rest.; tel. (403) 979–2801 Finto Motor Inn, between airport and city centre, 51 r.; tel. (403) 979–2647 Inuvik Inn, Marine Bypass/Mackenzie Rd., Sh., Rest.; tel. (403) 979–2631 Mackenzie, 33 r., Rest.; tel. (403) 979–2861
Iqualuit	Frobisher Inn, 50 r., Rest.; tel. (819) 979–5241
Norman Wells	Mackenzie Valley, 22 r., Sh., Rest.; tel. (403) 587–2511
Yellowknife	Discovery Inn, 41 r., CC, Rest.; tel. (403) 873–4151 Explorer, 110 r., Rest.; tel. (403) 873–3531 Northern Lites, near the centre, 20 r.; tel. (403) 873–6023 Twin Pine Motor Inn, Franklin Ave., 44 r.; tel. (403) 873–8511 Yellowknife Inn, Franklin Ave., 150 r., CC, Rest.; tel. (403) 873–2601

Nova Scotia

Antigonish	Best Western Claymore Church St., SP; tel. (902) 863–1050
Baddeck	Auberge Gisèle, Shore Rd., 65 u., Rest.; tel. (902) 295–2849 Inverary Inn, Shore Rd., 137 u., B., Rest.; tel. (902) 295–2674 Silver Dart Lodge, 88 u., Rest., SP; tel. (902) 295–2340
Bridgetown	Bridgetown, 83 Granville St.E, 33 u., Rest., SP; tel. (902) 665–4491
Bridgewater	Best Western Bridgewater, 35 High St., 50 u., SP; tel. (902) 543–8173 Wandlyn Inn, 50 North St., 75 u., Rest., Sh, SP; tel. (902) 543–0000
Chester	Big Oaks Inn B & B, on the Chester Basin, 5km/3 miles west of the city, 4 r.; tel. (902) 275–4542 Windjammer, Rte. 3, west of the city, 15 u.; tel. (902) 275–3567
Cheticamp	Park View, at the entrance to Cape Breton Highlands National Park, F, SP; tel. (902) 224–3232
Digby	Harbourview Inn, Smith's Cove, 23 u., T; tel. (902) 245–5686 Pines Resort Hotel, Shore Rd., 150 u., G, SP, T; tel. (902) 245–2511

Halifax	★Chateau Halifax, 1990 Barrington St., 300 r., 18 suites, Rest., SP;
	   tel. (902) 425–6700
	Chebucto Inn, 3151 Lady Hammond Rd., 32 r.; tel. (902) 453–4330
	Citadel Inn, 1960 Brunswick St., 270 r., Rest.; tel. (902) 422–1391
	Delta Barrington Inn, 1875 Barrington St., 200 r., Rest., SP;
	   tel. (902) 429–7410
	Halifax Hilton, 1181 Hollis St., 307 r., CC, Rest., SP; tel (902) 423–7231
	Halliburton House Inn, 5184 Morris St., 30 r., Rest.; tel. (902) 420–0658
	Holiday Inn, 1980 Robie St., 232 r., Rest., SP; tel. (902) 423–1161

Lord Nelson, 1515 St. Park St., 320 r.; tel. (902) 423–6331
Nova Scotian, 1181 Hollis St., 316 r.; tel. (902) 423–7231
Prince George, 1725 Market St., over 200 r., Rest., SP; tel. (902) 425–1986
Sheraton Halifax, 1919 Upper Water St., about 350 r., Rest.;
 tel. (902) 421–1700
Waken's Eggs Bed and Breakfast, 2114 Windsor St.; tel. (902) 422–4737

Anchorage House and Cabins, 6612 Shore Club Rd., 12 u., F, WS;   Hubbards
 tel. (902) 857–9402

Glenghorm, Ingonish, B, SP; tel. (902) 285–2604   Ingonish and
Keltic Lodge, Herman Falls, Ingonish Beach, G, T; tel. (902) 285–2880 Ingonish Beach

Inverness Beach Village, about ½km/¼ mile north of the town on Route 19, Inverness
 40 u.; tel. (902) 258–2653

Liscombe Lodge, Hwy. 7/Marine Dr., 35 u., F, T, WS; tel. (902) 779–2307   Liscomb Mills

Hopkins House, 120 Main St., 3 r.; tel. (902) 354–5484   Liverpool
Lanes Privatier, at the east end of the Liverpool Bridge, 28 r., Rest.;
 tel. (902) 354–3456

Fleur-de-Lis, Main St., 46 u.; tel. (902) 733–2844   Louisbourg

Bluenose Lodge, Falkland Ave. & Dufferin St., 9 r., Rest.; tel. (800) 565–8851   Lunenburg

Margaree Lodge, Route 19/Cabot Tr., 46 u., F, Rest., SP; tel. (902) 248–2193   Margaree Forks

Normaway Inn & Cabins, Egypt Rd. (3km/2 miles off the Cabot trail), 19 u.,   Margaree Valley
 9 r., F, Rest., R; tel. (902) 248–2987

Pictou Lodge, Braeshore Rd., 29 u., B, Rest., SP, WS; tel. (902) 485–4322   Pictou
The Walker Inn, 34 Coleraine St., 10 r.; tel. (902) 485–1433

Beachside, 20 u., F; tel. (902) 224–2467   Pleasant Bay

Auberge Wandlyn Inn, Reeves St., SP; tel. (902) 625–0320   Port Hawkesbury

Ox Bow Village, on Lake George, 50 r., SP; tel. (902) 875–3000   Shelburne

Milford House, Annapolis Royal, in the Kejimkujik National Park;   South Milford
 tel. (902) 532–2617

Best Western Glengarry, 138 Willow St., 115 u., SP; tel. (902) 893–4311   Truro
Howard Johnson's, 165 Willow St., 40 r., Rest.; tel. (902) 893–9413
Palliser, Rte. 102, 42 u., Rest; tel. (902) 893–8951

Best Western Oak Island Inn, 74 u, F, Rest., WS; tel. (902) 627–2600   Western Shore

White Point Beach Lodge Resort, 47 r., 43 chalets, B, CC, G, Rest., R, Sh., SP,   White Point
 WS; tel. (902) 542–5751

Old Orchard Inn, 140 u., Rest., SP, T; tel. (902) 542–5751   Wolfville

Gateway Farms B & B, Chegoggin Rd., 3 r.; tel. (902) 742–9786   Yarmouth
Rodd's Colony Harbour Inn, by the ferry, Rest.; tel. (902) 742–9194
Rodd's Grand Hotel, 417 Main St., 138 r., Rest; tel. (902) 742–2446

Ontario

Arowhon Pine, Huntsville, B, WS; tel. (705) 633–5661   Algonquin Park

Blue Haven, 680 Front Rd., 16 u., B, F; tel. (519) 736–5404   Amherstburg
Duffy's, 296 Dalhousie St., 17 r., Rest., SP. WS; tel. (519) 736–2101

Hotels and Motels

Aylmer	Aylmer, 300 Talbot St. W, 17 r.; tel. (519) 773–3262
Barrie	Continental, at the Dunlop St. intersection, 124 r., SP, T Journey's End, Exit Hwy. 400 on Dunlop St. at Hart Drive, 60 r.; tel. (705) 722–3600
Blenheim	Queens, about 5km/3 miles west of the town on Hwy. 3, 17 r.; tel. (519) 676–5477
Bracebridge	Aston Villa, on Route 118, 67 r., B, G, SP, T; tel. (705) 764–1111 Bangor Lodge, Golden Beach Rd., 101 u., G, SP, T; tel. (705) 645–4791
Cochrane	Northern Lites, Hwy. 11, 41 r., Rest.; tel. (705) 272–4281 Westway, 21 First St., 42 u.; tel. (705) 272–4285
Gananoque	Gananoque Inn, 550 Stone St., 34 u.; tel. (613) 382–2165 1000 Island, 550 King St., 38 r., SP; tel. (613) 382–3911
Geraldton	Park Bay View, Rte. 11, 20 r., B, Rest.; tel. (807) 854–1716 Wild Goose Lake Resort, Rte. 11, 12 cabins, F, WS; tel. (807) 854–0482
Gravenhurst	Pine Dale, Pinedale Rd., 22 u., B, F, WS; tel. (705) 687–2822
Huntsville	Deerhurst Inn, Muskoka Rd., 136 u., SP; tel. (705) 789–5543 ★ Deerhurst Resort, 370 u., F, G, R, Rest., SP; tel. (705) 789–6411 Hidden Valley, Hidden Valley Rd., 100 r. B, F, Sk., SP, WS; tel. (705) 789–2301

Ivy Lea	Caiger's, Thousand Island Pkwy., 35 r., B, F, Rest., SP;
	  tel. (613) 659–2266
	Ivy Lea Inn, 1.6km/1 mile west of Thousand Island Pkwy., 31 u., F, SP, T;
	  tel. (613) 659–2329

Kapuskasing	Apollo, Rte. 11, 37 u., SP; tel. (705) 335–6084 Two Bridges, Hwy. 11, 23 r.; tel. (705) 335–2281
Kingston	Beaver, Rte. 15, 22 r., SP; tel. (613) 546–6674 Confederation Place, 237 Ontario St., 101 r.; tel. (613) 549–6300 Highland, Rte. 14, near Fort Henry, 44 r., SP, T; tel. (613) 546–3121 The Prince George, 200 Ontario St., Rest.; tel. (613) 549–5440 Seven Oaks, 2331 Princess St., 40 u., F, SP; tel. (613) 546–3655
Kingsville	Adams Golden Acres, 1.5km/1 mile west of Route 18, 27 r.; tel. (519) 733–4496 Lakeshore Terrace, 84 Park St. E, 40 r.; tel. (519) 733–4651
Kirkland Lake	Commodore, 1 Duncan Ave. N, 27 r., T; tel. (705) 567–9386
Leamington	Pelee, south of the town on Rte. 33, 60 r., B, Rest, SP; tel. (519) 326–8646 Sun Parlor, 135 Talbot St. W, 17 u.; tel. (519) 326–2214 Wigle's, 133 Talbot St. E, 24 u., Rest.; tel. (519) 326–3265
London	Golden Pheasant, Hwy. 22, 1.6km/1 mile west of Route 4, 41 r., Rest., SP; tel. (519) 473–4551 Hyland, 750 Wharncliffe Rd. S, 33 r., SP; tel. (519) 473–4551 Rainbow, Southdale, 23 r., T, SP; tel. (519) 685–3772
Marathon	Peninsula, Rte. 17, 21 u.; tel. (807) 229–0651 Pic, Marathon Rd., 23 r., Rest.; tel. (807) 229–0130
Marten River	Land O'Lakes, Rte. 11, 13 cabins, B, F, Sh., SP; tel. (705) 892–2206

Ameri-Cana, 8444 Lundy's La., 110 r.; tel. (416) 356–8444   Niagara Falls
Brock, 5685 Falls Ave., 238 r., G, Rest., SP; tel. (800) 263–7135
Foxhead, 5875 Falls Ave., 400 r., Rest., SP; tel. (800) 263–7135
Michael's Inn, 5599 River Rd., 130 r., Rest., SP; tel. (416) 354–2727
Parkwood, 8054 Lundy's La., 32 r., SP; tel. (416) 354–3162

Angel Inn, Queen St., 12 r.; tel. (416) 468–3411   Niagara-on-the-
Oban Inn, 160 Front St., 23 r., CC; tel. (416) 468–7811   Lake
Pillar and Post, King St./John St., 90 r., Rest., Sh., SP;
    tel. (416) 468–2123
Prince of Wales, 6 Picton St., 104 r., Rest.; tel. (416) 468–3246

Chalet Lodge, Hwy. 17, 19 u., F, H, Rest.; tel. (807) 887–3030   Nipigon

Ascot, 255 McIntyre St. W, 31 r.; tel. (705) 474–4770   North Bay
Ramada Inn, 700 Lakeshore Dr., 130 r., Rest., SP.; tel. (705) 474–5800
Sunset Park, 641 Lakeshore Dr., B; tel. (705) 647–8370

Fern, Rama Rd., 104 u., CC, F, Sk., SP; tel. (705) 325–2256   Orilla
Friendship's Knight's Inn, 265 Memorial Ave., 40 r.; tel. (705) 326–3554
Sundial, 600 Sundial Dr., 94 r., SP, T; tel. (705) 325–2233

Beacon Arms, 88 Albert St., 158 r.; tel. (613) 235–1413   Ottawa
Best Western Macies Ottawan Motor Inn, 1274 Carling Ave., 105 r., SP;
    tel. (613) 728–1951
Cartier Place, 180 Cooper St., 132 app.; tel. (613) 236–5000
★ Château Laurier, 1 Rideau St., 450 r., 40 suites, Rest., Sh., SP;
    tel. (613) 232–6411
Four Seasons, 150 Albert St., 236 r., Rest., SP; tel. (613) 238–1500
Radisson, 100 Kent, 504 r., Rest., Sh., SP; tel. (613) 238–1122
Roxborough, 123 Metcalfe St., 150 r., Rest.; tel. (613) 237–5171
Skyline, 101 Lyon St., 450 r., Rest., SP; tel. (613) 273–3600
Talisman, 1376 Carling Ave., 300 r., Rest., SP; tel. (613) 722–7601
Westin, 11 Colonel By Dr., 475 r., Rest., SP, T; tel. (613) 560–7000

Anchor and Wheel, in the north-west of the island, 11 u., F, G, WS;   Pelee Island
    tel. (519) 724–2195
Brown's Beach, East Side Rd., WS; tel. (519) 724–2094
Pelee Island, West Dock, B, F; Rest.; tel. (519) 724–2912

Fireside Inn, 35 Bridge St., 30 r., SP; tel. (613) 476–2156   Picton
Isaiah Tubbs Inn, West Lake Rd., SP; tel. (613) 393–5694

Beacon Flag Inn, Beacon Blvd., B, SP; tel. (416) 562–4155   St Catherines
Highwayman, 420 Ontario St., 50 r., SP; tel. (416) 688–1646
Parkway Inn, 327 Ontario St., 125 r., Rest., SP; tel. (416) 688–2324

Cardinal Court, Hyw. 4, 15 r.; tel. (519) 633–0740   St Thomas
Sleepy Time, Hyw. 4, 11 r.; tel. (519) 633–0471

Empire, 320 Bay St., 120 r., SP; tel. (705) 759–8200   Sault Ste Marie
Holiday Inn, 208 St Mary's River Dr., 200 r., Rest., SP;
    tel. (705) 949–0611
Ramada Inn, 229 Great Northern Rd., 133 r.; tel. (705) 942–2500
Water Tower Inn, Rtes. 17 B/50, 150 r., Rest., Sk., SP; tel. (705) 949–8111

Circle Route, Rte. 17, 31 u., Rest.; tel. (807) 824–2452   Schreiber
Nor-West, Rte. 17, west of the town, 11 r.; tel. (807) 824–2501

Château Belmont, Regent/York intersection, 40 r., Rest.;   Sudbury
    tel. (705) 673–1131
Peter Piper Inn, 151 Larch St., 45 r., Rest.; tel. (705) 673–7801

Hotels and Motels

Terrace Bay
Imperial, Rte 17, 21 u., Rest.; tel. (807) 825–3226
Red Dog, Rte. 17, 39 r., Rest.; tel. (807) 825–3286

Thunder Bay
Airlane, 698 Arthur St. W, 170 r., Rest., SP; tel. (807) 577–1181
Landmark, Dawson Rd./Thunder Bay Expy., 103 r.; tel. (807) 767–1681
Ramada Inn Prince Arthur, 17 N Cumberland St., Rest.;
   tel. (807) 345–5411

Timmins
Best Western Colonial Inn, 1212 Riverside Dr., 28 r., Rest.;
   tel. (705) 264–1296
Ramada, 1800 Riverside Dr., 116 r., SP; tel. (705) 267–6241

Toronto
Bond Place, 65 Dundas St. E, 285 r.; tel. (416) 362–6061
Carlton Inn, 30 Carlton St., 536 r., Rest., SP; tel. (416) 977–6655
Delta Chelsea Inn, 33 Gerrard St. W, Rest., SP; tel. (416) 595–1975
Four Seasons, 21 Avenue Rd., 375 r., Rest., SP; tel. (416) 964–0411
Harbour Castle Westin, 1 Harbour Sq., 977 r., Rest., SP, T;
   tel. (416) 869–1600
Hilton International, 145 Richmond St. W, 601 r., Rest., SP;
   tel. (416) 869–3456
★L'Hotel, 225 Front St. W, 587 r., 29 suites, CC, Rest., SP, T;
   tel. (416) 597–1400
★Royal York, 100 Front St. W, 1408 r., 198 suites, CC, Rest., Sh., SP;
   tel. (416) 368–2511
Sheraton Centre, 123 Queen St. W, 1427 r., Rest., Sh., SP;
   tel. (416) 361–1000
Sky Dome Hotel, 45 Peter St. S, 346 r., 31 suites, Rest., SP;
   tel. (416) 360–7100
Toronto Airport Marriott, 901 Dixon Rd, 423 r., Rest., SP;
   tel. (416) 674–9400
Westbury, 475 Yonge St., 545 r., Rest.; tel. (416) 924–0611

Wawa
Camp High Falls, Hwy. 17, 3km/2 miles south of the town, 10 u.;
   tel. (705) 856–4496
Kinniwabi Pines, Route 17, 6km/4 miles south of the town, 15 u., F;
   tel. (705) 856–7302
Normandy, Rte. 17, 48km/29 miles north of Wawa, 14 u., F, Rest.;
   tel. (705) 856–2644
Wawa, 100 Mission Rd., 88 u., Rest., SP; tel. (705) 856–2278

White River
Continental, Rte. 17, 33 r.; tel. (807) 822–2500

Windsor
★Compri/Doubletree Club Hotel, 333 Riverside Dr. W, 207 r., Rest., SP;
   tel. (519) 977–9777
Hilton International, 277 Riverside Dr. W, 300 r., SP;
   tel. (519) 973–5555
Holiday Inn, 480 Riverside Dr. W, 251 r., Rest., SP; tel. (519) 253–4411
National Traveller, 675 Goyeau, 110 r., Rest.; tel. (519) 258–8411
Red Oak Inn, 430 Quelette Ave., 150 r., Rest., SP; tel. (519) 253–7281
Relax Plaza, 33 Riverside Dr. E, 150 r., SP; tel. (519) 258–7774

Prince Edward Island

Brackley Beach
Bayview Farm, Winsloe, R.R.1, 7 u.; tel. (902) 672–2328
Shaw's Hotel and Cottages, Rte. 15, near the National Park, 34 u., Rest;
   tel. (902) 675–2022

Cavendish
Shining Water, 10 r., SP; tel. (902) 963–2251

Charlottetown
Charlottetown, Kent St./Pownal St., Rest., SP; tel. (902) 565–0207
Court Bed & Breakfast, 68 Hutchinson Court, 2 u.; tel. (902) 894–5871

Duchess of Kent Inn, 218 Kent St.; tel. (902) 566–5826
Dundee Arms, 200 Pownal St., Rest.; tel. (902) 892–2496
Holiday Island, 307–309 University Ave., Rest.; tel. (902) 892–4141
Inn on the Hill, University St./Euston St., Rest; tel. (902) 894–7371
★Prince Edward, 18 Queen St., 211 r., 33 suites, G, Marina, R, Rest., Sh., SP;
  tel. (902) 566–2222

Dalvay-by-the-Sea, Rte. 6, in Dalvay Beach, Rest., T, WS;   Dalvay Beach
  tel. (902) 672–2048

Sea Breeze, Rte. 16, 16 u., Rest., F; tel. (902) 357–2371   Kingsboro

St. Lawrence Motel, Gulf Shore Rd., 15 u., F, G; tel. (902) 963–2053   North Rustico

Partridge's, Rte. 2, 7 r., WS; tel. (902) 838–4687   Panmure Island

Senator's House, Rte. 12, 2km/1 mile from Green Provincial Park, 8 r., Rest;   Port Hill
  tel. (902) 831–2071

Brudenell Resort, west of Georgetown, 50 chalets, G, SP, T;   Roseneath
  tel. (902) 652–2332, (902) 892–7448 (in winter)

Souris West Motel & Cottages, R.R.4, F, Rest.; tel. (902) 687–2676   Souris

McCrady's Shore Acres, Rte. 19, at Meadowbank, Rest.;   South Shore
  tel. (902) 566–2814

Cairn's Motel, 721 Water St. E; tel. (902) 436–2992   Summerside
Linkletter, 311 Market St., 82 r., Rest., F; tel. (902) 436–2157

Doctor's Inn, Rte. 167, 2 r.; tel. (902) 831–2164   Tyne Valley

Rodd's Mill River, by Rte. 2, G, Rest., SP, T; tel. (902) 859–3555   Woodstock

Québec

Cascades, 140 du Pont Nord Ave., Rest.; tel. (418) 662–6547   Alma
Dequen, 800 du Pont Nord Ave., Rest.; tel. (418) 662–6649

Caravelle, 202 Blvd. La Salle, Rest.; tel. (418) 296–4686   Baie Comeau
Le Manoir, 8 Rue Cabot, Rest.; tel. (418) 296–3391

Belle Plage, 192 Rue Ste-Anne, Rest.; tel. (418) 435–3321   Baie St Paul
Le Dery, 896 Blvd. Monseigneur de Laval, 27 r., SP; tel. (418) 435–5252
Maison Otis, 23 Rue St-Jean-Baptiste, 28 r., Rest.; tel. (418) 435–2255

Manoir Montmorency, 2490 Ave. Royale; tel. (418) 663–2877   Beauport

Auberge Le Château, 98 Port Royal Ave., Rest.; tel. (418) 534–3336   Bonaventure

Auberge Bromont, 95 Rue Montmorency, 55 r., Rest., SP;   Bromont
  tel. (514) 534–2378
Loft Acres, Rte. 139, near Bromont and Mont Sutton, Rest.;
  tel. (514) 263–3294
Menhir, near the Bromont skiing area, 20 r., CC, SP; tel. (514) 534–3790
La Petite Auberge, 360 Blvd. Pierre La Porte, 8 r.; tel. (514) 534–2707

Bellevue, 40 Rue Principale, 28 r., Rest.; tel. (418) 986–4477   Cap aux Meules
Château Madelinot, Rte. 199, 40 u.; tel. (418) 986–3695

Baie Bleue, 482 Blvd. Perron, 85 u., B, SP; tel. (418) 364–3355   Carleton
Shick Shock, 1746 Blvd. Perron, 25 u., Rest.; tel. (418) 364–3361

Hotels and Motels

Chandler	Fraser, Rte. 132, 40 u., Rest.; tel. (418) 689–2281
	St Laurent, 499 Réhel St., Rest.; tel. (418) 689–3355
Chicoutimi	Auberge des Gouverneurs, 1303 Blvd. Talbot, Rest., SP; tel. (418) 549–6244
	Chicoutimi, 460 Rue Racine, Rest.; tel. (418) 549–7111
	Universel, 250 Rue Des Sagueneens, 119 r., Rest., SP; tel. (418) 545–8326
Escoumins	Gagnon, 87 Rue Marcelinn, 14 r.; tel. (418) 233–2010
	Motel 138, Rte. 138, 25 u., Rest.; tel. (418) 233–2401
L'Esterel	L'Esterel, Blvd. Fridolin Simard, 135 r., CC, F, G, SP, T, WS; tel. (819) 228–2571
Forestville	L'An 2000, 164 Rue Principale, 20 u.; tel. (418) 587–4431
	Danube Bleu, Rte. 138, Rest.; tel. (418) 587–2278
Fort Prével	Auberge Fort Prével, Rte. 132, G, Rest.; tel. (418) 368–2281
Gaspé	Adams, 2 Rue Adams, 98 u., Rest; tel. (418) 368–2244
	Auberge des Commandants, 178 Rue de la Reine, 56 r.; tel. (418) 368–3355
Gatineau-la-Vérendrye	Auberge Le Domaine, Rte. 117; tel. (819) 435 2541
Granby	Bon Soir, 1587 Ave. Principale, 44 u., SP; tel. (514) 378 7947
	Le Castel de l'Estrie, 901 Ave. Principale, 125 u., Rest.; tel. (514) 378–9071
	Du Lac, 255 Rue Denison E, 36 u., Rest., Sk., SP; tel. (514) 372–5930
Grande Vallée	Frigault, Rte. 132, 21 u., Rest.; tel. (418) 393–2720
Havre aux Maisons	Des Îles, 29 r.; tel. (418) 969–2931
	Thériault, Dune de Sud, 20 u., Rest.; tel. (418) 969–2655
	Au Vieux Couvent, Rte. 199, 12 u., Rest.; tel. (418) 969–2233
Île aux Coudres	Auberge de la Roche Pleureuse, La Baleine, 238 Rue Principale, 90 r., Rest., SP, T; tel. (418) 438–2232
	Cap-aux-Pierres, 220 Rue Principale, 98 r., SP, T; tel. (418) 438–2711
	St. Bernard, 35 Rue Royale Ouest, 14 r., Rest.; tel. (418) 438–2261
Île d'Orléans	Auberge Le Chaumonot, 5129 Ave. Royale, St. François, 8 r., SP; tel. (418) 829–2735
Laurentides Park	Auberge l'Étape, Rte. 175, in the centre of the park, 21 r., Rest.; tel. (418) 846–2801
La Malbaie	Manoir Charlevoix, 1030 Rue St-Etienne, 42 r., Rest., SP, T; tel. (418) 665–4413
Matapédia	Restigouche, 3 Rue du Saumon, Rest.; tel. (418) 365–2155
Montebello	★ Chateau Montebello, 210 r., 22 suites, CC, G, Rest., R, Sk., SP; tel. (819) 423–6341
Mont Orford	Auberge Estrimont, 44 Ave. l'Auberge, 96 u., Rest., SP; tel. (819) 843–1616
	Auberge du Parc Orford, 42 u., Rest., Sh., SP; tel. (819) 843–8887
Mont-St-Pierre	Mont-St-Pierre, Rue Prudent Cloutier, Rest.; tel. (418) 297–2202

Auberge La Porte Rouge, in the centre; tel. (819) 425–3505   Mont-Tremblant
Cuttle's Tremblant Club, 32 r., F, G, R, Rest., S, Sk., T;
  tel. (819) 425–2734
Station Mont Tremblant, Sh., Sk.; tel. (819) 425–8711
Villa Bellevue, on Lac Ouimet, Rest., Sk., T, WS; tel. (819) 425–2734

Bonaventure-Hilton International, 1 Place Bonaventure, 395 r., CC, Rest.,   Montréal
  SP; tel. (514) 878–2332
Le Centre Sheraton, 1201 René Lévesque Ouest Blvd., 832 r., Rest., SP;
  tel. (514) 878–2000
★Château Champlain, 1 Place du Canada, 616 r., Sh., Sk., SP;
  tel. (514) 878–9000
Château Versailles, 1659 Sherbrooke Ouest, 70 r.; tel. (514) 933–3611
La Citadelle, 410 Sherbrooke Ouest, 182 r., SP; tel. (514) 844–8851
Delta, 450 Sherbrooke Ouest, 458 r., Rest., SP; tel. (514) 286–1986
Downtown Bed & Breakfast, 3458 Ave. Laval; tel. (514) 289–9749
Four Seasons (Quatre Saisons), 1050 Sherbrooke Ouest, 320 r., Rest., SP;
  tel. (514) 284–1110
Le Grand, 777 University, 768 r., Rest., SP; tel. (514) 879–1370
Holiday Inn, 420 Sherbrooke Ouest, 486 r., Rest., SP; tel. (514) 842–6111
De l'Institut, 3535 St Denis, 42 r.; tel. (514) 873–4163
Lord Berri, 1199 Berri St., 154 r., Rest.; tel. (514) 845–9236
De Luxe Shangrila, 3407 Peel St., 200 r.; tel. (514) 288–4141
Manoir LeMoyne, 2100 de Maisonneuve Blvd., 286 r., Rest., SP;
  tel. (514) 931–8861
Maritime Travelodge, 1155 Guy St., 214 r., SP; tel. (514) 932–1411
Méridien, 4 Place Desjardins, 604 r., SP.; tel. (514) 285–1450
De la Montagne, 1430 de la Montagne St., 130 r., Disco., Rest., SP;
  tel. (514) 288–5656
Du Parc, 3625 Av. du Parc, 465 r., Rest., SP; tel. (514) 288–6666
★Queen Elizabeth (Reine Elizabeth), 900 René Lévesque Blvd. W, 1040 r.,
  Rest., Sh.; tel. (514) 861–3511
Ramada Centreville, 1005 Rue Guy, 205 r., Rest., SP; tel. (514) 866–4611
★Ritz Carlton, 1228 Sherbrooke Ouest, 240 r., Rest.; tel. (514) 842–4212

Hatley Inn, Magog Hwy., 20 r., G, R, Rest., SP, WS; tel. (819) 842–2451   North Hatley
Le Manoir Hovey, Hovey Rd., 36 r., Rest., T, WS; tel. (819) 842–2412

Gîte du Mont Albert, Rte. 299, 21 u., Rest.;   Parc de La
  tel. (418) 763–2288   Gaspésie

Auberge du Gargantua, 222 Rte. des Falls, 11 u., Rest.;   Percé
  tel. (418) 782–2852
Bleu-Blanc-Rouge, Rte. 132, Rest.; tel. (418) 782–2142
Le Bonaventure sur Mer, Rte. 132, 124 u., Rest.; tel. (418) 782–2166
Manoir Percé, Rte. 132, 38 u., Rest.; tel. (418) 782–2022
Pic de l'Aurore, Rte. 132, 18 u., Rest.; tel. (418) 782–2166

Auberge au Petit Berger, 1 Côte Bellevue, 20 r.; tel. (418) 665–4428   Pointe-au-Pic
Manoir Richelieu, 181 Ave. Richelieu, 332 r., G, Rest., SP, T;
  tel. (418) 665–3703

Château, 30 Elie Rochefort St., Rest.; tel. (418) 766–3444   Port Cartier

Auberge des Gouverneurs, 690 Blvd. St-Cyrille, 361 r., Rest., SP;   Québec
  tel. (418) 647–1717
Auberge des Gouverneurs, Ste-Foy, 3030 Blvd. Laurier, 318 r., Rest., Sk.,
  SP; tel. (418) 651–3030
Auberge du Trésor, 20 Rue Ste-Anne, 21 r., Rest.; tel. (418) 694–1876
Auberge Ramada Inn, Ste-Foy, 1200 Rue LaVigerie, 100 r., Rest., SP;
  tel. (418) 651–2440
Bed and Breakfast in Old Quebec, 300 Rue Champlain; tel. (418) 525–9826

Hotels and Motels

Château Bonne Entente, Ste-Foy, 3400 Chemin Ste-Foy, 170 r., Sk., SP;
   tel. (418) 653–5221
Le Château de Pierre, 17 Ave. Ste Geneviève, 15 r.; tel. (418) 694–0429
★ Le Château Frontenac, 1 Rue des Carrières, 551 r., G, R, Rest., Sh., Sk., SP;
   tel. (418) 692–3861
Château Laurier, 695 Grande Allée Est, 55 r., Rest.; tel. (418) 522–8108
Clarendon, 57 Rue Ste-Anne, 93 r., Rest.; tel. (418) 692–2480
Fleurs de Lys, 115 Rue Ste-Anne; tel. (418) 694–4901
Hilton International, 3 Place Québec, 563 r., Rest., SP;
   tel. (418) 647–2411
Holiday Inn Ste-Foy, 3225 Hochelaga; tel. (418) 653–4901
Loews Le Concorde, 1225 Place Montcalm, 424 r., Rest., SP;
   tel. (418) 647–2222
Manoir Ste-Geneviève, 13 Ave. Ste-Geneviève, 9 r.; tel. (418) 647–9377
Mercure, 638 St Vallier W, 56 r.; tel. (418) 529–3787
Québec Hilton International, 3 Place Québec, 563 r., Rest., SP;
   tel. (418) 647–2411

Rimouski
Auberge des Gouverneurs, 155 René Lepage Blvd., 166 r., Rest.;
   tel. (418) 723–4422
Auberge Wandlyn Le Brasier, 130 Rue St. Barnabé, 63 r., Rest.;
   tel. (418) 724–6944
St Louis, 214 St Edmond St., 83 r., Rest.; tel. (418) 723–1170

Rivière du Loup
Auberge de la Pointe, Autoroute 20, Exit 507; tel. (418) 862–3514
Château Grandville, 94 Lafontaine St., Rest.; tel. (418) 862–3551
Lévesque, 171 Fraser St., Rest.; tel. (418) 862–6927
Universel, 311 Hôtel de Ville Blvd., 119 r., Rest.; tel. (418) 862–9520

St Jovite
Gray Rocks, G, Sk., SP, WS; tel. (819) 425–2771
Le St Jovite, 1011 Rue Ouimet, Rest.; tel. (819) 425–2751

Ste-Adèle
Altitude, Rte. 117, 55 u., Rest., Sk., SP; tel. (514) 229–6616
Auberge Bonne Nuit-Bonjour, 1980 Blvd. Ste-Adèle, 7 r.;
   tel. (514) 229–7500
Le Chantecler, Lac Rond, Chemin Du Chantecler, 224 r., B, G, R, Sk., SP, T;
   tel. (819) 229–3555

Ste-Agathe-des-Monts
Auberge du Lac des Sables, 230 St-Venant, 15 r., SP; tel. (819) 326–7016
Raymond, 30 Blvd. Morin, 37 u., SP; tel. (819) 326–3626

Ste-Anne de Beaupré
Château Mont-Ste-Anne, 500 Blvd. Beaupré, 258 r., Rest., Sk.;
   tel. (418) 827–5211
Le Manoir Gérard, 9776 Blvd. Ste-Anne, 36 u., Sk.; tel. (418) 827–4548
Au Pied du Mont, 2 Blvd. Belanger, Sk., T; tel. (418) 827–4543

Ste-Anne des Monts
Monaco des Monts, 90 Blvd. Ste-Anne, Rest.;
   tel. (418) 763–3321

Ste-Luce-sur-Mer
Auberge Ste-Luce, 52 Rue Bord du Fleuve, 29 r., Rest;
   tel. (418) 739–4955

Ste-Marguerite Station
Alpine Inn, T; tel. (819) 229–3516

Sept Îles
Auberge des Gouverneurs, 666 Laure Blvd., 124 r., Rest., SP;
   tel. (418) 962–7071
Sept Îles, 451 Arnaud Ave., Rest.; tel. (418) 962–2581

Shawinigan
Auberge L'Escapade, 3383 Rue Garnier, Rest.; tel. (819) 539–6911

Sutton
Centre Paulette Hiriart, McCullough Rd., 9 r., Rest., SP;
   tel. (514) 538–2903

Horizon, Chemin Mont Sutton, 48 r., Rest., SP; tel. (514) 538–3212
La Paimpolaise, Chemin de Ski, 28 r., Rest., T; tel. (514) 538–3213

Georges, 135 Du Bateau-Passeur St., 18 u., Rest.; tel. (418) 235–4393   Tadoussac
Tadoussac, Bord de l'Eau St., Rest.; tel. (418) 235–4421

Le Gîte, 1100 Blvd. Ducharme, Rest.; tel. (819) 523–9501   La Tuque

Auberge Le Rucher, 2368 Rue de l'Eglise, 13 r.; tel. (819) 322–2507   Val-David
La Sapinière, 1244 Chemin de la Sapinière, 70 r., G, Rest., Sk., T, WS;
    tel. (819) 322–2020

Saskatchewan

Beefeater Motor Inn, 13th Ave./9th St.; tel. (306) 634–6456   Estevan

Country Squire Motor Hotel, Hwy. 10/Bay St., Rest.; tel. (306) 322–5603   Fort Qu'appelle

Capri, 4615 50th Ave., 60 r., Rest.; tel. (403) 825–5591   Lloydminster
Cedar Inn, 4526 44th St, 50 r.; tel. (403) 825–6155
Imperial 400, 4320 44th St., 100 r.; tel. (800) 667–0400
Tropical Inn, 5621 44th St., 72 r., SP; tel. (403) 875–7000
Voyageur, 4724 44th St., 31 r.; tel. (403) 825–2248
Wayside Inn, Hwy. 16, 99 r., Rest; tel. (403) 875–4404

Maple Grove, Hwy. 21/1st Ave. W, 14 r.; tel. (306) 662–2658   Maple Creek

Best Western Downtown, 45 Athabasca St., 28 u.; tel. (306) 692–1884   Moose Jaw
Best Western Heritage Inn, 1590 Main St., 90 u., Rest., SP;
    tel. (306) 693–7550
Harwood's Moose Jaw Inn, 24 Fairford St. E, 89 r., Rest., SP;
    tel. (306) 692–2366

Moose Mountain Park Cabins, 30 u.;   Moose Mountain
    tel. (306) 577–2155   Provincial Park

Capri, 992 101st St., 97 r. (47 r. in adjacent motel), Rest.;   North Battleford
    tel. (306) 445–9425

Coronet Motor Hotel, 3551 Second Ave. W, 101 r., Rest., SP;   Prince Albert
    tel. (306) 764–6441
Imperial 400 Motel, 3580 Second Ave. W, Rest., SP; tel. (306) 764–6881
Marlboro Inn, 67 13th St. E, 112 u., Rest., SP; tel. (306) 763–2643

Northland Waskesiu, 13 u.; tel. (306) 663–5322   Prince Albert
Skyline, Waskesiu, 21 u.; tel. (306) 663–5461   National Park

Imperial 400, 4255 Albert St., 200 r., CC, Rest., SP;   Regina
    tel. (306) 584–8800
Landmark Inn, 4150 Albert St., 188 u., Rest., SP; tel. (800) 667–8191
Plains Motor Hotel, 1965 Albert St., Rest.; tel. (306) 757–8661
Regina Inn, 1975 Broad St., 247 r., CC, Rest., SP; tel. (306) 525–6767
Sandman Inn, 4025 Albert St., 181 u., Rest., SP; tel. (306) 586–2663
Seven Oaks, 777 Albert St., 105 r., Rest., SP; tel. (306) 757–0121
Sheraton Centre, Victoria Ave./Broad St., 251 u., Rest., SP;
    tel. (306) 569–1666
Vagabond Motor Inn, 4177 Albert St., 98 r., Rest.; tel. (306) 586–3443

Holiday House, 2901 Eight St. E, 107 u., Rest., SP; tel. (306) 374–9111   Saskatoon
Holiday Inn, 90 22nd St. E, 187 u., Rest., SP; tel. (800) 465–4329
King George Motor Hotel, 157 2nd Ave. N, 104 r., Rest., Sh.;
    tel. (306) 244–6133

Hunting

Park Town Motor Hotel, 924 Spadina Crescent E, 109 u., Disco., Rest., SP; tel. (800) 667–3999
Patricia, 345 2nd Ave., 48 r., Rest.; tel. (306) 242–8861
Ramada Renaissance, 405 20th St. E, 300 r., SP; tel. (800) 667–3020
Relax Inn, Airport/Circle Drive, 192 r., Rest., SP; tel. (800) 661–9563
Saskatoon Inn, 2002 Airport Dr., 257 r., Rest., SP; tel. (800) 667–8789
Sheraton-Cavalier Motor Inn, 612 Spadina Crescent, 250 u., Rest., SP; tel. (800) 325–3535
TraveLodge, 106 Circle Dr. W, 221 u., Rest., SP; tel. (306) 242–8881
Will Inns Saskatoon, 806 Idylwyld Dr. N, 171 r., CC, SP; tel. (800) 661–1331

Swift Current
Horseshoe Lodge, Hwy. 1 E, 50 u., Rest., SP; tel. (306) 773–4643
Imperial 400, 1150 Begg St. E, Rest., SP; tel. (306) 773–2033

Weyburn
Weyburn Inn, 5 Government Rd., 70 r., Rest., SP; tel. (306) 842–6543

Yorkton
Holiday Inn, 100 Broadway E, 91 u., Rest., SP; tel. (800) 667–1585

Yukon Territory

Beaver Creek
Alas/Kon Border Lodge, km 1934 Alaska Hwy., 179 r., Rest., Sh.; tel. (800) 544–2206

Burwash Landing
Burwash Landing Resort, km 1759 Alaska Hwy., 32 u., Rest., F, WS; tel. (403) 841–4441

Carmacks
Carmacks; tel. (403) 863–5221

Dawson
Downtown, 2nd/Queen, 60 u., CC, Rest.; tel. (403) 993–5346
Eldorado, 3rd/Princess, 53 u., Rest.; tel. (403) 993–5451
Westmark Inn-Dawson City, 5th/Harper, 52 r., Sh.; tel. (403) 993–5542, (403) 68–4700 (mid-May to mid-September)

Destruction Bay
Talbot Arms Motel, Rest.; tel. (403) 841–4461

Haines Junction
Kluane Park Inn, opposite Kluane National Park, 20 u.; tel. (403) 634–2261

Skagway, Alaska
Golden North, 33 r., Rest., Sh.; tel. (907) 983–2451
Irene's Inn, Sixth St./Broadway, 10 r., Rest.; tel. (907) 983–2520
Sgt. Preston's, Sixth St., 23 r.; tel. (907) 983–2521
Skagway Inn, 15 r.; tel. (907) 983–2289

Whitehorse
Capital, 103 Main St.; tel. (403) 667–2565
Goldrush Inn, 411 Main St., 39 u., Rest., Sh.; tel. (403) 668–4500
Regina, 102 Wood St., 53 r., Rest.; tel. (403) 667–7801
Westmark Klondike Inn, 2288 2nd Ave., 98 r., Rest., Sh.; tel. (403) 668–4747
Westmark Whitehorse, 2nd Ave./Wood St., 181 r., Rest., Sh.; tel. (403) 668–4700

Hunting

Hunting licence
Hunting is governed by federal, provincial and territorial laws. Non-residents must obtain hunting licences from each province or territory in which they plan to hunt. When hunting migratory game-birds a federal migratory game-bird hunting permit is also required. This is available from most Canadian post offices.

Visitors may bring a hunting rifle or shotgun and up to 200 rounds of ammunition into Canada, but they must be 16 years of age or older (19 in British Columbia) and the firearm must be for sporting or competition use. In many of Canada's provincial parks and reserves and adjacent areas, the entry of any type of weapon is forbidden. Regulations available from each province provide instructions in this regard.

Hunting firearms

As a rule, anyone wanting to go big-game or trophy hunting would be well advised to obtain the services of an outfitter (see Outfitters), who will fit them out with planes, horses, guides, etc. and also set up base camps, all of which can be quite a costly undertaking.

Big-game and trophy hunting

In most provinces and territories export permits are required to take out unprocessed game, i.e. any part of an animal, such as hunting trophies, hides and skins, and both large and small game, that has not been properly processed. Detailed information about this can be obtained from Canadian hunting tour operators or from the relevant provincial or territorial authorities.

Taking out game

Information about hunting and fishing licences can be obtained from the following:

Where to obtain information

Forestry, Lands and Wildlife, Alberta Energy and Natural Resources, 8th Floor, South Tower, 9915 108th Street, Edmonton, Alberta T5K 2C9
Information about the provincial parks:
Alberta Recreation and Parks, Standard Life Centre, 10405 Jasper Avenue, Edmonton, Alberta T5J 3N4

Alberta

Department of Fisheries and Oceans, 555 W. Hastings Street, Vancouver, B.C. V6B 5G3; tel. (604) 666 3545 (saltwater licences)
Fish and Wildlife Information, Ministry of the Environment, Parliament Buildings, Victoria, British Columbia V8V 1XE

British Columbia

Travel Manitoba, Department 7020, 155 Charlton Street, 7th Floor, Winnipeg, Manitoba R3C 3H8

Manitoba

Environment Canada, Ottawa, Ontario K1A OH3
(for information about the Canadian National Parks, the national historic parks and sites and historic waterways)

National Parks of Canada

Department of Natural Resources, Fish and Wildlife Branch, 349 King Street, Fredericton, New Brunswick E3B 5H1
Information about the provincial parks:
Tourism New Brunswick, P.O. Box 12345, Fredericton, New Brunswick E3B 5C3

New Brunswick

Tourist Services, Department of Development and Tourism, Box 2016, St John's, Newfoundland A1C 5R8

Newfoundland and Labrador

Wildlife Service, Renewable Resources, P.O. Box 2668, Northwest Territories X1A 2P9

Northwest Territories

Department of Lands and Forests, P.O. Box 698, Halifax, Nova Scotia B3J 2T9 or Department of Natural Resources, Box E8 , Truro, NS B2N 5B8

Nova Scotia

Ministry of Natural Resources, Wildlife Branch, Queen's Park, Toronto, Ontario M7A 1W3

Ontario

Fish and Wildlife Division, Department of Community and Cultural Affairs, P.O. Box 2000, Charlottetown, Prince Edward Island C1A 7N8

Prince Edward Island

Ministère du Loisir, de la Chasse et de la Pêche, Direction des communications, 150 St Cyrille St., Québec, Québec G1R 4Y1

Québec

Saskatchewan   Tourism Saskatchewan, 1919 Saskatchewan Drive, Regina, Saskatchewan
S4P 3V7

Yukon   Tourism Yukon (CG), P.O. Box 2703, Whitehorse, Yukon Y1A 2C6

Indians and Inuit

Canada's native peoples, the Inuit (the term Eskimo is considered an insult, since it means "eater of raw flesh") and the Indians, actually cover more of the country's vast lands, despite there only being about half a million of them, than the European Canadians, who tend to be mostly in southern Canada. Anyone wanting more detailed information about such peoples as the Inuit, the Kwakiutl, the Dene Nation, the Blackfoot, and the Micmac should contact: Indian and Northern Affairs Canada, Ottawa, Ontario, Canada K1A 0H4.

Information

Canada as a whole   Tourisme Canada, 235 Queen Street, 4th floor, Ottawa, Ontario, Canada
K1A 0H6; tel. (613) 993–7021

Canadian Official Tourist Offices

London   Tourism Programme, Canadian High Commission, Canada House,
Trafalgar Square, London SW1Y SBJ; tel. (071) 629 9492
Visit Canada Centre, 62–65 Trafalgar Square, london WC2N 5DT;
tel. (0891) 715000, fax (0171) 389 1149
Ontario Tourism, UK Office, 21 Knightsbridge, London SW1X 7LY;
tel. (0171) 245 1222
Québec Tourism, Québec House, 59 Pall Mall, London SW1Y 5JH;
tel. (0171) 930 8314, fax (0171) 930 7938

Provincial Tourist Offices in Canada

Alberta   Travel Alberta, Box 2500, Edmonton, Alberta T5J 2Z2;
tel. (403) 427–4321, freefone 1800 661–8888

British Columbia   Tourism British Columbia, Ministry of Tourism, Parliament Buildings,
Victoria, British Columbia V8W 2Z2;
tel. (604) 356–9932

Manitoba   Travel Manitoba, 7th Floor, 155 Carlton Street, Winnipeg, Manitoba
R3C 3H8; tel. (204) 945–3777

New Brunswick   Department of Economic Development & Tourism, P.O. Box 12345, Fredericton, New Brunswick E3B 5C3; tel. (506) 453–8742, fax (506) 453 5370

Newfoundland   Department of Tourism, Culture & Recreation, P.O. Box 8730, St John's,
Newfoundland A1B 4K2; tel. (709) 729–2830

Northwest
Territories   TravelArctic, Department of Economic Development & Tourism, Yellowknife, NWT X1A 2L9; tel. (403) 873–7200, fax (403) 873 0294

Nova Scotia   Nova Scotia Marketing Agency, P.O. Box 519, Halifax, Nova Scotia B3J
2R7; tel. (902) 424–4045

Ontario   Ontario Travel, Queen's Park, Toronto, Ontario M7A 2E5;
tel. (416) 314–0944, fax. (416) 314 7372

Visitor Services Division, Department of Tourism and Parks, P.O. Box 940, Charlottetown, Prince Edward Island C1A 7M5; tel. (902) 368–4444 — Prince Edward Island

Tourisme Québec, C.P. 20000, Québec, Québec G1K 26X2 — Québec

Saskatchewan Tourism Authority, 500–1900 Alberta Street, Regina, Saskatchewan S4P 4L0; tel. (306) 787–2300 — Saskatchewan

Tourism Yukon (CG), P.O. Box 2703, Whitehorse, Yukon Y1A 2C6; tel. (403) 667–5340, (403) 667–3546 — Yukon

National Parks

Parks Canada, Ottawa, Ontario K1A 1G2 — Head office

Parks Canada, Upper Water Street, Halifax, Nova Scotia B3J 1S9; tel. (902) 426–3457 — Atlantic Region

Parks Canada, 1141 Route de l'Eglise, Ste-Foy, Québec G1V 4H5; tel. (418) 694–4177 — Québec Region

Parks Canada, 132 Second Street E, Cornwall, Ontario K6H 5V4; tel. (613) 933–7951 — Ontario Region

Parks Canada, 291 York Avenue, Winnipeg, Manitoba R3C 0P4; tel. (204) 949–2110 — Prairie Region

Parks Canada, 134 11th Avenue SE, Calgary, Alberta T2G 0X5; tel. (403) 231–4745 — Western Region

Insurance

Visitors are strongly advised to ensure that they have adequate holiday insurance, including loss or damage to luggage, loss of currency and jewellery. — General

It is essential for visitors to take out some form of short-term health insurance providing complete cover, since medical consultations and hospital treatment can be very expensive. — Health
See also Medical Attention.

Language

Under the 1969 Official Language Act Canada has two official languages, English and French. More than 60% of the population have English as their mother tongue, while French is the language of about 25%, most of whom (about 85%) live in Québec.

Lodges

Located far from civilisation and often only reached by light aircraft, lodges (hunting boxes, log cabins, converted logging camps) are ideal bases for touring in the remote areas. They can usually provide guides and equipment as well.

Lodges are very much a Canadian speciality, mostly with first-rate facilities. Further information can be obtained from travel agents and tourist offices.

Measurements

Canada has recently adopted the metric system of weights and measures, exchanging miles, feet and inches for kilometres, metres and centimetres, Fahrenheit for Celsius, gallons for litres, pounds for kilos, etc. However, clothing sizes and food amounts may still be given in either the metric or the British/American system.

Medical Attention

Doctors, dentists, hospitals

Canada has good medical services, both as regards its hospitals and its dental and medical practitioners.

For the European visitor the problem is one of cost, rather than quality of care. A stay in hospital will usually be very expensive, particularly since some provinces impose a surcharge on care for non-residents. It is therefore strongly recommended that visitors obtain sufficient medical insurance before leaving for Canada.

Medicines

Visitors taking prescribed medication should bring a copy of the prescription in case it needs to be renewed by a doctor in Canada.

Medical insurance, accident insurance

Visitors to Canada should find out before leaving home how much cover they have from their own medical and accident insurance when in the country. It will usually pay to take out special medical insurance for the duration of the stay in Canada. "Ontario Blue Cross" is a name worth remembering if it is necessary to take out insurance while in Canada.

It is also wise to get travel accident insurance for the time in Canada, and this can be done, if necessary, through automatic dispensers in airports and bus and train stations.

Opening Times

Shops

In most places stores are open Monday to Saturday from 9.30am until 6pm. Town centre shops stay open until 9pm one or two evenings in the week; many open on Sundays as well.

Places of Entertainment

For cinemas, concert halls, theatres, etc. enquiries can be made by telephone.

Banks

Normal banking hours in Canada are 10am to 3pm Monday to Friday, with extended hours until 6pm one day a week, usually Thursday or Friday.

Post offices

See entry

Outfitters

"Outfitters" and bush-pilots act as the go-betweens twixt civilisation and the untamed wilderness and make adventure holidays possible. They deal in goods and services, supply sailing dinghies, canoes, horses, diving equipment, food, fuel, tools and whatever else may be required for a "civilised" adventure holiday.

The bush-pilot works closely with, if not, as is often the case, in personal partnership, with the outfitter, making it possible with their (occasionally ancient) hydroplanes and helicopters to penetrate into the deepest, untouched wilderness. The passenger sits next to or behind the pilot and sees clearly what is happening outside.

Quite a few outfitters and bush-pilots operate in and out of fly-in camps and lodges – clusters of tents or cabins, often surprisingly well-appointed, and used by holiday hunters, anglers and comfort-loving adventurers as bases for their expeditions.

Fly-in camps, lodges

Parks, National and Provincial

Canada currently has 34 National Parks and a great many Provincial Parks. These are mostly nature reserves or particularly scenic areas, where the ecosystem is left in its natural state.

Fees are charged in many national parks to use the roads, trails, campsites, etc., while there are also such commercial recreational facilities, as hotels, swimming pools, golf courses, horseback-riding in some places (see also Information, National Parks).

These parks have reception centres for informing the visitor, usually through audio-visual presentations, of that particular park's special features, besides providing literature such as maps and trails. There are also trained guides who can impart specialist information for those with particular interests.

The best views and observation points can be reached by pathways, and there are some forms of shelter that can be used overnight, but this needs approval from the park authorities.

Aulavik National Park (Banks Island), Box 1840, Inuvik, N.W.T. X0E 0T0; tel. (403) 979–3248

The principal National Parks

Auyuittuq National Park, Box 1720, Iqaluit, N.W.T. X0A 0H0; tel. (819) 979–6277

Baffin Island National Park, Box 1720, Iqaluit, N.W.T. X0A 0H0; tel. (819) 979–6277

Banff National Park, Box 900, Banff, Alberta T0L 0C0; tel. (403) 852–1500

Bruce Peninsula National Park, Box 189, Tobermory, Ontario N0H 2R0; tel. (519) 596–2233

Cape Breton Highlands National Park, Ingonish Beach, Nova Scotia B0C 1L0; tel. (418) 285–2270

Dinosaur Provincial Park, Alberta

Elk Island National Park, Fort Saskatchewan, Alberta, T8L 2N7; tel. (403) 992–6380

Ellesmere Island National Park, Box 1720, Iqaluit, N.W.T. X0A 0H0; tel. (819) 979–6277

Forillon National Park, 122 blvd. Gaspé, Gaspé, Québec G0C 1R0; tel. (418) 368–5505

Fundy National Park, Box 40, Alma, New Brunswick E0A 1B0; tel. (506) 887–2000

Georgian Bay Islands National Park, Box 29, Honey Harbour, Ontario P0E 1E0; tel. (705) 756–2415

Glacier National Park, Box 350, Revelstoke, B.C. V0E 2S0; tel. (604) 837–7500

Grasslands National Park, Box 150, Val Marie, Saskatchewan S0N 2T0; tel. (306) 298–2257

Gros Morne National Park, Box 130, Rocky Harbour, Newfoundland A0K 4N0; tel. (709) 458–2417

Gwaii Haanas, Anthony Island (South Moresby), Box 37, Queen Charlotte City, B.C. V0T 1S0; tel. (604) 559–8818

Head-Smashed-In Bison Jump Provincial Historic Resource, Alberta

Jasper National Park, Box 10, Jasper, Alberta T0E 1E0; tel. (403) 852–6161

Kejimkujik National Park, Box 236, Annapolis, Nova Scotia B0T 1B0; tel. (902) 242–2772

Kluane National Park, Box 5495, Haines Junction, Yukon Territory Y0B 1L0; tel. (403) 634–2251

Kootenay National Park, Box 220, Radium Hot Springs, B.C. V0A 1M0;
   tel. (604) 347–9615
Kouchibouguac National Park, Kouchibouguac, Kent County,
   New Brunswick E0A 2A0; tel. (506) 876–2443
L'Anse aux Meadows National Historic Park, Newfoundland
Mauricie National Park, Box 758, Shawinigan, Québec G9N 6V9;
   tel. (819) 536–2638
Mingan Archipelago National Park, Box 1180, Havre-St-Pierre, Québec
   G0G 1P0; tel. (418) 538–3331
Mount Revelstoke National Park, Box 350, Revelstoke, B.C. V0E 2S0;
   tel. (604) 837–7500
Nahanni National Park, Box 300, Fort Simpson, N.W.T. X0E 0N0;
   tel. (403) 695–3151
Northern Yukon National Park, Box 5495, Haines Junction, Yukon Territory
   Y0B 1L0; tel. (403) 634–2251
Pacific Rim National Park, Box 280, Ucluelet, B.C. V0R 3A0;
   tel. (604) 726–7721
Pointe Pelee National Park, Leamington, Ontario N8H 3V4;
   tel. (519) 322–2365
Prince Albert National Park, Box 100, Waskesiu Lake, Saskatchewan
   S0J 2Y0; tel. (306) 663–5322
Prince Edward Island National Park, Box 487, Charlottetown, P.E.I. C1A 7L1;
   tel. (902) 566–7050
Pukaskwa National Park, Box 39, Heron Bay, Ontario P0T 1R0;
   tel. (807) 228–0801
Québec National Historic District
Riding Mountain National Park, Wasagaming, Manitoba R0J 2H0;
   tel. (204) 848–2811
St Lawrence Islands National Park, Box 469, Mallorytown Landing, Ontario
   K0E 1R0; tel. (613) 923–5261
Terra Nova National Park, Gloverton, Newfoundland A0G 2L0;
   tel. (709) 533–2801
Waterton Lakes National Park, Waterton, Alberta T0K 2M0;
   tel. (403) 859–2224
Wood Buffalo National Park, Box 750, Fort Smith, N.W.T. X0E 0P0;
   tel. (403) 872–2349
Yoho National Park, Box 99, Field, B.C. V0A 1G0;
   tel. (604) 343–6324

Post

Post offices	Canadian post offices are generally open from Monday through to Friday 9am to 6pm. Some are also open on Saturday. In the main cities head post offices are also open on Sundays and public holidays.
Stamp automats	Automats are a convenient source of stamps in many towns, being found particularly at airports, bus and train stations, and newspaper kiosks.
Mail to Europe	The current cost of a stamp for a letter under 20 g. or a standard postcard to Europe is 86 cents.
General delivery/ poste restante	Canadian post offices will keep mail marked "General Delivery", as poste restante, up to 15 days, after which, if not collected, it will be returned to sender. Letters should be addressed to the recipient c/o General Delivery, Main Post Office, then the name of the town, the province, Canada and postcode.

Public Holidays

A number of Canada's public holidays are taken on a particular Monday in the month or the nearest Monday to the date in question so that Canadians get several long weekends during the year.

The same applies to some of the public holidays that are celebrated only by certain provinces.

New Year	**National holidays** January 1st
Good Friday and Easter Monday	March/April
Victoria Day	Monday before May 25th
Canada Day	July 1st
Labour Day	1st Monday in September
Thanksgiving	2nd Monday in October
Remembrance Day	November 11th
Christmas Day and Boxing Day	December 25th/26th
St. Patrick's Day (Newfoundland & Labrador)	**Provincial holidays** March 17th or Monday before
St. George's Day (Newfoundland & Labrador)	April 23rd or Monday before
St-Jean Baptiste (La Fête Nationale) (St John the Baptist, Québec)	June 24th
Discovery Day, St John's Day (Newfoundland & Labrador)	Monday nearest to June 25th
Memorial Day (Newfoundland)	Beginning of July
Orangeman's Day (Newfoundland & Labrador)	Monday nearest to July 10th
Heritage Day (Alberta) British Columbia Day (British Columbia) New Brunswick Day (New Brunswick) Civic Holiday (Manitoba, Northwest Territories, Ontario, Saskatchewan)	1st Monday in August
Discovery Day (Yukon)	3rd Monday in August

Public Transport

Canada has a good public transport system. Buses operate on scheduled routes in all the main built-up areas, and in the major cities the local transport network is particularly close-knit. Toronto and Montréal have underground (subway), systems, while Calgary, Edmonton and Vancouver have light rail transit (LRT) mass transportation systems.

Compared with Europe fares in most Canadian cities are relatively cheap. Usually the exact money has to be given – bus drivers don't sell tickets manually or carry any change.

Fares

© *Baedeker*

Rail Transport
Passenger Services
of VIA Rail

	Via Rail
	Other Bus Services
	British Columbia Railway
	Algoma Central
	Ontario Northland
	Limited service
	Amtrak
. . . . . .	Ferries

St. John's
Gander
Corner Brook
Ardentia
Port-aux-Basques
Gaspé Percé North Sydney
Matapédia Sydney
Mont-Joli
Jonquière Campbellton Charlottetown
Edmundston Borden
Moosonee Hervey Truro
Cochrane Rivière- Fredericton
du-Loup
Hearst Senneterre Halifax
Kapuskasing Val d'Or Québec Moncton
Rouyn-Noranda Trois- Levis Bar Digby
Capreol Rivières Harbour Yarmouth
White River Ottawa Sherbrooke Saint John
nder Bay North Bay Montréal
Sault Ste. Marie Sudbury
Havelock
Kitchener Toronto Brockville
Stratford Kingston
Sarnia Niagara Falls
London Hamilton
hicago Windsor New York
Detroit

Radio and Television

Rush-hour travel	In many places it costs extra to travel in the morning and evening rush-hour, but fares are lower for travel outside the peak periods.
Concessionary fares	Public transport in many provinces operates concessionary fares, at substantially reduced rates, for school-children, students and senior citizens (over 65), subject to the usual proofs.
City tours	Every Canadian city has guided bus tours and local excursions. Details from travel agents, hotel reception, or the local tourist information centre.

Radio and Television

Canada has broadcasting to suit every taste, from the bilingual radio and TV broadcasts of the Canadian Broadcasting Corporation to innumerable local stations, as well as American network television.

Radio
AM and FM radio stations carry on round the clock, transmitting news, music, sport, etc. put out by CBC and local and national independents.

Television
Canadian TV uses the NTSC system, not PAL or SECAM as in Europe, so anyone wanting to play videotapes from Europe could encounter problems.

There are TV sets in almost every hotel room. The public service stations are free, but other channels are "Pay TV", so have to be paid for.

Rail Travel

Canada's passenger train network of nearly 43,000 miles of line is operated by VIA Rail, the national system of VIA Rail Canada Inc., which uses the tracks of Canadian Pacific and Canadian National, who function solely as freight carriers. Together with VIA Rail Canada, some smaller railways offer scenic journeys as well, such as the "Rocky Mountaineer", operated by Mountain Vista Railtour Services of Vancouver, and Blyth & Company of Toronto's "Royal Canadian". The American rail company Amtrak also operate some services on Canadian routes. Rail reservations abroad can be made only through a travel agent. The relatively leisurely passenger journey by rail from coast to coast takes about four days (see also Suggested Routes: Canada by rail).

Canrail pass
VIA Rail's Canrail pass, which must be purchased prior to departure for Canada, offers unlimited coach class travel for up to 30 consecutive days.

Concessionary fares
Children under the age of two accompanied by an adult travel free; those aged 2 to 11 pay half fare. For the over 60s there is a reduction of 10%. No reductions on the cost of sleepers or couchettes.

VIA Rail
VIA Rail was set up as a Crown Corporation in 1977 to act as Canada's national passenger train service, although the rails and rolling stock still belong to the former rail companies. It has to cover its costs, and was forced to limit its operations considerably in 1990 by such factors as competition from the airlines. Concentrating on passenger comfort and good service delivery, it continues to operate a number of routes in eastern Canada, including Québec/Montréal, Montréal/Ottawa, Montréal/Toronto, Ottawa/Toronto, Toronto/Niagara Falls and Toronto/Windsor. Passenger services also operate out of Vancouver and Prince Rupert over the Rockies to Edmonton and from Winnipeg to Churchill on Hudson Bay. A high-speed stretch is planned for Montréal/Toronto to take advantage of the increased use, but it has to be said that ultimately the income from passenger travel is only a fraction of that earned from carrying freight.

There are some regional carriers around the main cities who use part of the rail network for passenger services, and are subsidised by the provincial and local authorities in question.

Regional passenger trains

Several provinces, such as Ontario, also maintain rail lines for economic and social purposes.

Since most of Canada's rail system, apart from in the Rockies and around the major cities, is single-track, while Canadian freight-trains are longer, heavier, and slower than those in Europe, passenger trains and scenic railtours often have to be shunted into sidings to wait for freight to pass, causing considerable delays. The Canadian rail corporations are also not good at ploughing their quite considerable profits back into the system, and have no compunction in closing down any lines that have become unprofitable.

Problems

VIA Rail Canada Inc., C.P.8116, 2 place Ville-Marie, Montréal, Québec H3B 2G6; tel. (514) 871–6000

Rail carriers

Algoma Central Railway, 129 Bay Street, P.O. Box 7000, Sault Ste Marie, Ontario P6A 5P6

Amtrak National Railroad Passenger Corporation, 400 North Capital Street NW, Washington, C.C. 20001, USA

British Columbia Rail Ltd., P.O. Box 8770, Vancouver, British Columbia V6B 4X6

Ontario Northland Transportation Commission, 555 Oak Street East, North Bay, Ontario H3C 3N3

Ranch and Farm Holidays

Holidays on a ranch or farm are rapidly increasing in popularity. Accommodation can range from small, simple farms to the most splendid of ranches, where there are opportunities for horseback riding, fishing, sailing and canoeing, not to mention golf in some cases. Further details can be obtained from travel agents.

Restaurants

Eating out in Canada covers the whole spectrum from fast-food outlets to gourmet restaurants, and reflects the ethnic diversity of the Canadian people. Salmon, lobster, steak and other national delights can be found on the menu of every quality establishment, as well as a variety of more exotic dishes depending on where the chef comes from.

Canada's individual regions have their own specialities (see Food and Drink), so a visit to a restaurant can be an excursion into the culinary unknown. Montréal is traditionally the country's gastronomic capital, owing to its French cuisine, while the four Maritime provinces – Newfoundland, Prince Edward Island, New Brunswick and Nova Scotia – specialise in seafood, especially lobster. Toronto ranks third for good food on the east coast. Although here too there is a strong French influence, a great many other ethnic groups are represented among its restauranteurs. In Manitoba, Saskatchewan and Alberta good hearty meals are served, often with a flavour of the Ukraine. On the West Coast there is superb fish and seafood, while the best gastronomic choice is to be had in Vancouver and Victoria, from a international cuisine and regional specialities.

Sales tax, at varying rates, is charged on food in restaurants in almost all Canada's provinces.

Tax

Alcoholic drinks are only available in establishments with the appropriate licence. This means going without a beer in many fast-food eating places,

Alcoholic drinks

or often finding that it is only possible to get a drink with a meal during certain hours.

The following list of restaurants is clearly only a selection, listed in alphabetical order by province or territory. The Hotels section also includes a number of restaurants.

Abbreviations   Ch. = Chinese, Cr. = Creole, D = Danish, F = French, g = game, Gr. = Greek, H = Hungarian, In. = Indian, It. = Italian, J = Japanese, K = Korean, loc. = local, M = Mexican, res. = reservation required, S = Spanish, Sc. = Scandinavian, sf. = seafood, stk. = steak, V = view, Y = Yugoslav.

Alberta

Banff	Caboose, Elk/Lynx Sts., stk.; tel. (403) 762–3622
	Sukiyaki House, 211 Banff Ave., J; tel. (403) 762–2002
Calgary	Calgary Tower, 9th Ave.; tel. (403) 266–7171
	Cannery Row, 317 10th Ave. SW, Cr.; tel. (403) 269–8889
	La Chaumière, 121 17th Ave. SE, F; tel. (403) 228–5690
	Dilettante, 225 7th Ave. SW, Scotia Centre, sf., stk.; tel. (403) 228–6882
	Greek Village, 1212 17th Ave. SW, Gr.; tel. (403) 244–1144
	Karouzo's, 2620 4th St. NW, It.; tel. (403) 277–0096
	Japanese Village, 302 7th Ave. SW, sf., stk.; tel. (403) 262–2738
	The Saddle Room, in the Stampede Park Saddledome, V; tel. (403) 261–0573
	Three Greenhorns, 503 4th Ave. SE; tel. (403) 264–6903
	Wellington's Fine Restaurant, 10325 Bonaventure Dr. SE; tel. (403) 278–5250
Camrose	Bono's Family Restaurant; tel. (403) 672–5614
Claresholm	The Flying N, loc.
Drumheller	Roman's Restaurant; tel. (403) 823–6564
Edmonton	Bistro Praha, 10168 100A St.; tel. (403) 424–4218
	Bruno's, 8223 109th St., It.; tel. (403) 433–8161
	Cook Country Saloon, 8010 103rd St., stk.; tel. (403) 432–0177
	Cucci's, 99th St./Jasper Ave., Sun Life Bldg.; tel. (403) 421–1551
	Four Seasons, Four Seasons Hotel, 10235 101st St., sf., res.; tel. (403) 428–7111
	Hy's Steak Loft, 10013 101st St., res., stk.; tel. (403) 424–4444
	Merryland, 7006 109th St., K; tel. (403) 435–6495
	Red Diamond House, 7500 82nd Ave., Ch.; tel. (403) 465–0755
	Unheardof, 9602 82nd Ave.; tel. (403) 432–0480
	Waldens, 10245 104th St., sf.; tel. (403) 420–6363
Fort Macleod	Scarlet & Gold Inn, sf., stk.; tel. (403) 553–3063
Grande Prairie	Grand Prairie Inn, 11633 100th St; tel. (403) 532–5221
Hinton	Husky House; tel. (403) 865–2833
Jasper	L & W, Hazel/Patricia Sts.; tel. (403) 852–4114
	Tonquin Prime Rib, Juniper/Connaught Dr.; tel. (403) 852–4966
Lethbridge	El Rancho; tel. (403) 327–5701
	Sven Eriksen's Restaurant, Mayor Magrath Dr., loc.; tel. (403) 328–7756
	Treats Eatery; tel. (403) 328 4818
Medicine Hat	Continental Inn; tel. (403) 527–8844
	Old Mill Inn, sf.; tel. (403) 526–7500
	Westlander Inn, 13th Ave. SE; tel. (403) 526 7500
Pincher Creek	Oasis, sf., stk.

Capri Centre   Red Deer
Ranch House, stk.

Pearl's Pantry   Waterton Lake

British Columbia

China Village, 165 Victoria St., Ch.; tel. (604) 372–2822   Kamloops
David Thompson Dining Room, 650 Victoria St., sf., stk.;
   tel. (604) 372–5282

Pilgrim House Motor Hotel, 1056 Eckhardt Ave.; tel. (604) 492–8926   Penticton

The Achilion, 422 Dominion, Gr.; tel. (604) 564–1166   Prince George

Smile's Seafood Cafe, 112 George Hills Way, sf.; tel. (604) 624–3072   Prince Rupert

Old Dutch Inn, 100 17th St.; tel. (604) 338–5406   Qualicum Beach

Bishop's, 2183W 4th Ave., sf., res.; tel. (604) 738–2025   Vancouver
Bridge's, Granville Island, 1696 Duranleau St., V, sf.; tel. (604) 687–4400
Café de Paris, 751 Denman St., F,; tel. (604) 687–1418
Café Splash, 1600 Howe St.; tel. (604) 682–5600
The Cannery, 2205 Commissioner St., V, sf.; tel. (604) 254–9606
La Côted'Azur, 1216 Robson St., F; tel. (604) 688–3504
Le Crocodile, 818 Thurlow St., F; tel. (604) 669–4298
Delilah's, 1906 Haro St.; tel. (604) 687–3424
India Gate, 616 Robson St., In.; tel. (604) 684–4617
Kamei Sushi, 811 Thurlow St., J; tel. (604) 684–4823
Kegs, stk.: Keg, Granville Island; tel. (604) 685–4735; Keg, Coal Harbour;
   tel. (604) 682–5608; Keg Boathouse; tel. (604) 669–8851
A Kettle of Fish, 900 Pacific St., sf.; tel. (604) 682–6661
The Only, 20 East Hastings, sf.; tel. (604) 681–6546
The On On Tea Garden, 214 Keefer St., Ch.; tel. (604) 685–7513
Quilicum, 1724 Davie St., In.; tel. (604) 681–7044
Salmon House on the Hill, 2229 Folkestone Way, V; tel. (604) 926–3212
Umberto's, La Cantina, Il Giardino, 1376–82 Hornby St., It.;
   tel. (604) 687–6316
William Tell, 765 Beatty St.; tel. (604) 688–3504

Bengal Room, Empress Hotel, 721 Government St.; tel. (604) 384–8111   Victoria
Blethering Place, 2250 Oak Bay Ave.; tel. (604) 598–1413
Captain's Palace, 309 Belleville St.; tel. (604) 388–9191
The Chantecler, 4509 West Saanich Rd., g; tel. (604) 727–3344
Chauney's, 614 Humboldt St., sf.; tel. (604) 385–4512
Chinese Village, 755 Finlayson St., Ch., res.; tel. (604) 384–8151
Chez Daniel, 2522 Estevan St., res.; tel. (604) 592–7424
Deep Cove Chalet, 11190 Chalet Dr., Sidney, V, sf.; tel. (604) 656–3541
Chez Denis, 1548 Fort St., F; tel. (604) 592–2611
Foo Hong's, 564 Fisgard St., Ch.; tel. (604) 386–9553
Herald Street Café, 546 Herald St.; tel. (604) 381–1441
Hy's, 777 Douglas St., sf., stk.; tel. (604) 382–7111
Japanese Village, 734 Broughton St., J, res.; tel. (604) 382–5165
Perikilis, 531 Yates St., Gr.; tel. (604) 386–3313
Chez Pierre, 512 Yates St., F; tel. (604) 388–7711
Sam's Deli, 805 Government St.; tel. (604) 382–8424
Taj Mahal, 679 Herald St., In., res.; tel. 383–460062
Tomoe, 726 Johnson St., J; tel. (604) 386–4522
Victoria Harbour House, 607 Oswego St., sf., stk.; tel. (604) 386–1244
Windsor Park Tea Room, 2540 Windsor Rd.; tel. (604) 595–3135

Vernon Lodge Hotel, 3914 32nd St., sf.; tel. (604) 545–3385   Vernon

Restaurants

Manitoba

Brandon	North Hill Inn, 10th/Braecrest Dr., V; tel. (204) 727–4455
	Kokona's Restaurant, 1011 Rosser Ave., Gr.; tel. (204) 727–4395
Churchill	Trader's Table, loc.; tel. (204) 675–2001
Falcon Lake	Falcon Lake Resort and Club, Lake Blvd.; tel. (204) 349–8400
Flin Flon	Kelsey Trail Motor Inn, Hwy. 10N; tel. (204) 687–7555
Gimli	Golden Falcon, 72 First Ave.; tel. (204) 642–8868
The Pas	Wescana Inn, 439 Fisher St.; tel. (204) 623–5446
Portage La Prairie	Midtown Motor Inn, 177 Saskatchewan Ave.; tel. (204) 857–6881
Wasagaming	Elkhorn Ranch Resort, Mooswa Dr.; tel. (204) 848–2802
Winnipeg	Amici's, 326 Broadway; tel. (204) 943–4997
	Bistro Dansk, 63 Sherbrook St., D; tel. (204) 775–5662
	Cibo's, 283 Bannatyne, lt.; tel. (204) 943–4922
	Chi-Chi's, 1460 Maroons Rd., M; tel. (204) 775–0351; 1590 Regent St.; tel. (204) 661–6776
	Churchill, Marlborough Inn, 331 Smith St.; tel. (204) 942–6411
	Dubrovnik, 390 Assiniboine Ave., Y; tel. (204) 944–0594
	Kronborg, 1875 Pembina Hwy., D; tel. (204) 261–1448
	Tokyo Joe's, 132 Pioneer, K/J; tel. (204) 943–5796
	La Vieille Gare, St. Boniface, 630 Rue des Meurons, F; tel. (204) 237–7072
	Victor's, 454 River Ave.; tel. (204) 284–2339

New Brunswick

Bathurst	La Fine Grobe, Nigadoo, F; tel. (506) 783–3138
	Danny's Restaurant, Rte. 134; tel. (506) 548–6621
	The Galleon, Line Motel, 855 Ste. Anne St., sf.; tel. (506) 548–8803
Edmundston	Le Baron, 174 Victoria St.; tel. (506) 739–7822
	The Wandlyn, 919 Canada Rd.; tel. (506) 735–5525
Fredericton	BarBQ Barn, 540 Queen St., sf.; tel. (506) 455–2742
	The Coffeemill, Prospect St., Shopping Mall, sf.; tel. (506) 459–3463
	Eighty-Eight Ferry, 88 Ferry St.; tel. (506) 472–1988
	The Luna Steakhouse, 168 Dundonald St.; tel. (506) 455–4020
	Martha's, 625 King St., H; tel. (506) 455–4773
	The Maverick Room, Queen St., ground floor of the Lord Beaverbrook Hotel; tel. (506) 455–3371
	Mei's Chinese Restaurant, 74 Regent St., Ch.; tel. (506) 454–2177
	Pat's Gourmet, Lower St. Mary's St.; tel. (506) 472–0992
	Victoria and Albert, 634 Queen St., sf.; tel. (506) 458–8310
	La Vie en Rose, 594 Queen St.; tel. (506) 455–1319
Grand Manan	The Compass Road, North Head, sf.; tel. (506) 662–8570
	The Marathon, North Head; tel. (506) 662–8144
Moncton	Le Cave à Papa, 236 George St., F; tel. (506) 855–0581
	Cy's, 170 Main St., sf.; tel. (506) 382–0032
	Ming Garden Restaurant, 797 Mountain Rd., Ch.; tel. (506) 855–5433
	Chez Jean Pierre, 21 Toombes St., F; tel. (506) 382–0332
	Two Brothers, Petitcodiac, 71 Main St., F, sf.; tel. (506) 756–8111

The Wandlyn Dining Room, 365 Water St.; tel. (506) 622–2847   Newcastle

Marshlands Inn, 73 Bridge St., loc.; tel. (506) 536–0170   Sackville

Café Creole, 14 King Square South, Cr.; tel. (506) 633–8091   Saint John
Grannan's, Market Square, sf.; tel. (506) 642–2225
The House of Chan, Hilyard Place; tel. (506) 693–7777
Incredible Edibles, 177 Prince William St., lt., Gr.; tel. (506) 693–0209
Mallard House, Delta Brunswick Inn, 39 King St.; tel. (506) 648–1981
Reggie's, 16 Germain St.; tel. (506) 657–6270
Turn of the Tide, Hilton Hotel, One Market Square, V; tel. (506) 693–8484

Chez Françoise, 93 Main St., F, sf.; tel. (506) 532–4233   Shediac

Conley's Lighthouse, sf.; tel. (506) 529–8823   St Andrews
Tara Manor, 559 Mowatt Dr.; tel. (506) 529–3304
Whale of a Café, 173 Water St., sf.

Auberge Wandlyn Inn, 99 King St.; tel. (506) 466–1814   St Stephen

Auberge Wandlyn Inn, Rtes.2/95; tel. (506) 328–8876   Woodstock

Newfoundland

The Carriage Room, Glynmill Inn, Cobb Lane, sf., loc.;   Corner Brook
  tel. (709) 634–5181
The Wine Cellar, Cobb Lane, lt., stk.

Albatross Motel, sf.; tel. (709) 256–3956   Gander
Sinbad's, Bennett Dr., loc.; tel. (709) 651–2678

Mount Peyton Hotel, 214 Lincoln Rd. loc.; tel. (709) 489–2251   Grand Falls

The Act III, Arts and Culture Centre; tel. (709) 754–0790   St John's
The Battery, Signal Hill, V, loc.; tel. (709) 762–0040
Cabot Club, Hotel Newfoundland, Cavendish Square, V; tel. (709) 726–4980
Captain's Cabin, Bowring's Department Store, V, loc.; tel. (709) 726–3290
Casa Grande, 108 Duckworth St., M; tel. (709) 553–6108
Colonial Inn, Topsail; tel. (709) 722–6933
The Flake House, Quidi Vidi Village, V, sf.; tel. (709) 576–7518
McGregor's, 28 Cochrane St.; tel. (709) 754–2413
Stone House Restaurant, 8 Kenna's Hill, res.; tel. (709) 753–2380
Victoria Station, 288–290 Duckworth St., sf.; tel. (709) 722–1290

Nova Scotia

Continental Kitchen, Granville Ferry, R.R.1, res.; tel. (902) 665–2287   Bridgetown

The Captain's House, 129 Central St.; tel. (902) 275–3501   Chester

Acadian Museum, Main St.; tel. (902) 224–2170   Cheticamp
Harbour Restaurant, Main St., sf., stk.; tel. (902) 224–2042

The Pines Resort Hotel Dining Room, Shore Rd., V; tel. (902) 245–2511   Digby

Clipper Cay, Historic Properties, end of Water St., V, res.;   Halifax
  tel. (902) 423–6818
Fat Frank's, 5411 Spring Garden Rd., res.; tel. (902) 423–6618
McKelvie's Delishes Fishes, 1680 Water St., sf.; tel. (902) 421–6161
O'Carrolls, 1860 Upper Water St., sf.; tel. (902) 423–4405
Old Man Morias, 1150 Barrington St., Gr.; tel. (902) 422–7960

Restaurants

La Perla, Dartmouth, 67 Alderney Dr., F, It.; tel. (902) 464–1223
Ryan Duffy's Steakhouse, 5640 Spring Garden Rd., M, stk.;
  tel. (902) 421–1116
Scanway, 1569 Dresden Row, Sc.; tel. (902) 422–3733
The Silver Spoon, 1865 Hollis St.; tel. (902) 422–1519
Thackeray's, 5435 Spring Garden Rd., res.; tel. (902) 423–5995

Ingonish beach   Keltic Lodge Dining Room, res.; tel. (902) 285–2880

Liscombe Mills   Liscombe Lodge Dining Room, Shore Rd., V, res.; tel. (902) 779–2307

Louisbourg   Anchors Aweigh, 1095 Main St., sf.; tel. (902) 733–3131
L'épee Royale, fortress, F; tel. (902) 733–2441

Sydney   Joe's Warehouse, 403 Charlotte St.; tel. (902) 539–6686

Truro   Glengarry Motel Dining Room, 138 Willows St., loc.; tel. (902) 895–5388

Wolfville   Blomidon Inn, 127 Main St., loc.; tel. (902) 542–9326

Yarmouth   Harris' Seafood Restaurant, Rte.1, sf., res.; tel. (902) 742–5420

Ontario

Algonquin Park   Arowhon Pines, on Hwy. 60; tel. (705) 633–5661

Barrie   Maude Koury's Steak House, 126 Collier St.; tel. (705) 726–6030

Bracebridge   Holiday House, 17 Dominion St., V; tel. (705) 645–2245

Gananoque   Golden Apple, res.; tel. (613) 382–3300

Kingston   Chez Piggy, 68 Princess St.; tel. (613) 549–7673

London   Auberge du Petit Prince, King St., F; tel. (519) 433–9394

Niagara Falls   Old Stone Inn, 5425 Robinson St., sf.; tel. (416) 357–1234

Niagara-on-the-Lake   Oban Inn, 160 Front St., V; tel. (416) 468–2165

North Bay   Champlain Trails, 300 Lakeshore Dr., Gr.; tel. (705) 476–3636

Ottawa   Friday's, 150 Elgin, sf.; tel. (613) 237–5353
Guadala Harry's, 18 York St., M; tel. (613) 234–8229
Café Henry Burger, 69 Laurier Ave., F; tel. (613) 235–9711
Chez Jean Pierre, 210 Somerset St. W, F; tel. (613) 235–9711
Japanese Village, 179 Laurier Ave. W, J; tel. (613) 236–9519
Le Jardin, 127 York St., F; tel. (613) 238–1828
Mamma Teresa, 300 Somerset St., It.; tel. (613) 236–3023
The Place Next Door, 320 Rideau St.; tel. (613) 232–1741
Ritz 3, 15 Clarence St.; tel. (613) 234–3499
226 Neppean St.; tel. (613) 238–8752
375 Queen Elizabeth Dr.; tel. (613) 238–8998
Yantze, 700 Somerset St., Ch.; tel. (613) 236–0555

Sault Ste Marie   Thymely Manner, 531 Albert St.; tel. (705) 942–5076

Sudbury   Peter Piper, 151 Larch St., Gr., It., sf.; tel. (705) 673–7801

Thunder Bay   Hoito, 314 Bay St., Finnish; tel. (807) 345–6323
Uncle Frank's Supper Club, RR4 Hwy. 61, loc.; tel. (807) 577–9141

Aida's, 597 Yonge St.; tel. (416) 925–6444   Toronto
Auberge du Pommier, 4150 Yonge St.; tel. (416) 482–6211
Barberian's, 7 Elm St., stk.; tel. (416) 597–0335
Blue Diamond, 142 Dundas St., Ch.; tel. (416) 977–3388
Byzantium, 401 Danforth Ave., Gr.; tel. (416) 466–2845
La Chaumiere, 77 Charles E, F; tel. (416) 922–0500
Cibo, 1055 Yonge St.; tel. (416) 921–2166
Don Quixote, 300 College St., S; tel. (416) 922–7636
Lobster Trap, 1960 Ave. Rd.; tel. (416) 787–3211
Metropolis, 838 Yonge St., loc.; tel. (416) 924–4100
Moghul, 563 Bloor W, In.; tel. (416) 597–0522
Old Fish Market, 12 Market St., sf.; tel. (416) 363–0334
Oliver's, 2433 Yonge St.; tel. (416) 485–1051
Palmerston, 488 College St.; tel. (416) 922–9277
Parrot, 325 Queen St. W; tel. (416) 593–0899
Poretta's Pizza, 97 Harbord; tel. (416) 920–2186
Scaramouche, 1 Benevenuto Pl., V, res.; tel. (416) 961–8011
Thai Magic, 1118 Yonge St.; tel. (416) 968–7366
West End Vegetarian, 2849 Dundas W, ; tel. (416) 762–1204
Young Lok, 122 St Patrick St.; tel. (416) 593–9819

Mason-Girardot Manor, 3203 Peter St.; tel. (19) 253–9212   Windsor

Prince Edward Island

Shaw's Hotel, res.; tel. (902) 672–2022   Brackley Beach

Chez Yvonne, loc.; tel. (902) 963–2070   Cavendish

Off Broadway Café, loc.; tel. (902) 566–4620   Charlottetown
Caesar's Italy, lt.; tel. (902) 892–9201
Cedar's Eatery, 81 University Ave., loc., Lebanese; tel. (902) 892–7377
Claddagh Room, 129 Sydney St., sf.; tel. (902) 892–9661
Confederation Dining Room, Charlottetown Hotel, Kent/Pownal Sts.;
  tel. (902) 894–7371
Griffin Dining Room, Dundee Arms Inn, 200 Pownal St., sf.;
  tel. (902) 892–2496
Lord Selkirk Dining Room, Prince Edward Hotel, 18 Queen St.;
  tel. (902) 566–2222
Pat's Rose and Grey Room, 132 Richmond St., lt., sf.; tel. (902) 892–2222
Queen Street Café, 52 Queen St., loc., res.; tel. (902) 566–5520
Town & Country, family; tel. (902) 892–2282

Seabreeze Motel, loc.; tel. (902) 357–2371   Kingsboro

Brudenell Resort Restaurant; tel. (902) 652–2332   Roseneath

Fisherman's Wharf Restaurant, sf.; tel. (902) 963–2669   Rustico

Platter House, Rte.2, V, sf.; tel. (902) 687–3340   Souris

Brothers Two, Water St., sf., stk; tel. (902) 436–9654   Summerside

Québec

Le Vivier, Rte. du Quai; tel. (418) 364–6122   Carleton

Ben's, 990 Blvd. de Maisonneuve Ouest; tel. (514) 844–1001   Montréal
Bonaparte, 443 Rue St-Françoise-Xavier, F, sf., res.; tel. (514) 844–4368
Briskets, 2055 Bishop St.; tel. (514) 843–3650
Le Caveau, 2063 Rue Victoria, F, res.; tel. (514) 844–1624
Les Chenêts, 2075 Bishop St., F; tel. (514) 844–2328

Restaurants

Le Commensal, 2115 St-Denis St., vegetarian; tel. (514) 845–2627
Restaurant d'Europe, 27 Rue Ste-Angèle, F, lt.; tel. (514) 692–3835
L'Exprèss, 3927 St-Denis St., F, res.; tel. (514) 845–5333
Le Fadeau, 423 St-Claude St., F, res.; tel. (514) 878–3959
Les Filles du Roy, 415 Rue Bonsecours, loc., res.; tel. (514) 849–3535
Les Halles, 1450 Crescent St., F, res.; tel. (514) 844–2328
Laurier, 394 Laurier St. W; tel. (514) 273–2484
La Marée, 404 Place Jacques-Cartier, F, res.; tel. (514) 861–8126
Le Mas des Oliviers, 1216 Bishop St., res.; tel. (514) 861–6733
La Mer à Boire, 429 Rue St-Vincent, loc., sf.; tel. (514) 397–9610
Chez la Mère Michel, 1209 Guy St., F, res.; tel. (514) 934–0473
Le Paris, 1812 Ste-Catherine Ouest, sf.; tel. (514) 937–4898
Chez Pauzé, 1657 Ste-Catherine Ouest, sf.; tel. (514) 932–6118
Le Piémontais, 1145A Rue de Bullion, lt., res.; tel. (514) 861–8122
Schwartz's Montréal Hebrew Delicatessen and Steak House, 3895 Blvd. St-Laurent; tel. (514) 842–4813
Les Trois Arches, Pierrefonds, 11131 Blvd. Gouin, F, res.; tel. (514) 683–8200

Mont Trembland	Auberge du Coq de Montagne, Lac Moore, lt.; tel. (819) 425–3380
Parc de la Gaspesie	Auberge Gite du Mont Albert, Rte.299; tel. (418) 763–2288
Percé	Auberge du Gargantua, 222 Rte. des Falls; tel. (418) 782–2852

Québec
　　　　Aux Anciens Canadiens, 34 Rue St-Louis, loc., res.; tel. (418) 692–1627
　　　　Le Champlain, Château Frontenac, 1 Rue des Carrières, F, res.; tel. (418) 692–3861
　　　　Le Continental, 26 Rue St-Louis, res.; tel. (418) 694–9995
　　　　Le Croquembroche, Québec Hilton, 3 Place Québec, F, res.; tel. (418) 647–2411
　　　　Le D'Orsay, 65 Rue Buade, pub, res.; tel. (418) 694–1582
　　　　Le Graffiti, 1191 Ave. Cartier, F; tel. (418) 529–4949
　　　　Chez Guido, 73 Rue Ste-Anne, F, lt.; tel. (418) 692–3856
　　　　Kyoto, 560 Grande Allée Est, J, res.; tel. (418) 529–6141
　　　　Le Marie Clarisse, 12 Rue Petit-Champlain, sf.; tel. (418) 692–0857
　　　　Café de la Paix, 44 Rue Desjardins, F, sf., res.; tel. (418) 692–1430
　　　　Café de Paris, 66 Rue St-Louis, F, lt.; tel. (418) 694–9626
　　　　Au Parmesan, 38 Rue St-Louis, F, lt.; tel. (418) 692–0341
　　　　Le Paris-Brest, 590 Grande Allée Est, F; tel. (418) 529–2243
　　　　Table de Serge Bruyère, 1200 Rue St-Jean, F, res.; tel. (418) 694–0618

St-Jovite	La Table Enchantée, Rte. 117 nord, Lac Duhamel, 5km/3 miles north of St-Jovite, loc.; tel. (819) 425–7113
Ste-Adèle	St-Trop, 251 Rue Morin, F; tel. (514) 229–3298
Ste-Marguerite	Le Clef des Champs, 875 Chemin Ste-Marguerite, F; tel. (514) 229–2857
Val-David	Auberge du Vieux Foyer, 3167 Montée Doncaster; tel. (819) 322–2686

Saskatchewan

Estevan	Old Homestead, 400 King St.; tel. (306) 634–6775
Lloydminster	Wayside Inn, Hwy. 16; tel. (403) 875–4404
Moose Jaw	Hopkins Dining Parlour, 65 Athabasca St. W; tel. (306) 692–5995 Grant Hall Inn, 24 Fair Food St. E; tel. (306) 692–2301

Amy's on Second, 2990 2nd Ave. W; tel. (306) 763–1515   Prince Albert
Venice House Restaurant, 1498 Central St.; tel. (306) 764–6555

Bartleby's Dining Emporium, 1920 Broad St.; tel. (306) 565–0040   Regina
Bonzini's, Albert St./Gordon R., lt.; tel. (306) 586–3553
The Brothers Theatre Restaurant, 1867 Hamilton St.; tel. (306) 522–1659
C. C. Lloyd's, 1907 11th Ave.; tel. (306) 569–4650
Celebrations, 669 Albert St.; tel. (306) 525–8989
Cellar Dining Room, Sheraton Centre, 1818 Victoria Ave.;
    tel. (306) 569–1666
Geno's, 1515 Albert St., res.; tel. (306) 522–6700
Diplomat, 2032 Broad St., sf., res., stk.; tel. (306) 359–3366
Roxy's Bistro, 1844 14 Ave.; tel. (306) 352–4737

Cousin Nik's, 1100 Grosvenor, Gr., res.; tel. (306) 374–2020   Saskatoon
Imperial 400 Motel, 610 Idylwyld Dr. N, family; tel. (306) 244–7722
Lucci's, 117 3rd Ave.; tel. (306) 653–0188
Shaheen's Curry, 135 20th St., In.; tel. (306) 244–8807
Villy's, 410 22nd St. E, 17th floor of Toronto Dominion Bank, V;
    tel. (306) 244–0955

Wong's Kitchen, South Service Rd.; tel. (306) 773–6244   Swift Current

El Rancho Pizza and Steak House, 53 Government Rd.; tel. (306) 842–1411   Weyburn

Gladstone Inn, 185 Broadway W, German; tel. (306) 783–4827   Yorkton
The Samovar and Coffee Shop, Holiday Inn, 110 Broadway E, stk., Russian;
    tel. (306) 783–9781

Yukon

Bonanza Dining Room, Eldorado Hotel, Third/Princess Sts.;   Dawson City
    tel. (403) 993–5451
Midnight Sun Hotel, Queen/Third Sts., Ch.; tel. (403) 993–5495

Cellar Dining Lounge, Edgewater Hotel, 101 Main St., stk.;   Whitehorse
    tel. (403) 667–2573
Mr Mike's, 4114 Fourth Ave., sf., stk.; tel. (403) 667–2242
Village Garden, Westmark Whitehorse Hotel, Second Ave./Wood St., stk.;
    tel. (403) 668–4700

Roads

Canada has a very good road system, considering the sheer vastness of the country. Urban Canada has virtually perfect road cover, with multi-lane ring-roads encircling the town centres. Generously proportioned highways connect all the major cities and open up the interior.

All the highways have numbers, and it is these numbers, rather than place names, that are the best indication of the route to follow. All are clearly signposted by the individual provincial highway authority, and each bears its provincial road number. The TransCanada Highway is also signposted throughout the ten provinces with the maple-leaf emblem. Signs to tourist amenities such as picnic sites and camp grounds are usually white on a brown background.   Road signing

Classification of roads

Expressways, which are the North American equivalent of Europe's urban motorways, are the main roads of metropolitan Canada. They are the quickest way to cover longer distances in the country's built-up areas.   Expressways

TRAFFIC SIGNS

Mandatory Signs

Only those signs which differ considerably from those customary in Europe are shown

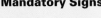

Warning change of lane

Maximum speed

Warning Schoolchildren

No right turn at red traffic light

Cul de sac

No overtaking

No Parking

No stopping

One-way street

No turning in direction indicated

Pedestrian zone

Parking allowed for 30 minutes

Lane indications

Traffic sign for drivers turning left

No through road for dangerous loads

No heavy goods vehicles

Overtaking lane

Warning Signs

 Beware traffic signals

Level-crossing crossing

Cycle-track crossing crossing

Snowmobile crossing

Maximum speed | Beware of deer, etc. | Bends

Road junction | Cross-roads | Slippery when wet | Maximum height | Steep hill | School-bus turning

Keep in lane | Road narrows | Lane ends | Uneven Carriageway | Maximum speed | DANGER

Drive slowly | Warning roadworks | End of metalled road | Roadworks | Vehicles turning | Diversion

Information

Tourist Information | Boat landing-stage

Hospital | | Provincial Park | Provincial Police | Road number | Signpost

Exit

Signpost

© *Baedeker*

Roads

Distances in kilometres	Calgary	Charlottetown	Edmonton	Fredericton	Halifax	Montréal	Ottawa	Québec	Regina	St. John's	Saskatoon	Thunder Bay	Toronto	Vancouver	Victoria	Whitehorse	Winnipeg	Yellowknife
Calgary		4917	299	4558	5042	3743	3553	4014	764	6183	620	2050	3434	1057	1123	2385	1336	1811
Charlottetown	4917		4949	359	232	1184	1374	945	4163	1294	4421	2878	1724	5985	6051	7034	3592	6460
Edmonton	299	4949		4598	5082	3764	3574	4035	785	6212	528	2071	3455	1244	1310	2086	1357	1511
Fredericton	4558	359	4598		346	834	1024	586	3813	1622	4070	2527	1373	5634	5700	6684	3241	6109
Halifax	5042	232	5082	346		1318	1508	912	4297	1349	4554	3011	1857	6119	6185	7168	3726	6593
Montréal	3743	1184	3764	834	1318		190	270	2979	2448	3236	1693	539	4801	4867	5850	2408	5275
Ottawa	3553	1374	3574	1024	1508	190		460	2789	2638	3046	1503	399	4611	4677	5660	2218	5086
Québec	4014	945	4035	586	912	270	460		3249	2208	3507	1963	810	5071	5137	6120	2678	5546
Regina	764	4163	785	3813	4297	2979	2789	3249		5427	257	1286	2670	1822	1888	2871	571	2297
St. John's	6183	1294	6212	1622	1349	2448	2638	2208	5427		5684	4141	2987	7248	7314	8298	4855	7723
Saskatoon	620	4421	528	4070	4554	3236	3046	3507	257	5684		1543	2927	1677	1743	2614	829	2039
Thunder Bay	2050	2878	2071	2527	3011	1693	1503	1963	1286	4141	1543		1384	3108	3174	4157	715	3582
Toronto	3434	1724	3455	1373	1875	539	399	810	2670	2987	2927	1384		4492	4558	5528	2099	4966
Vancouver	1057	5985	1244	5634	6119	4801	4611	5071	1822	7248	1677	3108	4492		66	2697	2232	2411
Victoria	1123	6051	1310	5700	6185	4867	4677	5137	1888	7314	1743	3174	4558	66		2763	2298	2477
Whitehorse	2385	7034	2086	6684	7168	5850	5660	6120	2871	8298	2614	4157	5528	2697	2763		3524	2704
Winnipeg	1336	3592	1357	3241	3726	2408	2218	2678	571	4855	829	715	2099	2232	2298	3524		2868
Yellowknife	1811	6460	1511	6109	6593	5275	5086	5546	2297	7723	2039	3582	4966	2411	2477	2704	2868	

King's Highways are the main trunk roads between the towns and cities. Although mostly dual carriageway and without junctions, they are the responsibility of the provincial highway authorities and in more sparsely populated parts of the country will be graded but also often loose-surfaced and single carriageway. Secondary Highways are mostly single carriageway provincial trunk roads, also with a graded road surface. | Highways

Tertiary roads are the minor roads linking the different districts, counties, etc., and may often just have metalled surfaces. | Tertiary Roads

These gravel highways are for getting around Canada's remote areas. They are mostly loose-surfaced logging roads, and call for very careful driving. Give way to any enormous juggernauts encountered – a collision could prove fatal. | Gravel Highways

Road conditions

Canadian road maintenance crews are constantly busy keeping the roads in good repair, and motorists have to comply with their instructions. | Road Maintenance

There can be some nasty surprises in store for drivers after a prolonged or heavy downpour. This particularly applies to the loose-surfaced roads. Parts of the carriageway can actually be washed away, or turned into treacherous mudslides, depending on the subsoil. The severe Canadian winter and heavy spring rains can mean that even the best of road surfaces will be potholed or hollowed out by the frost. | Road passability

Besides technical knowledge, several spare tyres, a well-stocked toolkit, sturdy windscreen wipers, broad sticky-tape, a solid towrope and the proper cleaning materials are all very useful. It also pays to have extra protection for headlights and possibly windscreens. Special precautions, such as encasing luggage in plastic bags, should also be taken to prevent dust getting into the vehicle and its contents. | Driving equipped for northern conditions

In cold weather motorists should also carry plenty of warm, waterproof clothing and appropriate footwear.

Shopping and Souvenirs

Canada's big cities, in particular, offer plenty of opportunity in their wide range of stores for shopping or just looking around.

Ultra-modern shopping malls, such as the Eaton Centre in Toronto or the West Edmonton Shopping Mall, are a maze of boutiques, restaurants, even streams and gardens, housed in arcades and subterranean passages, where it is possible to browse over bargains away from the vagaries of the weather and the extremes of hot or cold.

Anyone who prefers searching for souvenirs in a historic setting can explore the newly converted waterfronts of some Canadian cities, such as Granville Island in Vancouver or Queens Quays in Toronto.

Stores are usually open between 9am and 5.30 or 6pm, and in some of the bigger cities they often stay open until quite late at night, while some neighbourhood stores are also open on Sunday, selling groceries, personal items and newspapers (see also Opening Times).

There are strict limits on the export of objects over 50 years old and of historic, cultural or scientific significance. More precise information can be had from: | **Antiques**

The Secretary, Canadian Cultural Property Export Review Board,
Department of Communications,
Ottawa, Ontario, Canada K1A 0C8

Sport

Souvenirs Art	Craftwork by Canada's native peoples, the Inuit and the Indians, makes for souvenirs that have a lasting value, such as paintings, carvings and sculpture in the form of masks, soapstone figures and scrimshaw, with the price depending on the fame and reputation of the particular artist. It is worth making sure that the work is genuine and Canadian, and not some spurious imitation from the Far East.
Glass and pottery	Well-fashioned glassware and pottery are popular handmade souvenirs of a stay in Canada.
Handmade clothes	Favourite items include knitted or handwoven clothes made by the Canadian Indians such as mittens, heavy-knit Cowichan sweaters and well-lined parkas.
Moccasins	Inuit fur and sealskin boots and Indian moccasins, often trimmed with porcupine quills and glass beads, make memorable and unusual souvenirs.
Western clothing	Stetson hats and hand-tooled boots and belts, as well as typically Canadian hunting jackets and lumberjack shirts are also very popular as gifts and mementoes.
Maple syrup	Maple syrup and maple sugar products are very much a speciality of eastern Canada, and calculated to rekindle memories of the country after the holiday.
Alcoholic beverages	In Canada alcoholic beverages, including beer, are sold in special national Monopoly stores. The prices are strictly controlled and the advertising of alcoholic drinks is banned in many places. Drinks manufacturers can only promote themselves as sponsors of cultural and sporting events.
Whisky	See Food and Drink
Wine	See Food and Drink
Beer	See Food and Drink

Sport

Sports	See Canoeing, Cycling, Fishing, Golf, Walking, Winter Sports.
Spectator sports	Canada's favourite spectator sports are ice hockey, baseball and Canadian football, although the original national game, as played by the Indians, is lacrosse. Ice hockey, or simply hockey, as it's usually called, is to Canadians what football, i.e. soccer, is to Europeans. The top teams, such as Vancouver, Montréal, Toronto, Edmonton, Calgary, Québec and Winnipeg, play in the National Hockey League.

Taxes

Provincial sales tax	All provinces except Alberta, the Northwest Territories and the Yukon levy a sales tax, ranging from 6% to 12%, on most items purchased in shops, on food in eating establishments and, in some cases, on hotel and motel rooms. Alberta has a 5% sales tax but it only applies to accommodation. This provincial sales tax is recoverable, but only in Nova Scotia, Québec and Manitoba.
GST	There is also a general sales tax (GST), which is currently 7% on all goods and services. Visitors may reclaim tax on accommodation and goods purchased and taken out of the country, but GST is not reclaimable on food, drink, tobacco, car hire, transport and motorhomes. To claim rebate com-

plete the reclaim form, attach all receipts, and mail to the address on the form. GST must be claimed before applying for refunds of provincial sales tax.

Taxis

There are plenty of taxicabs in the towns and cities. Fares are usually slightly higher than in Europe.

Telephone

Unlike most of Europe, the North American telephone system is in the hands of private companies, with Bell Canada the biggest of these in Canada. This private system is integrated with that in the United States. The cheapest way to make a call is to use a public telephone or one of the many telephone company stores. Local and international calls can usually be dialled direct from hotel rooms, but the surcharges will be quite high.

Canadian numbers are seven-digit, preceded, if long-distance, by the area code. Dial 0 to get the operator when wanting to make personal or reverse-charge calls. Calls for information on local numbers are free and can be made on 411 or 1–+area code+555–1212. Freefone numbers usually have a 1–800 prefix. Further information will be found in the front pages of the local telephone directory.

From Canada the international dialling codes are:
International dialling codes

Australia	011 61, plus area code and number
New Zealand	011 64, etc.
Republic of Ireland	011 44 353, etc.
South Africa	011 27, etc.
United Kingdom	011 44, etc.

N.B. the first zero is dropped from the area code

From the United Kingdom to Canada dial 001 then the area code and the rest of the number.

Cheap rate is from 6pm to 9am local time. Local calls from a telephone box cost 25 cents. Long-distance rates will be announced automatically after dialling.
Rates

Time

Canada is divided into six time zones. These are measured against Greenwich Mean Time.
Standard Time Zones

Newfoundland Standard Time:	GMT minus 3½ hrs.
Atlantic Standard Time:	GMT minus 4 hrs.
Eastern Standard Time:	GMT minus 5 hrs.
Central Standard Time:	GMT minus 6 hrs.
Mountain Standard Time:	GMT minus 7 hrs.
Pacific Standard Time:	GMT minus 8 hrs.

The general rule when crossing from one time zone to another travelling across Canada from east to west is to put watches back an hour (half an hour for Newfoundland), and, clearly, to reverse the process when travelling in the opposite direction.

Daylight Saving Time (Summer Time) comes into effect in most of Canada on the first Sunday in April each year, when the clocks are advanced by one
Daylight Saving Time

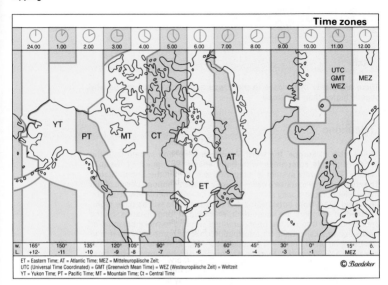

Time zones

| 24.00 | 1.00 | 2.00 | 3.00 | 4.00 | 5.00 | 6.00 | 7.00 | 8.00 | 9.00 | 10.00 | 11.00 | 12.00 |

UTC
GMT
WEZ

MEZ

YT

PT   MT   CT

AT

ET

| W. | 165° | 150° | 135° | 120° | 105° | 90° | 75° | 60° | 45° | 30° | 0° | 15° | ô. |
| L. | +12- | -11 | -10 | -9 | -8 | -7 | -6 | -5 | -4 | -3 | -1 | MEZ | L. |

ET = Eastern Time; AT = Atlantic Time; MEZ = Mitteleuropäische Zeit;
UTC (Universal Time Coordinated) = GMT (Greenwich Mean Time) = WEZ (Westeuropäische Zeit) = Weltzeit
YT = Yukon Time; PT = Pacific Time; MT = Mountain Time; Ct = Central Time

© *Baedeker*

hour. They then revert to standard time on the last Sunday in October. However, this practice is not observed over most of the province of Saskatchewan, so the transition from Central Daylight Time to Mountain Daylight Time occurs at the Manitoba/Saskatchewan border.

Tipping

Tips or service charges are not usually added to the hotel or restaurant bill in Canada. In restaurants the tip is usually left on the table. As a general rule, a tip of up to 15% of the total amount should be given. This also applies to barbers and hairdressers, taxi drivers, bellhops, doormen, redcaps (porters), etc., at hotels; porters at airports and railway stations generally expect $1 per item of luggage.

Traffic Regulations

Although Canadian traffic rules are basically similar to those found in Europe, they can be different in some respects, and may also vary from province to province. Speed limits tend to be enforced rather more rigorously as well.

Driving licence

A full British driving licence is valid for driving in Canada for up to three months in most provinces. For longer periods, an international driving licence is required as well. An international driving permit is also recommended for visitors from non-English speaking countries. A US drivers licence is also valid in Canada.

Third-party insurance

Insurance cover under a vehicle liability insurance policy against liability for bodily injury, death or damage to the property of others is compulsory in all provinces in Canada. The minimum liability insurance requirement is

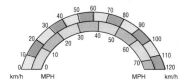

1 km = 0,62 mi
1 mi = 1,61 km

© *Baedeker*

$200,000 except in Québec and the Northwest Territories, where the limit is $50,000.

The rule of the road in Canada, as in the United States, is drive on the right. On multi-lane carriageways, outside built-up areas, it is possible to be overtaken on the left or the right, although people tend not to change lanes very often. Any lane-change should be clearly signalled. Overtaking is usually forbidden if there is poor visibility, e.g. on bends, the tops of hills, crossings, etc.

Drive on the right

All speed limits are clearly signposted and are in kilometres per hour. On freeways the limit is 100 kilometres per hour/62 miles per hour, on Trans-Canada routes 90kph/56mph, most rural highways and country roads 80kph/50mph, and in urban/populated areas from 40 to 60kph/25 to 37mph.

Speed limits

Right turns on a red light are legal, unless otherwise indicated, in all Canadian provinces except Québec. The motorist must come to a full stop at the light but may proceed with caution if the way is clear.

Right turns on red lights

Parking is strictly forbidden on the pavement (sidewalk), in front of hydrants, near traffic lights and within 15m/49ft of level crossings.

No Parking

School buses are usually painted bright orange, and it is an offence to overtake them when they are at a standstill with their warning lights flashing. This applies to oncoming traffic as well.

School buses

The use of seat belts by vehicle drivers and all passengers is compulsory throughout Canada. Child restraints are also mandatory in all provinces.

Seat belts

Driving under the influence of alcohol is illegal.

Drinking and Driving

Some Canadian provinces and territories have made it a statutory requirement to drive with vehicle headlights on for extended periods after dawn and before sunset. In the Yukon the law requires drivers to keep their headlights on at all times while driving on the Yukon highways. The use of side (parking) lights while driving is contrary to highway statutes.

Headlights

As in Europe, Canada has traffic lights on many crossroads. There are also flashing yellow lights at accident blackspots and on main through roads, and these are a signal to slow down and proceed with care.

Traffic lights

Give way immediately to police cars flashing their lights and sounding their sirens.
    If followed by a police car with flashing light and siren sounding, pull in immediately, stay in the car and show your driving licence without waiting to be asked. Questioning by the police should be responded to with scrupulous politeness.

Police cars

In the event of a breakdown make sure the vehicle is parked where it will not hold up the traffic. Raise the bonnet and fix a white cloth on the driver's side to indicate help is wanted. Emergency telephones are installed on most major trunkroads.

Vehicle breakdown

Travel Documents

Hitch-hiking   Most Canadian provinces do not allow hitch-hiking.

Canadian Automobile Association

The Automobile Association, the Royal Automobile Club, the Royal Scottish Automobile Club, and the Royal Irish Automobile Club are fully affiliated with the Canadian Automobile Association and its member clubs across Canada. Advance information on motoring in Canada can be obtained by members of the AA of Great Britain simply by contacting their head office before departure. In Canada the address is:

Canadian Automobile Association
1775 Courtwood Crescent
Ottawa, Ontario, Canada K2C 3J2

Travel Documents

Entry into Canada

British citizens must have a full valid British passport. A visitor's passport is not accepted. All visitors must also have a return ticket, and sufficient funds to cover their stay. The maximum length of stay is six months, but anyone wanting to stay longer than three months should clear this with the authorities on entry. No vaccinations are currently obligatory.

Visas

British citizens and citizens of the Republic of Ireland do not require a visa to enter Canada, nor is a visa required by citizens of the following countries: Australia, Austria, Belgium, Brazil, Denmark, Finland, France, Germany, Greece, Iceland, Israel, Italy, Japan, Liechtenstein, Luxembourg, Malaysia, Malta, Mexico, Monaco, the Netherlands, New Zealand, Norway, Saudi Arabia, Singapore, Spain, Sweden, Switzerland, United States, and Venezuela. Citizens of many other countries are also exempt from visa requirement, but regulations may change. Contact the visa section of the nearest Canadian diplomatic mission for more information.

Canada/US border

No visa is required to cross the Canada/US border provided a full UK passport is held. Visitors will be requested to complete a waiver form prior to disembarking by sea or air. If it is a surface crossing, this form will be completed at the border post.

Walking, Hiking, Backpacking, Trekking

Notwithstanding the fact that Canada is famed in many guises as a walker's paradise, anyone who wants to tackle its vast areas on foot needs to be well equipped and quite experienced.

National and provincial parks are the only areas with well-signed trails where walkers can take relatively danger-free hikes of varying timescales. The park reception centres will usually be able to provide them with all the information they require.

Walking

Walking is mostly on trails that are also suitable for children and hence not too strenuous, often in the parks with explanations along the way.

Hiking

Hiking tends to be for longer day trips, as opposed to leisurely walks or the more strenuous pastimes of trekking and backpacking.

Hitchhiking

Hitchhiking is not allowed in many Canadian provinces, so before doing this it is advisable to check first with the police or the local tourist office.

Backpacking

As in Europe, backpacking – taking off on foot into the backwoods just carrying a rucksack – has also become an increasingly popular Canadian pursuit. The necessary maps can be obtained from the Map Office in Ottawa or from one of the licensed shops found in most main towns and cities.

Trekking, taking off for days at a time, can be on horseback, mountainbike, even with a vehicle, as well as on foot, and often in groups with the help of a local guide. In every case the Canadian wilderness can provide Europeans with challenges of quite a special nature, not least confrontations with dangerous wild animals (see Bears).

For safety's sake there are a number of rules which should be observed:
– thoroughly plan trips in advance;
– go for the easier option rather than pressing on to the limits of
  endurance;
– stick to the established route;
– don't use up all the provisions;
– tell someone where you are going (the park warden, the pilot or a police
  station, or leave a note on the car windscreen if it is just an impromptu
  walk), and let them know when you get back;
– watch out for hypothermia;
– take precautions with campfires because of the danger of forest fires;
– take plenty of insect repellent to ward off the black flies and mosquitoes.

Weights and Measures

See Measurements

When to go

Vast country that it is, Canada experiences widely differing weather as between north and south, not to mention east and west. Hence, in the more southerly parts of the country there are actually four seasons – spring from mid-March to mid to late May, summer from then until the first half of September, followed by fall, to give autumn its transatlantic name, until the onset of winter about mid-November. In the north, particularly Yukon and the Northwest Territories, there are really only two seasons – the cold time of year from October to April, tempered only by the Chinook, or "snow eater", the warm dry southwesterly wind blowing down the eastern slopes of the Rockies, and the warmer weather for the rest of the year. The hottest part of the country is the south-western corner of British Columbia, but it also among the wettest.

Canada's size makes it difficult to give general advice, so it is worth reading the information on particular areas in the section on Climate in the Introduction section. The most pleasant time to visit the far north, other than for specific cold-weather reasons, is from June to August. So far as the rest of Canada is concerned, the best time to travel is between May and October.

May has quite warm days, but is cool at night. Victoria Day weekend, about May 22nd, heralds the start of the travel season. It also signals the opening of many national and provincial parks, and of tourist information centres throughout the country, as opposed to just those in the main cities. Starting with the west, the milder weather brings on the flowers and trees, and some fog can occur in the Atlantic provinces. June is a good time to travel, while July and August are the hottest months, when most people elect to take to the road. The sun also brings out the mosquitoes, so insect repellent is essential.

September's golden days are still pleasantly warm, but the cool evenings have already set in. The Indian summer at the end of the month and in early October is when the autumn colours are at their best, particularly in the forests of Québec and the Maritimes. By the end of October – earlier in the north – the first of the winter snow and frosts have arrived.

From November to April the bitter cold and heavy winter snowfalls put large parts of Canada out of bounds for most visitors other than winter sports enthusiasts. These will then be in their element in British Columbia and Alberta in the Rockies and in Québec's Laurentian resorts. The snows start to melt in March but skiing can carry on into the milder weather on the higher slopes, with April's warmer weather heralding the summer that is to come.

Winter Sports

Many skiing holiday tour operators recommend Canada as the ideal antidote to the overcrowding of Europe's traditional ski slopes. They are absolutely right. In western Canada, in the Rockies and the mountains along British Columbia's coast, and on the slopes of Ontario and Québec in the east, right through from November to April there is usually plenty of snow, and Europe-style ploughed-up pistes are only found around the big cities such as Québec, Montréal, Calgary and Vancouver. To the novice winter in Canada may simply conjure up images of ice and snow, but for the hardened European skier there is also the lure of the Canadian west, and not just the hectic life of Banff but particularly the remote slopes of the Rockies in Alberta and British Columbia, where heli-skiing is part of the attraction.

Skiing territory

Canada's ten province's offer skiing, be it downhill or cross-country, to suit just about any visitor, making it a skiers' paradise, ranging from the seemingly endless mountain chains of British Columbia in the west to the superb Laurentian ski-slopes of the east. And the Canadians ensure that there is the après-ski to match!

Many ski-resorts offer good packages, complete with accommodation, food and skipass. Further information on prices, seasons, etc. can be obtained from travel agents.

Ski resorts are not necessarily open seven days a week, so it pays to contact the local tourist office or the actual resort to find out about snow conditions, weather forecasts, opening times, etc.

British Columbia

British Columbia's mountains boast Canada's longest skiing season, from sunny Okanagan to the Rockies and the Alberta border. A few minutes by road from Vancouver is Grouse Mountain, where the fine floodlit pistes allow night-time skiing. Whistler Village, 125km/78 miles north of Vancouver, has, in Blackcomb mountain, the highest lift-serviced vertical in North America and incredible fall-line runs, while the Okanagan Valley, further east, has four ski resorts with a whole spectrum of pistes. Kootenay in the south has skiing on a variety of slopes without lifts packed to capacity. The scenic splendour of the Rockies also provides the skier with sun, deep snow and pistes seemingly without end, while for the more ambitious visitor British Columbia offers heli-hiking and snowmobile tours.

Alberta

Alberta's downhill ski slopes are all in the Jasper and Banff National Parks. Jasper National Park has excellent winter sports facilities and top-class hotels, while located within Banff National Park are three world-class ski resorts offering downhill skiing across the whole range of difficulty, as well as heli-hiking. Besides downhill skiing and all the other Alpine-style activities there are also good cross-country trails in many national and provincial parks, and close to the towns.

Yukon and Northwest Territories

Both of these northern provinces have landscapes and snow conditions that make them ideal for cross-country skiing. Whitehorse, Yukon, has top cross-country facilities, while there are ski-trails in Yellowknife Park and around Fort Smith, in Northwest Territories. The glaciers in Auyuittuq National Park and on Baffin Island in the north provide winter sport opportunities all year round, although the best conditions are from March onwards, when the days grow longer and powder snow awaits the enthusiast.

Sunshine and Snowfall

Region	Total hours of Sunshine				Annual Snowfall	Snow-cover days
	Juni	Juli	Aug.	Sept.	cm	(days)
British Columbia						
Kamloops	256	316	280	195	67	68
Prince Rupert	151	143	138	117	84	47
Vancouver	238	307	256	183	51	11
Victoria	258	329	274	195	32	3
Alberta						
Banff	204	256	211	163	251	149
Calgary	267	322	282	195	153	116
Edmonton	272	306	277	182	136	133
Lethbridge	284	345	299	214	176	114
Yukon						
Whitehorse	273	250	231	137	100	170
Northwest Territories						
Fort Simpson	281	289	246	134	142	193
Frobisher Bay	175	202	161	82	256	242
Inuvik	375	340	216	109	177	232
Saskatchewan						
Prince Albert	262	296	268	166	122	153
Regina	283	342	295	191	87	134
Saskatoon	294	341	293	191	114	133
Manitoba						
Churchill	234	285	232	111	196	211
Winnipeg	276	316	283	185	126	135
Ontario						
Hamilton	260	288	255	173	109	73
London	244	274	246	173	196	92
Muskoka	263	283	239	169	300	131
Niagara Falls	252	283	253	191	163	39
Ottawa	247	274	243	168	206	121
Sault Ste. Marie	256	288	249	157	305	138
Thunder Bay	262	304	256	168	213	132
Toronto	253	281	252	191	139	73
Québec						
Gaspé / New-Richmond	228	249	225	164	322	165
Montréal	249	275	240	169	243	116
Québec	224	248	219	153	288	146
Ste-Agathe-des-Monts	238	275	237	162	396	154
New Brunswick						
Fredeicton	206	233	221	167	290	119
Moncton	226	243	230	166	301	118
Saint John	203	218	212	166	224	104
Nova Scotia						
Halifax/Dartmouth	221	219	225	180	217	99
Sydney	226	243	226	167	318	101
Yarmouth	211	207	209	176	208	60
Prince Edward Island						
Charlottetown	221	241	218	176	275	122
Newfoundland/Labrador						
Goose Bay	187	200	176	121	445	188
St. John's	187	220	186	147	322	109

Young People's Accommodation

Saskatchewan and Manitoba	Although these two provinces have little downhill skiing there is plenty of cross-country. Most ski resorts are near the towns.
Ontario	Thunder Bay in northern Ontario is a winter sports centre good for both downhill and cross-country skiing, and equally famous for its ski-jumping. Collingwood, north-east of Toronto, has Canada's biggest skilifts. Muskoka, which is north of Toronto, is another ski playground. Cross-country skiing can be enjoyed in and around almost every park and resort area. Details of tours and other outdoor pursuits can be had from Ontario Tourism.
Québec	Québec Province has everything to gladden the heart of the winter sports fan. It has three major ski regions: the Laurentians, the Eastern Townships (or L'Estrie) and the Greater Québec Area, and over a hundred ski centres, most of them easily accessible from Montréal or Québec City. There are facilities for skiers of all abilities and a stylish variety of après-ski that is very French-Canadian.
Atlantic Provinces	Newfoundland, Nova Scotia, New Brunswick and Prince Edward Island have excellent cross-country skiing, but not much downhill.
Heli-skiing	Heli-skiing is a sport that is gaining in popularity, particularly with overseas visitors. An Austrian ski-instructor first chartered a helicopter in the 1960s to take deep snow enthusiasts to the higher regions. Ski-tourists can then master differences in altitude of between 500 and 2500m/1640 and 8200ft. This kind of what can hardly be described as environmentally friendly ski-tourism is carried on in several places, including Revelstoke National Park (Peter Schlunegger), Blue River (Mike Wiegele), Golden (Rudi Gertsch) and Panorama (Roger Madson). Anyone wanting to try heli-skiing must be very fit and be experienced when it comes to skiing in deep snow, as well as having the very best equipment and plenty of team spirit.

Young People's Accommodation

Canada has plenty of low-cost accommodation catering for young people, including youth hostels, YMCAs and YWCAs and college residences (both student and staff).

Youth hostels · YMCA hostels · YWCA hostels

Youth hostels	Canada's 80 youth hostels offer members simple inexpensive accommodation at a cost of between 8 and 20 Can.$ for the night. Hostels are found in all larger towns and cities and in some country areas of special tourist interest. Membership, individual or family, is open to everyone; there is no age limit. Intending visitors should take out membership before departure for Canada.
YMCA and YWCA hostels	There are YMCA and YWCA hostels in all the bigger cities. Overnight accommodation in a single room costs between 20 and 30 Can.$. In some cases accommodation can be booked in advance prior to leaving for Canada.
Information	For up-to-date information contact: Hostelling International Canada, 1600 James Naismith Drive, Suite 608, Gloucester, Ontario K1B 5N4; tel. (613) 748–5638, Fax (613) 748–5750 In the UK: Youth Hostel Association, 84 Highgate West Hill, London N6 6LU; tel. (0181) 340–1831

The Hostelling International handbook is available in bookshops throughout Canada.

College accommodation (student and staff residences)

Young people can find cheap accommodation between May and August in the residences (student and staff) of a great many colleges, where for a small additional charge they can also make use of sports and leisure facilities.

Comprehensive, detailed information can be obtained direct from the college concerned or from the appropriate local or provincial tourist office (see Information).

Index

Index

Index

Principal Sights of Tourist Interest

(Continued from page 4)

N.B.: For reasons of space only the most important locations in Canada which are worth visiting, either for themselves or for interesting places in the vicinity, can be included in the above list. In the A to Z section will be found many other sights distinguished by stars which are worthy of a visit.

Sources of Illustrations

Anderson (1); Archiv (5); Baumgarten (1); Beaulieu (1); Beedell (2); Bickell (1); Burger (6); Cochrane (1); Engel (30); Herold (10); Historia (1); Hydro-Québec (1); Jaraush (4); Klein (1); Law (3); Linde (26); McClosky (1); Parks Canada (2); Saint Jacques (1); Schäfer (3); Schäffer (1); Scherm (28); Stehle (1); Tourism Canada (13); Tourism Nova Scotia (3); Tourism Ottawa (1); Tourisme Québec (8); Tourism Saskatchewan (2); Ullstein (1); Walker (3); Zeruk (2)

Imprint

166 colour photographs, 74 maps, plans and drawings, 1 general map, 1 large map at end of book

Original German text: Dr Bernard Abend, Monika I. Baumgarten, Annette Bickel, Gisela Bockcamp, Birgit Borwski, Heinz Burger, Dr Helmut Eck, Rainer Eisenschmid, Brigitte and Elmar Engel, Carmen Galenschovski, Mattias Gaul, Görres Grenzdörffer, Prof. Dr Hassenpflug, Dr Cornelia Hermanns, Prof. Dr Alfred Herold, Klein, Barbara Kreissel, Markus Kunz, Helmut Linde, Martina Melk, Dr Christina Melk=Haen, Dr Roland Metz, Dr Madeleine Reineke, Dr Georg Scherm, Inge Scherm, Jutta Seeberger, Claudia Smettan, Lydia Störmer, Reinhard Strüber, Andrea Wurth, Dagmar Zimmermann

Editorial work: Baedeker, Stuttgart
English language edition: Alec Court
General direction: Dr Peter Baumgarten, Baedeker Stuttgart

Cartography: Christoph Gallus, Hohberg-Niederschopfheim; Franz Kaiser, Sindelfingen; Gert Oberländer, Munich, Travel Alberta, Edmonton; MapArt, Brampton; Mairs Geographischer Verlag, Ostfildern-Kemnat (large map)

English translation: Wendy Bell, David Cocking, Brenda Ferris (Babel Translations), Julie Waller

2nd English edition 1996

© Baedeker Stuttgart
Original German edition 1994

© 1996 Jarrold and Sons Limited
English language edition worldwide

© 1996 The Automobile Association
United Kingdom and Ireland

Published in the United States by:
Macmillan Travel
A Simon & Schuster Macmillan Company
1633 Broadway
New York, NY 10019–6785

Macmillan is a registered trademark of Macmillan, Inc.

Distributed in the United Kingdom by the Publishing Division of the Automobile Association, Fanum House, Basingstoke, Hampshire RG21 2EA

Licensed user:
Mairs Geographischer Verlag GmbH & Co.,
Ostfildern-Kemnat bei Stuttgart

Printed in Italy by G. Canale & C.S.p.A – Borgaro T.se –Turin

ISBN 0–02–0861350–3 USA and Canada
    0 7495 1396 9 UK